Human Resource Management

A Practical Approach

Human Resource Management

A Practical Approach

Michael Harris
University of Missouri-St. Louis

The Dryden Press
Harcourt Brace College Publishers

Fort Worth Philadelphia San Diego New York Orlando Austin San Antonio
Toronto London Montreal Sydney Tokyo

Acquisitions Editor	John Weimeister
Developmental Editor	Dona Hightower
Project Editor	Betsy Cummings
Production Manager	Carlyn Hauser
Senior Art Director	David Day
Picture and Literary Rights Editor	Annette Coolidge
Copy Editor:	Karen Carriere
Proofreader:	Thomas Torrans
Indexer:	Edwin Durbin
Compositor:	Graphic World, Inc.
Text Type:	10/12 Clearface Regular

Cover: "Rush Hour" by Diana Ong. Reprinted with permission of SuperStock.

Address for Editorial Correspondence: Harcourt Brace College Publishers, 301 Commerce Street, Suite 3700, Fort Worth, Texas 76102.

Address for Orders: Harcourt Brace & Company, 6277 Sea Harbor Drive, Orlando, Florida 32887-6777, 1-800-782-4479, or 1-800-433-0001 (in Florida).

ISBN:0-03-002067-0

Library of Congress Catalog Card Number: 96-84341

Printed in the United States of America

6 7 8 9 0 1 2 3 4 5 032 9 8 7 6 5 4 3 2 1

The Dryden Press
Harcourt Brace College Publishers

To my parents,
Monford and Rivkah Harris

The Dryden Press Series in Management

Anthony, Perrewé, and Kacmar
Strategic Human Resource Management
Second Edition

Bereman and Lengnick-Hall, Mark
Compensation Decision Making: A Computer-Based Approach

Bourgeois
Strategic Management: From Concept to Implementation

Bracker, Montanari, and Morgan
Cases in Strategic Management

Brechner
Contemporary Mathematics for Business and Consumers

Calvasina and Barton
Chopstick Company: A Business Simulation

Coston
Managing in the Global Economy: The European Union

Costin
Management Development and Training: A TQM Approach

Costin
Readings in Total Quality Management

Czinkota, Ronkainen, and Moffett
International Business
Fourth Edition

Czinkota, Ronkainen, Moffett, and Moynihan
Global Business

Daft
Management
Fourth Edition

Daft
Understanding Management

Dessler
Managing Organizations in an Era of Change

Foegen
Business Plan Guidebook
Revised Edition

Gatewood and Feild
Human Resource Selection
Third Edition

Gold
Exploring Organizational Behavior: Readings, Cases, Experiences

Greenhaus and Callanan
Career Management
Second Edition

Harris and DeSimone
Human Resource Development

Higgins and Vincze
Strategic Management: Text and Cases
Fifth Edition

Hills, Bergmann, and Scarpello
Compensation Decision Making
Second Edition

Hodgetts
Modern Human Relations at Work
Sixth Edition

Hodgetts and Kroeck
Personnel and Human Resource Management

Hodgetts and Kuratko
Effective Small Business Management
Fifth Edition

Holley and Jennings
The Labor Relations Process
Fifth Edition

Jauch and Coltrin
The Managerial Experience: Cases and Exercises
Sixth Edition

Kindler and Ginsburg
Strategic & Interpersonal Skill Building

Kirkpatrick and Lewis
Effective Supervision: Preparing for the 21st Century

Kuratko and Hodgetts
Entrepreneurship: A Contemporary Approach
Third Edition

Kuratko and Welsch
Entrepreneurial Strategy: Text and Cases

Lengnick-Hall, Cynthia, and Hartman
Experiencing Quality

Lewis
Io Enterprises Simulation

Long and Arnold
The Power of Environmental Partnerships

Morgan
Managing for Success

Ryan, Eckert, and Ray
Small Business: An Entrepreneur's Plan
Fourth Edition

Sandburg
Career Design Software

Vecchio
Organizational Behavior
Third Edition

Walton
Corporate Encounters: Law, Ethics, and the Business Environment

Zikmund
Business Research Methods
Fourth Edition

The Harcourt Brace College Outline Series

Pentico
Management Science

Pierson
Introduction to Business Information Systems

Sigband
Business Communication

PREFACE

TO THE STUDENT

Most of us spend a major portion of our lives at work. Whether you are a job applicant searching for your first full-time job or you are currently employed, human resource management practices affect you in a variety of ways. The premise of this book is that you, the reader, will want to know how human resource management affects your career. Consequently, each topic will be examined from a variety of perspectives. While the book focuses on the implications of human resource management issues for employees and job applicants, close attention is also paid to the managerial and supervisory perspective. Thus, regardless of your career stage or job responsibilities, this book will be of value to you. The nature of our jobs, the way in which we are paid, the type of benefits we receive, as well as many other aspects of our employment, have important implications for the quality of our lives and our personal happiness. This book addresses the features and conditions of work that are typically regarded as human resource management concerns, such as recruitment, employee selection, career management, compensation, benefits, training and development, health and safety, as well as others.

To the Instructor

This textbook is written for undergraduate students taking an introductory course in Human Resource Management, either as an elective or as a required credit. Below you will find a detailed outline of what this textbook offers, how it is organized, what support materials are available, and the features that make this book different and distinct from the others.

Most introductory HRM textbooks are written with a managerial focus. They assume that the reader is or will be hiring, supervising, rewarding, and terminating other employees. This book takes a slightly different approach, one that shares the focus of the managerial perspective with that of the employee perspective. The first reason for this shared vision is that the majority of students are more motivated to read and understand a textbook when they see its *immediate* application. Many students are not managers or supervisors; therefore, they may have a better understanding of the material by seeing the application and relevance of material which assumes they are employees/applicants. Second, supervisors and managers are also employees of the organization, and are consumers as well as managers of human resources. Although they may supervise employees, they are also applicants for jobs, affected by benefits, responsible for their own career management, and so on. This textbook allows for managers and employees alike to see the visible personal and professional relevance.

Addressing the Essential Issues

The Reality of Business Today

Today's managers are faced with a different workplace and workforce than that of 20, 10, even 5 years ago. Human resource managers especially feel the impact of organizational decisions that affect the workforce. Succeeding in business today requires skills above and beyond insurance benefits, employee evaluations, and staffing issues. HR managers and general managers alike must be able to address these and other important issues.

- Chapter 6 Career Management talks about organizational layoffs, downsizing, and rightsizing in today's organizational climate. It also addresses the changing nature of work and of organizations.
- Chapter 7 is devoted to the subject of Performance Management and discusses how to handle and conduct performance reviews, how to give and receive constructive feedback, and performance management and the law.
- Chapter 5 The Selection Process addresses the uses of job analysis, the factors used in choosing selection procedures, and the advantages and disadvantages of the different selection procedures.

Realistic Emphasis on Participative Management

The traditional way of managing people is a thing of the past. Managers are now required and many professors are being asked to teach students the "soft skills," such as managing a diverse workforce, how to team-build and utilize work teams, and how to develop employees' potential, both personally and professionally.

Today's business world needs participative managers to address these growing issues.

- Chapter 12 Work Redesign for Productivity and Quality Improvement includes such topics as quality circles, total quality management, the work team, employee empowerment, and reengineering.
- Chapter 11 is devoted to Employee Training and Development and covers how to maintain competitiveness and improve productivity by using training and development techniques.

Driving Forces that Impact the Complexities of HRM

Issues such as management and labor relations, current career patterns, and providing a safe, healthy working environment are the driving forces that affect the complexities of HRM. Learning how to balance the need for the company's success with the need for the employees' success is a skill that is in demand. We live and work in a complex world that needs managers equipped to solve these complexities in a positive, effective way.

- Two chapters concentrate on unions—Chapter 14 discusses the organizing process, while Chapter 15 covers negotiating and administering an agreement.
- Career development and the changing career patterns of today are discussed in Chapter 6 Career Management.
- Chapter 13 Safety and Health covers current topics such as repetitive stress injuries, drug/alcohol use, stress, and indoor air pollution, as well as OSHA regulations, employee assistance programs, maintaining a safe and healthful workplace by empowering, rewarding, training, and testing employees.
- The Family and Medical Leave Act of 1993 is covered in Chapter 10 Employee Benefits.

Social and Cultural Contexts

No HRM textbook would be complete today without addressing the issues of the social and cultural contexts in which we work. The workplace is now leaner and more efficient, more diverse, and more open to societal changes and challenges than ever before. These social and cultural contexts are the threads interwoven throughout our organization and our workforces.

- Alternative work arrangements such as flextime, shiftwork, the compressed work week, and telecommuting are discussed in Chapter 16 Employee Rights.
- Affirmative action, race discrimination, and other discrimination laws are discussed in Chapter 2 Employment Discrimination Laws, as well as women and the glass ceiling and sexual harassment in the workplace.
- The issue of workplace romance is covered in Chapter 16 Employee Rights.
- Cultural diversity is integrated into every chapter and in "Intercultural Issues in HRM" box.

Organized in a Simple and Efficient Way

The book is organized into five parts. Part 1 explores the context of human resources by addressing what human resource management is, the major discrimination laws that play a critical role at work, and issues and events that affect careers.

Chapter 1 introduces the student to the functions of HRM, evaluating the external and internal environments, determining the goals of HRM activities, the roles of the HRM professional, and the different careers available to the HRM student.

Chapter 2 details the employment discrimination laws and the effects of each on the workforce, the facts an HRM manager needs to know about proving a discrimination case, and other topical issues such as sexual harassment, the glass ceiling, and race and job loss.

Chapter 3 addresses the issue of planning for HR managers. Why is planning important? What are a company's capabilities and needs? These issues and a look at jobs in the future are covered.

Part 2 covers staffing, and examines recruitment, selection, and career management.

Chapter 4 discusses recruitment practices, who to recruit, internal and external recruitment sources, and also includes appendices on the job search and how to write a cover letter and resume.

Chapter 5 details the selection process, job analysis, typical selection steps, and miscellaneous selection devices.

Chapter 6 covers career management for the HRM professional. Issues such as why career patterns have changed, the different career stages, and organizational advancement systems are addressed.

Part 3 addresses the subject of evaluation and compensation.

Chapter 7 discusses performance management and measures, performance appraisal problems and solutions, performance feedback, performance reviews, and performance management and the law.

Chapter 8 covers compensation administration, compensation laws, maintaining equity among employees, conducting a job evaluation, and alternatives to traditional pay structures.

Chapter 9 details the pay-for-performance plans and why companies use them, the kinds of and alternatives to PFP plans, and the different kinds of incentive plans.

Chapter 10 discusses benefits, and covers legally required benefits, pension and health insurance programs, the different kinds of health insurance programs, miscellaneous employee benefits, and paid time off benefits.

Part 4 concentrates on improving the workplace.

Chapter 11 employee training and development discusses what training and development is and why it's important, current trends and practices, training techniques and principles, on-the-job and off-the-job training techniques, and evaluating the success of training programs.

Chapter 12 looks at work redesign for productivity improvement and alternatives to the classical work design model such as quality circles, work teams, TQM, and reengineering. A special section addresses the question, "Is work redesign the answer?"

Chapter 13 covers safety and health in the workplace. The laws concerning these issues are presented, as well as discussions about reducing workplace accidents, current safety and health issues in the workplace, and workplace violence.

Part 5 concerns maintaining effective employee-employer relationships.

Chapter 14 on unions discusses the organizing process. A brief history of unions is presented, as well as tactics to gain more members, manager's attitudes toward unions, and how companies become unionized.

Chapter 15 covers negotiating and administering agreements with unions. Information on negotiating and administering the union contract, current trends in contract negotiations, and developing harmonious relationships between labor and management is provided.

Chapter 16 details employee rights by looking at terminations, contracts, personnel files, searches and seizures, workplace romance, employee disciplinary procedures, and alternative work hours.

Features that Differentiate this Book

Human Resource Management: A Practical Approach covers all aspects of HRM, and focuses on the **practical approach** and emphasizes how human resource issues are relevant to everyone within an organization. Written in a **simple, conversational tone,** the text emphasizes the relevance of the material to employees, job applicants, managers and supervisors—not just future human resource managers—allowing students to answer the important question: **"How is this material relevant to me?"**

This textbook is **shorter** and more succinct. **Sixteen chapters** focus exclusively on the basics of HRM without distracting information from other disciplines such as economics, finance, or marketing. The textbook covers what an HRM professional needs to know, as well as information the consumer of HRM can apply to his or her own experience.

Chapter 1 immediately involves students in **real-life human resources situations** with its coverage of current topics and challenges. The historical information has been placed in an appendix for professors to cover in class or assign as outside reading. **Core concepts** are also identified at the beginning of each chapter, with a series of questions and then revisited at the end of each chapter for use as class discussions or individual team exercises.

The book covers a number of pedagogical techniques that help the reader to understand and apply the information. Each chapter begins with a **brief case** that provides a context for the core concepts and raises relevant questions. An **experiential exercise** is provided at the end of each chapter to enable readers to apply the concepts they have learned and to develop their critical thinking skills.

In addition to an opening chapter case and an end-of-chapter exercise, each chapter contains **numerous in-text examples** of how human resources are managed in different companies and by different individuals.

The following **boxed materials** are throughout each chapter:

- "Intercultural Issues in HRM" boxes highlight intercultural and diversity concerns

- "Tales From the Trenches" present actual stories from the work world of human resources and management in general
- "Your Turn" is a fresh, new feature that gives students a chance to evaluate how *they* would manage a situation or complete a task

Instructional Support Materials That Make a Difference

Instructor's Manual/Test Bank/Transparency Masters

Written by Edwin Arnold of Auburn University at Montgomery, the Instructor's Manual includes detailed lecture outlines, answers to the questions for discussion, suggestions for teaching concepts, research project suggestions, and detailed teaching notes for the experiential exercises written by the author himself. In addition, 100 transparency masters of the figures and tables from the textbook are included.

The Test Bank, written by Amit Shah of Frostburg State University, contains more than 50 questions per chapter, including true/false, multiple-choice, short-answer, and essay questions. A computerized test bank is available in IBM 3.5", Mac, and Windows versions. Special functions allow an instructor to add, delete, edit or scramble questions (to create up to 99 versions of the same test). A phone-in testing service for creating test masters is also available with a 48-hour turnaround period.

Overhead Transparencies

Charles Beem of Bucks County Community College has written and prepared fifty original overhead transparencies for use in the classroom. These two-color acetates provide additional classroom resource materials for reinforcing and expanding on textual materials. The teaching notes to accompany the acetates are included in the IM-TB-TM.

Videos

Demonstrating the breadth of the video program in the human resource series, eight videos are now available for classroom viewing. Each video contains several class-tested questions by Amit Shah of Frostburg State University to encourage discussion and thought.

University National Bank—A very innovative financial institution, University National Bank follows progressive human resource policies and has a compensation policy, organizational structure, and employee benefits to enable employees to provide excellent service. (10 minutes)

Wainwright Industries, Inc.—This video shows how a company transformed itself to win the coveted Malcolm Baldrige National Quality Award in 1994. (10 minutes)

Valassis Communication, Inc.—This video focuses on Valassis' application of teams through the organization, its strict JIT system, and communications within and among teams. (10 minutes)

Harley-Davidson—Labor and management come to the realization that they have to work together and this video shows how they made the transition to a cooperative management/labor climate. (10 minutes)

Fighting for the Rights of Workers with Disabilities—How an AFMSME employee who is legally blind copes with her workday and counsels others with disabilities. She also talks about issues of managing those with special needs. (18 minutes)

ADA . . . The Time to Understand—An AFSCME (Association of Federal, State, County, and Municipal Workers) profile of one compelling case in North Dakota of a mentally disabled county employee tormented by his co-workers and supervisor. (18 minutes)

Southwest Airlines People Department—Southwest has a different management style, including a manager who calls his style "Management by Fooling Around." He feels it is better to rule by love than by fear and instills confidence in his employees by treating them as people instead of as employees. (10 minutes)

La Madeleine French Bakery—The story of how La Madeleine treats its employees and the community like family and supports both in tangible and intangible ways. The owner extends his open arms philosophy of managing people to his community by weekly trips to Dallas to feed the homeless freshly made French onion soup and croissants. (10 minutes)

Acknowledgments

I would like to acknowledge the help of many individuals in this project. In terms of The Dryden Press staff, I would like to thank Ruth Rominger, who served as acquisitions editor, for her encouragement and support, and Dona Hightower, developmental editor, who also deserves much credit for her advice, encouragement, support, and most importantly, for her listening ear. John Weimeister, acquisitions editor, also helped oversee the end of the process. I would also like to thank the people who worked so hard on the production side of this book, namely Betsy Cummings, project editor; Carlyn Hauser, production manager; David Day, senior art director; and Annette Coolidge, picture and literary rights editor. Without their support and expertise this book would not have become a reality.

The assistance and help of the following reviewers and survey respondents is also greatly appreciated:

Reviewers:

Edwin Arnold
Auburn University

Charles Beem
Bucks County Community College

Ralph Braithwaite
University of Hartford

Win Chesney
St Louis Community College—Meramec

Elizabeth Cooper
University of Rhode Island

Satish Deshpande
Western Michigan University

Jean Forray
University of Massachusetts

Thomas Lloyd
Westmoreland County Community College

David Murphy
Madisonville Community College

John Pappalardo
Keene State College

Pamela Pommerenke
Michigan State University

Survey Participants:

Ellen J. Frank
Southern Connecticut State University

Gary C. Raffaele
University of Texas at San Antonio

Alan Cabelly
Portland State University

Sandy J. Wayne
University of Illinois at Chicago

Jon Monat
CSU Long Beach

Jerry B. Madkins
Tarleton State University

Yohannan T. Abraham
Southwest Missouri State University

Jeff Mello
Golden Gate University

Walter E. Greene
University of Texas—Pan American

Edwin C. Leonard, Jr.
Indiana University—Purdue University at Fort Wayne

Lynn Hoffman
University of Northern Colorado

Charles J. Capps III
Sam Houston State University

Vicki Kaman
Colorado State University

Marcus Sandver
Ohio State University

Acknowledgments are also due to my teachers, students, colleagues, and friends who encouraged me during the writing of this book. A very special thanks to Jennifer Dennis and Karen Wagster for their hard work during the development of this book. While I cannot list all of these individuals by name due to space limitations, I would like to single out two persons in particular: Fred (Fischel) Mael and Rabbi Chona Muser. Both of these individuals have been the source of much help, encouragement, and advice in all of my life endeavors and I owe them a great deal.

Last, but not least, I wish to thank my wife, Sharon, and my children, David, Anne, and Yonah for their companionship and love.

Contents

part 1

The Context of Human Resources

chapter 1 An Introduction To Human Resource Management

Core Concepts

After reading this chapter, you should be capable of:

1. Identifying the major areas of human resource management.
2. Understanding the factors that affect human resource management practices and programs.
3. Identifying major human resource management goals and their determinants.
4. Explaining what a human resource manager job entails.

Opening Case

Consider the following situation. Sandy Sanazaro is being interviewed for a financial analyst job. After the interviewer introduces herself to Sandy, she asks her the following question, "Tell me about a time when you were under a great deal of stress. How did you handle the situation? What did you learn from it?" Following several similar questions, she asks Sandy whether she is married, single, divorced, or engaged. After about an hour of questioning, she says to Sandy, "I have one last question—What starting salary do you expect?" How would you answer these questions? Are all of these questions legal?

Now consider this situation. Douglas Weir is supervising an employee, Phil Stone, who has been working for the company for one month. So far, Phil has made numerous errors, such as billing the wrong client, erasing an important file, and turning in a report late. For the first few weeks, Douglas assumed it would just take a while until Phil caught on. Now he is beginning to realize that experience alone may not improve Phil's performance. Douglas has decided that he must meet with Phil to discuss these problems, in order to try to improve Phil's performance. How should Douglas go about giving Phil the feedback? If Phil's performance does not improve, can Douglas discipline him? Can he fire Phil? Are there restrictions on Douglas' ability to discipline or terminate him?

Now consider this situation. Tonya Powell has been given the responsibility of teaching new employees how to use a computerized cutting machine. The last employee to use this machine ended up breaking it, and the repair work was quite expensive. How should Tonya instruct the new employees? Do some training techniques work better than others?

Finally, what would you do in this situation? You have been with your company for about one month. Three days after you began working, the area manager approached you and said, "Hey, how about a drink after work?" You politely answered, "No, thanks, I'm busy tonight." The invitation for a drink after work was repeated each day, until yesterday, when the area manager became more persistent, and said, "If you want to keep your job, I'm going to insist you go out for a drink with me so that we can get to know each other better—know what I mean?" You wonder whether this is considered sexual harassment under the law; if so, what do you need to do to stop the area manager's behavior?

All of these situations describe common human resource management (HRM) problems faced by managers, supervisors, employees, and job applicants. These, and other issues, are obviously important for both employees and organizations. What did you think was the best strategy in each situation? You will learn more about these situations throughout the book. The remainder of this chapter is divided into three sections. First, we will define more precisely what HRM is. After that, we will present a model of HRM, which will provide an overview of different HRM activities, key HRM goals, and the factors that affect HRM activities and goals. Finally, you will read about careers in human resource management. We begin first with a definition of human resources managment (HRM).

What Is Human Resource Management?

Human resource management (HRM) may be defined as programs, policies, and practices for managing an organization's workforce.[1] Consider, for example, a company that manufactures electronic devices, such as VCRs, televisions, and radios. Employees must be hired by the company and then trained in specific areas where they lack expertise. Production workers, for example, may need to be instructed in how to use various tools and machines in the manufacturing processes. In return for their employment, the workers must be paid an appropriate wage. The company must also provide certain required benefits to the employees, such as workers' compensation (in case they become injured as a result of the job) and unemployment compensation (if they are terminated). The company may also offer additional benefits as well, such as health insurance. During the course of employment, workers are likely to receive feedback on their performance, particularly if their performance is below expectations. At some point in time, top management may introduce a productivity improvement program, which changes the way in which the work is performed. For example, rather than having each worker perform one simple task (for example, packing the product as it comes off the production line), the productivity improvement program may have workers responsible for a complete order (for example, taking the order, setting up the machinery, packing the product, and so forth). Some employees eventually may be promoted to the position of shift supervisor, and from there to a managerial job. Other employees may be terminated by the organization for poor performance. Certain employees and job applicants may feel they were discriminated against, and file a complaint with the Equal Employment Opportunity Commission (EEOC). The Occupational Safety and Health Agency (OSHA) may conduct an inspection of the facilities and issue citations charging violations of safety conditions, which the company will need to address.

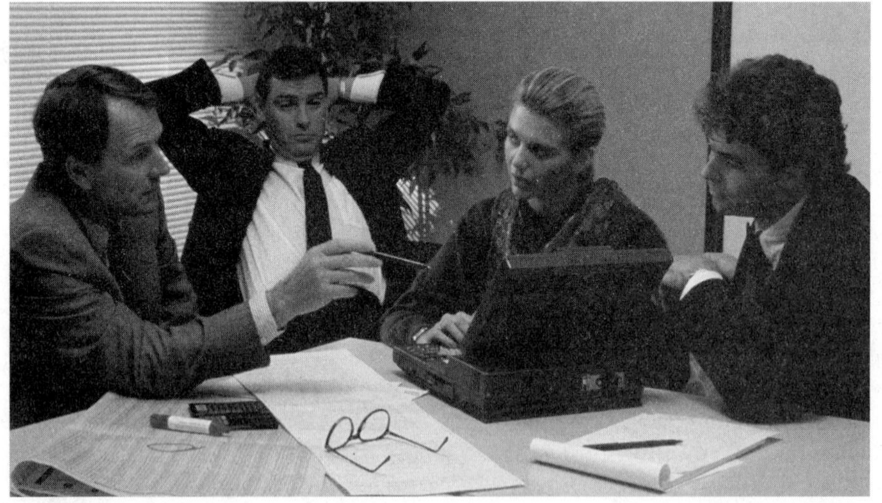

A productivity program is being discussed and modified by the managers of this company using a laptop computer. The advent of technology allows presentations, graphs, and charts to be created and updated as well as displayed to widen the employee audience when human resource issues arise.

All of the activities described are included in what this book calls human resource management, or in previous years, personnel. While most medium and large size organizations have a specific department responsible for human resources, many small organizations do not. The company just described, for example, may employ one or two individuals who are responsible for general administrative issues, including human resource management.

At this point you may be thinking, "Well, my major is marketing (or finance, management information systems, accounting, management science, or even liberal arts), and I certainly don't *ever* plan on being an HRM manager!" If that is what you are thinking, you are probably right—most companies only have one HRM employee for every 100 or so employees. But HRM staff are *not* the only people responsible for HRM programs, policies, practices, and decisions. Consider, for a moment, your current job or a job you have had in the past. Who was responsible for hiring, pay raises, performance management, and training? In most cases, the supervisor or manager was responsible—not an HRM staff person. Supervisors and managers, then, play an extremely important role in HRM. Even if you are not an HRM manager, then, you are likely to be responsible for HRM activities. Supervisors and managers who have a good grasp of HRM programs and practices will make much better HRM decisions, which in turn will enable them to be more effective in their jobs.

Now you might be saying to yourself, "I don't plan to be a supervisor or manager of any kind. I'd rather not be responsible for any subordinates. So how does a book on HRM pertain to me?" The answer to this question goes back to the situations presented in the beginning of this chapter. Remember how the first situation involved interview questions? What about the potential sexual harassment incident described in the fourth situation? Even employees without any supervisory responsibility face these situations. In that way, HRM affects all of us, regardless of whether we are HRM managers, line supervisors or managers, or employees. Regardless of what job you have, HRM affects you.

Now that you know what HRM is, you will learn more about the different areas of HRM, as well as the issues that affect HRM activities and HRM goals. As you can see in Figure 1.1, HRM activities may be divided into the following categories:

1. Planning
2. Staffing
3. Evaluating and Compensating
4. Improving the organization
5. Maintaining effective employer-employee relationships.

We will describe each of these categories in greater detail next.

Figure 1.1 **Model of Human Resource Management**

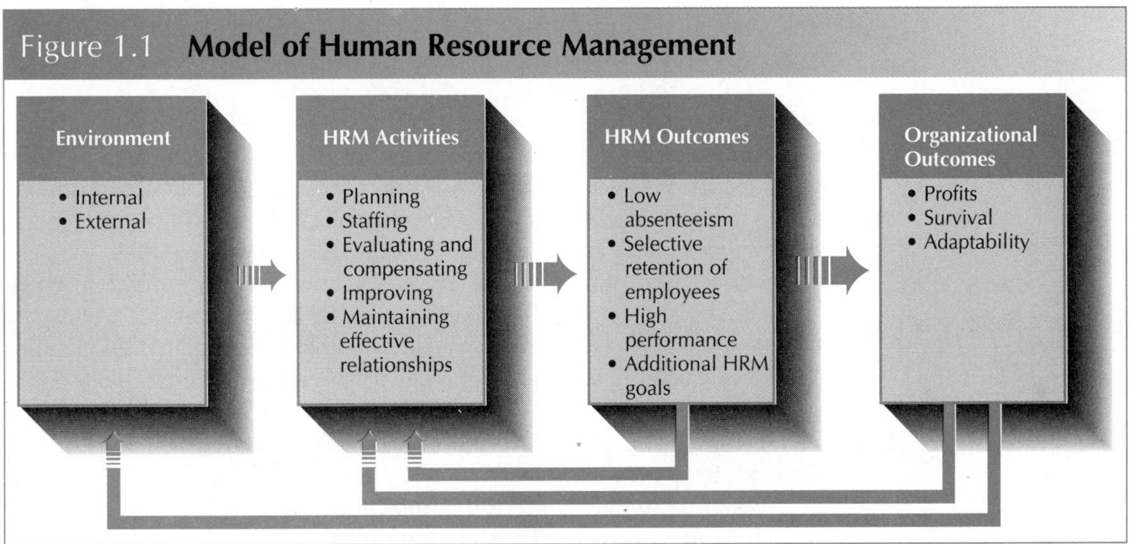

Box 1.1 The Ethics of International Human Resource Management

Although U.S. workers may suffer when companies manufacture products in other countries, U.S. consumers are happy because productions costs are usually lower in places such as Mexico, China, and India, making the products less expensive to purchase. But lower costs are often attained in an ethically questionable way, because laws that protect workers in the United States are often nonexistent in other countries of the world. Consider, for example, a plant in Mexico, where the workers (all of whom were women) worked with vats containing the poisonous environmental pollutants PCBs. Their only protection from the chemicals? Rubber gloves, which did little to protect their arms and faces from being splashed with the liquids. The children borne to these workers often had birth defects, including Down's syndrome, webbed feet, and deformed hands. In many other countries, children are often employed in jobs requiring heavy physical labor.

Some U.S. businesses are beginning to take action. Reebok, the athletic shoe company, recently stopped using a Pakistani contractor that had been employing workers under 14 years old; and, the U.S. government is encouraging companies to voluntarily adopt guidelines for foreign companies in regard to HRM practices.

Some consumer groups are taking notice as well. One such group is urging Asian rug makers to use a stamp to identify products that are not made by children; another group is urging Starbucks (a coffee company) to improve work conditions for workers in Guatemala.

Would you pay more for products if they were produced under humane conditions? Would you boycott a firm that does business with a plant in another country that mistreats its workers even if you paid 10 percent less for the goods? What if the goods were 25 percent cheaper?

Source: Adapted from G. P. Zachary, "The Outlook: Multinationals Can Aid Some Foreign Workers," *The Wall Street Journal,* April 24, 1995, A1; and M. Butler, and M. Teagarden, "Strategic Management of Worker Health and Safety Issues in Mexico's Maquiladora Industry," in *Readings and Cases in International Human Resource Management,* ed. M. Mendenhall and G. Oddou, (Cincinnati: South-Western, 1995), pp. 418–432.

Human Resource Activities

Planning

If there is one aspect in today's business world that you can count on, it is constant change (or, as a colleague of the author says it, "The only certainty is uncertainty"). In turn, this necessitates careful HRM planning. Consider, for example, the United States Army. Like most organizations of the 1990s, the army must operate under cost constraints, though, in this case, the constraints are imposed by Congress and the president. Unlike many other organizations, the U.S. Army can only guess where its next "business" (that is, military action) will come from and what the nature of that "business" will be. HRM planning with regard to the types of employees needed and their job requirements is therefore critical. For instance, if a major military action is fought on desert terrain, and the available troops cannot operate in this venue, failure may result. Another reason that HRM planning is critical to the army is because technology plays a major role in military operations. For example, some military strategists predict that wars in the future will involve very few, if any, actual soldiers. Instead, military action in the future may be conducted by technicians armed only with computers, in positions hundreds or even thousands of miles away from the front lines. Think of the implications for human resources under this futuristic scenario. First, how many military personnel will be needed? Perhaps only a few thousand "combat troops" would be necessary. Conversely, perhaps hundreds of thousands of computer technicians will be needed. Second, what types of skills and abilities will the soldiers of the 21st century need? Rather than physical fitness, marksmanship, and courage, it may be that high-level computer, analytical, and tactical skills will become most important. In essence, soldiers in the 21st century may need many of the skills and abilities that a *general* from the 20th century needed. From an HRM perspective, the army must engage in careful planning to ensure that sufficient numbers of the properly trained staff will be available at all times. When you think about it, this is no small task.

Finally, HRM planning is not just something that organizations need to do. You, as an employee, need to plan for the future to ensure that you have the necessary abilities and experiences to succeed as your job and career change. In today's world, no employee can sit by passively; you must do your own HRM planning.

Staffing

Staffing refers to recruiting, hiring, promotions, and the termination processes. If you have ever been hired for a job, you probably completed an application, responded to interview questions (perhaps some that were used in the first situation described in the beginning of this chapter), and maybe even took a drug test. Although you may have been completely unaware of it, the company that hired you

Box 1.2 Changing the Human Resource Management Function at Lands' End

Tales from the Trenches

Do you like wearing khaki pants, oxford shirts, and loafer shoes? If you do, chances are that you have heard of Lands' End. A 5,000-employee company headquartered in a small town in Wisconsin, it is now the top specialty-catalog business in the United States. Up until a few years ago, the company was run much like a small, family-owned business. But in 1991, the founder and chairman, Gary Comer, hired William End, formerly a manager at L.L. Bean, as the new chief executive officer (CEO). End immediately began implementing many new HRM policies and practices, such as the team concept, formal performance management systems, and extensive employee training. Employees' reactions to many of these new programs, however, were negative. With regard to the team concept approach, the number of meetings increased, so much so that some employees protested that they no longer had time to do their work. Employees in the monogramming department reported being coerced to increase their productivity, even though they were doing an excellent job. Other employees felt that the new performance management system, which involved assigning numerical ratings to employees, undermined the personal nature of management-employee relationships. Three years later, End was asked to resign, and Michael Smith, who had worked for his entire career at Lands' End, was promoted to CEO. While many of the HRM programs that End introduced have since been eliminated, the new pension plan, as well as other new benefit programs, have been retained. End believes that the company felt threatened by change, and therefore backed away from the new HRM programs. The company apparently believed that the changes were undermining the company's culture, which had been quite successful so far. Who do you think was right?

Source: Adapted from G. Patterson, "Bad Fit." *The Wall Street Journal,* April 3, 1995, A1, A4.

may have also contacted some of your previous supervisors. Do you recall any other steps in the hiring process, such as taking a paper-and-pencil or computer-administered test? Consider again the U.S. Army. Given that the U.S. Army has hundreds of thousands of applicants for jobs each year, the army must make hundreds of hiring decisions each day. Moreover, the army must decide what job each qualified candidate is best suited for. Not surprisingly, then, the army uses an objective, computer-based test to facilitate these decisions.

So far, we have emphasized a very large organization. But even small organizations must pay close attention to staffing decisions. While one poorly qualified employee will have a relatively small effect on an organization as large as the U.S. Army, the same poorly qualified employee will have a much larger impact on an organization that only has ten employees. Small organizations, then, must be even more careful about their staffing procedures.

As you will see in subsequent chapters, there are a variety of recruiting sources to generate job applicants and selection methods to choose the most qualified candidate. Regardless of whether you are a job applicant or the hiring manager, it will be helpful for you to know the advantages and disadvantages of different recruiting sources and the strengths and weaknesses of various selection devices.

Promotions and terminations are increasingly important HRM issues in the 1990s. Compared to previous years, promotions are increasingly rare. Companies are attempting to refocus employees' attention away from advancement and toward other rewards, such as interesting work and learning new skills. At the same time, given frequent mergers, changes in business conditions, and various other issues, companies often end up reducing the size of their workforces. Being terminated is a far more common experience today than it was 15 or 20 years ago. Whether you are a supervisor or manager in charge of making promotion or firing decisions, or an employee who will be affected by those decisions, it is in your interest to learn more about those aspects of the staffing process as well.

Like all HRM decisions, staffing decisions have legal ramifications. If applicants or employees feel they have been discriminated against in recruiting, hiring, promotions, layoffs, or any other staffing decisions, they have the right to file a complaint and pursue a lawsuit. For this reason, companies have become extremely cautious whenever they make a staffing decision. You will read about the basic HRM discrimination laws in Chapter 2.

Evaluating and Compensating

Organizations evaluate their employees for several different reasons, including determining pay raises, giving feedback, and assessing training programs. Organizations compensate employees through wages and salaries, bonuses, and benefits, such as health insurance, vacation time, and pension programs. These activities are obviously important for achieving HRM goals. Without evaluations, for example, employees have a difficult time knowing how they are performing compared to company expectations, or where they can make improvements. Recall the second situation that was described in the beginning of this chapter. How would you have given performance feedback to Phil? If you have had to give performance feedback to a poorly performing employee, you know that it can be a stressful and difficult experience. Have you ever been given performance feedback by your supervisor? How did you act during the feedback session? Many employees are uncomfortable receiving feedback, too. Chapter 7 provides some suggestions for how you can effectively give feedback to others as well as get helpful performance feedback.

Everyone has heard of lottery ticket winners who became instant millionaires, yet said they would continue working in the same job. Although a significant number of employees at Microsoft are millionaires as a result of stock options, they continue to work. There is obviously more to working than just the pay. But for most of us, who are not millionaires, our compensation is extremely important. Chapter 8 describes how companies determine your base pay and offers some suggestions for how you as an employee might negotiate your salary. Chapter 9 discusses some of the programs companies use to link some amount of pay to the employee's performance. As you will see in that chapter, some of these programs are very rewarding to both the employees and the organization. Finally, Chapter 10 discusses issues related to nonmonetary compensation, namely, employee benefits. The benefits your company provides can be extremely valuable to you, even if they are not in the form of direct cash.

Improving the Organization

In today's world, organizations are constantly on the lookout for ways to improve the organization, including employee training, implementing work redesign programs, and enhancing safety and health in the workplace. Organizations must constantly improve themselves for several reasons. First, technology is always changing, which in turn requires that employees receive training for these new procedures and equipment. Second, new ideas regarding organizational productivity are constantly emerging. Third, competition from other organizations forces companies to improve continually. Finally, failure to maintain a safe and healthy workplace may lead to legal sanctions, negative publicity, increased accidents, and employee time off from work.

Recall the third situation described in the beginning of this chapter. What would you recommend that Tonya do to train workers? If you have ever been responsible for a company training program, you know that there are many different approaches to this subject. More and more companies are now moving to computer-based techniques, which is changing the way that training is being conducted. Productivity improvement programs are being implemented in many organizations today, often with major implications for jobs and workers. Finally, many organizations now pay closer attention to safety and health matters, as the costs associated with injured and ill workers have steadily increased over the years.

Maintaining Effective Employer-Employee Relationships

Maintaining effective employer-employee relationships is important to companies for two reasons. First, employees who are dissatisfied are more likely to quit. If they are not unionized, dissatisfied employees may seek out a union to represent them, a move that most organizations will oppose. If they are already unionized, the employees may file many grievances and in some cases even go on strike. In short, poor employer-employee relationships can create many problems for the organization. Second, there are dozens of laws pertaining to the employer-employee relationship. For example, can your employer listen in on your phone calls? Can your employer terminate you because you are having a romantic relationship at work? Do you have the right to examine your personnel file? If your department or company is unionized, additional regulations exist that the organization must comply with. For these reasons, maintaining effective employer-employee relationships is an important aspect of HRM. Do you remember the fourth situation described in the beginning of this chapter? In that incident, the manager threatened to terminate an employee who refused to go out after work for drinks. As you will see in various chapters, such behavior can lead to much trouble for both the manager and the organization.

In sum, human resource management covers a wide range of activities. Regardless of whether you are an employee, supervisor, or manager, it behooves you to become knowledgeable in this area. We now turn to an overview of some of the environmental factors that affect an organization's HRM activities.

Environmental Factors

As shown in Figure 1.1, environmental factors may be divided into internal and external categories. The external environment refers to conditions that are outside of the organization, including business conditions, workforce characteristics, laws, unions, and technology. The internal environment refers to those factors that are within the organization and under its control, such as the work structure and business strategy. Although many external and internal factors are discussed in greater detail in Chapter 3, some preliminary comments will be made next.

External Environment

HRM activities are highly affected by the external environment. One of the primary factors affecting HRM activities is business conditions. You probably have heard the term "globalization of business" many times. So it will not surprise you that the international nature of the workplace has many implications for HRM. For example, consider the experience of Gillette Company, which recently introduced a worldwide stock plan for its employees. Much to its surprise, the company discovered that what works in the United States may not work in other countries. Employees in Belgium were prevented from participating because of national wage controls. Workers in China and Brazil were barred from the program because of laws prohibiting the purchase of stocks listed on the New York Stock Exchange. Mexican employees rejected the plan because stocks are viewed as risky, and cash is favored over investments.[2]

Workforce characteristics is another external factor that affects HRM activities. As described in greater detail in Chapter 3, profound changes are occurring in the composition of the U.S. workforce in terms of race, ethnicity, gender, and age.[3] In turn, these changes have many implications for HRM activities. As an example, what would you conclude if a subordinate you were giving feedback to kept staring down at the ground? You kept trying to make eye contact with him, but he continued to look at the ground. Would you conclude that he was embarrassed or that he was hiding something? In most Western countries, failure to make eye contact is viewed as a sign of insincerity or embarrassment. In other cultures, particularly the Asian culture, people are taught to lower their eyes when talking with a superior; it would be considered disrespectful to make eye contact with one's supervisor.[4]

As shown in Figure 1.2, the workforce is also changing in terms of educational levels, skill levels, and representation by unions. While the increasingly highly educated, skilled, and nonunionized workforce presents advantages for HRM managers, it also provides for challenges. One major trend is that employees are becoming more independent and motivated by the opportunity to take risks, and they are less interested in becoming a manager and moving up the corporate ladder.[5]

Laws comprise another external factor that has a major effect on HRM practices. As you will see, there are laws that protect employees from discrimination, laws that protect employees from potential abuses of work conditions (such as wages that are too low), laws that provide employees with the right to unionize, and laws that protect employees from health and safety hazards on the job. Undoubtedly, these laws have a significant impact on HRM activities.

Unions also have a major effect on HRM practices. The possibility of a union has a significant effect on an organization's HRM practices; for example, the nonunionized organization may maintain relatively high wages and benefits so that workers are not tempted to seek out a collective bargaining agreement. A company that has a union (a characteristic of the internal environment) often must use a much different approach to HRM issues than a company without a union. For example, most unionized organizations base HRM decisions far more on seniority than organizations that are not unionized.

Finally, as mentioned earlier, technology often has a major effect on HRM practices. The production facility of yesterday, for instance, relied far more on the sheer physical stamina and strength of its workforce than the highly automated production facility of today, which relies far more on mental abilities and teamwork. Many companies are forced to change the skills and abilities of their workforce accordingly. Barden Corporation, for example, purchased computerized numerical control (CNC) machines, which in turn required machine operators to possess knowledge of trigonometry and elementary computer programming. To ensure that employees were properly trained, the company developed an extensive apprenticeship program.[6]

Internal Environment

According to experts, one of the biggest revolutions in business today is changed thinking about organizational structure. Every business has at least contemplated eliminating the familiar departmentally based hierarchical structure with something quite different. The move away from the traditional organizational structure has many implications for HRM activities. As one example, when much of the hierarchy is removed, thereby eliminating many opportunities for promotion, how will workers continue to be motivated? As a second example, consider the responsibilities of the HRM department. If the organization no longer has a separate department for human resources, how might this change the HRM manager job? These are just two of the many issues that must be addressed when organizational structures change.[7]

An organization's business strategy also has major implications for HRM activities. Consider Cable & Wireless Communications, a company that sells

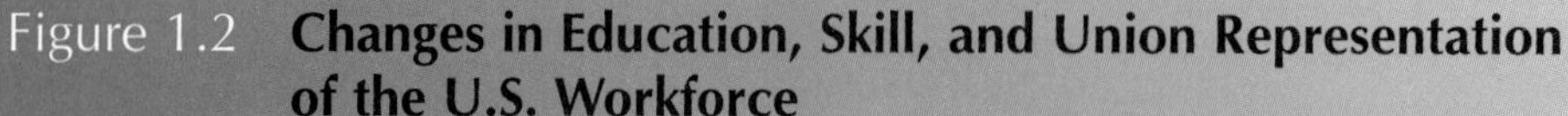

Figure 1.2 **Changes in Education, Skill, and Union Representation of the U.S. Workforce**

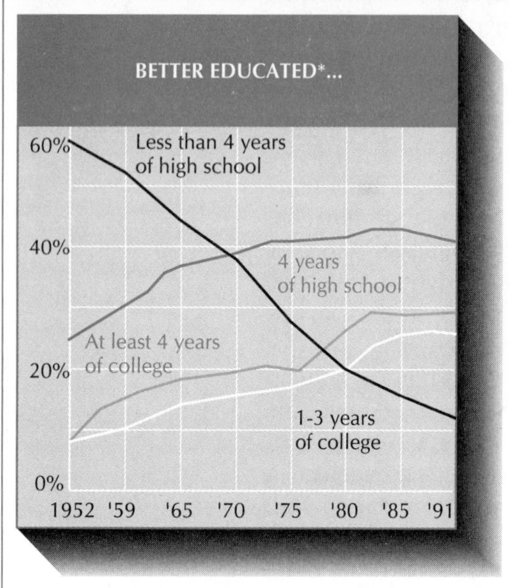

SOURCE: US BUREAU OF LABOR STATISTICS

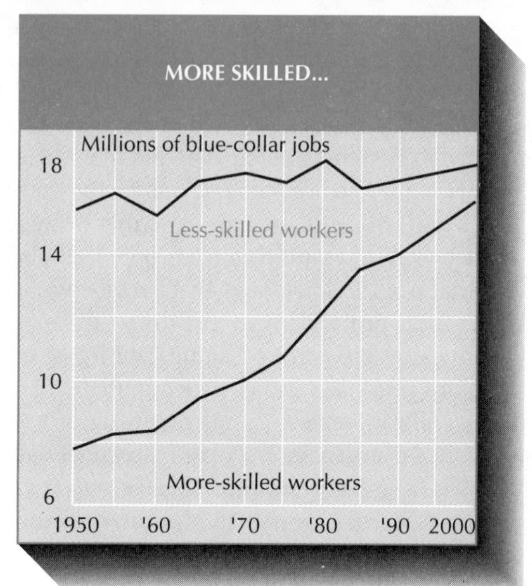

*1952-65 age 18 and older, 1970-91 age 25 through 64.

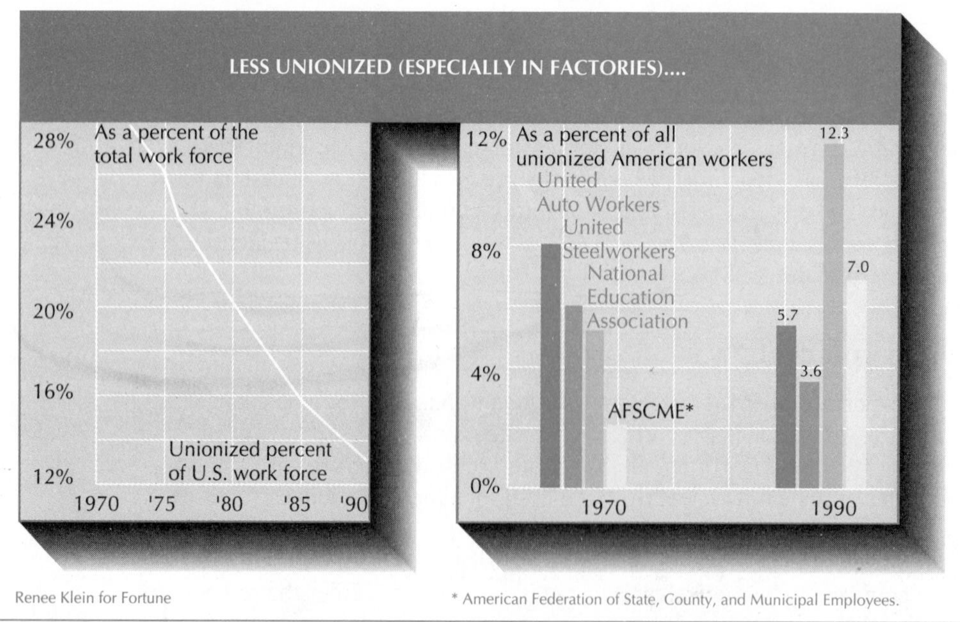

Renee Klein for Fortune

* American Federation of State, County, and Municipal Employees.

Source: M. Magnet. "The Truth About the American Worker," *Fortune,* May 4, 1992, 48–65.

long-distance telephone service to other businesses. For a variety of reasons, the company cannot compete on price, so it emphasizes customer service. As part of that business strategy, all sales personnel have the authority to determine the price at which will they sell, as well as control over budget decisions for advertising and trade shows. This enables sales staff to give personal attention to customers and to make the best decisions about pricing. Successful performance depends heavily on how well customers are handled, how successfully personal relationships are maintained, and how effective salespeople are in meeting the unique needs of the customers. Compare this to a very different company, Price/Costo, a nationwide chain of warehouse club stores. The company has a highly centralized purchasing department that carefully chooses one brand in each product category. Pricing decisions are made at the corporate office; individual stores have little discretion over pricing, because the company is competing over price. Successful employee performance at Price/Costo involves following directives, keeping costs down, and improving efficiency. Clearly the employee behaviors that are rewarded are going to be very different depending on the company, which in turn affects staffing, compensation, and training. Can you think of some ways in which HRM activities would differ in the two companies?[8]

In sum, an organization's internal and external environments have major effects on HRM practices. We now turn to consideration of HRM goals and objectives.

Goals of HRM Activities

As shown in Figure 1.1, HRM has a number of goals. We will discuss these goals in greater detail next.

Technology affects employees, which in turn affects human resource policies. The highly automated production facility and use of robotics relies more on mental abilities and teamwork than on physical strength and stamina. Technological progress has led to companies developing and investing in extensive apprenticeship and training programs for its employees.

Low Absenteeism

Workers who fail to attend work on an unscheduled basis are considered absent. Absenteeism poses a major problem for many organizations. To understand why, think about a time when one or two of your coworkers were absent from work. What were some of the problems you experienced? One of the biggest problems was that you probably had a heavier workload. You may also have had to work overtime, when you would rather have gone home. The company also is likely to be negatively affected—productivity may be lower and, in some cases, the company may still have to pay the absent employee. If the absenteeism becomes more frequent, the supervisor or manager may have to take time from work to counsel the employee. On the other hand, there may be some advantages for you and the company when workers are absent. When your coworker is away, you may be forced to perform that person's job, which helps develop your skills. Your organization may save money, since some workers will not be paid when they are absent. Finally, have you ever been absent from work to extend your weekend, take a longer vacation, or do some other pleasurable thing? Have you ever missed work because your children were on vacation from school? Absenteeism sometimes serves legitimate personal needs and may help reduce job-related stress and tension. In general, however, absenteeism creates more problems than it solves for organizations.[9]

Why are employees absent from work? Two basic factors determine whether an employee will have an unplanned absence:[10]

1. Motivation to attend work.
2. Ability to attend work.

Motivation, or willingness, to attend work is determined by several factors. Certain individuals and organizations have a strong set of norms regarding absenteeism; in some cases, those norms eschew absenteeism. In other cases, the norms may encourage high absenteeism. Other factors that contribute to motivation to attend work include organizational policies about absenteeism (companies that enforce penalties have lower absenteeism) and job satisfaction (more satisfied employees are more likely to show up for work).

Ability to attend work is generally affected by three things: illness, family responsibilities (such as a sick child), and transportation problems (for example, a car that won't operate). If you wish to find a reason for not coming to work, these are some of the most popular ones used!

In order to reduce absenteeism, organizations have used a number of different approaches. To increase workers' motivation to attend work, some organizations have introduced rewards, including participation in company lotteries, for workers with excellent attendance records. To improve workers' ability to attend work, organizations have implemented wellness programs, on-site day care centers that have facilities for sick children, and special transportation arrangements (for example, van pools).

Selective Retention of Employees

How do you think your organization would react if you decided to quit and go to work for another company? Do you think your supervisor would beg you to stay and offer you a large salary increase? Or would your supervisor shake your hand

and wish you good luck? Your answers to these questions probably depend on various considerations. Table 1.1 lists some circumstances under which your company would be disappointed if you left, as well as some circumstances under which your employer might be pleased with your departure.[11]

What about from your perspective as an employee? Will changing jobs be good or bad for you? Table 1.2 provides some thoughts about the positive and negative aspects of changing jobs.

Have you ever thought about changing jobs? If you had a job offer from another company, what factors did you consider in deciding whether to change jobs? Employees generally consider three basic factors when deciding to change jobs:[12]

1. Job satisfaction of current job.
2. Expected job satisfaction of alternative employment.
3. Investments.

Job satisfaction refers to how pleased you are with your present job. Although there are many aspects to job satisfaction, pay, coworkers, your supervisor, and the work itself are among the most important considerations. Obviously, the more satisfied you are, the less likely you are to change jobs.

Expected job satisfaction with alternative employment refers to how content you predict you will be with the other job opportunity; in other words, how satisfied do you think you will be with the new job? The less satisfied you believe you will be, the less likely you are to change jobs.

Table 1.1 **Circumstances under Which Turnover Is Good versus Bad for the Organization**

Turnover Is Good When	Turnover Is Bad When
1. Poor performer leaves.	1. Company must spend money hiring replacements.
2. New employees with innovative ideas can be hired.	2. Company must spend time and money training replacements.
3. New employees can be hired at lower wages and benefits.	3. Remaining employees become demoralized.
4. Remaining employees have new promotion opportunities.	4. Former employee takes away business from company.

Source: Adapted from P. Hom and R. Griffeth, *Employee Turnover,* (Cincinnati: South-Western, 1995).

Table 1.2 **Positive and Negative Effects for Employees Who Change Jobs**

Positive Effects	Negative Effects
1. Relocate to better community.	1. Forfeit seniority.
2. Obtain better job (higher pay, more interesting work, etc.).	2. May reduce value of pension.
3. Improve spouse's job.	3. Relocation costs.
4. Change may be energizing.	4. Transition stress.
	5. New job may not meet one's expectations.

Source: Adapted from P. Hom and R. Griffeth, *Employee Turnover,* (Cincinnati: South-Western, 1995).

Investments refer to various aspects of your job that are not sources of satisfaction but are factors that commit you to staying, such as seniority rights and pension plan considerations. A major investment may occur over time because psychologically many people are reluctant to change jobs simply because a known quantity (their present job) is often preferred over an unknown quantity (the alternative job). Unfortunately, then, people sometimes stay in a job they are dissatisfied with simply because they feel safer remaining rather than trying something new.

Organizations that wish to reduce turnover must be sure that they are appropriately rewarding their employees. If, for example, other organizations are paying more money, the company must either increase the salaries offered or provide other rewards that are valued by job applicants. A company may also need to consider how to increase employees' investments in the organization through pension plans and by promoting more from within the organization. Of course, some turnover is inevitable and may be beneficial for the organization. From both an employee's and a company's perspective, then, turnover is sometimes good and sometimes bad.

High Performance

High employee performance is obviously one of the most important goals of HRM, both from the organization's and the employee's viewpoint. Generally, when we think of performance, we tend to emphasize the *amount* of work produced (that is, the number of widgets or sales made). But in recent years, organizations have expanded their evaluation of performance to include two additional aspects: customer satisfaction and quality of work.

Box 1.3 What Does It Pay? Salaries for HRM Employees

Wondering what HRM employees earn? The pay ranges from about \$80,000 (for compensation and benefits directors) to about \$18,000 for training clerk-typists. But some HRM employees earn more than \$250,000! The HRM executive who earns that salary is a corporate human resources director for a financial services, merchandising, health care, or manufacturing company employing more than 25,000 workers and having more than \$1 billion in sales, assets, or net annual premiums. Furthermore, he or she possesses either an MBA or PhD and has at least 25 professional-level subordinates. In terms of experience, this highly paid professional has been in the field at least 25 years or more and works for a business located in a major metropolitan area such as Washington, D.C., or Los Angeles.

Besides which HRM job you have, several other factors will determine your pay level. The size of the company that you work for is likely to affect how much you earn; in general, HRM employees at the largest companies tend to make about 20 percent more than employees at smaller companies. Manufacturing companies also tend to pay more than nonmanufacturing companies. Among nonmanufacturing companies, educational organizations, food and beverage companies, and tobacco companies generally pay the lowest salaries. The region of the country you live in is yet another factor affecting pay—the lowest-paying regions are in the southern and Rocky Mountain states. Finally, if you are wondering whether going to school is worth it, the answer is yes. The higher your degree, the higher your salary is likely to be.

Source: Adapted from S. Langer, "Incomes Inch Up," *Personnel Journal,* January 1994, 67–71.

Let us begin by examining the factors that determine your performance in any given job. The three primary determinants of job performance are shown in Figure 1.3. We will discuss each of these in greater detail next.

Knowledge, Skills, and Abilities. Knowledge refers to the basic facts and information that is necessary to perform the job. As an example, consider the type of person needed to teach an algebra course. To be effective, the instructor would need to understand algebra. Similarly, to be effective, a lawyer would need to understand basic legal principles; a brain surgeon must have a thorough understanding of various anatomical and physiological reactions. For most jobs, then, a successful employee will need to know certain basic facts to be effective.[13]

Skills refer to psychomotor aptitudes, such as eye-hand coordination, physical agility, and manual dexterity. To be effective, a brain surgeon probably needs a high level of eye-hand coordination and finger dexterity. Other jobs that need skills include taxi drivers, professional athletes, and dentists.

Abilities are defined as the mental aptitude for such things as making decisions, communicating, reading, and interacting effectively with other people. To be successful as a trial lawyer, verbal communication ability is extremely important. To be an effective salesperson, the ability to persuade others is quite useful.

From an HRM perspective, the two most important activities to ensure adequate levels of knowledge, skills, and abilities (KSAs) are effective staffing systems

Figure 1.3 **Determinants of Employee Performance**

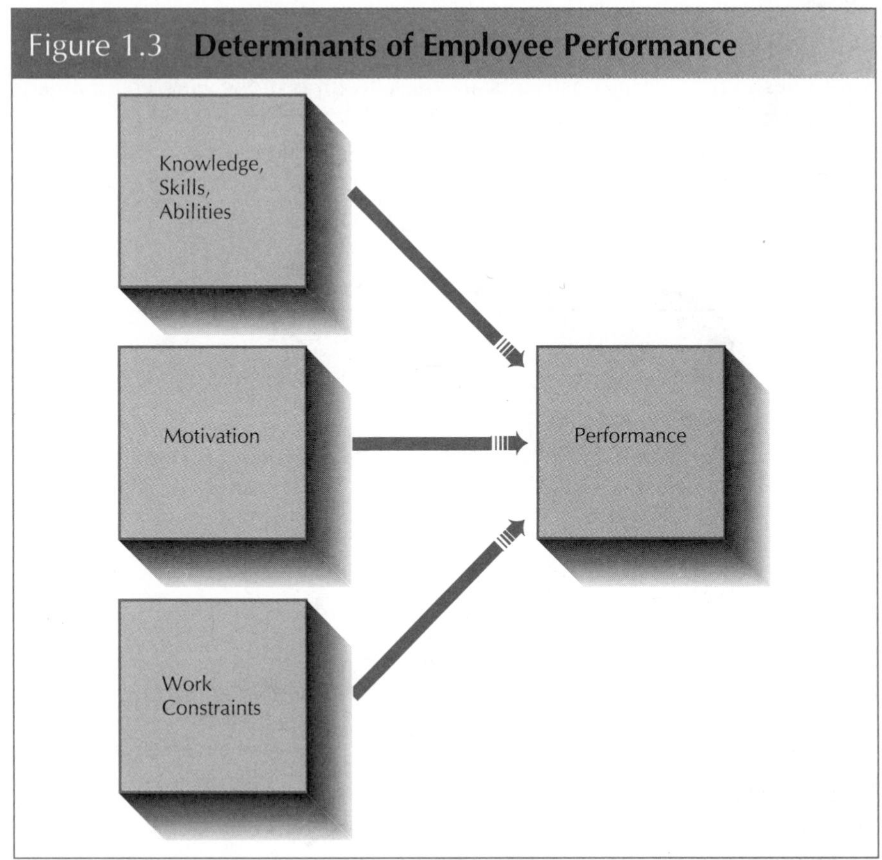

and training and development programs, topics that will be examined in much greater detail in subsequent chapters. What can you, as an employee, do in this regard? First, be sure that you choose a career and job that provides a good match with your KSAs. Second, be sure that you seek out training and development programs that will benefit your career. We now consider the second determinant of job performance—employee motivation.

Motivation. Even people with the necessary KSAs will be poor performers unless they are motivated, or willing, to devote the time and effort to the work. Table 1.3 lists a number of different rewards that might motivate an employee to achieve higher performance. Which of the aspects listed in Table 1.3 motivate you to be a productive worker? Does your job provide those rewards? Does your company provide other rewards? Because of the importance of motivation, a major HRM activity is developing effective employee reward programs.[14]

While many HRM programs focus on extrinsic (that is, financial) rewards to motivate employees, organizations are increasingly recognizing the importance of intrinsic rewards (such as the nature of the work itself) as a motivating factor. To understand the importance of intrinsic rewards, think about a college course you had that involved many interesting and fun assignments. Was that a course in which you were motivated to perform well? Now think about a course that involved dull and uninteresting assignments. Did you find it more difficult to do the work? In sum, both intrinsic and extrinsic rewards are useful motivators. Effective organizations use both intrinsic and extrinsic means to motivate their employees to be successful performers. From your perspective as an employee, it is critical that you choose a job involving work you enjoy.

Work Constraints. Work constraints are those features of the work environment that negatively affect job performance.[15] Table 1.4 provides a list of some of the more common work constraints that employees experience. As you can see from Table 1.4, these include insufficient information and inappropriate tools and

Table 1.3 **Some Factors That Motivate Job Performance**

1. Pay increases
2. Bonuses and related financial incentives (for example, company stock)
3. Extra vacation time
4. Verbal compliments from your supervisor
5. Promotion to a better job
6. Free tickets to sports events
7. More interesting work
8. Special projects
9. Better office (for example, one with a window)
10. Employee of the month award
11. Your name in the company newsletter
12. All-expenses paid vacation
13. Free movie tickets
14. Better job title

What other factors motivate you to increase your job performance?

Table 1.4 **Common Work Constraints That Affect Productivity**

1. Insufficient information
2. Inappropriate tools and equipment
3. Missing materials or supplies
4. Limited budget
5. Insufficient support from others
6. Insufficient task preparation
7. Limited time
8. Poor physical conditions
9. Poor scheduling

Source: Adapted from L. Peters, E.J. O'Connor, and J. Eulberg. "Situational Constraints: Sources, Consequences, and Future Considerations," in *Research in Personnel and Human Resources Management,*. vol. 3, ed. K. Rowland and G. Ferris, (JAI Press: Greenwich, CT, 1985).

equipment. Total quality management (TQM) programs often address these concerns and develop solutions to them.[16] Although TQM will be discussed in much greater detail in Chapter 12, a brief description is appropriate here. TQM is a program that focuses on continuous improvement of the organization's product or service quality. A key emphasis in TQM is enhancement of customer satisfaction. Toward that end, TQM programs employ teams of employees to search for ways to eliminate barriers to quality and improve work processes.[17]

Now that you understand the factors that determine job performance, you will read about three additional HRM outcomes, namely, cost containment, meeting legal requirements, and counterproductivity.

Additional HRM Goals

Cost Containment. Especially in today's competitive business environment, cost containment, or keeping expenses down, is a critical HRM goal. As you will see in subsequent chapters, compensation and benefit costs can be extremely high. This is particularly true in organizations that are labor intensive, such as educational institutions, consulting firms, and service businesses.

Legal Requirements. Meeting legal requirements is one of the most important HRM goals. As mentioned previously, virtually every HRM decision—including hiring, promoting, firing, starting pay and pay raises—has legal ramifications. Many additional regulations must also be met, such as safety and health rules. Because supervisors and managers make many HRM decisions, it is also critical that they have a basic understanding of these laws. And, as an employee, knowing your legal rights will help you deal with problem situations.

Violations of legal requirements can be costly to an organization. Aside from lawyers' fees and employee time and energy spent handling legal complaints, an organization may be required to pay various fines and implement special training programs. An organization that neglects to stay abreast of legal developments may, therefore, pay dearly.

Counterproductivity. Counterproductive behaviors include a wide range of possible problems such as stealing on the job, engaging in fights, and sabotaging company equipment. The cost of counterproductive behavior to businesses and organizations has been estimated in the billions of dollars annually.[18] Certain industries, such as retail stores, are particularly susceptible to employee theft. For example, it is estimated that employee stealing accounts for twice as much loss in retail stores as shoplifting by customers.[19] From an HRM perspective, several things can be done to reduce counterproductive behavior, including the careful selection of employees, surveillance of the workplace, and thorough investigations of possible employee misconduct. As you will see, however, these activities are fraught with legal restrictions, and therefore organizations must operate carefully here.

Finally, Figure 1.1 indicates that HRM goals and outcomes will affect organizational goals and outcomes, such as profitability, survival, and adaptability. Most businesses today recognize that achievement of HRM goals is necessary for the organization as a whole to succeed.[20]

If you examine Figure 1.1, you will observe arrows pointing from organizational outcomes to HRM activities and the environment; similarly HRM outcomes have arrows pointing back to HRM activities and the environment. The reason for these arrows is that organizational outcomes and HRM outcomes also affect HRM activities and the environment to some degree. For example, a highly profitable organization will have different HRM programs and policies than an organization that is struggling to survive. An organization that has a high absenteeism rate may change its disciplinary procedures. Thus, much interplay goes on between the environment, HRM activities, HRM goals, and organizational outcomes.

We now turn to a discussion of the roles HRM staff play in performing their jobs.

HRM Roles

Traditionally, the HRM function has emphasized two roles: administrative and advisory. In the administrative role, the human resource department has served as a record-keeper (by performing such tasks as maintaining personnel files and updating benefit enrollment information) and as a distribution center (for example, by delivering paychecks and dispensing application blanks). In the last 30 years, the human resource function has also played an increasingly important advisory role by providing information, guidance, and procedures for use by line managers. For example, the HRM function has become more involved in updating line managers on recent court decisions, recommending new preemployment testing procedures, and helping counsel problem employees. Table 1.5 lists some typical tasks performed by HRM staff that reflect these roles.

Changes in the 1990s, however, have resulted in the need for HRM to take on additional roles as well. These roles include the following:[21]

1. **Business Expert.** All too often the human resource specialist has only a limited understanding of the organization's business. Not only will this hurt his or her credibility with others, but it may limit his or her ability to make sound HR decisions. HRM staff members may improve their understanding of the business in many ways, including taking courses in finance, marketing, and strategic

Table 1.5 **Typical HRM Staff Tasks**

1. Answer employee questions about the benefits program.
2. Contract with health providers to provide medical service.
3. Provide orientation programs for new employees.
4. Conduct employee attitude surveys.
5. Give advice to line managers on problem employees.
6. Respond to EEOC investigations.
7. Create newspaper advertisements for job openings.
8. Screen resumes responding to job openings.
9. Approve salary raise recommendations made by managers and supervisors.
10. Create a sexual harassment policy.
11. Design performance appraisal forms.
12. Conduct preretirement workshops.
13. Implement an affirmative action program.
14. Maintain records on employee hours and pay.
15. Develop a human resource information system.
16. Review company policies and procedures.
17. Write rejection letters to applicants who were not hired.
18. Interview job candidates.

planning; participating in business task forces; and rotating into line management positions.

2. Change Facilitator. This is a new critical role played by human resource managers and, indeed, all managers and supervisors. As discussed previously in this chapter, many organizations are changing the way they are structured and designed. As the change facilitator, HRM staff will have an impact on how to change, assist in facilitating the change, and monitor reactions to change. To prepare for this role, HRM employees should take workshops and seminars in organizational change, read books on the change process, and talk with other professionals about such programs.

3. Strategy Consultant. Human resource experts are more frequently being called upon to participate in making major, long-term decisions regarding the organization's business direction, plans for opening new facilities or closing existing facilities, and so forth. Toward that end, HRM staff will play a more active role as the strategy consultant to managers and executives. To prepare for this role, HRM employees should learn more about the business through conversations with a variety of people from different functions of the organization, read books and magazine articles about business strategy, and take seminars in the area of strategic human resources.

In sum, regardless of whether you are a full-time HRM employee or have several responsibilities, including HRM, you will need to fulfill an increasingly diverse set of roles. Your ability to serve effectively in each of those roles will greatly affect your career. We now turn to the last section of this chapter, a brief discussion of careers in HRM.

Careers in Human Resource Management

Many different types of HRM jobs are available, ranging from interview specialist to training manager and including generalist positions such as manager of human resources. Most medium and large companies have a vice president or director of human resources as well. As you read through this book, think about whether certain areas seem particularly interesting to you. For example, the chapter on safety and health issues may intrigue you; if so, consider a career in that area. If you want further information about careers in HRM, contact the Society for Human Resource Management (1-800-283-SHRM or write to 606 North Washington Street, Alexandria, Virginia 22314). In addition to providing career information, this organization sponsors student groups on many college and university campuses. You should contact the student organizations office at your campus to see if a chapter has been organized.

Pursuing a Career in HRM: Tips for Students

If you are interested in a career in HRM, here are some suggestions for you.[22]

1. **Work Experience Is as Important as Education.** In order to enter the human resource field, it is extremely important to have some work experience. This is especially true if you plan to obtain a master's degree—get some work experience first. A good internship program may suffice.

2. **Obtain a Well-Rounded Educational Background.** A basic understanding of business (marketing, finance, and so forth) will be important to succeed in the human resource field. If you are an undergraduate business major, there will be considerable overlap with course work you receive in an MBA program, unless you enter a more specialized master's program in human resources or organizational development.

3. **The "Soft" Skills Will Become Increasingly Important.** Although traditional areas of HRM, such as compensation and benefits, remain important, changes in both the internal and external environment have increased the importance of communication, conflict resolution, and interpersonal abilities. Consider other means of obtaining these abilities, including workshops and seminars, if these areas are not covered in your school. Your local chamber of commerce, community college, or management consulting firm may have additional information on such programs.

4. **Experience in Leadership Roles Will Be Helpful.** Serving in leadership positions in your school, your community, and volunteer organizations provides evidence that you are capable of managing and leading people in a variety of situations. More companies view such experiences as important for HRM positions.

Box 1.4 From Personnel Representative to Chief Executive Officer: The Story of Mike Bowlin

Tales from the Trenches

Although few chief executive officers (CEOs) begin their careers in human resources, Mike Bowlin did. His first job after graduating from college was a marketing position with R.J. Reynolds. But Bowlin soon left for a human resource job at Atlantic Richfield (ARCO), a Fortune 500 company. He quickly moved up through the ranks, serving as the manager of corporate college recruiting, followed by a stint as the manager of human resources for ARCO's Alaska operations. Bowlin eventually became vice president of human resources for ARCO Oil and Gas company. He then moved away from the human resources function when he was selected as vice president of finance, planning, and control. This position was the first stepping stone on a general management track that eventually led to the CEO job at ARCO.

When asked about his success in the HRM area, Bowlin emphasizes the importance he placed on being part of the management team, being intimately familiar with the company's operations and products, and being able to connect HRM with the company's operations. Neal Bondy, a human resource consultant and personal friend, says that Mike Bowlin's greatest strength is his ability to relate to everybody, including production workers, managers, and top executives. Given the many challenges facing the oil industry, including massive layoffs, public antipathy toward oil exploration in the United States, and the need to expand into other countries, Mike Bowlin's unique background is bound to be an important asset.

Source: Adapted from B. Leonard, "Mike R. Bowlin: HR Vet Leads ARCO," *HRMagazine,* December 1994, 46–51.

Box 1.5 Human Resource Management Systems in a Small Business

Tales from the Trenches

Cadet Uniform Services, a uniform supply company based in Toronto, Canada, with annual revenues of about $24 million, recently won an award for business excellence. The majority of the employees are truck drivers—but they do much more than just drive the delivery trucks. The workers, who incidentally are called customer service representatives (CSRs), also solicit new customers, handle complaints from existing customers, and are responsible for managing their own accounts. A major reason for their success is Nada Cian, the company's HR director. Cian emphasizes the importance of hiring the best applicants. For example, one of the company's recent hires was someone working in a local grocery store. Cian noticed how friendly, neat, and efficient he was and encouraged him to apply to Cadet. As a result, Cian hired both him and his wife. Cian uses several means of assessing job candidates, such as observing them while they walk from the parking lot to her office (for example, to see if they are neatly groomed) and escorting them back to their car after the interview to see how tidy they keep their vehicles. The reason for such careful selection of drivers is because the company considers them to be one of the most critical factors to its success. The compensation system also plays an important role in the HRM system at Cadet. The base pay is about $40,000 annually for the CSRs, which is about double the average for the industry. This enables the company to be extremely selective with regard to whom it hires. Pay is closely tied to customer satisfaction, and if a customer defects (fewer than 1 out of 100 do so annually), the CSR's pay will be reduced. The end result? Cadet has very low employee turnover, double-digit profit margins, and rapid growth.

Source: Adapted from R. Henkoff, "Finding, Training, & Keeping the Best Service Workers," *Fortune,* October 3, 1994, 110–122.

5. **Exposure to International Issues and Cultural Diversity.** HRM issues increasingly must be addressed at a global level, and more HR positions will appear in countries other than the United States. In addition, the United States is becoming more culturally diverse. Knowledge of a foreign language, such as Spanish, Japanese, or Russian, will be invaluable. Does your school provide an opportunity for you to go overseas for a semester or a year? Does your school provide any international business courses? Participation in these activities will be helpful for those seeking a career in HRM.

Careers in HRM: Becoming an Independent Consultant

Have you thought of going into business on your own as a human resource consultant? Because many companies have begun outsourcing their human resources function, many new opportunities are arising in this area. Before you become an independent consultant, however, here are some suggestions you should consider.[23]

1. **Most HRM Consultants Have Extensive Previous Work Experience.** Prior experience is important for two reasons. First, it gives you credibility with potential clients; second, former employers may be an initial source of business. You are best off working in the HRM department of several companies before you start your own consulting business.

2. **A Diverse Set of Skills Is Essential.** If you are a private consultant, you need to have more than just knowledge of HRM. You will need to manage your time well, have considerable patience, and enjoy working alone. Marketing ability is most essential. Experts recommend that consultants spend at least 30 percent of their time engaged in marketing activities, such as making presentations, developing materials, and so forth. New consultants may need to spend as much as 80 percent of their time doing marketing.

3. **Acquire the Proper Materials.** In addition to business cards, you will probably need a fax machine, a computer, and a separate telephone line and answering machine. You should also develop a business plan and obtain information on how to set up your business.

4. **Obtain Information.** Numerous books and articles provide guidelines on how to establish and run a consulting business. Some of the recommended ones are the following:

   Flawless Consulting, by Peter Block (University Associates, San Diego, CA)

   Do-It-Yourself Publicity, by David Ramacitti (AMACOM Books, American Management Association, New York)

   Become an Outside Consultant, from the American Society for Training and Development, March 1994, Issue 9403, Alexandria, VA.

Finally, talk with people. Meet other successful consultants, and learn what they do. Talk with potential customers and learn what their needs are. See what niche you could fill as a consultant.

Conclusion

Human resource management is a complex area, with many environmental factors that must be taken into account. Among the activities included in HRM are planning, staffing, evaluating and rewarding, improving the organization, and maintaining effective employer-employee relationships. The major goals of HRM include low absenteeism, selective retention of employees, and high job performance; additional goals include compliance with legal requirements and reduction of counterproductive employee behavior. Compared to years ago, it is not surprising that the role of the HRM staff has become much more complex. Today's business environment demands that HRM play more than just an administrative and advisory role; the human resource manager must serve as a business expert, change facilitator, and strategy consultant as well. Students planning a career in HRM are encouraged to plan wisely and to take a diversity of college courses, supplemented by additional experiences such as work, international exposure, and volunteer positions.

Applying Core Concepts

1. Think of a new technology or concept, such as the World Wide Web. How might it affect HRM activities such as staffing, evaluating, and improving?
2. What do you think are the most important HRM outcomes at the organization you work for? How about at the school you attend?
3. What kinds of HRM activities have you participated in or expect to participate in soon?
4. What do you think is the most interesting aspect of human resource management?
5. Contact a human resource professional (there is probably a human resource department at the college or university you attend) and interview that person about his or her job. Be sure to ask (a) what he or she does on a typical workday, (b) what he or she enjoys most about the job, (c) what he or she enjoys least, and (d) how he or she expects the field to change in the next five years.

Chapter 1: Experiential Exercise

Making Changes at Electrik, Inc.

Introduction Electrik, Inc. is a highly sophisticated electronics manufacturer. Given the increasing competition, it is in the process of making many changes. One major change is the new chief executive officer (CEO), who comes from a much more progressive company. Given the apparent low morale among employees, high turnover, and concerns about a possible buyout by another company, the new CEO asked you to conduct an employee survey. Based on the results of the survey, the top executives have brainstormed a brief list of possible changes. Assume for the case that all changes will take the same amount of time and cost. You must recommend only two (2) of the possible changes. You should be prepared to:

1. Discuss which two changes you would recommend. Explain why these two. Explain why you did not choose the other five changes.
2. Explain what problems you anticipate in implementing those two changes, and what you will do to successfully implement them.

Electrik, Inc. Corporate Structure Electrik Inc. has a traditional hierarchical structure. Reporting to the CEO are 5 executives. Reporting to the executives are 35 managers. About 75 supervisors report to these managers. There are approximately 500 clerical, professional, technical, and production employees. In the past, a formal reporting structure has been used, with most decisions made by the executives.

Electrick, Inc. Business Conditions When the company was founded 20 years ago, it experienced very rapid growth. However, recent trends have combined to begin to reduce profits. There are several reasons for the changing business conditions. First, more companies are shifting their work to production facilities in Asia. Second, there has been a major increase in the amount of automation in this industry (so far, Electrik, Inc., has had little automation). Third, Electrik, Inc. has spent relatively little money on research and development (R & D), particularly compared to their competitors, who tend to be much larger and can afford more R & D. Fourth, Electrik, Inc. has always been an extremely high quality producer (even though the company's products are slightly more expensive than the competitors); however, other competitors have begun to improve their quality, and thus have become more competitive on that dimension as well, while not raising their prices.

Results of the Employee Survey

Pay and Benefits: A frequent complaint by employees was low pay. A major problem seemed to be a sense of internal unfairness (e.g., some people in the company were being paid more than other employees felt they were worth). Clerical and production employees, in particular, felt they were underpaid relative to managers and professional employees. On a positive note, employees felt very positive about their basic benefits package (e.g., retirement, health insurance, etc.).

Management Style: Many complaints were leveled at the management style exhibited by managers and supervisors. In general, managers and supervisors were perceived to be "heavy-handed," indifferent to employee feelings, and often tactless. On the positive side, the existing grievance system seemed well-regarded, and the "open door" policy of the new CEO appeared to be working well.

Promotions: Despite Electrik Inc.'s heavy emphasis on internal promotions, there were many complaints leveled against the promotion procedures. First, it was felt that there was far too little guidance and advice regarding career development. This was particularly true for technical employees. Second, employees criticized the fact that they were generally not informed when a position became open. Third, in many cases they were completely unaware of how promotion decisions were made, what criteria were used, and why they were not promoted. In some cases, employees felt that discrimination was occurring.

Performance Evaluations: Although performance appraisals were supposed to be conducted once a year for each employee, several employees indicated they had never received any performance appraisal. Most employees felt that the performance appraisals provided no useful feedback, and were simply "another piece of paper to fill out." A significant portion of employees related the lack of career development and limited information about pay raises, etc. to the lack of an effective performance appraisal system.

Employee Input: Without exception, employees felt that they had far too little input on important issues relevant to their jobs and the company. Even on minor decisions (such as where to have the annual company party), employee input was considered nonexistent. Everyone desired to have more "say," particularly given the changes in business conditions.

Quality of Work Life: Despite the problems with supervisors noted above, employees were fairly positive about work conditions. The work sites were perceived to be clean, safe, and pleasant. The company's flextime schedule and maternity/paternity leave policy were well-liked by the people who used them.

The Possible Changes

1. Devise and implement a new (mandatory) performance appraisal system that is more specific and formalized, and focuses on career development.
2. Conduct a systematic review of the pay system to address any potential inequities.
3. Implement supervisory training programs.
4. Create and implement an employee committee to address specific issues and problems.
5. Develop and implement a *subordinate appraisal of boss program* that will provide feedback to all supervisors and managers..
6. Develop and implement a job posting system for company job openings.
7. Institute a company-wide profit-sharing program to cover all employees. The profit-sharing plan would give the employees a yearly share of the company's profits (the company must make a profit for employees to get a share). As presently conceived, the profit-sharing could produce as much as a 15% bonus for the employees.

Chapter 1 References

1. M. Beer, B. Spector, P. Lawrence, D.Q. Mills, and R. Walton, *Managing Human Assets* (New York: Free Press, 1984).
2. T. Parker-Pope, "Culture Clash," *The Wall Street Journal,* April 12, 1995, R7.
3. P. Harris, and R. Moran, *Managing Cultural Differences* (Houston: Gulf Publishing, 1991).
4. J. Segal, "Stop Making Plaintiffs' Lawyers Rich," *HRMagazine,* April 1995, 31–36.
5. M. Magnet, "The Truth about the American Worker," *Fortune,* May 4, 1992, 48–65.
6. R.S. Schuler, "Repositioning the Human Resource Function: Transformation or Demise?" *Academy of Management Executive,* 4 (1990), 49–60.
7. T. Stewart, "Welcome to the Revolution," *Fortune,* December, 13, 1993, 66–80.
8. M. Treacy and F. Wiersema, "How Market Leaders Keep Their Edge," *Fortune,* February 6, 1995, 88–98.
9. S. Rhodes and R. Steers, "Managing Employee Absenteeism," (Reading, MA: Addison-Wesley, 1990).
10. Ibid.
11. P. Hom and R. Griffeth, "Employee Turnover," (Cincinnati: South-Western, 1995).
12. C. Rusbult and D. Farrell, "A Longitudinal Test of the Investment Model: The Impact of Job Satisfaction, Job Commitment, and Turnover of Variations in Rewards, Costs, Alternatives, and Investments," *Journal of Applied Psychology,* 68 (1983), 429–38.
13. J. Campbell, "Modeling the Performance Prediction Problem in Industrial and Organizational Psychology," in *Handbook of Industrial/Organizational Psychology,* vol. 1, ed. M. Dunnette and L. Hough, (Palo Alto, CA: Consulting Psychologists Press, 1990).
14. R. Kanfer, "Motivation Theory and Industrial and Organizational Psychology," in *Handbook of Industrial and Organizational Psychology,* vol. 1, ed. M. Dunette and L. Hough (Palo Alto, CA: Consulting Psychologists Press, 1990).
15. L. Peters, E.J. O'Connor, and J. Eulberg, "Situational Constraints: Sources, Consequences, and Future Considerations," in *Research in Personnel and Human Resources Management,* vol. 3, ed. K. Rowland and G. Ferris, (Greenwich, CT: JAI Press, 1985).
16. G. Dobbins, R. Cardy, and K. Carson, "Examining Fundamental Assumptions: A Contrast of Person and System Approaches to Human Resource Management," in *Research in Personnel and Human Resources Management,* vol. 9, ed. G. Ferris and K. Rowland, (Greenwich, CT: JAI Press, 1991).
17. H. Costin, *Management Development and Training: A TQM Approach* (Fort Worth, TX: Dryden, 1996).
18. P. Sackett and M. Harris, "Honesty Testing for Personnel Selection: A Review and Critique," in *Personality Assessment in Organizations,* ed. H.J. Bernardin and D. Bownas (New York: Praeger, 1985).
19. D. Cherrington, and O. Cherrington, "The Climate of Honesty in Retail Stores," in *Employee Theft: Research, Theory, and Applications,* ed. W. Terris (Chicago: London House, 1985).
20. N. Napier, "Strategy, Human Resources Management, and Organizational Outcomes: Coming Out from Between the Cracks," in *Human Resources Management: Perspectives and Issues,* ed. G. Ferris and K. Rowland, (Boston: Allyn & Bacon, 1988).
21. Schuler, "Repositioning Human Resource Function."
22. B. Kaufman, "What Companies Are Looking for in Graduates of University HR Programs," *Labor Law Journal,* 45 (1994), 503–10.
23. N.C. Tompkins, "How to Become a Human Resources Consultant," *HRMagazine,* August, 1994, 94–98.

chapter 2 Employment Discrimination Laws

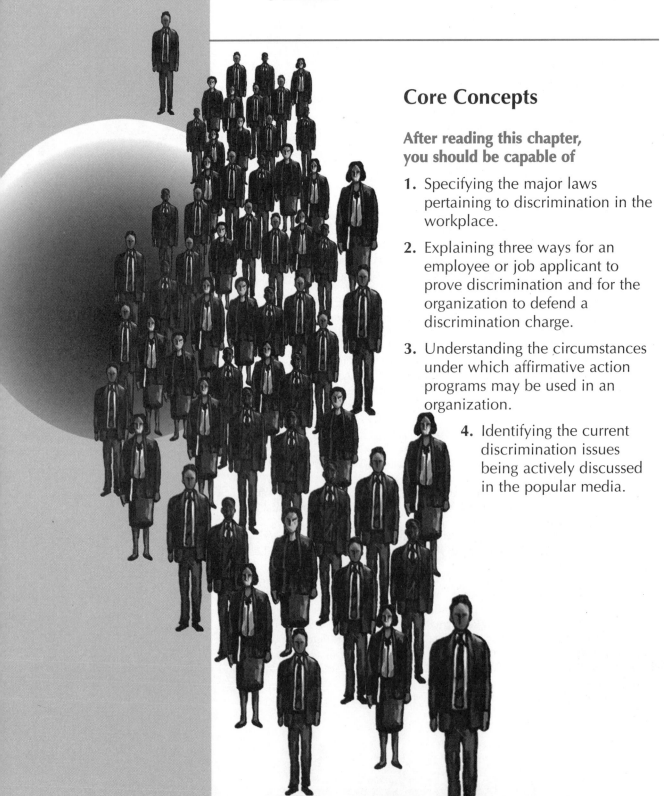

Core Concepts

After reading this chapter, you should be capable of

1. Specifying the major laws pertaining to discrimination in the workplace.
2. Explaining three ways for an employee or job applicant to prove discrimination and for the organization to defend a discrimination charge.
3. Understanding the circumstances under which affirmative action programs may be used in an organization.
4. Identifying the current discrimination issues being actively discussed in the popular media.

Opening Case

Yesterday, when you went out to lunch with Maria Martinez, both of you took turns complaining about your jobs. But after about 20 minutes of complaining about the unpleasant customers, the low pay, and the difficult deadlines, Maria lowered her voice and said, "I think that I'm being mistreated because I'm young and female. For example, three other employees who were hired the same week I was have long since been promoted—and all three of them were men older than me. But the worst of my problems is my boss, Pat. About twice a day, I catch him staring at me in a strange way. A couple of times he has said to me that he really likes the shirt I'm wearing or the dress I have on. And yesterday he asked me to go out after work with him for a drink at Down Under, the bar across the street from the office. When I hesitated, he said something about discussing ways I might advance in the company. I really don't like it when he looks at me that way, and I'm very uncomfortable with the comments he makes. Frankly, I have no interest in any romantic relationship or even friendship after work. I'm afraid if I say something, though, he will be angry and will hinder my attempts for a promotion. What do you think I should do?"

Now that you are have thought about what Maria said, you are wondering what you should recommend she do. Certainly the fact that other people are being promoted while she stays in the same job doesn't seem fair. But isn't it possible that her performance hasn't been as good as theirs? What her boss, Pat, is doing certainly seems unethical. But is it illegal? If it is illegal, you wonder what laws would Pat's actions violate? And what should Maria do?

The purpose of this chapter is to discuss employment discrimination laws. As you will see, employment discrimination laws apply to virtually all employment decisions, including hiring, firing, promotions, and transfers. Even behavior on the job, such as Pat's activities, may be prohibited by employment discrimination laws. You will learn who is covered by these laws, what you would have to prove and how you would go about showing you were discriminated against, and how companies go about defending themselves in a lawsuit. You will also read about affirmative action, as well as several current issues in the discrimination area. We begin first with an overview of the discrimination laws.

Discrimination Laws: An Introduction

Laws prohibiting racial discrimination in the United States go back to the 1860s, just after the Civil War. But it was not until the 1930s that Congress first introduced any discrimination laws within the more general workplace context.[1] However, Congress did not pass a comprehensive law banning workplace discrimination, the Civil Rights Act of 1964, for another 30 years. One of the major forces behind this law was the increasingly recognized disparity in the economic health of blacks and whites. In the early 1960s, black unemployment was about twice as high as white unemployment; the average black family's income was about half of the income of the average white family. The civil rights movement of the 1960s had much to do with bringing the plight of African Americans to the attention of the public. Many Americans began to feel that it was necessary to pass a comprehensive, federal law that would, among other things, ban race discrimination in the workplace. The result was the passage of the Civil Rights Act of 1964.[2]

Civil Rights Act of 1964 A comprehensive law banning workplace discrimination (which covers race, color, religion, sex, and national origin) passed in 1964.

It may surprise you to learn that the Civil Rights Act of 1964 was a controversial law, which produced a great deal of debate and discussion within Congress. The debate within the Senate lasted more than 500 hours. The bill passed the Senate by a vote of 76 to 18. It passed the House by a vote of 289 to 126. President Lyndon B. Johnson then signed the bill into law. Subsequently, a number of additional laws providing coverage against such acts as age discrimination were passed.[3]

Major Discrimination Laws

The major federal fair employment laws, along with the types of discrimination banned and the organizations that are covered by each law, are summarized in Table 2.1. You should also be aware that many states have laws that provide additional protection to employees. Because these laws are quite numerous and often change, they will only be mentioned briefly in subsequent sections. Some laws and cases pertain to compensation specifically; they will be addressed in Chapter 8. The key points of the laws summarized in Table 2.1 are discussed in greater detail next.

Discrimination on the Basis of Race, Color, Religion, Sex, and National Origin

Civil Rights Act of 1866 The first of many laws banning race discrimination in private companies, unions, and employment agencies, passed in 1866.

Although the Civil Rights Act of 1866 was passed almost 100 years earlier, it was not until the Civil Rights Act of 1964 that employment discrimination laws had much impact. The Civil Rights Act of 1991 clarified a number of subsequent issues that arose. Why wasn't the Civil Rights Act of 1866 more helpful in combating em-

Table 2.1 **Summary of Key Federal Employment Discrimination Laws**

Law	What is Covered	Employers Covered
CRA 1866	Race discrimination	Private companies, unions, employment agencies
CRA 1871	Anyone deprived of equal rights under state law	State and local governments
CRA 1964, CRA 1991	Race, color, religion, sex, national origin	Private companies with 15 or more employees, government unions, employment agencies
Rehabilitation Act of 1973	Physical and mental disabilities	Federal contractor, federal government
Americans with Disabilities Act of 1990	Physical and mental disabilities	Employers with 15+ employees
Executive Order 11141	Age discrimination	Federal contractors and subcontractors
Age Discrimination in Employment Act (ADEA) of 1967	Age discrimination	Private companies with 20 or more employees; unions, employment agencies

Source: Adapted from J. Ledvinka and V. Scarpello. *Federal Regulation of Personnel and Human Resource Management* (Boston PWS-Kent, 1991).

ployment discrimination? Examination of the Civil Rights Act of 1866 may provide some clues. This law states that "All persons within the jurisdiction of the United States shall have the same right in every State and Territory to make and enforce contracts . . . as is enjoyed by white citizens." What exactly does that law cover? For many years this law was interpreted very narrowly by the courts. For example, this law was initially understood to apply only to cases involving a governmental organization discriminating against someone, but not to a private company (for example, General Motors). A person charging discrimination by a private-sector company therefore could not win under this law. In addition, the Civil Rights Act of 1866 only prohibits racial discrimination, not other forms of discrimination.[4]

Civil Rights Act of 1991
A further delineation of civil rights, resulting from several controversial Supreme Court decisions during the late 1980s. Some key changes include making it easier for employees and job applicants to win lawsuits; prohibiting the use of different norms, based on race or sex, for scoring tests; permitting use of jury trials; expanding coverage of discrimination laws to U.S. citizens working for U.S. companies based in other countries; and allowing employees and job applicants to win punitive damages.

The Civil Rights Act of 1964 was, therefore, the first comprehensive, broad federal law banning employment discrimination in the United States. This law has many different parts. The section of the Civil Rights Act of 1964 that is most applicable to the employment area is known as Title VII. The highlights of Title VII are as follows:

1. Prohibits discrimination on the basis of race, color, religion, sex, or national origin (it doesn't matter what race, color, religion, sex, or national origin you are);
2. Provides for an agency, the **Equal Employment Opportunity Commission** (or, as it is usually referred to, the EEOC), to process discrimination charges and write regulations pertinent to congressional laws. One of the most well-known set of regulations is called the Uniform Guidelines on Employee Selection Procedures, which outlines technical requirements for defending employment tests in a discrimination charge. In addition to these responsibilities, the EEOC is responsible for receiving EEO-1 reports, which companies with 100 or more workers must complete annually. These reports provide information as to the number of women and minorities employed at the organization. Other organizations, such as employment agencies, apprenticeship programs, and labor unions, must file similar reports.

Equal Employment Opportunity Commission (EEOC)
Created by Title VII of the Civil Rights Act of 1964, the agency that processes discrimination charges and writes regulations pertinent to congressional laws.

A number of amendments and changes have been applied to the Civil Rights Act of 1964 over the years. One of these amendments is the **Pregnancy Discrimination Act of 1978,** which Congress passed to overturn a related Supreme Court decision. Under this law, an employer must comply with the following:

1. Cannot require a maternity leave of a particular length, unless specifically related to ability to perform the job.
2. Must provide the same terms and conditions for a leave of absence for childbirth as is provided for other medical conditions.
3. Must offer those returning from medical leave the same or equivalent job and employment conditions.[5]

Pregnancy Discrimination Act of 1978
An amendment to the Civil Rights Act of 1964, which states that an employer cannot require maternity leave of a particular length; must provide the same terms and conditions for a leave of absence for childbirth as is provided for other medical conditions; and must offer those returning from medical leave the same or an equivalent job and employment conditions.

The impetus behind the Civil Rights Act of 1991 was a number of controversial Supreme Court decisions during the late 1980s. Some of the key changes resulting from the Civil Rights Act of 1991 include the following:[6]

1. Making it somewhat easier for employees and job applicants to win lawsuits (unlike some Supreme Court decisions which had made this more difficult).

2. Prohibiting the use of different norms, based on race or sex, for scoring tests (which in some cases had become commonly used).
3. Permitting use of jury trials (which was not allowed under the Civil Rights Act of 1964).
4. Expanding coverage of discrimination laws to U.S. citizens working for U.S. companies based in other countries (who previously were not covered in that case).
5. Allowing employees and job applicants to win punitive damages in certain circumstances (this was not allowed under the Civil Rights Act of 1964).

Immigration Reform and Control Act
Provides additional protection against discrimination on the basis of national origin, and even protects certain noncitizens of the United States such as individuals who are permanent residents of the United States or who have declared an intention to gain citizenship in the United States.

In addition to the Civil Rights Acts of 1866, 1964, and 1991, other laws prohibit discrimination on the basis of national origin. The **Immigration Reform and Control Act (IRCA)**, for example, provides additional protection against discrimination on the basis of national origin and even protects certain noncitizens of the United States, such as individuals who are permanent residents of the United States or who have declared an intention to gain citizenship in the United States.[7]

Discrimination on the Basis of Disabilities

Rehabilitation Act of 1973
Prohibited discrimination against disabled individuals, applying only to government employees or businesses having contracts with the federal government.

Americans with Disabilities Act of 1990
Prohibits most other employers from discriminating against the disabled. Also addresses the definition of what disability means. Also requires that employers offer reasonable accommodations.

It was not until the early 1970s that a law, the **Rehabilitation Act of 1973**, was passed prohibiting discrimination against disabled individuals. Even so, as you can see in Table 2.1, this law was relatively limited in coverage, as it only applies to government employers or businesses having contracts with the federal government. It took almost 20 more years to pass the **Americans with Disabilities Act (ADA) of 1990** to prohibit most other employers from discriminating against the disabled. That it took so long for a comprehensive law of this nature is surprising, given that it has been estimated that 8.6 percent of Americans between the ages of 16 and 64 have some kind of disability, and almost one-third of these either work or are actively seeking work.[8]

One of the interesting issues addressed in the Rehabilitation Act of 1973, and in large part adopted by the more recent Americans with Disabilities Act of 1990, is the definition of what a disability is. As you might imagine, the decision as to who is covered by these laws could have important implications for people charging discrimination. Table 2.2 summarizes who is covered under the ADA. You should note that the law covers applicants and employees who are thought to have a disability, as well as those who have a disability. Potentially, then, *anybody* could be covered under the ADA. As you can also see in Table 2.2, certain conditions are explicitly not protected from employment discrimination, such as temporary disabilities (for instance, a broken leg that will heal in a few months) and current illegal drug use.

Reasonable accommodation
A modification or adjustment to a job, the work environment, or the way things usually are done that enables a qualified individual with a disability to enjoy an equal employment opportunity.

In addition to protecting applicants and employees from discrimination on the basis of a disability, both the Rehabilitation Act of 1973 and the ADA require that employers offer **reasonable accommodation**. Simply put, a reasonable accommodation is "a modification or adjustment to a job, the work environment, or the way things usually are done that enables a qualified individual with a disability to enjoy an equal employment opportunity."[9] A reasonable accommodation must be provided for the following purposes:

1. To provide equal opportunity in the application process.
2. To enable a qualified individual with a disability to perform the job.

Table 2.2 **Who Is and Who Is Not Covered by ADA**

The Following Individuals *Would* Be Covered by ADA:	**The Following Conditions Are *Not* Covered by ADA:**
1. An individual with a physical or mental impairment that substantially limits one or more major life activities of the individual (e.g., someone confined to a wheelchair).	1. Various sexual disorders, such as pedophilia and transvestitism.
2. An individual with a record of such an impairment (e.g., someone who used to have a heart disease).	2. Compulsive gambling, kleptomania, or pyromania.
3. An individual who is regarded as having such an impairment (e.g., someone who the interviewer believes has a learning disability, even though the individual has no such disability).	3. Psychoactive substance use disorders.
4. An individual who has a business, family, or social relationship with someone with a disability (e.g., the individual has a physically disabled child).	4. Homosexuality and bisexuality.
5. *Former* drug addicts.	5. Current illegal drug use.
	6. Temporary disabilities (e.g., a broken leg that will heal soon).

Source: Adapted from the U.S. Equal Employment Opportunity Commission, *Technical Assistance Manual on the Employment Provisions (Title I) of the Americans with Disabilities Act* (Washington: U.S. Government Printing Office, 1992).

3. To enable an employee with a disability to have equal benefits and privileges of employment.[10]

An example of each of these purposes is provided in Table 2.3.

Table 2.3 **Reasonable Accommodations: Some Examples**

1. *Providing equal opportunity in the application process.* An applicant who is visually impaired ("blind") applies for a job. The company must provide an accommodation to enable this applicant to complete the application blank, take written tests, and fill out other necessary paperwork.
2. *Enabling the applicant or employee to perform the job.* The job requires the employee to read brief reports. The applicant, who is visually impaired, but qualified for the job, cannot be denied the job on the basis of the disability if access to the reports can be provided through such means as braille, tape recordings, or a reader.
3. *Enabling the employee to have equal benefits and privileges of employment.* The employee cannot be treated differently because of his or her disability. For example, he or she cannot be denied health insurance. Due to insurance companies' policies, this may create problems for employers and disabled employees.
4. Some specific examples and costs of accommodations enabling companies to accommodate disabled employees include the following:
   - Providing a drafting table, page turner, and special tape recorder to a sales agent paralyzed by a broken neck ($950).
   - Supplying a telephone amplifier for a computer programmer who was hard of hearing ($56).
   - Providing padded wrist-rests under a computer keyboard to alleviate repetitive motion strain ($35).

Source: Adapted from information from the Job Accommodation Network (JAN) and C. Koen, S. Hartman, and S. Crow, "Health Insurance: The ADA's Missing Link," *Personnel Journal,* November 1991, 82–87.

According to the EEOC, more than half of the accommodations cost nothing to a company. More than 80 percent of the accommodations will cost the company less than $500. Under what circumstances could an employer deny an accommodation? Under ADA, a company could refuse to accommodate if it could prove that to do so would create an **undue hardship**. An undue hardship would exist if the accommodation would involve considerable expense or difficulty to the company. Just what constitutes too much expense or difficulty is not clearly defined under ADA. It will probably take several court decisions to clarify this issue. Given the previous information about the relatively low cost of many accommodations, though, it is unlikely that EEOC will willingly accept this as a defense.[11]

Undue hardship
Exists if the accommodation to enable a qualified individual with a disability to enjoy an equal employment opportunity would involve considerable expense or difficulty to the company.

At this point you may be wondering, "What if the reasonable accommodation creates a danger to safety or health?" For example, what if a person with a visual impairment applies for a factory assembly-line job involving various power saws, drills, and other dangerous equipment? Under the ADA, a company may refuse to hire and accommodate such an individual if it can be shown that a *direct threat* exists to the health or safety of the person or to other workers. However, if the company was charged with discrimination, the employer would need to show objective evidence that there was a specific risk involved, that it could result in substantial harm to individuals, and that a reasonable accommodation reducing or eliminating the risk could not be applied.[12] The President's Committee on Employment of People with Disabilities, in conjunction with a private organization, has established a free service that provides help to companies with accommodations (the telephone number is 1-800-526-7234).

One disability that is covered by both the Rehabilitation Act and the Americans with Disabilities Act is AIDS. Consider the story of Drew Hickman, who worked as a flight controller for the Federal Aviation Administration (FAA) in California. In June of 1992, the FAA declared Hickman unfit for duty because of AIDS and reassigned him to a clerical job. Even though his base salary remained the same ($38,000 annually), Hickman became ineligible for overtime pay and lost out

HR managers must accommodate all physically challenged employees. Workers such as the one shown here are entitled to office space and equipment, restroom facilities, and other accommodations that enable them to work.

on large raises he would have received had he remained a flight controller. After being harassed by coworkers, Hickman filed for disability-related retirement. As of yet, he has not received any disability payments from the government. The FAA claims that people with AIDS frequently develop central nervous system disorders, and therefore Hickman would have created a risk to public safety had he remained a flight controller. His lawsuit charges that the FAA violated the Rehabilitation Act by removing him from a job he was able to perform.[13] Figure 2.1 provides a summary of the nature of ADA violation charges.

Discrimination on the Basis of Age

Age discrimination was prohibited in the broader context by the **Age Discrimination in Employment Act (ADEA) of 1967** and in the federal government by Executive Order 11141. An executive order is a law passed by the president of the United States. Unlike congressional acts, such as the Civil Rights Act of 1964, an executive order does not require approval by Congress. Executive orders in the employment context, though, generally only apply to federal employees and companies doing business with the federal government. When first passed, the ADEA applied only to individuals between the ages of 40 and 65. So, when this law was first passed in 1967, once you turned 65, a company could require that you retire or discriminate against you in other ways (for example, pay you less). After changing the coverage to include individuals under 70 years old in 1978, Congress abolished the age cap in subsequent years for almost all jobs, with the exception of

Age Discrimination in Employment Act of 1967
Prohibits age discrimination. When first passed, it applied only to individuals between the ages of 40 and 65. In 1978, it was changed to include individuals under 70 years of age. In subsequent years, Congress abolished the age cap in subsequent years for almost all jobs.

Figure 2.1 **Reasons for ADA Violation Charges**

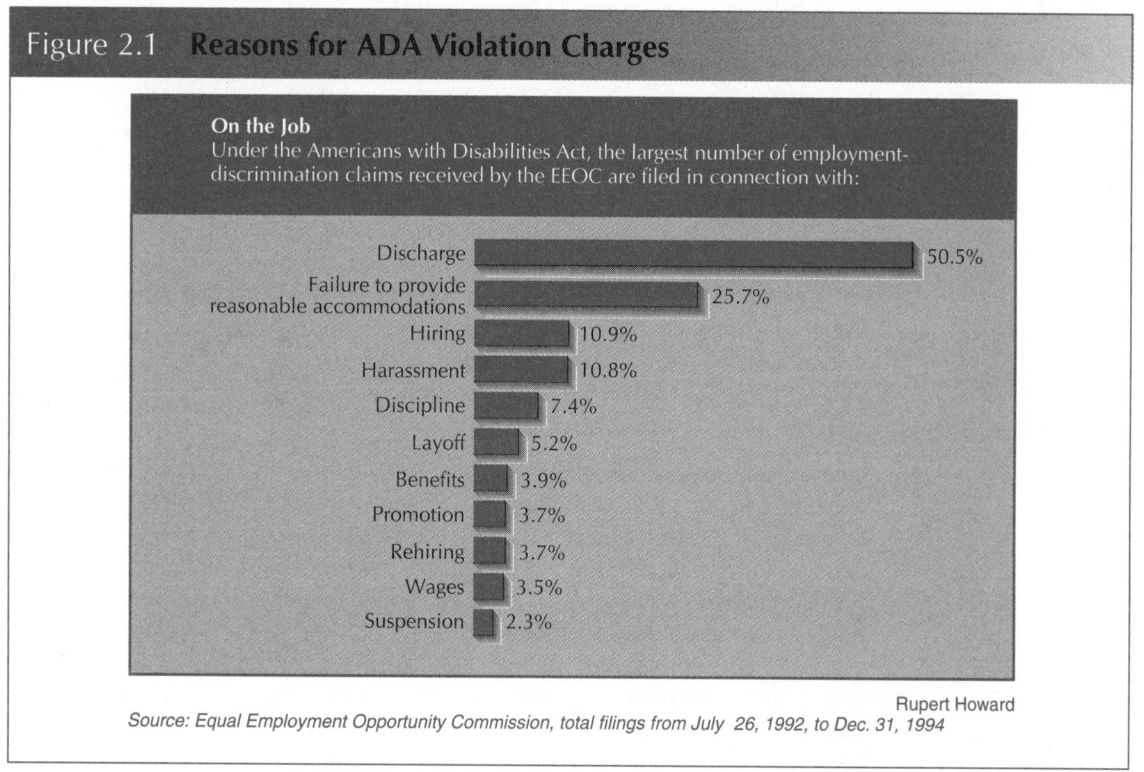

Source: *The Wall Street Journal,* Feb. 17, 1995, B12.

Box 2.1 An Age Discrimination Case

Tales from the Trenches

Frank Wilhelm was a field sales representative for Blue Bell, a manufacturer and marketer of clothing, including Wrangler jeans. He was fired from the company on February 2, 1982. At the time of his termination, Wilhelm was 49 years old and had worked at Blue Bell for more than eight years. Wilhelm asserted that he was terminated because of his age, and therefore sued under the federal age discrimination law. During the trial, he testified that his manager, Bill Wise, told him that "eventually Blue Bell is going to have $15,000-a-year college boys for salesmen . . . Blue Bell cannot stand these five and six percent commission rates, so, in time they will have all young college guys on a salary." Wilhelm's supervisor also was quoted as saying he believed that "older people tend to become complacent whereas younger people generally have more drive and ambition." Moreover, when Wilhelm discussed some of these and other statements with the president of a Blue Bell division, the president allegedly said, "You have to understand that Bill Wise is of the opinion that the younger salesmen do a much better job than you older fellows." Contrary to these disparaging remarks, Wilhelm testified that he had obtained four new accounts prior to being terminated and was the top salesperson in his region. In response, the company provided information suggesting that Wilhelm's performance on other measures (for example, salesperson efficiency) was quite low. Furthermore, the company asserted that other, younger sales people (under age 40) were terminated at the same time, evidence that the company was not simply targeting older employees. Despite the company's defense, the court viewed negatively the age-related statements made by various managers at Blue Bell and ruled in favor of Wilhelm.

Source: Adapted from *Wilhelm v. Blue Bell, Inc.*, 773 F.2d 1429 (1985).

certain executives. Under current laws then, a discrimination charge could be brought by an employee who was 102 or even older! Nonetheless, ADEA still only applies to employees or applicants who are at least 40 years old. Does that mean that under ADEA your company could discriminate against you on the basis of age if you were 25? If you answered yes, you are right. However, some states (Minnesota, Florida, and Michigan, to name a few) have laws that ban discrimination on the basis of age at even younger ages. This is a good example of how some states have laws that provide more protection to employees than does the federal law.[14]

Discrimination on the Basis of Other Demographics

Other factors that a company may take into account in employment decisions could be considered discriminatory. Use of sexual orientation to treat employees differently, for example, is considered discrimination in eight states (such as Minnesota and New Jersey) and more than 100 municipalities (such as Washington, D.C.). To date, however, the courts have concluded that none of the federal civil rights acts covers sexual orientation.[15]

Dress and grooming regulations imposed by organizations is another issue that in some cases has led to discrimination lawsuits. Alma Dolores Reardon, for example, who converted to Islam in the early 1980s, was barred from working as a substitute teacher in the Philadelphia public school system because she wore a head scarf and long flowing dresses. The school asserted that this was a violation of its dress code. Simcha Goldman, a Jewish officer in the U.S. Air Force, was prohibited from wearing a skullcap while on duty. The U.S. Air Force argued that use of distinctively different clothing would diminish cohesiveness and encourage disobedience. As a final example, consider two police officers, Jerry and Marion Cupit, who converted to the Assembly of Yaweh religion. This religion requires members to wear beards, yet the Baton Rouge police department where they worked had a regulation requiring that officers be clean shaven. Although not all of these cases were filed under civil rights laws (some were filed under the U.S. Constitution), it may surprise you to know that the employees lost in all three cases. Given the increasing diversity of the workforce, challenges to dress and grooming rules are likely to increase in the future.[16]

Proving a Discrimination Case

Now that you have learned about the different laws banning discrimination in the workplace, and who is covered by those laws, you may be wondering how you would prove you were discriminated against. You probably are also wondering what the company would need to defend itself if you were charging discrimination. Just how one proves that discrimination has occurred is not an easy matter. Consider for a moment the company's perspective. There may be hundreds, perhaps thousands, of applicants for a particular job. But only a handful can be hired. Or, in the case of a large reduction in the workforce, hundreds of thousands of employees may work for the company, and due to business losses, the company may need to reduce the workforce by 10 percent. As a result, a large number of people will lose their jobs. Typically, the company doing the hiring or the layoff will want to consider qualifications, such as education, work experience, skills, and other job-related factors, such as past performance. Some of these factors may be quite objective, such as a college degree; others may seem quite subjective to you, such as an applicant's communication skills. Factors such as seniority may seem best to you because of their objectivity. Subjective factors, like work motivation and customer relations, however, may be far more important to the company, even though they are less quantifiable. Therefore, what might seem to the rejected applicants or terminated employees to be a clear case of discrimination may be nothing more than the company making the best decision given limited and often subjective information.

Now consider the applicant/employee perspective. There is substantial data (some of which is discussed later in this chapter and some of which is reviewed in other chapters) that suggest that, at least in the past, women and minorities, as well as other groups, have suffered from lower wages and limited employment opportunities. And, no doubt people of both sexes, all races, colors, religions, and backgrounds have experienced discrimination at some point in time. It is probably safe to say that discrimination does occur sometimes. It is also safe to say that at times what might have seemed like discrimination was not. The major point here is that it is often not clear whether or not discrimination has occurred. Over the years, several approaches have evolved for bringing and defending discrimination cases. These can be referred to as *evil intent, disparate treatment,* and *adverse impact.* Each of these approaches will be described in greater detail next.[17]

Evil Intent

Evil intent
An earlier practice, where employers would refuse to hire applicants of a particular race, religion, or gender simply out of prejudice.

Bona fide occupational qualification (BFOQ)
Suitable defense against a discrimination charge only where age, religion, sex or national origin is an actual qualification for performing the job.

In earlier times, employers often would refuse to hire applicants of a particular race, religion, or gender simply out of prejudice, a practice referred to as evil intent. Can you think of any situations where a company might *legitimately* exclude people of a certain religion, sex, or national origin? What about a model for men's clothing or a women's bathroom attendant? In fact, under the Civil Rights Act of 1964, an organization may defend the decision to hire people of a certain religion, sex, or national origin where this characteristic constitutes a bona fide occupational qualification (BFOQ).[18] The courts have accepted the BFOQ defense in cases such as a model for clothing and an Asian restaurant wishing to ensure authenticity (and therefore only hiring Asian servers). On the other hand, the courts have rejected the company's BFOQ defense in cases such as a refusal to hire men as flight attendants and the exclusion of fertile women from jobs involving contact with toxic chemicals, which potentially could harm a fetus. In general, it is safe to say that an organization that openly excludes persons on the basis of their religion, sex, or national origin will have a difficult time defending the action.

Rather than having a formal policy not to hire applicants from a certain racial group, age, gender, and so on, representatives of the company may make statements that suggest such a policy exists in a more informal fashion. In one case, for example, Otis Felton, a black machine operator, was denied a promotion to production supervisor. Witnesses testified that managerial employees responsible for the promotion decision had made various derogatory statements in the past, such as "if it was . . . [my] company, . . . [I] wouldn't hire any black people."[19] Once it can be proven that such statements were made, the plaintiff must show that there is a link between the statement and the employment decision. For example, in one case, the employer allegedly made statements that "women are not good sailors." When a woman was denied a job requiring work on a ship, this statement was used as evidence of discrimination.[20]

Finally, what would you say as the judge if a company argued that even though some discriminatory remarks had been made, the applicant would have been rejected anyhow, based on job-related factors? This was the company's response in a recent case where a woman rejected for promotion to the partnership level charged the company with making a variety of discriminatory statements about her. The company's defense was that regardless of the sexist comments, the same decision would have been made, because there were sufficient work-related problems to warrant her not being promoted. Because there were both job-related, legitimate as well as non–job related, discriminatory reasons involved, this is referred to as a *mixed motive* case. The Civil Rights Act of 1991 states that a company would lose a mixed motive case, overturning a Supreme Court decision in 1989.

Turning back to the hypothetical situation posed at the beginning of this chapter, the first question to ask is what law(s) could Maria use to file a discrimination charge? If Maria believes that sex or race discrimination was occurring, she could file a charge under the Civil Rights Acts of 1964 and 1991. Second, recall that Maria did not mention that any specific discriminatory statements or comments had been made. Nevertheless, it is possible that examination of documents or statements made to others could be used to advance a discrimination case. Given the limited information presented in the opening case, it may be difficult to prove evil intent. The next approach to bringing a lawsuit may therefore be more relevant.

Disparate Treatment

A classic form of discrimination involves disparate treatment, in which the employer treats people differently, depending on their age, sex, race, or other protected categories. For example, employers in the past often asked women if they had children, but did not ask the same question of male applicants. In general, treating people differently in the employment context is discrimination. In 1973, in the McDonnell-Douglas v. Green Case, the Supreme Court of the United States described a somewhat more elaborate three-step process for examining hiring or promotion discrimination under the disparate treatment concept.[21] The three steps are as follows:

Disparate treatment When an employer treats people differently or evaluates them by different standards, depending on their age, sex, race or other protected categories.

***McDonnell-Douglas v. Green* Case Standards** A 1973 case that outlined a more elaborate three-step process for examining hiring or promotion discrimination under the disparate treatment concept.

Step 1. The plaintiff (the employee or applicant) must show that he or she is from a protected class (that is, a racial or ethnic minority, female, or over 40 years old), applied for a job for which a vacancy existed, was qualified for the job, was rejected, and the employer continued to seek other persons or selected a person of a different class. This is often referred to as prima facie evidence (meaning evidence sufficient to establish a fact or presumption of a fact). For example, a woman might establish that she applied for promotion to a mid-level management position, had three years of relevant experience, was rejected, and that ten other males were promoted.

Step 2. If the plaintiff can prove all of the required points in Step 1, the defendant or company must provide a *legitimate, nondiscriminatory reason* for rejecting the plaintiff. Legitimate reasons may include seniority, education, experience, and other job-relevant factors. For example, following along with the previous example, the company might defend their failure to promote her by stating they had a policy of promoting only employees who had an MBA or equivalent graduate degree.

Step 3. If the defendant can provide an acceptable "legitimate, nondiscriminatory reason" for rejecting the plaintiff, the plaintiff has the opportunity in Step 3 to show that this reason was simply a pretext or cover-up for discrimination. Following the above example, the female plaintiff may show that there were some other employees who were promoted (e.g., males) who did not have an MBA or equivalent graduate degree. Alternatively, the plaintiff may show that her gender somehow played a role in the rejection decision. It is noteworthy that in a recent Supreme Court decision (St. Mary's Honor Center vs. Hicks), the Court concluded that even if the plaintiff can show pretext, it may still be necessary for the plaintiff to prove the company was motivated to discriminate against him or her.[22] So, in the future, disparate treatment cases may become more similar to the evil intent approach.

Returning to the opening situation in this chapter, Maria would have to show that she belonged to a protected class (that she was a woman, racial or ethnic minority, or over 40 years old, for example), a vacancy existed (even though it was not advertised, the company made promotions, indicating vacancies existed from time to time), she was at least minimally qualified for promotion, and she was rejected for the position (that is, not promoted). Would she meet all these criteria? Even if she did, the company usually has a great deal of leeway in the legitimate, nondiscriminatory reason offered. For example, it may be able to show that the other people who were promoted had higher performance appraisal ratings. Or,

Box 2.2 "You're Overqualified": Legitimate, Nondiscriminatory Reason or Pretext?

Have you ever applied for a job and been told you were "overqualified"? In today's competitive job market, where there are many applicants for most jobs, it is not unusual for employers to reject applicants because they appear to be "overqualified." That is exactly what happened to Thomas Taggart, who was hired to serve as a print production manager for a magazine owned by a subsidiary of Time, Inc. At the time of hire, Taggart was 58 years old and had more than 30 years of experience in the printing business. Six months after being hired, employees of the company, including Taggart, were told that their jobs would be eliminated, but they could apply for other jobs at Time, Inc. Taggart applied for 32 positions at a number of different divisions of Time and failed to receive a job offer from any of these applications. In defending the failure to hire Taggart, the company said he was underqualified for some jobs, interviewed poorly, had typographical errors in his cover letters, received some negative references from other employers, among other reasons. For some of the jobs, though, the company's "legitimate, nondiscriminatory reason" was that he was overqualified based on his previous experience and jobs. Despite the fact that no evidence of evil intent was shown (for example, Time never mentioned age in its decision process), the court felt that "overqualified" was not a "legitimate, nondiscriminatory reason." Its conclusion was based on the following logic, "overqualified has a connotation that defies common sense: How can a person overqualified by experience and training be turned down for a position given to a younger person deemed better qualified?" In addressing the unstated fear an employer may have that the overqualified person might continue to seek employment that was more consistent with his or her qualifications, the court noted that for someone over 40 years old, "loss of employment late in life ordinarily is devastating economically as well as emotionally. Instead, an older applicant that is hired is quite unlikely to continue to seek other, mostly nonexistent employment opportunities." Thus, the court felt that overqualified was simply a pretext for discrimination. This, as well as other court decisions, suggest that "overqualified" may not be accepted as a legitimate, nondiscriminatory reason in an age discrimination lawsuit.

Source: Adapted from *Taggart v. Time, Inc.* 924 F2.d 43; (1991) and M. Levine "Age Discrimination in Employment: The Over Qualified Older Worker," *Labor Law Journal,* 44 (1993). 440–44.

perhaps the people promoted had obtained an MBA. Then, it would be important for Maria to try to show that the company was inconsistent in their promotion policy. Finally, a key issue is whether remarks were made suggesting they intentionally discriminated against people of Maria's protected class. Clearly, much more information would be needed to determine whether she had a reasonable chance of proving discrimination under the disparate treatment approach.

Adverse Impact

Adverse impact
The selection process or procedure has a disproportionate effect on a protected group (e.g., women).

Unlike disparate treatment which focuses on the *individual* who may have been discriminated against, adverse impact focuses on the plaintiff's *group* as a whole. The adverse impact approach is perhaps the most controversial way to advance a discrimination case. This concept was first articulated by the Supreme Court of the United States in the *Griggs v. Duke Power* case, shortly after the passage of the Civil Rights Act of 1964.[23] Griggs was a part of a *class action* suit, in which a large group of people in a similar situation, allow a representative to sue on their behalf. In this particular case, the suit involved charges of race discrimination against Duke Power, a power-generating facility located in North Carolina. The suit charged that race discrimination was occurring with regard to hiring and job assignment as blacks were employed only in the lowest-paying department of the facility. In order to qualify for placement in the other departments, an applicant had to have a high school degree or pass two professionally developed tests: the Wonderlic Personnel test, which measures general cognitive ability, and the Bennett Mechanical Comprehension Test, which measures knowledge of mechanical principles. The first black person to be employed in the other departments was not hired until after the race discrimination charge had been filed. A lower court had ruled in favor of the company, pointing out that the Civil Rights Act of 1964 specifically allows use of professionally developed ability tests and there was no evidence of *intention* to discriminate against blacks.

The Supreme Court, however, issued a different interpretation of the Civil Rights Act of 1964 and ruled against the company. In explaining this decision, the Supreme Court asserted that the goal of the Civil Rights Act of 1964 was to remove discriminatory barriers that had existed in the past and to actively advance the employment opportunities of minorities. Therefore, tests or other procedures that were "neutral on their face, and even neutral in terms of intent" would be deemed discriminatory if they served to maintain the status quo of prior practices. Because the selection procedures were serving as a barrier to the employment of blacks, albeit unintentionally, the Supreme Court ruled that the company was guilty of discrimination. Over the next 20 years, in conjunction with EEOC's Uniform Guidelines on Employee Selection Procedures and the Civil Rights Act of 1991, an adverse impact case has been determined to involve the following three steps:

Step 1. The plaintiff must show that his or her protected class was disproportionately affected by the selection practice, procedure, or test. Like disparate treatment, this constitutes the prima facie evidence that must be established. Two popular approaches are used by plaintiffs to establish prima facie evidence.[24]

- Applicant Flow. This method of assessing whether the plaintiff's group was adversely affected by the selection procedure involves comparison of the hiring rate of the plaintiff's group to the hiring rate of the majority group. Although several means of comparing the two selection rates are applied, a commonly used rule of thumb is the *four-fifths (or 80 percent) rule.* A specific example of this approach is shown in Box 2.3.

- Stock Analysis. An alternative approach for showing that the selection procedure had an adverse effect is to compare the percentage of the protected group members in the organization's workforce to the percentage of the protected group members in the labor market. Although some ambiguity may exist regarding the calculation of the percentage of the protected group members in the organization's workforce (for example, should part-time employees be counted?), things become far more complex when trying to calculate the percentage of protected group members in the labor market. The difficulty arises when one attempts to calculate precisely what the relevant labor market is (for instance, does it cover the entire city or county, the larger metropolitan area, the state, or the nation?) and who should be included in the relevant labor market (Should it include only qualified individuals? What constitutes "qualified"?). Given that decisions about such matters could have a tremendous effect on conclusions about the disproportionate effect of a hiring procedure, such issues are the source

Applicant flow
A method of assessing whether the plaintiff's group was adversely affected by the selection procedure that involves comparison of the hiring rate of the plaintiff's group to the hiring rate of the majority group.

Stock analysis
An alternative approach for showing that the selection procedure had an adverse effect is to compare the percentage of the protected group members in the organization's workforce to the percentage of the protected group members in the labor market.

Box 2.3 Assessing Applicant Flow Using the Four-Fifths Rule

EEOC's Uniform Guidelines on Employee Selection Practices suggest that one way to establish the disproportionate effect required in Step 1 of an adverse impact case is to use the 80 percent or four-fifths rule. Briefly stated, this rule establishes that the percentage of protected group members who are hired (or, in a promotion case, promoted) should be at least 80 percent of the percentage of majority group members who are hired (or, in a promotion case, promoted). In one case, for example, a test was administered as one step in the promotion process. Of the employees taking this test, 48 were African American and 259 were white. Twenty-six African Americans and 206 whites passed the test. Four African Americans failing the test sued on grounds of race discrimination. To assess whether or not the test met the 80 percent rule, you would divide 26 by 48 to obtain the minority pass rate, and divide 206 by 259 to determine the majority pass rate. Did you calculate these two figures? You should have arrived at a pass rate of . 54 or 54 percent for minorities, and . 80 or 80 percent for majority employees. Now, divide .54 by .80 (that is, the pass rate of minorities by the pass rate of the majority), you should get a figure of .675 or, rounding off, 68 percent. In other words, the percentage of minorities that pass the test is 68 percent of the percentage of majority group members who pass the test. Because 68 percent is *less than* 80 percent, the organization fails to meet the 80 percent rule. In turn, this provides prima facie evidence of discrimination. In the actual case, though, the organization defended its actions by focusing on the "bottom line." That is, the organization stated that the more appropriate number to look at was the percentage of minorities who were actually promoted after going through all the stages of the process. Because 11 blacks were promoted at the end, and 35 whites were promoted, the bottom line pass rate for minorities was .23 and .14 for whites. Because .23 divided by .14 is 1.6 (or 160 percent), the organization would meet the 80 percent rule based on these figures. So, in the end, which set of numbers did the court accept? Ultimately, the court felt that the first set of figures, wherein the 80 percent rule was not met, were the relevant ones, and the organization therefore lost the case.

Source: Adapted from *Connecticut v. Teal,* 102 S.Ct. 2525, 73 (1982).

of much argument in the courts. Box 2.4 gives an example of one legal case in which the labor market was carefully examined by the courts.

Step 2. As in a disparate treatment case, if the plaintiff is able to successfully demonstrate prima facie evidence as described in Step 1, the company must provide a defense in Step 2. In an adverse impact case, the company must show that the selection or promotion procedures are "job related for the position in question and consistent with business necessity." The law does not define precisely what this entails. However, an organization has several possible ways to demonstrate this. One way is through a validation study.[25] Although Chapter 5 will describe a validation study in greater detail, one way a test can be shown to be valid is by statistically examining its relationship with job performance. That is, if scores on the test vary in tandem with measures of job performance, this is evidence that the test is valid. In cases not involving a test, such as an educational requirement (for example, a college degree), the company might explain the connection between the requirement and the job on logical grounds. For example, it would probably be legally acceptable to require applicants for an attorney's position to have a law degree.[26] Other defenses might be useful here as well, including a properly implemented seniority system.[27]

Validation study
A method of demonstrating that a test is valid by statistically examining its relationship with job performance.

Step 3. Even if the company is able to successfully prove that the procedure used is job related, the plaintiff may attempt to show that there is an alternative selec-

Box 2.4 Determining the "Right" Labor Market

One of the more interesting cases involving a determination of the proper labor market was *Hazelwood School District* v. *United States,* which was heard by the Supreme Court of the United States in 1977. This school district was located in the northern part of St. Louis County in Missouri. The plaintiff maintained that blacks were disproportionately affected by the hiring process. Indeed, fewer than 2 percent of the teachers were black. In order to prove that the selection process had a disproportionate effect on blacks, the plaintiff attempted to show that the percentage of black teachers was far lower than the percentage of black teachers in the labor market. The plaintiff argued that in the appropriate labor market, which would include both St. Louis County and the city of St. Louis, 15.4 percent of all teachers were black. The school, in defending itself, argued that the city of St. Louis should be excluded from the labor market. If only St. Louis County was considered, 5.7 percent of teachers in the labor market were black. The Supreme Court pointed out that a number of considerations were critical in deciding what the correct labor market figure was, including such factors as the extent to which black teachers would prefer to work in Hazelwood if its employment policies were perceived to be fair. One factor that appeared to receive little weight in the Court's thinking was the percentage of black students enrolled in the Hazelwood school district at the time, which was 2.3 percent. What figure(s) would you use if you were the judge deciding the case?

Source: Adapted from *Hazelwood School District v. United States,* 97 S.Ct. 2736 (1977).

tion procedure that has less adverse impact and yet is equally useful to the organization. For example, if an alternative test can be shown to have less adverse impact, but is equally effective in screening applicants, the organization may be required to adopt this alternative procedure in place of the original procedure.

There are several things organizations can, and should, do to avoid discrimination charges. To avoid disparate treatment charges, organizations must be careful to avoid inconsistent decisions. For example, personnel policies must be applied uniformly. Every personnel decision must be based upon carefully documented job-related information. Non-job-related factors, particularly those related to sex, race, age, and so forth, should play absolutely no role in personnel decisions. Finally, to avoid adverse impact lawsuits, organizations should carefully monitor the hiring and promotion rates of classes that traditionally have suffered discrimination. In addition, organizations should compare their workforce to labor market surveys to ensure comparability.

Companies concerned about reducing the likelihood of a lawsuit should be sure that each job requirement and selection procedure can be clearly justified as to its importance. The legal history of many common selection procedures, as well as a discussion of legally inappropriate interview questions, is provided in Chapter 5.

Do you think that an adverse impact approach might be an effective way for Maria to bring a lawsuit in the opening situation of this chapter? Indeed, it might be. If it could be shown that Maria's protected class was underrepresented among area-level managers, the burden would shift to the company to show that a job-related procedure was being used. However, given the statistics involved, the case might require an expert witness, which could become quite expensive for Maria.

Now that you have read about the different approaches to proving a discrimination case, you will read about affirmative action, which has generated quite some controversy over the years.

Affirmative Action

Affirmative action Emphasis on recruitment of traditionally underrepresented groups; altering managerial and supervisory attitudes to eliminate prejudice; removing discriminatory barriers in hiring and promotions; and using a quota, or giving preferential treatment in hiring and promotion, to groups that have been underrepresented in the organization's workforce.

Depending on whom you talk with, you may get different explanations of what affirmative action means, including the following:

1. Emphasis on recruitment of traditionally underrepresented groups, such as women, for executive positions.
2. Altering managerial and supervisory attitudes to eliminate prejudice.
3. Removing discriminatory barriers in hiring and promotions.
4. Using a quota, or giving preferential treatment in hiring and promotion, to groups that have been underrepresented in the organization's workforce.[28]

None of these explanations is wrong, different companies and different people simply use the term "affirmative action" differently. The first three explanations, however, are fairly noncontroversial. You would probably agree that these three are reasonable actions for a company to undertake. The fourth explanation, on the other hand, may surprise you. After all, didn't the Civil Rights Act of 1964 bar discrimination and preferential treatment on the basis of race, sex, religion, color, and national origin? Wouldn't a quota hiring plan (for example, one female must be hired for each male hired) therefore be illegal? Because of the controversy that has arisen regarding it, this section will cover only the fourth explanation of affirmative action. As you will see, certain affirmative action programs have evoked much attention and have been addressed in several major Supreme Court cases. There are three ways in which an affirmative action (AA) program may become part of the organization's staffing system:

1. The organization may *voluntarily* choose to implement an AA program.
2. The organization may be *required* to implement an AA program because it does business with the government.
3. The organization may be *required* to implement an AA program because it has been found guilty of discrimination or as the result of an out-of-court settlement.

We begin with a discussion of the first situation, where a company voluntarily adopts an affirmative action program. To understand this concept, it is useful to review a famous Supreme Court decision that was handed down in the late 1970s. Following this, you will read about the two situations where affirmative action will be required.

Affirmative Action: Can A Company Voluntarily Adopt Quota Hiring?

Perhaps the most controversial affirmative action situation is one where a company voluntarily adopts a quota hiring or promotion plan. The first major court case involving such a plan in the workplace was brought by a white male, Brian Weber. Weber was working as a production employee for Kaiser Aluminum &

Chemical Corporation. As a member of the Kaiser workforce, Weber was eligible for entry into a highly sought-after, skilled-craft training program. Entry into this program was based on seniority at Kaiser. However, due to the AA plan, several black production workers with less seniority were admitted into the training program prior to Weber. From Weber's perspective, this action was a clear violation of the 1964 Civil Rights Act because the decision to deny his entry into the training program had been based solely on his race. From the company's perspective, the percentage of black crafts workers was extremely low. At the time of the lawsuit, only 1.83 percent of the skilled crafts workers were black, even though blacks constituted 39 percent of the workforce in the labor market surrounding the plant. Thus, the company's goal was to establish a more equitable workforce (and perhaps to avoid a lawsuit by blacks for racial discrimination). Do you think Kaiser was violating the Civil Rights Act of 1964 by not admitting Weber? At the end, the Supreme Court ruled in favor of the company and against Weber. In justifying this decision, the majority opinion of the Supreme Court focused on two points. First, based on records of the debate that took place when Congress discussed the 1964 Civil Rights Act, the Supreme Court felt that the intent of Congress was to help further the employment of blacks in the workforce. Thus, the Supreme Court majority opinion asserted that the purpose of the act was not only to remove barriers and discrimination, but to also encourage the advancement of minorities in the workforce. Voluntary AA plans, such as the one implemented by Kaiser, were therefore perceived to be in keeping with the spirit of the Civil Rights Act. A second point raised by the Supreme Court was the wording of the section in the Civil Rights Act of 1964 that pertains to AA programs. The major statement regarding affirmative action here was as follows:

> Nothing contained in this title shall be interpreted to require any employer . . . to grant preferential treatment to any individual or to any group because of the race, color, religion, sex, or national origin of such individual or group on account of an imbalance which may exist.

Do you see the term "require"? The majority opinion on the Supreme Court pointed out that the term "require" implies that an organization may *choose* to adopt such a plan. Had Congress intended to ban a voluntary affirmative action plan, the word "permit" would have been used. Although the Supreme Court ruled in favor of Kaiser's AA plan, the Court indicated that not just any affirmative action plan would pass court muster. Specifically, the Supreme Court outlined several features of Kaiser's plan that made it acceptable:

1. The plan did not seriously violate the rights of the majority (in this case whites); (one white would be admitted for each black), and no whites would be terminated as a result of the plan.
2. The plan was temporary in nature, it was designed to end when its purpose was achieved.
3. The plan had a specific, reasonable purpose in mind, namely, to correct a racial imbalance.[29]

Voluntary AA plans in other organizations have also been accepted by the courts. In cases where layoff situations have been the focus, however, the courts have generally ruled in favor of seniority systems and against AA principles. For example, in one case, the Supreme Court decided that even though a reduction in

Box 2.5 Sex Discrimination: A Global Comparison

Although sex discrimination in the workplace occurs around the world, the experience of women differs from country to country. Consider Japan, where powerful cultural norms dictate that women should remain housekeepers, while their husbands devote both their work life and social life to the company. A majority of Japanese women continue to accept that norm, as indicated by a 1992 poll showing that 56 percent endorsed a statement that the man should be the wage earner while the wife stays home. In comparison, only 24 percent of American women and 13 percent of Swedish women approved of that statement. Thus, despite the existence of a national law banning discrimination, women in Japan continue to face many hurdles, especially in light of the current economic problems. Male college graduates, for example, are twice as likely to get jobs as females. Many newspaper job ads specify whether a man or woman is desired; being less than 35 years old is sometimes an explicit "qualification" listed in the ad. Only 1 percent of women who work hold managerial jobs.

Although different in certain ways, working women in Mexico have had a similar experience as working women in Japan. On the surface, though, women in the workplace have far more rights than in Japan. An equal rights law for women has existed for more than 20 years, and working women are legally provided three months of paid maternity leave, as well as extra rest time for nursing mothers. But companies regularly run afoul of the law by firing pregnant women and requiring married women to take pregnancy tests before being hired. Apparently, existing laws are of little or no help to women who feel they have been discriminated against. But this may change in the future, as the number of women in the Mexican Senate tripled in the most recent year, and about twice as many women serve now in the lower house.

Women in Sweden have experienced far fewer problems than in most countries of the world, but even there problems remain. On the positive side, there are many laws supporting working women in their child care efforts, including more than one year of paid maternity leave and a guaranteed equivalent job upon return. Companies must also allow working mothers to work part-time for up to 12 years after the birth of a child (men are also eligible for these benefits). At the same time, differences between men and women persist. Only 8 percent of managerial jobs are held by women, and practically no women are in top management jobs. Some critics feel that the generous leave policies too often encourage working women to maintain traditional roles and forego career advancement.

Source: Adopted from V. Reitman, "Japan: She Is Free, yet She's Alone in Her World," *The Wall Street Journal,* July 26, 1995, B1, B12; D. Solis, "Mexico: A Pioneer in the Land of Machismo," *The Wall Street Journal,* July 26, 1995, B1, B12; and D. Milbank, "Sweden: Laws Help Mom, but They Hurt Her Career," *The Wall Street Journal,* July 26, 1995, B1, B12

workforce based on seniority would be more harmful to blacks (most of whom were hired on the basis of a recently implemented AA plan and therefore had only worked a short time), the seniority principle was more important. Hence, although voluntary AA plans have been ruled legal by the courts, it is imperative that organizations considering their implementation pay careful attention to the characteristics mentioned here, and be prepared to justify their affirmative action plan if challenged.[30]

Affirmative Action: Presidential Mandate

Executive Order 11246 A law passed by President Johnson in 1965

Executive orders, as defined earlier, refer to laws enacted by the president of the United States. The most well-known is **Executive Order 11246**, which was initially signed into law by President Lyndon B. Johnson in 1965 and which prohibits discrimination on the basis of race, color, religion, sex, and national origin. Private businesses that have government contracts and subcontracts of more than $10,000 are covered by this law. Firms with contracts of $50,000 or more and 50 or more employees also must engage in "affirmative action" to remedy underutilization of women and minorities. The guidelines for AA under this law are contained in a document referred to as "Revised Order No. 4," which was written and is enforced by the Office of Federal Contract Compliance Programs (OFCCP). A company covered by this document must engage in affirmative action planning, which involves the following steps:

covering government contractors that prohibits discrimination.

Office of Federal Contract Compliance Programs (OFCCP)
Wrote and enforces a document referred to as "Revised Order No. 4," which contains the guidelines for affirmative action to remedy the underutilization of women and minorities in firms that have government contracts.

Utilization analysis
A method of affirmative action planning where the employer must compare the race, sex and ethnic composition of the workforce to the race, sex, and ethnic composition of the labor market.

1. Utilization Analysis. The employer must compare the race, sex, and ethnic composition of the workforce to the race, sex, and ethnic composition of the labor market; this is called a utilization analysis. A list of eight factors is used to determine the composition of the labor market (for example, general availability of minorities having requisite skills in the immediate labor market), which are combined using a formula. A job group in which the percentage of women or minorities in the workforce is significantly lower than in the labor market indicates underutilization.
2. Establishment of Goals and Timetables. For any areas in which there is an underutilization, the organization must establish a goal (such as a target percentage of women or minorities to be attained) along with a timetable for when that goal will be reached.
3. Action Steps to Be Taken. The organization must specify in writing the steps that will be taken to achieve the goals within the specified timetables. Steps may include publicizing its affirmative action plans, participating in minority outreach programs, advertising in minority newspapers and magazines, and so forth.[31]

Affirmative Action: Required Due to Court-Ordered or Out-of-Court Settlement

An affirmative action program may be court imposed if the company is found guilty of persistent and serious discrimination. Or, the company may agree to implement an affirmative action program as part of a settlement with EEOC or OFCCP. As an example, in 1984 the Prudential Insurance company agreed to implement such an AA program as a result of an agreement with the OFCCP. As part of the AA program, Prudential agreed to provide training to nearly 10,000 minority applicants who were denied jobs between 1978 and 1983. Further, the company agreed to hire some of those completing the training and to provide additional training to 438 women and minority employees who had not advanced as far as others. Participants were offered the opportunity to take as many as 260 hours of training, for which they would be paid a minimum wage.[32]

Most recently, affirmative action has come under a great deal of public scrutiny and debate, as the political mood of the country turns more conservative and critical of government regulations. Some experts speculate that the genre of affirmative action programs described above will soon be either eliminated or deemed illegal by the Supreme Court. Whether affirmative action programs are completely discontinued in the workplace remains to be seen.[33]

Bringing a Lawsuit

So far, you have learned about who is covered by the laws, the procedures for proving and defending a legal charge, and the conditions under which an organization may implement an AA plan. But, what if you have had a bad experience in your job or in applying for a job, and you would like to bring a discrimination charge. What happens next? Here are the basic steps you would need to follow.[34]

1. Most of the federal fair employment laws require you to first file the complaint with the EEOC or the state agency responsible for processing such complaints. Check your phone book for the address and phone number. You should be aware of the following issues in filing your charge:
   a. You may file a charge either in person or by mail.
   b. You do not have to identify yourself in the charges you file, but in many cases your company may be able to figure out who you are. It is, however, against the law for your company to retaliate against you for filing a charge.
   c. There are strict time limits for filing charges. Although the limit depends in part on whether a state agency or the EEOC is handling the complaint, it is safe to say that you should file your complaint within six months of the act you are challenging. So, if you feel you have been discriminated against, and plan to file a charge, don't wait too long!
2. What will the EEOC do with your complaint? A summary of the steps is provided in Figure 2.2.
   a. The EEOC must notify the organization within 10 days that you have filed a charge.
   b. The EEOC has the authority to conduct an investigation of your charge. Toward that end, the EEOC may inspect company records, interview other employees, and request other information from the company such as job descriptions, tests, and so forth.
   c. Based on its initial investigation, the EEOC may feel that your case has merit (or **reasonable cause**). The EEOC is obliged to first try to reach a *reconciliation,* or settlement, between you and the organization.
   d. If no reconciliation can be agreed upon, the EEOC can sue the organization on your behalf. If the EEOC feels there is insufficient evidence of discrimination, it will issue you a **right-to-sue notice.** This gives you the right to have a lawyer take your case. Given that many discrimination charges are filed each year, the EEOC usually concentrates only on the most promising cases. So even though your charge may have merit, there is a good chance that the EEOC will not pursue your case.
3. If the EEOC has issued you a right-to-sue notice, or if you are filing a charge under a law not requiring you to go to the EEOC first, you will need to hire a lawyer to represent you. Here are some things you should know about hiring a lawyer:
   a. There are tens of thousands of lawyers in practice today; choosing an effective lawyer you can work with is not easy. You are encouraged to obtain a referral from a reliable source, such as the state bar association, or a publication, such as "Best Attorneys in America" or the Martindale-Hubbell directory, which provides background information on many lawyers.

Reasonable cause
Based on their initial investigation, the EEOC may feel that a case has merit, or reasonable cause, to pursue a settlement or a suit.

Right-to-sue notice
A notice issued from the EEOC that gives you the right to have a lawyer take your case in a discrimination suit.

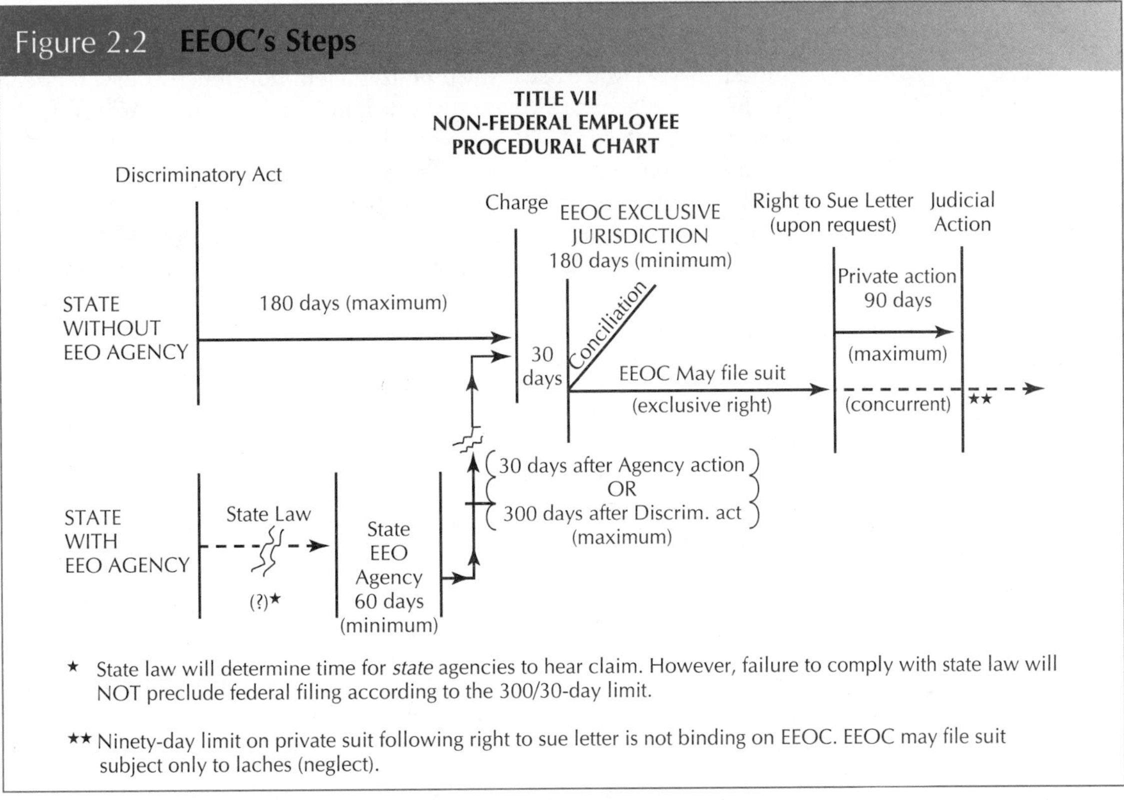

Source: M.A. Player (1992). *Federal Law of Employment Discrimination.* St. Paul, MN: West.

Sexual harassment comes in many forms—inappropriate touching, suggestive comments, unwanted advances, lewd language, or paraphernalia. As shown here, sexual harassment can be either a male harassing a female, or a female harassing a male. Any unwelcome advances can be considered sexual harassment, and should be reported to a supervisor or a human resource manager.

b. Carefully interview several potential lawyers. Because they may charge an initial fee, use the time carefully to explain your case, and get their advice. Honest lawyers won't make any promises about how much money they can win for you. Make sure you ask who would handle the case. Will it be the person you are talking with (who may be a partner) or an associate (usually a junior lawyer with less experience)?
c. Be sure to determine the fee structure. Depending on the nature of the case, there may be an hourly fee (typically this will range between $100 to $250 per hour, depending on the cost of living in the area), or a contingency fee, which is based on winning the case. In either situation, you may also have to pay for various expenses, such as travel, filing costs, and so forth. So be sure you fully understand the fee structure.

The bottom line in hiring a lawyer is this: Choose carefully and make sure you understand what you are getting into.

Remedies for Discrimination: Or What You Can Get If You Win

What you may be wondering at this point is whether it is worth it to even file a discrimination complaint or talk with a lawyer. Although the remedies you might win differ depending on the specific law you are suing under, you may be awarded the following:[35]

1. The promotion or job that you were denied as a result of discrimination.
2. Back pay (the amount of money you lost as a result of being discriminated against).
3. Attorney's fees (and fees of certain other parties, such as expert witnesses who testified on your behalf).
4. In a case of intentional discrimination, punitive damages, which could amount to hundreds of thousands of dollars.
5. An agreement that the organization will no longer engage in the practice(s) you have complained about.

Of course, in many cases, the company simply settles out of court, so you may win something even though the case never goes to trial.

Current Issues in Workplace Discrimination

Several current issues in workplace discrimination have captured the attention of interested observers. We will address three of these in further detail, namely, women and the glass ceiling, sexual harassment, and the impact of recent layoffs on African Americans.

Women and the Glass Ceiling

The term glass ceiling refers to an invisible barrier preventing women from advancing to higher levels within the organization. Recent surveys indicate that

Box 2.6 How One Woman Sued Her Company for Discrimination

Katharine Stone once worked as a news director for a television station. After several years on the job, she was called into the station manager's office and told she was fired. Most of the reasons given for her termination were quite vague and none of them had ever been mentioned in any previous feedback sessions. The major reason seemed to be insubordination. In an ironic twist, Stone in the past had protested the termination of other female managers. Now it was her turn to be fired. Stone was shocked; she had received the maximum raise each year and had always been praised for her work performance. Her boss thought so highly of her work that he once told her she would be employed "forever."

As a result of the termination, Stone contacted a lawyer, who encouraged her to try to reach an amiable settlement without filing a discrimination charge. However, when Stone met with the CEO of the television station, he informed her that if she brought a lawsuit, she would never again be able to work in the broadcast industry. Stone therefore decided to bring a sex discrimination lawsuit.

Little did Stone know at the time what she was getting into when she filed the lawsuit. As preparation for the trial began, both sides began the discovery process, during which the attorneys attempt to uncover evidence pertinent to the case. In addition to interviewing coworkers, obtaining company memos, and examining Stone's tax returns (to determine if she experienced a reduction in income as a result of discrimination), Stone's personal diary was examined. Particularly surprising and upsetting to Stone was that lawyers spoke with her therapist, because her attorney was arguing that she suffered emotionally from the discrimination. All in all, the discovery process was a very stressful and difficult experience for her.

At the end, the case did not go to trial. After months of investigation by the attorneys, the company made an out-of-court settlement offer, which Stone accepted. How much money do you think Stone received in the settlement? Well, your guess is as good as anybody's, because as is typical, part of the settlement is that Stone was not allowed to tell others what she received. Do you think Stone would have still sued, had she known all of the stress it would produce? Her answer to this question was, "My fight was worth it. Even if I had received nothing, I'd still believe I had done the right thing."

Source: Adapted from K. Stone, "How and Why I Sued My Boss for Sex Discrimination," *Glamour,* June 1987, 228–29, 258–59, 262.

while the percentage of women managers nearly doubled from 1981 (27 percent) to 1991 (41 percent), the percentage of women who are senior executives barely budged from 1981 (when they represented a mere 1 percent) to 1991 (when women represented only 3 percent of senior executives).[36] As Ann Morrison, coauthor of a recent book on the glass ceiling, noted, "Because women represented 15 percent of all managers in 1968, you might expect 15 percent of today's senior managers to be female. . . . Instead they make up about 3 percent."[37] Perhaps even more startling, a recent survey of 201 CEOs from large U.S. companies showed only 16 percent believed that they would very likely be or somewhat likely be succeeded by a female CEO within the next ten years—and a shocking 40 percent indicated that this event was not likely at all to occur! When asked why they felt a female CEO was unlikely to succeed them, a major barrier was simply discrimination. As John Bryan, CEO of Sara Lee, put it, "It shouldn't be this way, but too many senior managers, and particularly CEOs, tend to want to pass their jobs along to someone who's the image and likeness of themselves." The CEOs provided a number of specific reasons as to why women have such low chances of becoming CEO. The top five reasons, along with the percentage of CEOs indicating each, were the following:

Glass ceiling
Refers to an invisible barrier preventing women from advancing to higher levels within the organization.

1. Lack of enough experience (64 percent).
2. Work in positions that typically don't lead to CEO position, such as communications (50 percent).
3. Lack broad enough experience (45 percent).
4. Lack of networks (31 percent).
5. Personal lives and obligations to families get in the way (29 percent).[38]

But the obvious question is, How do women get enough experience and of the right kinds, as indicated by reasons 1, 2, and 3 above? William Ruckelshaus, CEO of Browning-Ferris Industries, summed it up this way, "It really isn't a question of what else women should be doing. It's a question of what *companies* should be doing to ensure that women are getting the opportunities men get."[39]

So, what can companies do to deal with these problems? Several things can be done.[40]

1. Reduce bias in the workplace. There are numerous ways to reduce bias, including use of unambiguous policy statements, diversity training, and disciplinary actions leveled against those managers who engage in sex discrimination. Monsanto, the diversified chemical company, holds workshops for employees that are designed to identify and eliminate stereotypes about women. Almost 5,000 employees have taken the workshop, which lasts six days. In one of the exercises, participants are instructed to write down every stereotype they believe about women. These stereotypes are then posted for discussion.

2. Track highly qualified women and provide appropriate experiences and skills. Anheuser-Busch, the beer company, has a highly regarded management development program for wholesaler positions where employees progress from inventory analysts to inventory management specialists. This program makes a point of involving qualified women. American Airlines started a program, called the Supertrack, that circulates evaluations of promising managers to senior officers in the company. This is one reason the percentage of women in middle- and upper-level positions rose at American Airlines from 12 percent in 1986 to 21 percent in 1991.

3. Provide mentoring and coaching programs for women. Pacific Bell, based in San Francisco, started its two-year mentoring program in 1989. One of the early mentorees, D.J. Hulet, was matched with 48-year-old John Seymour, a vice president and general manager. Because some of her male coworkers felt she was too aggressive, Seymour coached Hulet on how to influence people without coming across too forcefully. As a result, Hulet received a promotion to regional marketing manager. Women are also establishing their own networks. For instance, a group of women who graduated from the University of Pennsylvania have formed a council that provides female seniors and business school students with a list of highly successful businesswomen to contact for career advice. The council also developed a program that enables students to observe a female executive at work. As Constance Duckworth, a partner at Goldman Sachs, the investment banking firm, puts it, "This is something I didn't have when I was starting out in business. . . . It's an 'old-girls' network, in an embryonic stage."

Sexual Harassment

Almost everyone has heard of sexual harassment. Various surveys show that sexual harassment at work has, at least in the past, been quite prevalent. For example, a 1988 survey indicated that 42 percent of federally employed women reported some form of sexual harassment. A random telephone survey of private-sector women in Los Angeles reported that more than half had experienced at least one incident of sexual harassment in their careers. Maria's experience, as described in the opening case of this chapter, is not unique. But what exactly is considered sexual harassment? What can companies do to avoid sexual harassment lawsuits? These issues will be discussed in greater detail next.[41]

What Is Sexual Harassment? One reason that companies have been particularly concerned by sexual harassment is that the definition of this term can be quite vague. Initially, sexual harassment was understood to occur only in a **quid-pro-quo** (a Latin phrase meaning something in exchange for something) situation, meaning when a supervisor offered to provide a subordinate's job or raise or other personnel action in exchange for sexual favors. But a case in 1986, *Meritor Savings Bank v. Vinson,* changed that situation. In that case, the Supreme Court identified a second type of sexual harassment, known as **hostile environment**. A hostile environment is created by unwelcome sexual advances, requests for sexual favors, and other verbal or physical conduct of a sexual nature. Table 2.4 gives some specific examples of hostile environment cases where the plaintiff won. As you can see from Table 2.4, a hostile environment can be created by even nonsupervisors (such as coworkers). In fact, there have been cases where actions taken by a nonemployee (for example, a vending machine operator) served as grounds for a sexual harassment charge. So, what behaviors are okay? And what behaviors should you avoid so that *you* are not charged with sexual harassment? Table 2.5 gives a list of do's and don'ts in this regard. Be sure to note that sexual harassment charges can be made against women as well as men. Next, we discuss what an organization can

Quid-pro-quo sexual harassment
A Latin phrase meaning something in exchange for something else, such as a supervisor offering an employee a promotion or raise or other personnel action in exchange for sexual favors.

Hostile environment sexual harassment
An environment created by unwelcome sexual advances, requests for sexual favors, and other verbal or physical conduct of a sexual nature.

Table 2.4 Typical Sexual Harassment Cases Where Plaintiff Won

Photographs, Graffiti, and Comments:

1. The shipyard in which a woman welder worked had pictures of nude and partially nude women in a variety of posters. These pictures were affixed to walls throughout the shipyard. In addition, sexually offensive words, phrases, and drawings appeared. Male employees continuously made sexually offensive comments to the woman.
2. A female police office was subjected to frequent sexually oriented incidents by fellow officers and other local officials, including kissing and moaning noises over the police radio. Various pictures and graffiti were also written on police department walls.
3. A female agent with the Internal Revenue Service was asked to lunch by a male coworker, which she accepted. Subsequently, the coworker began to spend much time talking with the female agent, and one day he asked her to go out for a drink. She refused. A few days later, the coworker wrote a note to her, expressing his deep feelings toward her. After refusing to talk with the coworker, he sent her an emotionally charged letter in the mail, which frightened her further.

Source: Adapted from *Sexual Harassment Manual for Managers and Supervisors* (Chicago: Commerce Clearing House, 1991).

Table 2.5 The Do's and Don'ts of Sexual Harassment

Here's What You Can Do	Here's What Might Be Seen as Sexual Harassment	Here's What Would Probably Be Seen as Sexual Harassment
1. Hug or pat on the back *if the recipient doesn't flinch, scowl, or object* (better yet, play it safe, and don't hug or pat anyone on the back). 2. Shake hands. 3. Request a date.	1. Sexually suggestive conversation if the other person objects. 2. Sexist remarks about the person's body, clothing, or personal activities. 3. A request for a date after the person says no. 4. A dirty joke if a person objects. 5. Leering, ogling.	1. Demands (subtle and blatant) for sexual favors. 2. Pictures of nude and seminude bodies, including possibly the swimsuit issue of *Sports Illustrated.* 3. Repeated leering or ogling. 4. Repeated requests for a date after a person says no. 5. Repeated brushing against a person's body.

Source: Adapted from R. Sharpe, "Acceptable Behavior: Sexual Harassment Message Swift and Clear," *St. Louis Post-Dispatch,* November 14, 1993, B1.

do to avoid charges and reduce the likelihood of losing a sexual harassment suit.

What Can Organizations Do to Avoid Sexual Harassment Problems? Companies can do a number of things to avoid sexual harassment problems.[42]

1. **Establish a formal, written policy regarding sexual harassment.** This policy should clearly define and prohibit sexual harassment, outline a grievance procedure for employees who believe they have been sexually harassed, and describe the disciplinary actions that will be taken against an employee who engages in sexual harassment.

2. **Educate employees about sexual harassment.** Employees should be trained on how to deal with sexual harassment and instructed on how to go about filing a grievance. Managers and supervisors should be trained to identify such situations and enforce the policy.

3. **Establish an effective grievance procedure.** The presence of an effective grievance procedure is evidence that the company did its best to eliminate sexual harassment. An effective grievance procedure will have a designated person (other than one's direct supervisor) handling any complaints, an alternative person if the grievant feels the complaint was not handled fairly, and a promise of confidentiality.

4. **Conduct prompt, thorough investigations.** It is critical for the company to promptly conduct a complete, careful investigation of any charges of sexual harassment. Once a complaint has been received, and the details obtained (for example, who was involved, when and where did the events occur, and so forth), it is critical to interview potential witnesses and attempt to verify the events from independent sources. Of course, in many cases there are no other witnesses.

5. **Take quick, but carefully considered, disciplinary action against harasser(s).** In some court cases, the court ruled in favor of the company because it had taken immediate disciplinary action. In addition, taking the appropriate disciplinary action is a clear sign that such behavior will not

be tolerated. At the same time, the organization should be sure not to unjustly punish persons for things they did not do.

In sum, Maria's comments in the opening case suggest that sexual harassment is occurring in her company. She has the legal right to end the behaviors and verbal statements that her boss, Pat, is making. Given both potential liability, as well as ethical and moral considerations, organizations must take an active role in weeding out this problem.

Race and Job Loss

Losing one's job is quite common in today's workplace. But do some racial or ethnic groups suffer more job losses than others? In a 1993 *Wall Street Journal* study, it was reported that African Americans suffered disproportionately more job loss during the last recession than did other racial and ethnic groups. Based on an analysis of EEOC reports filed by more than 30,000 companies, African Americans lost nearly 60,000 jobs in the 1990–1991 recession. By contrast, Asians gained more than 55,000 jobs, Hispanics gained 60,000 jobs, and whites gained more than 70,000 jobs. Why this effect on African Americans? Company spokespeople generally assert that it is due merely to company restructuring, not racially motivated decision making. Sears Roebuck, for example, from which a large percentage of African American employees lost their jobs, blamed the closure of several expensive distribution centers located in urban areas, which were heavily staffed by African Americans. At W.R. Grace, several businesses such as restaurants (which employed substantial numbers of African Americans) were sold off, which, according to company spokespeople, explains the high job loss of African Americans. Another, related explanation is that African American employees are concentrated in the four job categories that have suffered the greatest losses: office/clerical, skilled, semiskilled, and laborers. Proportionately few African Americans are employed in job categories that suffered little, if any cuts, such as technicians or professionals. Critics point to alternative explanations for the job loss of African Americans. Frank Bellow, a machinist at one of W.R. Grace's plants, maintains the company is simply prejudiced and deliberately sought to cut minority employment. Wesley Poriotis, head of Wesley, Brown & Bartle, a minority search firm, maintains that, "There's a deep sourness in corporate America that they had to hire minority professionals. Downsizing has been their first opportunity to strike back."

But African Americans did not suffer at all companies. American Telephone & Telegraph company, for instance, was careful not to adversely affect minorities. So, rather than cut employees, AT&T began trimming its payroll by offering employees two-year unpaid leaves of absence. The company also helped these employees find other jobs, as temporary employees in the firm or elsewhere. As a result of this effort, of the nearly 20,000 AT&T employees who lost jobs during the recession, about 16 percent were African American, almost exactly matching the percentage of African American employees in the company. At Louisiana-Pacific, the percentage of African Americans on the workforce actually grew during the recession, from 6.1 percent to 7.7 percent. What was the reason for the growth? The company shut down plants in rural Northern California—which have few minorities—and added workers in southern states that have a large African American population. Regardless of which explanation you believe for the disproportionate job loss among African Americans, the numbers from these companies do suggest a potential social problem.[43]

Conclusion

You have read about the various federal laws regarding employment discrimination, as well as the procedures relevant to proving a discrimination charge. You have also learned about affirmative action, and some conditions under which it may be required. Finally, you learned about some major issues in the discrimination area today. You should have gathered several key points from this chapter. First, discrimination laws have a major effect on the human resource management function today. To be an effective line manager, you will need to have a basic understanding of the legal aspects of any personnel decisions you make. If you wish to be a successful human resource manager, of course, you will need to have a much more in-depth understanding of the law. Relatedly, it is in your best interest as an employee to be aware of your protection from discrimination. That way, you will be better able to identify and deal with potentially unfair employment decisions. Second, employment discrimination issues are related to some major societal problems. Such issues as disproportionate job losses by African Americans suggest more careful consideration of our various laws, as well as various social policies. At the same time, given the trend toward reducing government regulation, a move toward reducing some of these laws may gain momentum. The final result on employment discrimination will be seen in the next few years.

Applying Core Concepts

1. Jose Sanchez recently applied for a job where he was one of the three final candidates. Although he had the necessary skills, abilities, and education, the manager told him that he lacked the necessary experience. What type of lawsuit might Jose pursue? What would he need to show to prove discrimination? What would the company need to show to defend itself?
2. Mary Lao applied for a job as a secretary. The job involves using a personal computer to type letters and memos, answering the phone, and filing papers. Although Mary is qualified in every way, she is legally blind. What would you do if you were the hiring manager?
3. What does your company or organization do to help prepare women for senior executive positions? What should your company or organization do to help prepare women for these jobs?
4. Do you think what is happening to Maria in the opening case constitutes sexual harassment?
5. Should a federal law protecting workers from discrimination on the basis of sexual orientation be passed? Why or why not?
6. If you felt you were discriminated against in your job, what laws might protect you?
7. Does your company that you work for now or plan to work for in the future have an affirmative action program? Why or why not?

Key Terms

- Civil Rights Act of 1866
- Civil Rights Act of 1964
- Civil Rights Act of 1991
- Equal Employment Opportunity Commission (EEOC)
- Pregnancy Discrimination Act of 1978
- Immigration Reform and Control Act
- Rehabilitation Act of 1973
- Americans with Disabilities Act of 1990
- Reasonable accommodation
- Undue hardship
- Age Discrimination in Employment Act of 1967
- Evil intent
- Bona fide occupational qualification (BFOQ)
- Disparate treatment
- *McDonnell-Douglas* v. *Green* Case Standards
- Adverse impact
- Applicant flow
- Stock analysis
- Validation study
- Affirmative action
- Executive Order 11246
- Office of Federal Contract Compliance Programs (OFCCP)
- Utilization analysis
- Reasonable cause
- Right-to-sue notice
- Glass ceiling
- Quid-pro-quo sexual harassment
- Hostile environment sexual harassment

Chapter 2: Experiential Exercise

The Case of Paula Kind

Microtone Products (not its real name) is a small (200 employees) company located in the midwest, near a large city. It produces electrical machinery. Paula Kind (not her real name) began working for the company several months ago. She is one of the maintenance staff, responsible for machine repair. Most of the workers are men, and she is the only woman in her department. During the first month, the workers would occasionally whistle at her, and once or twice, someone had made a crude, sexually suggestive remark. At the end of the first month of her employment, Paula talked to you, the area supervisor, about the whistles and the remarks. After she told you what had happened, you replied:

"Well, that's what it is like working in a predominantly male workforce, especially in a factory. Some of the men resent having a woman around, but mostly they are trying to lighten the place up. If you just ignore them, I'm sure they'll stop."

Paula seemed to follow your advice, and the whistles and remarks began to end. A few months later, however, Paula came back to you with the following story. She had been repairing some equipment on the second shift when Bill "Wild Man" Smith came over to her and said: "You look foxy tonight, Paula! I've been meaning to ask you to have a drink with me at the end of the shift." She replied: "No thank you, I'm busy tonight." He then said: "How about tomorrow night?" to which she again replied: "No, thank you, I'm busy tomorrow night as well." According to Paula, Bill stood there looking her "up and down" in a very suggestive way, winked, and then left.

The next day, you called Bill in to your office to hear his version. He admitted asking her to have a drink with him after the shift, but said that he likes to socialize with the new employees (male and female) just to get to know them better. When you asked him about the "suggestive look," he smiled and said that she is attractive and it's only natural to admire beauty.

The next day, when you met with Paula, she began by saying: "Unless some immediate action is taken against Bill and some significant changes are made in this company as a whole, I intend to press sexual harassment charges against this company."

The questions for you to address are as follows:

1. What should you say now to Paula? To Bill? Do you think she is being harassed?
2. What should you do now? What would you have done differently in the case?
3. What actions could you take to avoid this situation in the future?

Chapter 2 References

1. United States Equal Employment Opportunity Commission, *Legislative History of Titles VII and XI of Civil Rights Act of 1964* (Washington: U.S. Government Printing Office [no date]).
2. H. Graham, *The Civil Rights Era* (New York: Oxford University Press, 1990).
3. United States Equal Employment Opportunity Commission, "Legislative History of Titles VII and XI of Civil Rights Act of 1964," (Washington: U.S. Government Printing Office [no date]).
4. J. Jones, W. Murphy, and R. Belton, *Discrimination in Employment* (St. Paul: West, 1987).
5. L. Joel, *Every Employee's Guide to the Law* (New York: Pantheon, 1993).
6. D. Bennett-Alexander and L. Pincus, *Employment Law for Business* (Chicago: Irwin, 1995).
7. J. Ledvinka and V. Scarpello, *Federal Regulation of Personnel and Human Resource Management* (Boston: PWS-Kent, 1991).
8. U.S. Census Bureau, *Labor Force Status and Other Characteristics of Persons with a Work Disability 1981–1988* (Washington: U.S. Government Printing Office, 1989).
9. U.S. Equal Employment Opportunity Commission, *Technical Assistance Manual on the Employment Provisions (Title I) of the Americans with Disabilities Act* (Washington: U.S. Government Printing Office, 1992).
10. Ibid.
11. *Equal Employment Opportunity for Individuals with Disabilities,* 29 CFR Part 1630 Federal Register, July 26, 1991.
12. M. Wilson, "Defenses to Discrimination Actions Filed under the Americans with Disabilities Act," *Labor Law Journal* 42, (1991) 732–46.
13. E. Fenner, "A Real-Life Philadelphia Case," *Money,* April, 1994, 134–45.
14. Joel, *Every Employee's Guide to the Law.*
15. Bennett-Alexander & Pinus, *Employment Law.*
16. H. Schachter, "A Case for Moving from Tolerance to Valuing Diversity," *Review of Public Personnel Administration,* Spring 1993, 29–44.
17. M. Player, *Federal Law of Employment Discrimination* (St. Paul: West, 1992).
18. Ibid.
19. *EEOC v. Alton Packaging Corporation,* 901 F.2d 920 (1990).
20. Player, *Federal Law of Employment Discrimination.*
21. *McDonnell-Douglas Corporation v. Green,* 93 S.Ct. 1817 (1973).
22. *St. Mary's Honor Center v. Hicks,* 113 S.Ct. 2742 (1993).
23. *Griggs v. Duke Power Co.,* 91 S.Ct. 849 (1971).
24. Ledvinka and Scarpello, *Federal Regulation of Personnel.*
25. R. Gatewood and H. Feild, *Human Resource Selection,* (Fort Worth, TX: Dryden, 1994).
26. Player, *Federal Law of Employment Discrimination.*
27. Ledvinka and Scarpello, *Federal Regulation of Personnel.*
28. Ibid.
29. *Weber v. Kaiser Aluminum and Chemical Corporation,* 443 S.Ct. 193 (1979).
30. L. Kleiman and R. Faley, "Voluntary Affirmative Action and Preferential Treatment: Legal and Research Implications," *Personnel Psychology* 41, (1988), 481–96.
31. Ledvinka and Scarpello, *Federal Regulation of Personnel.*
32. C. Trost, "Prudential, U.S. Agree on Plan for Minorities," *The Wall Street Journal,* August 22, 1984), 2.
33. D. Terpstra, "Affirmative Action: A Focus on the Issues," *Labor Law Journal* 46 (1995), 307–13.
34. Joel, *Every Employee's Guide to the Law.*

35. Player, *Federal Law of Employment Discrimination.*
36. "Corporate Women," *Business Week,* June 8, 1992, 74–83.
37. Ibid., 76.
38. A. Fisher, "When Will Women Get to the Top?" *Fortune,* September 21, 1992, 44–56.
39. Ibid., 47.
40. U.S. Department of Labor. (1992). *Pipeline of Progress: A Status Report on the Glass Ceiling Initiative* (Washington: U.S. Government Printing Office, 1992); and Fisher, "When Will Women Get to the Top?"
41. S. Riger, "Gender Dilemmas in Sexual Harassment Policies and Procedures," *American Psychologist* 46 (1991) 497–505; and P. Popovich, "Controlling Sexual Harassment in the Workplace," in *Applying Psychology in Business,* ed. J. Jones, B. Steffy, and D. Bray (Lexington, MA: Lexington Books, 1991).
42. Anonymous, *Sexual Harassment Manual for Managers and Supervisors* (Chicago: Commerce Clearing House, 1991).
43. R. Sharpe, "Losing Ground: In Latest Recession, Only Blacks Suffered Net Employment Loss," *The Wall Street Journal,* September 14, 1993, A1.

chapter 3 Human Resource Planning

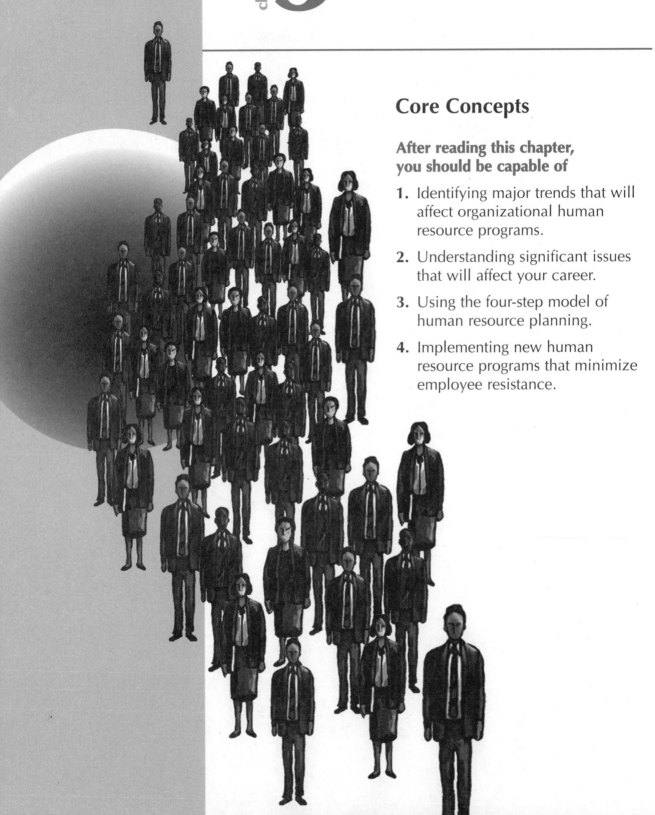

Core Concepts

After reading this chapter, you should be capable of

1. Identifying major trends that will affect organizational human resource programs.
2. Understanding significant issues that will affect your career.
3. Using the four-step model of human resource planning.
4. Implementing new human resource programs that minimize employee resistance.

Opening Case

Imagine that your supervisor told you that your organization was initiating a new program called the Career Assessment and Planning System (or CAPS). Using a personal computer (PC) software package, the employee would complete an inventory of his or her skills, experience, education, and training, as well as his or her interests in other jobs and other areas within the organization. After completing the inventory, someone from the human resources department would meet with the employee and provide feedback and suggestions for future career opportunities within the organization.

About one month later, you receive the CAPS software. The package contains detailed instructions about how to complete the PC-generated program. As shown in Figure 3.1, the program requests information regarding a variety of topics, including experience with specific tasks (such as typing, statistical analysis, and cost accounting), different positions or areas held in the organization, and various functional areas (for example, finance, sales or human resources) in which you wish to gain experience.

After reading the materials, you begin to think about career issues. So far, you have done little career planning. After graduating from high school, you went directly to college. During college you worked several part-time jobs, including working as a ticket collector at an amusement park, a food server at a restaurant, and a telephone marketer. Since graduating from college, you have worked as a management trainee with a large consumer products company and as a salesperson for your current employer, a medical products company. Three months ago, you were assigned to work as a marketing researcher for the company. You generally have given little thought to each of these moves, and you certainly don't have any game plan or even career direction. Rather, opportunities have arisen, and you have decided whether or not to accept them. You are beginning to wonder, however, whether you should develop a formal career plan. If you do choose to do this, how should you go about developing the plan?

This chapter is about human resource planning. A four-step model of human resource planning will be described that both organizations and individual employees should use, and some important issues that will affect everyone will be discussed. This chapter concludes with information on recent job trends and some thoughts on emerging jobs. First, however, you will learn why HR planning is important for both organizations and employees.

Why Is Human Resource Planning Important?

Human resource planning is important for helping both organizations and employees to prepare for the future. But you might be thinking, "Aren't things always changing?" For example, a few years ago, the law field seemed to be a good profession. But now it is very crowded. So what is the value of planning? The answer is that even an imperfect forecast of the future can be quite helpful. Consider weather forecasts. You can probably think of occasions when it snowed, even though the television weather forecaster predicted there would be no snow. Conversely, you can probably think of times when it did not snow, even though the weather forecaster predicted a foot of snow by the next morning. You may be surprised to learn that as inaccurate as weather forecasts sometimes seem to be, many organizations pay a forecasting service for regular weather updates. The reason for this is quite simple. Even a prediction that is sometimes wrong is better than no forecast or prediction at all. Perhaps the best example is the stock market.

Figure 3.1 **Career Assessment and Planning System Menu**

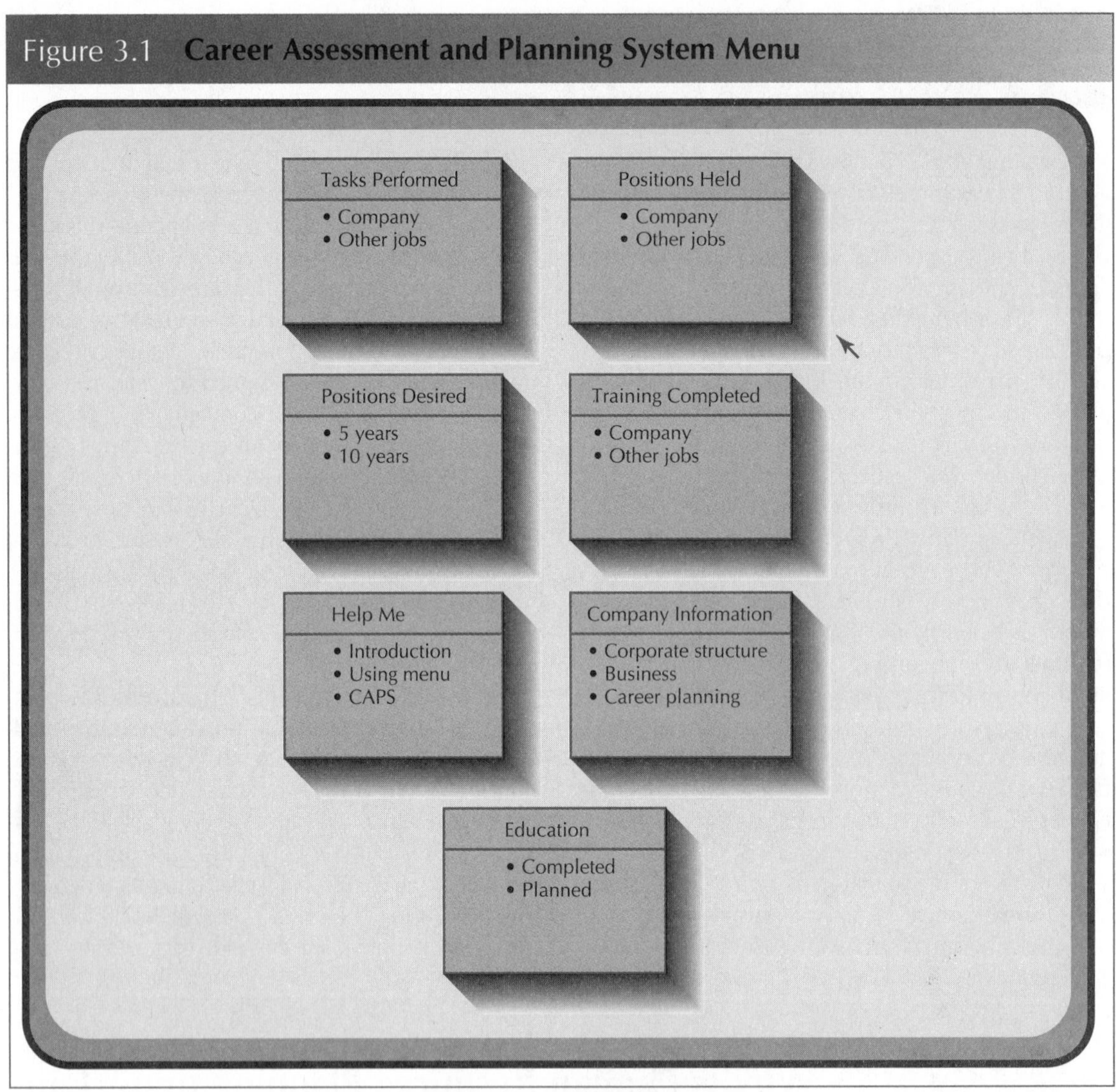

Human Resource Planning
The process of examining an organization's or individual's future human resource needs compared to future human resource capabilities, and developing human resource policies and practices to address potential problems.

If someone had even a fairly accurate way to predict which stocks would go up and which stocks would go down, that person could make a great deal of money investing in the stock market, even though there would be some mistakes. The key is whether one's prediction tool *improves* the chances of making the right decisions. Even though the predictive tool may not be always accurate, as long as it is more accurate than random guessing, it will result in better decisions.

The same point applies to human resource planning. Even though neither organizations nor employees can see into the future, making predictions can be quite helpful, even if they are not always accurate. The basic goal of human resource planning, then, is to predict the future and, based on these predictions, implement programs to avoid anticipated problems. Very briefly, human resource planning is the process of examining an organization's or individual's future human resource needs (for instance, what types of skills will be needed for jobs of the future) compared to future human resource capabilities (such as the types of skills employees or you already have) and developing human resource policies and practices to address potential problems (for example, implementing training programs to avoid skill deficiencies). We turn now to a four-step approach to human resource planning and discuss some important trends that will affect organizations, employees, and job applicants alike.

A Four-Step Approach to Human Resource Planning

Human resource planning typically involves four steps, which are shown in Figure 3.2.

Each of these steps is discussed in greater detail next.

Step 1: Examining External and Internal Issues

External and internal issues are the forces that drive human resource planning. An issue is any event or trend that has the potential to affect human resource outcomes, such as employee motivation, turnover, absenteeism, the number and types of employees needed, and so forth. External issues are events or trends outside of the organization, such as workforce demographics and technology. Internal issues refers to events or trends within the organization, such as business strategy, organizational structure, and company profitability.[1] Next, you will read about some external and internal issues that are currently affecting human resource planning, followed by a review of issues that will be of particular interest for your career.

External Issues
Events or trends outside of the organization, such as workforce demographics and technology.

Internal Issues
Events or trends within the organization, such as business strategy, organizational structure, and company profitability.

Figure 3.2 **A Model of Human Resource Planning**

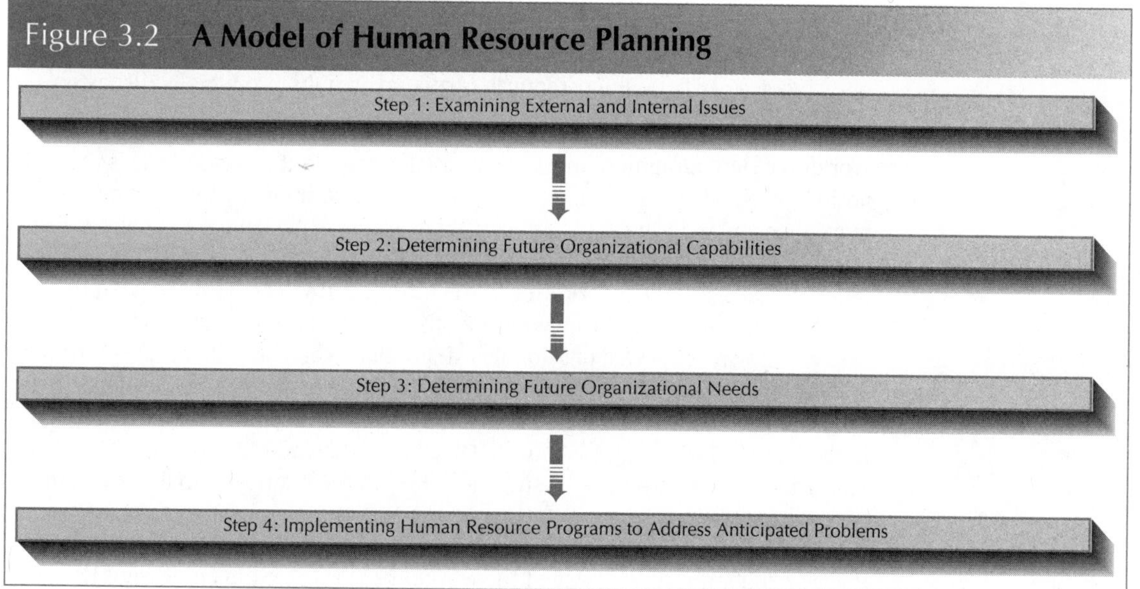

External Factors

Competition. Most businesses today compete on a global basis and therefore face fierce competition. In turn, this has led to four dramatic changes in many organizations and businesses.[2]

1. *Increased automation.* Consider, for example, Solectron Corporation, a circuit board manufacturer located in Silicon Valley, which has invested more than $80 million in automation. According to the president of the company, almost twice as many workers would be needed without the new equipment.
2. *Movement of production and service to countries with lower cost of labor.* Yolanda Navarro, who worked for 20 years at a Pillsbury frozen vegetable plant in California, recently lost her job due to layoffs. Compare her wages at the Pillsbury plant ($8.10 per hour plus benefits) to the wages paid to workers at another Pillsbury plant that produces the same product in Mexico. Workers there earn $7.58 per *day*.
3. *Increased outsourcing of work to other companies.* Many companies save money by **outsourcing** their work to other companies that do it cheaper. General Motors, for instance, recently discontinued bumper production at its Livonia, Michigan, plant and began contracting with other companies to provide the bumpers. A major reason is GM's high hourly wages, which average more than $17 per hour. The other companies pay far lower wages, which in turn has provided an incentive for GM to outsource more and more work.

Outsourcing
When companies contract their work to other companies and individuals to save money.

4. *Fewer workers, with higher workloads.* Many companies are pushing their employees to work much harder. Take J. Walter Thompson North America, the well-known advertising agency. Even though it has 650 fewer employees than in 1986, billings are up more than 20 percent since 1986. Employees are simply working longer hours.

Inasmuch as global competition has affected such changes, there are indications that more is yet to come. Some worry that the North American Free Trade Agreement (NAFTA), which reduces tariffs on various products, will hasten the loss of manufacturing jobs in the United States.[3]

Workforce Demographics. Another potentially important external issue is the composition of the national workforce. Specifically, there are likely to be changes in the racial, gender, and age composition of the workforce. As Table 3.1 shows, in terms of racial composition, African Americans, Hispanics, and Asians will comprise a larger percentage of the workforce in the future. Women are also expected to comprise a larger segment of the workforce than in the past. The number of married women who are employed has doubled since 1960, when only about one-third were employed, to nearly 70 percent in 1990. The average age of the workforce is expected to increase as well. Baby boomers, that large group of people who were born in the late 1940s through the late 1950s, all reached working age by the late 1970s. The "babybusters," who are the next generation, are relatively smaller in number. Given these two factors, it is not surprising that the average age of the workforce fell to a low of 34.3 years by 1980, and has been steadily increasing since then. By the year 2005, the average age of the workforce is expected to be nearly 41![4]

Table 3.1 **The Changing Racial Composition of the U.S. Workforce Group**

	Percentage of Workforce in 1990	Percentage of New Employees in 2005
African Americans	10.7	13.0
Hispanics	7.7	15.7
Asians and others	3.1	6.0

These are all interesting figures and facts, but what are some of the possible implications for human resources? The increased participation of women, for example, means there will be pressure on organizations to provide pro-family policies, such as flextime and child care, to support working mothers. Increased representation of minorities will result in more emphasis on diversity programs to ensure harmonious relations between workers from different racial and ethnic groups. The aging workforce also has important implications for many human resource practices. Consider, for example, the Big Three automobile manufacturers (General Motors, Ford, and Chrysler) in the United States. Experts say that nearly half of their production workers will retire in the next 20 years. On the short term, it is predicted that 200,000 workers will have to be hired within the next ten years to replace the new retirees. The need to hire so many new employees in this relatively short time frame may create worker shortages, particularly since the job requirements are likely to be much higher than in the past. According to Doug Rothwell, director of the Michigan Jobs Commission, the current K–12 public school system may not be effective in training workers for such jobs. Accordingly, the state of Michigan is applying for federal grants and is considering other options to ensure that public school students obtain the requisite preparation for automobile production work.[5]

Technology. U.S. companies invested more than $1 trillion in information technology (such as computers) during the 1980s. Given the size of this investment, a variety of changes in the human resource area can be expected. Take, for example, United Parcel Service of America (UPS). In 1983, UPS employed fewer than 90 information-technology (IT) workers. Today, UPS employs several thousand IT personnel. For the most part, though, advances in technology lead to major reductions in the number of employees needed. Consider Pacific Bell, the West Coast telecommunications company. This company has recently been testing the use of a $10 device that may save the company more than $700 million each year. Currently, when a customer's telephone line fails, Pacific Bell sends out a repairperson (at a cost of $140 to the company) to determine whether the problem lies with the customer's connection or the company's connection. In the former case, it is the customer's obligation to make the repair. Use of the device, however, will enable Pacific Bell to determine where the problem exists without sending out a technician. Along with other technological changes, this change will result in a workforce reduction of 10,000 employees.

American Telephone and Telegraph (AT&T) recently announced plans to reduce its workforce by 15,000 employees as a result of technological changes. AT&T has also used automation to reduce the number of long-distance operators by two-thirds. Most experts do not expect the number of new jobs to match the number of jobs lost through technological changes.[6]

Now that you have read about some of the external issues that affect human resource planning, you will learn about some important internal issues.

Internal Factors

While several internal issues may affect human resource planning, we will discuss only two of these: organizational structure and business strategy.

Organizational Structure Refers to how work tasks are assigned, who reports to whom, and how decisions are made

Organizational Structure. Many businesses today are changing their organizational structure. **Organizational structure** refers to how work tasks are assigned, who reports to whom, and how decisions are made.[7] As part of their restructuring, some companies are creating teams to perform the work. At General Mills' cereal plant in California, for example, the use of teams has increased productivity by as much as 40 percent. Part of the increased productivity is a direct result of the teams being responsible for such decisions as scheduling and maintaining equipment, which in turn means fewer supervisors are needed. At night no managers are at the facility. Use of a team structure has a number of implications for human resources. One of these implications is that employees will need a different set of skills than do employees in a traditional assembly-line production process, including the ability to work as a team.[8] A second implication is that compensation plans must emphasize team cooperation, rather than individual effort.

Business strategy Refers to the approach that companies take in conducting business.

Business Strategy. The approach that a company takes in conducting business is referred to as its **business strategy**. As Table 3.2 shows, an organization may choose from three basic business strategies:[9]

1. Innovation
2. Quality enhancement
3. Cost reduction

Each business strategy, in turn, has implications for human resource practices. As an example, consider Grand Union, a large grocery chain on the East Coast. In terms of business, Grand Union represented the traditional small, discount-oriented 40,000-foot grocery store. But in the mid-1980s, Grand Union faced a new kind of competition: the superstore food market. The smallest of the competition's new superstores was double the size of Grand Union's largest store. To avoid going out of business, Grand Union's management decided to refine its business strategy by adopting a quality-enhancement strategy, which would be highly customer oriented. This new business strategy had numerous implications for human re-

Table 3.2 Three Business Strategies

1. Innovation. The organization develops a product or service that is different from those offered by other organizations. Companies such as Hewlett-Packard, 3M, and PepsiCo typify this strategy.
2. Quality enhancement. The organization emphasizes improving quality of product or service. Companies such as Xerox, Corning Glassware, and Honda typify this strategy.
3. Cost reduction. The organization emphasizes tight cost controls and minimization of overhead costs. Companies such as Emerson Electric, Texas Instruments, and Du Pont typify this strategy.

General Mills finds work teams effective for increasing productivity in their cereal plant in California. Teams affect human resource planning because they require a different set of skills and compensation plans that emphasize cooperation rather than individual effort.

sources. Whereas previously employees could ignore customers, interaction with customers was quite important under the new business strategy. This new emphasis, in turn, required numerous changes in human resource activities such as performance appraisals (which now would incorporate customer service dimensions), training and development (which would now cover customer service), and compensation (which would now cover more than just speed and efficiency).[10]

In sum, it is important for organizations to monitor both the internal and external environment to anticipate and understand the issues that will affect human resources in the future. It is equally important for you as an employee to engage in similar activities to anticipate and understand how these issues will affect your career. A more detailed discussion of some key issues that are likely to affect your career is provided next.

Issues Likely to Affect Your Career

Whether you are just beginning your career, or have worked for many years, certain issues are likely to affect you. We discuss six of these next.

1. *Business is increasingly service oriented.* In the past, the dominant U.S. industry was manufacturing (for example, steel). Today, 75 percent of the U.S. gross domestic product (GDP) is created by the service sector. In the future, service businesses are likely to account for an even greater proportion of the GDP. Even in the auto industry, which is the classic manufacturing business, some experts wonder whether car manufacturers should begin to think of themselves as service providers (providing mobility services). One of the many implications of being a service provider is that customer satisfaction becomes increasingly important. What do you think are some of the implications of the service focus for your career? Certainly, the ability to deal with customers will become much more important. Can you think of other implications?[11]

2. *The economy is increasingly based on the combination of telecommunications and computer technologies.* Both of these technologies are rapidly

changing, and their impact on the workplace is growing. For example, the percentage of employees who reported using a computer in their job rose from 25 percent in 1984 to 37 percent in 1989. What are the implications for your career? At a minimum, experience with and training in these technologies is likely to become critical for a successful career. You should also consider whether advances in these fields have the potential to make your present or expected job obsolete. It should not surprise you, for example, that the number of secretaries has dropped dramatically (from nearly 4 million in 1984 to fewer than 3.6 million in 1993) at the same time that the number of computers in the workplace has increased. Similarly, as the number of automated teller machines has grown in the United States, the number of bank tellers has begun to decline.[12]

3. *Teams are becoming more widely used.* Have you had team projects in school? Team projects are no longer a view of the future in the workplace, they are heavily emphasized now. Again, what are some of the implications for your career? One consequence is that you will need at least a rudimentary understanding of many different areas in order to communicate effectively with different specialists on your team.[13]

4. *There are fewer managers.* With increasing technology, greater use of teams, and emphasis on cost cutting, fewer managers and supervisors will be necessary. Their replacement will be referred to as a team leader (or as a coordinator or facilitator). As these terms suggest, this job will involve coordinating, facilitating, and advising, as opposed to directing, controlling, and supervising. Therefore, don't plan on a career of telling others what to do. You must be able to provide some direct service or function. Should you become one of the few team leaders, you can expect to operate in a far different manner than the supervisor of the past.[14]

While all of the changes we have discussed so far are happening now, the next two are mere possibilities. But as you read them, you will realize that should they come true, they will have a tremendous impact on your career.[15]

Courtesy of International Business Machines Corporation

Planning calls for looking into the future and meeting the needs you see there. The electromechanical Mark I was technologically obsolete almost upon completion, demonstrating that managers and employees are called to be visionaries in every aspect of their jobs—from the technology needed, to the management techniques used.

5. *Few traditional jobs will exist.* This doesn't mean that there will no longer be work. Rather, this means that the "traditional job," defined as work with a specific, regular list of responsibilities, hours, and predetermined pay within a specific place in the organizational structure, may become increasingly rare. In its place, individuals will be hired to perform a specific project or task. As you will read in a later chapter, the number of freelancers, temporaries, and independent contractors is rapidly growing in line with this trend. What are some implications for your career?

6. *Very small (perhaps one-person) organizations will dominate.* The age of the large company seems to be over. Small companies are the rage. But some experts say even smaller companies, perhaps with only one employee (you), will dominate. Take, for example, the design of a new car. Rather than having a design team composed of regular, permanent employees, the company will contract with a panel of experts from around the world (for example, it may contract a bumper designer from one country and an engine expert from another country), who will work together to design the new car. Once it completes the project, the panel will disband. The use of various high-tech advances (such as fax machines and video conferencing) will keep the costs of meeting and communicating down. A new career that emerges in light of the one-person organization is the information broker, who locates specialists around the world and links them with the organizations needing their services.

Finally, various internal or personal events, such as getting married, having a child, or experiencing health problems, may affect your career. What types of other personal events do you think will affect your career?

In sum, you have read about some of the major external and internal issues that are likely to affect careers. It is critical that you stay attuned to trends in business, technology, and the world around you. There are many vehicles for learning about issues, including newspapers, trade magazines, conferences and seminars, as well as conversations with suppliers, competitors, and coworkers. Returning to the opening case, can you think of some current issues that are likely to affect the medical products industry? How might those issues affect the career of the employee described in the opening story?

Step 2: Determining Future Organizational Capabilities

The second step of the human resource planning process involves an analysis of future organizational or personal capabilities. Capabilities include the skill levels of employees, the number of employees, productivity rates, and so forth.

In the past, most of the focus was on predicting the number of employees, or human resource supply, the company was likely to have in the future. Organizations may use a number of procedures to estimate the *supply.* These procedures are generally categorized as either quantitative, which use mathematical or statistical procedures, or qualitative, which use subjective judgment approaches.[16]

Human resource supply
The number of employees the company is likely to have in the future.

The quantitative procedures generally use past information about job categories and the numbers of people retiring, being terminated, leaving the

Markov analysis
A quantitative procedure of determining supply that uses historical rates of promotion, transfer, and turnover to estimate future availabilities in the workforce.

Replacement planning
A method of forecasting human resource supply, which involves an assessment of potential candidates to replace existing executives and other high-level managers as they retire or leave for other organizations.

Succession planning
Similar to replacement planning, except that it is more long term and developmentally oriented and is likely to involve input from several managers and the recommendation of various developmental activities for the candidates to ensure the ability to fill positions as they open.

organization voluntarily, and being promoted.[17] One of the most well-known quantitative procedures is the **Markov analysis**. This technique uses historical rates of promotion, transfer, and turnover to estimate future availabilities in the workforce. Based on the past probabilities, one can estimate the number of employees who will be in various positions within the organization in the future. Of course, the Markov analysis is based on various assumptions, which may not necessarily be correct. One assumption is that the same patterns and probabilities will apply in the future as they have in the past, when various unforeseen events (such as new technologies) and trends may affect the actual supplies.[18] Other quantitative techniques for measuring supply include computer simulations, trend extrapolation, and various operations research techniques.

Qualitative or judgmental approaches are much more popular in forecasting human resource supplies. Among the most frequently used methods are replacement planning, succession planning, and vacancy analysis. **Replacement planning** involves an assessment of potential candidates to replace existing executives and other high-level managers as they retire or leave for other organizations. **Succession planning** is similar to replacement planning, except that it is more long term and developmentally oriented. Table 3.3 summarizes other differences between replacement and succession planning. A succession planning program is likely to involve input from several managers and the recommendation of various developmental activities for the candidates to ensure that the organization will be able to

Table 3.3 Comparison of Replacement and Succession Planning

CONTRASTS BETWEEN REPLACEMENT AND SUCCESSION PLANNING

Variable	Replacement Planning	Succession Planning
Time frame	0–12 months	12–36 months
Readiness	Best candidate available	Candidate with the best development potential
Commitment level	Designated preferred replacement candidate	Merely possibilities until vacancies occur
Focus of planning	Vertical lines of succession within units or functions	A pool of talented candidates with capability for any of several assignments
Development planning	Usually informal, a status report on strengths and weaknesses	Specific plans and goals set for the individual
Flexibility	Limited by the structure of the plans, but in practice a great deal of flexibility	Plans conceived as flexible, intended to promote development and thinking about alternatives
Basis of plans	Each manager's best judgment based on observation and experience	Result of inputs and discussion among multiple managers
Evaluation	Observation of performance on the job over time; demonstrated competence; progress through the unit	Multiple evaluations by different managers on different assignments; testing and broadening early in careers

Source: J. Walker, *Human Resource Strategy* (New York: McGraw-Hill, 1992).

fill positions as they open. Finally, vacancy analysis is much like the Markov analysis, except that it is based on managerial judgments of the probabilities. If knowledgeable experts provide these estimates, the vacancy analysis may be quite accurate.[19]

Vacancy Analysis Similar to the Markov analysis, except that it is based on managerial judgments of the probabilities of promotion, transfer, and turnover rates.

Recall the opening case where the company was having employees provide information using the CAPS program about their interests in working various functions, as well as their past experience and current skills. This was probably part of a replacement or succession planning effort to determine current qualifications of the workplace and future rosters of employees in terms of positions they could move to within the company.

One organization that has conducted extensive human resource planning for many years is Quebec-Telephone, one of the largest Canadian businesses. An early issue that particularly prompted the company's attention was the rapid technological change, which resulted in the need for fewer telephone operators. Based on its estimates, the task force decided to decrease the number of new operators hired and to expedite the retraining of current telephone operators. Another objective of the human resource planning committee was to develop a forecast of human resource supplies. Based on reports from various divisions of the company, the committee compiled a large database that contained information on staffing practices, turnover, and promotions for more than nearly 20 years. This database was then used to develop early retirement programs and estimate the number of engineers needed in the future. In light of the earlier comments regarding the telecommunications industry and technological advances, Quebec-Telephone's extensive use of human resource planning should not surprise you.[20]

In recent years, organizations have become concerned with a broader range of issues under the rubric of future capabilities. For example, organizations have begun to estimate their future productivity levels. Toward this end, benchmarking is a technique that has recently become popular. **Benchmarking** involves comparing an organization's human resource practices and programs to other organizations. Security Life, an insurance company located in Denver, Colorado, recently used benchmarking to review its compensation system. One of the issues that prompted the benchmarking study was an internal issue, namely, a change in management philosophy, which was placing much greater weight on creativity, teamwork, and performance than in the past. In conducting the study, the human resource department solicited information from outside sources, as well as from internal sources (employees, for instance). Some of the most valuable information came from Security Life's competitors.[21]

Benchmarking Involves comparing an organization's human resource practices and programs to other organizations.

Although benchmarking often focuses on an organization's competitors, *best-practices benchmarking* focuses on the programs and policies used by outstanding organizations.[22] For example, Federal Express' leadership evaluation system, employee survey program, and total quality management efforts are frequently studied by other organizations because of their reputation.[23] Box 3.1 describes the basic steps, as well as some general advice, for conducting a benchmark study.

Yet another means of analyzing current programs and policies is to obtain reactions from various parties, such as employees, business partners, and customers. Employee attitude surveys, used for years for a variety of purposes, may be quite helpful for human resource planning as well. More recently, techniques such as the use of focus groups have been employed to obtain feedback from suppliers and vendors.[24]

Box 3.1 Conducting a Benchmark Study

A benchmark study may be broken down into five basic steps.

Step 1. The first step involves preparing for the benchmark project. It is highly recommended that a team be formed for the project, to ensure greater commitment to the findings. Other issues to be addressed at this step include the focus of the project and the expected time frame.

Step 2. Decide which companies to include and how to obtain the necessary information. In terms of the companies to examine, it may be worthwhile to include organizations that are outside of the industry, as organizations in a completely different industry may have the most effective practices. As an example, when Federal Express was examining the use of bar codes, employees benchmarked supermarkets, which are the leaders in this technology.

Step 3. Establish relationships with relevant companies, and plan how information will be collected and shared. Companies don't like to give away information for free, so be prepared to answer questions that are asked of you during the visits or inquiries that you make.

Step 4. Collect the relevant information. There are a variety of means of collecting information, including making site visits and paper-and-pencil surveys. One of the leading experts in benchmarking, Michael Spendolini, recommends using telephone calls. He suggests preparing specific questions ahead of time, contacting a specific person, explaining who you are and why you are calling, and giving a realistic estimate of how much time the phone call will take. Spendolini recommends that you send a thank-you note afterwards, preferably with a summary of the results you found.

Step 5. Analyze the results, and determine what to do based on the findings.

You should also be aware that benchmarking raises a variety of legal and ethical questions, including possible violation of antitrust laws, which restrict companies from working together or cooperating in business; property rights laws, which establish ownership of certain acts or business secrets by the organization; and confidentiality agreements, which may provide ethical constraints on your ability to use information you glean in a benchmark study. Be sure, therefore, to obtain legal advice with regard to these and related matters.

Sources: J. Main, "How to Steal the Best Ideas Around," *Fortune,* October 19, 102–04, 106, 1992.
H.L. Richardson, "Measure up with Benchmarking," *Transportation and Distribution,* June, *34,* 32–35, 1993.
"The benchmarking boom," *HR Focus,* April, *70,* 1, 6, 1993.

Analyzing Your Future Capabilities

There are a variety of different ways for you, as an employee, to analyze your future capabilities. Capabilities refer to your experience, qualifications, skills, and training. At a minimum, you should list all of the basic job-related experiences, qualifications, skills, and training that you have or will have in the near future. After you have made this list, devote some time to thinking about them. One way to organize this task is to develop a chart that lists each of the jobs you have held, the activities you performed in each, and the skills that were required to perform each activity. Once you have developed this chart, update it on a regular basis.

Step 3: Determining Future Organizational Needs

In this step, the organization must determine what its human resource needs will be in the future. This includes the number of employees that will be needed, the types of skills that will be required, productivity rates needed to compete successfully, and so forth.

Just as there are methods for examining the future number of employees, there are several procedures for predicting the number of employees that will be needed in the future. Typically, this is referred to as the human resource demand. Once again, two basic approaches to estimating human resource demand are available: quantitative and qualitative methods.

Two quantitative techniques for estimating human resource demand are *ratio analysis* and *regression analysis*.[25] Ratio analysis involves comparing the number of employees to some index of workload. For example, a recent study of well-managed companies indicated that the ratio of training and development (T&D) staff to employees in the company was 4.1 to 1,000.[26] In other words, the well-managed companies averaged 4.1 T&D staff for every 1,000 employees. If your organization was planning for its future T&D staffing demand in five years, you could estimate the number of employees likely to be employed by the company in five years, and then use this ratio to determine the number of T&D employees needed in five years. For example, if your company was expecting to have 5,000 employees in five years, this ratio would suggest that 20½ T&D employees would be needed.

Regression analysis relies on factors or predictors that determine the demand for employees, such as revenues, degree of automation, and so forth. Information on these predictors from past years, as well as the number of workers employed in each of those years, is used to produce an equation or formula. The organization can then enter expected figures for the predictors, such as revenues and degree of automation into the formula, to obtain an estimated number of employees needed in future years. Regression analysis is more sophisticated than ratio analysis and should lead to more accurate predictions of employee demand. Although both procedures are widely used, they have their potential weaknesses. A major potential problem is that the factors that were related to workforce size may not be relevant factors in future years.[27]

Turning now to qualitative tools for estimating the demand for employees, the most common tool is the bottom-up forecast where department managers make estimates of future human resource demands based on issues described in Table 3.4. Like any other technique, bottom-up forecasting has its shortcomings. For instance, line managers may overestimate the demand in order to ensure that they don't find themselves understaffed. A more traditional approach, referred to as the position allocation and control procedure, uses rules determined by top management in estimating future needs. Typically, a predetermined payroll budget is the determining factor in how many employees will be hired and retained in the future.[28]

Human resource demand
The procedure for predicting the number of employees that will be needed in the future, usually by using quantitative and qualitative methods.

Ratio analysis
Involves comparison of the number of employees to some index of workload.

Regression analysis
Relies on factors or predictors that determine the demand for employees, such as revenues, degree of automation, and so forth.

Bottom-up forecast
Involves the department managers making estimates of future human resource demands based on issues such as new positions needed, positions to be eliminated, expected overtime, hours worked by temporary, part-time, or independent contractors, and expected changes in workload by department.

Position allocation and control procedure
A more traditional approach to estimating the demand for employees, position allocation and control procedure uses rules determined by top management in estimating future needs.

Table 3.4 **Factors Considered in a Bottom-up Forecast**

1. New positions needed
2. Positions to be eliminated or not filled
3. Expected overtime
4. Hours to be worked by temporary, part-time, or independent contractor employees
5. Expected changes in workload by department

Source: Adapted from J. Walker, *Human Resource Strategy* (New York: McGraw-Hill, 1992).

Determining Your Future Needs

One of the most difficult challenges for you, as an employee, will be to assess future career needs. To do this well, you will need to read about issues in your field constantly, talk with knowledgeable people, and generally monitor what is going on in your area of expertise. It is also important to think in broad terms, because the immediate implications for your job are not always obvious. The simplest example is computers. Given the rapid changes in this area, all kinds of things that were not possible a few years ago are happening today. As one example, consider the possible effect of the World Wide Web on marketing and sales. Is it possible that individual banking conducted over this medium may increase? How about airplane tickets—will many ticket purchases eventually occur over the Web? How might the Web affect the career of the employee described in the opening case of this chapter?

By way of summary, it is important to point out that although the value of generating predictions has been emphasized here, they will not always be accurate. A good example is a report published in 1987, called *Workforce 2000: Work and Workers for the 21st Century,* which predicted a number of significant changes would occur in the U.S. workforce by the beginning of the next millennium. Table 3.5 provides a summary of the major predictions from this report, along with a more recent set of predictions. As you can see, changes in the workforce are still predicted for the 21st century, but by and large the changes are less dramatic than the 1987 report indicated.

Step 4: Implementing Human Resource Programs to Address Anticipated Problems

In Step 4, the organization must determine the gaps between future capabilities and future needs and then implement the necessary human resource programs to

Table 3.5 **Predicted Workforce Characteristics in the 21st Century**

Prediction	1987 Report	1992 Report
1. Racial/Sex composition of new employees	Only 15% white males	Only 33% white males
2. Percentage of new employees who are women	66%	52%
3. Racial/Sex composition of current worforce compared with future workforce	Radically different	Somewhat different
4. Match between worker skills and job requirements	Many workers underqualified for jobs	No major mismatch
5. Demand versus supply of workers	Demand greater than supply	Demand about equal to supply

Source: The 1987 predictions are from W.B. Johnston, *Workforce 2000: Work and Workers for the 21st Century* (Indianapolis: Hudson Institute, 1987); the 1992 predictions are from the U.S. General Accounting Office, *The Changing Workforce: Demographic Issues Facing the Federal Government* (GAO/GGD-92-38), (March 1992).

avoid the problems arising from these gaps. Because much of this book is devoted to the various human resource programs and practices that might be used to address anticipated problems, we will focus only on implementation issues here.

Implementing new human resource programs often sounds much easier than it actually is because employees tend to resist change. Consider the case of Navistar International. Known for more than 100 years as International Harvester, a manufacturer of engines, trucks, and related equipment for construction and farming, the company ran into serious financial problems in the late 1970s. The financial problems were caused by environmental factors, such as a declining farm economy, two severe recessions, and the failure of management to react properly. After selling off various parts of its businesses, closing down numerous facilities, and changing its strategic focus, Navistar's top management realized that effective human resource planning was necessary for future success. Accordingly, the CEO, Don Lennox, assigned Roxanne Decyk, vice president of administration, the responsibility of comparing future human resource capabilities with future human resource needs and determining critical gaps. Decyk came to the conclusion that the most important problem was the existing management style. That is, Navistar's management style continued to be bureaucratic and hierarchical. This was completely contrary to the organization's new emphasis on teamwork, innovation, and continuous improvement. Hence, the problem was an incompatibility between management style, human resources, and business strategy. Once Decyk determined that the major problem was management style, the next step was to choose and implement the human resource practices that would enable the company to deal with the problem. But in this case, the problem lay with the people who would be involved in making the necessary changes. So the CEO could not simply tell the managers they must encourage innovation, teamwork, and worker autonomy.

In order to pave the way for such changes, then, Decyk and Don Lennox decided that it was critical for the top executives in the company to become actively involved in all future human resource planning. Accordingly, an outside consultant conducted a team-building program to provide the necessary communication skills and to improve trust among the top executives. Following this, the executives worked on developing a statement of corporate values. Drafting such a statement might seem like a simple, straightforward task. In reality, however, it was a controversial, conflict-laden process, which nevertheless led to a highly productive airing of differences between the top executives. Moreover, by participating in creation of the value statement, the executives had committed themselves to a very different management style. Excerpts from the final statement are provided in Table 3.6.

In implementing a new human resource program, four basic steps are recommended to obtain employee acceptance.[29]

1. *Communicate need for the program.* Employees will want to know why the program is being introduced. Many people believe the old saying: "If it ain't broke, don't fix it." It is imperative to explain, then, exactly why the change is needed.

2. *Explain the program.* Management must explain precisely what the program is, how it will be implemented, and what its effects will be on other practices and programs.

Table 3.6 **Excerpts from Navistar's Corporate Value Statement**

The Company will [provide] . . . an environment which . . .

- promotes teamwork and ethical behavior among its employees and dealers,
- recognizes the contribution of its employees and encourages the full use of their abilities,
- challenges all employees to achieve continuing improvement in quality, productivity, and service to customers.

Source: C. Borucki, C. Barnett, Restructuring for Self-Renewal: Navistar International Corporation, *The Academy of Management Executive* 4 (1990), 36–49.

3. *Explain what is expected of the employees.* Management must discuss how the behaviors of employees are expected to change as a result of the new program. For example, implementation of a new pay-for-performance system may also redirect employee activities.

4. *Establish feedback mechanisms.* No matter how carefully planned and implemented, almost any new policy or practice is likely to lead to questions and problems. It is critical, therefore, for mechanisms to be established to resolve problems and answer concerns that arise. Such mechanisms may include a telephone hotline, an ongoing survey program, as well as a dispute resolution policy.

Choosing and implementing programs is a critical component in the human resource planning process. Because organizational resistance can defeat even the most effective programs, special attention must be paid to ensure that the program is accepted by all affected parties.

Utility analysis
A relatively recent approach to choosing which, if any, human resource programs should be implemented, utility analysis considers the financial benefits versus the costs of any human resource program and attempts to base the choice of program on its dollar value to the organization.

Finally, utility analysis is a relatively recent approach to choosing which, if any, human resource programs should be implemented. Utility analysis, and related approaches such as human resource accounting, consider the financial benefits versus the costs of any human resource program and attempt to base choice of a program on its dollar value to the organization. Using such techniques, organizations are able to determine the best way to invest money in employees.[30]

Now that you have read about Step 4 from the organization's perspective, let us consider this step from an employee's perspective. Once you, as an employee, have determined your future capabilities as compared to future needs, you must determine and implement programs to address any expected gaps. There are many different ways to address gaps. A key method is called *lifelong learning.* Lifelong learning refers to constant learning, through seminars, reading, talking with knowledgeable individuals, participating in task forces, and so forth. Some of the other ways to address gaps are described elsewhere in this book, including formal training programs. You may even need to change jobs or careers. You should probably conduct career planning on a yearly basis, perhaps writing an informal report that covers each of the four basic steps. Find a time each year that will be convenient. This will motivate you to really think about the future and plan accordingly. Finally, Table 3.7 provides some suggestions for you, as an employee, in the human resource planning process.

Box 3.2 Estimating the Supply versus Demand for College Graduates

Have you ever wondered about the future job market for college graduates? If you have, you were probably thinking about whether the number of jobs that will be available for college graduates in the future (or, as we have called it here, the demand) will outweigh the number of college graduates (or, as we have called it here, the supply). Recently, researchers at the United States Bureau of Labor Statistics conducted a careful study of this question, and you may find the results quite interesting. As explained by Kristina Shelley, who reported the results of the study, the supply of college graduates is determined by the size of the college-age population and the percentage that attends college. In turn, these numbers are affected by such things as financial aid, immigration laws, and so forth. Based on historical trends, it was estimated that almost one-third of young people, or about 1.2 million, will earn a bachelor's degree in the year 2005. Interestingly, even though the number of 22-year-olds is expected to be lower than it was in 1980, a large increase in the percentage of 22-year-olds obtaining a bachelor's degree means that there is an expected 35 percent increase in the number of bachelor's degrees awarded in 2005. Of course, there is a second source of new bachelor's degrees: individuals returning to college later in life, older immigrants, and so forth. According to the study, though, these numbers will stay roughly the same (214,000 per year). All in all, the study predicted an increase in supply of college graduates. Now that you have read about the estimated supply of college graduates, let us turn to the demand for college graduates.

The demand for college graduates, or the number of jobs which require a college degree, is based on factors such as the country's rate of economic growth, the growth of jobs that specifically require a college degree, the number of college graduates who leave the workforce, and so forth. Because of the complexity of these factors, and the difficulty in accurately predicting them, estimates of demand are likely to be quite rough. In terms of general economic growth, the study assumed moderate job growth between 1990–2005 and that nearly 22 percent of all jobs would require a college degree. Putting all of these estimates and assumptions together, the study came to a rather surprising conclusion, namely, that the job market would be somewhat *less favorable* to college graduates in the future than during the 1980s.

Wondering whether you should leave this class and drop out of college? Before you do, consider the following facts:

1. The previous information is based on a number of educated guesses about the future, any one of which may prove to be wrong, thereby changing the conclusions.
2. College graduates, on average, earn considerably more than high-school graduates. For example, in 1990, men with a college degree earned on average more than $40,000 annually compared with the average of slightly more than $25,000 for men with only a high-school diploma.
3. The job market in the 1980s has been referred to as a "disaster" for less educated, blue-collar workers. As bad as the job market may be for college graduates, it is likely to be even worse for those with less education.

The bottom line is don't make a rash decision. You must plan carefully if you wish to have a successful career in the years to come. While obtaining a college degree will certainly not be a guarantee of a good job, the alternatives may be worse.

Source: K. Shelley, "The future of jobs for college graduates," *Monthly Labor Review,* June, 1992, 13–21.
N. Alsalam, "Communications: Interpreting conditions in the job market for college graduates," *Monthly Labor Review,* February 1993, 51–53.
D. Hecker, "Reconciling conflicting data on jobs for college graduates," *Monthly Labor Review,* July, 1992, 3–12.

In sum, human resources planning is an important activity for organizations and employees. Although time-consuming, careful advance planning may save an organization and you considerable time, effort, expense, and problems later. Next, we discuss some predictions about job trends.

Box 3.3 Perspectives on Labor Supply and Demand: Europe's Experience

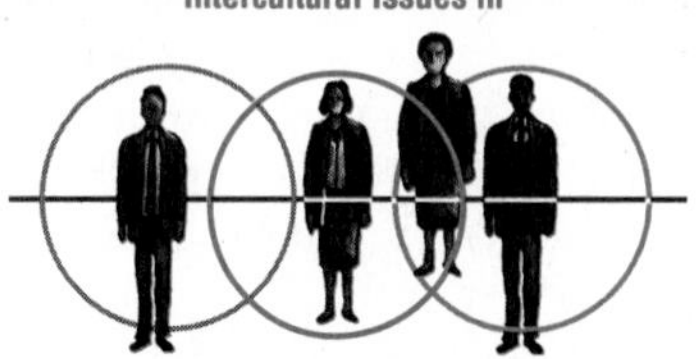

Although most of what you have read concerns the United States, other countries are experiencing problems regarding labor supply as well. European countries, for example, face problems in the workplace—due to the changing nature of the population—that are perhaps more severe than those in the United States. Specifically, for Europe as a whole, unemployment for people under 25 is 16 percent; in countries such as Italy, nearly one-third of those under 25 are unemployed. There are many reasons for the high unemployment rate in Europe. One explanation is the generous unemployment policies found in many European countries. Consider Klaus Beilisch, who lives in Berlin, Germany. While he is unemployed, Beilisch receives the equivalent of more than $275 per week, free comprehensive health insurance, and a rent-free apartment. While Beilisch regularly checks job listings, he finds that few will pay more than his unemployment program does, which will continue as long as he does not have a job. Many of the jobs pay less than he earns with unemployment.

In the long term, Europe may face extreme labor shortages. For example, the number of 15- to 29-year-olds in Italy is expected to decline more than 30 percent between 1990 and 2010, while Spain is expected to experience a 20 percent decline. With reunification, Germany has experienced a large increase in the number of young workers. As a result, some countries may experience major worker shortages, while other European countries may experience large surpluses. Despite such forecasts, unpredictable factors come to play. For example, the introduction of new technology may completely eliminate labor shortages. Meanwhile, European countries plan a variety of national policies, such as new training programs, to handle labor supply and demand imbalances.

Source: D. Wessel and D. Benjamin, "Looking for Work," *The Wall Street Journal,* March 14, 1994, A1, A6.

Table 3.7 Treating Your Career Like a Business

1. Define your product or service. Define your target market—in other words, who are your customers? Your customers may include your boss, coworkers, people outside of the organization, and so forth.
2. Understand why your customer does business with you. For example, are you a low-cost provider (that is, you cost less than the competition), or do you have a specialized skill that is difficult to find elsewhere? Why might your customer(s) go elsewhere? In other words, what might your competition (for example, other employees) do that threatens your business?
3. The emphasis in today's business is on quality and customer satisfaction. Even if your only customer is your boss, you need to provide these two elements. There are several techniques to help you in this regard, including total quality management (see Chapter 12) and continuous improvement (also see Chapter 12). Apply these concepts to your career.
4. Invest in research and development (R&D), just like any business would. In the career context, this means obtaining books, magazines, training programs, and other products and services that will enhance your marketability (you may even be able to obtain a tax deduction in some cases).
5. Consider restructuring or changing businesses. Sometimes, you must change your business or seek new customers. It is unlikely you will remain with the same company or even within the same job for 30 years. Expect change and prepare for it.

Source: Adapted from W. Kiechel, "A Manager's Career in the New Economy," *Fortune,* April 4, 1994, 68–72.

Jobs in the Future: What's Hot and What's Not

You have probably always wondered which jobs are hot and which are not. Figure 3.3 provides some predictions as to growth in various occupations between now and the year 2005. Several features of Figure 3.3 are noteworthy. For example, the biggest predicted job losses are in the production category (for example,

Figure 3.3 Predictions about Job Growth

	Jobs in Thousands in 1990	Projected Growth 1990 to 2005
Executive, Administrative, and Managerial		
General managers & top executives	3,100	14 to 24%
Accountants & auditors	985	25 to 34%
Financial managers	701	25 to 34%
Other managers	701	N.A.
Restaurant & food service managers	557	25 to 34%
Personnel & labor relations managers	456	25 to 34%
Marketing, advertising, & PR managers	427	35% or more
Wholesale & retail buyers	361	14 to 24%
Education administrators	348	14 to 24%
Engineering & data-processing managers	315	25 to 34%
Purchasing agents & managers	300	14 to 24%
Health services managers	257	35% or more
Property & real estate managers	225	25 to 34%
Administrative services managers	221	14 to 24%
Inspectors & compliance officers	216	25 to 34%
Industrial production managers	210	14 to 24%
Construction contractors & managers	183	25 to 34%
Cost estimators	173	14 to 24%
Loan officers & counselors	172	25 to 34%
Management analysts & consultants	151	35% or more
Marketing and Sales		
Retail sales workers	4,754	25 to 34%
Cashiers	2,633	25 to 34%
Manufacturers' & wholesale sales reps	1,944	14 to 24%
Service sales representatives	588	35% or more
Insurance agents & brokers	439	14 to 24%
Real estate agents, brokers, & appraisers	413	14 to 24%
Counter & retail clerks	215	25 to 34%
Securities & financial services sales reps	191	35% or more

Source: W. Woods, "The Jobs Americans Hold," *Fortune,* July 12, 1993, 54–55.

(continued)

Figure 3.3 Predictions about Job Growth

(continued from previous page)

	Jobs in Thousands in 1990	Projected Growth 1990 to 2005
Professional		
Registered nurses	1,727	35% or more
Kindergarten & elementary teachers	1,520	14 to 24%
Engineers	1,519	25 to 34%
Secondary-school teachers	1,280	25 to 34%
Other professionals	865	N.A.
College & university faculty	712	14 to 24%
Lawyers & judges	633	25 to 34%
Social & human services workers	583	25 to 34%
Physicians	580	25 to 34%
Adult-education teachers	517	25 to 34%
Computer systems analysts	463	35% or more
Physical, speech, & other therapists	382	25 to 34%
Musicians and other performing artists	356	14 to 24%
Designers	339	25 to 34%
Ministers, priests, & rabbis	312	14 to 24%
Architects & surveyors	236	14 to 24%
Reporters, announcers, & PR specialists	233	14 to 24%
Writers & editors	232	25 to 34%
Visual artists	230	25 to 34%
Social scientists	224	35% or more
Coaches & sports instructors	221	14 to 24%
Recreation workers	194	14 to 24%
Dentists	174	5 to 13%
Pharmacists	169	14 to 24%
Physical scientists	157	14 to 24%
Transportation and Material Moving		
Truck drivers	2,700	14 to 24%
Other transportation workers	698	5 to 13%
Bus drivers	561	25 to 34%
Industrial truck & tractor operators	431	5 to 13%
Operating engineers	157	25 to 34%
Technical Support		
Engineering technicians	755	25 to 34%
Licensed practical nurses	644	35% or more

(continued)

Figure 3.3 Predictions about Job Growth

(continued from previous page)

	Jobs in Thousands in 1990	Projected Growth 1990 to 2005
Technical Support, *continued*		
Computer programmers	565	35% or more
Other health technicians	522	35% or more
Other technicians	346	24 to 35%
Drafters	326	5 to 13%
Medical technologists and technicians	258	14 to 25%
Science technicians	246	14 to 25%
Production		
Miscellaneous production workers	1,997	5 to 13%
Supervisors	1,800	5 to 13%
Metal- & plastic-working machine ops.	1,473	−4 to 4%
Apparel workers	1,037	−5 or more
Inspectors, testers, & graders	668	−4 to 4%
Welders, cutters, & welding machine ops.	427	−4 to 4%
Machinists	386	5 to 13%
Butchers & meat cutters	355	−5% or more
Precision assemblers	352	−5% or more
Woodworkers	349	5 to 13%
Textile machinery operators	289	−5% or more
Printing press operators	251	14 to 24%
Electrical & electronic assemblers	232	−5% or more
Prepress workers	186	14 to 24%
Laundry & drycleaning machine ops.	173	14 to 24%
Painting & coating machine ops.	160	−4 to 4%
Repairs and Installation		
General maintenance mechanics	1,128	14 to 24%
Automotive mechanics	757	14 to 24%
Other mechanics	718	5 to 13%
Industrial machinery repairers	474	5 to 13%
Electronic equipment repairers	444	5 to 13%
Diesel mechanics	268	14 to 24%
Line installers & cable splicers	232	−5% or more
Automotive body repairers	219	14 to 24%
Heating, a/c, & refrigeration mechanics	219	14 to 24%

(continued)

Figure 3.3 **Predictions about Job Growth**

(continued from previous page)

	Jobs in Thousands in 1990	Projected Growth 1990 to 2005
Unskilled Labor		
Miscellaneous unskilled workers	2,082	5 to 13%
Freight, stock, & material movers	881	5 to 13%
Packers & packagers	667	5 to 13%
Construction trades helpers	549	5 to 13%
Machine feeders & loaders	255	5 to 13%
Service station attendants	245	−5% or more
Vehicle & equipment cleaners	240	14 to 24%
Agriculture and Forestry		
Farm operators & managers	1,223	−5% or more
Farm workers	837	−5% or more
Other farm & forestry workers	338	5 to 13%
Construction Trades		
Carpenters	1,077	14 to 24%
Other trades & miners	863	N.A.
Electricians	548	25 to 34%
Painters & paperhangers	453	14 to 24%
Plumbers & pipefitters	379	14 to 24%
Bricklayers & stonemasons	152	14 to 24%
Highway maintenance workers	151	14 to 24%
Administrative Support		
Record clerks	3,761	5 to 13%
Traffic, shipping, & stock clerks	3,755	5 to 13%
Secretaries	3,576	14 to 24%
General office clerks	2,737	14 to 24%
Word processors & data-entry keyers	1,448	−4 to 4%
Information clerks	1,400	35% or more
Clerical supervisors & managers	1,218	14 to 24%
Adjusters, investigators, & collectors	1,088	14 to 24%
Teacher aides	808	25 to 34%
Postal clerks & mail carriers	607	5 to 13%
Bank tellers	517	−5% or more
Other clerical workers	501	5 to 13%
Telephone operators	325	−5% or more

(continued)

Figure 3.3 Predictions about Job Growth

(continued from previous page)

	Jobs in Thousands in 1990	Projected Growth 1990 to 2005
Administrative Support, *continued*		
Computer operators	319	5 to 13%
Mail clerks & messengers	280	5 to 13%
Credit clerks & authorizers	240	14 to 24%
Duplicating & office machine operators	169	5 to 13%
Miscellaneous Service		
Food & beverage service workers	4,400	25 to 34%
Chefs, cooks, & kitchen workers	3,100	25 to 34%
Janitors & cleaners	3,000	14 to 24%
Nursing & psychiatric aides	1,374	35% or more
Preschool workers	990	35% or more
Guards	883	25 to 34%
Gardeners & groundskeepers	874	35% or more
Private-household workers	782	−5 or more
Other service workers	727	14 to 24%
Barbers & cosmetologists	713	14 to 24%
Police, detectives, & special agents	665	14 to 24%
Home health & housekeeping aides	391	35% or more
Firefighters	280	14 to 24%
Correction officers	230	35% or more
Amusement & recreation attendants	184	14 to 24%
Dental assistants	176	25 to 34%
Medical assistants	165	35% or more
Armed Forces		
Enlisted personnel	1,742	−5% or more
Officers	295	−5% or more

machine operators and assemblers). This should not surprise you. As mentioned in the beginning of the chapter, much production work has gone to other countries or has been replaced by automation. On the other hand, professional jobs will experience some of the largest growth. For example, the demand for registered nurses, computer systems analysts, and health services managers is expected to rise dramatically. Finally, note that a large rise in demand for management analysts and consultants is expected. Can you guess why? One likely explanation is that more companies will contract with outside specialists to perform functions and tasks that used to be done by regular employees, but are now done less expensively by nonpermanent employees. Indeed, if you are interested in a consulting career, there will be some interesting opportunities in the future.[31]

While Figure 3.3 contains information about expected demand for a variety of occupations, Figure 3.4 provides predictions as to the highly sought-after, trendy jobs of the future. Take home-entertainment marketer, for example. Given the number of Americans owning VCRs, advances in cable television, and the proliferation of personal computers in the home, the home-entertainment marketer may become a hot job in the future. If it involves commission sales, it could provide well-paid jobs. Or, take biotech salesperson. With the new advances in biotechnology, it is estimated that in the next few years, the number of sales and marketing employees will triple.[32]

Figure 3.4 **Trendy Jobs of the Future**

Actuary
Actuaries determine that a company charges a fair price to insure their employees despite the risk level and still operate profitably. Education: Undergraduate degree in math or economics is required; examinations are administered by the Society of Actuaries and the Casualty Actuarial Society.

Bankruptcy Attorney
More than 900,000 corporate and individual bankruptcies were filed in 1991, and the number is steadily increasing. Companies no longer have to be insolvent to file for Chapter 11, thus bankruptcy is used as an acceptable method for restructuring debt and reorganizing businesses. Education: In addition to a law degree, some background in economics and finance is needed.

Biotech Salesperson
The biotechnology industry, although only ten years old, is essential to the field of medical technology. Biotech companies develop new drugs from DNA, monoclonal antibodies and enzymes that target diseases more effectively than synthetic drugs. The shortage of sales personnel who can understand and sell this type of service will be critical within the next five years, when the biotech industry is expected to double or even triple its business. Education: A B.S. or its equivalent and two years' related sales experience.

Certified Financial Planner
Financial planners manage and advise individuals' financial goals and needs. Certification requires a six-course program, a comprehensive examination, and a few years' experience working in a financial institution. Education: The College for Financial Planning in Denver, CO, provides information and classes for certification.

Employment Attorney
Employment attorneys are hired by either an organization's management or by its employees due to the increase in litigation among employees, especially since the passage of the 1991 Civil Rights Act. Education: In addition to a law degree, concentration in labor and employment law is desirable.

Environmental Engineer
Because of the increase in environmental legislation and the need for personnel who can interpret the various regulations of the EPA, environmental engineers are greatly needed. Education: A B.A. or B.S. in science or engineering, a master's in environmental engineering is recommended.

50-Plus Marketer
Because of the graying of America, marketers, account executives, and consultants are needed to meet the needs of the fifty-plus consumer. By the year 2010, thirty-four percent of the country will be over fifty, and mature marketing experts will be hired to meet the changing demands of the graying Boomers. Education: The Andrus Gerontology Center at USC gives courses on the mature market, and Wolfe Resources Group in Reston, VA, gives training seminars around the country.

(continued)

Figure 3.4 **Trendy Jobs of the Future**

(continued from previous page)

Health Designer/Architect
With the exploding growth of the health care industry, demand is high for health-care-related construction, according to the Department of Commerce. Health designers, who are architectural specialists, will be called upon to create outpatient and special-care facilities and to upgrade existing hospitals. Education: A degree in architecture, usually a five- to six-year program, is required; specialization in health care architecture is ideal, although few universities offer such programs right now; interning at a firm that specializes in health-care design is recommended.

Home-Entertainment Marketer
Because of the great emphasis and increase in the home-entertainment business—VCRs, movie rentals, cable—marketers are increasingly needed to market and sell services, products, and other home-entertainment-related products to consumers. Education: A degree in marketing is a plus; experience or an internship at a media company is recommended.

Home Health-Care Specialist
Because so many senior citizens want to remain at home until they die, home health-care specialists and managers are needed to advise people on sorting out their home health-care options. Managers advise patients on the best long-term and short-term treatment available to them. Education: A master's or Ph.D. in nursing and/or public health or social work is preferred; business training is helpful.

Human Resources Manager
Human Resources managers are taking on a more strategic role in companies in light of the increased attention on labor law, benefits and pension planning, day care, elder care, and wellness programs. Continued growth is expected in the coming years due to increased diversity and personnel issues and their importance to companies. Education: A business-oriented undergraduate degree is the minimum entry-level requirement; an MBA is becoming essential to reach a top spot.

Information Systems Specialist
Companies are now trying to determine how to use their information systems the most efficient way, and are in need of specialists who can see the larger picture of the company and know where information systems fit into it. Education: A bachelor's degree in computer science is required; an MBA may be necessary for some management positions.

International Accountant
As American companies expand abroad, accountants who specialize in tax, management consulting, and auditing are needed both in America and in foreign countries to analyze tax liabilities and to help companies comply with foreign tax structures. The demand for international accountants has increased 200 percent since 1990, and will continue at that pace. Education: A degree in accounting is required; an MBA, knowledge of international business practices, and proficiency in a foreign language are highly desirable.

International Entrepreneur
The global marketplace, European Community 1992, and corporate downsizing are all factors that have led to the increased demand for international entrepreneurs. Education: Entrepreneur classes are available at many universities; a background in owning or managing a business is useful.

Loan Workout Specialist
A loan workout specialist is hired by a bank to reshape a loan that is not performing, either by lowering the interest rate, splitting up the loan or restructuring the debtor's books. This is one specialty that combines a working knowledge of finance, banking, and investment. Education: A business, banking, commercial, or real estate lending background is helpful.

Managed Health Care Manager
With the increase in health maintenance organizations, preferred provider organizations, physician group practices and the consumers who are members, managers are needed to advise consumers on where to find the highest-quality care at the lowest cost. Education: An MA in health

(continued)

Figure 3.4 Trendy Jobs of the Future

(continued from previous page)

administration or public health is generally required.

Meteorologist

The need for educated, experienced meteorologists is fast replacing the weather technicians of the past. The National Weather Service hires meteorologists, but other companies such as the Department of Energy and NASA do also, as well as private firms and engineering firms. Education: A BS in meteorology is required, with a master's degree necessary for advancement; for research work, a Ph.D is a must.

Nurse Anesthetist

Certified Registered Nurse Anesthetists (CRNAs) perform the same function as anesthesiologists at a fraction of the cost. Those CRNAs who choose to specialize in such areas as open-heart surgery or obstetrics are even more desirable. Education: A BS in nursing or an RN, plus at least one year of clinical experience, is required for acceptance into a nurse-anesthetist program. Graduates must pass a national certification examination. Advanced degrees are helpful for management and teaching positions.

Ombudsman

Working as representatives of the people, ombudsmen are employed in all types of organizations, to act as impartial go-betweens for employees and employers with job-related concerns. Education: Some mediation training is preferable; there are also ombudsman associations around the country.

Physical Therapist

One of the fastest growing industries, physical therapists have expanded their skills to include sports injuries and prevention as well as therapy for the elderly and disabled. Education: A BS in physical therapy is preferred; graduates must pass a licensing exam to practice in each state.

Physician Assistant

Physician assistants are able to perform seventy-five to eighty percent of a doctor's usual duties, which include taking medical histories, physical exams, and ordering and examining lab results. The need for this service has expanded into the home health-care market and nursing homes. Education: The minimum requirement for a physician assistant certificate is one to two years of college; most physician assistants have a bachelor's degree in a health-related field. Physician assistants must pass a national certifying exam in order to practice.

Radiologic Technologist

The shortage of radiologic technologists has caused salaries and demand to increase. Technologists not only administer X-rays and ultrasound, but nuclear medicine technologists administer radioactive drugs to diagnose various illnesses, and radiation therapy technologists treat cancer patients. Education: Hospital programs last two to three years; individual certificate programs take six months.

Special Education Teacher

Teachers are needed for all grades who can teach dyslexic, emotionally disturbed, or mentally retarded children. Due to the passage of the Education for All Handicapped Children Act of 1975, the supply can hardly keep up with the demand for these teachers. Education: Check state requirements. Usually a standard teacher's certification is the minimum; a master's is desirable.

Technical Writer

Technical writers translate the scientists' and manufacturers' jargon for manuals, operating instructions, studies and research reports for the professional and the consumer. They are also increasingly used in new products development, especially in the computing, consumer electronics, and medical industries. Education: A BA or BS with an additional technical-writing course is helpful; continuing education in developing technologies is recommended.

Telecommunications Manager

Telecommunication specialists advise companies on how to best utilize their telecommunication systems, which now include PCs with modems, electronic mail, multifunction phones, fax machines, teleconferencing, and databases. Education: A degree in electrical engineering, computer science, or a related math field is required; a master's degree is preferred; an EE degree with an MBA is ideal.

Although investigating emerging trends can be a successful means of choosing a career, be aware that new jobs do not always materialize.[33] First, a new technology may fail in the marketplace (perhaps customers don't purchase it). More often, however, new technology does not create new jobs; rather, existing jobs are modified. Take for example the printing industry. Compared to the past when typesetters worked manually, computers have fundamentally changed how typesetting is done. Rather than creating a new occupation, however, the job of the typesetter simply changed. Sometimes, predictions about new jobs never materialize. For example, during the oil crisis of the early 1970s, many predicted that occupations involving new sources of energy would be in demand. Instead, synthetic fuels were found to be far too expensive to produce, so the new occupations never emerged. Finally, take the case of the health care industry. While this industry created a large number of jobs during the 1980s and 1990s (some say it accounts for 1 out of every 6 new jobs), recent health care changes (such as mergers) have caused layoffs, and job growth in this area will probably slow.[34] In sum, historical trends and future predictions may give you some ideas for new careers. But be aware that the past does not always predict the future, nor do predictions always come true.

Conclusion

This chapter discussed a number of major issues and trends in today's workplace that will affect organizations and employees alike. Models for conducting human resource and career planning were also provided. Although change is occurring very rapidly in the work world, it is important for both organizations and employees to monitor issues and events continuously, and consider their potential effects. The Boy Scout's motto says it all: Be prepared!

Applying Core Concepts

1. Discuss some key trends that are likely to affect the organization you currently work for or hope to work for in the future.
2. Discuss how three of the trends identified in this chapter will affect your career plans.
3. Using the four-step model of human resource planning, describe how you would go about conducting a human resource plan for the organization you work for or an organization you are familiar with (for example, the high school you attended or college).
4. Answer the questions in Table 3.7 in terms of your career.
5. Assume your boss would like you to implement a new pay-for-performance plan. How would you go about implementing the program so that employees accept it?
6. Discuss three ways in which you currently do or will stay abreast of issues in your chosen career field.

Key Terms

- Human resource planning
- External issues
- Internal issues
- Outsourcing
- Organizational structure
- Business strategy
- Human resource supply
- Markov analysis
- Replacement planning
- Succession planning
- Vacancy analysis
- Benchmarking
- Human resource demand
- Ratio analysis
- Regression analysis
- Bottom-up forecast
- Position allocation and control procedure
- Utility analysis

Chapter 3: Experiential Exercise

Preparing for Changes at Electrik, Inc.

After hearing the class discussion of Making Changes at Electrik, Inc. in Chapter 1, the CEO decided that it was critical to perform a human resource planning report for the company. Use the four-step model of human resource planning presented in Chapter 3 to develop your report for Electrik, Inc. (information regarding the company was provided in the experiential exercise for Chapter 1).

Chapter 3 References

1. J. Walker, *Human Resource Strategy* (New York: McGraw-Hill, 1992).
2. J. Fierman, "What Happened to the Jobs?" *Fortune,* July 12, 1993, 40–41.
3. B. O'Reilly, "How to Keep Exports on a Roll," *Fortune,* October 19, 1992, 68–72.
4. General Accounting Office, *The Changing Workforce: Demographic Issues Facing the Federal Government* (GAO/GGD-92-38), March 1992.
5. R. Haglund, "Hiring Boom Is Forecast for Big 3," *St. Louis Post-Dispatch,* May 1, 1994, E1.
6. J. Rigdon, "Retooling Lives: Technological Gains Are Cutting Costs, and Jobs, in Services," *The Wall Street Journal,* February 24, 1994, A1, A5.
7. S. Robbins, *Organization Theory: Structure, Design, and Applications* (Englewood Cliffs, NJ: Prentice-Hall, 1990).
8. B. Dumaine, "Who Needs a Boss?" *Fortune,* May 7, 1990, 52–60.
9. M. Porter, *Competitive Strategy.* (New York: The Free Press, 1985); R. Schuler and S. Jackson, "Linking Competitive Strategy with Human Resource Management Practices," *Academy of Management Executive* 1, (1985), 207–19.
10. R. Schuler, "Strategic Human Resources Management: Linking the People with the Strategic Needs of the Business," *Organizational Dynamics* 21 (1992), 18–32.
11. W. Kiechel, "How We Will Work in the Year 2000." *Fortune,* May 17, 1993, 38–52.
12. T. Stewart, "The Information Age in Charts," *Fortune,* April 4, 1994, 75–79; W. Kiechel, "A Manager's Career in the New Economy," *Fortune,* April, 4, 1994, 68–72.
13. Kiechel, "A Manager's Career in the New Economy."
14. Ibid.
15. Ibid.

16. C. Greer, *Strategy and Human Resources: A General Managerial Perspective* (Englewood Cliffs, NJ: Prentice-Hall, 1995).
17. H. Heneman and R. Heneman, *Staffing Organizations* (Middleton, WI: Mendota House, 1994).
18. Ibid.
19. Greer, *Strategy and Human Resources.*
20. T. Wils, C. Labelle, and J. Le Louarn, "Human Resource Planning at Quebec-Telephone," *Human Resource Planning* 11, (1988), 255–69.
21. S. Overman, "In Search of Best Practices," *HRMagazine,* December 1993, 48–50.
22. H.L. Richardson, "Measuring Up with Benchmarking," *Transportation and Distribution* 34 (1993), 32–35.
23. M. Harris, "The Benchmarking Boom," *HR Focus* 70 (1993), 1, 6.
24. J. Walker, "Human Resource Planning: 1990s Style," *Human Resource Planning* 13 (1990), 229–40.
25. Heneman and Heneman, *Staffing Organizations.*
26. D. Ford, "Benchmarking HRD," *Training & Development* 47 (1993), 36–41.
27. Heneman and Heneman, *Staffing Organizations.*
28. Greer, *Strategy and Human Resources.*
29. Walker, "Human Resource Planning."
30. J. Boudreau, "Utility Analysis for Decisions in Human Resource Management," in *Handbook of Industrial and Organizational Psychology,* Vol. 2 M. Dunnette and L. Hough, ed. (Palo Alto: CA: Consulting Psychologists Press, 1991).
31. L. Richman, "Jobs That Are Growing and Slowing," *Fortune,* July 12, 1993, 52–53.
32. L. Anzelowitz, "The 25 Hottest Careers," *Working Woman,* July 1992, 45–51.
33. E. McGregor, "Emerging Careers. *Occupational Outlook Quarterly,* Fall 1990, 22–25.
34. D. Hiles, "Health Services: The Real Jobs Machine," *Monthly Labor Review,* November 1992, 3–16.

part 2

Staffing

Chapter 4 Recruitment

Core Concepts

After reading this chapter, you should be capable of

1. Identifying different sources of job candidates.
2. Understanding the advantages and disadvantages of different recruitment sources.
3. Designing a recruitment program.
4. Developing a job-hunting strategy.
5. Creating a cover letter and resume.

Opening Case

Imagine that yesterday you realized you were beginning your third year of full-time employment since graduating from college. For the last six months, you have had the feeling that you should begin looking for a job at a different company. It's not that your current job is bad in any way. Rather, you have learned all you can from this position, there are few promotion opportunities, and even worse, the company has announced some layoffs for next year. But how should you go about applying for other jobs? The last time you searched for a job was when you graduated from college. As you think back about those times, your attempts to find a job were not well planned and you became quite frustrated. It was not until about one month before your graduation date that you began applying for jobs. As you recall, the first thing you did was go to the college placement office, where you attended a one-hour session on job hunting. Initially, someone spoke about submitting your resume to the placement office resume bank. Then a recruiter talked about proper conduct during the campus interview, and afterwards a counselor discussed other means of job hunting (such as answering newspaper ads). The assistant director then asked how many of the attendees had begun their search at least a year prior to graduation; nobody responded. She asked how many attendees had begun the job search six months prior to graduation; a few hands were raised. Incredibly, several attendees indicated they were within a week of graduation and had yet to initiate a job search. What surprised you the most was when the recruiter said, "Most experts recommend you begin your job search six months prior to graduation. But you should begin *planning* the job search two years before graduation!"

Things did not go too well for you after that. Despite having several campus interviews, not a single job offer materialized from them. You also sent out 300 resumes to local companies, answered 75 newspaper ads, and called several managers at companies you had worked at during summer breaks. Although you did not end up using them, you talked with several employment agencies, who promised that over 95 percent of their clients found jobs within six months. After all of those inquiries, mailings, and telephone calls, a friend of yours who had graduated from college the previous year informed you of a job at her company. You interviewed and were made an offer the same day. You accepted this job the next day and are still employed there.

As you think about your current situation, you wonder how you should go about job hunting now. Perhaps answering newspaper ads would work better this time, particularly since you have gained some valuable job experience (that was the most common explanation you were given for not receiving a job offer). Also, you wonder if there are other sources of job leads that you have overlooked. What about such sources as employment agencies? Can they really help you find a good job? You also realize that it's time to make a new resume, which you have not updated since your job hunt three years ago. How should you write a resume? What should you include on the resume? Do you need a cover letter to go with the resume?

This chapter concerns the recruitment process or—from the applicant's perspective—the job search process. Recruitment refers to the process of generating job applicants. Obviously, if an organization fails to obtain applicants who are qualified for the job, it will face a problem in the selection phase. Likewise, if too few applicants apply, an organization may be unable to fill all of its vacancies. It is therefore critical for organizations to identify and properly utilize effective recruitment practices.

In this chapter, you will first read about what type of applicants organizations seek, followed by an examination of the sources companies use to obtain applicants. The chapter discussion provides suggestions for supervisors and managers who are recruiting job applicants. You will also learn how to conduct a job search and create a cover letter and resume that will be useful in finding employment.

Who Is Recruited

Once an organization has decided through a job analysis (see Chapter 5) what kind of skills, knowledges, and abilities are needed for the position, the *type* of employee sought must be carefully considered. Among these considerations are the status of the employee (for example, does the company seek a full-time employee, a part-time employee, or a temporary employee?) and the experience level of the employee.

Considering first the status of the employee, it has been estimated that by the year 2000, 50 percent of working Americans will be either self-employed, temporary workers, or independent consultants. Manpower, the largest temporary agency in the United States, has about 600,000 employees on its payroll. That's larger than General Motors (which employs about 400,000 workers) and IBM (which employs about 255,000). In fact, more than 1.5 million U.S. workers are employed by temporary agencies. Most people think of temporary employees (or, as they are often called, temps) as the people who serve as secretary when the regular secretary is on vacation. But the role of temporary employees has changed a great deal in the last decade. Consider Matthew Harrison, for example. Harrison is a temporary employee who works for Imcor, a firm that provides temporary executives. What is his current position? He heads a manufacturing operation in Queens, New York. Companies will therefore make greater use of short-term employees, at increasingly higher levels in the organization.[1]

Temporary employees Employees who are hired for short-term projects or to fill a position created by personnel who are on leave, and so on. Temporary employees are often less expensive for businesses, can be added or dropped without having to terminate them, and the task of recruiting, hiring, disciplining, and so forth is the responsibility of the placement agency, not the company.

Temporary employees offer several basic advantages for companies. One major advantage is that temporary employees are often less expensive for businesses. Kolmar Laboratories, for example, found that temporary workers paid $5.60 per hour were significantly less expensive than the $9.00 per hour plus benefits paid to regular full-time employees. A second advantage of temporary workers is that they can be added and dropped without having to terminate them, depending on business demand. Third, the task of recruiting, hiring, disciplining, and so forth,

Box 4.1 Recruitment Changes in Japan

As a result of the increasingly older workforce and the relatively small number of college graduates, along with the changing culture, Japanese companies are radically changing their recruitment practices. Traditionally, workers in Japan followed the womb-to-tomb concept—they joined a company immediately after graduation and remained there until retirement. But changes occurring in Japan have affected the traditional recruitment patterns. For one thing, more Japanese workers are willing to switch organizations during their careers. John Harlow, managing director of an executive search firm office based in the Asian region, attributes this to the fact that Japanese students have greater exposure to Western countries, where job changing is much more common. By attending graduate school in the United States or Europe, the Japanese employee is exposed to a very different career system and organizational structure. In turn, this affects his or her expectations. To keep up with this trend, 250 new employee search firms opened for business in Tokyo during a recent three-year period.

Source: Adapted from J. McCune, "Japan Says Sayonara to Womb-to-Tomb Management," *Management Review* 79 (1990), 12–16.

of temporary workers is the responsibility of the temporary agency, not the company.[2]

On the other hand, there are significant disadvantages to temporary employees. One disadvantage is that the turnover rate among temporary workers can be extremely high. Because temporary employees need training to perform their jobs, the high turnover rate can hike the costs. Second, use of temporary employees along with permanent full-time employees can lead to conflicts. For example, Kolmar Laboratories found that temporary workers, who had no share in the company's incentive program, frequently conflicted with permanent full-time employees, who participated in an incentive program based on output. Ultimately, Kolmar Laboratories found that the disadvantages of the temporary employees outweighed their advantages.[3]

In terms of worker experience, organizations must consider several trade-offs. On the one hand, an experienced applicant should be more effective in the short term than an inexperienced applicant. Moreover, there is no guarantee that the inexperienced applicant will be able to achieve an acceptable level of performance. On the other hand, the experienced worker will probably command a higher salary, and some companies would rather not hire an employee who has worked for other organizations that have a different culture or work style.

Once an organization has decided whom to recruit, it is necessary to decide what recruitment sources to use. A major decision at this point is whether to use internal recruitment sources, which provide applicants who already are employed by the organization, or external recruitment sources, which tap applicants from outside of the organization. Each has both advantages and disadvantages.

Internal recruitment sources
Provide applicants who already are employed by the organization. Advantages include less expense, greater speed in completing the recruitment process, less orientation time for new employees, and an effective motivator for employees.

External recruitment sources
Tap applicants from outside of the organization. Advantages include they offer new perspectives by bringing in new employees, offer a large pool of applicants, and may be necessary for increasing minority and female representation in the workforce.

Internal versus External Recruitment Sources

As shown in Table 4.1, the basic advantages of internal recruitment include less expense, greater speed in completing the recruitment process, less orientation time for new employees, and an effective motivator for employees. Finally, and perhaps most importantly, because internal candidates have worked for the

Table 4.1 **Pros and Cons of Internal versus External Recruiting**

Internal Recruiting		External Recruiting	
Pros	**Cons**	**Pros**	**Cons**
1. Less expensive	1. Limits new ideas	1. Large pool of candidates	1. May increase employee resentment
2. Faster	2. Encourages in-breeding	2. Will help increase workforce diversity	2. More expensive and time-consuming
3. Orientation time is shorter 4. Serves as a motivator	3. Smaller pool of potential applicants is available	3. Will encourage new ideas	3. Requires lengthier orientation period
5. More accurate assessment of skills and abilities is possible	4. May hinder efforts to increase workforce diversity		

Box 4.2 Life as a Temp: Boon or Bane?

Given the large number of employees who work as temps, you might wonder what it is like to work in this capacity. On the positive side, temp work provides a means of trying out different career opportunities. Some temps view this as a way to earn money, while still not committing themselves to a given field. Other temps enjoy the flexibility. As an example, consider Laura Masurovsky, who stopped working at a prestigious law firm when she gave birth to her third child. She now works as an independent lawyer and also takes work from Attorneys Per Diem, a firm that provides temporary lawyers. Laura values the ability to take care of other responsibilities and commitments, while still doing the work she enjoys and earning money. Some temps make high wages. Take Amy Schroeder, a former corporate treasurer, who used to earn nearly $90,000. Schroeder now works for J & A Corporate Financial Solutions, a temporary agency that pays its employees between $30 and $50 per hour. Some temps enjoy the constant change associated with working for different companies. Finally, many temp jobs lead to permanent jobs. In fact, the National Association of Temporary Services estimates that about one-third of temporary assignments lead to a permanent job.

Convinced you want to be a temp? There are plenty of disadvantages as well. Rita Gallagher, for example, typically works three to five days per week for J & A Corporate Financial Solutions. Last year, Gallagher was assigned a one-month project, slated to take 140 hours. At the last minute, the client modified the work so that it took only 90 hours. Then a second job was delayed. As a result, Gallagher was unable to work for three weeks. So temping is no guarantee of a steady paycheck. Further, most temporary agencies do not provide benefits, such as a pension or health plan. Another frequent problem is that some managers have a negative opinion of temps. Some feel they are not very effective in filling in for an absent worker, since the temp will take a while to learn the procedures and equipment. Sometimes coworkers resent the temps. And many companies limit the use of temps to only the simplest of jobs. As one "career" temp put it, temporary work is "wonderful, exhilarating, rewarding and challenging. And it is horrible, demeaning, thankless, and boring."

Source: Adapted from J. Fierman, "The Contingency Workforce," *Fortune,* January 24, 1994, 30–36.

organization, a more accurate assessment of their job qualifications should be possible than for external candidates. On the negative side, internal recruitment reduces the influx of new ideas and encourages in-breeding. Furthermore, internal recruitment means a smaller pool of potential candidates and may hamper efforts to increase minority and female representation in the workforce. External recruitment has a number of advantages for the organization. Employees from other organizations often bring with them a new perspective. External recruitment also offers a large pool of applicants and may be necessary for increasing minority and female representation in the workforce. In terms of its disadvantages, external recruitment may increase dissatisfaction felt among current employees, who will resent an outsider being hired. Moreover, external recruitment is generally more time-consuming, more expensive, and requires longer orientation time for the new hires.[4] For these reasons, many companies use both internal and external recruitment methods.[5] Regardless of whether the organization chooses to use internal or external methods for recruitment, there are many different sources that can be used. As you will see, each of the sources has its own strengths and weaknesses. We first discuss internal sources, followed by a discussion of external sources of recruitment.

Internal Recruitment Sources

Companies rely on several commonly used sources or methods to conduct internal recruitment. In a **closed internal recruitment system**, employees are unaware of job openings and therefore do not have the opportunity to formally apply. The simplest, most informal closed system is based on managerial nominations, wherein employees are simply nominated by managers when there is a job opening. The major problem here is that nominations may be based on favoritism toward specific individuals or bias against various protected groups. Or, perhaps unintentionally, highly qualified candidates will be overlooked due to the capriciousness of the recruitment system. Other organizations use closed systems that are more systematic and objective. IBM, for example, has designed a system known as the Recruiting Information System, whereby employees complete a long questionnaire describing their background and qualifications. When a manager has an opening, he or she can access a computer base that contains these listings.[6]

Closed internal recruitment system
Employees are unaware of job openings and therefore do not have the opportunity to formally apply.

Given the many problems associated with closed systems, some organizations have moved to **open internal recruitment systems**, wherein employees are made aware of potential openings. Perhaps the most well known is **job posting**, where the organization publicizes job openings on bulletin boards, electronic media, and similar outlets. A major purpose of an open system is to avoid the "good old boy network," by providing all employees the opportunity to apply for job openings. Another advantage of job posting is that it provides employment opportunities within the company for highly qualified applicants who might otherwise leave the organization in search of external opportunities. The basic disadvantages of job posting include a great deal of administrative time and expense. Another common problem is that the job postings may be tailored to fit a particular employee. Thus, in some cases, the job posting may only increase the perceived sense of inequality among employees who are not promoted.[7]

Open internal recruitment system
Employees are made aware of potential openings and have the opportunity to formally apply.

Job posting
When an organization publicizes job openings on bulletin boards, electronic media, and similar outlets.

External Recruitment Sources

There are many different external sources of job applicants. We begin with a discussion of newspaper ads, followed by a discussion of television and radio ads, employee referrals, college campus recruitment, employment agencies, applicant-initiated sources, and miscellaneous sources. In each case, you will learn about the pros and cons from the company's perspective, as well as some suggestions from a job applicant's viewpoint. As illustrated in Figure 4.1, the many different job sources can also become quite confusing to an applicant, especially when no offers are forthcoming. At the same time, as shown in Figure 4.1, employment experts recommend that job applicants also use nontraditional methods for locating work.

Newspaper Advertisements

When you look at the Sunday edition of a major newspaper such as the *Chicago Tribune,* you will find page after page of job ads. Another major source of jobs, primarily for managerial and professional employees, is the *National Business Employment Weekly,* which provides ads from all regional *Wall Street Journal* editions. It has been estimated that more than $2 billion is spent annually

Figure 4.1 **Traditional versus Nontraditional Methods for Job Search**

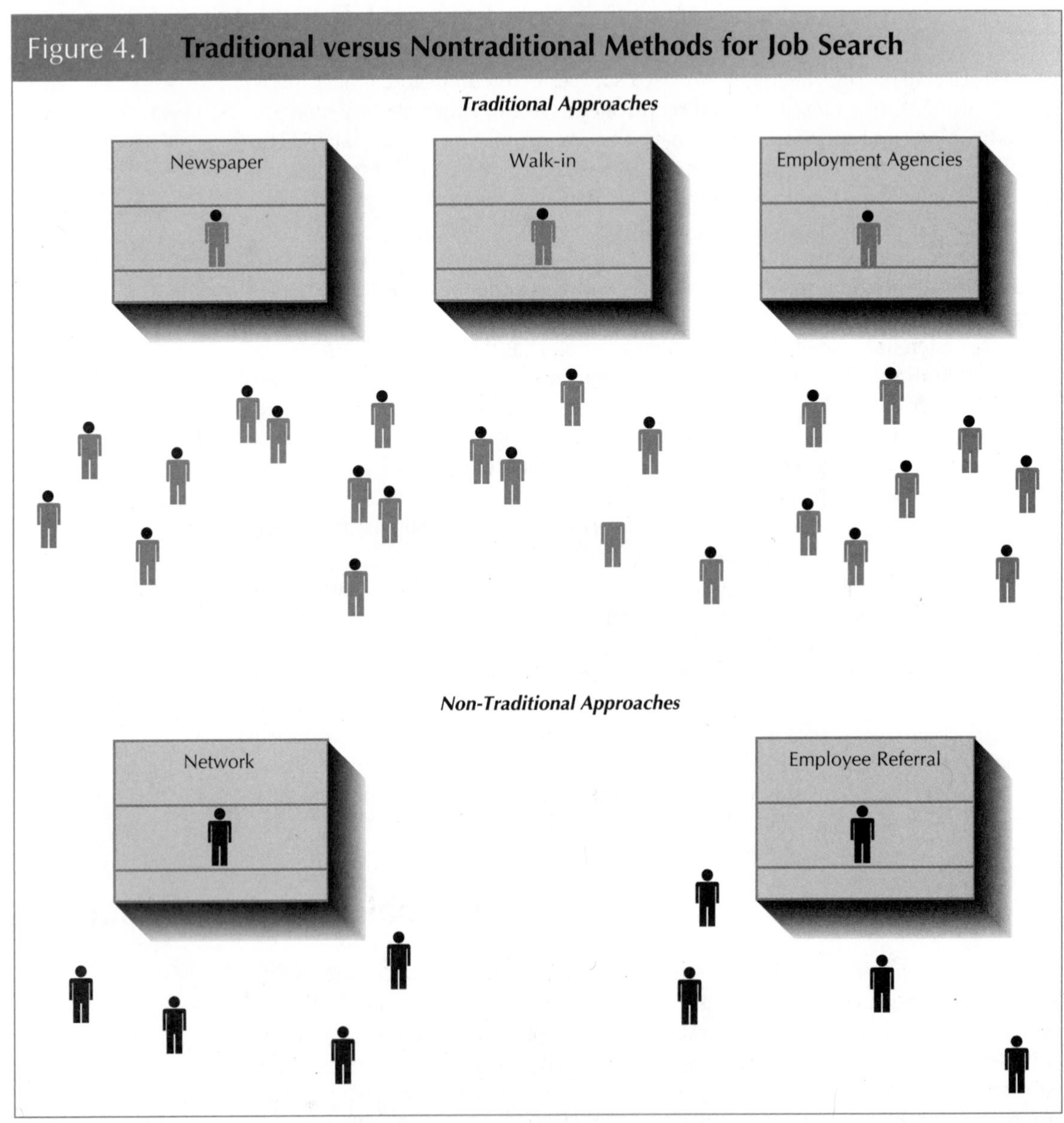

Newspaper advertisements
A method of job recruitment by advertising in newspapers. Advantages include quick placement of ads, flexibility in terms of information, and the ads can target a specific geographic area.

for newspaper ads.[8] An example of what is referred to as a "box ad" is shown in Figure 4.2.

Given the popularity of newspaper advertisements, it is not surprising that this source has several advantages. First, job ads can be placed quite quickly, with very little lead time. Newspaper ads permit a great deal of flexibility in terms of information; they can also target a specific geographic area.[9] For example, Stegall Security and Protective Services, a small security services company, recently was faced with a shortage of job applicants for security guard positions. To recruit applicants, they placed an ad in a local newspaper serving a nearby county with a high unemployment rate. The ad generated almost 100 applicants, of whom 12

Figure 4.2 Example of a Box Ad

VP of Marketing

We are a large, well-known food products company located in a pleasant, medium-size Midwestern city. We have had steady profit growth over the last 20 years and offer promotion opportunities and career challenges for an experienced candidate.

The qualified candidate should have an MBA or equivalent; at least 10 years of experience in the food products industry, and extensive experience in all phases of marketing.

Compensation is commensurate with experience. In addition to a competitive benefit package, we offer a lucrative bonus program.

Interested parties should mail or fax a resume to our consultants (801-666-5555) Attention: R. James, 22 Herringbone Trails, Fairfax, VA.

We are an Equal Opportunity Employer; Diverse candidates are encouraged to apply.

were hired within a few weeks.[10] On the negative side, newspaper ads tend to attract only individuals who are actively seeking employment, while some of the best candidates, who are well paid and challenged by their current jobs, fail to even be aware of these openings. Also, a company may get many applicants who are marginally qualified or completely unqualified for the job. Thus, this source may generate a great deal of administrative work for the organization, with little in return.

A major question is whether to include the name of the organization in the ad. An organization may choose not to have its name listed in the ad (known as a "blind" ad) for several reasons, including the fact that someone may be working currently in the job, the organization may not wish to respond to every person who applies because of the administrative time and expense, the organization may not wish to signal new strategic directions to its competitors, and the organization

Job posting boards can be found in every human resource office listing the positions available within the company. In today's competitive job environment, employment experts recommend that job applicants use the more nontraditional methods for locating work, such as networking or employee referrals.

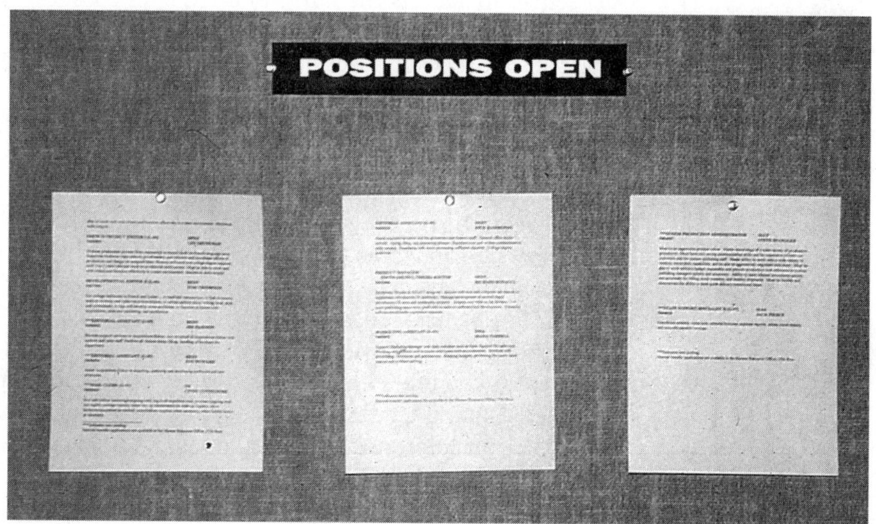

HB Photo/Annette Coolidge

may be concerned that too many job ads will reflect negatively on the organization.[11]

In sum, newspaper advertisements are a popular source for organizations to use in conducting an external recruitment campaign. Although many organizations use newspaper ads, from an applicant's perspective, this is not the most effective source of jobs, as a job ad may produce anywhere between 150 to several thousand resumes. A recent newspaper ad, for example, placed by Ford Motor Company for production workers in Louisville, Kentucky, produced more than 100,000 inquiries, of which the company planned to hire at most 1,300 individuals.[12] It should not surprise you, then, that somewhere between 24 percent and 5 percent of applicants find jobs this way. Like the employee in the beginning of this chapter discovered, newspaper ads are often a poor source for job hunters.[13]

Television and Radio Ads

Television and radio ads
Methods of job recruitment by advertising open positions using television and radio spots. Advantages include that these ads are more likely to reach individuals who are not actively seeking employment, ads are more likely to stand out, they enable the organization to target the audience more carefully, and a considerable amount of creativity can be used in designing the ad.

Television and radio ads are gaining in popularity among employers such as Ford Motor Company and Six Flags over Georgia. This recruitment source offers several potential advantages, particularly compared with newspaper ads. First, television and radio ads are more likely to reach individuals who are not actively seeking employment. Likewise, because relatively few organizations use this approach, job ads are more likely to stand out. Television and radio ads also enable the organization to target the audience more carefully, by selecting the channel or station and the time of day the advertisement is aired. Finally, a considerable amount of creativity can be used in designing the ad.[14] Einstein Medical Center is an example of an organization that successfully used television and radio ads to recruit registered nurses (RNs). The organization began first by surveying RNs as to what features they considered in choosing a job, and it found that three very important factors were nurse-to-patient ratio, flexible scheduling, and the hospital's reputation. But the most important factor was proximity to home. Based on this survey, a recruitment campaign was designed. Because no other hospitals used television or radio ads, Einstein Medical Center felt that these media would be particularly effective. To address the nurse-to-patient ratio issues, three 30-second television ads were designed to highlight this feature. In each ad, a nurse from the hospital described a special aspect of the job (for example, the satisfaction of seeing patients leave).[15]

On the negative side, television and radio ads are rather expensive. In addition to design costs, airtime may be quite costly. For example, a 30-second television commercial may cost as much as $40,000. Einstein Medical Center found that its entire recruitment program for RNs (which included a variety of features besides the television and radio ads) cost more than one million dollars. Also, because the television or radio ad is simply seen or heard, potential candidates may have a difficult time remembering the information, making application difficult. For this latter reason, some employers choose to use the television or radio ad as a supplement to a more traditional newspaper ad. In addition to using newspaper ads, Einstein Medical Center also developed brochures and even created a five-minute videotape for interested applicants. In sum, despite their costs, television and radio ads may be highly effective recruitment sources. Einstein Medical Center, for instance, found that compared to alternative recruitment sources, its program saved more than two million dollars.[16]

Box 4.3 Answering Newspaper Ads: Tips for the Savvy Job Hunter

Although newspaper ads provide relatively few jobs, it is still possible to obtain employment through this source. Before you respond to a job ad, however, consider the following points.

1. *Be extremely careful in applying for a job that does not list the company's name.* If the job ad seems to mesh exactly with your current responsibilities, it may be your own job! Or, if an ad describes a job that sounds like the perfect growth opportunity, it may be in your department. Even if the company doesn't appear to be yours, you never know who will see the resumes received. Perhaps your supervisor's best friend is in charge of the recruiting. He or she may tell your boss something like, "You wouldn't believe it, but someone from your department applied for the job." Even if that seems very unethical to you, it does happen, and it could negatively affect your current employment.

2. *Some job ads are fraudulent.* You probably are wondering why someone would put a phony job ad in a newspaper. Some individuals place an ad so that they can get your social security or driver's license number, which is then used for various illegal purposes. Other companies put ads in the paper to sell their services. For example, some contain a 900 number; when you call, someone will attempt to sell you information of little or no value. Other ads are placed by unscrupulous employment agencies, who are merely attempting to get resumes and names of potential job candidates for other positions.

3. *Write an effective cover letter.* Although Appendix 2 contains suggestions for writing an effective cover letter, here are two basic suggestions for responding to a newspaper ad. First, be sure that your cover letter contains no spelling mistakes. Second, be sure that you put control of the next step of the process in your hands by ending the letter with a statement like, "I look forward to hearing from you. In order to make sure you have received this letter, I will contact you in a week or so."

4. *Consider calling ahead of time.* You may sometimes obtain useful information about the job if you call the company. But be aware that some companies are annoyed by such calls, and, in fact, some job ads specifically say "no phone calls." It is recommended that you call only if you have a specific question to ask that will put you in a positive light. Don't call if the ad says not to call.

5. *Consider sending the resume via Federal Express.* If you want your resume to stand out from the pack and get special attention, you may wish to spend the money needed to send it by Federal Express or another overnight service. On the other hand, it will get expensive to send it this way, and only the secretary may notice what you have done.

Source: Adapted from R. Bolles, *What Color Is Your Parachute?* (Berkeley, CA: Ten Speed Press, 1994).

Employee Referrals

Almost everyone has heard of the expression "networking," which means using personal contacts to locate job opportunities. If you have heard that networking is an effective means of finding a job, it will not surprise you that employee referrals have the reputation for being an excellent source of job applicants. Several reasons have been offered as to why applicants referred by employees tend to be superior to applicants garnered from other sources. First, employees are likely to refer only highly qualified applicants who they think will reflect well on them. Another explanation is that applicants obtain information about the organization from the employees, which enables them to self-select and to have realistic expectations about the job and organization.

Employee referrals An excellent source of job applicants, employee referral means using personal contacts to locate job opportunities.

Given that employee referrals often produce excellent candidates, some organizations have made much use of this source. T.J. Maxx, the fashion retail store chain, pays employees $100 for each hired applicant they refer. The University of Kentucky Hospital instituted a lottery for employees who refer candidates, in which the grand prize is an all-expense paid trip for two to any island in the world. Given the value many companies place on employee referrals, it is not surprising that the employee in the opening case of this chapter obtained employment through a personal contact.[17]

Despite the advantages of employee referrals, they have some potential disadvantages. First, there have been lawsuits involving companies with predominantly

Box 4.4 How to Network for Job Leads

There are many networks you can, and should, tap into when you are searching for a job. You have probably heard the old saying "network, network, network." Unlike many such sayings, this one is true. Surveys indicate that jobs are obtained through friends in about 34 percent of cases and through relatives in about 27 percent of cases. Other sources for networking include acquaintances (for example, your lawyer, banker, insurance agent, and so forth), neighbors, members of professional organizations, individuals in volunteer organizations, and members of your temple, church, or synagogue. A network is also useful when you need references for potential employers to contact. You should speak with your contacts prior to beginning your job search for at least two reasons. First, it will enable you to update them on your recent experiences and accomplishments, as well as your future plans, so they are better informed in case a potential employer contacts them. Second, you can utilize their knowledge of any job openings or contacts.

Here are some recommended steps in talking with these contacts:

1. In most cases, you should telephone the person. Depending on your relationship, you might begin by mentioning how you know one another ("As you probably remember, we worked together for two years at company xyz"). In any case, begin with some small talk by asking the other person how he or she is doing or talking about some other topic you know is of interest to him or her (for example, sports).
2. Briefly explain your situation ("As you may have heard, John Doe and Associates had a big workforce reduction, and unfortunately, I was let go").
3. Describe why you are contacting him or her. You should probably not come out directly and ask whether the person has any openings in his or her organization; this might put your contact on the spot. Rather, you should focus on two basic things. First, you want to know if she or he has any general suggestions for you in regard to job hunting (for instance, you could say, "I'm calling to see if you have any career advice for me as to where job opportunities are or what the future holds for the profession"). Most people love being asked for advice, and you may get some excellent ideas. Second, you want to know if he or she is aware of any job openings at other companies ("I'm also wondering whether you know of any job openings or any jobs you expect will open in the near future in any organizations"). If you word your request carefully, the person will also think of any jobs at his or her organization, without being put in an awkward position.
4. Follow through to obtain specific information from the contact. If the contact indicates that Widget Manufacturing is hiring salespeople, ask him or her for the name of the hiring manager. Also, ask if you may use your contact's name. Presumably, your contact will agree, but asking indicates your professionalism.
5. If you would like to use the contact as a reference, you should ask whether he or she has any reservations about this. Even if you are disappointed by the answer, you are better off finding that out now than ruining your chances at getting a job later.
6. Next, briefly describe your accomplishments and experiences, and offer to send an updated resume.
7. Thank the person, and finish the conversation on a positive note ("Let's try to get together for coffee one of these days").
8. Be sure to follow up in writing with a thank-you note, and offer to return the favor one day.

Source: Adapted from M. Yate, *Knock 'Em Dead: The Ultimate Job Seeker's Handbook* (Holbrook, MA: Bob Adams, 1994).

white workforces and few minority employees. In those instances where employee referrals were heavily used for recruiting purposes, the courts have tended to rule against the company, arguing that this recruitment practice was used in a discriminatory fashion. Thus, employee referrals may create legal problems. Second, employee referrals may not produce enough applicants to fill job vacancies.[18]

College Campus Recruitment

If you are currently enrolled in a university or college, you are almost certain to be aware of the placement center. From the employer's perspective, college campus recruitment offers several advantages, as well as several shortcomings. On the positive side, many organizations find the college campus an effective source of applicants. The placement center typically helps locate applicants and provides their resumes to organizations. Often these resumes are organized by type of work sought, and they may even be computerized. Most placement offices now allow the organization to prescreen applicants, thereby giving the organization control over which candidates will be interviewed. Because all applicants are on campus, an interviewer may be able to meet with as many as 16 candidates each day. Also, applicants have at least some qualifications, since they have demonstrated the ability and motivation to complete a college degree. Furthermore, in most cases, these applicants will not have to be enticed away from a current job. Another advantage of the college campus is that students generally have lower salary expectations than more experienced applicants. Finally, in some fields, such as the computer industry, where technology is continuously changing, the college campus may be the source with the largest number of well-qualified candidates.[19]

College campus recruitment
A method of recruiting by visiting and participating in college campuses and their placement centers. Advantages include the placement center helps locate applicants and provides resumes to organizations, applicants can be prescreened, applicants will not have to be enticed away from a current job, and lower salary expectations.

On the negative side, the college campus suffers from several distinct disadvantages compared with other recruitment sources. First, most of the applicants have little or no work experience. Thus, the organization must be prepared to provide some kind of training, even if informal, to the applicants they hire. This is likely to be more of a problem on some campuses than others; urban campuses

The college campus placement center is one method of finding a job in your career field. The center provides applicants' resumes to organizations seeking workers and sets up prescreening interviews for the organizations. Resource material is also available to help students find information about the different careers available.

with a large evening studies program will have students with more experience (though they may not necessarily be seeking jobs through the placement service). A second disadvantage to this source is the amount of timing and preplanning that must be undertaken. Although this too will depend on the particular college campus, in some cases organizations must register several months prior to interviewing. Third, college campus recruiting tends to depend on the season. For example, a few students seek jobs during the summer. An organization that is hiring during the months of July and August may find very few qualified applicants at college campuses. Fourth, college campus recruiting can be quite expensive for organizations located in another city. Costs such as airfare, hotels, and meals for recruiters as well as applicants invited for a site visit can become quite high for organizations located at a distance from the university. On the other hand, for organizations located in the same city as the university, college campus recruiting may be a highly cost-effective source.[20]

In recent times, given the amount of time invested in college campus recruitment, organizations have begun to more carefully evaluate these programs and, in many cases, institute changes. One of the biggest changes in recent times has been the decline in college campus recruiting by large companies and an increase in college campus recruiting by small companies. Some organizations, such as TRW, have developed close relationships with a select number of universities by providing faculty grants and student scholarships and by donating money for equipment such as computers.[21]

Companies using college campuses as a recruitment source should consider the following guidelines.[22]

1. **Prescreening Applicants as Early as Possible.** The earlier that candidates with top potential can be identified, the more likely the organization will be in the position to attract them. Aside from prescreening at the placement office, internships, co-ops, and summer jobs can be effective in identifying candidates early.

2. **Utilize a Variety of Means for Attracting Applicants.** There are many ways for an organization to advertise and enhance its image on college campuses. Among the more popular means are having company managers and executives offer guest lectures on campus, providing research funds and consulting opportunities for faculty, and offering money to the university for buildings, computers, and other capital improvements.

3. **Make Effective Use of Recruiting Materials.** Some companies use slick brochures, films, and even computer diskettes. While these materials may be beyond the budget of smaller organizations, it is important to note that even basic correspondence can affect company image. For example, the rejection letter is often brief and impersonal, and students may find out about these letters from peers. So if a student has been rejected in a curt and unfriendly fashion, this may negatively affect the company image in the eyes of other applicants.

4. **Evaluate the Cost-Benefits of the Recruitment Program.** Although there are no fixed rules, it is suggested that an organization spend no more than two-thirds of the recruiting budget on applicants who don't end up working for the company. In other words, if the total budget for the campus re-

cruiting program is $18,000, and $14,000 is spent on applicants who either reject offers or are rejected by the company, the recruiting program needs to change. Organizations should be aware that recruiting costs involve more than just travel and the price of materials; costs also include time for interviewers, telephone calls, secretarial time, and so forth. Organizations that are successful in the campus recruiting programs are able to hire more than 70 percent of the applicants that they conduct follow-up interviews with.

In sum, college campus recruiting can be a cost-effective, efficient way to hire well-qualified candidates at readily affordable salaries. Whether the organization can utilize and train applicants with relatively little experience, however, must be considered carefully.

Employment Agencies and Search Firms

Organizations known as **employment agencies** serve as a third party by matching applicants to jobs. The U.S. Employment Service (USES), a federal agency, operates a network of public employment offices, which serve as a liaison for individuals receiving unemployment compensation. These individuals must register with the state employment agency in order to receive payments. The employment service also obtains information from the individuals regarding their work histories and abilities and attempts to find them appropriate work. Because neither the applicant nor the organization is charged a fee, this is often seen as a low-cost recruiting source. A major drawback, however, is that the available applicants often have neither the motivation nor the ability to work, and frequently they are not well-matched to the job requirements. Nevertheless, especially in high unemployment areas, such agencies can be a useful source of job applicants. If you are an applicant, be aware that public employment agencies place only about 15 percent of those who enroll.[23]

Employment agencies Organizations that serve as a third party, matching applicants to jobs.

There are two types of private employment agencies. One type of private employment agency charges the applicant. This type of agency will help you in your job search by training you on how to write an effective resume, coaching you on how to interview, and informing you about job opportunities. Fees can run into the thousands of dollars.

A second type of private employment agency, often known as a **search firm** or headhunter, is paid by the organization. Search firms often have lists of qualified candidates, many of whom may not actively be seeking a new job. They are particularly important for organizations seeking to fill high-level jobs (such as a CEO or a physician), where there is a scarcity of qualified applicants, and when the search must be conducted with a great deal of discretion to protect potential applicants who may fear their company finding out. In addition, the search firm does prescreening, therefore better candidates should be produced. The major disadvantage of the search firm is cost: search firms tend to work either on a retainer basis, where they will fill any openings that appear within a given year, or on a contingency basis, when the need arises. In the latter case, a typical fee is between 25 and 33 percent of the hired applicant's yearly salary, plus expenses. Given the fees charged and the need to use such firms for higher-level positions, it is not surprising that nearly 2,000 search firms exist in the United States.[24]

Search firm A private employment agency that works for the employer and maintains lists of qualified candidates.

For job applicants, be careful that you utilize a reputable employment agency. Numerous employment agencies have been charged with bad business practices, so you may wish to check with a consumer agency (such as the Better Business Bureau) to determine the history of the agency. Agencies that have the National Association of Personnel Consultants (NAPC) and the Certified Personnel Consultant (CPC) designations are recommended. Also, be aware of company claims regarding their success in placing individuals. Finally, don't be pressured into signing a contract. If you do choose to use an employment agency, you are generally advised to use a fee arrangement that charges by the hour. That way, you can stop whenever you like.[25]

Search firms that contact you are an entirely different matter, since they are paid by the company. Although they will often accept resumes, their best candidates generally come from personal contacts (referrals from others). If you choose to send your resume to them, be selective. You want to make sure that your application does not get back to your current employer. On the other hand, even if a search firm doesn't have a possible position for you at the moment, keep in touch. A position may materialize later. The best way for a search firm to become interested in you is for you to establish an excellent work record and to re-

Box 4.5 Think Your Job Competition Is in the Same Classroom as You? Don't Bet on It!

Because many students come from other countries to study in U.S. colleges and universities, you might think that North American institutions of higher learning are far superior to those in other parts of the world. Many recruiters believe otherwise. Consider for a moment what Stuart Reeves, senior vice president of EDS (the information technology company), says about college graduates from other countries:

"If you're hiring college types, there isn't a lot of difference in quality among nations. The difference among college graduates by countries is a lot less than the difference among day laborers and high-schoolers. And there's a lot of pent-up talent out there."

Texas Instruments has set up a software programming operation in a city called Bangalore. Never heard of it? Do you think Bangalore is located somewhere in Texas? If you do, you couldn't be more incorrect. Bangalore is a city of four million inhabitants, located in southern India. Why set up this operation overseas? Wages are low enough that the work gets done for half of what it costs back in the United States. Still not convinced? Albert Hoser, president of Siemen's U.S. subsidiary, explains his evaluation of Indian computer programmers this way: "They are less expensive, but that's not why we went there. They do some of the best work in the world."

Workers in other countries are also reaping the benefits of the new global job market. The University of Limerick, located in Ireland, is considered by many to produce outstanding graduates. That is one reason Ireland is rapidly becoming a major international service center. Initially, Quarterdeck Office Systems, a U.S. software company, opened a facility in Ireland to develop software for Europe. As the quality of the work there became apparent, increasingly sophisticated projects were assigned to that facility. More recently, late-night U.S. customer inquiries are routed to Ireland (where it is daytime). U.S. companies are finding that costs are approximately one-third lower, turnover is extremely low, and employees are highly dedicated to their jobs.

The lesson is that you compete for jobs with people around the world.

Source: Adapted from B. O'Reilly, "Your New Global Work Force," *Fortune,* December 14, 1992, 52–66.

main visible in your field. Join professional organizations and network. Take the case of Joyce Golden, a 44-year-old African-American woman. Several years ago, she decided to leave the banking industry. Through her contacts with various search firms, she was able to land a job as controller with a San Francisco–based newspaper company. A short time later, she was promoted to her current position, where she earns more than $100,000 annually and supervises more than 100 employees.[26]

Applicant-Initiated Recruitment

Many applicants search for jobs either by walking into the organization and completing an application blank or by mailing a resume in the hope that a position is available. Have you ever tried to get a job this way? Referred to as **applicant-initiated recruitment**, many retail, fast-food, and production facilities hire employees this way. Some applicants have been successful in obtaining managerial and technical jobs this way as well. The major advantage to companies of this source is the relatively low cost, because the company is not spending money to gather the resumes. On the other hand, there are several disadvantages. First, although there are no advertising costs, there is a cost associated with processing and storing the resumes and application blanks. Second, minorities are less likely to apply for jobs that have not been advertised.[27] Thus, heavy reliance on this approach may lead to the underrepresentation of minorities in the workforce, which could result in legal problems. This source tends to favor applicants who are actively job searching; highly qualified applicants who are satisfied with their current jobs are unlikely to be applying. Given all of these reasons, companies tend to differ on the value of this recruitment source. Some organizations will simply discard any mailed resumes unless they are submitted for a specific job opening. Other organizations may save the resumes for future consideration, even if no position is open at the time.[28]

Applicant-initiated recruitment
Applying for a job by either walking into the organization and completing an application blank, or by mailing in a resume in the hope that a position is available.

Miscellaneous Recruitment Sources

As Table 4.2 shows, there are many other recruitment sources that deserve at least a mention.

Table 4.2 **Miscellaneous Recruitment Sources**

- Job fairs
- Computer networks
- Trade publications
- Transit advertisements
- Billboard advertisements
- Direct mail
- Open houses
- Professional organizations' placement rosters
- Point-of-purchase
- Trade associations' directories

Job fairs, for example, provide a forum for many different employers to conduct recruiting with large numbers of applicants. Computer networks are also being used more frequently for advertising job opportunities. Trade publications are yet another source of applicants. Both organizations and job hunters are encouraged to use these as well as other sources to meet their needs.[29]

In sum, we have reviewed a large number of sources for applicants (see Figure 4.3). Each source has its advantages and disadvantages. From a company's perspective, there is no one best source of job applicants; the best source will depend on the type of employee needed, the nature of the job, and similar considerations. From the job hunter's perspective, personal contacts are the best way to get a job. The more contacts and acquaintances you have, the more employment opportunities you will find. We now turn to ways for companies to improve their recruitment practices. The appendices at the end of this chapter provide information on the job search, how to write a cover letter, and how to create a resume.

Improving Recruitment Practicies: Suggestions for Managers and Supervisors

Organizations can improve their recruitment practices by implementing the following suggestions.[30]

1. Plan the Recruitment Process. Too many companies approach the recruitment process in a haphazard, cavalier fashion. As a result, ineffective hiring decisions are made. Some factors to consider in the planning stage include the skills, abilities, and experiences needed to perform the job in question, the number of candidates needed to fill the open positions, when to conduct the recruitment process, and who should be in charge of the recruiting. With some careful planning, the recruitment phase can be greatly improved.

2. Carefully Train or Select Recruiters. Although the recruiting process can have a major effect on job candidates' impressions of an organization and willingness to accept a job offer, surveys indicate that few companies offer training in this area. Quite often, line managers take turns serving as a recruiter. To improve the effectiveness of line managers responsible for recruiting, it is recommended that companies provide training in the recruitment area. Or, at a minimum, those managers responsible for recruiting should be chosen carefully, to ensure that only employees who are effective communicators and aware of basic discrimination laws participate in this process. A training program at Exxon, for example, provides guidelines to recruiters on what information to ask of applicants, what information to share with applicants, how to plan a site visit, and other relevant issues.

3. Provide Realistic Information to Applicants. All too often, job candidates have an overly positive perception of the job and organization. This may be partly due to the candidate, who simply has limited information or may overlook the negative aspects, and partly due to the interviewer, who often feels reluctant to provide negative information for fear that applicants will

Figure 4.3 **The Job Search**

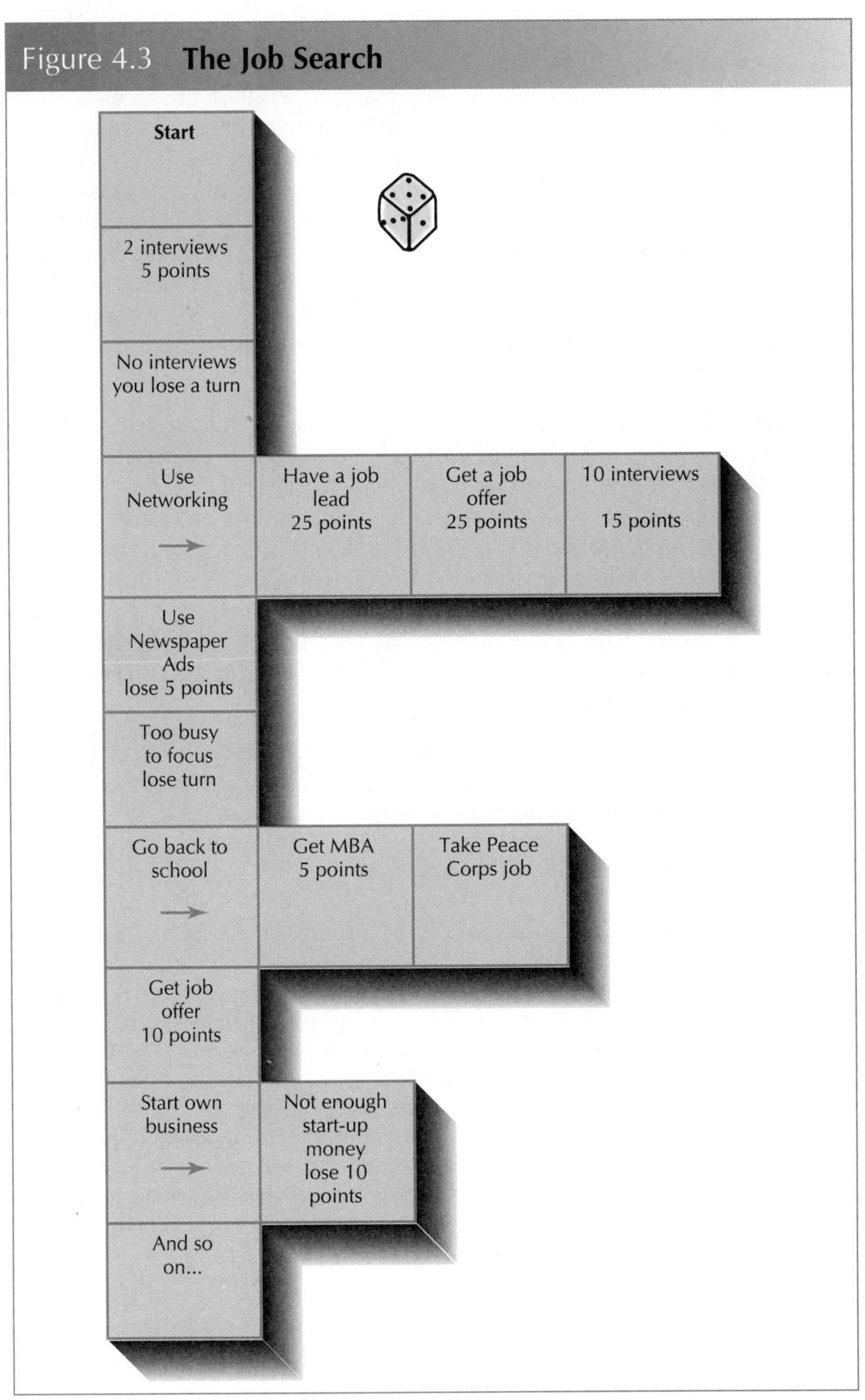

reject job offers. In reality, however, unrealistic expectations held by employees can create excessive turnover. This is particularly problematic if the organization has invested considerable time, effort, and money in hiring and training the employees. To reduce unrealistic expectations, organization are encouraged to develop a **realistic job preview (RJP)** program. An RJP is simply a mechanism for providing information about the more difficult or challenging aspects of a job. Merrill Lynch, for example, developed a tape recording to simulate the kind of phone calls a stockbroker can expect to receive. Included in the tape recording are responses from people answering a sales inquiry. Other ways to provide an RJP include a film, a "walk-through" of the job site, informal conversations with coworkers, and brochures describing the job.

Realistic job preview (RJP)
A mechanism for providing information about the more difficult or challenging aspects of a job that organizations can provide to reduce unrealistic expectations.

4. **Avoid Time Delays and Offensive Practices.** Research indicates that there are two things organizations do that are particularly exacerbating to applicants. Time delays, despite their frequency, are often seen by job applicants as a negative sign. The most highly qualified job applicants will view delays as an indication that there are problems in the organization. A second major problem, especially for women, is offensive recruiting incidents. Among the offensive incidents frequently encountered are letters that address women as Mr. even after an interview was conducted, being interviewed in a man's hotel room, and hearing inappropriate comments about dress or appearance.

In sum, organizations can take many steps to improve their recruitment processes. Careful preplanning can do much to improve the effectiveness of this process and to reduce the discrimination charges that may arise.

Conclusion

In sum, regardless of whether you are seeking to hire new employees or are trying to find a job, the recruitment process is critical to success. From a job applicant's perspective, employee referrals and job leads from people who know you are the best way to find jobs. Be sure to develop a thorough job hunt, and devote the necessary time to it. From the perspective of an employer, there are many different applicant sources; which one will be most useful depends on the nature of the job and the type of employee you seek to find. There are many things that you, as a manager or supervisor, can do to improve the effectiveness of your recruitment process, including developing an accurate job description, conducting a fair interview, and providing realistic information about the job and company.

Appendix 1

The Job Search: General Strategies

There are many different strategies and ways for you to find a job. There are also many books, computer software packages, and businesses (such as employment agencies) that provide assistance in your job search. The specific strategies for finding a job will depend much on your occupation, experience, education, and qualifications. Nevertheless, here are some general pointers for job hunting.[31]

1. A Job Search Takes Much Time and Effort. How long do you think it generally takes to find a job? Two days? Two weeks? Four weeks? Ten weeks? The truth is that it generally takes between 2 to 8 months to find a job. Because that's only the typical length of time, it can take much longer too. How many hours each week do you think you should devote to the job search? Most experts recommend 20 or more hours, even though the majority of job searchers spend fewer than 5 hours per week. The point is that a job search takes a great deal more time and effort than most people think.

2. Try to Talk with as Many Hiring Managers as Possible. Because the hiring manager is the one who determines if there is a need to hire someone and whom to hire, you need to find out who this person is and meet with him or her. If you have a mutual acquaintance who can serve as a contact with the person, you are even more likely to be successful in finding a job. As an analogy, consider a salesperson. Who do you think is going to be the most successful—the salesperson who merely sends flyers about the product, the salesperson who talks on the phone to a receptionist without control over the purchasing, or the salesperson who meets with the purchasing manager? As you probably guessed, the salesperson who meets in person with the purchasing manager is most likely to sell the product. You, the job hunter, are similar to a salesperson—you are selling yourself.

3. Pursue Small Businesses. Every survey shows that large companies are downsizing and reducing their workforces. A great deal of job growth, on the other hand, is coming from small businesses. Although small businesses may seem less prestigious, they often offer many more opportunities. In a small company, you will generally have a wider variety of responsibilities, because a small company does not need and cannot afford many specialists. As a human resource employee, for instance, you may well be responsible for all compensation, benefits, hiring, and training. Such broad responsibilities would be rare in a large firm. Not only are there many more job openings in small businesses, then, but the learning and growth opportunities abound.

4. Use All Possible Recruitment Sources. In this chapter, we described many of the different recruitment sources companies use, ranging from newspaper advertisements to employee referrals. While you need to be much more careful and discreet if you are currently employed, if you are unemployed, throw caution to the wind. And don't forget networking. As described in the chapter, anyone can serve as a potential job lead, including friends, neighbors, doctors, professors, and so forth.

5. Cast a Wide Net. The worst thing you can do in today's extremely competitive job market is be narrow either in terms of the type of companies you are pursuing or in the type of job you are pursuing. You must be more willing to consider companies that are not your ideal and be willing to consider jobs that are not your "dream job."

6. Seek Support. If you search earnestly, you will get turned down from jobs. There is only one way to have a perfect batting average—by not going up to bat! But what batting average would that give you? A .000! But job hunting is different from baseball in one key way. The job seeker who hits a home run (that is, gets an excellent job offer) one time out of 1,000 at bat is just as successful as the job seeker who gets 300 home runs out of 1,000 times at bat. So, like any successful salesperson, you will get rejections. What you need, therefore, is a support group, friend, or relative who will serve as a cheering squad. You will probably need to work at keeping your morale and self-esteem up. The worst is to come across to a prospective employer as a frustrated person with low self-esteem. So, keep your chin up and keep hunting!

Appendix 2

Writing the Cover Letter

In almost every case, you will want to include a cover letter with your resume. The basic purpose of the cover letter is to introduce the resume, highlight any key points, and grab the attention of the reader. While the content of the cover letter will depend to some degree on the particular circumstances (for example, how well you know the recipient or whether you are responding to a specific job ad or not), here are five basic steps to assist you in writing the cover letter.[32]

1. Use a standard business letter format, in which your name, address, and phone number appear in the top left-hand corner, followed by the date on the far right-hand side of the page, and the addressees's name and address on the left-hand corner. Begin with the salutation "Dear Ms.:" or "Dear Mr.:".

2. Begin the body of the letter with a strong opening sentence or two, such as "I was recently encouraged by a mutual acquaintance, Richard Green, to write to you regarding a potential job opening in your firm." If you are responding to a job ad, be sure to mention that ("I am writing in response to the job advertisement in *The Wall Street Journal* for a position in financial management").

3. Now that you have told him or her why you are writing, you want to explain in a short paragraph why the reader should be interested in *you.* Therefore, what you want to do is explain briefly (in one or two paragraphs) why you are qualified for the job (for instance, "In my seven years of experience in the field of financial management, I have produced a consistent track record of cost reduction, . . .").

4. To wrap up the letter, you want to close on a strong note. In fact, the ending may be the most important part of the letter. Say something like "I hope to speak to you further, and I will call next week to follow up."

5. Review the letter very carefully for typos, mistakes, and clarity. The cover letter should be no more than one page long.

Appendix 3

Chronological resume The type of resume that lists each of your jobs, beginning with the most recent and ending with the first job you held.

Writing the Resume

There are basically three kinds of resumes:[33]

1. The **chronological resume** is the type you are probably most familiar with. The chronological resume lists each of your jobs, beginning with the most recent and ending with the first job you held. The chronological resume is considered ideal for someone who has worked primarily in one profession, has had few periods of unemployment, and has had few job changes. The chronological resume tends to be ineffective for someone who is changing occupations or is just out of school and has little job experience.

2. The **functional resume** emphasizes your skills and experiences. It is ideal for someone with many different jobs and areas of expertise, military employees who are applying for civilian jobs, people closer to retirement age, and individuals who are returning to the work world after a long absence (such as women who have been housewives for a number of years and who are now beginning to work outside the home).

3. The chrono-functional resume combines both the chronological and functional approaches. It is ideal for someone with a strong career record who desires to use the advantages of both approaches. Some people encourage a unique style of resume, such as a videotape. You should be warned that with few exceptions, use of an unconventional resume format will merely indicate that you lack good taste, good business sense, and resist conformity. Except possibly for certain highly creative jobs, these attributions will not serve you well.

Functional resume
The type of resume that emphasizes your skills and experiences.

Regardless of the type of resume you have, the resume should be no more than two pages long. Any longer than that, and the hiring manager will seriously question your business judgment and ability to communicate successfully. Now that you have read about the different kinds of resumes, let's talk about the basic components of any resume.

All Resumes Should Have the Following Elements

1. Your Name. It is suggested that you give your first and last names only (for example, Michael Harris); avoid initials (D.Z. Dean). Generally, there is no need to mark Mr. or Ms., though you may wish to if your name does not indicate your gender (Mr. Chris Sanders).

2. Your Address. Avoid abbreviations (for instance, use "Street" rather than "St."). The only exception is the state, where postal standards stipulate the use of the postal abbreviation (Missouri is MO, for example).

3. Your Telephone Number. Always include your area code, even if you apply for a local company. While you will always want to include your home phone number, the question is whether to include your work number. The problem with including a work number is that a prospective employer may call you at a bad time, or even more critically, may tip off your manager that you are job hunting. One recommended solution is to put your work number in the cover letter, with a comment about using discretion if he or she contacts you there. Regardless of which number you provide, be sure there is always someone to answer the phone or there is an answering machine. Otherwise, the recruiter may simply proceed to the next person on the list without trying again.

4. Education. Typically, this section should contain the degree awarded from each school, the name of the school, and the date of graduation (unless that will mark you as possibly too old or too young for the position). If the grade-point average was between 3.0 and 4.0, you should list that information, otherwise you are better off not listing it. If applicable, you should include any scholarships or honors given. Whether the education section comes before or after the experience section will depend on several factors. In general, though, the education section should come first only if you have just graduated from school and you have a limited job history.

You Should Consider Having the Following Elements in Your Resume

1. Job Objective. There is considerable debate among experts as to whether you should include a job objective or desired position. On the positive side, this information will help focus the resume and clarify for the company why your application is appropriate. On the other hand, a job objective that is too specific will exclude you from other opportunities. Therefore, you should keep the objective fairly general or avoid a job objective altogether on the resume. Or, some job hunters use two or three resumes, each with a different objective. Just don't get mixed up if you get a call!

2. Personal Interests. Do any of your hobbies or interests mesh with the job? If they do, you may wish to include them. If there isn't an obvious link, it's probably not worth it to include them.

3. **Personal Information.** Facts such as your marital status and relocation flexibility are often not pertinent or conceivably could hurt you. In other circumstances, these facts may help increase your chances of employment. Generally, personal information should be avoided, since many issues, such as your marital status, are not job related.

Things Never to Include in Your Resume

There are several things that you probably should never provide in your resume. These include the following:

1. **Reasons for Leaving a Job.** It can only hurt you. This topic will be covered in the interview anyhow, so there is no value in addressing it here.

2. **References.** It is considered unprofessional to put the names of actual references on the resume. Most employers will assume you have references anyhow. But you should note at the end something like "References Available Upon Request." If for no other reason, this forces you, the job hunter, to make sure you have informed these references of your plans.

3. **Exaggerations.** Don't lie or stretch the truth on your resume. There is a good chance that a thorough, smart interviewer will catch it.

Now that you have read about some basic considerations, let's address the actual writing of a resume. First, we will review some general writing style considerations, followed by specific suggestions for writing a chronological resume. After that, you will learn some tips on writing a functional resume.

Writing the Resume: General Points

The writing in any resume must be clear, concise, and direct. To meet these guidelines, follow these general suggestions:

1. Use action verbs: acted, adapted, installed, performed, edited, and produced.
2. Avoid the pronoun "I" since the reader will assume that you did whatever you have described (for example, Designed and installed new computer system).
3. Use incomplete sentences, especially since you do not need the pronoun "I."
4. Use quantitative terms wherever possible. It is much more convincing to have "Increased sales volume 50 percent" than to have "Greatly increased sales volume."
5. Use one long sentence rather than several short sentences and avoid any extraneous words.

Chronological Resume: Describing the Jobs

Recall that the chronological resume focuses on each job that you have worked, in the order that you have worked in them. For each job, then, you should list the following:

1. **Job Title.** You should use the most general, meaningful job title. This may not be the actual title your company used, but you want to make sure that the screening manager understands what your previous job was. For example, "Senior Associate" may be what your company called the job, but the more meaningful title might be "Account Representative." Also, avoid using titles that designate level, such as junior, intermediate, or trainee. Such titles might imply a lower status than was the case.

2. Responsibilities. Rather than merely providing a brief description of the basic tasks you performed, you should report the major achievements in the job. For example, rather than saying "responsible for monitoring inventory, negotiating contracts, and making purchasing decisions" you might say "implemented new JIT inventory system, negotiated 30 percent reduction in charges, and decreased purchase decision time by 20 percent." If you managed a budget or supervised people, be sure to include the actual figures ("managed a $500,000 budget").

3. Employment Dates. Failure to include the dates of employment for each job is an immediate red flag to the hiring manager. If you have no significant gaps in your employment record, you should probably use the month and year (such as "August 1988–July 1992"). If there are short gaps in employment, you may wish to insert only the years ("1988–1992"). If there are gaps of several years, you probably should be using a functional resume.

Functional Resume: Describing the Skills and Experiences

Recall that the functional resume focuses on your skills and experiences. To design the functional resume, you should determine the major responsibilities and functions of the job(s) you are applying for. Then, rank the importance of each of those major responsibilities and functions. Once you have done that, you should determine which of those responsibilities and functions you have had experience with and what your major accomplishments have been in each. For example, you might determine that "cost reduction" is a major responsibility for the kind of work you are seeking. Although you have never worked in the position of office manager, you may have engaged in cost reduction in other positions you had, such as production supervisor. List any related accomplishments under the cost reduction heading (for example, "reduced scrap rate, resulting in a 20 percent cost reduction").

For a combination resume, you will probably list the skills and experiences first, followed by a brief section on work history. In that case, the work history might include only the dates of employment, the name of the employers, and the positions.

Preparing the Resume for Copies

Nothing is worse than using a resume that is sloppy, contains spelling mistakes, or has a poor visual appearance. To avoid such problems, you are encouraged to do the following:

1. Have several people proofread your resume. It is easy to overlook spelling mistakes, typos, and missing words. No matter how many times you read and reread your resume, you are bound to miss one or two of these errors. Any one of those mistakes can cost you a job. You must therefore have as many individuals proofread your resume as possible.

2. Once you have had the resume proofread, you will need to have it typed up. It is recommended that you use a word processor and have the resume printed on a laser printer or letter-quality printer. Above all, don't scrimp on this. Appearance is extremely important. You may even wish to have the resume typeset. The difference in cost may well be worth it. If you don't have the proper word processor or laser printer, have a printing company do it.

3. Use the proper paper. You should have the resume printed on high-quality (16 to 25 lb.) paper. In most cases, white or cream color is highly recommended. Again, aim for a professional businesslike appearance. Be sure to obtain envelopes that match.

In conclusion, your resume is an important tool for job hunting. Many paperback books are available at a relatively low cost that will provide additional information as well as examples on how to create a resume. Also, a number of computer software programs are now available for resume writing that you might wish to consider.

Applying Core Concepts

1. If you were responsible for hiring someone for your job, which recruitment sources would you use? Why? Which recruitment sources would you avoid? Why?
2. Which recruitment sources described in this chapter have you used in job hunting? How well did they work?
3. Ask a friend or relative for a recent copy of his or her resume. Based on the suggestions in Appendix 3, provide comments on the resume. How can your friend or relative improve her or his resume?
4. Think about your current job or a job you were hired for previously. How effective was the employer's recruitment process? How would you have improved it?
5. Thinking about your current employer or an organization that a friend or relative works for, would internal or external recruitment sources be more valuable? Explain your thinking.
6. Design a job hunting program for the person described in the opening vignette of this chapter.

Key Terms

- Temporary employees
- Internal recruitment sources
- External recruitment sources
- Closed internal recruitment system
- Open internal recruitment system
- Job posting
- Newspaper advertisements
- Television and radio ads
- Employee referrals
- College campus recruitment
- Employment agencies
- Search firm
- Applicant-initiated recruitment
- Realistic job preview (RJP)
- Chronological resume (Appendix 3)
- Functional resume (Appendix 3)

Chapter 4: Experiential Exercise

Technosoftware Company: Part 1

On Monday morning, Walter Chipnowsky looked concerned as he took his first sip of coffee. Walter had spent the weekend examining the ledgers and status reports for the small computer firm, Technosoftware, that he had founded with his two college friends, Darrell D. Rive and Benjamin B. White. Although the three of them had operated the company for the last three years with little more than some part-time clerical help and the services of an occasional consultant, Walter had recently concluded that the company had grown much more rapidly than he originally expected and that they desperately had to hire another full-time employee. The impending release of their latest product made this need even more apparent.

As Walter thought more about the need to hire another full-time, professional employee, he realized that this would create new concerns and potential problems. Over the years that Technosoftware had been in existence, the three partners had grown accustomed to having complete control over decisions. Moreover, they believed that this was a major strength of the company. And, although they had occasionally had major disagreements, they had known each other for many years and trusted each other completely. Bringing in an outsider could change all of that.

Company History

The history of Technosoftware is not unlike other entrepreneurial firms. It was a company that developed out of the dreams and frustrations of three ambitious computer experts. Walter, Darrell, and Benjamin (usually called Ben) graduated from Purdue University in the early 1970s. Although all three had received master's degrees in mathematics or computer science, each had a somewhat different personality. Walter was the "people person," who enjoyed interacting with others and working out interpersonal problems. Darrell was the technical-oriented one; he preferred to work on computer or math problems, and tended to avoid dealing with people. Ben was the more business-oriented one, who enjoyed the financial aspects of Technosoftware. Even though they each had their particular strengths, none of them had any formal training or experience in areas besides computer and software development.

After graduating from Purdue, each of the three partners began a career in a large computer company, slowly working their way up to a middle management position (Walter and Ben) or moving up to a highly regarded research and development job (Darrell). Eventually, though, all three became tired of the politics and lack of challenge in their jobs. This led to the creation of Technosoftware.

Technosoftware: Current Projects

Technosoftware focuses on software development for business applications. In the past, they have dealt primarily with other companies on a contract basis to modify existing software and to implement and train companies on various software packages. But over the last year, the partners have been spending many weekends working on a new software program, called Sparks. Walter and his partners feel that Sparks, which the partners are keeping a closely guarded secret, could be a revolutionary product.

The Job

After drinking his second cup of coffee for the day, Walter began to write a brief description of the responsibilities of the person to be hired, along with some basic characteristics of the ideal candidate. His lists follow.

Responsibilities: The person would be involved in all phases of product management and product introduction, including packaging, user manual writing, pricing, product announcements, positioning strategy, promotion, advertising, and sales.

Characteristics of the Employee: Given the size of Technosoftware, the ideal candidate would be highly motivated, self-sufficient, be familiar with personal computers, and be prepared to do his or her own clerical work (e.g., typing, copying). The person would have a master's degree in a technical field, and considerable experience in computer software.

Compensation: Because most of the partners' energy and time has been devoted to Sparks, their cash flow is rather poor. The person they hire would not be highly paid. They prefer to set up some kind of bonus plan with the individual, so that his or her pay would be related to sales of Sparks. They feel they would probably have to pay someone about $35,000 annually, but if sales of Sparks were successful, they would be prepared to pay as much as $100,000 annually in a bonus. Also, because they are a very small firm, they offer no health insurance or pension plan.

Walter's Question: Walter's question for you to answer is how should he go about getting interested people to apply for this job. He realizes that if he does a poor job of getting qualified applicants to apply, he will not be able to hire an effective person for the job. He would like you to come up with a recruitment plan for this position. Offer as many relevant recruitment sources as possible. For each source, be prepared to explain the pros and cons.

Chapter 4 References

1. J. Fierman, "The Contingency Workforce," *Fortune* January 24, 1990, 129, 30–36.
2. Ibid.
3. B. Marsh, "A Consulting Business Thrives by Hiring Mothers Part-Time," *The Wall Street Journal* February 23, 1994, B1–B2; Fierman "The Contingency Workforce."
4. R. Heneman and H. Heneman III, *Staffing* (Middleton, WI: Mendota House, 1994).
5. J. Breaugh, *Recruitment: Science and Practice* (Boston, MA: PWS-Kent, 1992).
6. Ibid.
7. B. Schneider and N. Schmitt, *Staffing Organizations* (Glenview, IL: Scott, Foresman, 1986).
8. Breaugh, *Recruitment: Science and Practice.*
9. Ibid.
10. D. Huntley, "Security Firm Beats Bushes for Workers." *Personnel Administrator* 34, (1989), 50–52.
11. R. Half, *Robert Half on Hiring.* (New York: Crown, 1985).
12. N. Templin, "Dr. Goodwrench: Auto Plants, Hiring Again, Are Demanding Higher Skilled Labor," *The Wall Street Journal,* March 11, A1, A4.
13. R. Bolles, (1994). *What Color Is Your Parachute?* (Berkeley, CA: Ten Speed Press, 1994).
14. Breaugh, *Recruitment: Science and Practice.*
15. R. Kimmell, "Health Care Marketing Minicase: Market Research Guides an RN Recruitment/Retention Campaign," *Journal of Health Care Marketing,* (1991), 11, 69–73.
16. Kimmell, "Health Care Marketing" and Breaugh *Recruitment: Science and Practice.*
17. S. Rynes, "Recruitment, Job Choice, and Post-Hire Consequences: A Call for New Research Directions," in *Handbook of Industrial and Organizational Psychology,* vol. 2, ed. M. Dunnette and L. Hough (Palo Alto, CA: Consulting Psychologists Press, 1991), 399–444.
18. Breaugh, *Recruitment: Science and Practice.*
19. J. Hawes, "How to Improve Your College Recruiting Program," *Journal of Personal Selling and Sales Management* 9, (1989), 47–52; Breaugh, *Recruitment: Science and Practice.*
20. Ibid.
21. R. Blumenthal, "Entrepreneurs Vying for Graduates the Giants Recruit," *The Wall Street Journal,* February 4, 1994, B2; Breaugh, *Recruitment: Science and Practice.*
22. M. Hanigan, "Seizing the Competitive Edge on Campus," *Managers Magazine,* August 1991, 13–17.
23. Bolles, *What Color is Your Parachute?*
24. Ibid.
25. Ibid.
26. S. Harrison, "Star Search," *Black Enterprise,* April 1990, 74–78; Breaugh, *Recruitment: Science and Practice.*
27. J. Kirnan, J. Farley, and K. Geisinger, "The relationship between recruiting source, applicant, and hire performance: An analysis of sex, ethnicity, and age," *Personnel Psychology, 42,* (1989), 293–308.
28. Breaugh, *Recruitment: Science and Practice.*
29. Ibid.
30. Breaugh, *Recruitment: Science and Practice.*
31. Bolles, *What Color Is Your Parachute?*
32. R. Beatty, *The New Complete Job Search* (New York: John Wiley, 1992); M. Yate, *Knock 'Em Dead: The Ultimate Job Seekers Handbook* (Holbrook, MA: Bob Adams, 1994).
33. Ibid.

The Selection Process

chapter 5

Core Concepts

After reading this chapter, you should be capable of

1. Understanding the uses of job analysis.
2. Explaining what factors organizations use in choosing selection procedures.
3. Describing the features of different selection procedures.
4. Identifying the advantages and disadvantages of different selection procedures.

Opening Case

Five minutes ago, Tom Brown received a phone call from Mike Clayton, the human resource employment manager of Federal Bank. Mike began by saying that he was pleased to inform Tom that he was one of three finalists for the commercial loan officer job, and that he was now being invited to the bank for a series of interviews, tests, and background checks (including a review of his credit history). Tom was excited to get the call. Not only had he had only two interviews so far (despite applying for more than 50 jobs), but Federal Bank was one of his top choices. However, when Mike Clayton told him that he would be taking some tests and would be subject to a background check, Tom became apprehensive. Tom has always disliked taking tests, and does not feel that tests reflect what he is capable of doing. Tom believes that a face-to-face interview provides a much better assessment of his qualifications. Nonetheless, of the two interviews he has participated in so far, neither has gone particularly well for Tom. Midway through his first interview, Tom was asked to describe his greatest weakness. He was not expecting this question, and so he blurted out, without thinking: "It sometimes takes me a while to learn a new routine or procedure. But once I catch on, I really become good at it." By the look on the interviewer's face, Tom could tell that he had lost any chance of getting that job. So, before his interview with the next company, Tom went to the library and checked out a book on interviewing. But his interview with the second company was completely different. In that interview, the manager asked questions about Tom's different work experiences. One question in particular really unnerved Tom. The interviewer asked if Tom had ever persuaded his boss to adopt a new technique or procedure. It was the third question in a row that Tom answered, "I never had that experience," and it was then clear to him that he didn't stand a chance of getting a job offer from that company either. So, as Tom continued to think about the upcoming interview at Federal Bank, he was worried that he would not do well there once again. Furthermore, he wondered, what tests would he be given? And what information would Federal Bank obtain from a background check? Is such a procedure even legal? What if his credit record has a mistake on it?

What kinds of selection procedures do companies use? Are there different kinds of interviews and tests? The purpose of this chapter is to discuss the procedures that companies use in hiring applicants and promoting employees. First, however, you will read about job analysis, which is a way to determine what qualifications the employees will need. Following this, you will read about the critical factors companies look for when they choose selection procedures. After that, we will review the major features of commonly used selection procedures, including application forms, interviews, tests, background and reference checks, and drug screens.

Job Analysis

What Is Job Analysis?

Job analysis
The process of collecting information about two basic issues: What the job entails, and what knowledge, skills, abilities and other requirements are needed to perform the work.

Job analysis may be defined as the process of collecting information about two basic issues:

1. What the job entails (what tasks and functions are performed by the employees).
2. What knowledge, skills, abilities, and other (KSAOs) requirements are needed to perform the work.

As an example of the first issue, a job analysis may reveal that the tasks performed by a commercial loan officer include generating new clients, evaluating loan applications, and maintaining relationships with existing clients. With regard to the second issue, a job analysis might reveal that the KSAOs needed to perform these tasks effectively include the ability to interact with others, knowledge of financial concepts, oral communication skills, and a four-year college degree.

There are, as you will soon see, many different approaches to doing a job analysis. Which approach is best will depend on the purpose of the job analysis and the nature of the job. Before we discuss different types of job analyses, however, you will first learn why organizations do job analyses.

Why Do a Job Analysis?

While a superficial job analysis may take only an hour or so to conduct, an extensive, thorough, and detailed job analysis covering many different positions can be very expensive and time-consuming. In fact, some organizations spend as much as $4 million annually for this purpose. Why do companies spend the time and money doing job analyses? The answer is that job analysis is a basic building block for many human resource management (HRM) activities. As you can see in Table 5.1, job analysis provides useful information for many HRM programs and practices, including training, career development, performance management, and work design, to name just a few. Job analysis is particularly helpful from a legal standpoint, because it helps to justify the criteria upon which hiring, promotion, and termination decisions were made. A job analysis would also be useful in clarifying expectations for both the employee and his or her supervisor so that both parties are clear as to what the job involves. Now that you know what job analysis is and why it is done, you will read more about how to do a job analysis.[1]

Conducting a Job Analysis

There are many different approaches to conducting a job analysis. These approaches differ in terms of the three factors:

Table 5.1 **Uses of Job Analysis**

1. Hiring
2. Training
3. Career development
4. Performance management
5. Work design
6. Compensation
7. Human resource planning
8. Safety
9. Vocational guidance
10. Recruitment
11. Rehabilitation counseling
12. Engineering design

Source: Adapted from W. Cascio, *Applied Psychology in Personnel Management.* (Englewood Cliffs, NJ: Prentice-Hall, 1991).

1. The *type* of information collected.
2. *How* the information is collected.
3. The *form* of the information.

Job description
A list of the tasks and functions performed by each employee.

Job specification
A list of knowledge, skills, abilities, credentials, and experiences needed to successfully perform the job.

What Type of Information Will Be Collected? Are you interested in determining the tasks and functions performed in the job, the KSAOs required to perform the job, or the basic behaviors performed in the job? The answer to this question is determined in part by the purpose of the job analysis. Suppose that the purpose of the job analysis is to clarify job responsibilities. For example, Mike Clayton from the opening case of this chapter may perform a job analysis so that the commercial loan department understands who is responsible for which tasks. In that case, Mike Clayton would determine the tasks that are performed in the department, and the final result would be a job description, or list of the tasks and functions performed by each employee. If, however, Mike Clayton wanted to determine which candidate to hire as a commercial loan officer, he would focus on determining the KSAOs required for the job. The final result would be a job specification, or list of knowledge, skills, abilities, credentials, and experiences needed to successfully perform the job. Finally, if Mike Clayton was conducting the job analysis to establish career counseling programs, the emphasis might be on broad behaviors (for example, dealing with outside customers) underlying performance in different jobs.[2]

How Will the Information Be Collected? There are many ways for the job analysis information to be collected. How the information is collected will in large part be determined by the nature of the work. For instance, if the job involves production work, you might simply observe workers and record the tasks that they perform over a period of a week. Thus, observing employees at work is one way to collect information. Consider, however, a computer programmer. Because a computer programmer's work is primarily mental, you would probably learn little about the tasks involved simply by observation. Instead, you may need to interview computer programmers and ask them to describe the tasks they perform. Another way to collect information is by using a questionnaire. An example of a questionnaire used to collect job analysis information is provided in Figure 5.1. Questionnaires are commonly used for job analysis because they enable one to obtain information in an efficient fashion from many different people, and if done properly they will withstand legal scrutiny. Because of their popularity, you will learn about questionnaires in greater detail later.[3]

Additional means of gathering job analysis information include using work logs, videotapes, and meetings with customers.[4]

In What Form Will the Information Be Collected? Information may be collected in either a qualitative or quantitative form. An example of a questionnaire used to collect qualitative information was shown in Figure 5.1. As you can see in Figure 5.1, employees are asked to provide a narrative description of the tasks they perform, the tools and equipment they use, and the conditions under which they work. Figure 5.2 shows a questionnaire used to collect quantitative information. A person completing the questionnaire in Figure 5.2 rates each task on a 0– to –4 scale, indicating the importance of and the frequency with which each task is performed. The purpose of the job analysis often determines whether a qualitative or quantitative approach is used. If the purpose of the job analysis is to clarify what a subordinate's responsibilities are, then a qualitative approach might be best. If

Figure 5.1 **Sample Job Analysis Questionnaire**

Name: ______________________________

Position: ______________________________

Department: ______________________________

Supervisor: ______________________________

1. Briefly describe your job: ______________________________
____
____
____

2. Describe the specific tasks that you are responsible for in your job: ______________
____
____
____

3. Name the person that you report to, along with his or her job title: ______________
____

4. List the equipment, tools, or machines that you use in your job: ______________
____
____
____

5. List any outside customers you deal with: ______________________________
____
____
____

6. List any internal departments or units you deal with: ______________________________
____
____
____

7. List any physical hazards that you face in your work (for example, heavy lifting): ______
____
____
____

8. How many employees report to you? ________ List their names: ______________
____
____
____
____

Figure 5.2 Sample of a Quantitative Job Analysis Questionnaire

Directions:

Step 1—Significance

Indicate how significant each activity is to your position by entering a number between 0 and 4 in the column next to it. Remember to consider both its importance in light of all the other position activities and frequency of occurrence.

0–**Definitely not** a part of the position
1–**Minor significance** to the position.
2–**Moderate significance** to the position.
3–**Substantial significance** to the position.
4–**Crucial significance** to the position.

Dimension: Controlling

Step 2—Comments

Use this space to clarify or comment on any aspects of **Controlling** that you feel are not adequately covered by the questions.

____
____
____
____
____
____
____
____

The Duties of This Position Require You to

1. Review proposed plans for adequacy and consistency with corporate policies/objectives.
2. Track and adjust activities to ensure that objectives/commitments are met in a timely fashion.
3. Develop milestones, due dates, and responsibilities for projects, plans, and activities.
4. Monitor product quality and/or service effectiveness.
5. Develop evaluation criteria to measure the progress and effectiveness of a unit.
6. Evaluate and document the effectiveness of plans, projects, and/or operations upon their completion.
7. Analyze at least monthly the effectiveness of operations.
8. Analyze operating performance reports.

Source: Sample items from the Management Position Description Questionnaire.

the purpose is to determine the appropriate wage for different jobs, a quantitative approach might be best (see Chapter 8).

Now that you have learned about some ways in which job analysis procedures differ, you will read about the questionnaire method in greater detail. Because many questionnaires use a quantitative approach, we will focus our attention there.

Quantitative Job Analysis Questionnaires

Although employers use many different quantitative job analysis questionnaires, we will discuss just two of them: the PAQ and the Task/KSAO Inventory.

PAQ
A standardized job analysis questionnaire that may be used for nearly any job.

PAQ. The Position Analysis Questionnaire, or PAQ, is a standardized job analysis questionnaire that may be used for nearly any job. The PAQ consists of 194 items, the majority of which concern work behaviors and use of equipment and tools. A few items concern work conditions, such as the physical environment and pay practices. The items on the PAQ are grouped into 32 specific scales and 13 overall dimensions for scoring purposes. Some examples of the items on these scales are "making decisions," "using machines/tools/equipment," and "performing service-related activities."[5]

Some sample PAQ items are provided in Figure 5.3. If you examine Figure 5.3, it should not surprise you that the job analyst (the person performing the job analysis) must receive training in how to use the PAQ. Indeed, the PAQ is a relatively complex job analysis tool.

The PAQ has two advantages. Because the PAQ is a standardized questionnaire, results can be compared across different organizations. To assist in this comparison, a large database with ratings of many different jobs from many different organizations has been gathered by the firm that owns the PAQ copyright. Another advantage of the PAQ is that it is scored by computer, thereby producing more objective results. In turn, these features have facilitated the use of the PAQ for several different HRM purposes. We will briefly describe two applications of the PAQ.[6]

Using the PAQ for Choosing Selection Tests. In earlier research studies using the PAQ, the relationships between PAQ scores, test scores on some popular selection tests, and job performance ratings were calculated for many different jobs. By statistically comparing the PAQ scores for jobs in your organization with the PAQ scores from this database, you can estimate how useful these tests would be in hiring workers for your organization. The PAQ, then, can be used to choose tests for hiring purposes.

Using the PAQ for Compensation Decisions. The PAQ may also be used to perform an analysis of an organization's pay structure. Toward that end, PAQ scores for each job are statistically analyzed in relationship to their base pay. Deviations from what a job is actually paid to what the statistical analysis indicates the job should be paid will pinpoint where pay adjustments may be needed.

Now that you understand what the PAQ is and what it may be used for, we will discuss another quantitative job analysis questionnaire: the Task/KSAO Inventory.

Task/KSAO Inventory. The **Task/KSAO inventory** is a job analysis technique that focuses on both the tasks performed in the job and the KSAOs needed to perform them. This approach has been widely used in both public-sector and private-sector organizations. Unlike the PAQ, there is no standardized Task/KSAO inventory. Rather, each organization develops its own unique list of tasks and KSAOs for each job. Another difference from the PAQ is that the Task/KSAO inventory is usually completed by the employees themselves, rather than by a trained job analyst.

Task/KSAO Inventory
A job analysis technique that focuses on both the tasks performed in the job and the KSAOs needed to perform them.

A typical Task/KSAO inventory consists of a list of 100 tasks and 10 to 15 KSAOs, which are then rated by subject matter experts (SMEs). The SMEs are usually supervisors and job incumbents. The tasks are typically rated in terms of the frequency with which they are performed and their overall importance. The KSAOs are usually rated on how important they are for successful job performance, as well as other aspects. Task/KSAO inventories are particularly helpful in developing selection procedures, as well as designing training programs.[7]

Now that you know how organizations determine the necessary KSAOs for a particular job, you will learn how organizations choose selection procedures to assess those KSAOs.

Choosing Selection Procedures

Companies consider several factors in choosing selection procedures: job relatedness, utility, legality, and practicality. In some cases, particularly in very large companies, formal research studies may be conducted to examine these factors. In

Figure 5.3 Position Analysis Questionnaire (PAQ)

Organization of the PAQ

The job elements in the PAQ are organized in six divisions as follows (examples of two job elements from each division are included):

1. *Information input.* (Where and how does the worker get the information he or she uses in performing his or her job?)
   Examples: Use of written materials
   Near-visual differentiation
2. *Mental processes.* (What reasoning, decision-making, planning, and information-processing activities are involved in performing the job?)
   Examples: Levels of reasoning in problem solving
   Coding/decoding
3. *Work output.* (What physical activities does the worker perform and what tools or devices does he or she use?)
   Examples: Using keyboard devices
   Assembling/disassembling
4. *Relationships with other persons.* (What relationships with other people are required in performing the job?)
   Examples: Instruction
   Contact with public, customers
5. *Job context.* (In what physical or social contexts is the work performed?)
   Examples: High temperature
   Interpersonal conflict situations
6. *Other job characteristics.* (What activities, conditions, or characteristics other than those described above are relevant to the job?)

Rating Scales Used With the PAQ

There is a provision for rating each job on each job element. Six types of rating scales are used:

Letter Identification	Type of Rating Scale
U	Extent of Use
I	Importance to the Job
T	Amount of Time
P	Possibility of Occurrence
A	Applicability
S	Special Code (used in the case of a few specific job elements)

A specific rating scale is designated to be used with each job element, in particular the scale considered most appropriate to the content of the element. All but the "A" (Applicability) scale are 6-point scales, and "0" (which is coded as "N") is for "Does not apply," as illustrated below:

Rating	Importance to the Job
N	Does not apply
1	Very minor (importance)
2	Low
3	Average
4	High
5	Extreme

Modified and reproduced by special permission of the Publisher, Consulting Psychologists Press, Inc., Palo Alto, CA 94303 from *Position Analysis Questionnaire (PAQ) from Job Analysis: Methods and Applications* by Ernest J. McCormick.

other cases, particularly in small companies, there may be no formal study regarding these factors. Of course, without a careful examination, a company may be in error with regard to the characteristics of its selection procedure.

Job Relatedness

Job relatedness refers to whether the selection procedure is related to job requirements (for example, professional license) or job outcomes (performance, attendance, and so forth). There are several possible ways for an organization to demonstrate that a selection procedure is job related. One way is by conducting a criterion-related validity study. In a criterion-related validity study, the organization uses the selection method, or *predictor,* with a large number of applicants (known as a *predictive study*) or current employees (known as a *concurrent study*). The organization would also obtain measures of job behavior, or *criteria,* such as absenteeism, turnover, accident rate, or productivity level for each hired applicant or employee.[8] Next, the organization would use statistics, usually correlation coefficients, to calculate the relationship between the predictor and the criteria. Be sure that you read Table 5.2, which describes what a correlation is in

Job relatedness
Refers to whether the selection procedure is related to job requirements or job outcomes.

Criterion-related validity study
One method of demonstrating that a procedure is job-related. The organization would use the selection method, or predictor, with a large number of applicants or current employees to obtain measures of job behavior, then use statistics to calculate the relationship between the predictor and the criteria.

Correlation coefficient
A statistic that summarizes the relationship between two variables or measures.

Table 5.2 **The Magic of the Correlation Coefficient**

A correlation coefficient is a statistic that summarizes the relationship between two variables or measures. A correlation can range anywhere between (and including) +1.00 and −1.00. Let's first start with what a +1.00 correlation would mean. Figure A shows a scatterplot of average daily temperatures in St. Louis during 1994. The x axis plots the temperature in Fahrenheit; the y axis is in centigrade. Because Farenheit and centigrade are simply two measures of the same thing, they correlate perfectly, namely, +1.00. This also means that if you know the temperature in Farenheit, you can completely accurately determine the temperature in centigrade, and vice versa.

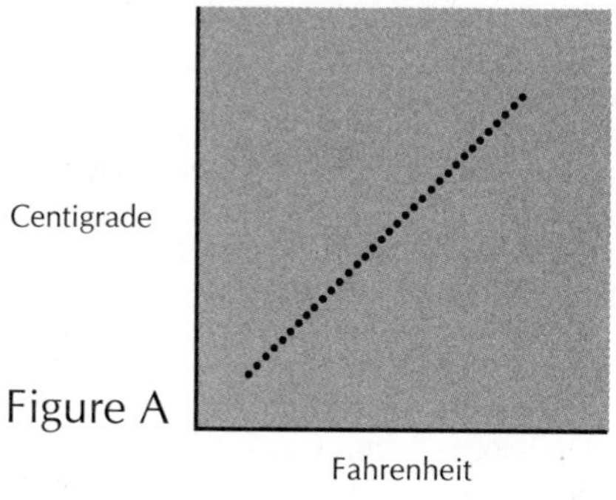

Centigrade

Figure A

Fahrenheit

A −1.00 represents a perfect *inverse* relationship between the two variables. Figure B shows a scatterplot of the amount of daylight for each day in St. Louis in 1994 and the length of the night during this time frame. This comprises a −1.00 correlation, indicating that the longer the daylight, the shorter the night, and vice versa. As in the previous example, a −1.00 means that you can accurately predict one variable (for instance, the amount of daylight) from the other variable (the length of the night). The fact that the correlation is a negative one means that high numbers on one variable are associated with low numbers on the other variable, and vice versa.

(Continued)

Table 5.2 **The Magic of the Correlation Coefficient (continued)**

(continued from previous page)

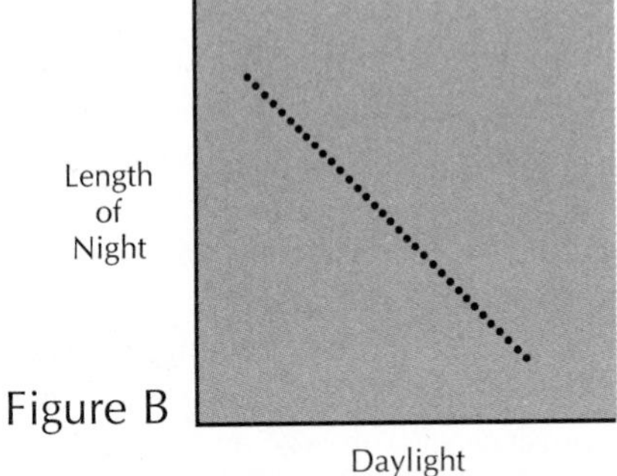

Figure B

Figure C illustrates a zero correlation between two variables. A zero correlation means that there is no relationship between the two variables. A zero correlation also means that knowing the score on one variable is not the least bit helpful in predicting the score of the second variable. Shoe size, for example, would probably have a zero correlation with grade point average.

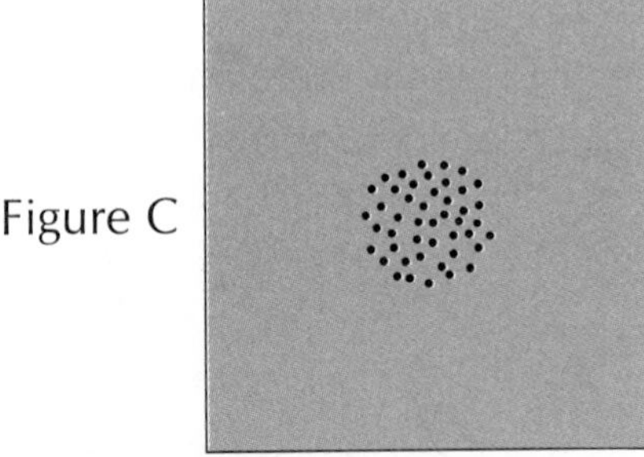
Figure C

The examples given here representing a +1.00, −1.00, and a zero correlation were, of course, fairly artificial. In reality, when you read about the correlations between selection methods and job outcomes, you will see that they rarely exceed .40, and they often hover around .30. In other words, job outcomes such as performance and turnover are difficult to predict with a great deal of accuracy. Nevertheless, a selection method that correlates at .30 or .40 with job outcomes will lead to better decisions than a selection method that has a zero correlation with job outcomes. While the predictions will not be completely accurate, a selection method with a correlation coefficient of .30 or .40 will lead to better decisions than a selection method with a zero correlation. Why is the correlation coefficient referred to here as being "magical"? Because it is a simple statistic, one that is easy to understand, and it can be used to compare the predictive accuracy or validity of different selection methods.

Content validity
Another method of demonstrating job relatedness, where the selection procedure should: Comprise a simulation of the job, have scores based on concrete and observable behavior by the test taker, represent important aspects of the job, and assess activities for which the person will not receive training if hired.

greater detail, as we will be discussing this statistic more specifically throughout the chapter.[9]

Another way to demonstrate job relatedness is through content validity. While criterion-related validity is shown through statistics, content validity is primarily judgmental in nature. In order to be considered content valid, a selection procedure should meet the following stipulations:

1. Comprise a simulation of the job.
2. Have scores based on concrete and observable behavior by the test taker.
3. Represent important aspects of the job.
4. Assess activities for which the person will not receive training if hired.[10]

A good example of a content valid test is a typing test for a typist job. The typing test would meet the first rule, because a typing test would simulate the job. Assuming the score on the test is based on something like the number of words typed per minute minus errors, the score would be based on highly concrete and observable behavior, thus meeting the second rule. The third rule would be met if the typist job, as suggested by the job title, involves a significant amount of typing. Finally, the fourth rule would be met if in fact the typist hired would be expected to know how to type and would not receive typing training.

Another approach, particularly for procedures other than standardized tests, is to judge the job relatedness of a particular selection procedure on the basis of logical arguments. For example, while few companies conduct a formal criterion-related validity study on their reference checking procedure, most people would probably consider this a job-related practice on logical grounds.[11]

Now that you have read about these different methods of demonstrating the job-relatedness of a selection procedure, which do you think would be best in a discrimination lawsuit? If you answered the first, namely, criterion-related validity, you are probably right. Recall from Chapter 2 that the two basic approaches to bringing a lawsuit are disparate treatment and adverse impact. The "logical argument" may not be acceptable to the courts in an adverse impact case, though it may well be sufficient for a disparate treatment case, where the company only presents a "legitimate, nondiscriminatory reason."

Utility

Utility refers to the benefits versus the costs of using a particular selection procedure. As was emphasized in earlier discussions of HRM, today's focus on cost cutting and remaining competitive means that a company must ensure that each program and practice provides satisfactory financial gains. Not surprisingly, most selection procedures also have a cost associated with them, whether it is direct (for example, a test may cost as much as $200 to purchase) or indirect (an interview takes a certain amount of time for the manager to conduct, for example). Utility is an increasingly important concept in HRM, not just for selection procedures. While there are several different ways to calculate the utility of a selection procedure, the commonly accepted way is to use the Schmidt-Hunter formula. Given the many factors that go into this formula, such as the number of employees being hired, the utility of any given selection procedure could vary widely from company to company. In most cases, however, systematic selection procedures such as paper-and-pencil tests provide at least some financial gain over costs to organizations. An example of the utility of a drug test as calculated by one organization is provided in Box 5.1.[12]

Utility
Refers to the benefits versus costs of using a particular selection procedure.

Legal Concepts

As you know from reading previous chapters, laws have a major effect on all HRM practices. Some of the legal principles and regulations covered earlier will be referred to here again. Some new principles and regulations will be introduced as

Box 5.1 Utility of a Drug Test

Tales from the Trenches

In order to examine the utility of a preemployment drug test, the U.S. Postal Service conducted a large-scale, carefully designed predictive validation study in 21 locations nationwide. Drug tests were administered to more than five thousand applicants, of whom 4,396 were ultimately hired. The study focused on differences between drug positives (those hired whom the test identified as drug users) and drug negatives (those hired whom the test had not identified as drug users) in absenteeism, turnover, injuries, and accidents. The statistical analyses showed that significant differences existed between drug positives and drug negatives on absenteeism and involuntary turnover. Because it was possible to calculate the financial gain of reduced absenteeism and involuntary turnover, the Postal Service could determine the utility of the drug test in dollar terms. More specifically, it was estimated that more than 60,000 new employees would need to be hired each year, from a total of 180,000 applicants. Approximately 9 percent of the applicants taking the test would show up as drug positives. In addition, the benefit of the drug-test program would last beyond one year, because the average Postal Service employee stays for 10 years.

On the cost side, the Postal Service estimated that the total cost of testing each applicant would be $11. Since the test would be given to all 180,000 applicants, this would result in a total cost of nearly two million dollars in any given year. Do you think the costs outweighed the benefits? If you answered no, you are right! According to the formula, the Postal Service would *gain* more than three million dollars the first year alone from the reduced absenteeism. With the reduction in involuntary turnover from using the drug test, the gain would be even higher in the first year, and the Postal Service would continue to reap benefits over the years. As you can see from this example, even an expensive test may have great utility for an organization.

Source: Adapted from J. Normand, S. Salyards, and J. Mahoney, "An Evaluation of Preemployment Drug Testing," *Journal of Applied Psychology* 75, (1990), 629–39.

well. Our discussion will address both legally restricted and legally recommended selection practices.

Restricted Selection Procedures/Questions. There are laws that restrict or ban a variety of selection procedures and questions. Most preemployment questions and inquiries regarding age, sex, race, national origin, religion, disabilities, and marital status, for example, are directly prohibited or discouraged by federal or state laws and various court cases. Table 5.3 provides a list of questions that would probably be considered discriminatory if asked during the hiring process. However, certain questions may be necessary to ask at some point in the hiring process. For example, to meet the requirements of certain laws, it may be necessary to ascertain that employees are over 16 years old. Table 5.3, therefore, also lists acceptable ways to ask some of the otherwise illegal questions.[13]

In addition to questions about age, sex, race, and so forth, medical and physical inquiries (for example, examinations or health-related questions) *prior to making a job offer* are illegal under the Americans with Disabilities Act. Until an organization makes you a job offer, it is illegal for the company to have you undergo a medical or physical examination.[14]

Finally, lie detectors or polygraphs, which are mechanical or electrical tests designed to assess whether you are lying in response to various questions, are re-

Table 5.3 **Do's and Dont's of Interviewing**

Subject	**Unlawful Inquiry**	**Lawful Inquiry***
Name	If your name has been legally changed, what was your former name?	Have you ever worked for this company under a different name? What is your maiden name? (May be asked of married female applicants, if necessary, to check educational or employment records.) Have you ever been convicted of a crime under another name?
Age	[Any question that tends to identify applicants age 40 or older.]	Are you over eighteen years of age? If hired, can you furnish proof of age? [Statement that employment is subject to verification that applicant's age meets legal requirements.]
Citizenship	Are you a citizen of the United States (varies by state)? Are your parents or spouse citizens of the United States? On what dates did you, your parents, or your spouse acquire U.S. citizenship? Are you, your parents, or spouse naturalized or native-born U.S. citizens?	If you are not a U.S. citizen, do you have the legal right to remain permanently in the United States? What is your visa status (If No to above)? Do you intend to remain permanently in the United States? [Statement that employment is subject to verfication of applicant's identity and eligibility for employment as required by immigration laws.]
National origin/ Ancestry	What is your nationality/lineage/ancestry/national origin/descent/parentage? How did you acquire the ability to speak, read, or write a foreign language? How did you acquire familiarity with a foreign country? What language is spoken in your home? What is your mother tongue?	What language do you speak, read, or write fluently? Do you have special familiarity with any foreign country? What is the nature of that familiarity (If Yes to above)?
Race or color	[Any question that directly or indirectly relates to race or color]	[None]
Religion	Do you attend religious services or a house of worship? What is your religious denomination or affiliation, church, parish, or pastor? What religious holidays do you observe?	[None]
Sex	[Any inquiry as to sex, such as the following:] Do you wish to be addressed as Mr., Mrs., Miss, or Ms.? What are your plans regarding having children in the future? Do you have the capacity to reproduce?	[None]
Relatives/Marital status	What is your marital status? (If over 18) What is the name or address of relative/spouse/children? With whom do you reside? Do you live with your parents? What are the ages of your children?	What are the names of relatives already employed by the company?

*Lawful only if job related.

Source: S. Kahn, B.B. Brown, M. Lanzarone, *Legal Guide to Human Resources,* (Boston, MA: Warren, Gorham & Lamont, 1995).

(Continued)

Table 5.3 **Do's and Dont's of Interviewing *(continued)***

Subject	Unlawful Inquiry	Lawful Inquiry
Physical condition	Do you have any physical disabilities? What is your disability? What caused your disability? What is the prognosis of your disability? Have you had any recent serious illness?	Do you understand the requirements of the job and can you perform the job with or without reasonable accommodation? Explain how you would go about doing the job applied for. {The Americans with Disabilities Act (ADA) prohibits preemployment-offer medical examinations or inquiries into an individual's disability status. Even where a disability is evident to an employer, the employer cannot make inquiries into the nature or severity of the disability.]
Education	{Any question asking specifically the nationality, racial, or religious affiliation of a school.]	[Statement that employment offer may be (is) made contingent on passing a medical evaluation.] [Questions related to academic, vocational, or professional education of an applicant, including schools attended, degrees/diplomas received, dates of graduation, and courses of study.]
Experience	[Questions related to military experience in general.]	[Questions related to applicant's work history.] [Questions related to applicant's military experience in the armed forces of the United States or in a U.S. state militia.]
Organizations	To what organizations, clubs, societies, and lodges do you belong?	To what organizations, clubs, societies, and lodges do you belong? (Exclude those whose names or character indicate the race, religious creed, color, national origin, or ancestry of its members.)
Character	Have you ever been arrested?	Have you ever been convicted of any crime?* If so, when, where, and disposition of case? Have you been convicted under any criminal law within the past five years (excluding minor traffic violations)?
Work Schedule/ Traveling	[Any question related to childcare, ages of children, or other subject that is likely to be perceived by covered group members, expecially women, as discriminatory.]	Do you have any family, business, health, or social obligations that would prevent you from working consistently/working overtime/traveling? Are there any reasons why you would not consistently arrive for work on time and work according to the company's (location's) work schedule?
Relocation	[Any question related to spouse's attitudes or other subject that is likely to be perceived by covered group members, especially women, as discriminatory.]	Do you have any family, business, health, or social obligations that would prevent you from relocating? Would you be willing to relocate?
Miscellaneous	[Any inquiry that is not job-related or necessary for determining an applicant's potential for employment.]	[Statement or notice to applicant that any misstatements or omissions of significant facts in written application forms or in an interview may be cause for dismissal.]

*In some states, such as California and New York, such a question must be accompanied by a statement that a conviction will not necessarily disqualify an applicant from a job. In Delaware, one *may* ask if the applicant has ever been arrested; in Massachusetts, one may ask if the applicant has been arrested for a felony. Some states put a time limit on convictions that may be inquired about (e.g., Massachusetts [ten years]). Minnesota suggests that the best practice may be to obtain conviction information through local police departments, rather than from applicants.

stricted by law. The **Employee Polygraph Protection Act of 1988** prohibits most private-sector organizations from having an applicant take a polygraph test as a condition of employment (security companies and drug and pharmaceutical companies are allowed to test for certain positions). In addition, this law prohibits covered organizations from the following:

Employee Polygraph Protection Act of 1988
Prohibits most private-sector organizations from having you take a polygraph test as a condition of employment.

1. Discharging or disciplining an employee based on a refusal to take a polygraph test.
2. Using or obtaining information about the results of a polygraph test given to an applicant or employee.
3. Retaliating against an employee or applicant filing a complaint on the basis of this law.

However, this law does permit organizations to require employees to undergo a lie detector examination when there are specific, legitimate circumstances (for example, theft has occurred, and there is reasonable suspicion that the employee was somehow involved).[15]

Legally Recommended Practices. Certain selection practices may be legally recommended or even required. One legal concept that would encourage employers to conduct careful background and reference checks is known as **negligent hiring**. In a negligent hiring lawsuit, an organization could be held liable for things done by an employee that should have been foreseen. Some examples where negligent hiring charges were filed against the company are the following:

Negligent hiring
A finding that an employer is responsible for using poor selection procedures after an employee inflicts harm on the customer or other third party.

- A service station employee shoots a customer to death.
- A truck driver sexually assaults a hitchhiker.
- An apartment manager rapes a tenant.
- A doorman shoots a customer being chased by a bouncer.
- A bond salesman threatens a customer into buying bonds.
- A hospital orderly hurts a patient when removing a catheter.[16]

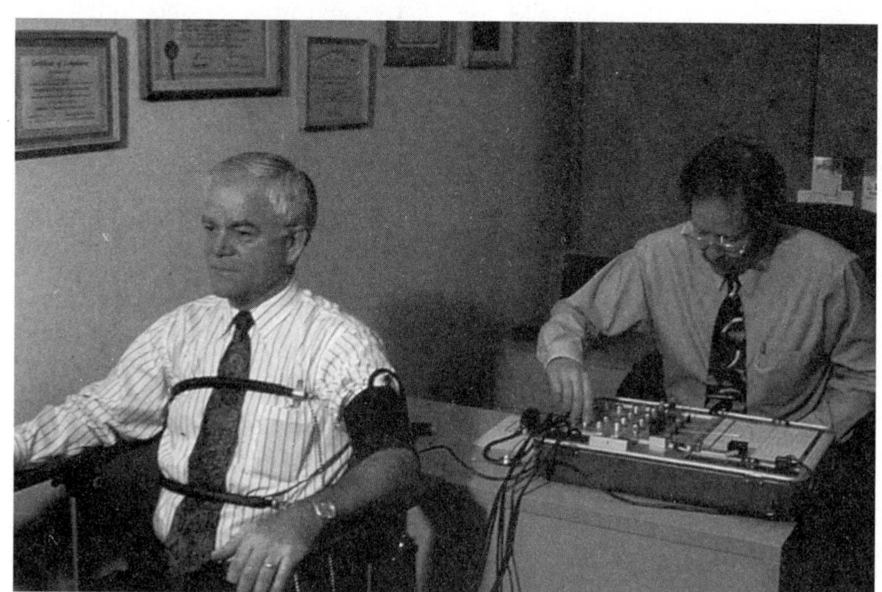

Taking a polygraph test as a condition of employment is no longer legal according to the Employee Polygraph Protection Act of 1988. Polygraph tests can be given only when there are specific, legitimate circumstances, such as if a theft has occurred.

As you can see from these examples, a negligent hiring suit can arise in many different occupations. Because of the negligent hiring concept, organizations are encouraged to conduct reference and background checks much more diligently in order to screen out applicants who may present a risk. Depending on the nature of the job, organizations may also be encouraged to perform conviction record checks and drug testing.

Certain regulated industries also have substantial numbers of laws that require background checks, drug testing, and other selection procedures to be performed. For example, Executive Order 12564, also known as the Drug-Free Federal Workplace order, requires government agencies to drug-test employees in sensitive positions. Similar laws are in place for other industries, such as the transportation industry.[17]

Practicality

There are several practical matters that an organization should consider in choosing selection devices. One of these is the *face* validity of each procedure. Face validity refers to perceptions held by various affected parties as to the job relatedness of the selection procedure. For example, if hiring managers feel that a test is not really job related (that is, it does not have face validity), they may not use test results properly. Similarly, if a selection procedure is not considered face valid by applicants, the organization may have difficulty getting them to accept job offers. Other practical considerations include the administration of the procedure (for instance, is it very time-consuming?) and scoring procedures for tests (are the tests difficult to score?).[18]

Typical Selection Steps

Although organizations differ in terms of which selection methods they use, many companies use a fairly standard set of steps in the hiring process. The common steps are as follows:

1. Review application blanks and/or resumes.
2. Select best applicants for interview.
3. Interview.
4. Administer tests.
5. Conduct reference and background checks.
6. Perform drug tests.

Of course, not all organizations use all procedures. Other organizations may have somewhat different steps. For example, an organization may have far too many applicants to interview first. In that situation, an organization may use a paper-and-pencil test in Step 3, and then follow up with interviews in Step 4.

Now that you have read about some of the considerations that companies use in choosing selection methods, we will discuss some of these different procedures in more detail. We begin first with a discussion of the application blank and related techniques, followed by a discussion of the interview and various tests. We conclude with a discussion of background checks, drug screens, and several miscellaneous procedures.

The Application Blank

Nearly every organization requires you, as an applicant, to complete an application blank at some point in the employment process. Figure 5.4 provides an example of an application blank. Notice the fairly lengthy sentence near the end of the form in Figure 5.4, just above the signature area. If you read this statement carefully, you will see that among other things, the company has retained the right to terminate you at any time, for any reason. Most application blanks have a similar statement, and there is little an applicant can do to get around this. Furthermore, as you will read in Chapter 16, even without such a statement, most employees have little protection from arbitrarily being terminated. You may also observe a warning on the application blank that falsification or omission of information is grounds for dismissal. This warning is an attempt to combat applicants' attempts to misrepresent themselves, given that as many as 30 percent of all resumes and application blanks contain some false information.[19]

Figure 5.4 **Sample Application Blank**

Name: ______________________________

Address: ______________________________

Home Phone Number: ______________

Education

College/University Attended: ______________________ Highest Degree: BA/BS MA/MS/MBA PhD

High School Attended: ______________________

Work Experience (List most recent jobs first)

Name of Organization: ______________________

Final Salary: ______________ (annual; be sure to include any bonuses or commission earned)

Job Title: ______________________

Name of last supervisor: ______________________

May we contact this supervisor? Yes No

Reason for Leaving: ______________________________

____

Name of Organization: ______________________ Dates of Employment: from ________ to ________

Final Salary: ______________ (annual; be sure to include any bonuses or commission earned)

Job Title: ______________________

Name of last supervisor: ______________________

May we contact this supervisor? Yes No

Reason for Leaving: ______________________________

____

(Continued)

Figure 5.4 Sample Application Blank *(continued)*

Name of Organization: ______________________ Dates of Employment: from ________ to ________

Final Salary: ______________ (annual; be sure to include any bonuses or commission earned)

Job Title: ______________________

Name of last supervisor: ______________________

May we contact this supervisor? Yes No

Reason for Leaving: ______________________

____

Name of Organization: ______________________ Dates of Employment: from ________ to ________

Final Salary: ______________ (annual; be sure to include any bonuses or commission earned)

Job Title: ______________________

Name of last supervisor: ______________________

May we contact this supervisor? Yes No

Reason for Leaving: ______________________

____

Work skills

1. List any job-related languages you are able to speak or write: ______________________
2. List any job-related clerical (e.g., typing) or technical skills (e.g., computer programming) that you have:

   A. ______________________

   B. ______________________

   C. ______________________

Additional Information

In case of an emergency, please contact.

Name: ______________________

Address: ______________________

Telephone: ______________________

____

____

I understand that falsification of information is grounds for dismissal.

I understand that my employment at the company may be discontinued at any time for any reason either by myself or by the company.

I agree to submit to a drug and/or alcohol test as a condition of employment.

____

Signature Date

For the most part, organizations use information from the application blank as an initial screen to reduce the number of potential candidates. In larger organizations, the human resources representative may perform an initial screen of the application blanks, and decide which candidates should be invited for an interview.

An alternative to the application blank is the Weighted Application Blank (WAB). Typically, the standard application blank is reviewed in a subjective fashion. The WAB is really nothing more than an *objectively* scored application blank. Rather than having the HRM manager or hiring manager make a judgment concerning the application blank on the basis of "gut feel," the WAB provides a score for each applicant, based on an answer key that was developed through research. The WAB is best suited for jobs where there are many workers, and it is particularly useful for reducing turnover. As such, WABs appear to be most commonly used for clerical and sales jobs, where traditionally there is high turnover.[20] Although the research on the WAB suggests it can be a valid selection device, it is not commonly used by employers.[21]

Weighted application blank (WAB)
An objectively scored application blank.

Another related technique is the Biographical Information Blank or BIB. The BIB extends the concept of the WAB one step further. That is, the aim of the BIB is to utilize a broader range of questions, particularly those pertaining to past achievements and personal goals and aspirations, which are scored with a standardized key.[22] Some examples of BIB items are provided in Table 5.4.

Biographical information blank (BIB)
Utilizes a broader range of questions on an application blank, particularly those pertaining to past achievements and personal goals and aspirations, which are scored with a standardized key.

Research on the BIB has been generally favorable with regard to its criterion-related validity.[23] The criterion-related validity of the BIB is about .30.[24] However, a number of concerns have been raised with this selection method.[25] One criticism is that a person's employment opportunities may be permanently affected by earlier (even childhood) experiences. Responses to BIB items such as #1 and #2 in Table 5.4 cannot be changed, regardless of a person's subsequent accomplishments. A second criticism is that BIB items often seem rather intrusive. Do you think, for example, that item #3 in Table 5.4 constitutes an invasion of your

Table 5.4 **Sample BIB Items**

1. Check each of the following activities you participated in by the time you were 18.
   a. Shot a rifle
   b. Driven a car
   c. Worked on full-time job
   d. Traveled alone over 500 miles from home
   e. Repaired an electrical appliance
2. While growing up, did you collect coins?
3. Are you satisfied with life?
   Yes
   No
4. How often did you feel a teacher was unfair in a decision she or he made?
5. How often did you go to your parents for advice when you were in school?

Source: Items 1, 2, and 3 are from R. Gatewood and H. Feild, Human Resource Selection, (Fort Worth, TX: Dryden, 1994). Items 4 and 5 are from C. Russell, J. Mettson, S. Devlin, and D. Atwater, "Predictive Validity of Biodata Items Generated from Retrospective Life Experience Essays," *Journal of Applied Psychology* 75 (1990), 569–80.

privacy? Indeed, the face validity of biodata appears to be quite low.[26] These concerns may explain why relatively few companies use BIBs. We turn now to the interview, which is one of the most popular selection methods.

The Interview

The interview is such a common selection practice that you would probably be suspicious if a company hired you without one. It is indeed rare to find a company that does not use at least one interview in its selection procedure. Many companies have applicants go through two or more interviews. As suggested by the opening case, there are many different kinds of interviews. Four basic kinds of interviews, namely the traditional interview, the structured interview, the stress interview, and the panel interview, are described next.

Traditional Interview

Traditional interview The most common type of interview, which allows the interviewer a great deal of discretion in terms of which questions are asked and in what order.

Most people at one time or another have experienced a traditional interview, which is probably the most common type of interview. Table 5.5 contains a list of questions that are often asked in the traditional interview. The traditional interview format also allows the interviewer a great deal of discretion in terms of which questions are asked and in what order. In other words, using a traditional interview, the hiring manager might ask completely different questions of each candidate.[27]

You can probably guess why an interviewer would want to ask most of the questions listed in Table 5.5. In general, the traditional interview is used to assess factors such as job motivation, "fit" with the organization, and ability to

Table 5.5 **Questions That May Be Asked in the Traditional Interview**

1. What did you like most about your last job?
2. What did you like least about your last job?
3. What are your career goals?
4. What is your greatest strength?
5. What is your greatest weakness?
6. What kind of boss do you work best with?
7. What is most important to you on the job?
8. What were your favorite courses at school?
9. What extracurricular activities did you participate in during school?
10. How did you choose this particular field of work?
11. What do you think your current supervisor's greatest strength is?
12. Why did you leave your last job?
13. Do you prefer to work alone or in a team?
14. What are your hobbies?
15. Who was your favorite teacher? Why?
16. Who paid your tuition in college?

Box 5.2 "What Do I Say If They Ask . . .?"

Because certain questions are commonly asked in the traditional interview, experts recommend that you prepare carefully ahead of time to answer these. Below are some suggested answers to some of these questions.

1. *"Tell me about yourself."* You should have planned an answer to this question. Your answer should consist of a brief speech, containing about 300 words and taking approximately one to one-and-a-half minutes. This speech should be an oral presentation of the highlights of your resume, along with the highlights of a cover letter you would write for this employer. In other words, your speech should emphasize your key achievements, key strengths, and an explanation of how these achievements and strengths are pertinent to the position. If possible, you should end your speech with a question to the interviewer (for example, "What new strategic directions is the company taking?"). Experts say the key to a successful answer here is to demonstrate your confidence, communication skills, and match between the job and your qualifications.

2. *"Why do you want to work for our company?"* This is the kind of question that makes you pleased you did some library research on the company. And this is a way for companies to see if you showed initiative. A good answer, then, reveals that you know something about the company and its products. For example, you may have read that the company is restructuring, and is in the process of redesigning the sales department into teams. You might respond by saying that you enjoy the team approach to sales (and hopefully you can demonstrate some experience working with teams) and describe why that sales approach makes sense given the company's product line.

3. *"What's your greatest weakness?"* Gulp! That's the question you probably dread most. This can be a "damned if you do and damned if you don't" question. If you say you have no weaknesses, the interviewer may believe you are being evasive (everybody has a weakness). If you say something like, "I work too hard" or "I'm very demanding of myself" your answer may also sound artificial. Experts advise you try to offer something that won't disqualify you (for instance, if you have never supervised anyone and the job doesn't involve supervising others, you can answer, "I have not supervised anyone.") or something that sounds reasonable (for example, "I offered several innovative ideas, but my boss was worried the ideas would lead to radical changes in the department").

4. *"Describe the best boss and worst boss to work with."* This is obviously a tough question. If you say the worst boss is one who checks on everything you do, and that's the prospective supervisor's style, your answer may not work in your favor. One response is to play it safe and say something like, "I've worked with a variety of different styles of bosses, and am able to adjust to different styles."

5. *"Are you married?"* or *"What religion do you practice?"* or *"How old are you?"* are questions that are probably illegal and certainly inappropriate. But how should you answer them? If you refuse to answer that kind of question, the interviewer may feel offended (he or she may not be aware such questions are inappropriate). If you challenge the interviewer by saying the question is illegal, you may be perceived as offensive. Experts suggest that you answer a question about religion or similar area by saying something like, "Do I look like I practice some unusual form of religion? I assume you are joking, because that is considered an illegal question." Or, "I'm happy to discuss any job-related questions, but in my human resources course we learned that questions pertaining to race, religion, age, disabilities, and so forth are illegal. I don't think questions related to my religion (or marital status, or age) are job related. Do you?"

6. *"What questions do YOU have?"* If you don't have any questions, the interviewer may take this as a lack of interest in the company or a lack of savvy, both of which may hurt you in the hiring process. Some good questions to ask include the following:

- Does this job typically lead to other jobs in the company? Describe those other jobs. How are staffing decisions made about those other jobs?
- What new products or services is the company thinking of introducing in the next few years?
- What changes do you expect in the company's business strategy over the next few years?

Whatever you do, do not ask about the company's vacation plans, personal days, and so forth! It will seem as though you are most worried about time away from the organization.

Source: Adapted from H. Medley, *Sweaty Palms: The Neglected Art of Being Interviewed* (Berkeley, CA: Ten Speed Press, 1984); R. Fry, *Your First Job* (Hawthorne, NJ: Career Press, 1993); and A. Ludmer, "Watch Out for Deadly Interview Traps," *St. Louis Post-Dispatch,* October, 3, 1993, 19G.

The traditional interview, such as the one shown here, is still the most common preferred method of selecting employees. Interviewers are able to ask a variety of questions in any order, and usually do not address the issue of your job-related abilities and skills. Questions relate to job motivation, "fit" with the organization, ability to work with others, and the like.

work with others, as well as to identify major problems (such as unreliability). As you read the questions in Table 5.5, you may also note that few of them seem to focus on the skills and abilities needed to perform the job. Questions that more directly assess job-related abilities and skills are found in structured interview formats.

Despite its popularity, many experts have been skeptical as to the value of the traditional interview. First, from a criterion-related validity viewpoint, the traditional interview generally is believed to have a relatively low correlation with job performance, perhaps as low as .14. Second, the traditional interview is susceptible to a wide variety of biases and errors. Hiring managers may use the traditional interview to select someone who seems similar to them or is likable, rather than the candidate who is most qualified for the job. Third, because the traditional interview permits complete discretion over which questions to ask, illegal inquiries sometimes are used. From the organization's standpoint, then, the traditional interview has a number of shortcomings. Many companies have therefore turned to the structured interview approach.[28]

Structured Interviews

Structured interview Uses a predetermined set of questions that are clearly job-related, such as the behavior description interview and situational interview.

The basis of a structured interview is a predetermined set of questions that are clearly job related. Although the interviewer may have a choice of questions from which to choose, he or she may not use a question that is not on the list. Although several different kinds of structured interviews are available, the two most popular are the behavior description interview (BDI) and situational interview (SI).[29] BDI questions address past experiences (they may begin with "Tell me about a time when . . . "), whereas SI questions address how the applicant would handle a situation in the future ("What would you do if . . . ?") Sample BDI and SI questions are provided in Table 5.6. As you can see, the questions are clearly job related and

Box 5.3 Interviewing Applicants in Other Countries

Depending on which country a job candidate is from, the wording of interview questions may be quite important. Consider first the Japanese. Because of cultural norms that encourage teamwork and de-emphasize individual achievements, Japanese managers would be very uncomfortable answering a question such as "How do you compare your skill level to that of your coworkers?" A question such as "From the time you were in high school through your time at the university, what skills did you exhibit that enabled you to excel?" would be far more appropriate. Nevertheless, Japanese managers tend to give brief responses to such questions, due to a concern that a lengthy answer will be less well understood. Therefore, probing questions, such as "Could you provide some more specific details on how you used those skills on a daily basis?" are usually needed to obtain further information.

If you are interviewing a Korean manager, however, this question would be considered highly appropriate: "What skill do you most enjoy using?" For a Japanese manager, this question might appear odd, because in Japan there is little concept of work enjoyment. In Korea, though, it is assumed that work should bring personal satisfaction. Another question that would be appropriate in Korea is "What was the most difficult decision you ever had to make on your own without your boss's input?" While Korean managers must sometimes make independent decisions, this would be very rare in Japan.

Interviewing in Europe will also reveal interesting cultural differences. French managers often operate within the "Napoleonic Code," which is patterned after the famous military general. This style of management is similar to the traditional bureaucratic management approach, which emphasizes close supervision and constant reaction to problems. To assess a French manager's type of management style, an effective question is: "Which of your skills do you employ that best demonstrates your leadership ability?" Yet another question that is very revealing of a French manager is "Describe your formal education and how that helps you in your current position?" The rationale behind this question is that the French culture places tremendous value on formal education and degrees. The answer given by a French applicant will provide insight into his or her ability to learn new things and the degree to which the applicant can utilize education in the job.

Clearly, depending on the country in which an interviewer is operating, different approachs to questions may be needed.

Source: Adapted from J. Artise, "Selection, Coaching, and Evaluation of Employees in International Subsidiaries," in *Global Perspectives of Human Resource Management,* ed. O. Shenkar, (Englewood Cliffs, NJ: Prentice-Hall, 1995), 71–111.

Table 5.6 Structured Interview Questions for a High School Teacher's Job

Behavioral Description Interview Questions	Situational Interview Questions
■ Tell me about a time when you had a student who was clearly having trouble keeping up with your class material, and was falling far behind. Describe how you handled the situation, and what the outcome was.	■ What would you do if a student was having a great deal of trouble keeping up with the class, and was beginning to fall further and further behind?
■ Tell me about a time when students were talking or engaging in other very disruptive behaviors during class. How did you handle it?	■ What would you do if you were in the middle of a lecture and several students began to whisper, laugh, and generally disrupt class?

probably more challenging to answer than many of the traditional questions found in Table 5.5.

There are several advantages to the structured interview approach. As you may have guessed, structured interviews are more valid than the traditional interview. Their criterion-related validity has been estimated to be as high as .60.[30] Second, by having highly structured interviews, managers are using preestablished questions that are job related, which in turn discourages biases and errors. Third, having a structured interview prevents managers from asking illegal questions. On the other hand, designing a structured interview may take a good amount of time and energy. Furthermore, some managers resent being restricted in terms of the questions they may ask.

Stress Interview

Stress interview
An interview technique that is an attempt by the interviewer to see how a candidate fares under duress.

On occasion, you may encounter the **stress interview**. A stress interview is simply an attempt by the interviewer to see how you fare under duress. There is little evidence that such interviews are valid. An interviewer may justify them on the grounds that the job involves highly volatile situations, where it is important to remain calm. In any case, the key is to remember that nearly any interview situation involves some degree of stress, and it is always important to maintain your self-composure. So, if you think the interviewer is deliberately trying to shake you up, you may be right. Just don't become flustered.[31]

Panel Interview

Panel interview
A group of interviewers interviewing a candidate at the same time. This type of interview is used to reduce personal biases any individual interviewer may have.

The **panel interview** is just a group of interviewers interviewing you at the same time. Although you may think the purpose of the panel interview is to make you uncomfortable, in most cases the actual purpose is to reduce the personal biases any individual interviewer may have. Nevertheless, as an applicant, a panel interview may make you feel more stressed than usual. Here are two suggestions for you as an interviewee:

1. Imagine you are talking to only one person; in fact, in some cases, only one person on the panel will be doing the talking. The others may be there only to listen and take notes.[32]
2. If different people do start asking questions, and do not let you finish giving your answers, pause and then say something like, "Let me answer one question at a time. First . . . ." Then, respond to the next question. In other words, don't let the questioning get out of hand, but at the same time, be polite.

Legal Considerations

In terms of legality, the interview has a mixed record. Most recent research suggests that the interview varies greatly in terms of whether protected groups, such as older workers and minorities, are adversely affected or not. Recent studies indicate that women, on average, do not fare worse than men in the interview.[33] In terms of court cases concerning the interview, most have involved organizations that used discriminatory questions. For instance, in one lawsuit, an African American woman applied for the position of kitchen helper. During the interview, she was asked about her recent pregnancy and future plans pertaining to children, her marital status, and her relationship with an employee of the company. However, such questions were not asked of other applicants, and the interviewer had a history of discriminating against women. Thus, companies seem particularly vulnerable to charges against their interviewing procedure when inappropriate questions are asked.[34] Table 5.7 provides some additional suggestions for companies that wish to increase the likelihood that their interviews will pass legal muster if challenged in court.

Considering the opening case, then, job seekers are encouraged to prepare for a variety of interview questions, many of which were provided in this section. As you participate in more interviews, you will become more comfortable and generally will perform better. Consider role-playing various possible questions with a friend. Try to anticipate all types of questions that might arise, and think ahead of time as to how you might answer them. Finally, recall that Tom Brown was unable to come up with previous experiences in one of his interviews. You should know that in some cases, you may be able to use experiences outside of the workplace, including school, volunteer experiences, and possibly even family situations.

In sum, the interview is a popular selection procedure, and all signs indicate it will remain so. As an applicant, you are encouraged to prepare carefully for every interview. From an organizational perspective, given the importance of the interview, it is critical that selection interviews are carefully planned and that only job-related questions are asked. Questions not directly related to the job, particularly inquiries that address areas such as age, religion, marital status, and so forth, should not be asked under any circumstances.

We now turn to a discussion of paper-and-pencil tests and work samples.

Paper-and-Pencil Tests

There are many different kinds of paper-and-pencil tests, but most can be sorted into two basic categories: personality measures and cognitive ability measures.

Personality Tests

Do you think a personality test would be a good predictor of job performance? It seems reasonable to expect that personality tests would predict job performance

Personality test
A test given to an applicant that will supposedly predict the type of personality a candidate has, and how that personality will affect job performance.

Table 5.7 Suggestions for How Organizations Can Avoid Legal Problems with Interviews

1. Base interview questions and ratings on job analysis.
2. Use interviewers representing diversity in terms of race, sex, national origin, and age.
3. Train interviewers regarding appropriate and inappropriate questions.
4. Use structured interviews.
5. Require interviewers to take notes and to document in writing why they made their hiring decisions.
6. Monitor interview decisions for adverse impact.

Source: Adapted from J. Campion and R. Arvey, "Unfair Discrimination in the Employment Interview," in *The Employment Interview: Theory, Research, and Practice,* ed. R. Eder and G. Ferris, (Newbury, CA: Sage, 1989), 61–73.

at least somewhat. After all, everybody has heard of personality conflicts, "bad" personalities, and other personality-related problems that often seem to take place at work. Table 5.8 provides some examples of questions found on a typical personality test. Although you might think that personality tests would be good predictors of job performance, early studies of the validity of these tests often produced low correlations with job performance, leading many experts to conclude that such tests were of little value in the workplace. Using more sophisticated research methods, the last few years has seen a change in conclusions about the validity of personality tests. A recent estimate placed the validity of personality tests at .24, but it found that when the personality test was chosen on the basis of a careful job analysis, the validity of the personality test climbed to .38.[35] Of course, many different personality tests are in use, and some may be more valid than others.

Honesty test
Two types of honest tests: Overt and personality-based. The overt test asks questions that directly address test-takers' perceptions and feelings about honesty, while personality-based tests tend to be somewhat less obvious as to what they are assessing, and focus on personality traits associated with dishonesty.

One of the more interesting types of personality tests, which has received some attention in the last few years, allegedly measures honesty. Because paper-and-pencil honesty tests are not considered polygraph tests, companies in most states may use them as part of the selection process. Two types of **honesty tests** are used: the overt test and the personality-based test. The overt test asks questions that directly address the test-taker's perceptions and feelings about honesty, such as "Do you ever think about stealing?" "Do you know people who steal?" and "Should someone who steals from his or her company be fired?" Personality-based honesty tests tend to be somewhat less obvious as to what they are assessing and focus on personality traits associated with dishonesty. Typical items include "Do you like to do dangerous things?" and "Do you sometimes do things without thinking?" Do you think such tests demonstrate good validity? A recent summary of research found a criterion-related validity of .55 for overt tests and .32 for personality-based tests. Such tests appear to have utility, then, particularly when the cost (which is only about $10 per test) is considered.[36]

Legally, personality tests have generally fared well, particularly because they produce little, if any, adverse impact.[37] The same is true for honesty tests.[38] The face validity of personality tests, on the other hand, may be somewhat low.[39] All in all, personality tests appear to be making a comeback in industry, though they may never become as popular as cognitive ability tests, which are reviewed next.

Table 5.8 **Typical Personality Test Items**

1. I like to win in any activity I try.
2. I have many friends.
3. I sometimes get upset when I'm criticized.
4. I prefer to work in a team than to work alone.
5. It's more important to me to do a thorough job on one thing than to complete many things.

Cognitive Ability Tests

Cognitive ability tests, or intelligence tests, have a long history of use in the workplace. The use of cognitive ability tests in the United States for selection purposes goes back to the early part of the 20th century. Both private- and public-sector employers began using such tests extensively in the 1950s and 1960s. But in the 1970s, public outcry against such tests in educational settings, as well as in business settings, led many organizations to reduce their reliance on them. Even more importantly, court cases based on the Civil Rights Act of 1964 (for example, *Griggs* v. *Duke Power,* 1971), in which cognitive ability tests fared poorly, led to a marked decline in their use.[40] A major problem, which continues even today, is that on average, blacks and Hispanics obtain lower scores on these tests than do whites, which in turn often creates adverse impact.[41] To compound the problem, early researchers found contradictory results regarding the criterion-related validity of such tests. Sometimes the tests appeared to have sufficient criterion-related validity, while other times they did not, making it difficult for companies to defend the job relatedness of such tests. As a result, the use of cognitive ability tests began to wane in the 1970s. Two things happened that created a revival in the use of cognitive ability tests in the 1980s. First, a new research method known as **meta-analysis** was developed by Frank Schmidt and John Hunter.[42] Meta-analysis, which is a statistical procedure for summarizing past research, indicated that cognitive ability tests have adequate validity across virtually all jobs. In fact, this research suggested that when used properly, cognitive ability tests would have a criterion-related validity of .53.[43] The validity of cognitive ability tests therefore is much higher than earlier HRM experts had thought. In terms of adverse impact, experts suggested that one way around this problem was to use **race norming.**[44] In using race norming, companies would use separate norms for different racial and gender groups, thereby eliminating adverse impact.

Many companies continue to use cognitive ability tests today. In addition to their validity, they are fairly inexpensive. Thus, their utility is likely to be high. The major shortcoming of these tests is that the Civil Rights Act of 1991 explicitly prohibits the use of race and gender norming. Companies that had previously used race or gender norming to eliminate adverse impact must therefore decide whether they have sufficient validity evidence to defend a lawsuit if one arises. In spite of their general validity, then, cognitive ability tests may result in legal problems. Table 5.9 provides some sample items from a cognitive ability test. Figure 5.5 provides examples of a nonverbal cognitive ability test.

Cognitive ability test
Intelligence test given to applicants.

Meta-analysis
Developed by Frank Schmidt and John Hunter, this is a statistical procedure for summarizing past research, and has indicated that cognitive ability tests have adequate validity across virtually all jobs.

Race norming
A method used to eliminate adverse impact by separating norms for different racial and gender groups.

Table 5.9 **Typical Cognitive Ability Test Items**

1. Which of the following is the opposite of sanguine?
   a. pessimistic b. happy c. melodic d. rapid
2. If it takes three employees to complete each widget produced, how many employees would it take to complete 120 widgets?
   a. 300 b. 360 c. 36 d. 40
3. What is the next number in the following series of numbers: 1 3 7 15 31?
   a. 4 b. 63 c. 92 d. 103

Figure 5.5 **Typical Nonverbal Cognitive Ability Test Items**

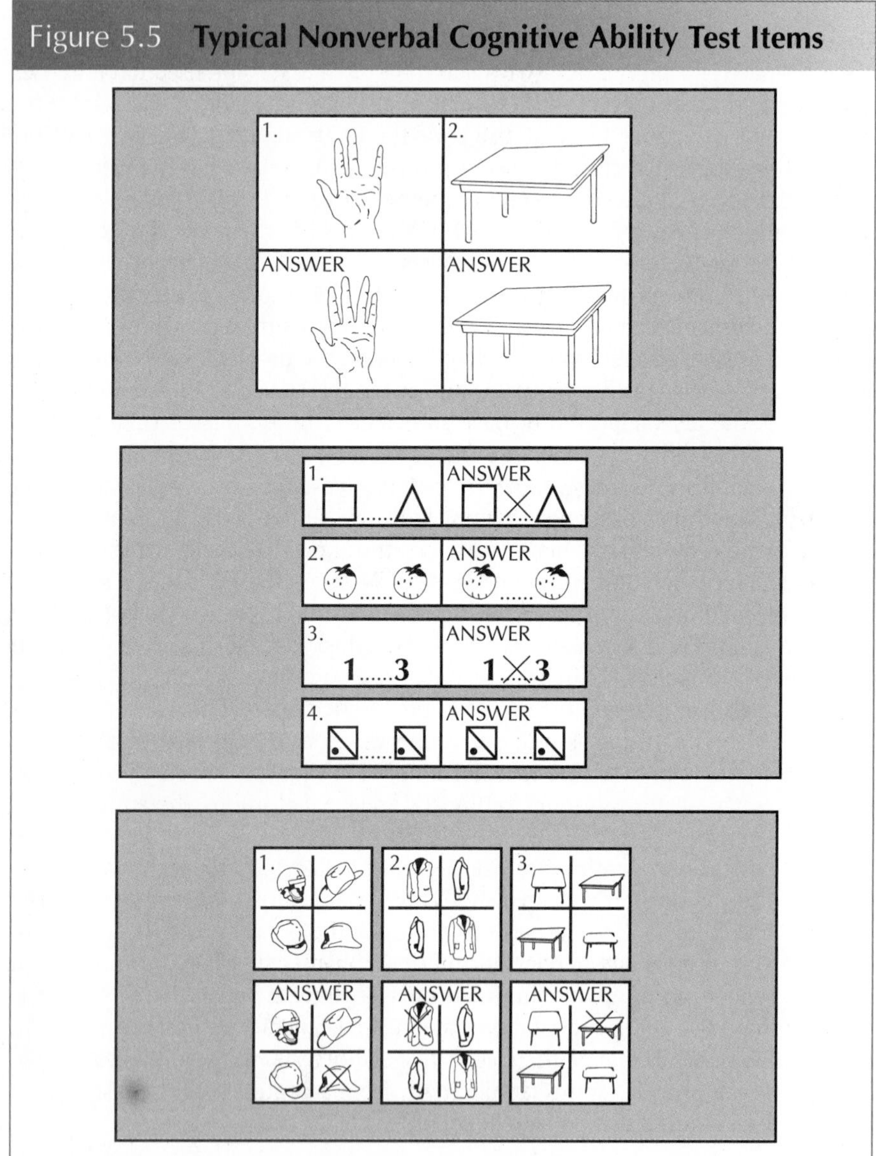

Source: From the Beta-II Examination. Copyright by the Psychological Corporation (Harcourt Brace).

Work Samples

Most managers will tell you that the best way to assess someone's job qualifications is to let them work on a trial basis for a few weeks. This method, however, is generally not feasible for at least two reasons. First, hiring someone on a trial basis might pose significant risks for the organization. For example, a production worker who is poorly qualified might be injured while operating a drill press. An unqualified salesperson could cause the loss of valued customers. Second, many applicants would be reluctant to accept a job that they may lose shortly after they begin. Therefore, some organizations and businesses use work samples, which are basically a brief simulation of major job activities. Work samples are commonly used for secretarial and clerical positions, where typing skills can be assessed using an objective method. The actual work sample depends on the particular job one is being hired for. An applicant for a sales position, for example, might be asked to simulate a meeting with a potential customer. A well-designed work sample would provide information about a hypothetical organization and product. Following a brief preparation period, the applicant would be given an opportunity to meet with the prospective "buyer," usually role-played by the interviewer. After the role-play, the interviewer would rate the applicant on job-related abilities, such as communication skills and persuasiveness. Work samples have been developed for every imaginable job, including bakers, auto mechanics, managers, army recruiters, customer service personnel, supervisors, police officers, and computer programmers, to mention just a few.[45]

Work samples
A brief simulation of major job activities.

An assessment center is an extended work sample. A typical assessment center consists of several different exercises, measuring various job-related abilities (see Table 5.10 for a list of common job-related abilities that are evaluated in assessment centers). Applicant behavior is observed by several assessors, usually employees from the organization. In many organizations, assessors meet together after the exercises are completed to make consensus-based ratings on the dimensions and to make an overall assessment rating.[46]

Assessment center
An extended work sample.

In terms of the validity of work samples and assessment centers, findings have generally been quite positive. A recent review of assessment centers reported that the average criterion-related validity was .37.[47] The assessment center technique has a number of additional advantages. First, the assessment center may also be content valid. Second, the assessment center has an excellent legal history. In at least one case, the court even recommended the use of assessment centers. Overall, the evidence suggests that assessment centers do not produce adverse impact on the basis of sex or race.[48] Third, when the assessment center closely simulates the actual jobs of the organization, it may provide a realistic job preview (see Chapter 4). Finally, because the assessment center relies on ratings made by

Table 5.10 **Common Dimensions Evaluated in Assessment Centers**

1. Oral communication
2. Written communication
3. Sales ability
4. Analysis and judgment
5. Planning
6. Delegating
7. Initiative
8. Conflict management
9. Organizational sensitivity
10. Tolerance for stress

multiple assessors from different parts of the organization rather than one supervisor, it is often viewed as a more objective procedure than interviews and performance ratings. The assessment center may therefore be an excellent device for promotion decisions, as well as for career development purposes.

Despite many virtues, the assessment center method has two potentially significant drawbacks. First, it is expensive to design and administer. In fact, it can cost thousands of dollars to assess each applicant. Second, although it is valid, other selection methods reviewed earlier, such as cognitive ability tests, interviews, and BIBs, appear to be equally valid. Viewed in this light, it may be difficult to justify the expense of the assessment center.[49]

In sum, work samples, and particularly assessment centers, offer several major advantages to organizations as a selection device. The major drawback is that the assessment center is likely to be more expensive and more time-consuming than other selection devices that are equally valid. We now move to two selection methods that are usually reserved only for candidates to whom the organization plans to make a job offer: background/reference checks and drug screening.

Background and Reference Checking

In today's highly litigious workplace, employers are increasingly interested in uncovering information about such factors as an applicant's credit record, prior employment history, and past criminal convictions. A credit record may be viewed as important for two reasons. First, employers often believe that a poor credit history is an indication of irresponsibility, which may also affect work. Second, poor credit history may indicate that the individual is financially strapped, which could encourage stealing from the organization. Recall in the opening case that Tom Brown expressed concern as to what information would be obtained from the credit check. Indeed, credit checks are notorious for errors; when the author was buying a house, the credit check incorrectly indicated an unpaid bill from a major retailer that supposedly was more than four years past due! However, some protection is available for the job applicant and employee. The Fair Credit Reporting Act requires an employer to notify an applicant in writing within three days of requesting a credit check. This law also requires that an applicant be informed if the credit report played a part in the decision to reject, and the applicant must be provided with the name and address of the agency that ran the check.[50] Returning to the opening case, then, the Fair Credit Reporting Act does provide a vehicle for correcting misinformation.

Fair Credit Reporting Act
Requires an employer to notify the applicant, in writing, within three days of requesting a credit check.

Another popular selection method is the reference check. This procedure involves contacting previous employers to verify employment information and obtain independent assessments of an applicant's qualifications. In recent years, reference checking has become much less useful to companies. This is the result of defamation lawsuits, which may be filed if a past supervisor makes statements about a former employee that cannot be proved to be true and that damage the reputation of the former employee. If such information is provided in writing (such as on a written reference form), it is called libel. If such information is given in oral form (for example, over the telephone), it is referred to as slander.

Defamation
Slander or libel which can result in a lawsuit.

In order to win a defamation case, the past employee would have to show the following:

1. The statement was made to another party.
2. The statement is false. Generally, the defendant has the burden of proving the statement was true.
3. The employee's reputation was harmed.[51]

In order to avoid lawsuits, companies are advised to be very cautious about providing information to other parties. Many companies have written policies that prohibit managers from discussing past employees with other individuals. Companies may also require that reference requests be handled by the HRM department, which in many cases will only verify employment dates and perhaps final salary. In cases where past supervisors do provide information about former employees, they tend to say very little that is negative. If you are a supervisor, be extremely careful concerning the information you release to other parties about past employees.[52]

In terms of criterion-related validity, the reference check has not fared well. Typical estimates of the criterion-related validity range between .13 and .26.[53] The relatively low validity is probably due to the reluctance on the part of supervisors to provide negative information. With regard to adverse impact, there have been few court cases in which the reference check was examined.[54] In one lawsuit, though, there was no evidence of adverse impact.[55] Moreover, most people would probably say that reference checking seems like a reasonable selection procedure. From a legal standpoint, then, reference checking does not appear problematic and, as mentioned earlier, may be encouraged.

Box 5.4 Former Boss Giving You a Bad Reference? What You Can Do to Fight Back

Do you ever worry that a former boss is giving you a negative reference? Documented Reference Check (DRC), a company located in California, now offers you a way to fight back. As explained in its brochure, DRC uses the same procedure as any HRM manager would in contacting past employers. The company calls or writes former employers and obtains information regarding your employment dates, salary, and job title, as well as any other information that your past employer releases. DRC then provides you with a written report. If negative or erroneous information is obtained, DRC will offer additional services to you so that you can prevent the information from being given to others.

Other former employees are fighting the effects of bad references in a different way, by invoking a legal concept known as "compelled self-publication." A lawsuit of this nature would arise if the employee was asked by the prospective employer why he or she was terminated. In certain industries, applicants are even required to explain in writing why they left a particular job. Applicants may then claim they were forced to provide the reason, which they felt was untrue, thus creating a kind of self-slander. In a 1986 lawsuit in Minnesota, for example, several claims processors were awarded nearly half a million dollars in such a case.

Source: Adapted from J. Woo, "Quirky Slander Actions Threaten Employers," *The Wall Street Journal,* November 26, 1993, B1, B5.

Drug Tests

Drug screening is commonly used in business, industry, and government today. About 50 percent of Fortune 500 companies use drug screening as part of their preemployment procedures. Drug screening has become widespread for several reasons, including industry laws, the belief that such programs help combat drug abuse in the United States, and concern with company safety and productivity. Drug testing has also received some negative publicity, particularly from such groups as the American Civil Liberties Union (ACLU), who feel that this procedure is an unfair invasion of people's privacy.[56] The remainder of this section will address various drug screening procedures, as well as their validity and legality.

Drug Screening Procedures

Urinalysis
A urine sample that is tested for drugs.

Have you ever applied for a job where a drug screen was administered? Chances are that if you were drug-tested, you were administered a urinalysis—that is, you were asked for a urine sample. You may have had several questions with regard to this test:

False positive
Occurs when you are mistakenly identified as a drug user even though you do not use drugs.

1. How long will the presence of drug traces (or, as they are usually called, metabolites) stay in your urine?
2. What is the likelihood of a false positive? A false positive occurs when you are mistakenly identified as a drug user even though you do not use drugs.
3. About what percentage of job applicants are identified as drug users?

What did you guess about Question 1? You may be surprised to learn that most drug metabolites, including cocaine and heroin, leave your urine within one to four days. Only marijuana can remain as long as several weeks, particularly for a heavy drug user.[57] Question 2 has led to controversy as a result of some widely publicized stories in which people eating a poppy-seed bagel or taking over-the-counter cold medicines were mistakenly identified as drug users when they took a drug test. Also, several early studies on the accuracy of drug tests found a great many false positives; in one test, as many as 66 percent of the drug samples were false positives! How could the false positive rate be so high? There are at least two answers. One, some laboratories are not very careful and may make mistakes. Two, certain drug tests are not highly accurate. To get around this problem, many companies use a two-step drug screening procedure. In the first step, an initial screen is used; that is, a relatively inexpensive, but occasionally fallible test is employed (for example, the Enzyme Multiplied Immunoassay Test (EMIT) test). If the urine sample indicates drug use, a second, *confirmatory* procedure is applied, such as the GC/MS (or, the gas chromatography/mass spectrometry) test, which when used properly is extremely accurate.[58]

Finally, if you guessed about 5 percent in answering the third question, you are right. Although the number of drug positives varies from location to location, nationwide about 5 percent of job applicants are identified as drug users.[59]

Validity of Drug Testing

Because drug testing seems to make so much sense to many employers who accept its validity as a matter of faith, there have actually been few good criterion-related validity studies of drug tests. The few good validation studies that have been conducted indicate that drug testing seems to have fairly low validity (perhaps a correlation of .10).[60] You may be rather surprised by this low validity. One reason it is probably so low is that relatively few people in the working population are found to be drug users. As you read earlier, only about 5 percent of applicants and employees tested are drug positive. In this type of situation, a test will have limited validity. Companies considering implementing a preemployment drug testing program should therefore consider carefully whether the benefits of such a program will outweigh the costs.

Legal Considerations in Drug Testing

Given the popularity of drug testing, it is not surprising that it has faced many legal challenges. In terms of discrimination laws, practically all permit drug testing. Most of the legal challenges to drug testing, then, have come from other laws and regulations. The most well-known lawsuits involving drug testing focused on constitutional rights to privacy and due process. Basically, these laws do place restrictions on the use of drug screening by organizations, especially for government employees. Because of their complexity, however, these laws will be discussed in greater detail in Chapter 16. You should be aware, however, that there are myriad industry, state, and government laws that regulate drug testing. Some states, for example, require that companies doing drug testing use a con-

Box 5.5 Alternatives to Urinalysis Testing

Given the many problems associated with urinalysis screening for the presence of drugs (for example, traces of the drug disappear quickly), some companies have developed alternative devices. One such alternative is the hair test, in which a lock of the applicant's hair is clipped and submitted for analysis. The advantages cited for the hair test include that it is less invasive of privacy than taking a urine sample, drug traces stay in the hair longer than in the urine, and the applicant has less opportunity to switch samples. One company now using the hair test is Blockbuster Video, the video rental chain. Experts, however, remain skeptical as to the accuracy of the hair test. Another device that has been marketed is a brain scan test, which allegedly can detect drug use from brain wave activity. Again, very little research regarding the accuracy of this device has been conducted.

Groups such as the ACLU have endorsed a technique generally referred to as an *impairment test*. An impairment test is not unlike the police officer asking a suspected drunk driver to walk a straight line. One such impairment test is similar to a video game. The "player" must line up a cursor with a moving target that appears on a video screen. Proponents of this approach argue that urinalysis, and similar devices such as the hair test, are too narrowly focused on the one hand and too broadly focused on the other hand. They maintain that urinalysis is too narrowly focused in that an individual may be unfit to work on a particular day for a variety of reasons, such as a hangover from alcohol abuse, lack of sleep, or stress, none of which would be detected by a urinalysis. On the other hand, maintain proponents of the impairment test approach, a person may use illegal substances only on the weekend and experience absolutely no negative effects during the workday. Therefore, it is argued, the impairment test is best at assessing whether the employee is capable of working on that particular day. Which device do you think would be best?

Source: Adapted from M. Harris and L. Heft, "Alcohol and Drug Use in the Workplace: Issues, Controversies, and Directions for Future Research," *Journal of Management* 18 (1992), 239–66.

"For cause"
Means if there is good reason to believe you may have been under the influence of drugs during work, your company may require you to take a drug test.

firmatory test, inform applicants ahead of time that they will be tested, and employ a properly certified laboratory. Finally, it should be noted that drug testing is not limited to job applicants. Many firms have a policy of "for cause" testing. "For cause" means if there is good reason to believe you may have been under the influence of drugs during work (maybe you were in an accident or were behaving erratically), your company may require you to take a drug test. Also, some organizations either currently do or have considered doing random drug testing of employees.[61]

Miscellaneous Selection Devices

In addition to the methods described above, there are several others, including medical examinations and physical strength and agility tests. Two particularly interesting evaluations—psychological assessments and graphology—are described briefly here.

Psychological Assessment

Psychological assessment
Conducted by a psychologist, this assessment lasts between 4 to 8 hours, and involves an hour-and-a-half interview as well as personality and cognitive ability tests.

Many companies, particularly in manufacturing and banking, use a psychological assessment to evaluate candidates for middle- and upper-level management positions. Generally, this assessment is conducted by a psychologist, and the average fee per candidate is more than $500. A typical session lasts from four to eight hours and involves an hour-and-a-half interview, as well as personality and cognitive ability tests. Information gathered is generally used to produce a written summary of the candidate's strengths and weaknesses, with a specific recommendation regarding the hiring or promotion decision. If you are ever assessed in this fashion, you should know that the majority of psychologists in this business will provide individual feedback to you, and in some cases, they may even share a copy of the report they gave the organization. Very little research has been done regarding the validity and adverse impact of psychological assessments.[62]

Graphology

Graphology
Handwriting analysis.

Graphology, or handwriting analysis, was first developed in 1622, but the most well-known work on this technique was published in France in 1875. It may surprise you to learn that while only a few companies in the United States use graphology as a selection device, it is quite popular in Europe. One estimate indicates that as many as 80 percent of companies in Western Europe use it as a selection tool. Although there are different approaches to analyzing handwriting, most focus on the size of letters, the slant, width, pressure, and spacing of letters, and connections between letters.[63] Despite its popularity in some circles, graphology has not fared well in carefully designed research studies. One well-designed study found that although the two handwriting analysts were in reasonably high agreement on their ratings of personality traits of employees, correlations of their ratings with employees' job performance ratings were practically zero.[64] Most HRM experts in the United States, at least, do not favor graphology as a selection device.

Conclusion

You have read about the factors that companies consider in deciding which employee selection methods to use. To be beneficial, the selection method should be practical to use, job related, legally acceptable, and provide sufficient utility. As you have seen, many different selection procedures are available to organizations. Although interviews, reference and background checks, and application blanks are the most common methods, each of these methods has its limitation. Some suggestions were also provided here for improving the value of the interview. Many companies supplement their hiring decisions with various additional methods, including paper-and-pencil tests, work samples, and psychological assessments. Only with careful selection procedures will organizations be assured of hiring and promoting the most qualified candidates.

Applying Core Concepts

1. Describe how you would go about conducting a job analysis for either your own job or a job with which you are very familiar.
2. What selection process was used to hire you or a friend of yours for a recent job? What selection procedures described in this chapter might have been used to improve the process?
3. Develop a structured interview to hire people for a job with which you are very familiar.
4. If you were hiring a college instructor, would you want to use any paper-and-pencil tests? Why or why not?
5. Do you think that a drug screen should be used to hire people for a job? Can you think of some jobs where a drug test might be irrelevant?

Key Terms

- Job analysis
- Job description
- Job specification
- PAQ
- Task/KSAO Inventory
- Job relatedness
- Criterion-related validity study
- Content validity
- Correlation coefficient
- Utility
- Employee Polygraph Protection Act of 1988
- Negligent hiring
- Weighted application blank (WAB)
- Biographical information blank (BIB)
- Traditional interview
- Structured interview
- Stress interview
- Panel interview
- Personality test
- Honesty test
- Cognitive ability test
- Meta-analysis
- Race norming
- Work samples
- Assessment center
- Fair Credit Reporting Act
- Defamation
- Urinalysis
- False positive
- "For cause"
- Psychological assessment
- Graphology

Chapter 5: Experiential Exercise

Technosoftware Company: Part 2

Two Months Later . . . . Based on his recruiting effort, Walter received a total of 150 resumes. He managed to narrow down the list of potential applicants to three. Walter, Darrell, and Ben reviewed their resumes, conducted brief telephone interviews, panel interviews, and gave several paper-and-pencil tests to the three candidates. In order not to affect your judgments, Walter, Darrell, and Ben have tried to be as objective as possible in writing up this information. The results of these selection devices are summarized next.

Background Information Based on an examination of resumes, an initial phone conversation, and preliminary questions in the interviews, educational, work, and experience information were obtained from each candidate. This information is summarized below.

Candidate 1: Jack Smith Has B.S. in engineering and M.B.A. from Harvard (1967); worked for last 20 years in a large, computer products firm. Began as product manager, ended as VP marketing. Terminated due to reduction in workforce. Prior to this worked as salesperson for several manufacturers. Has had broad range of experience in all phases of marketing. Computer experience limited to experience with a few, commonly used spreadsheets. Appears to be about 50 years old.

Candidate 2: Ann Real Has B.S. in mathematics; M.S. in information systems (1990) from Purdue University. Also took some business courses in marketing. From 1990 to present, has worked in developing computer software for very large computer firm. During last year, worked with a team responsible for designing and marketing of a new product. Also, did summer internship a few years ago with company very similar to Technosoftware. Experience and familiarity with computer software is very extensive. Appears to be about 30 years old.

Candidate 3: Tom VanFleet Has B.S. in computers; M.B.A. with concentration in marketing (1984) from University of Illinois at Chicago. From 1984 to present, has worked at 4 different firms. In each case, was a marketing position. Each job involved slightly broader responsibilities. Second job was for a computer products firm, which involved marketing of computer hardware; other jobs have been with office supply companies. Appears to be about 35 years old.

Interview Results Each of the three candidates was then interviewed in a panel session with Walter, Darrell, and Ben. Each candidate was asked the same set of questions, with follow-up probes. A summary of each candidate's responses is provided below.
The key questions were:

1. What strengths can you bring to this company?
2. Describe your managerial style.
3. Describe your ideal job.
4. What are your career plans?
5. Describe a time when you had a major disagreement with a coworker . . . What was the situation: How did you resolve the conflict?
6. Why are you interested in this job?
7. What salary would you expect to make?
8. What is your current (or most recent) salary?

Candidate 1

1. A great deal of experience in the marketing of computer products (but primarily hardware); many contacts in the marketing world, which will help in the introduction and promotion of a new product; exposure to other functions, including production and accounting.
2. Believes in open communication, delegation, ongoing feedback, and frequent goal-setting sessions.
3. Ideal job would be one with a great deal of responsibility, challenging assignments, and a great deal of influence over marketing decisions.
4. (Candidate chuckled when asked this question.) "To stay employed."
5. Several years ago, candidate had a major disagreement with VP of sales regarding some promotional plan. After days of heated debate, they agreed to present their arguments in a 1-hour session to the Executive VP of sales and marketing. He agreed, listened carefully to their arguments, and candidate lost.
6. Job offers many of the points raised in response to question #3.
7. Salary less important than potential share in company. Willing to even forego base pay for first year or two as long as can get ownership in company.
8. $100,000 plus "substantial" bonus ($15,000 but not sure).

Candidate 2

1. Great knowledge of computer software products; well-versed in user needs.
2. Although she never has managed anyone . . . very open style, judge on the basis of results, very democratic, encourage participation in all areas.
3. Ideal job would have lots of responsibility, challenging assignments, involve computer software in some way, lots of opportunity to learn.
4. Career plan is to be involved in all aspects of computer software, including marketing, design, R&D, etc.
5. Got into major disagreement with a coworker regarding some software development project. Had ongoing debate for weeks about it; finally, came to work over an entire weekend to resolve disagreement. In the end, found they were both wrong.
6. Allows candidate to devote full time to marketing. Also, want opportunity to work for small firm, where one can have much impact.

7. At least $65,000.
8. $59,000.

Candidate 3

1. Have worked several phases of product management and introduction as they relate to software, including pricing, product announcement, market research, and positioning strategy. "Outstanding performance in every job."
2. Establish close supervision, careful monitoring of subordinate performance, give on-going feedback.
3. Ability to achieve ongoing advancement in the marketing area through increasing responsibility, continuous development of new products, and innovation.
4. Advance into a senior marketing position in a small computer software firm.
5. "Have never had such a situation . . . Always able to deal with such situations before they became major conflicts."
6. Position offers a "fast track" opportunity to learn about a whole lot of marketing tasks that a larger company cannot offer.
7. Mid to upper $50s.
8. $50,000 plus bonus.

Test Scores Each of the three candidates was then sent to a management psychologist, who had each candidate take three tests. One test, the Thurstone cognitive ability test, provides a verbal ability (V) and mathematical ability score (M). The second text, the Guilford-Zimmerman Temperament Survey (GZTS) is a standard personality measure—the psychologist only relies on four scales, so only four scales are reported here, namely, energy (E), emotional stability (ES), thoughtfulness (T), and personal relations (PR). Finally, the psychologist had each candidate complete the Computer Programmer Aptitude Battery, which measures one's ability to write computer programs (CP). Provided below are the scores for each candidate, in terms of their percentile (a percentile score indicates the percentage of test-takers that the individual did as well as, or better than. For example, a percentile score of 50 indicates that the individual did as well as or better than about half the people who have taken the test).

Candidate	V	M	E	ES	T	PR	CP
1	80	15	50	99	40	95	5
2	90	99	99	50	99	70	99
3	80	50	80	40	25	90	40

Questions

1. Rank order your choices from best candidate for the job to worst candidate for the job.
2. Be prepared to defend your rank order; you may choose to ignore any information you want, but be prepared to explain why you did not use that information.
3. What additional information would you have obtained from the candidates (e.g., additional interview questions, tests)?

Chapter 5 References

1. E. Levine, F. Sistrunk, K. McNutt, and S. Gael, "Exemplary Job Analysis Systems in Selected Organizations," in *Applying Psychology in Business,* ed. J. Jones, B. Steffy, and D. Bray (Lexington, MA: Lexington Books, 1991).
2. W. Cascio, *Applied Psychology in Personnel Management* (Englewood Cliffs, NJ: Prentice Hall, 1991).
3. R. J. Harvey, "Job Analysis," in *Handbook of Industrial and Organizational Psychology,* vol. 2, ed. M. Dunnette and L. Hough (Palo Alto, CA: Consulting Psychologists Press, 1991).
4. Cascio, *Applied Psychology.*
5. R. Gatewood and H. Feild, "Job Analysis Methods: A Description and Comparison of the Alternatives," in *Applying Psychology in Business,* ed. J. Jones, B. Steffy, and D. Bray (Lexington, MA: Lexington Books, 1991).

6. R. Gatewood and H. Feild, *Human Resource Selection* (Fort Worth, TX: Dryden, 1994).
7. B. Schneider and N. Schmitt, *Staffing Organizations* (Glenview, IL: Scott, Foresman, 1986).
8. Gatewood and Feild, *Human Resource Selection.*
9. R. Guion, "Personnel Assessment, Selection, and Placement," in *Handbook of Industrial and Organizational Psychology,* vol. 2, ed. M. Dunnette and L. Hough (Palo Alto, CA: Consulting Psychologists Press, 1991).
10. Uniform Guidelines on Employee Selection Procedures, 29 CFR, Part 1607.
11. M. Player, *Federal Law of Employment Discrimination* (St. Paul, MN: West, 1992).
12. J. Boudreau, "Utility Analysis for Decisions in Human Resource Management," in *Handbook of Industrial and Organizational Psychology,* vol. 2, ed. M. Dunnette and L. Hough (Palo Alto, CA: Consulting Psychologists Press, 1991); F. Schmidt, J. Hunter, R. McKenzie, and T. Muldrow, "Impact of Valid Selection Procedures on Work-Force Productivity," *Journal of Applied Psychology* 64 (1979), 609–26.
13. L. Joel, *Every Employee's Guide to the Law* (New York: Pantheon, 1993).
14. U.S. Equal Employment Opportunity Commission, "A Technical Assistance Manual on the Employment Provisions (Title I) of the Americans with Disabilities Act," 1992.
15. J. Bible, "When Employers Look for Things Other Than Drugs: The Legality of AIDS, Genetic, Intelligence, and Honesty Testing in the Workplace," *Labor Law Journal,* 41 (1990), 195–221.
16. A. Ryan and M. Lasek, "Negligent Hiring and Defamation: Areas of Liability Related to Pre-Employment Inquiries," *Personnel Psychology* 44 (1991), 293–319.
17. Joel, *Every Employee's Guide to the Law.*
18. Schneider and Schmitt, *Staffing Organizations.*
19. Gatewood and Feild, *Human Resource Selection.*
20. F. Mael, "A Conceptual Rationale for the Domain and Attributes of Biodata Items," *Personnel Psychology* 44 (1991), 763–92; G. England, *Development and Use of Weighted Application Blanks,* rev. ed. (Minneapolis, MN: University of Minnesota, 1991).
21. E. Hammer, and L. Kleiman, "Getting to Know You," *Personnel Administrator* 34 (1988), 86–92.
22. C. Russell, J. Mettson, S. Devlin, and D. Atwater, "Predictive Validity of Biodata Items Generated from Retrospective Life Experience Essays," *Journal of Applied Psychology* 75 (1990), 569–80.
23. J. Hunter and R. Hunter, "Validity and Utility of Alternate Predictors of Job Performance," *Psychological Bulletin* 96 (1984), 72–98.
24. H. Rothstein et al., "Biographical Data in Employment Selection: Can Validities Be Generalizable?" *Journal of Applied Psychology* 75 (1990), 175–84.
25. Gatewood and Feild, *Human Resource Selection.*
26. J. Smither et al., "Applicant Reactions to Selection Procedures," *Personnel Psychology* 46 (1993), 49–76.
27. R. Fear, *The Evaluation Interview* (New York: McGraw-Hill, 1984); B. Smart, *Selection Interviewing* (New York: J. Wiley, 1983).
28. R. Eder and G. Ferris, *The Employment Interview: Theory, Research, and Practice* (Newbury Park, CA, Sage, 1989); M. Harris, "Reconsidering the Employment Interview: A Review of Recent Literature and Suggestions for Future Research," *Personnel Psychology* 42 (1989), 691–726.
29. T. Janz, L. Hellervik, and D. Gilmore, *Behavior Description Interviewing* (Boston: Allyn & Bacon, 1986); G. Latham, L. Saari, E. Pursell, and M. Campion, "The Situational Interview," *Journal of Applied Psychology* 65 (1980), 422–27; M. Campion, E. Pursell, and B. Brown, "Structured Interviewing: Raising the Psychometric Properties of the Employment Interview," *Personnel Psychology* 41 (1988), 25–42.

30. W. Wiesner and S. Cronshaw, "A Meta-Analytic Investigation of the Impact of Interview Format and Degree of Structure on the Validity of the Employment Interview," *Journal of Occupational Psychology* 61 (1988), 275–90.
31. H. Medley, *Sweaty Palms: The Neglected Art of Being Interviewed.* (Berkeley, CA: Ten Speed Press, 1984).
32. Ibid.
33. Harris, "Reconsidering the Employment Interview."
34. J. Campion and R. Arvey, "Unfair Discrimination in the Employment Interview," in *The Employment Interview: Theory, Research, and Practice,* ed. R. Eder and G. Ferris (Newbury, CA: Sage, 1989).
35. R. Tett, D. Jackson, and M. Rothstein, "Personality Measures as Predictors of Job Performance: A Meta-Analytic Review," *Personnel Psychology* 44 (1991), 703–42.
36. D. Ones, C. Viswesvaran, and F. Schmidt, "Comprehensive Meta-Analysis of Integrity Test Validities: Findings and Implications for Personnel Selection and Theories of Job Performance," *Journal of Applied Psychology* 78 (1993), 679–703; P. Sackett, L. Burris, and C. Callahan, "Integrity Testing for Personnel Selection: An Update," *Personnel Psychology* 42 (1989), 491–529.
37. Joel, *Every Employee's Guide to the Law.*
38. Ryan and Lasek, "Negligent Hiring and Defamation."
39. Gatewood and Feild, *Human Resource Selection.*
40. M. Tenopyr, "The Realities of Employment Testing," *American Psychologist* 36 (1981), 1120–27.
41. F. Schmidt, "The Problem of Group Differences in Ability Test Scores in Employment Selection," *Journal of Vocational Behavior* 33 (1988) 272–92.
42. F. Schmidt, and J. Hunter, "Development of a General Solution to the Problem of Validity Generalization," *Journal of Applied Psychology* 62 (1977), 529–40; J. Hunter, F. Schmidt, and G. Jackson, *Meta-Analysis: Cumulating Research Findings Across Studies (*Newbury Park, CA: Sage, 1982).
43. Hunter and Hunter, "Validity and Utility."
44. Schmidt, "The Problem of Group Differences in Ability Test Scores."
45. J. Asher and J. Sciarrino, "Realistic Work Sample Tests: A Review," *Personnel Psychology* 27 (1974), 519–33.
46. G. Thornton, *Assessment Centers in Human Resource Management (*Reading, MA: Addison-Wesley, 1992).
47. B. Gaugler, D. Rosenthal, G. Thornton, and C. Bentson, "Meta-Analysis of Assessment Center Validity," *Journal of Applied Psychology* 72 (1987), 493–511.
48. R. Arvey and R. Faley, *Fairness in Selecting Employees (*Reading, MA: Addison Wesley, 1988).
49. Gatewood and Feild, *Human Resource Selection.*
50. Joel, *Every Employee's Guide to the Law.*
51. Ryan and Lasek, *Negligent Hiring and Defamation.*
52. Joel, *Every Employee's Guide to the Law.*
53. P. Muchinsky, "The Use of Reference Reports in Personnel Selection: A Review and Evaluation," *Journal of Occupational Psychology* 52 (1979), 287–97; Hunter and Hunter, "Validity and Utility."
54. Arvey and Faley, *Fairness in Selecting Employees.*
55. *EEOC v. National Academy of Sciences,* 12 FEP 1690 (1976).
56. M. Harris and L. Heft, "Alcohol and Drug Use in the Workplace: Issues, Controversies, and Directions for Future Research," *Journal of Management* 18 (1992), 239–66.
57. B. Potter, and J. Orfali, *Drug Testing at Work* (Berkeley, CA: Ronin Publishing, 1990).
58. D. Crown, and J. Rosse, "A Critical Review of the Assumptions Underlying Drug Testing," *Journal of Business and Psychology* 3 (1988), 22–41.

59. Bureau of Labor Statistics, *Survey of Employer Anti-Drug Programs,* U.S. Department of Labor, Report 760 (Washington: Government Printing Office, 1989).
60. M. Harris and L. Heft, "Preemployment Urinalysis Drug Testing: A Critical Review of Psychometric and Legal Issues and Effects on Applicants," *Human Resource Management Review,* in press.
61. Ibid.
62. A.M. Ryan and P. Sackett, "A Survey of Individual Assessment Practices by I/O Psychologists," *Personnel Psychology* 40 (1987), 455–88.
63. Gatewood and Feild, *Human Resource Selection.*
64. A. Rafaeli and R. Klimoski, "Predicting Sales Success Through Handwriting Analysis: An Evaluation of the Effects of Training and Handwriting Sample Content," *Journal of Applied Psychology* 68 (1983), 212–17.

Career Management

chapter 6

Core Concepts

After reading this chapter, you should be capable of

1. Understanding why career patterns have changed in the last 20 years.
2. Defining the three basic career stages.
3. Explaining various strategies both organizations and individuals can use to maximize effectiveness at different career stages.
4. Discussing the four types of career advancement systems that organizations use.
5. Solving some common career issues.

Opening Case

Yesterday, at her first day at Drafco, Julie Cheng attended an orientation program for new employees. As she thought back over things, it wasn't much different from what she had expected. First, Julie and about 25 other new management trainees had breakfast together. All wore badges with their names on them, and went around introducing themselves. After 30 minutes, the human resources manager introduced the CEO of Drafco, who welcomed them and wished the group much luck and success. Next, the human resources manager showed a film about the company, which described the company's history, including when it was founded (1957), its original business (selling chocolate novelties), and who the original owners were (Mary and Beth Townsend). Mr. Gooden, the vice president who oversees the management trainee program, spoke next. He described the type of job the management trainees would have, the assignments they would experience, and typical career paths in the company. Most of what he had to say Julie had already heard when she interviewed for the job. When he was done, several of the new employees asked questions regarding the company's performance expectations, the new computer system, and current business conditions.

The presentation that followed this was the most intriguing. Employees who had been through the management trainee program last year, 10 years ago, 20 years ago, and even one who had gone through the program 30 years ago took turns talking about their careers in the company. While it was interesting to hear what the different employees had to say, Julie began to wonder about several things. First, what did one really have to do to succeed in this company? While the employee who had been a management trainee 30 years ago was now second in charge (only the CEO had a higher position), none of the speakers explained what one needed to do to get ahead. Second, Julie wondered if there were some common career problems people encountered at Drafco and how they were handled. All of the speakers had been very upbeat about the company and talked enthusiastically about their personal successes, but had said virtually nothing about difficulties or frustrations that they had experienced. These and other questions continued to circulate in her mind as the final part of the program began. Perhaps, she thought, this will be the part where she would learn some answers to these questions. Much to her disappointment, however, the remainder of the program dealt with such things as choosing the most suitable benefit program, and learning more about different departments in the company. The program concluded with a walking tour of the entire facility.

This chapter concerns career management issues. Career management is important both for organizations and employees. From an organizational standpoint, an understanding of these issues is helpful in managing employees and providing appropriate programs to support productive careers. From an employee perspective, an understanding of career stages and common career issues will help you perform more effectively. The remainder of this chapter, then, is divided into four sections. First, you will read about why careers have changed a great deal over the last 20 years. Next, you will learn about typical career stages in the 1990s. Third, you will read about career advancement systems that companies use. The chapter concludes with information on several common career issues, such as job burnout, and provides strategies for dealing with them.

Why Have Career Patterns Changed?

Prior to the 1980s, careers in the United States were characterized by much stability and continuity. Managerial and professional employees, in particular, often worked their entire careers in the same organization. In the 1980s, however, careers became much less stable and subject to far more disruption. What follows next is a discussion of some factors that have led to these changes.

Organizational Layoffs

It is almost commonplace now to hear about mass layoffs by organizations. Regardless of whether the term used is "downsizing," "reduction in force" or "rightsizing," nearly every large organization in the United States has terminated workers for reasons other than their poor performance during the last five years. Nor do layoffs only happen when organizations report a decline in profits. In 1994, for example, over 500,000 jobs were lost in the United States, despite corporate profits rising on average 11 percent. In fact, the number of layoffs was nearly as high as the number of layoffs during the last recession (1991), when more than 550,000 jobs were lost. Major companies that have had recent layoffs include Xerox (almost 10 percent of its people were laid off in 1994), Procter & Gamble (over 10 percent of its people were terminated in two years), and AT&T (almost 10,000 jobs were lost in 1994). It is particularly common for organizations to eliminate middle management and staff jobs, while maintaining production and customer

Box 6.1 **Career Anchors: What Makes You Tick?**

Experts have suggested that people have a career anchor or orientation that characterizes them. Eight primary anchors have been identified and are defined next.

1. *Technical/Functional Competence.* If this is your anchor, your career interests focus on working in a specific technical or functional area, such as finance, marketing, accounting, and so forth. People with this interest tend to avoid supervising others. They generally prefer to develop their skills rather than being promoted for the sake of a higher-level position.

2. *General Managerial Competence.* If this is your anchor, your career focuses on climbing to the highest level possible and being responsible for output of a specific business unit. You desire accountability for results and view your experiences in specific functions or technical area as a means to that end.

3. *Autonomy and Independence.* If this is your anchor, you strive to be independent at work and prefer a minimum amount of rules and regulations concerning your work. You like to establish your own hours and dress code and dislike supervision.

4. *Security and Stability.* If this is your anchor, you prefer to have stability in your job. You will avoid taking risks at work and seek to have as secure a future at work as possible.

5. *Entrepreneurial Creativity.* If this is your anchor, your desire is to create a business of your own. You will work for others only insofar as you feel you are gaining important experience. You seek risks and enjoy overcoming obstacles.

6. *Dedication to a Cause.* If this is your anchor, you focus on a cause that you believe is important, such as discovering a cure for a disease or helping bring about world peace. You will seek out jobs that can help you in your cause, particularly nonprofit or volunteer work.

7. *Pure Challenge.* If this is your anchor, you seek to meet and overcome difficult barriers or obstacles. For a medical researcher, this may be finding a cure for the common cold; for a business consultant, this may be taking over companies going through bankruptcy. You seek novelty and variety in your work.

8. *Lifestyle.* If this is your career anchor, you seek to integrate personal, career, and family goals. You define success in terms greater than just your career. You will choose a job that enables you to fit all parts of your life together.

Which career anchor fits you best? Of course, it is possible that a combination of two or three anchors describes you.

Source: E.H. Schein, *Career Anchors: Discovering Your Real Values* (San Diego, CA: Pfeiffer, 1990).

service positions. As a result of these layoffs, many employees have had successful careers end abruptly and have been forced to start their careers over again.[1]

Changed Nature of Work

Careers in most organizations have been defined in terms of a ladder or set of steps. Take, for example, a traditional human resources career pattern. One might begin in the HRM field as an interviewer, followed by a promotion to HRM staffing supervisor. Next, one might be promoted to manager of college placement, followed by a promotion to manager of human resources, and then to vice president, of human resources. But in the 1990s, work is less frequently designed along specific job responsibilities and more and more commonly designed around projects. In the human resources area, for example, projects might include redesigning the pay-for-performance plan, developing an integrated training program, and conducting an annual employee satisfaction survey. The workers assigned to these

Box 6.2 The Japanese Career Model: An Alternative Approach

In strong contrast to the U.S. career model, which minimizes job security and heavily weights performance rather than seniority in promotions, the Japanese career model emphasizes lifetime employment and promotions based on seniority. The Japanese career model may seem to be ineffective for organizations (though highly desirable for employees), but some experts are now saying that the Japanese system is much more beneficial than previously thought. First, however, a brief history of the Japanese career system is in order.

Contrary to what you might think, Japanese workers were quite unreliable prior to World War II. The 1920s, for example, were characterized by many work stoppages, and turnover was often a significant problem. All of this changed after World War II, as business and political leaders realized that a stable workforce was a prerequisite for Japan to compete globally. To increase stability, many laws were passed that reduced companies' power over employees in such areas as firing. Hence, one reason for the lifetime employment practice is that Japanese companies have many legal restrictions regarding terminations.

Aside from legal restrictions, there are many other reasons why the Japanese career system thrives in that country. Consider, for a moment, that Japan has made extensive use of automation and robotics in the workplace. One reason for the widespread embrace of such technology is that employees know they will not lose their jobs. In fact, just the reverse is true—workers understand that new technology will lead to competitive advantage, thereby benefiting them in the long run. Furthermore, while many U.S. companies refrain from expensive training and development programs on the grounds that workers often leave, Japanese companies know their employees will stay. Not surprisingly, then, Japanese companies provide far more training than do U.S. companies.

What about seniority-based promotions? In the United States, there is a great deal of emphasis on performance—rather than seniority—in making promotions. But a seniority-based system has some advantages. First, there is less intergenerational conflict than in the United States. Second, because they feel less threatened, supervisors will be more likely to mentor an employee than in the United States.

Finally, despite lifetime employment, Japanese companies do have a mechanism for discharge, namely, early retirement. Even workers in their late 40s may be given early retirement. Because the company usually offers generous severance pay and help locating another job, most people take early retirement if offered.

In sum, the Japanese career model offers several advantages over the U.S. model. Clearly, there is no one best approach.

Source: Adapted from E. Fingleton, "Jobs for Life," *Fortune,* March 20, 1995, 119–25.

projects would depend far less on position in the hierarchy, and much more on their abilities and experience as well as developmental needs. In turn, position in the hierarchy has become less important than in the past, thereby changing the way in which careers progress.[2]

Changing Nature of Organizations

A third factor that has changed careers is the way in which organizations are being designed today. Organizations in the 1990s typically have far fewer managers and supervisors than organizations did 20 years ago. The organization of today, therefore, is usually far flatter than organizations in the past. As such, there is generally far less room for advancement than there was 20 years ago. Many companies therefore are downplaying promotions and are rethinking their fundamental assumptions about careers.[3]

In sum, several factors have changed careers. As a result, many successful career management practices of the past are no longer appropriate today. What you will read about next is a description of typical career stages that many employees go through in the 1990s, along with a brief discussion of how these stages differ from the past.

Career Stages

Career stages refer to points or phases in one's career. Career stages today are different in several fundamental ways from career stages of earlier times. One difference is that many people today will change occupations a number of times in the course of their lifetime. Within the 61–65 age group, where you would expect the least amount of occupational change, 22 percent of people in the United States have changed occupations.[4] This experience is not unique to the United States; most British managers experience a major job change every three years, and fewer

Organizational layoffs are a reality in the 1990s. Nearly every large organization in the United States has terminated workers for reasons other than their poor performance during the last five years, leaving facilities, such as the production plant shown here, empty and abandoned.

than 10 percent work for a single company through their entire career.[5] A second difference is that achievement today is defined much more broadly than in years past. In the 1990s, career success must also take into account degree of preparation for the next job or career, balance between personal and work life issues, and the extent to which one experiences a sense of personal fulfillment. A third difference between today's career stages and career stages of previous years is that in the former case, one is likely to experience several cycles through the career stages. In the past, one would enter through each stage only one time.[6]

As shown in Figure 6.1, we will discuss three career stages. Each stage is described in greater detail next.

Entry Stage

Entry stage
The point at which the individual begins a new job.

The entry stage is the point at which the individual begins a new job. In the past, the entry stage was primarily experienced by young workers, typically in their early 20s. Today, however, individuals may pass through the entry stage several times, as they make radical transitions into completely different jobs. Workers in the entry stage face several challenges. First, particularly for young and inexperienced employees, the entry stage is fraught with unrealistic expectations regarding the type of work they will perform, the amount of feedback they will receive, the rewards they will obtain, their capacity to apply on the job what they have learned at school, and the balance between personal goals and organizational demands. Table 6.1 lists some typical expectations that young and inexperienced employees have and how they compare to the reality that the employees often find. Hence, one important challenge in the entry stage is for the individual to adopt more realistic expectations of work.[7]

A second challenge in this stage is for employees to learn more about their career goals and interests as they discover what they enjoy and what knowledge, skills, and abilities (KSAs) they have. Finally, a major challenge employees face during this stage is to determine the important goals of the organization and to become accepted by their peers and supervisors.[8]

Next, you will read about some steps that organizations can take to help employees in the entry stage.

Entry Stage: Suggestions for Organizations

Organizations and managers can help their employees to succeed in the entry stage in a number of ways.

Figure 6.1 **Today's Career Stages**

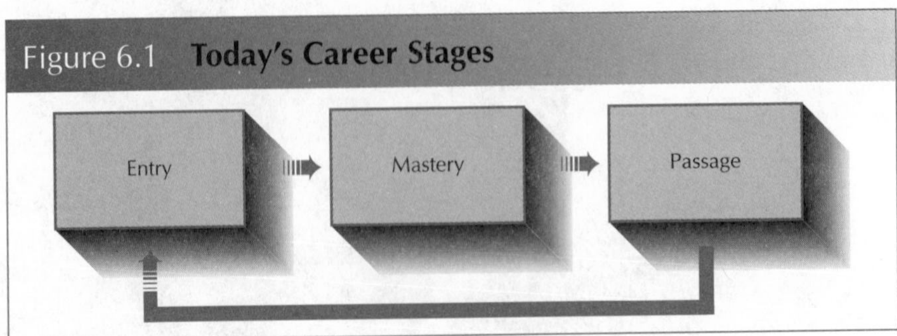

Table 6.1 **Typical Entry-Level Employee Expectations versus Reality**

Expectation	**Reality**
"I will have much freedom to work as I please."	My boss tells me what to do and how to do it."
"Most of my work projects will be fun."	"I have much boring, routine work."
"I will receive a lot of helpful feedback from my boss."	"I really don't know how well I'm doing."
"If I do well at work, I will get good raises and promotions."	"Money and promotions are limited and factors other than performance count."
"I can apply the latest techniques that I learned at school."	"People resist the new ideas I suggest."
"I will be able to balance my personal needs and work life."	"My job and personal goals often conflict."

Source: Adapted from J. Greenhaus, *Career Management,* (Fort Worth, TX: Dryden, 1987).

1. Early Interactions with the Organization Have Lasting Effects. Research shows that a new employee's earliest encounters with the organization, perhaps as early as the recruitment phase, have a lasting effect on the employee's experience of the entry stage. Organizations and managers must be sure to do as much as possible to help employees even before they formally begin work. Early opportunities for contact with the new employee's coworkers and supervisor become very important in this regard.[9]
2. Emphasize Informal Orientation Programs. While the opening case described a formal, structured orientation session for new hires, employees tend to rate such programs as being of little help.[10] Instead, orientation programs that provide significant early, informal on-the-job interaction with peers or experienced coworkers appear to be far more effective in facilitating the transition for entry stage employees.[11]
3. Provide Opportunities to Learn about Other Areas in the Organization. General Electric, which is famous for its employee development programs, sends new employees to its education unit located near New York City. As part of the extensive training program, new employees meet in small groups with top managers from different parts of the company. Not only does this enable the new employees to learn about different segments of the organization, but it also enables them to develop networks.[12]
4. Establish Formal Mentoring Relationships. Although some employees will establish mentoring relationships on their own (see the next discussion), in other cases, a mentoring relationship will only develop if the organization establishes a formal program. Mentoring programs are particularly helpful in increasing workplace diversity. Consider Dianna Green, an African-American woman in her 40s, who was employed at Xerox Corporation. A key reason she left her job at Xerox to join DQE, a small, male-dominated utility, was because of the person who recruited her, Wesley von Schack, CEO of the company. From the start of her employment at DQE, von Schack made it clear that he would play a key

role as her mentor. Among the things he has done to enhance her career have been to praise her to outsiders, help her get invited to various board of director positions, and make sure that she received key assignments at DQE.[13]

Entry Stage: Suggestions for Employees

Now that you know what organizations can do, here are some suggestions for you, as an employee, to achieve success in the entry stage.[14]

1. **Actively Seek Information.** There are two sources of information you need to draw from in learning about the people and the organization: written, formal sources and unwritten, informal sources. Take, for example, your assigned responsibilities. While you may have been shown a job description that listed your responsibilities, do not assume that it was completely accurate. Many organizations have outdated or incomplete job descriptions, and you need to determine what your actual job responsibilities are. If you want to learn about the written rules, seek out the relevant documents or sources (for instance, the employee handbook). To learn the unwritten rules, however, you will need to ask the appropriate questions. For example, if there are two different ways to order equipment, ask your boss about the advantages and disadvantages of both. You may also wish to check with a few coworkers. Be careful when you seek out information that you do not naively accept everything you are told. Sometimes you may intentionally be given the wrong information.

2. **Develop Networks.** Networks within the organization are useful for obtaining information, equipment, key assignments, as well as other resources. Again, organizations will have formal, written networks and informal, unwritten networks from which you may be able to tap. You need to identify those individuals who control important resources, and develop effective relationships with them.

3. **Learn about Your Boss, Coworkers, and Department.** You need to determine early on what the needs of each of these parties are and how you can meet their needs. Actively seek out this information. You may need to do some careful detective work, because these parties may not be fully aware as to their own needs.

4. **Develop Mentors.** Although some organizations have formal mentoring programs, most organizations do not, and you must acquire a mentor on your own. A mentor is a person who is higher up the organization and who can provide career advice and support to you. The mentor might be your immediate supervisor; but in many cases, it is to your advantage to have a mentor to whom you do not report. An effective mentor will be helpful in many ways, including recommending you for important assignments, protecting you from controversial issues, and coaching you for better performance.[15]

Mentor
A person who is higher up the organization and who can provide career advice and support to a less senior employee.

Individuals who have a mentor report higher salaries than individuals who do not have a mentor.[16] Those employees who have mentors also experience greater career success.[17] Hence, mentoring relationships are helpful in a variety of ways.

While there are many advantages to having a mentor, particularly in the entry stage, beware of some problems that may arise from a mentoring relationship. These include the following:

1. The Mentor May Experience Disappointment or Even Anger When the Relationship Ends. Typically, the protégé outgrows the relationship after two to five years. This can create a sense of disappointment or even anger on the part of the mentor. In the worst case, the mentor may turn against the protégé.[18]

2. Cross-Gender Relationships Create Difficulties. Tension sometimes arises when the mentor is a man and the protégé is a woman. One source of the tension is that mutual liking may lead to issues of intimacy and romantic involvement. Second, there may be a tendency for both the mentor and the protégé to assume stereotypical roles within the relationship. Third, other employees may look upon the relationship with greater suspicion than a relationship where the two parties are of the same gender.

3. Your Mentor Has a Poor Reputation. Your mentor may have or develop a poor reputation in the organization, as a result of performance problems or unethical behavior. As his or her protégé, you may have your reputation tarnished as well.[19]

In sum, there are many steps that both organizations and employees can take to ease the transition in the entry stage. Assuming the individual demonstrates basic competency in the entry stage, he or she moves to the next phase: the mastery stage.

Mastery Stage

In the mastery stage, employees seek to attain a high degree of success in their work. This stage represents a major departure from careers of the past. In years past, this stage consisted of two separate stages: an achievement stage and a mid-career stage. The achievement stage typically involved workers in their late 20s and 30s, and marked the period of time during which one was most likely to achieve success and advance up the organization hierarchy. Success in this stage was typically measured by and rewarded with promotions to higher positions, and employees assessed their level of achievement by how high they climbed the staircase toward the penthouse (the CEO's office). The mid-career stage, on the other hand, was characterized by a period of career reassessment, frequently marked by self-doubt and uncertainty on the part of the employee. That stage was typically experienced by employees between the ages of 40 and 55 who had stopped advancing in the hierarchy and sometimes were experiencing diminished motivation. The phenomenon was often referred to as plateauing.[20] There were three basic reasons for the reassessment often experienced by mid-career employees:[21]

Mastery stage
The next stage after entry when employees seek to attain a high degree of success in their work.

1. Fewer Career Opportunities. Unlike entry, in which there were typically more jobs, as an individual moved up the organizational hierarchy, he or she often found fewer and fewer job opportunities.

2. Much Greater Uncertainty about the Future. In the past, many companies focused resources on early career stages, but devoted far less effort to mid-career development activities.

3. Changing Perspective toward Careers. In the past, employees in the mid-career stage began to explore different definitions of career success. Furthermore, unlike the entry stage, where new employees often experienced a set of concerns

shared by many other new employees, mid-career employees often perceived their concerns to be unique.

The mastery stage of the 1990s is not associated with any specific age and is no longer closely associated with promotions. Instead, success is measured by and rewarded in a wide variety of ways including assignment to important or special projects, receiving training opportunities, and being granted time off to pursue other work-related interests.[22] Unlike the career ladder of the past, success in many companies today may be thought of as a moving sidewalk, with exits to various outlets. Thus, career success is measured not by how high you have climbed, but by how many different outlets (projects, assignments, learning opportunities, and so on) you have experienced. This model has long been common in some occupations, such as consulting, law, and research/development. In these occupations, star performers often earn handsome rewards and large bonuses. As Mel Warriner, the head of human resources at Walt Disney Imagineering, explains, performance is assessed in terms of successful projects. Success at an important project is rewarded with an opportunity to participate in the next project.[23]

Mastery Stage: Suggestions for Organizations

Organizations can take several steps to facilitate employees' progress in the mastery stage.

1. Develop Effective Promotion Systems. Although it was observed earlier that fewer promotion opportunities exist today than 20 years ago, organizations will continue to promote employees, albeit in fewer numbers and at a slower rate. Accurate promotion systems are notoriously difficult to develop because favoritism and politics often abound. Attempts to build objectivity into promotions, such as using seniority as an explicit factor, may lead to promotion of less qualified individuals. At the same time, candidates who are skilled in dealing with organizational politics may be more successful in their jobs than candidates who are ineffective at organizational politics. One manager described the ideal candidate for a promotion as someone who has the ability to successfully navigate the politics of our organization. Who you know and who knows you is important.[24]

   General Electric has one of the most thorough and well-regarded promotion systems in the world. As part of the process, the organization has internal consultants called Executive Manpower Consultants (EMCs) whose job involves assessing top managers, designing development plans, and disseminating this information when a promotion is being considered. To assess the candidates, the EMCs spend many hours talking with a candidate's current supervisor, past supervisors, and subordinates and then they write a lengthy report of their findings. This information becomes part of each top manager's record and plays a prominent role in promotion decisions.[25] Finally, several of the selection methods described in Chapter 5, such as structured interviews, simulation exercises, and assessment centers, have been used successfully for promotion purposes. Organizations that are designing promotion systems should carefully consider the use of such standardized, well-regarded practices.

2. Organizations Must Provide Appropriate Developmental Experiences. Research has identified a number of employee assignments and experiences that are use-

ful in developing employee abilities. You may be surprised to hear that some of the most valuable learning experiences involve difficult, stressful situations.[26] Two examples of important developmental experiences are provided in Table 6.2.

3. Provide Effective Career Programs That Reflect New Reality. To facilitate their employees' success in the mastery stage, some organizations have begun to offer career programs that emphasize many of the new career concepts just described. Chase Manhattan Bank, for example, recently initiated the Career Vision Program, which offers employees such services as confidential assessment tests and training in the KSAs needed for team project work. Sun Microsystems provides information to new hires about its Career Resilience program. Initially started as an outplacement program, it has evolved into a career counseling system that provides help regarding career issues as well.[27] Chevron company contracted with Beverly Kaye, a consultant, to implement a career guidance program to help redefine career objectives for employees. Among the suggestions that her program gives to employees is that they can move through the organization in many ways besides up, including sideways (such as to a more interesting department, but in a job with the same pay and prestige), out of the organization, or down (to a job that has lower pay and status, but more opportunity for growth).[28]

Mastery Stage: Suggestions for Employees

From an employee's perspective, you must acquire three basic competencies during the mastery stage:[29]

1. Advanced Knowledge in a Speciality Area. This may be marketing, finance, computer programming, or whatever. You probably have such an expertise if you were hired, but you must update and improve upon it during the mastery stage.
2. An Understanding of How the Business That You Are in Operates and Succeeds. It is critical to learn this during the mastery stage. One of the common criticisms employers make is that inexperienced workers fail to comprehend how their specialty area can contribute to the business.
3. The Ability to Work with Others. This includes effective communication, the ability to resolve conflicts, and networking. While you will begin learning some

Table 6.2 **Examples of Two Developmental Experiences and the Abilities They Affect**

Experience	Abilities Affected
1. Stabilizing or correcting a troubled business operation or unit	Learning how business works, being decisive, motivating others, gaining cooperation, negotiating, persevering, ability to confront others
2. Starting a new job to deal with dissatisfaction with a previous job	Coping with new situations; persevering; self-awareness, handling new relationships

Source: From M. W. McCall, "Developing Executives through Work Experiences," *Human Resource Planning* 11 (1988), 1–11.

of these KSAs in the entry stage, you need to become an expert in them during the mastery stage.

The new rules in the mastery stage, then, emphasize success in projects. The most successful workers will be those in greatest demand to work on projects; in turn, they will not only receive the highest rewards (pay, bonuses, and so forth), but they will be asked to participate in the most interesting and challenging assignments. Seniority and favoritism will play a smaller role than in the past. Next, you will read about the passage stage.

Passage Stage

Passage stage
Refers to the point during which the employee prepares to change jobs or employers.

The passage stage refers to the point during which the employee prepares to change jobs or employers. This may involve a complete change of occupation. Sydney Wood-Cahusac, for example, worked as a treasurer for several organizations, and finally concluded that what he wished to do was become a clergyman. Ten years after retiring from the business world, he is an ordained priest and says he finally feels fulfilled.[30]

In previous years, the passage stage was often referred to as the late career phase and was typically faced by employees past age 55. Traditionally, this was seen as the time when an employee would be planning for retirement, while combating issues of declining productivity and growing technical obsolescence. Today, however, as a result of many organizational layoffs and other factors affecting careers, employees are likely to enter the passage stage more than once.[31]

One may enter the passage stage either voluntarily (the employee chooses to change jobs or companies) or involuntarily (the organization terminates the employee). Voluntarily exiting a job or career and beginning afresh is something many people dream of but often hesitate to do. Two factors account for an individual's reluctance to change jobs or careers: fear of failure and concerns over loss of pay. But as Stephen Paskoff, formerly a partner in a successful law firm and now owner of a supervisor-training business, explains, "In the long run would you rather have the risk in your own enterprise or that your company lays you off?" In today's world, as described previously, working for even a large, established organization is certainly no guarantee of a job.[32]

Most of what you read next, however, will focus on involuntary transitions to the passage stage.

Passage Stage: Suggestions for Organizations

Although layoffs create a stressful and unpleasant situation for organizations and managers, a number of recommendations are offered here to help organizations facilitate this process.[33]

1. Involve All Employees in the Downsizing Process. Although top management will initiate the downsizing, all levels of employees can have input. Some organizations, for example, have had employees form task forces for the purpose of identifying unnecessary expenses, redundant positions, and other cost-savings changes. In one organization, employees were informed that their jobs were being eliminated, but they were told that they would receive full pay for one more year. During that time, they were asked to create another job for them-

selves within the organization that would make a contribution, or seek a position elsewhere.

2. Develop Plans for Both the Employees Who Will Remain and Those Who Will Leave. In terms of the employees who are being terminated, organizations should consider a variety of programs to assist them in their job search. Providing outplacement support to help employees in writing resumes and locating alternative jobs is a common practice for organizations that are conducting large layoffs. Organizations must also consider the needs of employees who will remain at the organization. Given all of the sympathy for the employees who are being asked to leave, it is not uncommon for the remaining employees to develop "survivor syndrome." This syndrome is characterized by feelings of anxiety about potential job loss, guilty feelings regarding departing workers, and loss of commitment to the organization. To combat such feelings, organizations must be sure to provide frequent, detailed communication with remaining workers, and develop programs and practices to signal a new start.

3. Organizations Should Develop Alternative Work Arrangements to Help Individual Employees in the Passage Stage. Programs such as sabbaticals, job sharing, and leaves of absence to pursue different opportunities may be helpful for individuals in the passage stage. Rank Xerox, for example, developed a formal program to enable employees in its human resources and purchasing departments to become consultants. As part of this program, the company helped employees to become independent contractors by hiring them part time at their current salary, while saving money by not paying benefits. Employees were also able to consult with other companies.[34]

Passage Stage: Suggestions for Employees

Here are some suggestions for you as an employee in the passage stage:[35]

1. Do Not Be Tempted by Jobs That Conflict with Your Career Plan. While sometimes these apparent mismatches can turn into positive situations, be wary of them. The wrong move may be extremely costly. On the other hand, Mike Hernacki, currently a freelance writer, has had five different careers, ranging from schoolteacher to lawyer. Some of these careers lasted only two years. Although it may seem as though none of these careers is related to freelance writing, Mike would completely disagree. As he explains, his business and legal experience helps him when he writes about financial issues, and his experience in advertising is useful for promotional writing.[36]

2. Keep Moving Around in Order to Acquire the Experiences and KSAs You Are Seeking. While you need to be careful not to appear as a job hopper, you also want to make sure that you attain your goals. Kathy Reed, who worked for several years at Xerox Corporation, found that the program manager position at the company enabled her to acquire a wide variety of KSAs, including marketing experience and conflict resolution ability.

3. What Seems Bad May Not Be Bad After All. Kathy Reed was laid off less than one year after being hired by Compaq Computer. Although she was devastated at first, she ultimately was hired at Recognition International, which

manufactures document-processing materials. As she describes the experience, "it was scary as hell. . . . But it was terrific to learn there is life after a layoff."

4. Handling the Termination. Given the number of mass layoffs occurring in the 1990s, don't be surprised if you are terminated in a workforce reduction. Below are some suggestions of what to do if you are fired:

   Stay Calm. Quite understandably, you may become extremely upset when you find out that you have been terminated. If you lose your cool, however, you may end up saying things (such as, threatening to sue your supervisor) or doing things (like badmouthing the company) that you will regret later. Don't be so concerned about how the termination will be viewed by other companies. Employers' perceptions of terminated workers have changed quite a bit in the last 15 years. In the past, being terminated had much stigma attached to it; but given the many layoffs during the last decade or so, many highly qualified employees are now fired for reasons other than their job performance. Dennis Lunder, an executive director of marketing communications for a large greeting card company, has lost his job six times in almost 30 years.[37]

   Avoid the Emotional Roller Coaster. Once you accept the fact that you must find a new job, adopt a regular schedule and continue engaging in outside activities. Keeping a regular schedule and maintaining your outside interests will help prevent you from becoming depressed and will help you to keep a balanced perspective.[38]

   Negotiate with Your Company. There are many benefits that your company may either offer to you or that you may be able to obtain through negotiation. The number and amount of the benefits will depend in part on why you were fired (was it poor performance on your part, or is the company simply reducing the size of the workforce). One of the most important benefits is severance pay—money above and beyond that which the company owes you. A common rule of thumb is a minimum of one week's pay for each year of service. Your company may offer you the amount as a lump sum or as a continuation of salary. There are pros and cons to each of these arrangements. The conditions under which you leave the organization also have implications. If the company asks you to resign, you may be forfeiting unemployment compensation. However, unemployment compensation may not provide much money, and your organization may even fight your claim. Chances are your health and life insurance will end when you are terminated; but you may even be able to negotiate continuation of these benefits for some period of time (note that even if your company does not continue your health benefits, you have the right to pay to continue them [see chapter 10]). Finally, the company may decide to hire you as a consultant to do the same job you were doing. It pays, then, not to "burn the bridges" as you leave.[39]

In sum, the passage stage can be a difficult one for employees, particularly if entering this stage was the result of an involuntary decision, as it can take months for one to find a new job. In 1989, for example, executives who were terminated took on average 6 months to become reemployed. During the 1990 recession, it took an average of more than 8 months. Individuals who are most able to cope with a termination tend to maintain their regular activities, have strong social support (including from their family) and financial resources to draw from, and limit the amount of time they are without a job.[40]

Organizational Advancement Systems

So far, we have focused on career stages that employees experience. But how do organizations view careers? In this section, you will read about four different career advancement systems that organizations use. We begin with the most traditional approach: the vertical system.

Vertical System

As its name implies, the vertical career advancement system is characterized by job advancement up a clearly delineated path within a specific functional area. In a clerical path, one might enter the organization as a clerk-typist 1, move to clerk-typist 2, then move to secretary 1, and finally secretary 2. As shown in Figure 6.2, the vertical system is much like a series of telephone poles. One may climb up the telephone pole, but it is difficult to change to another pole without starting all over again. In a traditional vertical career system, there is limited opportunity to move to a different path. As an example, a study of a savings and loan organization with this type of advancement system revealed that 93 percent of employees remained in the same path they began.[41]

Vertical career advancement system
Characterized by job advancement up a clearly delineated path within a specific functional area.

The vertical career pattern is usually found in well-entrenched, stable organizations that seek continuity, stability, and a positive public image, such as

Box 6.3 General Tips for Career Success

Everyone has some favorite career tips. Here are some career tips you might find of use.

1. *Take reasonable risks.* To succeed in today's world, you will need to take some risks. But make sure that you have alternative plans if things don't go as planned. As an example, you may consider changing companies in order to improve your career options. But if you are worried that things won't work out at the new company, you should first consider whether the job market is good enough that you will have alternative opportunities with other organizations.

2. *Compensation should be much less important in the beginning of your career.* Think of the first ten or so years of your career as a learning process; the major reward should be the opportunity to learn and develop your skills. Pay, on the other hand, should be much less important. Some experts suggest that you not even consider the compensation offered for the first few years and concentrate solely on what you can learn and the experience you can acquire.

3. *Focus on making your boss successful.* If your boss is successful, he or she will help you. This doesn't mean you should neglect your own career. But it does mean that you need to be very attuned to your boss' goals and what it takes to achieve those.

4. *Recognize the contribution of others.* Giving credit to others does not reduce your contributions. People tend to remember and to reciprocate when their contributions are recognized by others. This is especially true today, when many companies are emphasizing teams and alliances. Giving credit when it is due is critical in developing a team spirit.

Source: Adapted from G. Graen, *Unwritten Rules for Your Career* (New York: John Wiley, 1989).

Box 6.4 The Move Away from Corporate Careers

Tales from the Trenches

One of the recent career trends is the move away from large corporations. In fact, a recent survey indicated that only 1 percent of adults indicated they would like to work as a corporate manager. The trend is particularly pronounced among recent MBA graduates from top programs. At Stanford University, for example, six years ago almost 70 percent of graduating MBAs went to work for a large manufacturing business; in 1994 only about 50 percent chose this career. While many MBAs from top schools become consultants or investment bankers, their real aim often is to save a lot of money so that they can become entrepreneurs at a later date.

The trend against working for a large corporation has in some cases created difficulties for university officials. In recent years, for example, recruiters from large corporations have arrived at campuses, only to find far fewer interested students than expected. Some manufacturers no longer recruit at Harvard University because so few students accepted their job offers. On the other hand, university officials are finding extremely strong demand for certain courses with a small-business focus, such as entrepreneurial financing. At University of Chicago, more than 300 students signed up for a course in this area. The school could only admit 130 of them.

So why the move away from corporate careers? Several reasons have been offered. First, large organizations have acquired a reputation for bureaucracy, limited autonomy, and minimal impact. In the past, however, these negatives were often outweighed by several positives, such as implicit job security and frequent promotions. In light of the many layoffs and flattened organizational structure, though, the benefits of working for a large corporation have greatly diminished. Take Robert Berg, who recently graduated with an MBA and now works for a large consulting firm. Asked about his former large employer, he responds, "when the time came to close the division I was working with, management left us with the feeling that they were going to take care of us. They didn't. Basically, they lied to us." Another reason for the growing decline in corporate careers lies with more women in the workforce. As Kristin Snowden, a second year MBA student, explains, "There is a way people are supposed to behave at work at large companies, and it's based on a male model that is hundreds of years old. Women cry more often than men, for example; we find that it is an effective way to relieve stress. But you are never, ever supposed to cry on the job if you work at a large company." Finally, the newest generation heading into the work world (often called Generation X) seems to value independence and interesting work much more than previous generations did; yet these are the very characteristics that jobs in large corporations usually lack. Whether the trend against large companies will change remains to be seen.

Source: Adapted from K. Labich, "Kissing Off Corporate America," *Fortune,* February 20, 1995, 44–52.

quasi-government organizations (for example, utilities). By having all employees go through identical experiences and assignments in the functional area, the organization instills a common purpose and understanding in its members.[42]

Some of the advantages and disadvantages of the vertical career system are described in Table 6.3. As you can see, this system can be effective, depending on various considerations. In most situations, however, the vertical system is probably not ideal for the employee or the organization.

Trunk and Branch System

Probably more common than the vertical pattern is the trunk and branch system. As shown in Figure 6.3, the trunk and branch system is much like a tree, with a trunk and many branches, which turn off into other branches. The trunk and branch model allows employees to move between different functions and areas. In

Figure 6.2 **Vertical System**

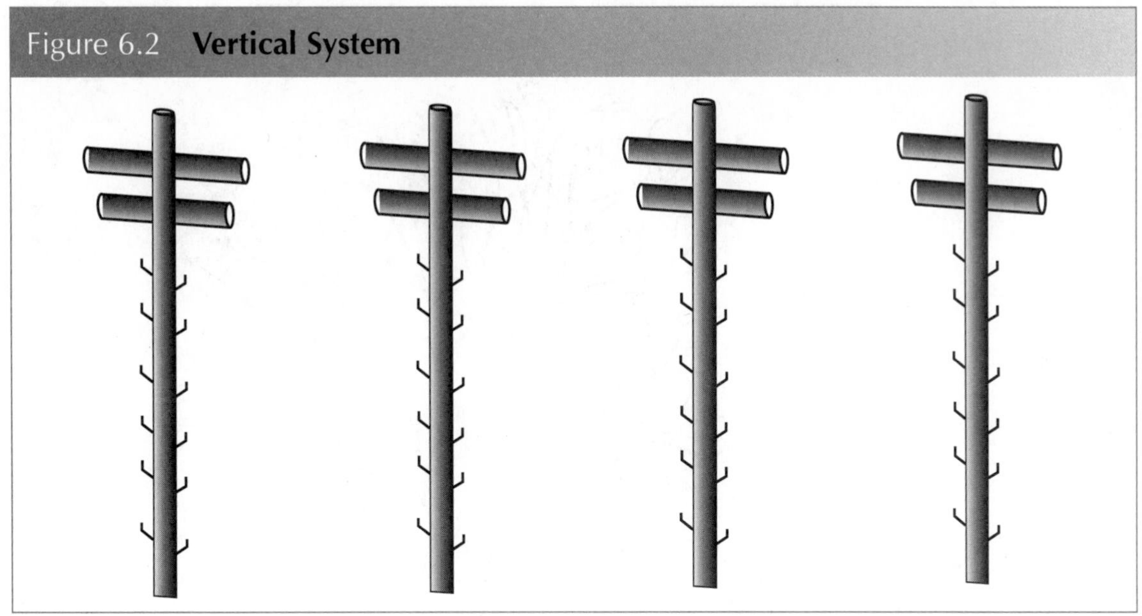

Table 6.3 **Advantages and Disadvantages of the Vertical Career System**

Advantages	**Disadvantages**
1. Employees have a clear idea of promotion steps.	1. If the organization is not growing or is in decline, employees will have limited promotion opportunities.
2. If the organization is growing, employees will have promotion opportunities.	2. Many employees may be competing for the few positions available.
3. Managers will understand subordinates' jobs and can be helpful to them.	3. Some lines of progression may be very short, limiting promotion opportunities.
4. The system provides reliable and thorough KSA development.	

Source: Adapted from H.D. Dewhirst, "Career Patterns: Mobility, Specialization, and Related Career Issues," in *Contemporary Career Development Issues,* ed. R.F. Morrison and J. Adams (Hillsdale, NJ: Lawrence Erlbaum, 1991), 73-107.

Figure 6.3 **Trunk and Branch System**

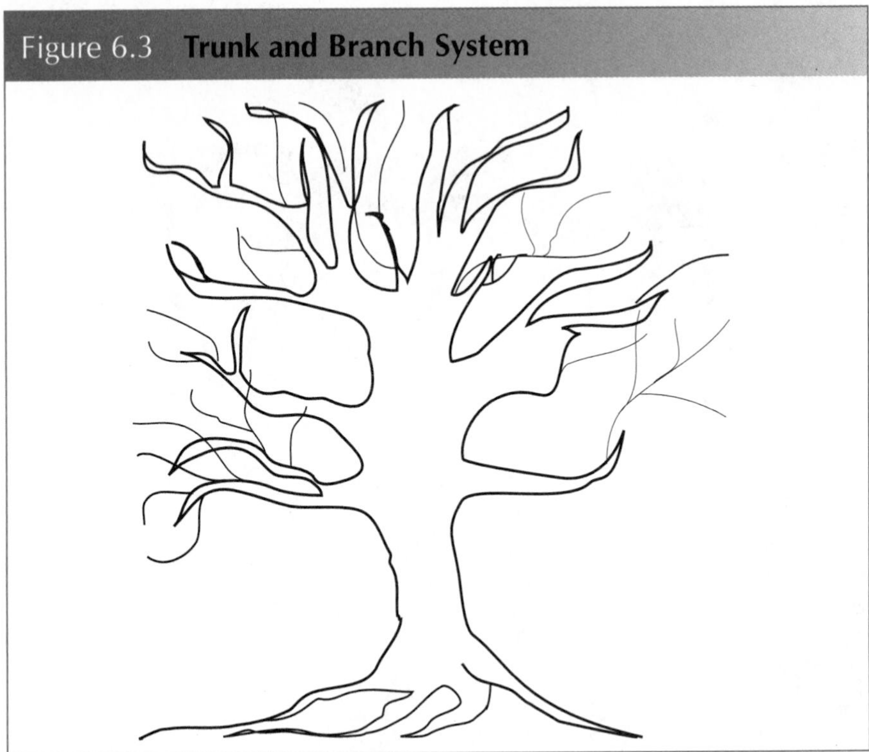

Trunk and branch career advancement system
This model allows employees to move between different functions and areas, just as a tree has a trunk and many branches that turn off into other branches.

keeping with the previous example of a clerical career, a trunk and branch approach might allow the clerical employee to move into a production hierarchy. This system is typical of many organizations, particularly those that face significant competition and operate in unstable environments. The primary advantage of this system is that it provides greater flexibility for both the employees and the organization. The employees have more than one set of promotion opportunities, and the organization has many more potential candidates to fill positions. Table 6.4 lists some additional advantages, as well as disadvantages, of the trunk and branch model.[43]

Table 6.4 **Advantages and Disadvantages of the Trunk and Branch System**

Advantages	Disadvantages
1. Employees can match their interests to more job opportunities.	1. Career paths can still become too competitive or can have too few applicants.
2. Employees can get experience in different areas.	2. Employees have more choices; more choices can produce more confusion and uncertainty.

Source: Adapted from H.D. Dewhirst, "Career Patterns: Mobility, Specialization, and Related Career Issues," in *Contemporary Career Development Issues,* ed. R.F. Morrison and J. Adams (Hillsdale, NJ: Lawrence Erlbaum, 1991), 73-107.

Planned Job Rotation System

The planned job rotation model is a carefully designed plan by the organization for employees to gain experience in specific functions for a predetermined amount of time. This system, then, is quite similar to the trunk and branch model, except it is much more carefully planned and designed. As shown in Figure 6.4, the planned job rotation system resembles a genetically grown tree, where the botanist designed the tree to have branches grow in a deliberate fashion. Job rotation is described in greater detail in Chapter 11, where the pros and cons of this system will be examined in greater detail.[44]

Planned job rotation model
A carefully designed plan by the organization for employees to gain experience in specific functions for a predetermined amount of time.

Planned job rotation is most commonly used by organizations that operate in an environment that has the characteristics of both a reliable, stable market and a market characterized by frequent change and rapid innovation. Drug companies are probably a good example of this type of industry today. The planned job rotation approach requires a great deal of time and effort on the part of companies, so they are clearly investing in their employees. This is also an excellent way of developing employees, and it provides employees with a thorough understanding of the organization's operations.[45]

We now turn to a new career advancement system, one that we will refer to as the diamond system.

Diamond System

The diamond career advancement system, which is relatively new, is used in an organization that is project based (see the section titled "Changed Nature of Work"

Diamond career advancement system
A relatively new career advancement system, the diamond system is used in an organization that is project based, and involves few upward, but potentially many sideways, moves.

Figure 6.4 **Planned Job Rotation**

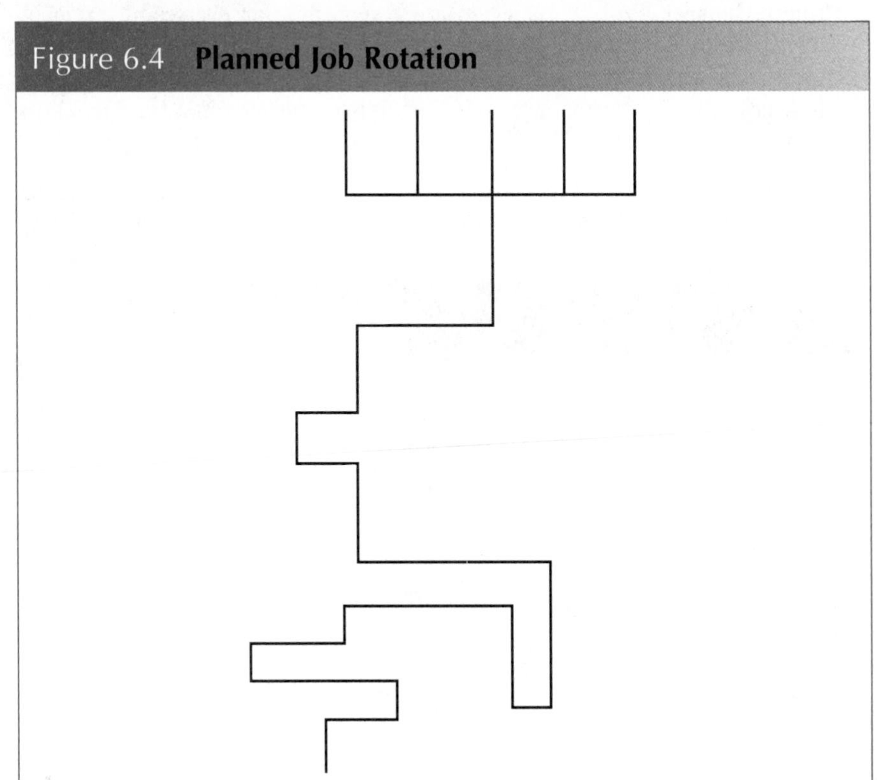

Organizations view career management differently than employees do. Companies like Packard-Bell may use the vertical or trunk and branch systems to characterize job advancement for their employees.

earlier in this chapter). Figure 6.5 displays the diamond shape, as well as the job types that constitute the diamond. Unlike the other systems, where employees progress in an upward fashion, the diamond system involves few upward, but potentially many sideways, moves. There are four basic job types in the diamond system.[46]

1. Project Manager. Project managers are responsible for overseeing projects. They coordinate the work, obtain the necessary resources, and interact with others, including clients and resource managers. Project managers perform many of the tasks that managers and supervisors perform in a traditional organization.
2. Strategist. Strategists are responsible for the "big picture" issues, such as the organization's long-term vision. They also have contact with major clients.

Figure 6.5 **Diamond System**

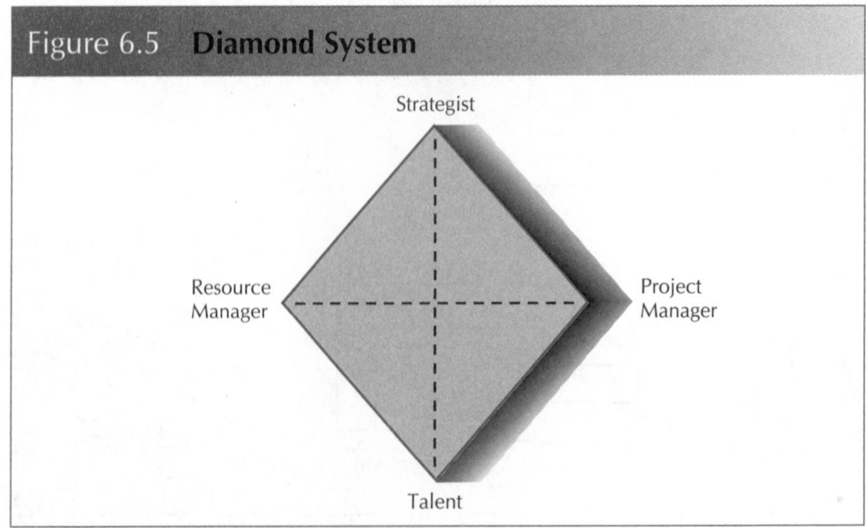

There are relatively few of these employees. They perform the work that CEOs and top executives do in a traditional organization.

3. Resource Manager. Resource managers are responsible for obtaining, developing, and allocating the resources that project teams need, such as people, money, equipment and materials. The employees who serve in this capacity do the tasks that human resources, finance, accounting and procurement staff perform in a traditional organization.

4. Talent. These are the people who perform the projects. Depending on the nature of the work, they may be computer programmers, scientists, statisticians, or other technical, professional, production, or clerical employees.

As shown in Figure 6.5, there are lines between these four job types, indicating that employees can move between these different positions. The strategist, for example, probably has had experience as a resource manager or project manager. There may even be flux between some of these roles; that is, the talent in one project may be project managers in the next project. Unlike the other systems reviewed above, however, employees do not advance in any traditional sense. Because the diamond system is relatively new, it is too early to know its advantages and disadvantages.

We now turn to consideration of some common career issues that many employees encounter, and discuss ways to handle them.

Common Career Issues

There are three common issues faced by many employees: being a specialist versus generalist, job burnout, and prioritizing managerial activities for success. Each is discussed in greater detail next, along with ways to address them.

Being a Specialist versus a Generalist

In many fields, such as computer programming and law, one begins working in one specific area, but after a few years one is faced with the question of whether to remain a specialist, and know a great deal about one topic, or to become a generalist, competent of handling several different areas. Research with scientists and engineers indicates that there is no one right answer as to which is best—some individuals have highly effective careers as specialists, while others have highly effective careers as generalists.

So what are some considerations that you should take into account in deciding whether to remain a narrow specialist or become more of a generalist? First, you can remain a specialist if you are in a highly sought-after field, especially where there is a shortage of qualified people. Certain computer fields, for example, are likely to always have a high demand for workers. You also need to evaluate the long-term picture, of course, in deciding how much demand there will be for your specialty. Is your specialty an area that is constantly changing or takes a high degree of training? Second, are you willing to work as a consultant, either independently or for a firm? If the answer is yes, then you may be able to succeed as a specialist. The reason why specialists will be more successful as consultants is that they will need more customers than someone who is a generalist. In other words, someone who is an expert on the Family and Medical Leave Act is unlikely to have enough work to do if she is employed by one organization; but she may have plenty of work if she is employed by a consulting firm that provides services to one hundred organizations that need help with this law. If you specialize, then, you should make sure that there will be sufficient demand for your skill over the long term, that you are extremely effective at what you do, and that you are willing to work as a consultant. If you don't meet these criteria, you should probably become more of a generalist. As Gary Kniser, an executive recruiter, says, "Never narrow your options. To the extent that technical expertise narrows your market, you've made a bad career decision."[47]

Burnout

Have you ever had a sense of emotional exhaustion, including a lack of energy and a perception that you were emotionally drained? How about a feeling of depersonalization toward coworkers or clients, or a sense of personal failure and limited progress at work? Practically everyone has had some of these feelings from time to time, but if you had one or more of those feelings for a longer period (such as a few weeks), you may be suffering from job burnout. Certain jobs are particularly susceptible to job burnout, particularly the helping professions, such as social workers, schoolteachers, and customer service representatives. Jobs that tend to create relatively little job burnout include laboratory technicians, researchers, and people who work alone. You will read next about some of the factors that contribute to job burnout, as well as some things you can do to avoid this symptom.[48]

Job burnout
A sense of emotional exhaustion, lack of energy, feeling of depersonalization toward coworkers or clients. A sense of personal failure and limited progress at work are all characteristics of burnout. One cause lies within the individual employee, whereas a second cause lies within the nature of the work.

Causes of Job Burnout. Job burnout has two primary causes. One cause lies within the individual employee; a second cause lies in the nature of the work. To understand the first cause, consider Nancy Parker, a new business graduate, eager to make her mark in the business world. She has set a number of goals for herself, including earning at least $100,000 by the time she is 30, and owning a BMW. She also expects to be a top executive by the time she is 35. Do you think these are realistic goals? Unless Nancy Parker is extremely talented, or works for a family-owned business, there is a good chance that she will not achieve these goals. She may begin to suffer from job burnout as she encounters setbacks. Job burnout, then, is particularly common for young employees who have set unrealistic goals for themselves and have inflated expectations as to what the organization will provide in the way of rewards and opportunities.

In order to understand work factors that contribute to burnout, consider Tom Richardson, a newly graduated business student who works for a collection agency. His job will be to try to get people to pay their debts. The people he is trying to collect from respond in a variety of ways, ranging from open hostility to crying. Because of the intensity (many people resist paying their debts to a collection agency) and frequency of these interactions, Tom Richardson is also likely to experience job burnout. Jobs with frequent, intensive contact with clients often lead to burnout. Other factors that contribute to burnout include having too much work to do and reporting to different supervisors with different expectations for work.

Avoiding Burnout. One of the most important ways to avoid burnout is to have access to social support. Social support means having one or more people who will listen to you when you want to complain, provide advice about issues that concern you, and generally make you feel valued as a person. Social support can come from several different sources, including your spouse, friends, and even your supervisor. Although there are also instances where your coworkers can provide social support to alleviate your feelings of burnout, at times social support from coworkers can actually increase your feelings of being burned out. Perhaps in talking with coworkers you may begin to feel even more negative about the situation than you did before.[49]

From the organizational perspective, another way to reduce burnout is to rotate jobs so that employees have a break from constant interaction with clients. Perhaps paperwork or other needed assignments can be performed each day by different employees, thereby providing a brief break from the tension associated with client contact. Similarly, reducing the workload to more manageable levels and reducing role conflict can in the long run save a great deal of turnover, and the necessary recruiting, hiring, and training that goes along with turnover.

In sum, burnout is a common problem. Be sure to set reasonable, achievable goals for yourself, and develop sources of social support. Finally, remember that there is more to life than just work.

Prioritizing Managerial Activities for Success

One question that often arises for managers is how to prioritize their supervisory activities to achieve maximum effectiveness. To answer this question, we need to first distinguish between four types of managerial activities:

1. Communication Activities. These involve such things as writing reports, answering telephone inquiries, contacting others, and so forth.

2. Traditional Management Activities. These include such activities as setting goals for employees, completing work schedules, inspecting work, assigning work tasks, and so forth.

3. Human Resource Activities. These include training employees, giving rewards (for instance, compliments), managing conflict between employees, mentoring employees, and so forth.

4. Networking. Activities in this category involve interacting, socializing, and politicking with others. It includes all types of informal interactions with others, including joking, gossiping, and discussing rumors.

Before we discuss which of these four activities is most related to success as a manager, it is important to note that there are at least two ways to define managerial success. One way, which we will refer to as career advancement, is based on how rapidly the manager has advanced in the organization. The second way, which we will refer to as unit performance, is based on how productive the manager's unit is in terms of quality and quantity of work, as well as subordinates' measure of job satisfaction. Interestingly enough, research has indicated that very few managers rate highly on both career advancement *and* unit performance.

Given this information, which of the four managerial activities do you think managers who demonstrate rapid career advancement spend most of their time doing? If you answered networking, you are correct. So, if you want to advance rapidly in the organization, spending your time on networking seems to be the key. On the other hand, what activities do you think the managers who have the highest unit performance tend to engage in most? If you answered communication and human resource management, you are right. Interestingly, the activity least related to unit performance was networking. Which activities you prioritize, then, will affect the type of success you experience. Based on earlier comments in this chapter, however, as organizations focus less on promotions and more on project management, it is likely that unit performance will become more important than career advancement. Given the choice between these activities, then, communication and human resource management should be given your highest priority as a manager.[50]

Conclusion

The nature of careers has changed dramatically in the last 20 years for several reasons, including the large number of corporate layoffs, the changed nature of work, and the changed nature of organizations. Accordingly, career stages are also different than in the past. Many individuals today will experience a three-phase cycle of entry, mastery, and passage several times around. Each stage will involve different challenges. There are several different types of organization advancement systems, ranging from the traditional vertical approach to the relatively new diamond system. You also read about three common career issues, including specializing versus generalizing, job burnout, and prioritizing managerial activities. With careful planning and foresight, organizations and employees should be able to foster career effectiveness.

Applying Core Concepts

1. Discuss how the career of someone 30 years ago may have differed from the career you are likely to have.
2. What career stage do you think you are in now? What issues have you dealt with so far? What issues do you expect to come up in the near future?
3. What types of programs and practices does your company or a company that a close friend of yours works for offer to deal with transitions to different career stages?
4. What advancement system does your company or a company that a close friend of yours works for use?
5. Which of the following career issues do you think you may experience in the career you have chosen or the career you hope to choose: being a specialist versus generalist, job burnout, and prioritizing managerial activities for success. Choose the one you think you are most likely to face, and explain how you would deal with it.

Key Terms

- Entry stage
- Mentor
- Mastery stage
- Passage stage
- Vertical career advancement system
- Trunk and branch career advancement system
- Planned job rotation model
- Diamond career advancement system
- Job burnout

Chapter 6: Experiential Exercise

The Controversial Promotion

Your instructor will assign you into groups of three people; each of you will be given a specific role. Read your role carefully before beginning the exercise; you should *not* read any other role besides the one given to you.

HRM Manager's Role

The Company: Kitchy Kitchens, Inc. sells consumer appliances, such as kitchen sinks, faucets, garbage compactors, and various other major kitchen appliances and hardware.

Background Information: Very recently, a manager of marketing job opened in your company. Because your company has a policy of hiring from within, a list of possible employees qualified for the job was generated. The two top contenders are Bill Smith and Mary Wells. Both have worked at the company for 10 years, and have spent most of this time in the marketing area. There are some differences between them as well. Bill Smith is a few years older, and had several years of prior marketing experience with a competitor. Bill has also had more varied experience than Mary in the marketing function, working on several different products in various different markets, including stores and individuals. Mary, on the other hand, has an undergraduate degree in business (Bill's degree is in philosophy), and has worked the entire time on marketing to retail stores, which is where the growth is. Your examination of the personnel files indicates that Mary and Bill have received on average identical performance ratings over the last 3 years, which is when performance ratings were first formalized.

The Issue: At issue is whether Bill or Mary should be promoted to Manager of Marketing. The VP of Marketing and Sales, to whom the person would report, wants to promote Bill. As far as you can tell, Mary and Bill are fairly evenly matched in terms of qualifications and experience. You interviewed both Mary and Bill, and were convinced that both are good communicators, and would be effective with subordinates. Given that they are fairly evenly matched, you felt strongly that Mary should be promoted because there are far too few females in management at Kitchy Kitchens. In fact, you have heard recent rumblings about a lawsuit regarding sex bias in promotions. Given the new law, Kitchy Kitchens could lose some actual money if such a lawsuit were successful. You are not quite sure what the VP's reasoning is, so you and the VP are going to meet to discuss this matter. Your task, then, is to explain why Mary should be promoted over Bill.

VP of Marketing and Sales Role

The Company: Kitchy Kitchens, Inc. sells consumer appliances, such as kitchen sinks, faucets, garbage compactors, and various other major kitchen appliances and hardware.

Background Information: Very recently, a manager of marketing job opened in your company. Because your company has a policy of hiring from within, a list of possible employees qualified for the job was generated. The two top contenders are Bill Smith and Mary Wells. Both have worked at the company for 10 years, and have spent most of this time in the marketing area. There are some differences between them as well. Bill Smith is a few years older, and had several years of prior marketing experience with a competitor. Bill has also had more varied experience than Mary in the marketing function, working on several different products in various different markets, including stores and individuals. Mary, on the other hand, has an undergraduate degree in business (Bill's degree is in philosophy), and has worked the entire time on marketing to retail stores, which is where the growth is. For the past three years, the company has had a yearly formal performance appraisal for all employees. You took an active role in monitoring those conducted by the previous manager of marketing, even attending some of the feedback sessions. From your observations, Bill is the more qualified of the two top candidates.

The Issue: At issue is whether Bill or Mary should be promoted to Manager of Marketing. As the manager to whom the position reports, you feel it is your "call." You have met with all five candidates. You even called the prior Manager of Marketing, who said Bill and Mary were both well qualified (but from the tone of his voice, you were pretty certain he would pick Bill). You have no doubt that Bill should be promoted. However, rumor has it that the HRM manager would like to promote Mary, and has called a meeting with you to discuss whether Bill or Mary should be promoted. Given that you are going to

Chapter 6: Experiential Exercise *(continued)*

be the one who has to work with the Manager of Marketing, it seems logical that you should be the one to make the decision. Your task, then, is to explain why Bill should be promoted.

President's Role

The Company: Kitchy Kitchens, Inc. sells consumer appliances, such as kitchen sinks, faucets, garbage compactors, and various other major kitchen appliances and hardware.

Background Information: Very recently, a manager of marketing job opened in your company. Because your company has a policy of hiring from within, a list of possible employees qualified for the job was generated. The two top contenders are Bill Smith and Mary Wells. Your examination of their personnel files revealed the following facts. Both have worked at the company for 10 years, and have spent most of this time in the marketing area. There are some differences between them as well. Bill Smith is a few years older, and had several years of prior marketing experience with a competitor. Bill has also had more varied experience than Mary in the marketing function, working on several different products in various different markets, including stores and individuals. Mary, on the other hand, has an undergraduate degree in business (Bill's degree is in philosophy), and has worked the entire time on marketing to retail stores, which is where the growth is. For the past three years, the company has had a yearly formal performance appraisal for all employees. The ratings indicate that Bill and Mary have had nearly identical ratings; sometimes Bill was rated a shade higher, sometimes Mary was rated a shade higher.

The Issue: At issue is whether Bill or Mary should be promoted to Manager of Marketing. Since you are not directly involved in the decision of who gets hired, you have not interviewed any of the candidates. You assume that the VP of Marketing and Sales will make the final decision, with the approval of the HRM manager. However, in this case, you have heard that there may be some disagreement between the two. The HRM manager has requested that you attend a meeting they are having, where this issue will be discussed. Both the HRM manager and VP have been with the company for a number of years, and you have a very high regard for both. Though you are less familiar with the HRM manager's work, you know that the VP is one of the best in the business. You also know that lawsuits are on the rise, and that the HRM function is critical in avoiding such things from happening.

Chapter 6 References

1. M. Murray, "Thanks, Goodbye," *The Wall Street Journal,* May 5, 1995, A1, A4.
2. T. Stewart, "Planning a Career in a World Without Managers," *Fortune,* March, 20, 1995, 72–80.
3. W. Kiechel, "How We Will Work in the Year 2000," *Fortune,* May 17, 1993, 38–52.
4. H.D. Dewhirst, "Career Patterns: Mobility, Specialization, and Related Career Issues," in *Contemporary Career Development Issues,* ed. R.F. Morrison and J. Adams (Hillsdale, NJ: Lawrence Erlbaum, 1991).
5. N. Nicholson, "The Transition Cycle: A Conceptual Framework for the Analysis of Change and Human Resources Management," in *Research in Personnel and Human Resources Management,* ed. K. Rowland and G. Ferris (Greenwich, CT: JAI Press, 1987).
6. E. Schein. *Career Survival: Strategic Job and Role Planning* (San Diego, CA: Pfeiffer, 1993).

7. J. Greenhaus, *Career Management* (Fort Worth, TX: Dryden, 1987).
8. Ibid.
9. T. Bauer and S. Green, "Effect of Newcomer Involvement in Work-Related Activities: A Longitudinal Study of Socialization," *Journal of Applied Psychology* 79 (1994), 1994, 211–23.
10. M. Louis, B. Posner, and G. Powell, "The Availability and Helpfulness of Socialization Practices," *Personnel Psychology* 36 (1983), 857–66.
11. G. Jones, "Socialization Tactics, Self-Efficacy, and Newcomers' Adjustments to Organizations," *Academy of Management Journal* 29 (1986), 262–79.
12. R. Morrison, "Meshing Corporate and Career Development Strategies," in *Contemporary Career Development Issues,* ed. R. Morrison and J. Adams (Hillsdale, NJ: Lawrence Erlbaum, 1991).
13. C. Hymowitz, "How a Dedicated Mentor Gave Momentum to a Woman's Career," *The Wall Street Journal,* April 24, 1995, B1.
14. G. Graen, *Unwritten Rules for Your Career.* (New York: John Wiley, 1989).
15. R. Noe, "An Investigation of the Determinants of Successful Assigned Mentoring Relationships," *Personnel Psychology* 41 (1988), 457–79.
16. G. Dreher and R. Ash, "A Comparative Study of Mentoring Among Men and Women in Managerial, Professional, and Technical Positions," *Journal of Applied Psychology* 75 (1990), 539–46.
17. D. Turban and T. Dougherty, "Role of Protégé Personality in Receipt of Mentoring and Career Success," *Academy of Management Journal* 37 (1994), 688–702.
18. K. Kram, *Mentoring at Work* (Glenview, IL: Scott Foresman, 1985).
19. R. Noe, "Mentoring Relationships for Employee Development," in *Applying Psychology in Business,* ed. J. Jones, B. Steffy, and D. Bray (Lexington, MA: Lexington Books, 1991).
20. Greenhaus, *Career Management.*
21. D. Hall, "Breaking Career Routines: Midcareer Choice and Identity Development," in *Career Development in Organizations,* ed. D. Hall and Associates (San Francisco, CA: Jossey-Bass, 1986).
22. J. Fierman, "Beating the Midlife Career Crisis," *Fortune,* September 6, 1993, 52–62.
23. Stewart, *Planning a Career.*
24. G. Ferris, M.R. Buckley, and G. Allen, "Promotion Systems in Organizations," *Human Resource Planning* 15 (1992), 47–68, 95.
25. S. Friedman and T. LeVino, "Strategic Appraisal and Development at General Electric Company," in *Strategic Human Resource Management,* ed. C. Fombrun, N. Tichy and M.A. DeVanna (New York: John Wiley, 1984).
26. M.W. McCall, "Developing Executives Through Work Experiences," *Human Resource Planning* 11 (1988), 1–11.
27. Stewart, *Planning a Career.*
28. Ibid.
29. Ibid.
30. J. Connelly, "How to Choose Your Next Career," *Fortune,* February 6, 1995, 145–46.
31. Greenhaus, *Career Management.*
32. Connelly, *How to Choose.*
33. K. Cameron, S. Freeman, and A. Mishra, "Best Practices in White-Collar Downsizing: Managing Contradictions," *The Executive* 5 (1991), 57–73.
34. T. Gilmore and L. Hirschhorn, "Managing Human Resources in a Declining Context," in *Strategic Human Resource Management,* ed. C. Fombrun, N. Tichy, and M.A. DeVanna (New York: John Wiley, 1984).
35. H. Lancaster, "Managing Your Career," *The Wall Street Journal,* February 14, 1995, B1.
36. Connelly, *How to Choose.*

37. D. Kirkpatrick, "The New Executive Unemployed," *Fortune,* April 8, 1991, 36–48; K. Salwen, "Decade of Downsizing Eases Stigma of Layoffs," *The Wall Street Journal,* February 8, 1994, B1.
38. Kirkpatrick, *The New Executive Unemployed.*
39. L. Asinof, "If Ax Falls, Know Your Benefits, Rights, and Don't Forget the Art of Negotiation," *The Wall Street Journal,* January 17, 1992, C1, C4.
40. Kirkpatrick, *The New Executive Unemployed;* J. Latack, A. Kinicki, and G. Prussia, "An Integrative Process Model of Coping with Job Loss," *Academy of Management Review* 20 (1995), 311–42.
41. Dewhirst, "Career Patterns."
42. J. Sonnenfeld and M. Peiperl, "Staffing Policy as a Strategic Response: A Typology of Career Systems," *Academy of Management Review* 13 (1988), 588–600.
43. Dewhirst, "Career Patterns."
44. Ibid.
45. Sonnenfeld and Peiperl, "Staffing Policy."
46. Stewart, *Planning a Career.*
47. Ibid.
48. C. Cordes and T. Dougherty, "A Review and Integration of Research on Job Burnout," *Academy of Management Review* 18 (1993), 621–56.
49. G. Kaufmann and T. Beehr, (1986). "Interactions between Job Stressors and Social Support: Some Counterintuitive Results," *Journal of Applied Psychology* 71, 522–26.
50. F. Luthans, "Successful vs. Effective Real Managers," *Academy of Management Executive* 11 (1988), 127-32.

part 3

Evaluating and Compensation

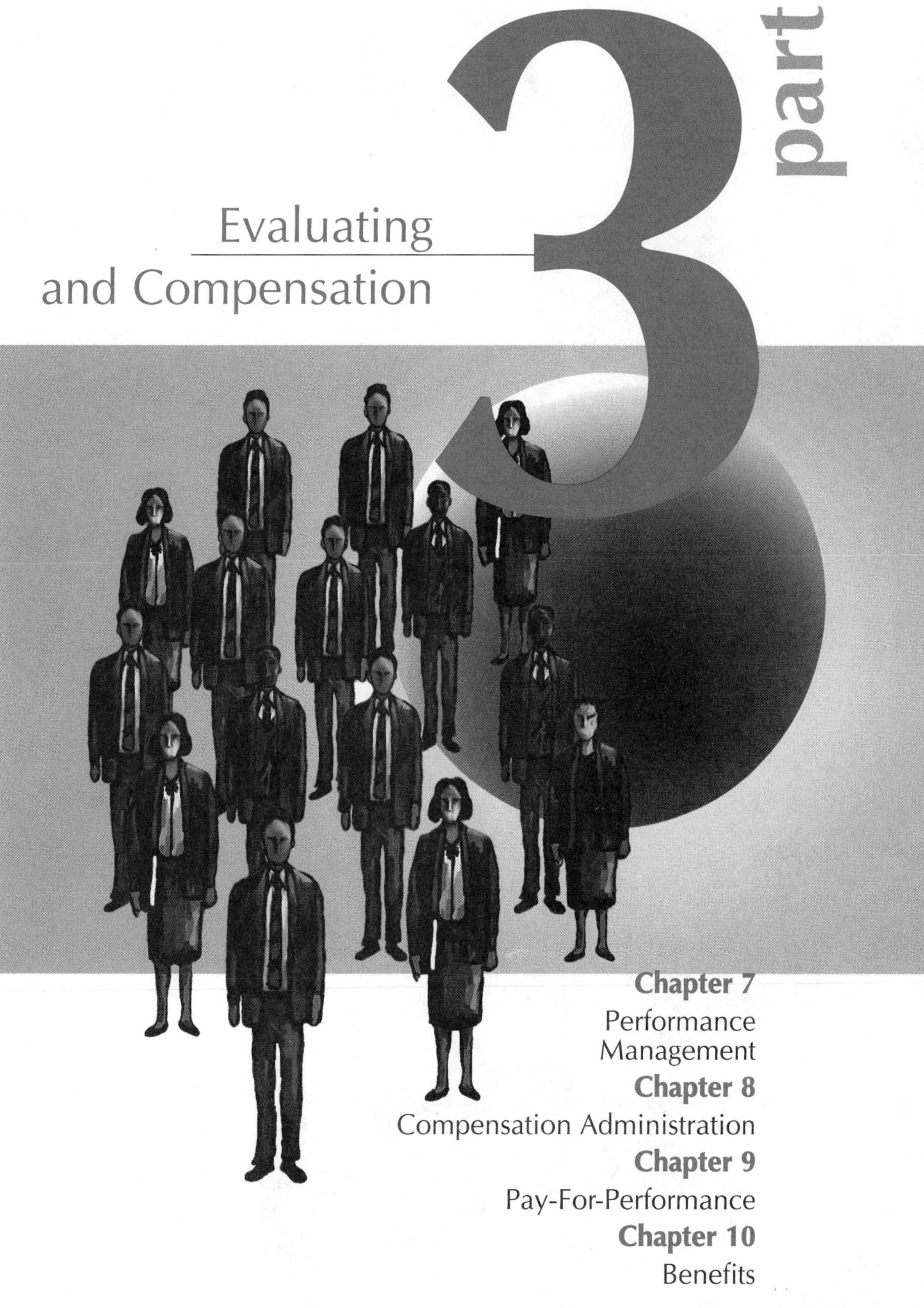

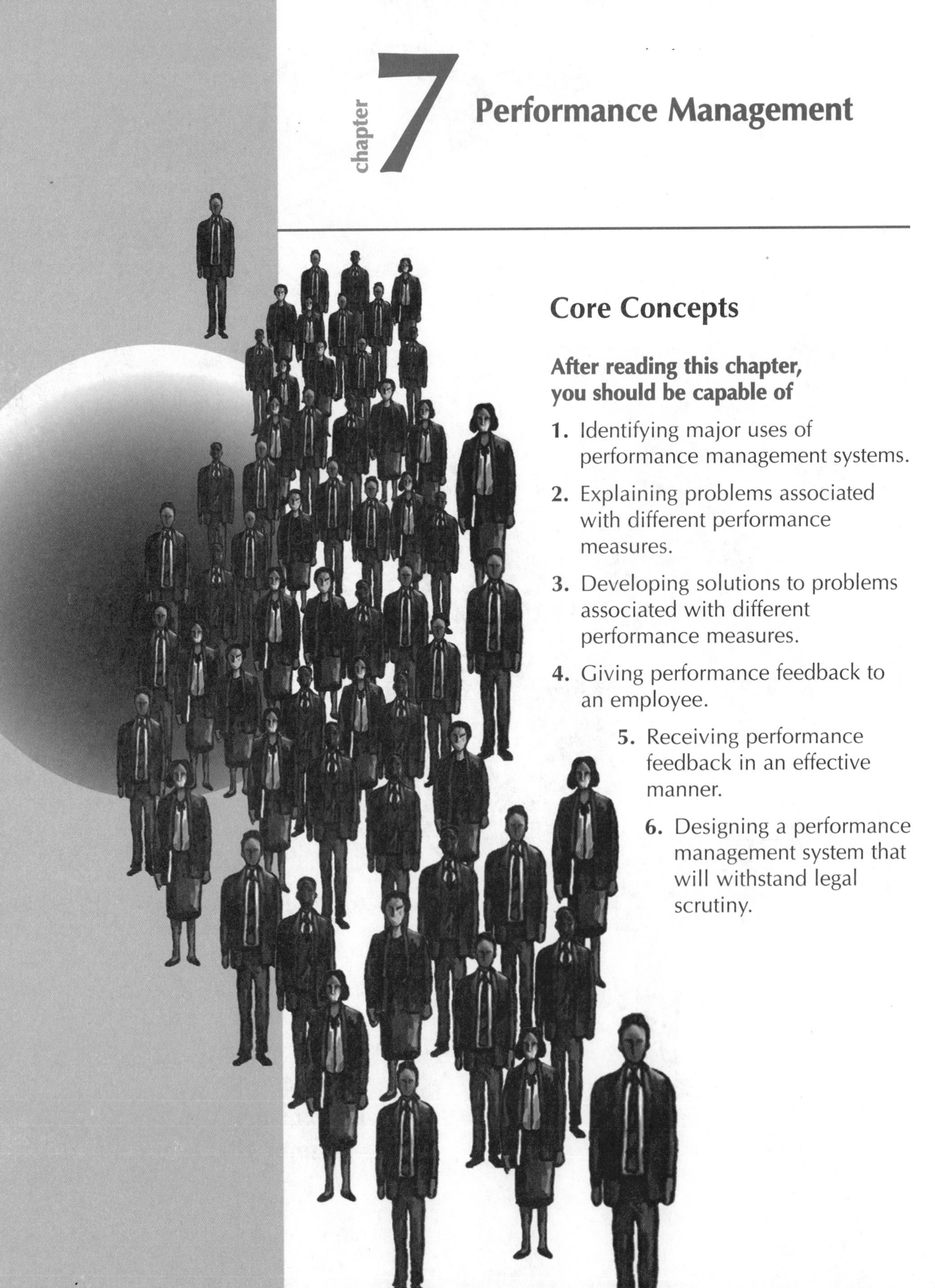

chapter 7 Performance Management

Core Concepts

After reading this chapter, you should be capable of

1. Identifying major uses of performance management systems.
2. Explaining problems associated with different performance measures.
3. Developing solutions to problems associated with different performance measures.
4. Giving performance feedback to an employee.
5. Receiving performance feedback in an effective manner.
6. Designing a performance management system that will withstand legal scrutiny.

Opening Case

Nicholas has been working as an inventory specialist at Runners' Gear, a company that designs and manufactures jogging apparel and equipment, for almost three years. Although he has worked there longer than many others, Nicholas has never been given much feedback about his work. He finds this particularly frustrating because he has always sought feedback from others. As far as he can guess, his performance must be at least adequate, because he has not been fired or demoted. In addition, his pay raises seem to be about what other employees are getting, assuming the office gossip is correct.

So far, the few formal performance appraisal meetings Nicholas has had have been practically fruitless. On all three occasions, his manager began by showing him the rating form (see Figure 7.1). Each time, Nicholas had been rated as being "average" on all aspects of performance. Although there was room for written comments, each time the manager had written: "Employee performs satisfactorily." Near the bottom of the page was an area for the employee's signature, indicating that he or she had seen the ratings. After showing Nicholas the form, the manager inevitably said, "You seem to have done a satisfactory job during the last year. Do you have any questions?" Nicholas would have liked to ask for some more specific feedback, but from the tone of the manager's voice, Nicholas could tell that his manager was thinking about other things he had to do and was hoping that Nicholas would simply say no.

What concerns Nicholas the most about the performance appraisals is his feeling that the ratings do affect promotions. Although no one has actually told him this, Nicholas also feels that if there were any layoffs, the performance ratings might be used to make decisions. Even though Nicholas' ratings have always been satisfactory, he is certain that some employees are getting higher ratings.

Nicholas also receives practically no informal feedback. Occasionally, after a particularly tough project is completed, his manager has said "nice work." The time when he received the most feedback was when he turned in a managerial report that apparently had not been well received by the department vice president. In that case, Nicholas' manager provided written comments about the report, and talked about his concerns for almost twenty minutes. Although the feedback was negative, he was glad to get some helpful input. As a result, Nicholas attended a ten-week writing program and a one-day seminar on multimedia presentations, both of which he felt would be helpful for his career.

Given all of the shortcomings that Nicholas indicated, why would Runners' Gear bother to maintain a performance management system? If the company wants to continue to have a performance management system, isn't there a better approach than the one used? Further, why does the manager seem so reluctant to give Nicholas feedback? If you were in Nicholas' place, how would you go about getting more feedback? This chapter will discuss performance management systems. Performance management refers to those activities that measure job performance and provide feedback to employees about their performances. This chapter will discuss why organizations use performance ratings, how organizations assess employee performance, the problems associated with performance ratings, and how organizations attempt to overcome these problems. You will also read about difficulties associated with giving and receiving feedback, and you will look at some solutions to these issues. As you will see, performance management systems play an important role in organizations; perhaps because of their importance, they produce a great deal of anxiety and concern for both managers and employees alike. We begin first with a discussion of why organizations have performance management systems.

Figure 7.1 A Performance Appraisal Form

Employee's Name: Nicholas Rozincksi
For each dimension, mark a number from 1–5, where 1 means poor, 2 means below average, 3 means average, 4 means above average, and 5 means outstanding. Provide written comments to support each rating.

A. Quality of work _3_ Comments:
B. Quantity of work _3_ Comments:
C. Customer service _3_ Comments:
D. Initiative _3_ Comments:
E. Leadership potential _3_ Comments:
F. Attendance _3_ Comments:
G. Overall _3_ Comments:

Additional Comments: *Employee performs satisfactorily.*

I have seen my performance ratings ____________________ (employee signature)

Performance Management: Organizational Uses

Organizations use performance management systems for four basic purposes:[1]

1. Human resource decisions, such as pay increases, promotions, and terminations.
2. Feedback to and development of employees.
3. Design and evaluation of various human resource systems, such as company training programs and human resource planning.
4. Documentation of personnel decisions.

Because all of these purposes are important, effective performance management systems take considerable time and effort to develop and operate. We now turn to a discussion of performance measures and the shortcomings associated with them.

Performance Measures: Objective and Subjective Approaches

There are many different measures of individual job performance. Generally these can be divided into two groups: objective measures and subjective measures. Although objective measures may seem as though they would be the best, they often have serious limitations.

Objective Performance Measures

For certain jobs, objective measures of performance, such as sales, units produced, or papers published, do exist. What about your current job? Are there objective measures of your performance? Certain occupations, such as those in production and sales, lend themselves to objective measures of performance. But if you have ever worked in these fields, you are probably aware that these seemingly objective measures often fail to accurately reflect an individual's performance. Consider, for example, a sales job. Although most sales organizations use an index such as sales volume or number of sales per unit time, other factors often play a role. In any given location, sales may be affected by the local economy, the nature of the businesses in the area, and so on. To take such differences into account, organizations often include a market potential factor in assessing an individual's performance. But the market potential is based on various subjective judgments, which may have shortcomings. Further, the sales volume or the number of sales is separate from the identification of new customers and the maintenance of relationships with existing customers. Even though the identification of new customers and the maintenance of existing customers may be difficult to measure in any objective way, they may be extremely important aspects of the job. In short, despite their apparent objectivity, measures such as sales volume and units produced may have serious shortcomings.[2]

Subjective Performance Measures

For many jobs, there simply is no objective measure of job performance. Particularly in the knowledge-based, service-oriented business world of today, relatively few employees produce a tangible, quantifiable product or service. Instead, they are generating knowledge, handling customer complaints, or various other intangibles. Or, in the case of an individual production worker, performance is affected by factors such as the machinery and other employees, over which he or she has no control. In these and many other cases, organizations must rely on subjective judgments of an employee's performance, usually made by the employee's supervisor. It is not surprising, then, that almost all organizations rely on subjective ratings to at least some extent. Despite their popularity, subjective performance ratings are also vulnerable to a myriad of problems. Next, you will read about these problems and some solutions to them.

Problems with Subjective Performance Appraisals

The problems inherent in performance appraisals can be divided into four categories: judgment errors, poor appraisal forms, lack of rater preparedness, and ineffective organizational policies/practices.

Judgment Errors

People are notoriously poor judges and decision makers, and we are subject to many biases and "judgment errors."[3]

Judgment errors
Errors made due to poor judgment, poor decision making, and biases.

1. Halo. The "halo" error occurs when one aspect of the subordinate's performance affects the rater's evaluation of other performance dimensions. An employee with highly effective interpersonal skills, for example, may be rated higher on other performance dimensions, such as written communication skills, than is appropriate. Conversely, an employee with poor interpersonal skills may be rated lower on other performance dimensions than he or she deserves.[4]

Halo
This error occurs when one aspect of the subordinate's performance affects the rater's evaluation of other performance dimensions.

Leniency
Many raters give higher performance evaluations than deserved, a practice often created by organizational policies and practices.

Severity
A bias in the opposite direction, in which a supervisor has a tendency to rate too harsly.

Central tendency
An alternative to the leniency effect where raters rate practically all employees about average.

2. Leniency/Severity. Many raters routinely give higher performance evaluations than are deserved. If the rating scale ranges from 1 to 5, with 5 being highest, it is not uncommon for 90 percent or more of the employees to be rated either a 4 or 5. This error, referred to as the "leniency" effect, is often created by organizational policies and practices, as is described later. The "severity" effect refers to a bias in the other direction, in which a supervisor has a tendency to rate too harshly.
3. Central Tendency. An alternative to the leniency effect is the central tendency, which occurs when raters rate practically all employees about average. This way, the manager "plays it safe" because all employees are rated the same.
4. Fallible Memory. What were you doing yesterday at this time? What were you doing a week ago at this time? For most of us, including supervisors, our memories tend to focus only on the most important issues and concerns. We usually forget the details of any situation. When asked to recall the minor (or perhaps even major) details, we may fill in the missing gaps based on how we think things ought to be. For example, if someone asked you today what you ate while watching television two months ago, you might say "potato chips," if that is what you generally eat while watching television, even though you had actually eaten popcorn that time. The same thing tends to happen to managers and supervisors when they are asked to rate a subordinate's performance. Moreover, managers and supervisors tend to remember more recent behaviors and results (known as the recency effect) and therefore more recent events generally have a greater effect on performance ratings. If your performance is going to be rated soon, it may be in your best interests to perform particularly well in the time frame prior to the performance appraisal.
5. First Impressions. Almost everyone has experienced a first impression of someone, whereby your subsequent interactions with this person were affected by things he or she said or did when you initially met. In the performance appraisal context, a manager may have a first impression (or primacy effect) that biases his or her evaluation of all subsequent behavior. In the case of a negative primacy effect, the employee may seem to do nothing right; in the case of a positive primacy effect, the employee can do no wrong.
6. Affect. Both the rater's general mood and his or her liking or disliking of the employee can affect the performance rating. In terms of general mood, a person who is in a bad mood often rates more harshly than someone in a good mood. There is also evidence that someone in a bad mood will give good performers even higher ratings than they deserve. In terms of your manager's liking for you, not surprisingly, your ratings are likely to be higher if your manager likes you and lower if he or she does not like you.[5]

Poor Appraisal Forms

As you will see in a later section, many types of appraisal forms are available. Some of these forms are more useful than others, but to a large degree, the best form will depend on the situation. Many appraisal forms, however, suffer from the following problems:[6]

1. Ambiguity. The scales may be quite vague and unclear. As an example, ask three people how they define leadership. You are likely to get three different answers as to what leadership is and what an effective leader does.

Ambiguity
The rating scales are vague or unclear.

2. Deficiency. Sometimes a performance appraisal form is missing key aspects of job performance. As you will see near the end of the chapter, one organization almost lost a lawsuit because only a few aspects of job performance were included on the rating form.

Deficiency
When a performance appraisal form is missing key aspects of job performance.

3. Contamination. On occasion, a rating form may have additional, irrelevant performance dimensions. Particularly in today's legal environment, where companies must be sure to include only job-related criteria in making personnel decisions, extraneous considerations are problematic.

Contamination
When a rating form has additional, irrelevant performance dimensions that may contaminate the performance appraisal.

4. Complexity. If the rating forms are too long and complex, managers may choose to either not fill them out or to complete them in a haphazard fashion.

Lack of Rater Preparedness

Managers and supervisors may be unprepared to conduct performance appraisals. Lack of preparedness can come about in several ways:[7]

1. Low Self-Confidence. Some raters feel thay are not competent to engage in performance management activities and therefore are reluctant to participate. Managers who have low self-confidence in this area will be particularly reluctant to give negative feedback.
2. Limited Familiarity. Particularly in today's workplace, where there are far fewer managers and supervisors than ever before, many raters have limited knowledge of how their subordinates are performing. If you work in a highly technical field, for example, you may report to an individual who has little more than a cursory understanding of your work. Your manager or supervisor therefore may have little knowledge as to your performance. It is therefore often incumbent upon you, the employee, to keep accurate records of your performance and achievements.
3. Lack of Time. Given that managers often have many responsibilities and subordinates, they may lack the time to gather sufficient information and to conduct thorough feedback sessions.

Ineffective Organizational Policies and Practices

Many of the problems with subjective performance appraisals are due to ineffective organizational policies and practices, which undermine performance management activities. Key issues here include the following:[8]

1. Lack of Rewards. What motivation does your supervisor have to conduct thorough and careful performance appraisals? In many organizations, there are few, if any, rewards for this activity. Given their many other responsibilities, then, doing performance appraisals may have very low priority for managers and supervisors. Recall that in the opening case, Nicholas' manager seemed unwilling to spend much, if any, time giving feedback. Do you think that manager was rewarded for doing performance appraisals? Probably not. Most organizations

offer few, if any, tangible rewards, such as pay raises, that are directly attached to performance management activities.

2. Norms Supporting Leniency. Rather than rewards for doing thorough and accurate performance appraisals, informal norms often penalize supervisors for giving low ratings. Low ratings may be viewed as a sign of managerial failure or as promoting employee discontent. As a result, most employees receive satisfactory ratings, even if they don't deserve them.

3. Lack of Appropriate Accountability. Although in most companies the rater's immediate supervisor must approve the ratings, the ratings are rarely challenged. As a result, the rater has little incentive to make accurate ratings, especially when subordinates are likely to become upset with low ratings.

Box 7.1 Performance Management Practices in the Pacific Rim

Contrary to what you might think, performance appraisal practices in Pacific Rim countries differ substantially from one another. Take Singapore and Hong Kong, for example. In an effort to bolster productivity, both of these countries emphasize the importance of performance appraisals, and like the United States, utilize the reviews for both HRM decisions and developmental feedback. The performance management systems in these countries are often more sophisticated than those found in some U.S. firms. The Fraser Neave and Malayan Brewery Company, headquartered in Singapore, uses a self-appraisal system, which the employee completes at least three days prior to the formal meeting. The self-appraisal form includes such questions as "What are the most important things you have achieved in the last twelve months?" and "In what way would you like to see your career develop within the next three years?" The Sime Darby company in Singapore uses performance appraisal forms that are geared toward the specific job. The dimensions on the form are behaviorally defined so that it is clear what high and low performance on each dimension represents. Goals are set for all areas of performance. Managers receive four hours of training in giving performance feedback, as well as training on how to avoid common human judgment errors. Like the United States, however, most companies in Hong Kong and Singapore use graphic scales, and most small companies have no mechanism for formal performance appraisals. As Yip Yu Bun, owner of a small company in Hong Kong observed, "My 40 employees have worked too long with one another to need a formal appraisal. We know each other extremely well."

Japan has traditionally taken a much different approach to performance appraisals than the United States has. The typical system used until very recently in Japan focused on personality factors, especially cooperation, and the ability to perform different jobs within the individual's work group. Both of these emphases are in keeping with the Japanese team culture. More recently, however, with Japan's changing economy as well as the increasing Westernization of its culture, there has been an increasing emphasis on individual job performance. Even here, however, there is a difference from many Western approaches—and indeed the approaches taken in other Pacific Rim countries—in that measures of individual job performance often take into account employee effort as well as achievement. In recent times, many Japanese companies have begun incorporating such measures into salary raise decisions.

Source: Adapted from G. Latham and N. Napier, "Chinese Human Resource Management Practices in Hong Kong and Singapore: An Exploratory Study, in *Research in Personnel/Human Resources Management* (Supplement 1; International Human Resources Management), ed. A. Nedd, G. Ferris, and K. Rowland (Greenwich, CT: JAI Press, 1989), 173–99; M.A. Von Glinow and B.J. Chung, "Comparative Human Resource Management Practices in the United States, Japan, Korea, and the People's Republic of China," in *Research in Personnel/Human Resources Management* (Supplement 1; International Human Resources Management), A. Nedd, G. Ferris, and K. Rowland (Greenwich, CT: JAI Press, 1989), 153–71; and T. Mroczkowski and M. Hanaoka, "Continuity and Change in Japanese Management, "*California Management Review* 31 (1989), 39–53.

Solutions to Performance Appraisal Problems

Because subjective performance ratings are very popular, organizations have applied a variety of tactics to reduce the problems just described.

Provide Training to Raters

To increase raters' self-confidence and reduce judgment errors, many companies train raters on how to conduct more effective performance appraisals. Effective training programs include help in understanding how to use the forms, how to give feedback, and so forth.[9]

Involve Users in the Development of Rating Forms

To make the rating forms more usable, some organizations have users participate in their development. In fact, some of the forms described later, such as the BARS, rely heavily on input from managers and supervisors. By being involved in their development, users will be more committed to the final product.[10]

Educate Managers on the Importance of Performance Appraisals

It is important to explain to managers *why* accurate ratings and thorough feedback are important. For example, managers must be persuaded that effective performance appraisals will improve their department's performance. Moreover, managers must be convinced that by giving the best performers the highest ratings, employees who are working hard will be motivated to continue. By the same token, managers must be informed that legal requirements (discussed later in greater detail) dictate that poorly performing employees must be given specific feedback and correspondingly low ratings.

Reward Managers for Performance Appraisals

Managers must be rewarded for conducting effective performance appraisals. At General Electric, for example, managers are held responsible for the development of their subordinates, which includes providing effective feedback. General Electric uses several mechanisms for monitoring a subordinate's development, including the independent evaluations of subordinates and tracking a subordinate's performance as he or she moves to different positions. Because subordinate development affects bonuses, a financial incentive is attached to performance management activities.[11]

Choose Appropriate Raters

Although most organizations involve only the employee's immediate supervisor in the performance evaluation, some organizations have begun to use other raters. In organizations that use teams, for example, coworkers may be the primary source of performance appraisals (see Box 7.2 for an example). Some organizations seek input from customers as well, much as universities and colleges obtain student evaluations of their instructors. Many companies have recently begun using a technique referred to as 360-degree feedback. A 360-degree feedback program involves a variety of different parties, including subordinates, completing performance appraisals.

360-degree feedback Information is gathered from a variety of sources, including subordinates who complete performance appraisals, then the results are summarized for the employee and areas needing improvement are discussed.

Box 7.2 How DEC Does Team Performance Appraisals

Tales from the Trenches

At Digital Equipment Corporation (DEC) in Colorado Springs, Colorado, manufacturing employees are organized into teams. Each team consists of about 40 members and one "consultant," who is responsible for facilitating and coordinating the team. Because there is very little direct supervision, team members provide performance evaluations for one another. The process of performance appraisal is as follows:

1. The team member, or "ratee," is notified that his or her performance appraisal is becoming due. The team member chooses a chairperson, generally another team member. The committee that will do the performance appraisal includes the ratee, the chairperson, the consultant and two other coworkers randomly chosen from the team.
2. The ratee prepares an outline of his or her achievements for the year. The committee collects additional information, which is provided to the ratee. The ratee then prepares a performance appraisal document based on all of the information.
3. The document is then given to the committee for review. The committee meets with the ratee, provides a formal rating, and sets goals with the ratee for the coming year. The chairperson provides a written summary of the meeting, which is then reviewed by the committee. The final document is sent to the human resources department.

This system has numerous advantages. First, multiple opinions are sought, so the ratee is not at the mercy of one person, who may have a personal bias. Second, the individuals who are most familiar with the employee's work have input. Third, the responsibility for getting the performance appraisal done is on the ratee's shoulders, so it is rarely late. The process also requires extensive participation by the ratee, which increases his or her commitment to the performance appraisal.

Of course, the system has several disadvantages as well. First, the process is very time-consuming. Because many parties are involved, team members spend considerable time in performance appraisals. Second, some employees are uncomfortable rating others. Third, internal team competition can bias coworkers' ratings. Clearly, this system will not work in all organizations.

Source: Adapted from C.A. Norman and R. Zawacki, "Team Appraisals—Team Approach," *Personnel Journal* 70 (1991) 101–4.

Results are summarized for the employee, and areas needing improvement are discussed. A distinct advantage of this procedure is that information is gathered from a variety of sources, providing a complete picture of one's performance.[12]

Even if your company only uses supervisors to give performance ratings, you might consider soliciting feedback from other sources on an informal basis. For example, the employee in the opening case might have sought feedback from other department managers or perhaps other coworkers.

Rating Forms

Due to the popularity of subjective performance ratings, many different types of rating scales have been designed. We will divide them into four categories:

1. Comparative approaches.
2. Graphic scales.
3. Behaviorally based scales.
4. Management-by-objectives.

Each of these is described in greater detail next.[13]

Comparative Approaches

Comparative approaches require the rater to compare each employee to the other employees. Practically everyone has heard of this type of approach in a school setting—the infamous bell-shaped curve that is particularly common in freshman and sophomore college courses is an example of the comparative approach. If you were in a class that used the bell-shaped curve, it meant that a certain percentage of the class would receive Fs, a certain percentage would receive Ds, and so on. Some companies use this type of approach for performance appraisals as well. In a **forced distribution,** a certain fixed percentage of employees must be given the highest rating, a certain percentage the next highest rating, and so forth. An even simpler procedure, the **rank order** method, merely requires the manager to rank order his or her employees from best to worst. The comparative approach has both advantages and disadvantages. The basic advantages include the fact that these systems force managers to assign low ratings or rankings to some employees. As you read earlier, managers are often too lenient in their ratings of employees. Use of comparative rating forms is one way to circumvent this problem. A second advantage is their basic simplicity and ease with which they are developed. The comparative approach has numerous disadvantages as well. A chief disadvantage is that this method tends to produce resentment and bickering among the employees and supervisors, and it makes comparisons between different departments difficult if not impossible. Another disadvantage is that the comparative approach usually provides little concrete information on which to make the comparisons. In terms of providing feedback to employees, then, this method is generally of limited use.

Comparative approaches Rating forms that require the rater to compare each employee to the other employees, also known as the bell-shaped curve that is particularly common in freshman and sophomore college courses.

Graphic Scales

A graphic scale is a type of form that has uses broad, relatively ambiguous work dimensions, such as quality, leadership, and reliability. As shown in Figure 7.2, many types of graphic scales are available. The major advantage of graphic scales is the ease in developing and using them. You could quickly and easily design four or five graphic scales—such as scales that rate quality of work, quantity of work, managerial effectiveness, and attendance—to rate all the employees in your company. Because the same scales could be used for nearly all jobs, comparisons between different departments, and even employees in different jobs, could be easily made. Given these advantages, it is not surprising that graphic scales are the most commonly used form.[14] These scales also have some potentially serious shortcomings. Due to the ambiguous nature of the scales, different supervisors may ascribe quite different meanings to the dimensions and may have different standards for what average, poor, and good performance is. These scales tend to be less useful for feedback purposes as well, because they do not specify what good, average, and poor performance entails.[15]

Graphic scales A type of performance evaluation form that uses broad, relatively ambiguous work dimensions, such as quality, leadership, and reliability.

Figure 7.2 **A Graphic Scale**

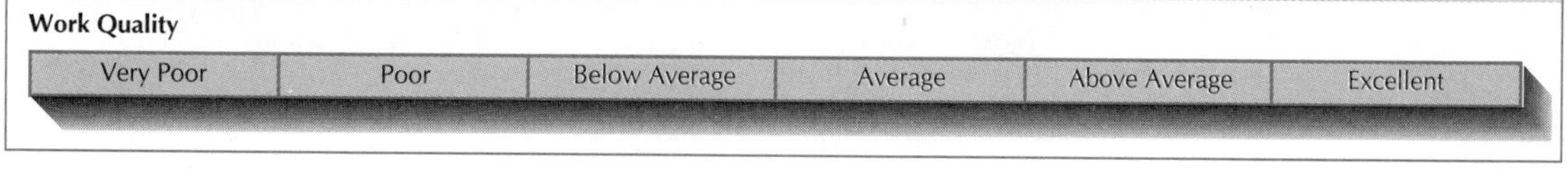

Work Quality

Very Poor	Poor	Below Average	Average	Above Average	Excellent

Behaviorally Based Scales

Behaviorally based scales
Developed as a response to the shortcomings of the graphic scale approach, the behaviorally based scale provides a set of scales that are defined in a precise, behavioral fashion.

Behaviorally Anchored Rating Scales
A rating system that defines the dimension and organizational skills in terms of behavior, and where the points on the scale are defined, or anchored, in behavioral terms.

Behavior Observation Scales
A behaviorally based approach that has the rater evaluate the frequency with which the employee engages in various behaviors.

Behaviorally based scales were developed as a response to the shortcomings of the graphic scale approach described above. The major aim of behaviorally based scales is to provide a set of scales that is defined in a precise, behavioral fashion. As an example, consider Figure 7.3, which displays a behaviorally anchored rating scale, or BARS. Note that the organizational skills dimension is defined in terms of behaviors. In addition, several points on the scale are defined, or anchored, in behavioral terms. For example, the instructor who is rated a 9 would be one who assimilates the present lecture into the previous one, an instructor rated somewhere between a 1 and a 2 would be one who spends a great deal of time talking about irrelevant topics. Raters should have a much clearer idea as to what is meant by good, average, and poor performance, which in turn should reduce differences caused by raters using different definitions and standards.[16]

There are several different behaviorally based approaches besides the BARS. With behavior observation scales (or BOS), the rater evaluates the frequency with which the employee engages in various behaviors. An overall rating for each dimension is obtained by adding the points assigned to each of the items that fall under that dimension. An example of the BOS form is provided in Table 7.1. If you

Figure 7.3 BARS Scale for a College Professor

9	Professor assimilates previous lecture into present one before beginning.
8	
7	
6	Professor announces at end of class the material that will be covered in next class.
5	
4	
3	Professor is sidetracked during lecture and does not cover much of the intended material.
2	
1	Professor lectures about irrelevant subjects.

Table 7.1 BOS Scale for College Professor

Rate how often the professor engages in each of these behaviors using the following scale (1 = never; 2 = occasionally; 3 = sometimes; 4 = often; 5 = all of the time):

1. Professor assimilates previous lecture into present one before beginning.
2. Professor announces at end of class the material that will be covered in next class.
3. Professor is sidetracked during lecture and does not cover much of the intended material.
4. Professor lectures about irrelevant subjects.

examine Table 7.1, you will see that the items are nearly identical to the behavioral anchors in the BARS scale in Figure 7.3.[17]

The major advantage of the behaviorally based approach is that the scales are more specific and less ambiguous. In turn, this should result in greater equivalence in the ratings of different supervisors. In practice, however, there is little evidence that behaviorally based ratings produce more accurate, or better, ratings than other approaches. That is, supervisors appear to assign the same ratings, regardless of the specific form used. On the other hand, behaviorally based scales should facilitate feedback to the ratees, because they force the supervisor to be more specific. Similarly, such scales should increase communication between subordinates and supervisors, because expectations and job requirements are more clearly delineated. On the negative side, the development of behaviorally based scales is much more time-consuming than the other forms discussed so far. And, because different scales and standards will exist for different jobs, it may become more difficult to compare employees with different jobs than it is when graphic scales are used.[18]

Management-by-Objectives

Management-by-objectives (MBO) was popularized in the 1970s as a means of removing much of the subjectivity in performance appraisals. Essentially, this form uses clearly defined objectives or goals and a specified time frame in which they will be reached. For example, a salesperson may have a goal of increasing sales volume by 20 percent within 9 months, as well as visiting 15 new customers and revisiting 200 previous customers. In many cases, the objectives are established by a joint planning session involving both the subordinate and the supervisor. The MBO approach aims to minimize the subjective judgments associated with other

Management-by-objectives
An evaluation system that uses clearly defined objectives or goals, with a specified time frame in which they will be reached.

When an employee sits down with his or her manager to establish performance goals, the open communication leads to more clearly defined objectives or goals with an established time frame in which they will be reached.

forms. Because the objectives are clearly defined and have a specified time frame, it should be clear to any observer at the end of the time period whether or not the goals were met. Moreover, the form encourages extensive participation by the employee, which should increase employee commitment to the objectives.

The MBO method was particularly popular for managerial and professional employees, who have considerable control over the objectives to be achieved and the specific behaviors needed to succeed are often ambiguous. Research shows that use of an MBO program can greatly increase productivity, particularly if top management actively supports and participates in the program.[19] Despite its potential advantages, MBO programs have several weaknesses.[20] One weakness is that different objectives may be set for different individuals doing the same job. Therefore, MBO probably would not be appropriate for determining promotions or pay raises. Second, the objectives may be set too low. Third, use of MBO tends to encourage short-term objectives that are simple to quantify, when in fact a longer-term perspective with more qualitative goals may be appropriate. Nonetheless, with proper modifications, MBO may be an important component in a performance management system. For example, by combining behaviorally based scales with an MBO approach, a complete performance management system might be developed.[21]

In conclusion, measuring job performance is a complex undertaking. Although there are both objective and subjective methods for measuring job performance, there is no one perfect method. As difficult as obtaining accurate measures of performance is, providing effective performance feedback is typically even more challenging. The next section provides some insight into why managers and subordinates generally dislike performance reviews. Following that, suggestions for both receiving feedback and giving feedback are offered. The chapter concludes with some guidelines for maintaining a legally sound performance management system.

Performance Feedback: Why Is It So Difficult?

While it may be difficult to obtain accurate measures of job performance, giving performance feedback poses an even great difficulty for many managers and supervisors. As one expert stated it, providing performance feedback is like approaching someone and saying "Here's what I think of your baby."[22] Recall that the manager in the opening case seemed to have no interest in giving feedback. Some possible reasons were already mentioned for this, including the lack of any rewards. It is also possible that the manager was uncomfortable at the mere thought of giving feedback. Why is giving feedback such an uncomfortable task for most managers? If you examine Figure 7.4, you will see that for both the supervisor and the employee, the performance feedback context contains certain inherent conflicts. Recall that from the supervisor's perspective, performance appraisals serve several major purposes, including helping the supervisor to make HRM decisions and develop employees. A manager may experience conflict between his or her role in developing an employee and the need to reprimand the employee for poor performance. From the employee's perspective, there is conflict in receiving performance feedback as well. On the one hand, most people do desire feedback about how they are doing. However, this desire may conflict with the need to maintain

Box 7.3 How Would You Feel If Your Boss Always Stood over Your Shoulder?

Consider, for a moment, Marie, who worked as a bill collector over the telephone (making $10 an hour) for a book publisher in Philadelphia. Although Marie likes her duties and her company, she has suffered from a nervous breakdown and sometimes cries about her work. Why? According to Marie, it's because of her boss standing over her shoulder. Her boss doesn't actually stand over her shoulder; rather, at any time without forewarning, her supervisor can listen in on her phone conversations. Throughout the day, a computer records the number of work-related calls and the length of each call she makes. In turn, the information recorded by the computer is used to generate a performance score, which is then posted for all employees to see.

Do you think Marie's company is an exception? If you answered no, you are right. It has been estimated that as many as 26 million employees are monitored through some kind of electronic device. Electronic monitoring may involve videotaping and listening in on phone calls, as well as other procedures. Take Blue Cross and Blue Shield of Missouri, for example. According to company spokespeople, employees are told before being hired that customer service calls at this company are monitored on a random basis, and employees are given immediate feedback about their performance.

As you probably could tell from Marie's story, some employees and their representatives resent electronic monitoring. Ben Turn, a union official, asserts that electronic monitoring increases employee stress and compromises the confidentiality of customer phone conversations. Many workers feel electronic monitoring is used against them. One employee, for example, said, "You can get a biased manager who is looking for the bad, rather than the good, in someone."

Not surprisingly, executives tend to support the use of electronic monitoring. For example, one senior executive said, "It has value inasmuch as it keeps employees on their toes. The more they are monitored, the more they realize there's a cop around the bend." The senior manager of the Tax Collection Division of the United States Internal Revenue Service put it this way:

> I think monitoring is absolutely vital. (1) Documentation of monitoring is the only method to ensure that you're telling the taxpayer the right information; (2) it's the only way that a manager can tell if an employee is using the techniques; and (3) it's important for the employee's positive and critical feedback, to develop the employee.

Interestingly, supervisors who use electronic monitoring may be less positive than senior executives. One supervisor, for example, noted that monitoring just ends up being negative management. Another supervisor disliked monitoring because "it takes so much time." On the other hand, supervisors tend to like the opportunity to give feedback and the ability to reward the workers who are doing a good job.

But even among those you might assume are opposed to electronic monitoring, namely, the employees who are monitored, not all reactions are negative. As one worker put it:

> We have to have monitoring. I'm sure we don't like to have it done to us all the time, but it's necessary for quality control and as a check on new procedures. It increases performance. I know when I get comments that say you forgot to do something, I try to do it the next time.

The limited scientific research that has been done on the effects of electronic monitoring suggest that its adverse effects can be reduced to the extent that the monitoring is tied to effective performance feedback. That is, when the monitoring is used for development purposes, employees' reactions are relatively positive, as indicated by the previous quote. At the same time, this research suggests that some employees have a negative predisposition toward monitoring which cannot be easily changed.

Currently, Congress is considering legislation to restrict the extent to which electronic monitoring can be used in the workplace. Given the popularity of electronic monitoring and the diversity of responses to this practice, the final outcome of this legislation will be interesting to observe.

Source: Adapted from J. Chalykoff and T. Kochan, "Computer-aided Monitoring: Its Influence on Employee Job Satisfaction and Turnover," *Personnel Psychology* 42 (1989), 807–34; L. Kabada, "The Unblinking Boss," *St. Louis Post-Dispatch,* February 2, 1994, F1; and S.A. Wood, "Monitoring Widespread in St. Louis," *St. Louis Post-Dispatch,* February 2, 1994, F1.

Figure 7.4 **Conflicts in Performance Management**

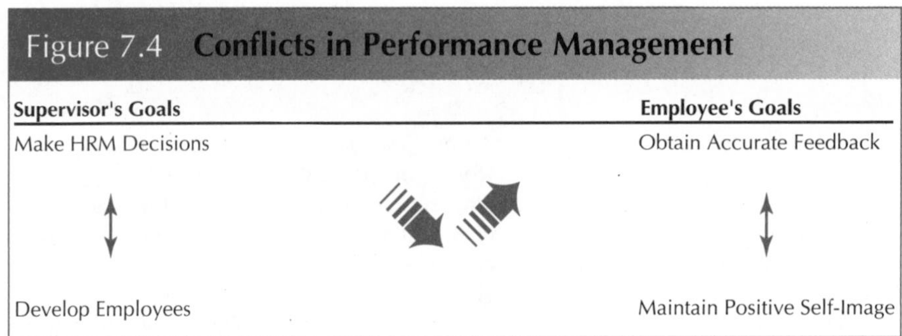

Source: Adapted from M. Beer, "Performance Appraisal: Dilemmas and Possibilities," *Organizational Dynamics* 27 (1981). 24–36.

positive self-esteem. Most employees, then, look forward to getting positive feedback but often dread the negative feedback they may hear. Coupled with the fact that many managers are not well prepared to give effective feedback, it is hardly surprising that conducting a performance feedback session is considered one of the most dreaded managerial tasks. In many cases, employees receive little constructive feedback and leave the feedback session even more confused than before. Moreoever, employees often perceive their supervisors more negatively after the feedback session than they did before the session. The situation described in the opening case, then, is certainly not unusual.[23]

Now that you have read about some reasons as to why the feedback process is often difficult for both parties, you will learn some strategies for improving these sessions. First, we will discuss what managers and supervisors can do to increase the effectiveness of the feedback process, and then we will examine some suggestions for employees preparing to receive feedback.

Handling Performance Reviews: The Managerial Perspective

This section provides guidelines for supervisors and managers conducting feedback reviews. You will read first about some general suggestions, followed by specific steps for giving feedback.

General Suggestions for Conducting Feedback Reviews

1. Distinguish between Formal and Informal Feedback Sessions. Effective managers use informal feedback sessions on an "as needed" basis. The primary purpose of an informal feedback session is to help a subordinate who is having performance problems. Most organizations also require the manager to meet with his or her subordinates once a year in a more formal manner to review their performances. As a manager, you should use the annual, formal session as an opportunity to summarize the employee's performance for the year, set goals for the next year, and discuss any general issues or concerns. If done

properly, there should be no unpleasant surprises for the employee in this meeting.[24]

2. Focus on Behavioral Examples. In giving performance feedback, be sure to use specific, behaviorally based examples of the employee's performance. Criticizing employees in terms of their personality traits or attitudes has two disadvantages. To understand this, imagine that someone told you that you were lazy. How would you feel? Compare that to someone saying that you completed your orders a day later than most of the other employees. How would you feel then? Do you see the difference? In the first approach, you probably took the criticism as a kind of personal attack. The latter approach was not an attack on you; it was a criticism of your *behavior.* In all likelihood, you would take the latter statement far less personally. Perhaps just as importantly, if someone tells you that you are lazy, it may not be at all clear to you why you are getting this feedback and what you need to change. If you were told that your orders are later than most of your coworkers, you would have a far better idea of what to change. Whenever you give feedback, it is critical to state the negatives, as well as the positives, using specific, behavioral examples.[25]

3. Seek the Employee's Input. No matter what the focus of the performance review session, it is critical for the manager to obtain input from the employee. There are several reasons for this, but two stand out. First, in today's workplace, most employees actively seek to participate in a variety of ways. Active participation in the performance review session is viewed by many employees as important. Second, active participation will help build commitment to the results of the review session. An effective manager is able to provide many participation opportunities during the feedback session.[26]

4. Carefully Plan the Feedback Session. As with any business activity, you should plan carefully and determine an agenda before the session. Be sure to obtain as much information about the person you are evaluating as possible. Consider what questions, issues, or even challenges he or she might raise. Of course, be sure to provide sufficient time and opportunity to address any issues your subordinate may bring up. Sometimes, particularly when there are many issues to discuss, it may be best to schedule a second or even third meeting.[27]

5. Use Effective Communication Skills During the Feedback Session. Good communication skills are essential to an effective review session. Given the discomfort and awkwardness typically felt by both the appraiser and the ratee, it is critical that both parties fully understand what has been said. One way to do this is to make frequent use of summary statements. By restating your point and paraphrasing the employee's reaction, you will ensure that you understand each other. Be certain to also use good nonverbal communication skills, such as nodding, leaning forward, and much eye contact. Those behaviors indicate that you are listening and taking the session seriously.[28]

6. Document Everything. Recall that our memories, especially on the long term, are quite limited. It therefore is helpful if you keep careful notes about the employee's performance and the discussion that you held. As you will also see later in this chapter, proper documentation is also helpful if there is a legal challenge.[29]

Now that you have read some general guidelines, we will discuss specific steps for giving feedback. As you will see, the approach a manager takes should depend on the nature of the situation.

Conducting Performance Reviews: Specific Steps for Managers

The nature of the performance review session depends heavily on the employee's general performance, as well as on the purpose of the session (that is, is this the formal, end-of-the-year session or an informal meeting for immediate feedback?). Generally speaking, the informal session is used to solve specific performance problems, while the formal session is used more to summarize the employee's performance for the year. Let's first start with a set of steps for an informal feedback session.[30]

Conducting the Informal Feedback Session

1. Summarize General Performance. If the employee is generally satisfactory, you may begin by informing the employee that you are generally quite satisfied with his or her work. Give specific examples of the employee's strengths or major achievements. In more serious cases (for example, the employee's overall performance is not satisfactory), you should skip this step.
2. Introduce Problem Area. If the employee's performance is generally acceptable, move to the problem area by saying something like, "But there is an area where there is room for improvement. . . ." If the employee's general performance is generally not acceptable, begin with a general statement like, "There are some job performance concerns that we need to discuss. Let me begin here. . . ." Give some specific examples of the employee's performance, then explain the company's expectations or standards (for instance, you might say, "As you know, the company maintains a scrap rate level of 1 percent or less, and your work clearly is above that"). This step is easier said than done; see Box 7.5 for handling two common employee reactions.
3. Determine Cause of Problem. In this step, the manager asks the subordinate what he or she thinks is the cause or source of the problem. Although you may have your own ideas as to what the causes are, there are several reasons to have the employee provide explanations. First, you may be wrong. Second, having the employee determine the causes will begin to establish commitment to the next steps. As the manager, feel free to probe the employee about the alleged causes, and clearly state your concerns to the employee if you disagree with the reasons brought forth. In some cases, the employee may say, "I didn't know that was the expectation." In most cases, however, once the possible causes are determined, you should go to the next step, which focuses on solutions to the problem.
4. Obtain Solutions. Once you have determined the probable causes of the problem, it is time to address solutions. As in Step 3, it is very helpful to turn to the

employee for possible solutions. The manager should say something like, "Now that we've discussed the causes, what can we do to solve the problem?" Again, if the employee comes up with the solution, he or she will be more likely to accept and follow through with it than if you come up with the solution. On the other hand, you should participate fully in discussing possible solutions. The final solution must be something that is acceptable to you, the manager, as well. If, for example, the proposed solution is going to be too costly or cause resentment among other employees, you may need to reject it. Be reasonable, though, and if you must reject it, don't sound overbearing. Say something like, "I think that you have proposed a good solution, but other employees will be resentful if you are always coming to work later. Is there some other way we can modify the solution to avoid such problems?"

Box 7.4 Handling Performance Feedback: A Quiz

For each of the situations, describe what you would recommend the manager do. Suggestions from Andrew Grove, president and CEO of Intel Corporation, are provided after the situations are presented.

Situation 1. Whenever criticized about job performance, the manager's assistant begins to look stubborn and upset, so the manager hesitates to continue. Instead, the manager simply corrects the assistant's work by himself.

Situation 2. A recently hired manager made some passing comments criticizing the quality of the work in her department. These comments have circulated throughout the department, and the manager is concerned she has alienated the staff.

Situation 3. In a recent feedback situation, the manager's subordinate began to cry. Since then, the manager has acquired the reputation of being an SOB. That didn't seem to be a problem until the manager's boss told him that his style was too abrasive and his promotion chances could be adversely affected. What should the manager do now?

Situation 4. An employee's supervisor recently got married and as a result is spending less time and focusing less on the workplace. The department's productivity has fallen somewhat as a result. What should the employee say to her supervisor?

Answers According to Andrew Grove

Situation 1. When discussing the employee's performance, ignore the assistant's facial expressions, and deal with the issues at hand. Find a later time, when things are going well, to bring up the matter of the employee's facial expressions, focusing on specific details (for example, "When we were discussing an error in the report last time, you began to frown and your face began to show anger") and discuss the implications for work (you might say, "That kind of expression sends a message to the other party that you don't really want to get the feedback, even though it may be crucial for work effectiveness"). Since the assistant's expression seems to affect the manager's ability to give needed feedback, it is important to discuss this.

Situation 2. Do not take back the comments. If indeed there are problems with the work quality, it is important that the feedback be given and the problems corrected. The manager must, however, plan a procedure for giving the feedback in a more effective, professional manner.

Situation 3. Having tough standards does not mean that one is an SOB. The manager must focus on giving feedback in a constructive and fair fashion. It is important to be consistent; being the "nice guy" won't work either. The expression "tough but fair" is where it's at.

Situation 4. The employee should have a private meeting with her supervisor and share these observations, using some specific examples. If the supervisor doesn't realize what's happening, there is no point in trying again. If the supervisor doesn't change, the employee shouldn't worry. Let the supervisor's boss take care of the problem.

Source: Adapted from A. Grove, "Criticism: Giving It Effectively," *Working Woman,* June 1993, 18–20.

Box 7.5 Handling Employee Responses to Criticism

Tales from the Trenches

Employees react differently to criticism. Although some employees readily accept negative feedback and will initiate a discussion on how to improve, some employees will respond either by denying the problem exists or by becoming angry. In the former case, the employee may respond by saying, "That's not my fault; that problem is caused by stations further down the production line!" In the latter case, the employee might respond by saying something like, "For what the job pays, you certainly can't expect perfection!" Here are some suggestions for dealing with those reactions.

Handling Denial. Provide additional evidence (such as specific examples) of the problem. Explain exactly why the employee's performance constitutes a problem and what the implications of the problem are for the organization (lost customers, more waste, and so on). If the employee persists in denying the problem, you may have to explain the consequences of not improving ("Given the importance of this issue, I may be forced to take disciplinary action if change is not forthcoming").

Handling Anger. You definitely do not want to get into a shouting match and say things you will regret later. Although it may be easy for you to lose your temper when the employee is hostile toward you (after all, the employee might really be affecting your department's success, so how dare the employee get angry?), it is most important that you stay calm. Further, you should try to calm the employee down and let him or her vent anger. Saying something like, "I can tell you're pretty angry. Why don't you give me your perspective in more detail" may be helpful. Or, you might say, "I'm rather surprised by your strong reaction. Perhaps there are some issues I'm not aware of that you would like to discuss." If the employee can't seem to calm down, you might consider requesting another time in the very near future to discuss the issue. A statement like, "You seem pretty upset by this. I'd rather schedule a meeting first thing tomorrow when we have both had more time to think about the issues." You can choose to meet at a later time, but don't back off. Delaying the meeting more than 24 hours is only going to work against you. Be sure to explain your persistence in dealing with the problem by emphasizing the importance to the department and organization. If the employee remains angry even after these attempts, you will have to consider possible disciplinary action.

Source: Adapted from S. Pollan and M. Levine, "Finding the Right Words: Criticizing an Employee's Work," *Working Woman*, November 1993, 18, 80.

5. Establish Goals. Now that you have agreed to a solution, set a goal to achieve the improved performance within a short, but reasonable, time frame. Be sure to have the employee participate in this phase as well. Finally, summarize your agreements, and set a time for a follow-up meeting. You will probably want to write down the solution and the goals, and consider having the employee sign this document and keep a copy for himself or herself. Arrange for another meeting in the near future so that you can both evaluate the improvement.

6. Encourage the Employee. End the meeting on a positive, upbeat note by indicating your confidence in the employee. Saying something like, "I have confidence that you will succeed, and I look forward to meeting you again on the date we've set." is usually a good way to end.

7. Document the Meeting. Take careful notes on everything said. This will be particularly critical if improvement does not occur and you need to discipline the individual.

8. If the Problem Persists. If the employee's performance has not come up to standards by the next meeting, you will need to decide what to do next. If you

feel that the employee simply needs a little more time to improve, you may indicate that his or her performance is still unsatisfactory, but you would like to know what could be done to bring it up to par. If, on the other hand, there is little or no improvement, you should summarize what you said at the initial meeting and go through the above steps once again. This time, however, you will probably need to mention that if improvement is not forthcoming, you will need to take disciplinary action (disciplinary action is discussed in greater detail in Chapter 16).

Conducting the Formal Performance Review Session

There are many different ways to conduct the formal annual performance review session. Some organizations have specific procedures that managers must follow; other organizations leave the conduct of this session largely to the manager. The more effectively you handle this session, the more productive your subordinates will be. As you read earlier, there should be no major surprises for the employee during the formal review if you have given appropriate informal feedback throughout the year. This session should focus on summarizing the employee's performance and setting an agenda for the next year. Here are some basic steps that should be followed:[31]

1. Summarize the Employee's Performance. Regardless of the specific rating form used, you should begin by summarizing how the employee has done. Be sure to provide specific examples of the employee's performance. Assuming the employee's performance is at least minimally acceptable, begin with the positives. After that, discuss any problem areas. You may also wish to ask how the employee feels about his or her performance.

2. Establish Objectives and Areas for Improvement for the Next Year. No matter how successful the employee, there are always areas for improvement. Although goals or objectives may not be part of the performance appraisal form, you are nevertheless encouraged to establish these with your employee. Ask the employee for input in setting those goals, and make sure that the employee actively participates in setting them. Depending on the nature of the job, this may be a large or small part of the focus of the session.

3. Discuss the Employee's Developmental Needs. In the case of an outstanding employee, this area might consume most of the feedback session. For an average employee in a job where there is little opportunity for promotion and advancement, this topic may take up far less time. Regardless, the focus here should be on further opportunities for career development, skills enhancement, and so forth. You might begin this part of the review session by turning to the employee and saying something like, "We've talked about your overall performance for the year, and established some directions for the next year. Now I'd like to talk about your career development plans. What activities or opportunities would be useful for you?"

4. Summarize the Session. This is a final opportunity to be sure that both the manager and the employee understood what has been said. As a manager, then, take the lead by summarizing the key issues that were covered in the session. Then, ask the employee if he or she has any additional comments or questions to ask.

In sum, despite its importance to successful organizations, performance feedback is often one of the most neglected aspects of management. Failure to successfully provide useful feedback will hurt the most effective organization.

Handling Performance Reviews: The Employee Perspective

Perhaps the best way for you, as an employee, to understand the importance of the performance management process is to compare it to visiting the dentist. Consider, for a moment, the consequences of skipping the annual visit to the dentist or waiting for your toothache to disappear by itself. In almost every situation, as uncomfortable and unpleasant as the visit may be, the alternatives (for instance, a root canal procedure) are far more painful. Similarly, although many employees dread the performance feedback sessions, the alternatives are only worse. Quite the contrary, an effective performance appraisal session can provide much information on other opportunities in the company, as well as a chance to get some accurate and helpful feedback about an employee's strengths and weaknesses. Here are some suggestions for how employees can enhance the value of the performance management process:[32]

1. The Performance Management Process Is a Joint Responsibility. As an employee you shouldn't view this session as only your manager's responsibility. Rather, view the performance appraisal as a joint effort. Take an active role in setting up meetings, establishing goals, and reviewing your performance.

2. Plan Carefully. Once you accept joint responsibility, you become equally responsible for planning. Some organizations have a formal mechanism to facilitate your preparation, such as a self-rating form. Even if your organization does not have a formal mechanism, it is important for you to make a list of your accomplishments, achievements, and any training programs you have completed during the last year. You should also conduct an honest evaluation of your own performance. That way, you will be prepared if your manager asks you for input on how you did or seems to have overlooked some aspect of your performance. Don't be surprised, however, if your self-rating is higher than your manager's rating of your performance. Research indicates that most people rate their performance higher than others rate them.

3. Take an Active Role. While some managers will run an effective session, you can't always count on that happening; you may need to ensure that key issues are covered. For example, if the manager fails to provide clear goals, you should raise this issue with the manager. Be sure that you understand what the goals are, how performance will be measured, and what resources (such as training) are available to meet those goals. Do *not* be embarrassed by or too humble about your performance. Because performance reviews are often used to make salary and promotion recommendations, it is important that your performance be properly evaluated. Be careful, though, in how you go about addressing these issues. You certainly do not want your supervisor to think you are being too aggressive or undermining his or her authority. Returning to the opening case of this chapter, recall that the employee wanted to get more feedback, but felt the manager was simply not interested. One sugges-

tion would be for the employee to try to schedule a different time, perhaps after work, to get more specific feedback. Another suggestion would be for the employee to explain why getting feedback would be useful (for example, "With some more specific feedback, I could contribute much more to the department and organization").

4. Handle Negative Feedback Effectively. Most managers are extremely uncomfortable giving negative feedback, and they are usually ineffective in handling such situations. Frequently, a manager will delay giving critical feedback, which may create more problems than advantages for the employee. In that sense, it is better to be told the negative feedback than to have your manager hide it from you. But for many of us, negative feedback is difficult to accept, and we have a tendency to become defensive when we hear it. Rather than learning from such feedback, many people tend to explain it in some way ("My boss doesn't like me, so she finds reasons to criticize my work"). Box 7.6 provides suggestions for dealing with criticism.

Box 7.6 **Suggestions for How Employees Can Deal with Negative Feedback**

Your Turn

1. Avoid Being Defensive. Even though the criticisms may be hurtful when you hear them, the negative feedback you receive may well contain important information that you are completely unaware of. It is therefore critical that you listen carefully and stay calm. Above all, don't get angry. Becoming hostile or aggressive toward the other person giving the criticism will only work against you.

2. Check Your Self-Esteem. If you do feel humiliated by the feedback, consider why you feel that way. Do you view the criticism as a threat to your self-esteem? Again, given that many managers are ineffective in giving criticism, your manager may simply be handling the situation poorly. But that does not mean that the feedback is unjustified.

3. Get Enough Information. You may have difficulty concentrating when you first hear the negative information, causing you to miss key points. Be sure you understand the feedback, and ask clarifying questions if you do not. It may be useful to request follow-up discussions, particularly after you have a chance to think about the feedback. So, one way to handle the feedback is to say something like, "You have given me some critical, but very constructive, feedback. I'd like to spend some time thinking about it more carefully and consider some ways to improve. Afterward, I would like to meet with you again to discuss some strategies and work out a mutually agreeable plan. Can we meet in, say, two days?"

4. Develop a Strategy. You will probably need some time to think privately about the feedback and develop a strategy for dealing with the information you have received. Along these lines, you may want to verify the criticism. For example, are there other individuals (for example, a coworker, a mentor outside of work) whom you can go to for a "reality check"? Is this the first time anyone has ever mentioned the problem(s), or have you received similar feedback before? Once you have determined whether there is merit to the feedback, you should begin to develop a plan. Focus on the most important issues first, and decide what you can do to change. Perhaps some type of training program or seminar would be helpful; your manager may even be willing to pay the costs. Whatever the case, be sure you respond to the person who provided the feedback.

The critical comments you get may be the most useful feedback you ever receive. Demonstrating to your manager that you are able to accept the feedback in a professional, effective manner may really change his or her mind about your abilities.

Source: Adapted from J. James, "Dealing with Criticism during an Evaluation," *Nursing,* September 1991, vol. 21, 103–104.

Performance Management and the Law

Like any other HRM practice, performance appraisals are subject to legal scrutiny. Many court cases, involving alleged violations of civil rights laws, have focused on the appropriateness of the performance appraisals. A number of recommendations are offered to organizations and managers to improve the chances the performance appraisal system will pass legal muster.[33]

1. Be Sure the Performance Measures Are Job-Related. Although this may sound obvious, some organizations are ineffective in measuring work performance. For example, in one case, a rank-order comparison was used that was based on only three performance areas. Although the organization eventually won the case, the court criticized the performance appraisal as being too narrowly focused. Clearly, all relevant aspects of the job should be addressed in a performance appraisal system. Use of job analysis (see Chapter 5) is strongly recommended as the basis for developing a performance management system.[34]

2. Use a Clearly Defined Form with Written Standards. While the use of behaviorally based forms is recommended by professionals, the court system does not appear to prefer them over other approaches, nor do the courts consider objective measures to be inherently superior. For example, in one lawsuit, an investigator was terminated by the Equal Employment Opportunity Commission (even the EEOC can be charged with discrimination!) for poor performance. The EEOC's defense was that it used an objective system whereby each investigator was required to complete four investigations per month.

To avoid litigation and courtroom battles, human resource departments need to serve as one of many checkpoints when decisions are made to terminate employees. When a board made up of several different parties is called upon to make a decision, it serves to eliminate bias by any one individual.

Upon careful examination, however, it was determined that the plaintiff had been given the most difficult assignments, and he ultimately won the case. Hence, no system is necessarily perfect; it will depend on the particular situation.[35]

3. Have the Performance Ratings Scrutinized by Other Parties. In several court cases, a major factor in a favorable decision for the organization has been the use of reviews by parties other than the supervisor. In one instance, the organization had terminated two employees for poor performance after they had completed a training program. In the courtroom, the organization demonstrated that the decision was based on reviews by four separate parties: the training supervisor, the line supervisor, the training director, and an executive board. Independent reviews by several different parties is often viewed as a vehicle for eliminating bias by any one individual. It is recommended that the manager's supervisor, as well as the HRM department, serve as independent checks.[36]

4. Require Documentation. It is essential to properly document the basis for performance ratings and the reasons why HRM decisions, particularly terminations, were made. Given that a lawsuit will generally require the managers involved in these activities to explain their decision, careful, accurate, and detailed notes are invaluable.

5. Provide Guidance and Counseling to Poor Performers. In some court cases, the judges have considered whether the plaintiff was provided an opportunity to improve his or her performance. For example, in one case, a sales representative working for Xerox was given written warnings regarding customer complaints and was placed on a one-month performance improvement program, which was extended an additional month at his request. When the performance was not forthcoming, the plaintiff was warned that he would be terminated if his performance did not improve. Although the employee sued after being terminated, the court ruled in favor of Xerox, given the attempts to improve his performance. At the other extreme, in some cases the plaintiffs have argued that they were completely unaware of any performance deficiencies up until the day they were fired. It is therefore critical that employees see their evaluations. One way many companies ensure awareness is to have each employee sign the form, indicating the ratings have been seen.

Conclusion

Performance management systems play an integral role in human resources. As you read, performance management systems are used for a variety of purposes, including salary raises, terminations, employee development, and program evaluation. Subjective rating approaches, which are quite popular, suffer from various problems, including rating errors, poor forms, lack of rater preparedness, and ineffective organizational policies and practices. A variety of suggestions were offered to overcome these problems. Although giving and receiving performance feedback can be difficult, numerous suggestions were offered for handling the review process. If done properly, both organizations and employees will profit.

Applying Core Concepts

1. Explain why organizations use performance management systems.
2. What performance management system does the company you work for (or a close friend works for) use? What are some problems the company has with the system? What could the company do to solve those problems?
3. Think of a time when an employee you supervised or interacted with as a customer did something wrong. How would you have given him or her feedback?
4. Think of a time when someone gave you feedback in an ineffective fashion. Given what you read in this chapter, how could you have reacted to improve the usefulness of the feedback?

Key Terms

- Judgment errors
- Halo
- Leniency
- Severity
- Central tendency
- Ambiguity
- Deficiency
- Contamination
- 360-degree feedback
- Comparative rating forms
- Graphic scales
- Behaviorally based scales
- Behaviorally anchored rating scales
- Behavior observation scales
- Management-by-objectives

Chapter 7: Experiential Exercise

This exercise involves a role-play of two different situations. In each situation, the supervisor must deal with an employee who has exhibited performance problems. Both situations pose somewhat different problems. The person who is the supervisor in situation A should take the role of employee in situation B.

Employee: A

You, CHRIS, have worked in the warehouse area for 25 years now, and have been doing a conscientious job the entire time. You know almost everyone in the company, and have not missed a day of work for ten years. Your work has been regularly praised by different bosses, and you know that it is mostly because of you that the warehouse area has been as effective as it has been. In the last few years, however, you have been upset that you keep getting passed over for promotion to supervisor, warehouse area. In your opinion, it is probably due to favoritism by the plant manager, who does NOT get along with you at all. Three months ago, someone much younger than you, no less, was hired from outside the company to be the warehouse manager. Now you're really upset! Who can blame you for occasionally complaining to the other employees about the new supervisor, JEAN, who has no idea as to how the warehouse operates? After all, you know your job performance is excellent.

When Jean meets with you, you should really blow off some "steam" about his/her lousy job performance so far!

Supervisor: B

You were recently hired to serve as a supervisor of receptionists and customer call handlers. The person you are meeting with has been with the company for 28 years now, and has informed the company that he/she will be retiring in two years. His/her job consists of routing customer telephone calls to the appropriate department within the organization. His/her performance ratings have been satisfactory for years, but your boss (the area manager) discussed the fact that this person recently has been rude to a large number of callers, who have complained to the customer service reps.

Chapter 7: Experiential Exercise *(continued)*

This exercise involves a role-play of two different situations. In each situation, the supervisor must deal with an employee who has exhibited performance problems. Both situations pose somewhat different problems. The person who is the supervisor in situation A should take the role of employee in situation B.

Employee: B

You have been working with this organization for 28 years now. Your job consists of routing customer telephone calls to the appropriate department within the organization. For years you have been reliably performing your job, but for the past few months, things seem different. The pay isn't great, the work isn't at all interesting—but then it never has been. What is really bothersome is the way management communicates. Occasionally you are abrupt with a caller who is annoying and irritating, and you are always blamed by the area manager, who says something like: "You have a real attitude problem and you'd better shape up or else." Your attitude is one of "What does it matter if you are curt to rude people?" You cannot just pretend to be nice to everyone. If someone is rude to you, you can't just roll over and play dead. The majority of callers you handle promptly and nicely. Besides, you are retiring in two years, and work does not matter as much to you anymore. Finally, given your age and closeness to retirement, what can the company do to you anyhow? Your supervisor is new to this company, and has called you to attend a meeting.

Supervisor: A

You are JEAN, the new supervisor of the warehouse area. You are new to the company and job. Recently, you heard Chris complaining loudly to other workers about your performance. This appears to be undermining the morale of the area, and you can tell that other workers are beginning to challenge your authority. You have decided to talk with Chris about this issue, because it is important that morale not become a problem. In general, Chris is effective and knows a lot about the operation. So it is just this one area that seems to be a problem.

Chapter 7 References

1. J. Cleveland, K. Murphy, and R.E. Williams, "Multiple Uses of Performance Appraisal: Prevalence and Correlates," *Journal of Applied Psychology* 74 (1989), 130–35.
2. W.C. Borman, "Job Behavior, Performance, and Effectiveness," in *Handbook of Industrial and Organizational Psychology,* vol. 2, ed. M.D. Dunnette and L.M. Hough (Palo Alto, CA: Consulting Psychologists Press, 1991), 271–336.
3. M. Stevenson, J. Busemeyer, and J. Naylor, "Judgment and Decision-making Theory," in *Handbook of Industrial and Organizational Psychology,* vol. 1, ed. M.D. Dunnette and L.M. Hough (Palo Alto, CA: Consulting Psychologists Press, 1991), 283–374.
4. H.J. Bernardin, and R.W. Beatty, *Performance Appraisal: Assessing Human Behavior at Work* (Boston, MA: PWS-Kent, 1984).
5. M.M. Harris, "Rater Motivation in the Performance Appraisal Context: A Theoretical Framework," *Journal of Management* (in press).
6. R.D. Gatewood, and H.S. Feild, *Human Resource Selection* (Orlando, FL: The Dryden Press, 1994).

7. Bernardin and Beatty, *Performance Appraisal;* and H.J. Bernardin, and P. Villanova, "Performance Appraisal," in *Generalizing from Laboratory to Field Settings,* ed. E.A. Locke (Lexington, MA: Lexington Books, 1986).
8. A.M. Mohrman, and E.E. Lawler, "Motivation and Performance Appraisal Behavior," in *Performance Measurement and Theory,* ed. F.J. Landy and J. Cleveland (Hillsdale, NJ: Lawrence Erlbaum, 1983), 173–89, and C.O. Longenecker, D.A. Gioia, and H.P. Sims, "Behind the Mask: The Politics of Employee Appraisal," *Academy of Management Executive* 1 (1987), 183–93.
9. D.E. Smith, "Training Programs for Performance Appraisal: A Review," *Academy of Management Review* 11 (1986), 22–40.
10. Bernardin & Beatty, *Performance Appraisal.*
11. S.D. Friedman, and T.P. LeVino, "Strategic Appraisal and Development at General Electric Company," *Strategic Human Resource Management,* ed C. Fombrun, N.M. Tichy, and M.A. DeVanna (New York: John Wiley, 1984), 183–201.
12. B. O'Reilly, *"360 Feedback Can Change Your Life,"* Fortune, *October, 17, 1994, 93–100.*
13. Bernardin & Beatty, *Performance Appraisal.*
14. R.D. Bretz, G.T. Milkovich, and W. Read, "The Current State of Performance Appraisal Research and Practice: Concerns, Directions, and Implications," *Journal of Management* 18 (1992), 321–52.
15. K.R. Murphy, and J. Cleveland, "Performance Appraisal: An Organizational Perspective (Boston, MA: Allyn & Bacon, 1991).
16. E. Pulakos, "Behavioral Performance Measures" in *Applying Psychology in Business,* ed. J. Jones, B. Steffy, and D. Bray (Lexington, MA: Lexington Books, 1991).
17. G. Latham, and K. Wexley, *Increasing Productivity through Performance Appraisal* (Reading, MA: Addison-Wesley, 1981).
18. R. Cardy, and G. Dobbins, *Performance Appraisal: Alternative Perspectives* (Cincinnati, OH: South-Western Publishing, 1994); Borman, "Job Behavior, Performance, and Effectiveness."
19. R. Rodgers, and J. Hunter, "Impact of Management by Objectives on Organizational Productivity," *Journal of Applied Psychology* 76 (1991), 322–36; and Bernardin and Beatty, *Performance Appraisal.*
20. Murphy and Cleveland, "Performance Appraisal."
21. C. Schneier and R. Beatty, "Developing Behaviorally Anchored Rating Scales (BARS)," *Personnel Administrator,* August 1979, 59–68.
22. B. Rice, "Performance Review: The Job Nobody Likes," *Psychology Today* 19 (1985), 30–36.
23. R. Henderson, *Performance Appraisal* (Englewood Cliffs, NJ: Prentice-Hall, 1984).
24. C. Green, "How to Turn Your Staff into Star Performers," *Black Enterprise,* July 1991, 61.
25. B. Armentrout, "Eight Keys to Effective Performance Appraisals," *HR Focus* 70 (1993) 13.
26. S. Bushardt, J. Jenkins, and P. Cumbest, "Less Odious Performance Appraisals," *Training and Development Journal* 44 (1990), 29–35.
27. Ibid.
28. Ibid.
29. M. Smith, "Documenting Employee Performance," *Supervisory Management* 24 (1979), 30–37.
30. W. Mahler, *How Effective Executives Interview* (Homewood, IL: Dow-Jones, 1976).
31. D. Pennock, "Effective Performance Appraisals (Really!)," *Supervision* (1992), 14–16.
32. A. LaPlante, "Making Performance Reviews Work for You," *Computerworld* 26 (1992), 119.

33. G. Barrett, and M. Kernan, "Performance Appraisal and Terminations: A Review of Court Decisions Since Brito v. Zia with Implications for Personnel Practices," *Personnel Psychology* 40 (1987), 489–503.
34. C. Miller, J. Kaspin, and M. Schuster, "The Impact of Performance Appraisal Methods on Age Discrimination in Employment Act Cases," *Personnel Psychology* 43 (1990), 555–78.
35. Barrett and Kernan, "Performance Appraisal and Terminations."
36. Ibid.

chapter 8 Compensation Administration

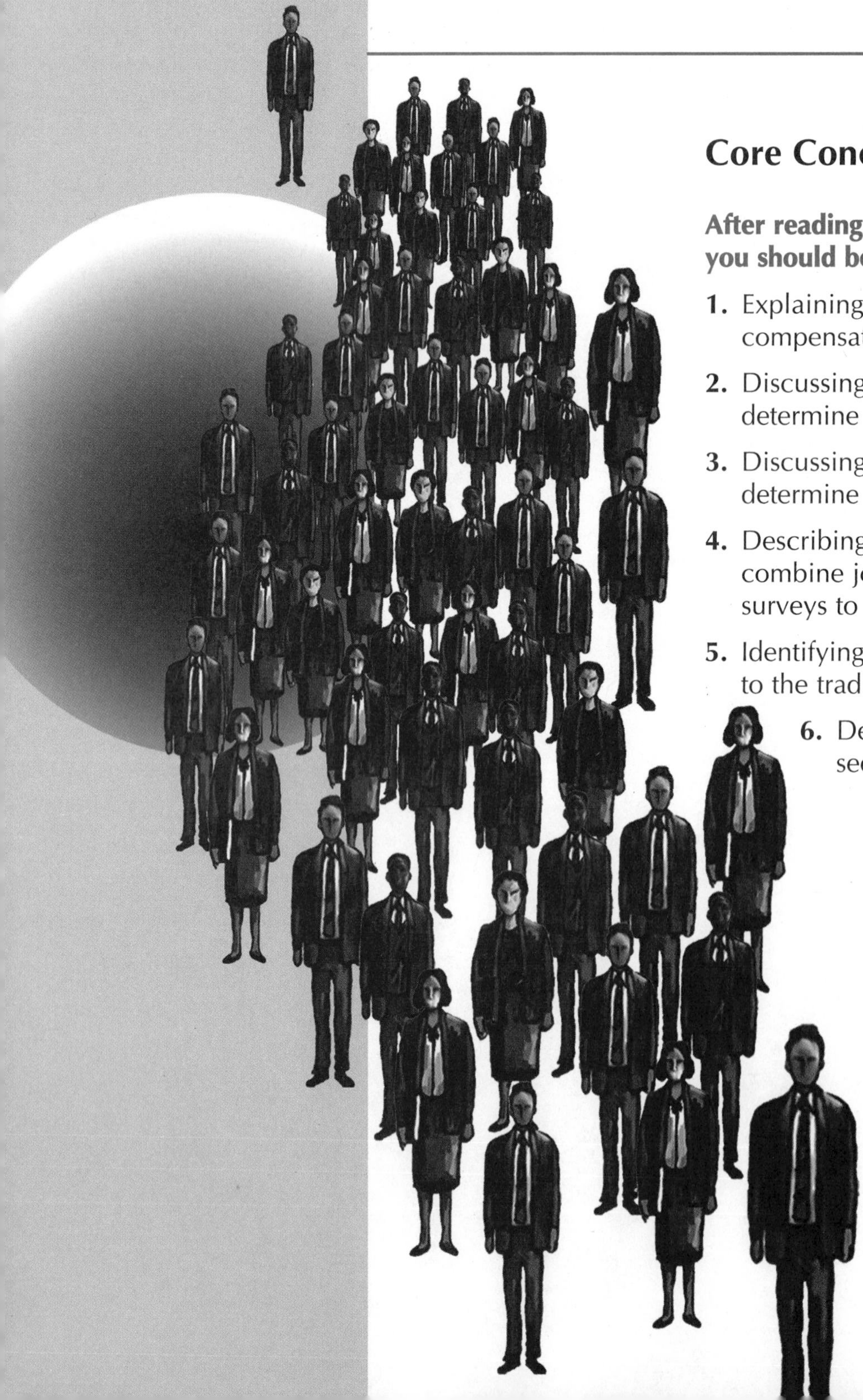

Core Concepts

After reading this chapter, you should be capable of

1. Explaining the laws that apply to compensation administration.
2. Discussing how organizations determine internal pay fairness.
3. Discussing how organizations determine external pay fairness.
4. Describing how organizations combine job evaluations and wage surveys to develop a pay structure.
5. Identifying alternative approaches to the traditional pay structure.
6. Developing a strategy for seeking a pay increase.

Opening Case

Laurie has been working at the same company for two years. Although she is satisfied with things at work, she cannot stop wondering whether she is underpaid. The most recent event that made her wonder is a conversation that she had with an old friend from high school last week. Much to her surprise, both Edward and she were in the same field of work. As they began talking, Laurie discovered that while their job titles differed, they both worked for different divisions of the same corporation and the actual work they performed was quite similar. Edward casually stated to Laurie that he made more than $35,000 anually. Laurie was so astonished that she blurted out, "What? More than $35,000? How do you make that much?" Edward responded by saying, "Even new employees in my department start off making about $31,000." After an embarrassing silence, another friend from high school came over and the conversation switched to another topic.

The next day, Laurie continued to think about her salary. She had once asked Dolly, a coworker who had been employed with the company for 20 years, what she thought about pay policies and practices, and Dolly replied in a whisper, "I don't talk about pay with anyone else. A number of years ago I asked another supervisor about pay raise policies, and he told me that they are a confidential issue that should only be discussed with your own supervisor. If you have questions, you are probably better off keeping them to yourself." As Laurie thought more about her pay, she could not help remembering a question that came up during her interview with this company two years ago. Near the end of the interview, the human resource representative asked her, "What are your salary expectations?" She was so unprepared for the question that she paused and then said, "I don't really know. I guess I haven't thought that much about it." The human resource representative smiled and said, "Well, how does $23,000 sound?" That seemed like so much more money than Laurie was earning in her part-time job that she nodded her head and said, "That sounds reasonable to me." The actual salary offer was slightly more ($24,000), but Laurie now wonders whether she handled the question properly. Should she have negotiated for a higher salary? Is she being paid fairly now? Could Edward really be making so much more in a different division of the company? And what can she do now to obtain a higher salary?

This chapter, and the next two chapters, address compensation issues. Total compensation packages for employees may be broken into three parts: (1) base pay, or the set amount for a given time period; (2) performance-based pay, or the part of one's pay that is based on job performance; and (3) benefits, or indirect pay, which would include such things as medical benefits that are paid by the company, contributions to the pension plan, and so forth. This chapter only addresses base pay. In particular, you will read about the goals of an organization's pay system, relevant laws, and how companies go about determining base pay. You will see that many of the concepts are useful for employees and job applicants, as well as supervisors and managers who are responsible for determining pay. We begin now with a discussion of the basic objectives that organizations consider in designing a compensation system.

Goals of Compensation Systems

What does an organization try to achieve in its compensation system? Understanding the answer to that question may help both the employee and the organization operate more effectively. As an employee, if you understand what the organization is trying to achieve, you may be able to concentrate your efforts better and therefore receive higher compensation. From an organization's perspective, the better the match between what is desired and what is actually rewarded, the more likely the business objectives will be met. Organizations attempt to achieve six basic goals with their compensation programs:

1. Complying with legal requirements.
2. Maintaining a sense of equity and fairness among employees.
3. Attracting new highly qualified employees.
4. Retaining current employees.
5. Motivating employees.
6. Controlling costs.[1]

Of course, most organizations will use other means, besides their compensation systems, to achieve these goals. For example, nonmonetary rewards, such as the nature of the work, interesting assignments, and flexible hours, are likely to be used as well. For most organizations, though, the compensation system is an important factor in recruiting, retaining, and motivating employees. But the compensation system is also a large part of most organizations' operating expenses. In fact, for most organizations, the payroll accounts for anywhere between 25 and 60 percent of operating expenses.[2] So, if not managed properly, an organization's payroll can severely reduce its profitability.

We now turn to a discussion of the first goal, complying with legal requirements. As you will see, there are a number of laws pertinent to the compensation area.

Compensation Laws: Complying with Legal Requirements

Virtually all compensation decisions—including starting pay, pay raises, and benefits—are covered by the discrimination laws. So, rather than repeating those laws here, you may wish to review those laws as described in Chapter 2. In addition to those laws, however, a number of laws pertain to the compensation area specifically. These can be divided into three areas:

1. The Fair Labor Standards Act of 1938.
2. Comparable worth.
3. Prevailing wage laws.

Fair Labor Standards Act of 1938

Fair Labor Standards Act of 1938
A congressional law passed with the intent of improving working conditions and living standards.

The Fair Labor Standards Act (FLSA) of 1938 was a congressional law passed with the intent of improving working conditions and living standards. Prior to this law, long work weeks, very low pay, and young children working in extremely hazardous conditions were common occurrences in the United States. In addition to requiring substantial record keeping and reporting to the government, the Fair Labor Standards Act of 1938 requires companies to do the following:

1. Provide overtime pay.
2. Pay a minimum wage.
3. Restrict the number of hours and the types of jobs children may work.
4. Pay equal wages to men and women doing the same job.

The hazardous working conditions are shown here by this child worker in the Chase Cotton Mill in Burlington, Vermont, in 1909. Such conditions led to the Fair Labor Standards Act of 1938 to improve working conditions and living standards of children and adults alike.

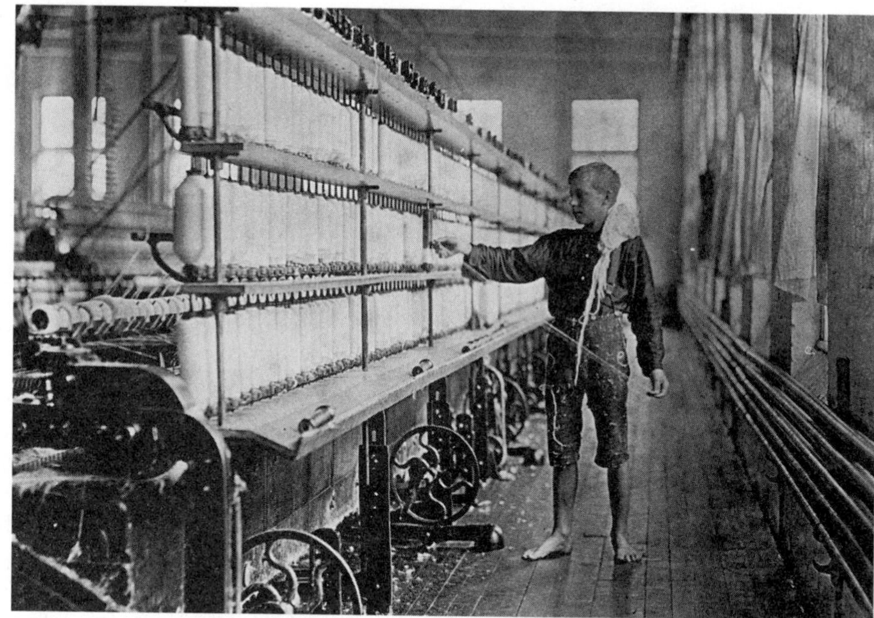

Chase Cotton Mill in Burlington, VT., May 1809. Photographed by Lewis Hine. Reproduced from the collection of the Library of Congress.

Each of these provisions can get quite complex, and organizations often get into trouble for alleged violations. Hence, whether you are a manager or employee, it is useful to have a basic understanding of these provisions.

Overtime Pay. This provision requires you as an employee to be paid time and a half (one and one-half of your regular pay) for each hour that you work more than 40 hours per week, as long as your job is covered by the law. A major determinant of whether your job is covered by the law—that is, whether your job is "nonexempt"—is the nature of your job. Specifically, executive, administrative, and professional employees are not covered, or are "exempt" from this law, as are certain other jobs (such as car salespeople, agricultural workers, and engineers). If you are employed in a hospital or other health care institution, a two-week period may be used to calculate overtime, such that you would not receive overtime wages unless you worked more than eighty hours during a two-week period. In today's world, many companies would rather have employees work overtime than hire additional workers. You may then wonder whether there is a maximum number of hours your company can require you to work. The answer is that many states do limit the maximum number of hours certain employees, such as bus drivers and mine workers, may work in a given time period.[3]

Nonexempt employees Employees who are covered by the law's provision that requires companies to pay time and a half for each hour that an employee works more than 40 hours per week.

Exempt employees Employees who are not covered by the law's provision that requires companies to pay time and a half for overtime; often applies to executive, administrative, and professional employees.

Minimum Wages. The FLSA requires that companies pay employees no less than the minimum wage. As stipulated by federal law, the minimum wage is $4.25 per hour. Some states, however, have higher minimum wages. Hawaii, which stipulates a minimum wage of $5.25, is the highest. You should note, however, that not all jobs are covered by this provision. Similar to the overtime provisions, if your job is considered an executive, administrative, or professional job, your company would not be required to pay you a minimum wage. Likewise, you would not be covered by this provision if you were employed as an apprentice (for example you were learning a skilled trade, such as electrician), trainee, or independent contractor.[4]

Child Labor Laws. Although technically not related to compensation, the FLSA also regulates the work hours and type of jobs employees under the age of 18 may work. This law focuses on three age groups: people between the ages of 16 and 18; people between the ages of 12 and 16; and people under the age of 12. Minors under the age of 12, for example, cannot be employed, with few exceptions (one common exception is delivering newspapers). Children between the ages of 12 and 16 are not allowed to work in a variety of dangerous occupations, including mining, manufacturing, and work involving heavy machinery. Children this age also have restrictions in the number of hours and the times they may work. Finally, people between the ages of 16 and 18 are restricted from certain hazardous jobs, such as meat packing, working with bakery machines, and coal mining.[5]

Equal Wages to Men and Women Doing the Same Job. The fourth provision of the Fair Labor Standards Act of 1938 was actually an amendment passed by Congress in 1963. This amendment, known as the Equal Pay Act of 1963, attempts to eliminate sex discrimination in pay. Although the primary intent was to help women who were frequently discriminated against on the basis of pay, men can sue for discrimination as well.

Equal Pay Act of 1963 An amendment to the Fair Labor Standards Act of 1938 that attempts to eliminate sex discrimination in pay.

In order to bring a lawsuit under the Equal Pay Act of 1963, the plaintiff would need to show the following:

1. That his or her work was essentially the same as the work performed by another employee of the opposite sex working in the same facility.
2. That his or her pay was less than that of the other employee.

If the plaintiff is able to successfully prove these two facts, the burden would shift to the organization to defend the pay difference in terms of one of the following factors:

1. Seniority (the lower paid employee has less seniority).
2. Merit or job performance (the lower paid employee is not as productive).
3. Differences other than sex.[6]

The third option, differences other than sex, allows the company many possible alternative defenses, some examples of which are provided in Box 8.1.

Recall in the opening case that Laurie wondered whether she was being paid fairly. If men were making more money in the same job, she might have grounds for a lawsuit. On the other hand, given that the friend from high school was working in a different division, the company would be able to defend the pay difference on the grounds that it was a "different facility." So unless there are sex differences within the same division and facility, the employee in the opening case would probably not be able to win a lawsuit under the Equal Pay Act.

Despite the Equal Pay Act of 1963, sex differences in salaries and wages persist. Women continue to earn significantly less than men in a wide variety of occupations and jobs. As you can see from Figure 8.1, women's earnings on average are only about 70 percent of those of men. In other words, for each $1.00 the average man earns, the average woman earns only 70 cents. Some critics assert that this is evidence that the Equal Pay Act of 1963 is of limited use in correcting sex discrimination pay, which only covers situations where women and men are working in the same job. These critics maintain that jobs that are stereotypically female

Box 8.1 How Companies Defend against Equal Pay Act Lawsuits

Organizations have used many different arguments to defend themselves in Equal Pay Act lawsuits. A common approach for organizations is to make use of the "differences other than sex" defense. Some of the following possibilities have been used here:

1. Shift Differentials. Different wages for different shifts (for example, night workers versus day workers) will be accepted by the courts, as long as they are applied equally to both men and women.

2. Salary Matching. It is legal for an organization to match or exceed salaries offered or provided by other organizations, even if this results in sex differences in pay. For example, if you had a competing offer from another employer, your company could choose to match the offer, even if it created a situation in which a member of the opposite sex doing the same job was paid less than you.

3. Profits. An organization may establish different commission rates for different products or services, even if this results in different earnings for men and women, as long as both men and women are permitted to sell the product or services. Likewise, different salaries can be paid for people in departments or units of different profitability. So, if men are working in a department that is profitable, their salaries may be higher than women working in a department that is losing money.

A completely different defense used by companies in some cases is to demonstrate that the jobs held by men and women are not really the same. For instance, in one court case involving a lawsuit by female janitors, the organization argued that male custodians (who were paid more) spent at least one-third of their time doing additional duties involving heavy lifting and moving. In a court case involving hospital orderlies, the organization successfully demonstrated that the men spent 70 percent of their time doing heavy work, unlike the women. One rule of thumb used by the courts is the frequency of the extra work being performed: if the extra duties are performed on a regular and frequent basis, the jobs may be deemed different. If, on the other hand, the extra duties are only performed occasionally (for example, less than 10 percent of the time), the courts may consider the jobs to be essentially the same.

Source: Adapted from E. Cooper and G. Barrett, "Equal Pay and Gender: Implications of Court Cases for Personnel Practices," *Academy of Management Review* 9 (1984), 84–94; and G. Milkovich and J. Newman, *Compensation* (Homewood, IL: Irwin, 1996).

(such as registered nurses, of which 93 percent were women in 1986) are systematically undervalued and therefore underpaid in our society, as compared to stereotypically male jobs (such as production supervisors, of which 85 percent were men in 1986).

According to some, then, the only meaningful way to eliminate sex bias in pay is to pass comparable worth laws. As you will see next, the comparable worth concept is controversial.

Comparable worth
The concept that jobs of equal worth or value should be paid the same, even if the jobs are completely different.

Comparable Worth

According to the comparable worth principle, jobs of equal worth or value should be paid the same, *even if the jobs are completely different.* This concept, then, is more sweeping than the Equal Pay Act, which requires that pay be the same only if the jobs are the same. As an example, consider two jobs in the state of Washington in the late 1970s, namely, a dental assistant and a stockroom attendant. The average monthly salary for a dental assistant, most of whom were women, was $608. The average monthly salary for a stockroom attendant, most of whom were men, was $816. But according to a study conducted for the state of Washington, there was evidence that the job of dental assistant and the job of stockroom

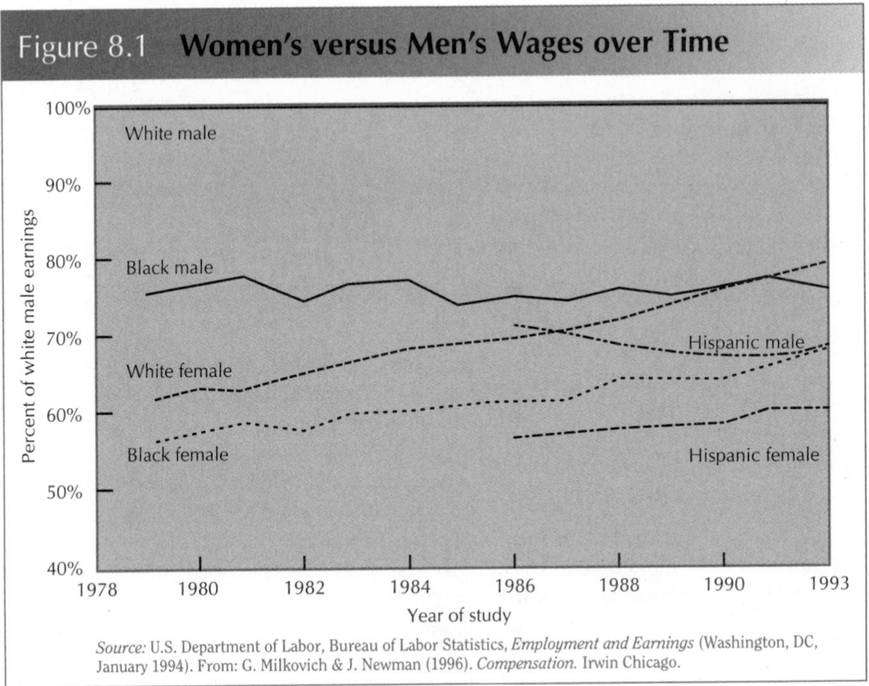

From G. Milkovich and J. Newman *Compensation.* (Chicago: Irwin, 1996).

attendant were equal in worth to the state. Based on the comparable worth principle, the average pay for dental assistant should have been the same as that for stockroom attendants. Comparable worth proponents advocate that each organization conduct an objective, unbiased analysis of the worth of every job that has a large majority of female employees. Then, for those jobs that are not paid according to their worth, the company would raise their wages or salaries to the proper levels (comparable worth proponents would oppose reducing the wages in male-dominated jobs to achieve equality).[7]

Not surprisingly, the comparable worth principle has generated a great deal of controversy. Critics of this principle raise several concerns, including the inherent additional pay costs, the difficulty of objectively determining the worth of jobs, the need to take into account other considerations besides job worth (for example, what other companies are paying for this job) and the additional litigation that would be generated if extensive comparable worth laws were passed.[8] The critics of comparable worth appear, in the United States at least, to hold the upper hand. To date, there are no comparable worth laws that cover private-sector businesses in the United States. Court cases have either ruled against this concept or have avoided addressing the issue. The one arena where there are many comparable worth laws is in state governments. Presently, nearly 20 states have made comparable worth pay adjustments, and require state employees be paid in accordance with comparable worth principles.[9]

Prevailing wage laws
Require companies with certain government contracts to pay workers the standard wage for the area, either the wage paid to a majority of workers in the area or a wage based on a weighted formula, which may be used if there is no single wage for the area.

Prevailing Wage Laws

Prevailing wage laws require companies with government contracts to pay workers the standard wage for the area. The original purpose was to prevent companies

Box 8.2 Comparable Worth: An International Perspective

Evidence from the international scene provides mixed evidence as to the effect of comparable worth laws. The International Labor Organization (ILO), a United Nations agency, officially endorsed the comparable worth principle in 1951. Since then, more than 100 countries have endorsed the ILO's position; the United States, however, has not. Although most of these countries have done little in the way of actually implementing the concept, a few noteworthy countries have passed laws that mandate comparable worth. Take Australia, which endorsed the comparable worth principle in 1974. Wages for Australian women were 65 percent of those for men in 1970, but they rose to almost 87 percent by 1977. However, the ratio slipped to 83 percent by 1982. The United Kingdom and Switzerland found that the difference between women's earnings and men's earnings decreased between 5 percent and 10 percent after acceptance of the comparable worth doctrine. Finally, in Sweden, adoption of comparable worth resulted in women making 90 percent of the earnings of men. The countries that have adopted comparable worth principles, such as Australia, United Kingdom, Switzerland, and Sweden, have created special boards, similar to the U.S.'s EEOC that handle comparable worth complaints. Ontario, Canada, recently passed legislation regarding comparable worth that covers even private-sector businessnes. The effects of this legislation remain to be seen, though it may be difficult to tell any time soon, given that Canada is suffering from high unemployment and a serious recession.

Source: Adapted from T. Linsenmayer, "Comparable Worth Abroad: Mixed Evidence," *The Wall Street Journal,* May 27, 1986, A26.

with large government contracts from unfairly depressing workers' wages. As of 1982, a prevailing wage is either (1) the wage paid to a majority of workers in the area, or (2) a wage based on a weighted formula, which may be used if there is no single wage for the area.[10] The following are the specific prevailing wage laws:[11]

1. The Davis-Bacon Act of 1931, which covers public construction projects.
2. The Walsh-Healy Public Contracts Act of 1936, which covers manufacturers and suppliers of goods to the government.
3. The Service Contract Act of 1965, which covers services (for instance, janitorial) to the government.
4. The National Foundation Arts and Humanities Act of 1965, which covers employees working on projects funded by the foundation.

If you are a manager employed by an organization with such a contract, be sure that your compensation practices are in compliance.

To summarize, organizations must conform with a great number of regulations and laws in administering their compensation programs. As was mentioned in Chapter 2, other discrimination laws—such as the Age Discrimination in Employment Act, the Americans with Disabilities Act, and the Civil Rights Acts of 1866, 1964, and 1991—also apply to pay issues. As of yet, comparable worth laws apply only to certain state governments. Finally, prevailing wage laws pertain to many companies with government contracts. As in other aspects of human resources, the laws play a major role in compensation administration. We now turn to a discussion of the second goal, maintaining a sense of equity and fairness among employees, which also relates to our third, fourth, and fifth goals of attracting, retaining, and motivating employees.

Maintaining a Sense of Equity among Employees: Internal and External Considerations

How would you go about determining whether your base pay was fair? In the opening case, Laurie seemed particularly troubled when she found out that a friend from high school who worked in a different division of the same company doing what seemed to be the same job appeared to be earning much more money than she was. Do you think Laurie was making an appropriate comparison? After all, the friend did work for a different division. What would you have done if you were in that situation? Would you have tried to find out what other employees in your department with the same job title were making? If that is what you would have done, be aware that some organizations have strict policies that prohibit employees from discussing salaries with coworkers. Some organizations might even terminate you for such discussions. So the coworker's refusal to discuss pay in the opening case is realistic. Would you have instead attempted to find out what other organizations pay employees doing your job? In that case, would you have tried to get information only from organizations in the same industry and same geographic location? You might even arrive at different conclusions regarding the fairness of your pay, depending on which comparison you use. There is no one "right" comparison. From an individual's perspective, then, pay fairness may all depend on whose salary you are comparing your pay with.[12]

Organizations face a similar dilemma in determining base pay. Organizations must determine what jobs are appropriate to compare to each other and what aspects of the jobs should be analyzed. By comparing jobs to one another within the organization, pay can be made *internally* fair. Organizations must also decide who the relevant companies are that should be used for comparison purposes. By basing compensation on what other companies are paying for the same job, an organization can make its wages and salaries *externally* fair.

As you might guess, internal and external fairness are determined quite differently. Internal fairness is determined by a job evaluation; external value is assessed using salary surveys. Each of these procedures is reviewed in greater detail next, followed by a discussion of how organizations combine the two approaches to determine the actual base pay for their employees.

Determining Internal Fairness: Conducting a Job Evaluation

Job evaluation
A systematic, objective procedure for determining the value of a group of jobs for the organization.

A job evaluation is a systematic, objective procedure for determining the value of a group of jobs for the organization. A job evaluation may be used for several purposes, some of which may be more important than others, depending on the organization's needs. Specifically, a job evaluation may be useful for the following:[13]

1. Explaining to employees how the base pay is determined.
2. Ascertaining the appropriate pay for jobs that are unique to the organization.
3. Defending the pay system from a legal challenge.
4. Helping design career paths.
5. Performing a comparable worth study.

Many different job evaluation procedures exist. You have read about one of these (the *Position Analysis Questionnaire,* or PAQ) in an earlier chapter; we will discuss two additional procedures in some detail: the point method system and the Hay system. Following that, the rank order and job classification methods are briefly mentioned.

Point Method System of Job Evaluation

The point method is one of the most commonly used job evaluation procedures. It involves the following basic steps:[14]

Point method job evaluation
One of the most commonly used job evaluation procedures that involves forming a committee, selecting and defining compensable factors, establishing and defining levels for each compensable factor, determining the total number of points for the system, dividing total points among compensable factors, distributing points to each level on every factor, and evaluating the jobs.

Compensable factors
The determinants of job worth.

1. Form a Job Evaluation Committee. The committee should include compensation experts, as well as managers, supervisors, and others who are familiar with the jobs being evaluated. Generally, anywhere between three to ten individuals should work on the committee.
2. Select and Define Compensable Factors. Compensable factors are the determinants of job worth. As an analogy, if you were considering how much to pay for an automobile, the relevant compensable factors might include safety ratings, fuel economy, resale value, and available options (such as antilock brakes). In the job evaluation domain, compensable factors often include the education required to perform the job, the amount of decision making performed on the job, the amount of responsibility involved in the job (such as budgetary responsibility), and the dangerousness of the work. In practice, the number of compensable factors used in the job evaluation can vary from 3 or 4 to as many as 15 or 20. Once determined, the compensable factors must be carefully defined.
3. Establish and Define Levels on Each Compensable Factor. It is not sufficient to merely define each compensable factor. Rather, like a ruler, each *level* or step must be clearly delineated. This is best explained by examining Table 8.1, which provides an example of the levels on education, a commonly used compensable factor. As you can see in Table 8.1, this compensable factor has four levels, ranging from a four-year college degree to an eighth-grade education. There is nothing magical about the number of levels or the particular levels chosen. The number of levels and the particular levels used should be a function of the jobs being evaluated. The levels should also be chosen such that each job to be evaluated will fall on one and only one level. While the levels in Table 8.1 might be appropriate for office workers, if the job evaluation was going to be used for a scientific laboratory, a different set of levels might be more appropriate, perhaps with the highest level being Ph.D., and the lowest level being two-year college degree.
4. Determine the Total Number of Points for the System. In this step, the committee must determine the total number of points (not dollars) to be allocated

Table 8.1 **Levels of the Compensable Factor of Education**

Level 1: Eighth-grade education.
Level 2: High school diploma or equivalent.
Level 3: Two-year college degree; technical/vocational school diploma.
Level 4: Four-year college degree.

in the job evaluation. This step is similar to your course instructor assigning a total number of points that can be earned through tests, projects, and class participation. Although this is an arbitrary number, it must be large enough to accommodate differences among even highly valued jobs. Many experts recommend that 1,000 points be used.[15]

5. Divide Total Points among Compensable Factors. In this step, the committee must decide how many points to assign to each compensable factor. This essentially weights the different factors, much as an instructor assigns a number of points for each test, quiz, and project in a course. The more important a given compensable factor is to the organization, the more points it should receive. For example, if our compensable factors were education, decision making, responsibility, and dangerousness, we might assign 200 points to education, 300 points to decision making, 350 points to responsibility, and 150 points to dangerousness. All things being equal, then, the job with a great deal of responsibility is likely to have a higher overall worth than a job with a great deal of danger.

6 Distribute Points to Each Level on Every Factor. Now that a total number of points has been assigned to each factor, the committee must determine the number of points each level will receive. There are several different ways to do this, but the simplest way is to divide the number of points assigned to the factor by the number of levels on the factor and assign this value to the lowest level. For example, since education was assigned 200 points and there are four levels, an eighth-grade education would receive 50 points. Each level receives 50 points more than the previous level. Thus, a high school diploma would receive 100 points, a two-year college degree 150 points, and a four-year college degree would receive 200 points. The development of the job evaluation system is now complete. All that needs to be done is to create a job evaluation manual or computer program to use in evaluating the jobs.

7. Evaluate the Jobs. In this step, relevant information must be gathered about the jobs so that they can be evaluated on each of the compensable factors. There are many ways to obtain this information, but among the most common are written questionnaires completed by supervisors and job incumbents that contain questions relevant to the compensable factors. The job evaluation committee may also interview supervisors and incumbents, and observe the jobs being performed. Committee members should first independently rate the jobs on each compensable factor, then discuss their ratings to reach agreement. Once the points on each compensable factor are determined, the points can be added up for each job to determine its overall value.

As you can guess, a properly performed point method job evaluation can take a great deal of time and energy to complete. On the positive side, the careful, systematic thinking involved should help employees to feel that the resulting pay decisions are fair.

Finally, it is important to note that most organizations will perform a separate job evaluation for different occupational groups. For example, most organizations will perform one job evaluation for clerical/office staff, a different job evaluation for managerial and professional staff, and yet a third job evaluation for other employees (for instance, manufacturing workers).

Hay Plan

The Hay Plan, or Hay Guide Chart-Profile method, is a preestablished job evaluation plan owned and copyrighted by the Hay Group, a management consulting firm. The Hay Plan is widely used for evaluating executive, managerial, and professional positions, but it can also be used for other positions, such as clerical jobs. A chief advantage of the Hay Plan is that is is based on preestablished compensable factors and points. A company choosing the Hay Plan will probably be able to complete the evaluation of jobs much more quickly than if a point method system was used.

Hay Plan
A preestablished job evaluation plan that is widely used for evaluating executive, managerial, and professional positions.

The Hay Plan assumes that three universal compensable factors can be used to evaluate all jobs.[16]

1. *Know-how,* which represents all skills, knowledge domains, and abilities that are required by the job.
2. *Problem solving,* which represents the degree to which analyzing, creating, and reasoning are required by the job.
3. *Accountability,* which represents the job's responsibility and impact on the organization.

Each of these three compensable factors is a function of several subfactors. For example, know-how is broken down into three subfactors: (1) breadth/depth of knowledge; (2) degree of integration of different functions, and (3) amount of human relations skill required for the job. An example of the know-how factor is provided in Figure 8.2.

To use the Hay Plan, a trained analyst would carefully review the jobs being evaluated (that is, the analyst would examine job descriptions, talk with supervisors, and so forth). Next, the analyst would find the appropriate levels on each of the subfactors underlying each of the three compensable factors.

A major advantage of the Hay Plan is that it is ready for immediate use. Another advantage of this method is that it is designed specifically for executive, managerial, and professional positions, which by their very nature are difficult to evaluate. On the other hand, because employees will have less involvement, they may be less inclined to accept the results than they would be with the point method plan.

Other Job Evaluation Procedures

In addition to the job evaluation procedures already mentioned, two other noteworthy procedures are ranking and job classification. The ranking method is among the simplest procedures. With this method, a committee ranks the jobs from most valued to least valued by the organization. No compensable factors are used; rank is based on the overall worth of the jobs to the organization. Although this method is quick and relatively easy to use, it suffers from several shortcomings. First, because it uses no compensable factors and no standards by which jobs are evaluated, bias may arise, particularly against stereotypically female jobs. Likewise, there is little documentation to explain why the jobs have been ranked as such. Therefore, this method may be of little value in convincing employees of the fairness of the pay system. Second, while a committee may have no difficulty deciding which are the most valuable and which are the least valuable jobs, the jobs in the middle may spark much more disagreement. Without clear standards,

Ranking method of job evaluation
Involves a committee ranking jobs from most valued to least valued by the organization.

Figure 8.2 Know-how from the Hay Plan

JMS MASTER GUIDE CHART

1992

KNOW-HOW

GUIDE CHART®

© HAY MANAGEMENT CONSULTANTS 1991

DEFINITION – Know-How is the sum total of every kind of skill, however acquired, needed for acceptable job performance. This sum total, which comprises the overall fund of knowledge, has three dimensions, the requirements for:

- • Depth and breadth of knowledge, ranging from basic knowledge of the most simple work routines, to unique and authoritative knowledge within learned disciplines.
- •• Know-How of integrating and harmonizing the diversified functions involved in managerial situations (operating, supporting, and administrative). This Know-How may be exercised consultatively as well as executively and involves, in some combination, the areas of organizing, planning, executing, controlling, and evaluating.
- ••• Active, practicing person-to-person skills in the area of human relationships.

MEASURING KNOW-HOW: Know-How has both scope (variety) and depth (thoroughness). Thus, a job may require some knowledge about a lot of things, or a lot of knowledge about a few things. The total Know-How is the combination of scope and depth. This concept makes practical the comparison and weighing of the total Know-How content of different jobs in terms of: "HOW MUCH KNOWLEDGE ABOUT MANY THINGS."

•• KNOW HOW OF

INTEGRATING AND HARMONIZING DIVERSIFIED FUNCTIONS

SCOPE OF TOTAL MANAGEMENT OF THE CHIEF EXECUTIVE OFFICER POSITION IS ESTABLISHED AFTER CONSIDERATION OF:

DIVERSITY (degree of integration; number of different businesses; dispersion of operations; organizational complexity; size)

POSITION IN INDUSTRY (degree of dominance and leadership — pace setter for the industry)

CHARACTER OF INDUSTRY (degree of regulation; effect on economy)

BUSINESS STRATEGY (response to challenge and environment; rate of change and growth)

		T. Performance of a task or tasks highly specific as to objective and content with limited awareness of surrounding circumstances and events.			I. Performance or supervision of an activity or activities specific as to objective and content, with appropriate awareness of related activities.			II. Operational or conceptual integration or coordination of activities which are relatively homogeneous in nature and objective.			III. Operational or conceptual integration of activities which are diverse in nature and objectives in an important management area or company-wide coordination of a function.			IV. Integration of major functions in an operating complex; or company-wide coordination of a strategic function which significantly affects corporate planning or operations.			V. Administration of an operating unit where size and character significantly augment managerial complexity or a corporate subfunction of wide and deep penetration or integration and coordination of a major function(s) in a major operating complex.			VI. Administration of a major operating unit or of a major corporate function of wide and deep penetration.			VII. Administration of a major operating complex or a major function which uniquely and comprehensively affects corporate planning and results.			VIII. Integration and coordination of the overall corporate activity with primary concern for assigned major operating complex and/or multiple function components.			IX. Total management of the enterprise.			
	••• Human Relations Skills →	1	2	3	1	2	3	1	2	3	1	2	3	1	2	3	1	2	3	1	2	3	1	2	3	1	2	3	1	2	3	
PRACTICAL PROCEDURES	L. LIMITED Basic instructions and simple work routines to carry out manual tasks.	29	33	38	38	43	50	50	57	66	66	76	87	87	100	115	115	132	152	152	175	200	200	230	264	264	304	350	350	400	460	L.
		33	38	43	43	50	57	57	66	76	76	87	100	100	115	132	132	152	175	175	200	230	230	264	304	304	350	400	400	460	528	
		38	43	50	50	57	66	66	76	87	87	100	115	115	132	152	152	175	200	200	230	264	264	304	350	350	400	460	460	528	608	
	A. PRIMARY Basic literacy and/or ciphering skills plus work indoctrination for performance of repetitive operational or clerical routines which may involve use of common tools and standard single purpose machines.	38	43	50	50	57	66	66	76	87	87	100	115	115	132	152	152	175	200	200	230	264	264	304	350	350	400	460	460	528	608	A.
		43	50	57	57	66	76	76	87	100	100	115	132	132	152	175	175	200	230	230	264	304	304	350	400	400	460	528	528	608	700	
		50	57	66	66	76	87	87	100	115	115	132	152	152	175	200	200	230	264	264	304	350	350	400	460	460	528	608	608	700	800	
	B. ELEMENTARY VOCATIONAL Familiarization with uninvolved, standardized work routines, and/or use of equipment and machines.	50	57	66	66	76	87	87	100	115	115	132	152	152	175	200	200	230	264	264	304	350	350	400	460	460	528	608	608	700	800	B.
		57	66	76	76	87	100	100	115	132	132	152	175	175	200	230	230	264	304	304	350	400	400	460	528	528	608	700	700	800	920	
		66	76	87	87	100	115	115	132	152	152	175	200	200	230	264	264	304	350	350	400	460	460	528	608	608	700	800	800	920	1056	
	C. VOCATIONAL Procedural or systematic proficiency, which may involve a facility in the use of specialized equipment.	66	76	87	87	100	115	115	132	152	152	175	200	200	230	264	264	304	350	350	400	460	460	528	608	608	700	800	800	920	1056	C.
		76	87	100	100	115	132	132	152	175	175	200	230	230	264	304	304	350	400	400	460	528	528	608	700	700	800	920	920	1056	1216	
		87	100	115	115	132	152	152	175	200	200	230	264	264	304	350	350	400	460	460	528	608	608	700	800	800	920	1056	1056	1216	1400	
SPECIALIZED TECHNIQUES	D. ADVANCED VOCATIONAL Some specialized (generally non-theoretical) skill(s), acquired on or off the job, giving additional breadth or depth to a generally single function.	87	100	115	115	132	152	152	175	200	200	230	264	264	304	350	350	400	460	460	528	608	608	700	800	800	920	1056	1056	1216	1400	D.
		100	115	132	132	152	175	175	200	230	230	264	304	304	350	400	400	460	528	528	608	700	700	800	920	920	1056	1216	1216	1400	1600	
		115	132	152	152	175	200	200	230	264	264	304	350	350	400	460	460	528	608	608	700	800	800	920	1056	1056	1216	1400	1400	1600	1840	
	E. BASIC SPECIALIZED Sufficiency in a technique which requires a grasp either of involved practices and precedents, or of scientific theory and principles, or both.	115	132	152	152	175	200	200	230	264	264	304	350	350	400	460	460	528	608	608	700	800	800	920	1056	1056	1216	1400	1400	1600	1840	E.
		132	152	175	175	200	230	230	264	304	304	350	400	400	460	528	528	608	700	700	800	920	920	1056	1216	1216	1400	1600	1600	1840	2112	
		152	175	200	200	230	264	264	304	350	350	400	460	460	528	608	608	700	800	800	920	1056	1056	1216	1400	1400	1600	1840	1840	2112	2432	
	F. SEASONED SPECIALIZED Proficiency, gained through wide exposure,in a technique which combines a broad understanding either of involved practices and precedents, or of scientific theory and principles, or both.	152	175	200	200	230	264	264	304	350	350	400	460	460	528	608	608	700	800	800	920	1056	1056	1216	1400	1400	1600	1840	1840	2112	2432	F.
		175	200	230	230	264	304	304	350	400	400	460	528	528	608	700	700	800	920	920	1056	1216	1216	1400	1600	1600	1840	2112	2112	2432	2800	
		200	230	264	264	304	350	350	400	460	460	528	608	608	700	800	800	920	1056	1056	1216	1400	1400	1600	1840	1840	2112	2432	2432	2800	3200	
	G. SPECIALIZED MASTERY Determinative mastery of techniques, practices, and theories gained through wide seasoning and/or special development.	200	230	264	264	304	350	350	400	460	460	528	608	608	700	800	800	920	1056	1056	1216	1400	1400	1600	1840	1840	2112	2432	2432	2800	3200	G.
		230	264	304	304	350	400	400	460	528	528	608	700	700	800	920	920	1056	1216	1216	1400	1600	1600	1840	2112	2112	2432	2800	2800	3200	3680	
		264	304	350	350	400	460	460	528	608	608	700	800	800	920	1056	1056	1216	1400	1400	1600	1840	1840	2112	2432	2432	2800	3200	3200	3680	4224	
• LEARNED DISCIPLINES	H. PROFESSIONAL MASTERY Externally recognized mastery of a complex professional or scientific field.	264	304	350	350	400	460	460	528	608	608	700	800	800	920	1056	1056	1216	1400	1400	1600	1840	1840	2112	2432	2432	2800	3200	3200	3680	4224	H.
		304	350	400	400	460	528	528	608	700	700	800	920	920	1056	1216	1216	1400	1600	1600	1840	2112	2112	2432	2800	2800	3200	3680	3680	4224	4864	
		350	400	460	460	528	608	608	700	800	800	920	1056	1056	1216	1400	1400	1600	1840	1840	2112	2432	2432	2800	3200	3200	3680	4224	4224	4864	5600	
	I. AUTHORITATIVE MASTERY Internationally recognized authority in an unusually complex professional or scientific field.	350	400	460	460	528	608	608	700	800	800	920	1056	1056	1216	1400	1400	1600	1840	1840	2112	2432	2432	2800	3200	3200	3680	4224	4224	4864	5600	I.
		400	460	528	528	608	700	700	800	920	920	1056	1216	1216	1400	1600	1600	1840	2112	2112	2432	2800	2800	3200	3680	3680	4224	4864	4864	5600	6400	
		460	528	608	608	700	800	800	920	1056	1056	1216	1400	1400	1600	1840	1840	2112	2432	2432	2800	3200	3200	3680	4224	4224	4864	5600	5600	6400	7360	
	J. PREEMINENT AUTHORITY Unique command of theory and principles at the pinnacle of an unusually complex professional or scientific field.	460	528	608	608	700	800	800	920	1056	1056	1216	1400	1400	1600	1840	1840	2112	2432	2432	2800	3200	3200	3680	4224	4224	4864	5600	5600	6400	7360	J.
		528	608	700	700	800	920	920	1056	1216	1216	1400	1600	1600	1840	2112	2112	2432	2800	2800	3200	3680	3680	4224	4864	4864	5600	6400	6400	7360	8448	
		608	700	800	800	920	1056	1056	1216	1400	1400	1600	1840	1840	2112	2432	2432	2800	3200	3200	3680	4224	4224	4864	5600	5600	6400	7360	7360	8448	9728	

•••HUMAN RELATIONS SKILLS

1. **BASIC:** Courtesy, tact and effectiveness in dealing with others in every day working relationships, including contacts to request or provide information.
2. **IMPORTANT:** Alternative or combined skills in understanding and/or influencing people are important to achieving job objectives, causing action or understanding in others.
3. **CRITICAL:** Alternative or combined skills in understanding, selecting, developing, and motivating people are important in the highest degree.

Source: 1992 Know-How Guide Chart from Hay Group © Hay Management Consultants. Reprinted by permission.

Box 8.3 **Are CEOs Overpaid?**

Tales from the Trenches

In today's era of mass layoffs and terminations, CEOs' pay may seem outrageously high. The average U.S. CEO makes more than $700,000 annually (this includes benefits and various incentive programs), which is far higher than CEOs in other countries. In fact, in 1991, Anthony O'Reilly, the highest paid CEO in the United States, made more than 70 million dollars. Hold on for a second. O'Reilly didn't make that much money from his salary—in fact, his salary was about 3 million dollars. Most of the money was made from stock options. Stock options are simply a right to buy a certain number of company stock in the future at a fixed price. For example, the CEO of Avon Products was once given the option to buy 50,000 shares of stock at $40.25 each. If the stock stays under the fixed price, the CEO makes nothing on the stock. However, for every penny above the fixed price, the CEO will make that much money for each stock purchased. Thus, some CEOs make money almost instantly, like Merrill Lynch and Companies' chairman, William Schreyer, who made a profit on paper at least of $9 million within a year of receiving stock options.

Defenders of high CEO pay contend that U.S. senior executives are more likely to be fired than their foreign counterparts and therefore are compensated for their riskier jobs. Moreover, stockowners, many of whom are retirees, want CEOs to have their compensation linked to stock price. The logic is that if the CEO has a financial incentive to increase the stock price, he or she will work to increase the stock price, which will also serve the shareholders' goals. Thus, even though CEO pay has been criticized in the past for not being based on company performance, emphasis on incentives such as stock options has increased the pay-for-performance nature of CEO pay.

Another common criticism of CEO pay is that U.S. businesses provide very little information to stockowners as to how much the compensation package provided to the CEO is worth. But new Securities and Exchange Commission (SEC) rules have begun requiring companies to provide much more information in a more readable form. The hope of many, then, is that such changes will result in better run, and more profitable, businesses.

Source: Adapted from A. Bennett, "A Little Pain and a Lot to Gain," *The Wall Street Journal,* April 22, 1992, R1, R2; and J. Lublin, "Higher Profits Fatten CEO Bonuses," *The Wall Street Journal,* April 21, 1993, R1, R2.

such disagreements may be difficult or impossible to resolve in a satisfactory manner.[17]

If you have ever worked in a government position, you are probably familiar with the job classification method. With this method, categories or classes are defined. A simple example of classes is provided in Table 8.2. As you can see in Table 8.2, each class is defined in terms of responsibility for subordinates, contact with other departments, amount of education required, and technical skills involved. Typically, there are about eight categories or classes, but some organizations will have as few as five and as many as fifteen. Because class definitions may be ambiguous, and disagreement may arise as to the proper class, it may become difficult to classify some jobs. In addition, the rationale for pay differences between classes is often limited, making such plans vulnerable to lawsuits.[18]

Job classification Categories or classes are defined in terms of responsibility for subordinates, contact with other departments, amount of education required, and technical skills involved.

After reading about these various job evaluation methods you may be wondering whether different job evaluation procedures will produce different results, or whether the conclusions would be the same regardless of which procedure you used. If different procedures do in fact produce different results, the job evaluation system used could have major policy implications, particularly in the case of

Table 8.2 **Sample Classes in a Job Classification System**

Class 1: No supervisory responsibility; minimal contact with other departments; high school diploma required, minimal technical skills.

Class 2: No supervisory responsibility; minimal contact with other departments; two-year college degree required; moderate technical skills.

Class 3: No supervisory responsibility; some contact with other departments; four-year college degree required; extensive technical skills.

Class 4: Supervisory responsibility; significant contact with other departments; four-year college degree required; extensive technical skills.

comparable worth adjustments. One study that compared the PAQ to the point method found relatively large differences in estimates of the underpayment of traditionally female jobs. Moreover, the way in which weights for the compensable factors for the PAQ and point method systems were developed made a difference.[19] Other studies have found similar results.[20] Thus, the job evaluation method used could have a large effect on one's conclusions. Unfortunately, there is no way to determine what the "right" job evaluation procedure is. As in beauty, it is ultimately in the eye of the beholder.

Box 8.4 **Compensation: An International Comparison**

Comparing compensation of different countries is a complex undertaking for several reasons. First, different countries have different costs of living. Second, the value of the U.S. dollar is always fluctuating, thereby changing one's comparison base. Third, different countries offer different compensation packages. Nevertheless, as you look at the following figures, you might be surprised to see that on average, U.S. manufacturing workers (earning about $27,000 annually) are paid less than their counterparts in Germany, Canada, Japan, Italy, and France. Only Britain pays manufacturing employees less (about $26,000 annually). Professional and managerial employees fare only somewhat better in the United States as they rank fifth out of seven comparison countries. CEOs are best off in the United States, earning an average of about $717,000 annually. Of the six other countries listed here, the next closest is France, where a CEO on average is paid close to $500,000 annually. A more careful look at other countries shows that there are big differences in the nature of the compensation package. Take a typical vice president of human resources, for example. Although the total income is about the same in Germany ($145,000) and the United States ($159,000), and slightly higher in Japan ($185,000), a breakdown of the sources of income shows great differences. Consider the bonus package. The typical VP of human resources in the United States gets nearly $14,000 a year from long-term incentives; his or her counterpart in Japan and Germany gets no long-term incentives. Instead, his or her counterpart in Japan gets nearly $10,000 in fixed bonuses. A counterpart in Germany is typically reimbursed more than $5,000 for automobile expenses. A major reason for the Japanese VP of Human Resources having a higher average salary is due to perquisites, such as a company car, club membership at an exclusive club (worth more than $5,000), and an entertainment allowance. The lesson: comparing pay between different countries can be very tricky.

Source: Adapted from A. Bennett, "Managers' Incomes Aren't Worlds Apart," *The Wall Street Journal,* October 12, 1992, B1.

Determining External Value: Using Wage and Salary Surveys

In order to assess external equity, organizations use wage and salary surveys, which report what other companies are paying their employees. An example of a page from a wage and salary survey is shown in Table 8.3. Organizations use wage and salary surveys for two purposes. A labor market survey provides information as to what other organizations that compete for employees are paying. The labor market survey, then, is used to determine what other companies are paying employees so that an organization can effectively recruit and retain its workers. A product market survey provides information as to what other organizations providing the same product or service are paying their employees. The product market survey, then, is used to make sure that the organization's payroll costs are not higher than its business competitors. Because the labor market and product market surveys have very different purposes, the information they contain may be based on completely different organizations. Consider, for example, the wage and salary surveys used by an automobile manufacturer located in central Indiana. The labor market survey may include all businesses within 100 miles of this factory, because those might be the organizations the automobile manufacturer competes with for employees. The product market survey, however, may be based on all automobile manufacturers worldwide, because those companies represent the business competition.[21]

Labor market survey Provides information as to what other organizations that compete for employees are paying; used to determine what other companies are paying employees so that an organization can effectively recruit and retain its workers.

Product market survey Provides information as to what other organizations providing the same product or service are paying their employees; used to make sure that the organization's payroll costs are not higher than its business competitors.

Wage and salary surveys can be obtained from a number of sources. Most organizations will use one or more of the following sources:

1. Federal Government. The federal government routinely conducts salary and wage surveys for major metropolitan areas in the United States.
2. Professional Associations. Many professional associations conduct wage and salary surveys as a service for their members. Graduating college students might be particularly interested in obtaining a copy of the Endicott Report, published by Northwestern University in Evanston, Illinois, which surveys starting salaries offered to graduating college students.
3. Consulting Firms. A number of well-known consulting firms conduct wage and salary surveys, including Hay Associates, Towers, Perrin, and William Mercer. Some consulting firms focus on a particular industry, such as health care, while others specialize in a particular occupational group, such as middle and top management. Prices for these surveys vary, but they generally cost several thousand dollars.[22]

The Pay Structure: Merging Job Evaluation and Salary and Wage Surveys

You may be wondering at this point why organizations do not simply conduct a salary and wage survey to determine how to pay their jobs. The answer is that wage and salary surveys have several limitations. First, most organizations have jobs for which there is no close match in the salary surveys. For any number of jobs, then,

Table 8.3 **Page from a Salary Survey (continued)**

Survey Report Prepared by Compensation Consulting Firm

REPORT PREPARED FOR COMPANY **P844** LOMELI PHARMACEUTICALS

Modifier (A=stronger match; B=exact match; C=weaker match)

Company's salary grade or job evaluation points

SIRS job family — *SIRS subfamily* — *Level of job (3=senior)*

0.9 . 04 TQ14 LEVEL 3 PROGRAMMING/ANALY-BUSINESS APPLICATIONS

Salary range minimum, midpoint or control point (*), maximum

Status under Fair Labor Standards Act

Company number — *Benchmark job code and title*

CO NO	MOD	JOB TITLE/INTERNAL JOB CODE		NO OF INC	—ACTUAL SALARIES— AVG	LOW	HIGH	RANGE MIN	MIDPT/ CNTRL	RANGE MAX	%SP	GR/ PTS	FL SA	TOTAL COMP
E067	B	PROG/ANALYST BUSINESS-SR		2	32396	32240	32500	25220	31564	37908	50	53	E	33692
E008	C	SR DATA PROC ANALYST		5	32656	28288	35464	25584	35464	45344	77	A4	E	34145
P023	B	PROGRAMMER ANALYST SR		13	34892	31980	39156	25584	37310	49036	92	45	E	34892
D032	B	MGMT SYSTEMS ANALYST SR		2	34892	33852	35880	31460	39520	47580	51	11	E	34892
E009	B	PROGRAMMER/ANALYST BUS		8	35388	31500	38400	29160	37860	46560	60	07	E	35388
E017	B	MCS 2-BUSINESS		297	35620	28756	45604	29380	39468	49556	69	12	E	35620
G002	B	PRINCIPAL BUSINESS PROG		1	36240	36240	36240	31740	39360	46980	48	A4	E	36240
P019	B	PRGRMMR/ANLYST SENIOR		12	36868	32240	43836	31460	41678	51896	65	73	E	36868
E231	B	PROGRAMMER ANALYST SR		3	37260	33000	39540	28896	37596*	45096	56	08	E	38750
E111	C	PROGRAMMER ANALYST SR		3	37536	34560	41520	28896	37002	45108	56	08	E	37536
P221	B	PROG/ANALY III		1	37980	37980	37980	30936	39600	48264	56	26	E	37980
E008	B	ADP ANALYST		4	38948	34840	43160	27144	39364	51584	90	A5	E	38948
E035	B	SR SYS ANALYST GEN		22	39204	27000	48195	33600	42000	50400	50	10	E	39204
P844	**B**	**SYSTEMS DEV SPEC III**	**4821**	**3**	**39252**	**37392**	**42300**	**27744**	**39636**	**51528**	**86**	**28**	**E**	**39252**
A012	B	ADMIN INFO SYS PROG/ANL		9	40040	35776	43628	33436	43498	53560	60	06	E	42442
K215	B	COMPUTING ANL SR		7	40196	31200	44096	31096	39676	48204	55	75	E	40196
E020	B	PROGRAMMER/ANALYST SR		1	40352	40352	40352	35880	46254	56628	58	14	E	40352

E015	C	PROGRAMMER ANALYST II	4	40417	39000	44200	31252	39052	46852	50	47	E	40417
C026	B	SR SYSTEMS ANALYST	13	40760	36312	47944	31100	40400	49700	60	09	E	40760
E003	B	PROGRAMMER/ANALYST SR	6	40812	37560	44100	31920	39900	47880	50	46	E	40812
E017	A	MCS 3-BUSINESS	125	41392	32916	50960	32136	42510	52884	65	13	E	41392
E111	B	PROG/SYS ANALYST (SR)	3	41520	40800	42600	32496	41646	50796	56	09	E	41520
B110	B	PROGRAMMER ANALYST III	103	41772	34560	51240	34560	43200	51840	50	09	E	41772
F007	A	SR PROGRAMMER/ANALYST	24	41988	29784	52740	34416	44748	55068	60	05	E	41988
P122	B	SR PROGRAMMER/ANALYST	1	42840	42840	42840	32400	41500	50600	56	13	E	42840
E009	A	PROGRAMMER ANALYST BUS	10	43080	39852	49116	33120	43260	53400	61	08	E	44803
S037	B	MGMT SYS ANALYST SR	2	43160	42276	43992	30680	40820	50960	66	47	E	43160
E034	B	ANALYST BUS SYSTEMS SR	1	44720	44720	44720	31564	42458	53352	69	17	E	44720
Q154	A	PROGRAMMER ANALYST SR	1	45032	45032	45032	35828	45136	54444	52	18	E	45032
E231	A	PROGRAMMER ANALYST STAFF	4	47436	44580	53040	36600	47604*	57096	56	10	E	47436
Q018	A	INFO SYS ANALYST SR	4	47700	46644	49008	32700	44790	56880	74	23	E	47700
E015	B	PROGRAMMER ANALYST I	1	48308	48308	48308	33540	41912	50284	50	49	E	48308
P005	B	SR MIS SPEC	1	50492	50492	50492	34216	45604*	54704	60	10	E	50492
		26 COMPANIES TOTAL INCUMBENTS	696										
		COMPANY P844 AVERAGE	3	**39252**	**37392**	**42300**	**27744**	**39636**	**51528**	86			**39252**
		MARKET WEIGHTED AVERAGE	693	38570			31179	40999	50801	63			38647
		MARKET SIMPLE AVERAGE		40360	36314	44659	31667	41143	50475	59			40596
		MARKET ARITHMETIC AVERAGE MIDPOINT						41071					
		LOW		32396	27000	32500	25220	31564	37908	48			33692
		HIGH		50492	50492	53040	36600	47604	57096	92			50492
		3 COMPANIES MATCHING MODIFIER C	12	36463	33949	40394	28577	37172	45768	60			37083
		23 COMPANIES MATCHING MODIFIER B	513	37531	36731	42817	31194	40530	49712	59			37587
		6 COMPANIES MATCHING MODIFIER A	168	41893	39801	49982	34133	44675	54962	61			41996

Your company's data, including internal job code, in boldface for easy reference

Number of incumbents reported to job

Salary range percentage spread minimum to maximum

Base salary plus bonus or incentive compensation

Source: Organization Resources Counselors, Inc. From G. Milkovich and J. Newman, *Compensation* (Chicago: Irwin, 1993).

Image 7015 © 1995 PhotoDisc, Inc.

Some companies determine salaries by looking at benchmark jobs, such as this forklift operator in a production warehouse. Because of the consistency in job responsibilities and tasks, the forklift operator's position and salary is the standard by which other production pay ranges are established.

there may be no salary survey information with which to determine pay. Second, even if there is a relatively close match for a particular job in the salary surveys, there may be some differences (for example, your organization uses the same job title, but the incumbent has additional duties and responsibilities not covered in the survey jobs). Third, for most jobs there is a range of pay across companies, not a single rate. Thus, a secretary may be paid as little as $6 per hour or as much as $12 per hour at different companies. Fourth, your organization may value some jobs more than the external market does.

For all of these reasons, most companies use the wage and salary surveys only to obtain information for benchmark jobs, and then use the results from a job evaluation to determine the pay for nonbenchmark jobs. Benchmark jobs have the following basic characteristics:[23]

Benchmark jobs
Jobs that are similar or comparable in content across firms.

1. Many workers in other companies have these jobs.
2. They will not be changing in the foreseeable future in terms of tasks, responsibilities, and so forth.
3. They represent the full range in terms of salary, such that some are among the lowest paid in the group of jobs, others are in the middle range, and some are at the high end of the pay scale.

At this point, the manager in charge of developing the pay structure has sufficient information to do so. For sake of example, let us assume that the manager has both salary information for 30 benchmark jobs and job evaluation points for all 100 managerial and professional jobs within the organization. Now the task is to determine the appropriate pay for all of these 100 jobs, not just the 30 benchmark jobs. In other words, the manager must determine the pay structure, which designates the base pay for each job. In designing the pay structure, the manager must make five decisions.

Pay structure
Designates the base pay for each job.

1. What Should the Pay Level Be Compared to Other Organizations? This question concerns how the organization's average salary or wage should compare to the average salary or wage paid by other organizations. Should the organization match (pay about average), lead (pay more), or lag (pay less) relative to other organizations? In deciding which of these three courses of action to follow, the manager must consider a number of factors, one of which will be the organization's ability to pay. If, for example, the organization is losing money it may be difficult to lead the market. Conversely, given evidence that pay level can increase the number of job applicants, the likelihood of an applicant's accepting a job offer, and the performance of employees, the benefits of higher salaries may outweigh the costs.[24]

2. Should Each Job Be Considered Separately or Should Jobs Be Broken Down into Grades? In most cases, the manager will choose to sort the jobs into a smaller number of job grades or classes. The reason for this is that it would be quite confusing administratively to try to establish pay rules for each job in the organization when there may be hundreds or even thousands of different jobs. Administratively, it is simpler to divide the jobs into anywhere from 10 to 20 different grades. How many grades are needed for a particular set of jobs depends on many factors, such as the number of managerial levels within the organization and how quickly employees are expected to progress from grade to grade. Depending on how many grades are desired, the manager may place all jobs rated between 100–120 points in grade 1, all jobs rated between 121–140 points in grade 2, and so forth.

Job grades
A manager may choose to sort jobs into a smaller number of grades or classes, usually into 10–20 different grades.

3. Should Each Grade Be Paid a Single Salary or Should There Be a Range of Pay for Each Grade? In most cases, the manager will choose to have a pay range within each grade. The logic behind that choice is that even within the same job, two people may need to be paid differently, depending on their seniority, performance, or other relevant factors. How large the range is depends on various factors, such as the amount of variation in job performance and the length of time a worker is likely to stay within the grade. To operationalize the range, each grade will have a minimum as well as a maximum salary. From an employee's perspective, this can be good news or bad news, depending on where you stand in the grade. The good news is that within a grade, you will earn at least the minimum wage designated for that grade. The bad news is that if you are at the top of your grade, you will not make more money, unless adjustments are made for inflation, the maximum is raised, or you are promoted to a higher grade.

Pay range
The range of pay a manager chooses within each grade, usually depending on seniority, performance, or other relevant factors.

4. How Much Overlap Should There Be between Grades? The amount of grade overlap, or the overlap that exists between grades, affects whether salaries in one grade will be more or less equivalent to salaries in higher grades. As shown in Figure 8.3, for any given set of grades, there may be no overlap (as shown in Figure 8.3a) between grades, some overlap between grades (as shown in Figure 8.3b), or nearly complete overlap between grades (as shown in Figure 8.3c). All else being equal, the less overlap between grades, the greater the incentive for the employee to move from grade to grade. Companies that wish to use promotions to motivate employees will have less overlap between grades.[25]

Grade overlap
The amount of overlap that exists between grades.

5. What Is the Midpoint Salary for Each Grade? The midpoint or salary corresponding to the middle point of the grade, must be determined. A quantitative

Figure 8.3 **Different Overlap between Grades**

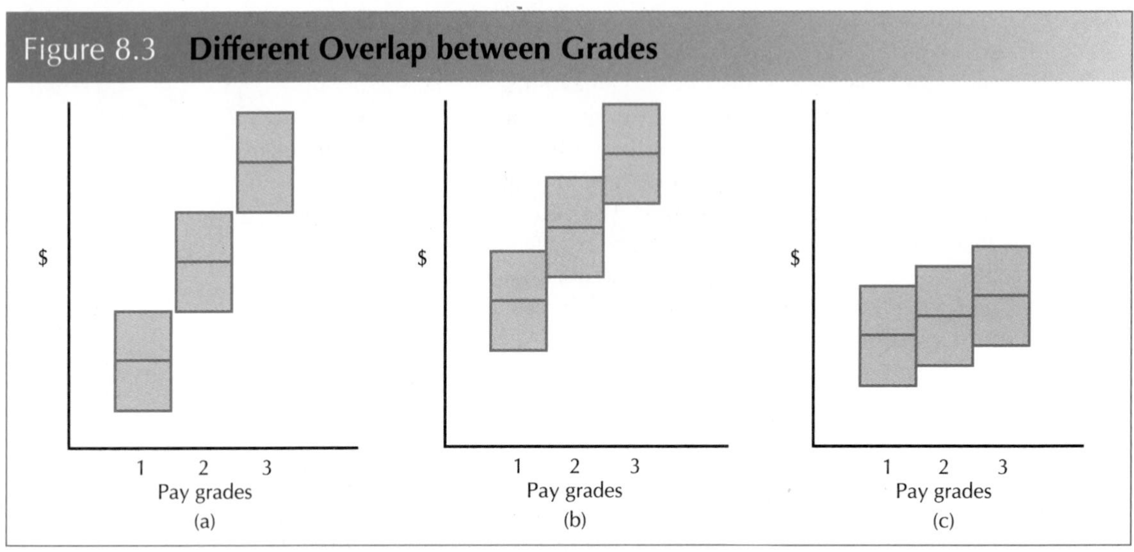

approach is to use regression analysis, a statistical technique that relates two variables. In the present situation, one would use job evaluation points and salary data from the benchmark jobs as the two variables. The regression analysis provides a formula based on this data. For example, the following formula might be produced by the regression analysis: weekly salary $= 410 + 2.0\,x$ (points). To use the formula to determine the midpoint salary in each grade, the manager could take the average number of job evaluation points for each grade and insert this number into the formula. For example, if jobs in grade 1 were worth an average of 110 points, the manager would multiply 2.0 by 110 and add 410, for a total of 630. Thus, the midpoint weekly salary for grade 1 would be $630. Based on the range that had been decided, the manager could then determine the minimum and maximum wage of grade 1. A similar procedure would be used for the remaining grades.[26]

Depending on the organization's particular objectives, quite different pay structures may be developed. Consider, for example, Organization A, whose pay structure is shown in Figure 8.4a. Assume that all new employees are hired in at grade 1, and then as they demonstrate effective performance, they are eligible for promotions to higher grades. As shown there, the pay in the entry-level grade is higher compared to Organization B, whose pay structure is presented in Figure 8.4b. All things being equal, Organization A may be more effective in attracting new employees than Organization B, because of the higher pay in grade 1. At the same time, Organization A's grades have more overlap than Organization B's grades. That means employees in Organization A will be less motivated to get promoted than employees in Organization B. Furthermore, all things being equal, Organization A will be less able to retain existing employees than Organization B, which on average pays employees in grades 4 and 5 more. From an employees' perspective, you should be careful about accepting an entry-level job merely because it pays more than other companies. It is quite possible that another company offering lower pay initially will pay potentially much more for higher level jobs.[27]

Figure 8.4 **Pay Structure from Two Different Organizations**

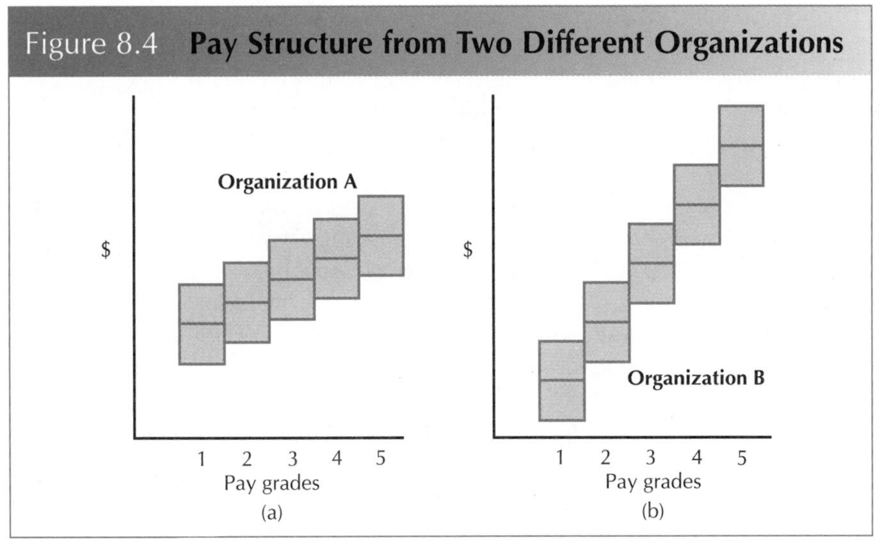

Once the pay structure is designed, adjustments are nearly always required. For example, unless the pay structure is being developed for an organization that does not yet exist, chances are some employees' salaries will be outside of their newly established grade. Green circle rates apply to employees whose salaries are below the minimum of their grades. Depending on the company's financial constraints, their pay may be increased immediately to the minimum of the grade, or it is more rapidly increased than that of other employees over a period of several years. Red circle rates apply to employees whose salaries exceed the maximum of their respective grades. Because of adverse reactions to pay being cut, most organizations will refrain from immediately reducing an employee's pay. Rather, over time, raises may be much smaller or nonexistent until the employee's pay is within the grade range. Another often needed adjustment is in regard to the grade a job is assigned. Sometimes a job will be misclassified, or its duties and responsibilities will change. A formal procedure for requesting a job grade review is therefore recommended to avoid perceived inequities that might otherwise result. As an employee, this might be one avenue for pursuing a pay raise.[28]

Green circle rates
Apply to employees whose salaries are below the minimum of their respective grade.

Red circle rates
Apply to employees whose salaries exceed the maximum of their respective grades.

In conclusion, an organization's pay structure can have an important effect on its ability to attract, retain, and motivate employees. Without a formal pay structure, an organization may face much confusion and make many mistakes in pay decisions. In turn, these matters can affect the organization's ability to survive and prosper. Despite the popularity of the traditional pay structure as described here, several alternative approaches are available, including broadbanding, market pricing, and skill-based pay. These three approaches are described in greater detail next.

Alternatives to Traditional Pay Structures

Boardbanding

Broadbanding may be defined as a pay structure that contains relatively few grades, with much greater range in each. As compared to the traditional pay

Broadbanding
A pay structure that contains relatively few grades, with much greater range in each as compared to the traditional pay structure.

structure, which consists of 10 to 20 pay grades, each with relatively little range, the broadbanding approach may use as few as three pay grades, with a great deal of range within each grade. The difference between the traditional pay structure and the broadbanding approach is illustrated in Figure 8.5.[29]

To understand why broadbanding may be preferred over the traditional system, recall from Chapter 6 that a number of changes have occurred in the workplace in recent years, including far fewer promotion opportunities and an increased emphasis on cross-training. Considering first the limited number of promotions in organizations, recall that the traditional pay structure emphasizes the value of promotions. The broadbanding approach, by having relatively few job grades, downplays the value of promotions. This is further reinforced by having a large range within each grade, allowing for considerable room for rewarding performance. With regard to the emphasis on cross-training, it may sometimes be critical for an employee to take a lower-level position as part of a developmental experience. With the traditional system, moving to a lower grade might require a pay cut. With the broadbanding approach, because there are few job grades, there is less of a chance that the other job is in a lower grade. Hence, the broadbanding approach facilitates job transfers and similar developmental experiences.

Although broadbanding has several advantages, it is not without problems. One problem that can arise is increased difficulty in controlling costs. Because jobs that might otherwise be in two or three different job grades are now all in the same grade, managers may be inclined to press for higher salaries for jobs that are not worth quite so much. Communication of the new "rules of the game" may also become more difficult, as the rules for obtaining a bigger salary are less clear. Nevertheless, depending on the particular circumstances, broadbanding may be a useful alternative to the traditional approach.

Market pricing
An approach to developing a pay structure that essentially downplays internal value and relies almost exclusively on external value to determine pay.

Market Pricing

The market pricing approach to developing a pay structure essentially downplays internal value. Instead, this approach relies almost exclusively on external value to determine pay. The underlying premise is that the organization should pay

Figure 8.5 **Traditional versus Broadbanding Pay Structure**

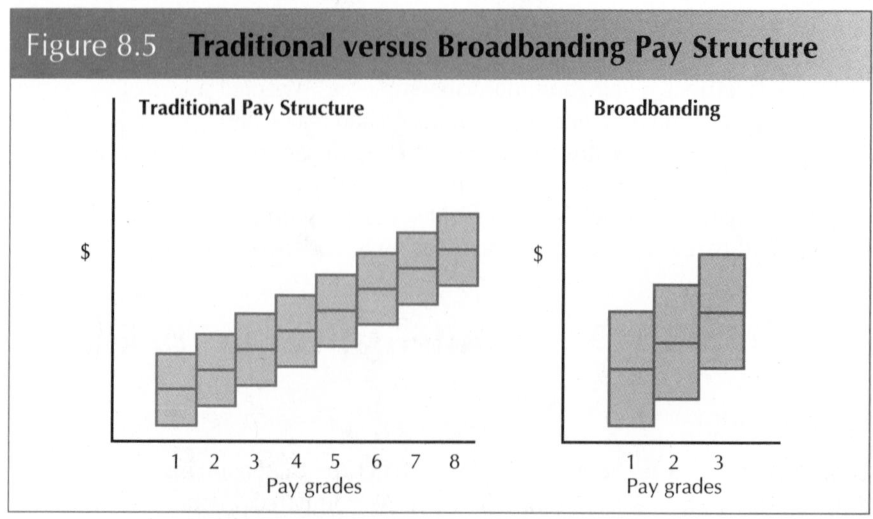

employees what it needs to hire and retrain them, with much less regard for internal fairness.[30]

Organizations that use this system obtain as much information on benchmark jobs as possible. Once that process is completed, the nonbenchmark jobs are priced in between, based on logical relationships. For example, assume the vice president of human resources and compensation analyst positions are two benchmark jobs for which we have external salary data. Now, we must decide how to "price" the manager of compensation job. Because this position reports to the vice president of human resources, while the compensation analyst reports to the manager of compensation, it is reasonable to "price" this position somewhere between the two benchmark jobs.

A market pricing strategy is likely to be particularly appropriate for an organization that is concerned with keeping costs down and does a great deal of hiring from the external labor market. Thus, this system should be best in attracting new employees and retaining high performers. The potential disadvantage is an increased likelihood that current employees will perceive internal unfairness.

Skill-Based Pay

Skill-based pay represents a significant departure from the traditional pay structure. Essentially, this procedure rewards workers for the skills or knowledge they have mastered. The more skills or knowledge an employee has mastered, the higher his or her pay. It is important to note that in a skill-based pay program, workers can only use one skill at a time; so skill-based pay is *not* job enlargement. Skill-based pay therefore pays the worker for what he or she knows, not what he or she is actually doing. Although relatively few companies use skill-based pay plans, new plants operated by Procter & Gamble, Honeywell, and TRW, to name a few, have adopted this kind of pay system.[31]

Skill-based pay
An approach that represents a significant departure from the traditional pay structure, this procedure rewards workers for the skills or knowledge they have mastered.

There are several different ways to set up this kind of pay plan. One way is to divide the relevant jobs into separate functions or modules. For example, suppose construction of a handmade suit involves four functions: arranging materials in accordance with the pattern, cutting materials, sewing materials, and assembling the finished product for packaging and shipping. Under a traditional pay plan, the person who sews might be paid the most, followed by the cutter. Perhaps the person who arranges the materials and the person who assembles the finished product for packaging and shipping are paid the least. Under the skill-based pay plan, however, employees will be paid for each job that they are capable of doing. The person who is capable of sewing and cutting would be paid more than the person who is just able to sew.

Companies that use the skill-based pay system cite a number of advantages to this approach. One advantage is greater workforce flexibility. If, for example, an employee is absent, it will be easier to move other workers around to fill the position. Similarly, if there is a bottleneck in one section (perhaps the cutting stage in the example above), everyone who is capable of doing that function can help complete the work. Another advantage is a complete understanding of the product or service being performed. Advocates of skill-based pay argue that the greater an employee's understanding of the work, the more likely the employee will be to offer work innovations and suggestions. Third, the ability to perform different jobs will enable the workers to use a variety of skills and rotate jobs. In turn, this should increase satisfaction with the work and help relieve boredom. Thus, skill-based pay systems have a number of potential advantages.[32]

Of course, there are several potential disadvantages to skill-based pay. One potentially unavoidable concern is that most skill-based pay plans will cost more than a traditional plan. This is primarily due to the fact that the company is paying people for what they know, not what they do. So the person who is capable of doing more than one job is paid more, even though he or she can only perform one job at a time. A second disadvantage is that the company will be required to spend a great deal of time training and developing employees to enable them to perform additional jobs. Finally, there are numerous situations where skill-based pay should not be used. Perhaps the worst situation for skill-based pay would be one where highly trained specialists are needed. Would you want surgeons, for example, to be on a skill-based pay system? Probably not.[33]

In sum, there are a number of alternatives to the traditional pay structure. Just as there are disadvantages to the traditional pay structure, however, the alternatives also have shortcomings. The specific pay plan your organization uses will depend much upon the particular circumstances involved.

Compensation Administration: Implications for Employees

You have read a great deal about basic compensation administration issues such as legal requirements, job evaluations, salary and wage surveys, and pay structures. As you read about salary negotiations next, you will see that an understanding of these topics will be helpful to you as an employee.

Negotiating a Pay Increase in Your Current Job

Negotiating for a large pay increase in your current job requires a great deal of careful planning and skillful negotiation. Let's start with the planning aspect first. There are several issues that you must carefully plan if you are to be successful in obtaining your desired pay increase. But even before that, you should be aware that some companies have strict policies about discussing pay. In fact, in some companies, discussing pay with a coworker is grounds for dismissal. Other organizations are more open about pay. Bell Labs, for example, publicly displays salaries (without names attached), so employees will know how their pay compares to others.[34]

1. How Much of a Pay Raise Should You Try For? Numerous factors come into play here, including what other people in your field are making, your worth to the company in terms of your performance and the importance of your position, the probability that you could get a job elsewhere, and the company's pay policies and practices. With regard to what other people in the field are making, be sure to gather salary survey information from reliable sources so that you have a good idea as to what other companies are paying, as well as information with regard to what other employees in your organization are being paid. Research shows that people often overestimate the amount of money both lower-level and same-level employees are being paid, so you may mistakenly believe that you are being underpaid. Check your facts carefully! You should also get a sense of the importance of your position (do you play a key role in regard

to the product or service or do you serve in a tangential role?), as well as the labor surplus or shortage in your job market. Try your best to learn about the company pay policies and practices. For example, you may be at the top of your grade level. In that case, your boss may simply respond that you have reached the maximum of your grade, and there is nothing else he or she can do. Finally, be careful that you don't ask for a raise that puts you at or above what your supervisor is making.

2. **Evaluate Your Supervisor's Style.** Perhaps almost as important as the issues mentioned above is to understand your supervisor's style. Some supervisors, for instance, enjoy give-and-take negotiations and will expect you to bargain hard for your raise. This type of supervisor may be impressed by an aggressive style. Others dislike conflict and will avoid confrontations. This type of supervisor might be more convinced by a rational and quiet approach.

3. **Consider Any Objections Your Supervisor May Have and How You Will Respond to Them.** Here are some common objections and possible responses:
   a. *"There is a pay freeze, so no raises are allowed."* Your response: "I realize there is a pay freeze, but if I received a promotion, I would be allowed a raise" or "I understand that pay raises are being allowed in exceptional cases, and I can show you that I should qualify as one."
   b. *"I can't give you that much of an increase; the maximum allowed is* x.*"* Your response: "I can accept that this year. But only if I can have a written promise that next year I will be raised by *y* amount" or "I understand that in exceptional cases, higher raises can be allocated."
   c. *"No one else in your position makes that much money—I can't justify you making more than other employees."* (Remember, as noted above, surveys show that people typically overestimate the salaries their coworkers are earning.) Your response: "Let me review for you the reasons why I should be making a higher salary." Be sure to emphasize your achievements—not your coworker's shortcomings—or your supervisor may conclude that you think he or she isn't monitoring your coworker's performance properly.

Carefully plan your strategy as to how you are going to approach the supervisor. Be ready to present your arguments in a coherent, logical fashion. Some suggestions for your meeting are as follows.

1. **Start by Explaining Several Reasons, All Equally Important, That Should Merit You Your Desired Pay Increase.** These may include what other people are being paid, but you must primarily emphasize your worth to the organization. That is your key bargaining chip; focusing too much on comparisons with other employees may work against you. Also, make sure that you cover all of your points. Avoid letting the supervisor cut you off; on the other hand, you don't want to appear rude by ignoring him or her.

2. **Give the Supervisor an Opportunity to Respond or Think about Your Request.** Offering your supervisor some time to consider your request might be a good way for handling a response like, "No way!" Likewise, "You might desire time to consider my counteroffer."

3. **Work Toward Agreement and Compromise.** Most supervisors are used to negotiating toward a compromise. A particularly effective way to proceed toward

a compromise is to summarize the supervisor's position, including any objections he or she has raised, and then summarize your position. This will be particularly helpful when the supervisor has made a counteroffer on the salary increase.

4. Avoid the Most Common Mistakes. During the meeting, beware of the following missteps:
   a. Settling on a counteroffer too quickly. If you are even a little hesitant to accept the counteroffer, you may get more than you bargained for.
   b. Negotiating when you are not completely prepared. If you don't have all of the facts in front of you, don't negotiate.
   c. Getting upset. It is imperative that you stay calm and relaxed. Getting upset or losing your temper will work against you.
   d. Meeting at a bad time in a bad place. Always arrange for a private meeting with the supervisor where there will be no interruptions (such as phone calls). Choose a time when your supervisor will be receptive to your request. You probably know the times when your supervisor is not in a good mood or is under pressure (for example, Monday mornings are usually not a good time).

Finally, be careful not to let your request for a salary raise backfire. Although research indicates that negotiating can increase your salary, being overly aggressive or demanding could negatively affect your relationship with your supervisor and your company, and it makes matters even worse over the long term. And, with tight times in the last few years, some experts recommend moving away from salary raise requests and focusing on other elements, such as stock options or bonuses.[35]

Conclusion

Compensation administration is an important issue to every organization. In addition to the discrimination laws described in Chapter 2, several additional laws affect compensation practices, including the Fair Labor Standards Act and prevailing wage laws. In determining base wages, organizations use a combination of job evaluation, which focuses on internal fairness, and wage and salary surveys, which address external fairness. A pay structure is ultimately developed, which establishes the wages that an organization will pay each job. Alternatives to the traditional pay structure include broadbanding, market pricing, and skill-based pay. With this basic information in mind, both organizations and individual employees should be able to make effective decisions about pay.

Applying Core Concepts

1. A commercial bakery that has a large contract to produce baked goods for a local army base has asked you what laws are likely to apply in terms of compensation. List all that may apply.
2. A company has asked you to design a job evaluation project. How would you go about this task?
3. The company you or a friend works for has decided to conduct a wage and salary survey. What organizations do you think should be included in the survey? Why?

4. Think of an organization you are very familiar with (if you are not familiar with any organization, use the university setting). Do you think a traditional pay structure, broadbanding, market pricing, or a skill-based pay system would be best? Why?
5. If Laurie from the opening case asked *you* how she should go about asking her boss for a pay raise, what would you suggest?

Key Terms

- Fair Labor Standards Act of 1938
- Nonexempt employees
- Exempt employees
- Equal Pay Act of 1963
- Comparable worth
- Prevailing wage laws
- Job evaluation
- Point method job evaluation
- Compensable factors
- Hay Plan
- Ranking method of job evaluation
- Job classification
- Labor market survey
- Product market survey
- Benchmark jobs
- Pay structure
- Job grades
- Pay range
- Grade overlap
- Green circle rates
- Red circle rates
- Broadbanding
- Market pricing
- Skill-based pay

Chapter 8: Experiential Exercise

Situation A

Background This exercise involves a manager and a job applicant. The manager works for a new technology company (Pi-Tree Industries), and is hiring a new manager of customer relations. The manager (Phil or Phyliss) will be making a salary offer to Chris, the top candidate for the job. The manager will make an offer, and Chris, the job applicant, can either (a) accept the offer; (b) try to negotiate for a higher offer; or (c) decline the offer and see if there is a counteroffer. The role-play ends either when an agreement as to the salary is made OR when either party withdraws from the negotiation.

Manager's Role: You, Phil (or Phyliss) are planning to make a job offer to Chris. Chris would be an *outstanding* manager from everything you can tell, and you would very much like to hire Chris as manager of customer relations. What you must now decide is how much salary to offer Chris. The following information is important in making your decision:

1. Other managers at your company at the same manager of customer relations level earn between \$40,000 to \$70,000 annually (everyone is eligible for a fifteen percent bonus, which has been given every year, anyhow. The bonus is a standard plan and cannot be changed). These managers have all been with the company for at least twenty years. Based on the salary structure, the most a manager at this level can earn is \$75,000. Because this maximum has not changed in several years, a manager who earns \$75,000 may not obtain a salary increase too quickly.
2. A salary survey from a major consulting firm indicates that the average industry pay for a manager of customer relations in your city is about \$70,000, plus a fifteen percent bonus. Most companies pay at least \$55,000 for this job, and a few pay \$90,000 or more.
3. Chris presently earns \$60,000 (plus a ten percent bonus), and indicated that it would take a good salary offer to move.
4. You are the vice president of administration, and you earn \$95,000 (plus a twenty-five percent bonus). From what you can see, you will need to offer Chris a good enough salary and yet at the same time not pay so much that the other managers will become upset and leave. Money for salaries is pretty tight now, and it will be very difficult to raise the other managers' pay.

Chapter 8: Experiential Exercise *(continued)*

Job Applicant's Role: You are Chris, a job applicant who is going to get a job offer to work as manager of customer relations at Pi-Tree Industries. Presently, you are paid $60,000 annually (plus a bonus, which varies from five–ten percent of your salary). You would really like to work for this new company, which (according to a friend at the company) apparently pays quite well and has excellent opportunities for promotion (in fact, the person who is hiring you seems to be nearing retirement age). The following information should be considered in evaluating a salary offer:

1. According to business contacts, the average industry pay for this job in your city is about $77,000. Bonuses of up to twenty percent are not uncommon. Some companies pay as much as $90,000 and you are hoping that is the case here.
2. A recruiter you know well told you that most people don't take another job unless the new job offers at least a fifteen percent salary increase, if not twenty percent.
3. You have outstanding experience and have been recruited by several companies. Getting jobs is not a problem for you. Pi-Tree, however, is an extremely exciting company with tremendous successes.

Situation B

Background: This situation involves an employee and a manager who are meeting about a raise. The employee is apparently upset by the raise he or she received.

Supervisor: As you examine your records about Jo(e), the employee, you find that the employee's starting salary was about five percent higher than other people doing the same job. So, for the first raise at the company, you assigned a slightly lower raise for Jo(e) (four percent versus six percent for the department average). Jo(e) must have found out about this lower raise, and is curious. It's clear to you that Jo(e) does a good job, but other employees will be upset if they find out that Jo(e) makes more money than them. Besides, at Jo(e)'s salary, a four percent raise is pretty close in actual dollar amount to the six percent that other people are averaging. Finally, if you give in to a bigger raise to Jo(e), every employee is going to try to do the same thing and you are going to have to say "no" to somebody!

Employee: You, Jo(e) are pretty upset about the first raise you have received from the company. While several of your coworkers received a seven percent raise, you only received four percent. You know your work is among the best in the unit, because your supervisor, whom you are meeting with next, told you several times this year that your work was excellent. And you know the company thinks highly of you because you were hired at a pretty good salary. You are pretty demoralized, then, by the raise you received, and are asking for another two percent (to make a total of six percent raise). You think it's very likely that the four percent was just an error anyhow.

Chapter 8 References

1. F. Hills, T.J. Bergmann, and V. Scarpello. *Compensation Decision-Making* (Fort Worth, TX: The Dryden Press, 1994).
2. M. Wallace and C. Fay, *Compensation Theory and Practice* (Boston, PWS-Kent, 1988).
3. L. Joel, *Every Employee's Guide to the Law* (New York: Pantheon, 1993).
4. Ibid.
5. Ibid.
6. M. Player, *Federal Law of Employment Discrimination* (St. Paul, MN: West, 1992).

7. E. Livernash, *Comparable Worth: Issues and Alternatives* (Washington: Equal Employment Advisory Council, 1980).
8. G. Milkovich and J. Newman. *Compensation* (Chicago: Irwin, 1996).
9. Ibid.
10. Ibid.
11. Ibid.
12. R. Scholl, E. Cooper, and J. McKenna. "Referent Selection in Determining Equity Perceptions: Differential Effects on Behavioral and Attitudinal Outcomes," *Personnel Psychology* 40 (1987), 113–124.
13. R. Henderson, *Compensation Management* (Englewood Cliffs, NJ: Prentice-Hall, 1994).
14. Wallace and Fay, *Compensation Theory and Practice;* and Hills, Bergmann, and Scarpello, *Compensation Decision-Making.*
15. Wallace and Fay, *Compensation Theory and Practice.*
16. Henderson, *Compensation Management.*
17. Wallace and Fay, *Compensation Theory and Practice.*
18. Milkovich and Newman, *Compensation.*
19. R. Madigan and D. Hoover, "Effects of Alternative Job Evaluation Methods on Decisions Involving Pay Equity," *Academy of Management Journal* 29 (1986), 84–100.
20. J. Collins and P. Muchinsky, "An Assessment of the Construct Validity of Three Job Evaluation Methods: A Field Experiment," *Academy of Management Journal* 36 (1993), 895–904.
21. Hills, Bergmann, and Scarpello, *Compensation Decision-Making.*
22. Ibid.
23. Wallace and Fay, *Compensation Theory and Practice.*
24. B. Gerhart and G. Milkovich, "Employee Compensation: Research and Practice," in *Handbook of Industrial and Organizational Psychology,* ed. M. Dunnette and L. Hough (Palo Alto, CA: Consulting Psychologists Press, 1992).
25. N. Bereman and M. Lengnick-Hall, *Compensation Decision Making: A Computer-Based Approach* (Fort Worth, TX: The Dryden Press, 1994).
26. Ibid.
27. Milkovich and Newman, *Compensation.*
28. Henderson, *Compensation Management.*
29. D. Hofrichter, "Broadbanding: A 'Second Generation' Approach," *Compensation and Benefits Review* 25 (1993), 53–58.
30. Ibid.
31. E. Lawler, *Strategic Pay* (San Francisco: Jossey-Bass, 1990).
32. Ibid.
33. H. Tosi and L. Tosi, "What Managers Need to Know about Knowledge-Based Pay," *Organizational Dynamics* 14 (1986), 52–64.
34. Adapted from G. Hartman, *"How to Negotiate a Bigger Raise,"* (Hauppauge, NY: Barron's Educational Services, 1991).
35. J. Rigdon, "I Want More: In Hard Times, the Old Rules on Pay Raises No Longer Apply," *The Wall Street Journal,* April 22, 1992, R5.

chapter 9 Pay for Performance

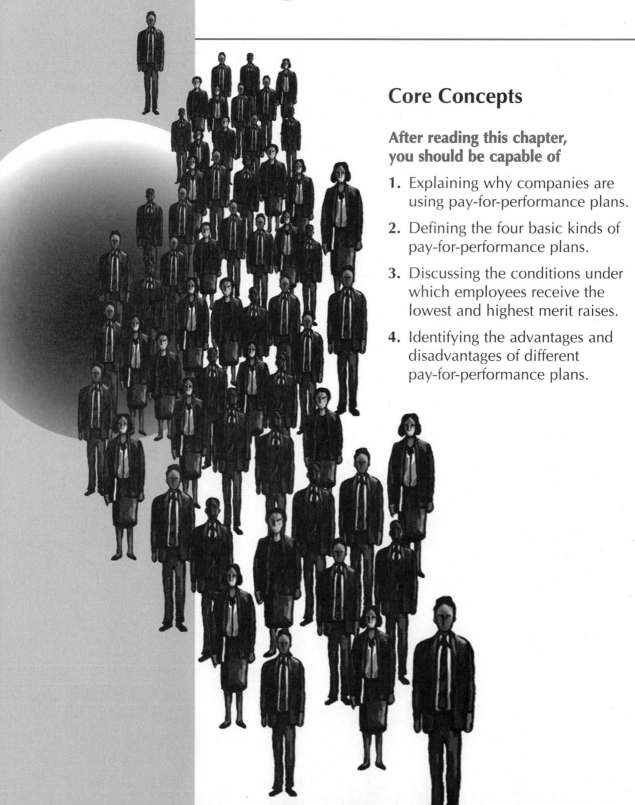

Core Concepts

After reading this chapter, you should be capable of

1. Explaining why companies are using pay-for-performance plans.
2. Defining the four basic kinds of pay-for-performance plans.
3. Discussing the conditions under which employees receive the lowest and highest merit raises.
4. Identifying the advantages and disadvantages of different pay-for-performance plans.

Opening Case

During the last month, Ricardo has received job offers from four different companies. Each job involves software sales for a medium-size computer products company, and in each case, the work is the same, the benefits are the same, and the coworkers seem quite similar. Even the type of software Ricardo would be selling is the same. The only difference between the jobs is the pay policy.

Stable Works, Inc. provides a fairly generous base pay. The company told Ricardo that pay increases will depend on the area manager's yearly review of Ricardo's work.

The second company, Fire Cracker Software, bases pay primarily on the salesperson's sales volume. Although Ricardo would be paid at least a minimum wage every month, he will earn a higher salary only to the degree that he is successful selling the software. This company even showed him the highest and lowest monthly salaries earned by sales associates for the last two years. While the average monthly salary was somewhat lower than the base salary at Stable Works, in some months a few sales associates earned double or even triple the monthly salary earned at Stable Works.

The third company, TeamWare Limited, offered yet a third type of pay plan. Under this plan, Ricardo would earn a modest base salary, roughly half of what Stable Works offered him. He would be part of a four-person sales team. The commission, based on sales volume, will depend on the team's performance. The team also decides how to distribute the commission. Usually, Vanessa Williams (the area manager) said, everyone shares equally in the bonus, which she said typically ranges from roughly one-quarter to double the base salary.

The fourth firm, Corporate Solutions, offered Ricardo a starting salary roughly 20 percent lower than what Stable Works offered, but had a profit-sharing plan based on company profitability. Over the past five years, the company has done extremely well, paying out yearly amounts equivalent to anywhere betwen 15 percent to 35 percent of sales associates' yearly salaries.

Clearly, each of these companies has a different pay policy, and Ricardo realizes that the policies have different consequences for him. While he likes the assurance of the high base pay offered by Stable Works, Inc., it seems as though he would have the most influence over his pay at Fire Cracker Software. But, under this plan his salary could change from month to month, and some months he might only get a minimum wage. TeamWare sounds as though it might be a nice mix of base and bonus pay, but Ricardo wonders what would happen if there were conflicts within the team. And at Corporate Solutions, it seems as though many different factors, many of which will be out of Ricardo's control, would affect his pay.

What would you do if you were in this situation? As you can probably guess, each of these pay-for-performance (P-f-P) policies has advantages as well as disadvantages for both the organization and the employee. Many organizations are trying to find the P-f-P plan that works best for them. The purpose of this chapter, then, is to examine why companies would implement a P-f-P plan, to identify what kinds of P-f-P plans there are, and to review some of the advantages and disadvantages for each plan. We begin first with a discussion of why companies implement P-f-P plans.

Why Do Companies Implement Pay-for-Performance Plans?

A P-f-P plan is a program in which the employee's pay is at least in part dependent upon job performance. As you will see a little bit later, P-f-P plans differ widely in terms of whether performance refers to the individual employee's success, his or her work group's success, or the success of the division, plant, or company.

Companies use pay-for-performance plans for several reasons. Each of these is described in greater detail next.[1]

1. **Pay Is a Powerful Motivator for Employees.** Not surprisingly, a properly designed and implemented P-f-P plan will be a strong motivator for employees. For example, a review of one type of P-f-P plan, profit-sharing, estimated an average productivity increase of 7.4 percent.[2] A study of gain sharing, a different kind of P-f-P plan, found that defects per 1,000 units fell from 20.93 to 2.31 once the plan was implemented.[3]

2. **Many Employees Support the Pay-for-Performance Concept.** Many employees believe that job performance should be a major determinant of pay. In one survey, for instance, respondents rated level of job performance as being the most important factor in determining the size of a salary increase. In contrast, seniority was rated the least important factor.[4] Thus, employees generally support the pay-for-performance concept.

3. **Pay for Performance Plans Attract and Retain Top Performers.** A successful P-f-P plan will attract and retain highly qualified applicants, who will view the plan as offering excellent opportunities for financial rewards. For example, one survey indicated that professional employees in U.S. Navy laboratories were less likely to quit when a pay-for-performance plan was in place.[5]

4. **Pay-for-Performance Plans Provide a Clear Signal.** An often overlooked advantage of a well-designed P-f-P plan is that it clearly defines what performance is desired and what the standards for performance are in the organization. As described in Chapter 7, performance dimensions and standards are often ambiguous. By developing a P-f-P plan, two things happen. First, the organization must decide what employee behaviors, processes, and goals are important, and it must communicate those expectations to the employees. Thus, the organization is compelled to consider its mission and goals. Second, employees will have a better understanding of what the company desires, and therefore should be more successful in their jobs.

In sum, an effective P-f-P plan may be useful for an organization for several reasons. Of course, much depends on how well designed and implemented the plan is. A poorly designed P-f-P plan can do more harm than no P-f-P plan at all.

Alternatives to Pay for Performance

Not all companies have a P-f-P plan. In some companies, seniority is the sole determinant of pay increases. Do you think that two employees doing the same job, with equal skills and identical job performance, should be paid differently if one has worked longer with the company? As noted earlier, one survey indicated that people consider seniority the least important factor in salary raises. Can you think of any logical reasons as to why seniority should be a determinant of pay increases? One answer might be that employees would be encouraged to stay with a company if their pay was related to seniority. Critics, however, would question what value seniority provides to the company, and they would probably argue that pay should

Box 9.1 **Pay-for-Performance in Other Parts of the World**

In the United States there is a deeply ingrained notion that high performers should receive greater pay than low performers. In Pacific Rim countries, that concept is considered quite alien. In fact, the entire pay-for-performance concept, even at the group or organization level, is hardly widespread. Moreover, Pacific Rim companies are slow to implement new pay-for-performance systems. There are, of course, a few exceptions. Countries such as Hong Kong, Taiwan, and Singapore make extensive use of individual incentive plans in the manufacturing sector. A few industries in Japan also use individual incentive plans. On the other hand, lump-sum bonuses are quite common in Pacific Rim countries. The size of this bonus may range from as little as 10 percent to as much as 30 percent of base pay. But unlike U.S. companies, the bonus is rarely tied directly to the employees' or company's performance. Instead, the bonus is virtually automatic, which is why it is often called an allowance. Only in cases of financial emergency is an organization likely to eliminate the bonus.

Cultural differences probably account for the tremendous variation in pay-for-performance practices between the United States and the Pacific Rim. In general, Pacific Rim countries value loyalty and cooperation a great deal, which in turn increases the likelihood that organizations in this part of the world would use a stable wage, rather than one that varies with performance. Second, Pacific Rim culture generally values certainty, which fits with the emphasis on guaranteed base wage rather than a contingency wage. Third, people in the Pacific Rim place much more emphasis on teams and groups than on individual achievements. Clearly, when it comes to pay-for-performance, U.S. managers should not automatically assume that practices that are effective in the United States will be successful in the Pacific Rim.

Other Western countries are far more similar to the United States in regard to their pay-for-performance plans. As an example, many organizations in Great Britain use merit pay systems, particularly for management and professional employees. Most recently, however, English companies have begun to apply merit pay concepts to office and administrative employees as well.

Although individual incentive plans were once quite common in British manufacturing facilities, the popularity of these plans has declined in Great Britain just as it has in the United States, and for similar reasons. Among the reasons mentioned in Great Britain are an increased emphasis on quality, as well as the growth of teams, which require more group cooperation. A third reason cited is the likelihood of carpal tunnel syndrome, which may become exacerbated under an individual incentive plan.

As an alternative to the individual incentive plan, two types of plans have flourished. As in the United States, some companies have turned to team incentives. But the biggest growth has been in profit-sharing plans, particularly for production workers. Nevertheless, English human resource managers express great concern regarding the motivational value of such plans. Many go so far as to say that profit-sharing does not constitute a pay-for-performance plan, since it does little to link individual efforts to outcomes. In addition, the size of the payout is generally felt to be too small to be of value. One major difference compared to the United States then is that companies in Great Britain appear more skeptical of the value of pay-for-performance plans.

Sources: Adapted from T.J. Atchison, "Impressions of Compensation Administration in the Pacific Rim." in *Research in Personnel/Human Resource Management* (International Human Resources Management), Supplement 2, ed. B. Shaw and J. Beck. (Greenwich, CT: JAI Press, 1990); G. McEvoy and W. Cascio, "The United States and Taiwan: Two Different Cultures Look at Performance Appraisal." in *Research in Personnel/Human Resource Management* (International Human Resources Management), Supplement 2, ed. B. Shaw and J. Beck. (Greenwich, CT: JAI Press, 1990); and M. Cannell and P. Long, What's Changed About Incentive Pay? *Personnel Management,* 23 (1991), 58–63.

be based on performance, not longevity on the job. Another alternative is to compensate employees for mastering additional skills or knowledge; this approach was discussed in Chapter 8. What other factors should affect pay increases? What about cost-of-living increases? Does it seem fair to you that your wages should increase in proportion to the inflation rate? It may surprise you to learn that fewer companies today would feel that salaries should be affected by the cost of living than was the case in the past. In fact, many companies would consider this a minor or even irrelevant factor. In the remainder of this chapter, then, we will discuss only performance-related pay differences. Next, you will read about different kinds of P-f-P plans and the advantages and disadvantages of each.

Kinds of Pay-for-Performance Plans

You have probably heard of many kinds of P-f-P plans, such as commission plans, individual incentive plans, bonuses, and so forth. For sake of simplicity, we will organize P-f-P plans into four basic categories. As shown in Figure 9.1, these categories are merit, individual incentive, team incentive, and organization-wide incentives. Before describing each of these categories in greater detail, however, several points are worth noting about P-f-P plans.

General Principles

1. The Best Plan Depends on the Context. As you will see in the next few sections, there is no one best P-f-P plan. Rather, the best P-f-P plan will depend on the nature of the job, the organization's business strategy, and other factors.
2. Many Organizations Use a Combination of P-f-P Plans. Although each type of P-f-P plan will be described separately, in reality, many companies use a combination of P-f-P plans. The reason, as you will see, is that no one P-f-P plan is perfect. In combination, however, many of the potential problems can be reduced.

Figure 9.1 **Types of Pay-for-Performance Plans**

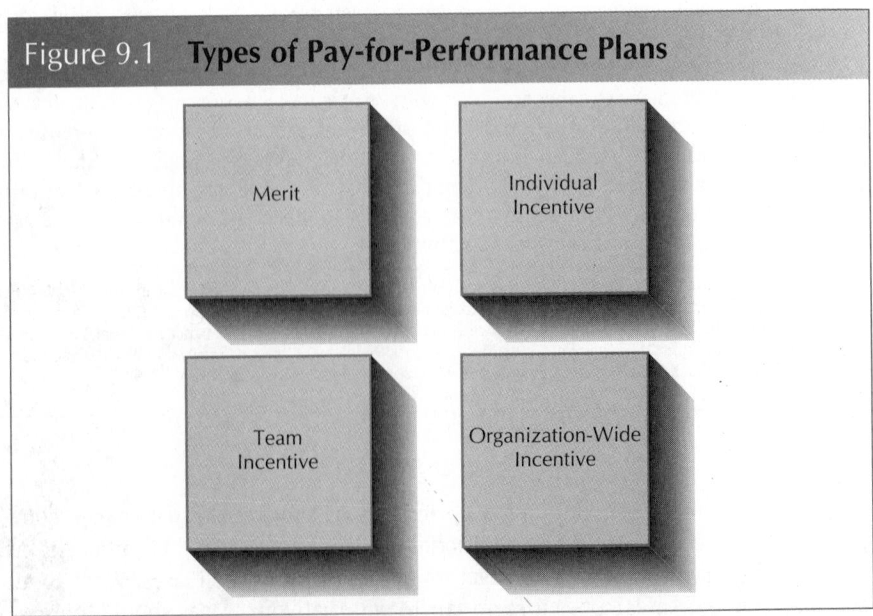

Some companies link salaries to employee productivity and output such as this catalog order operator. The more products sold or orders taken, the greater chance this worker has for increasing her base salary.

3. Pay Is Not the Only Motivator. Some critics of pay-for-performance systems have noted that an overemphasis on pay detracts from high performance and may even reduce certain desirable behaviors. Certainly, there is more to motivation than pay, and effective organizations use several means of motivating their employees. Nonfinancial rewards, such as flexible hours and interesting work assignments, may also be highly motivating. Keep in mind the following aphorism: "Men and women do not work for money only."

Now that you have read about some general principles involving P-f-P plans, we will define the four P-f-P plan categories.

Merit

Have you ever worked for an organization where you received a yearly salary increase that was based on your supervisor's recommendation? If you have, you were covered by a merit pay plan. This is the plan Stable Works used in the opening case of this chapter. Merit plans are quite common in the United States—at least 80 percent of organizations use them.[6] Essentially, a merit P-f-P plan has these features:

1. The payout is based on the individual employee's performance.
2. Performance is evaluated in a subjective fashion.
3. The payout is added to the employee's base salary.

Merit pay
The payout is based on the individual employee's performance, performance is evaluated in a subjective fashion, and the payout is added to the employee's base salary.

Individual Incentive

Have you ever worked in a sales job? If you have, how were you paid? Was your pay based on how much merchandise you sold? In certain industries, such as automobile sales, an employee's pay is directly tied to an objective measure of performance. This type of pay arrangement is referred to as an individual incentive, which is the approach Fire Cracker Software used in the opening case. An individual incentive plan, then, has two basic features:

Individual incentive
The payout is based on the individual employee's performance, and performance is evaluated using an objective standard.

1. The payout is based on the individual employee's performance.
2. Performance is evaluated using an objective standard.

Sales employees and production workers represent the occupations most likely to be covered by an individual incentive plan. This is not surprising, given that these jobs usually have an objective measure of performance.

Team Incentive

Team incentive
The payout is based on the team's level of performance, and performance is evaluated using an objective standard.

Have you ever been part of a classroom project in which you were a member of a team? If the answer is yes, how was the grade assigned? Typically, all members receive the same grade in a school team project. The same logic applies to a team incentive P-f-P plan. This is also the plan TeamWare used in the opening case. A team incentive plan, then, has these major characteristics:

1. The payout is based on the team's level of performance.
2. Performance is evaluated using an objective standard.

Organization-Wide Incentive

Organization-wide incentive
The payout is based on the performance of the plant, division, or organization, and performance is evaluated using an objective standard.

Profit-sharing plan
Pay is linked to some index of profitability.

Cost savings (gain-sharing) plan
Provides a payout when productivity improvements occur.

An organization-wide incentive is based on how one's plant, division, or company performs. This is the plan Corporate Solutions used in the opening case. The major characteristics of an organization-wide incentive plan are as follows:

1. The payout is based on the performance of the plant, division, or organization.
2. Performance is evaluated using an objective standard.

There are two basic types of organization-wide incentive plans. In a profit-sharing plan, performance is linked to some index of profitability. Typically, the payout is provided on a yearly basis and, in some cases, part of the payout is placed into a retirement fund for employees (see Chapter 10). In comparison, a cost-savings (often referred to as gain-sharing) plan provides a payout when productivity improvements occur. The assumption is that employees can increase productivity by suggesting improvements or by working more efficiently. Cost-savings plans generally provide cash payouts. The payout is usually made on a frequent, sometimes monthly, basis.[7]

Next, you will read about some advantages and disadvantages of each of these basic P-f-P plans.

Merit Plans: Advantages and Disadvantages

Merit P-f-P plans have a number of advantages and disadvantages. As shown in Table 9.1, from an organization's perspective, the merit approach is relatively easy to develop and implement. This is especially true if an effective performance management system is already in place, which can then be used to determine salary raises. Furthermore, because the merit system relies on a subjective performance evaluation, all aspects of the job can be considered in assigning raises. Take, for example, the sales job offered in the opening case of this chapter. One of the major

Table 9.1 **Advantages and Disadvantages of Merit Plans**

Advantages	Disadvantages
1. Is easy to develop	1. Costs snowball
2. Offers the ability to reward all aspects of job	2. Managers may not favor it
3. May be applied to any job	3. May not be highly motivating
4. Allows for flexibility within the company's budget	

Box 9.2 **Combining Pay-for-Performance Plans**

Tales from the Trenches

The NRL Federal Credit Union (NRLFCU) in Washington, D.C., is one organization that uses a combination of P-f-P plans to motivate employees. Designed by a seven-person multilevel task force, the plan provides monetary rewards beyond base pay for performance at the organizational, team, and individual level. The organizational level component ties employee bonuses to three factors: the credit union's income, the number of eligible members using the credit union, and growth in assets. Each year, target figures are established for these three components. If the minimum figure is not reached for income, no payout is provided. Interestingly, any payout is distributed among employees based on the number of hours they have worked (overtime hours do not count), rather than the more typical approach, which uses a percentage of salary. Why do you think the credit union bases the payout on number of hours worked rather than salary? The answer is that top management believes that the employees who deal directly with the customer (for example, the tellers) have at least as great an effect on success as do the managers and supervisors who do not deal as directly with customers. Basing the payout on the number of hours worked provides a proportionately greater payout to the direct service jobs than would a payout based on salary (which would provide a greater payout to managers and supervisors).

At the team level, a payout is based on measurable goals that are consistent with the organization's mission. An organizational incentive committee reviews each team's goals on a quarterly basis and frequently adjusts them. The goals must be approved by top management. A by-product of this process is that employees learn a great deal about how their department's work meshes with other departments and with the organization as a whole, which has also led to productivity improvements.

Finally, the individual incentive program is geared toward rewarding exemplary customer service. The program has established several criteria that may result in an individual reward, such as solving a unique or complex problem, proposing an innovative solution to a significant dilemma, or effectively handling a customer with a difficult problem. To be given an individual incentive award, employees must submit a self-nomination form, which requires a detailed description of the situation and the solution. The submissions are reviewed by the incentive committee, which makes the final decision regarding awards.

According to the president of the NRLFCU, the P-f-P plan has been extremely important to the success of this organization. From an employee perspective, the program has been successful as well, given that employees generally receive an additional 12 percent to 15 percent of their salaries. One employee even received a 20 percent increase during one quarter. NRLFCU demonstrates how multiple P-f-P plans can be used to achieve optimal results.

Source: Adapted from K. Cooke, "CU-Wide Incentive System Reaps Substantial Rewards," *Credit Union Management* 15, (1992), 14–17.

problems many companies face is motivating salespeople to perform activities besides straight selling. For example, salespeople may be reluctant to devote time to acquiring new product information if they have an established customer base, particularly when a large portion of their pay is based on sales volume. A company such as Stable Works (which uses a merit system) should be more effective in motivating salespeople to learn about new products than companies like Fire Cracker that reward salespeople primarily for sales volume.

Another advantage of a merit pay plan is that it can be applied to all jobs. The reason for this will become apparent when you realize that a subjective evaluation can be made for any job. An objective measure of job performance, however, cannot be provided for every job, which is a limitation of the individual incentive method. Finally, because of the way in which merit plans are typically developed, in the short term at least, such plans are advantageous in that they can be designed to fit within a company's budget. For instance, as Box 9.3 "Merit Pay at HBO," shows, an organization can decide how much of its budget to allocate to salaries and then divide this amount among employees based on their individual performances.

Despite the many strengths of a merit pay plan, it has several significant shortcomings that limit its effectiveness. One major shortcoming of this plan from the employer's perspective is that costs snowball from year to year as each year's payout becomes part of the base salary. From a long-term perspective then, use of a merit pay plan may create significant financial problems for an organization, particularly if profits are down at some point in time. This is one reason companies have begun to move away from merit pay plans toward other plans. A second

Box 9.3 Merit Pay at HBO

Home Box Office, Inc., or, as it is more commonly known, HBO, utilizes a carefully designed and monitored merit pay system for its employees. As with any merit pay system, HBO's program relies heavily on a performance management process. This particular performance management process revolves around goals established in the beginning of each year, which are reviewed midyear and at the end of the year. In the latter review, the manager rates progress on the goals using a ten-point scale, where 1 is clearly outstanding and 10 is unacceptable. Once the employee's overall rating is given, the human resources department generates a report containing the rating, as well as other information about each employee, including current salary, seniority, and so forth. After top-management reviews and approves that information, an analysis of the company's financial performance is conducted, along with predictions of the next year's growth, inflation rates, and pay increases for the nation as a whole and the entertainment industry specifically. Based on this information, top management allocates money for salary increases.

Following this, a matrix is created, which considers both performance rating as well as the individual's point in the grade. At the same time, grade minimums, maximums, and midpoints are adjusted to keep pace with inflation and industry changes. Each person's raise is then determined. Once all of these decisions are made, reports are generated for the human resources department, the department head, and top management. Each of these parties is able to review salaries to ensure that policies are being enforced and that decisions are fair.

Source: Adapted from M. Coleman-Carlone, "HBO's Program for Merit Pay," *Personnel Journal*, 69 (1990), 86–90.

major problem with this approach is that managers often dislike it. Recall from Chapter 7 that many managers are uncomfortable giving low performance ratings; leniency or central tendency is frequently the result. Managers often use the peanut butter approach to merit raises: pay increases are spread evenly so that relatively poor performers often receive raises that are similar if not identical to those obtained by top performers.

Finally, a likely outcome of these and related issues is that merit pay systems are often not effective motivators for employees. Consider for a moment that the average wage earner earns approximately $30,000 annually. Consider the results if you assume a 1986 average raise of 8.1 percent, with three-fourths of the raises between 6 percent to 10 percent.[8] Based on these figures, most employees would receive a raise between $1,800 and $3,000, a difference of only $1,200, or $100 per month. Once taxes (yes, raises are taxed, too!) are taken into account, the difference between receiving a 6 percent versus a 10 percent raise becomes even smaller. Not only are raise differences likely to be small under most merit pay plans, but many employees see little relationship between job performance and pay raises. One report indicated that fewer than half of the managers and professionals surveyed believed that top performers received higher raises than poor performers.[9] In more recent times, when raises have averaged closer to 4 percent, the difference in pay raises between top and poor performers has become even smaller.

Merit Pay Plans: Do They Work?

Given both the advantages and the disadvantages of merit pay plans, you may wonder if they are effective. There is some evidence that merit pay plans do improve both employee attitudes and job performance. Not all companies, however, report gains.[10] One large public transportation company, for instance, reported mixed results—employee performance improved; however, many participants reported dissatisfaction with their pay raises.[11] Clearly, then, merit pay systems are not always going to be effective in motivating employees. Where is a merit plan likely to work best? It would appear that this P-f-P plan is most likely to be effective in a large, traditional organization, particularly for employees where objective measures of job performance are not available.[12] Much of the success of a merit plan hinges on how well the performance management system works.

Maximizing Merit Raises: Tips for Employees

You may now be wondering whether there are certain factors that will affect the size of the raise you, as an employee, receive. Scientific research suggests that certain factors will affect your pay raises. In discussing these factors, it is simplest to organize them into three categories: employee characteristics, supervisor characteristics, and organizational characteristics.[13]

Employee Characteristics Affecting Merit Raises

Contrary to what you might think, research has found that there is at least some relationship between job performance and merit pay raises in many organizations.[14]

Thus, although it may not seem apparent to you as an employee, merit plans often do provide higher raises for superior performance. Furthermore, as you will see, even small raises can translate over time into big payouts. So, despite the negative comments earlier about the small size of pay differences, when considered over a long period of time, getting even a slightly larger raise than your coworker gets can mean much more money in your pocket.

What about seniority? Recall earlier that merit pay plans supposedly do not take senority into account. Although there is research indicating that, in some companies, seniority is related to higher raises, in other organizations seniority may work against the employee, as more senior employees are likely to be closer to the grade maximum. On the whole, though, more companies are ignoring seniority in making raise determinations than in the past.[15]

Other employee characteristics have been linked to higher pay raises. One such factor, which you will not find surprising, is the difficulty in replacing the employee. If you have a unique skill, for example, that would be difficult for the organization to replace, you are likely to obtain a higher raise than if you are easily replaceable.[16] There is also some evidence that "whom you know" in the organization will improve the raise that you receive, but only if it appears that you have other job opportunities.[17]

Finally, do you think that such factors as your sex, race, and age are related to size of raise? Contrary to what you might believe, few scientific studies have found evidence for such a relationship. You should also be aware that basing salary raises on sex, race, age, and certain other demographic characteristics is illegal and that organizations have been sued on this basis.

In sum, if you want to receive the highest raise possible, you will need to demonstrate superior job performance and provide a unique skill or experience that the organization will have a difficult time replacing. Knowing the right people will not hurt either.

Managerial Characteristics Affecting Merit Raises

Do some managers provide higher raises than other managers? The answer appears to be yes. Your chances for a higher raise are best under the following conditions:[18]

1. Your Manager Has Relatively Little Experience Giving Raises. Inexperienced managers are less comfortable giving raises and, to avoid controversy, will provide larger raises than will more experienced managers.

2. Your Manager Is Relatively Well Paid and Receives High Raises. Though it is not entirely clear why this would help you receive a higher raise, there is some evidence for a positive relationship between your raise and your manager's raise.

3. Your Manager Is More Altruistic and People Oriented. Logically, managers who are more concerned with the welfare of others are also more generous at salary raise time.

Despite these managerial factors being related to the size of your merit raise, you should not overemphasize their importance. It is clear that the employee factors described previously are much more critical.

Organizational Characteristics Affecting Merit Raises

Certain characteristics of the company or organization for which you work will affect the size of your raise as well. These include the following:

1. **The Other Employees in Your Department or Group.** Would you rather be a big fish in a small pond, or a small fish in a large ocean? At least in some organizations, you will receive a higher raise if the other members of your department or group are less effective, suggesting that it is better to be a big fish in a small pond. In other companies, however, a highly effective work group may get a higher raise than an ineffective work group. Which effect is found in your organization may well depend on the nature of the work and the way the merit plan is implemented.

2. **The Merit Pay Policies.** Certain pay policies will affect the magnitude of your raise, depending on whether you are a top performer or a poor performer. Specifically, when salary increase information is available to workers, and managers are attempting to promote work team harmony, there is less spread between the highest and lowest raises. If you are a top performer in this case, you will get a smaller raise. Conversely, if you are a poor performer, you would receive a higher raise under these circumstances.

3. **The Objectivity of the Performance Measures.** The more objective and precise the performance measures, the greater the difference between highest and lowest raises, because the managers will have more confidence in making salary raise decisions. The effect on your raise will again depend on whether your performance was relatively high or low. Poor performers will, all things being equal, receive higher raises the less objective and clear the performance measures are. Higher performers will, all things being equal, receive higher raises the more objective and clear the performance measures are.

Recall from the opening case that the applicant had a choice between a number of different jobs, each of which offered a different pay plan. One of the organizations, Stable Works, Inc., offered a merit pay plan. Now that you have read about merit pay plans, do you think this would be the best pay plan for Ricardo? You have read about the advantages and disadvantages from the organization's perspective. Let's now consider the employee's perspective. In terms of the advantages, because the payout becomes part of one's base pay, compensation will be much more stable from month to month and from year to year than other plans. Second, because the payout becomes part of one's base pay, Ricardo will continue to reap the rewards each year. Even a small difference in pay raises (for example, a 9.8 percent raise versus a 9.0 percent raise over a 20-year period) will therefore lead to major salary differences between two employees (a cumulative earnings difference of more than $200,000 if both employees begin with an annual salary of $40,000). The lesson for employees is that even small raise differences can add up to large differences over time. On the negative side, perhaps the biggest problem of the merit approach for employees is the payout may not be quite as big compared to an individual incentive plan. Merit pay plans, for the many reasons described earlier, tend to be fairly conservative in the size of the payout. So, if Ricardo is an outstanding salesperson, he may find Stable Work's plan to be less rewarding than Fire Cracker Software's plan.

In sum, many organizations use merit pay plans. Despite their simplicity and frequency of use, however, they have limited motivational value. Not surprisingly, many organizations are developing and implementing P-f-P plans that are based on more objective results. In a recent survey, for example, more than one-third of responding companies indicated they would implement a new or additional objective-based pay plan in the near future, while almost 75 percent of the respondents indicated that their company already had this kind of plan. Moreover, organizations were setting aside increasing amounts of payroll for objective-based P-f-P plans (from 5.7 percent in 1992 to 6.3 percent in 1993).[19] Clearly, many companies are giving other P-f-P plans more attention, and some companies are beginning to abandon the merit approach.

Individual Incentive Plans: Advantages and Disadvantages

As shown in Table 9.2, individual incentive plans provide several advantages over merit pay plans, but they also have a number of disadvantages compared to the merit pay system. In terms of their motivational impact, individual incentive programs are considered to be the most effective type of pay plan. Their motivational power stems from the fact that employees are in direct control of their performance and have a clear understanding of how they can attain rewards.[20] An equally important feature of these plans from a management viewpoint is that they allow the company to control costs over the long term. Compared to a merit pay plan, where each payout becomes part of the base salary, the individual incentive payout depends on the employee's performance within a given time period. As a result, an individual incentive plan can produce great savings for the organization.[21]

Finally, employees tend to embrace such plans because of their objectivity. Subjectivity will play much less of a role than it does in a merit pay plan, because the rules and standards are clearly spelled out in an individual incentive plan.[22] In turn, managers generally are more comfortable with individual incentive programs, because their judgments will only come into play in designing the plan. For the same reason, employees may view the system as being more fair.

Individual incentive plans also have several significant disadvantages. A critical feature is that they require a great deal of careful preplanning by the company.[23] The major issue that must be determined in the planning stages is what level of performance produces what amount of payout. Consider the following situation in which production workers assemble electrical parts. For the last three years, the average worker has produced 100 circuit boards per day. Should the bonus plan be established whereby 100 boards per day is the average? Or should

Table 9.2 **Advantages and Disadvantages of Individual Incentive Plans**

Advantages	Disadvantages
1. Is highly motivating	1. Requires much preplanning
2. Controls costs	2. May lead to the neglect of other desirable aspects of work
3. Reduces subjectivity	3. Encourages intragroup conflict
	4. May lead to burnout

the average be set at 120 boards per day? If you believe workers are easily capable of producing 150 boards per day, you may wish to set 150 as the standard. In many cases, the company will monitor workers prior to implementation to determine an appropriate rate. But workers may find out what is going on and deliberately reduce their pace in order to lower the standard. If preplanning is not carefully conducted, significant problems may result when the plan is implemented.

A second significant problem with the individual incentive plan is that it also motivates employees to neglect areas that are not directly linked to the incentives. In one large retail organization, the compensation for sales clerks was changed to an individual incentive plan linked to sales volume. Management discovered that the plan was indeed effective in increasing sales. But, at the same time, both inventory work and merchandise display activities were neglected. Realizing that additional income would be granted only through sales volume, the clerks had diminished the effort and time they devoted to other, nonselling activities. Another area that may suffer when an individual incentive is in place is product quality. Safety problems may also become more prevalent.

A third major problem with the individual incentive approach is that it may promote counterproductive intragroup competition. Use of an individual incentive plan encourages the "each man and woman for himself or herself" type of thinking. In the case of the retail clerks just mentioned, the use of the individual incentive plan also increased the number of times a sale was unfairly taken away from another retail clerk, as well as other problems. Internal conflict, then, can be a serious problem with an individual incentive plan.

Finally, in the long run, individual incentives may lead to employee burnout. One can be highly motivated only for so long; eventually, the value of an incentive tends to wear out.[24]

Given the potential problems associated with individual incentive plans, it is not surprising that their use is limited. Experts suggest that they are most effective for simple, highly structured jobs, where the objectives are not affected by other employees or departments and effective performance is quantifiable and clear.[25] In light of today's emphasis on teamwork and quality in manufacturing, it is not surprising that individual incentive programs have declined in popularity in manufacturing facilities, to a point where they are used by only about 20 percent of companies.[26]

On the other hand, many salespeople continue to be covered by individual incentive plans. Moreover, some organizations are beginning to use individual incentives for jobs other than sales and production, linking the payouts to broader organizational objectives. Consider, for example, Taco Bell, the fast-food chain, which starts 500 new restaurants a year. To choose sites for these new restaurants, the company employs real estate managers, who do everything from locating appropriate sites to obtaining building permits. Prior to 1990, the real estate managers had a base salary in the mid-50s, with a bonus of about 20 percent. But in 1990, the company changed the compensation program by cutting the base pay by about one-third, while increasing the incentive pay. Rather than having a single bonus, the company switched to a two-part incentive. First, for each new restaurant opened, the manager would receive a flat fee of $4,000. Once opened, the real estate manager would receive a second payout if the restaurant's return on investment (ROI) exceeded 15 percent. The higher the ROI, the higher the payout, which can be as high as $50,000. The result? Amy McConnell, whose area covers

North and South Carolina, earned well over $300,000 in 1992. If properly designed then, individual incentive plans can be highly effective.[27]

Now that you have read about some of the advantages and disadvantages of individual incentives from a company's perspective, you may be wondering what the advantages and disadvantages of this plan are from an employee's perspective. What were your reactions to Fire Cracker Software, which, as you may recall from the opening case, used this kind of plan? Probably one of the most significant advantages from your perspective would be the potential to really do well. That is, many individual incentive plans are set up so that the sky's the limit, as in the case of Amy McConnell described earlier. Had she been covered by a merit pay plan, she could not possibly have earned that much. Another advantage of the individual incentive plan is that your pay will be less influenced by your supervisor. If you have interpersonal conflicts with your manager, an individual incentive plan will be less affected. There are several disadvantages for an employee, however. A major disadvantage is, of course, that success in one month or year does not affect the next pay period. You will need to perform well continually. Relatedly, your pay may fluctuate; at times it may be high, at other times low. This may make financial planning difficult. Finally, although the individual incentive plan is more objective, inequities and unfairness can arise. For example, some sales territories may be far more profitable than others. In a manufacturing context, some machines or product lines may be superior. Because turnover is likely to be lower in lucrative territories or product lines, most hiring is likely to be for openings in the less lucrative areas.

Box 9.4 Changing from an Individual Incentive to a Unit Profit-Sharing Plan

Tales from the Trenches

Making changes is never easy, especially when workers' pay is affected. But sometimes, organizations are required to make changes in compensation, as was the case at West Bend Company. West Bend Company, located in Wisconsin, produces consumer appliances, including crock pots and woks. For many years, production workers were paid on an individual incentive basis. But, as in practically every industry, West Bend Company was affected in several ways by the increased global competition and the emphasis on quality. Now, objectives other than quantity were important, such as cost containment and speed. West Bend introduced several changes to meet these new objectives. One of these changes was to move to *just-in-time* production, whereby production would only work on existing orders. What was one of the effects on worker pay? In many cases, pay fell because workers could only produce as much product as was needed at that particular time. In fact, some workers' pay fell as much as $2 per hour. To address the workers' frustration with their decreasing pay, management formed a committee with the union to design and implement a new pay-for-performance plan. Management even permitted the committee to review accounting information. After one year, the committee agreed to a pay-for-performance plan that would focus on units (for instance, the beverage operation was a separate unit). Each unit established objectives regarding quality, costs, customer service, and so forth, which were put into a formula. A substantial amount of employees' pay was made "at risk," such that if the objectives are met, the employees receive 100 percent of their pay. To date, workers have received an average of 4 percent more than their base pay. According to management, inventory has been reduced 50 percent, scrap has been cut 70 percent, and quality has improved 70 percent.

Source: D.B. Hogarty, "New Ways to Pay," *Management Review 83,* (1994), 34–36.

In sum, individual incentive plans can be highly motivating. If properly designed, an individual incentive program can be quite effective. At the same time, a poorly conceived individual incentive plan can wreak havoc on the organization.

Team Incentive Plans: Advantages and Disadvantages

As you read in previous chapters, work teams are quite popular in industry today. Not surprisingly then, many organizations are modifying their P-f-P plans to motivate employees to work in teams. In the opening case, TeamWare used a team incentive to compensate salespeople. While the team incentive approach has some advantages over the individual incentive approach, it also has several disadvantages.

As shown in Table 9.3, a major advantage of the team approach is that it rewards work team cooperation. Recall that a significant disadvantage of the individual incentive approach is that it may encourage team conflict; the team incentive plan is the antidote to this problem. A second advantage of the team approach is that it is effective when performance differences between members of a team cannot be identified. Consider again the example provided earlier of the class team project. One person on the team may have conducted the library search, another member of the team may have contacted business professionals, and yet a third member of the team may have synthesized the information and written the report. Because each member of the team had a different task, it would not be possible to assess which person did better. Further, the instructor would have no way of knowing exactly who did what, so individual grades could not be assigned; all the instructor would be able to assess is the final product. And, if individual grades were assigned, there would be little incentive for one team member to assist another team member. Assignment of an overall grade or payout will motivate team members to help one another. Finally, in terms of motivational force, the team incentive plan is still relatively effective, although perhaps not quite as effective as the individual incentive approach.

Turning to the disadvantages of the team approach, almost everyone has worked on a class team project in which one or two team members failed to do their fair share. If you have ever been in this situation, you were probably pretty upset because not only would their behavior hurt your grade, but you might have had to do extra work to compensate for their lack of performance. Often referred to as social loafing, it has been long known that individuals are less motivated when they are part of a team or group than when they are working alone. Social loafing is a common problem and represents a major disadvantage of the team

Social loafing
The phenomenon in which one or two team members fail to do their fair share, leaving other team members to compensate for their lack of performance.

Table 9.3 **Advantages and Disadvantages of Team Incentive Plans**

Advantages	Disadvantages
1. Encourages team cooperation	1. Encourages social loafing
2. Is useful when the supervisor cannot identify individual performance levels	2. Repeats the other disadvantages of individual incentive programs
3. Is reasonably motivating	

A major disadvantage of the team concept is social loafing, which occurs when individuals are less motivated as part of a team or group than when they work alone. Social loafing can be one or two team members who fail to do their "fair share," work-related conversation dissolving into personal discussions, and time spent around the coffeepot, away from the project at hand.

incentive plan. To avoid social loafing problems, the team must have the ability to either formally or informally penalize the culprit. Like the individual incentive plan, other disadvantages of the team incentive plan include much pre-planning, possible neglect of other work responsibilities, and increased chances of burnout.

The major advantage of the team incentive plan is that it pulls the team together by providing the incentive for cooperation. This will be particularly important when individual contributions cannot be readily identified.

Now that you have read about the advantages and disadvantages of the team incentive from the company's perspective, what do you think some of the advantages and disadvantages are from an employee's perspective? Recall that, in the opening case of this chapter, TeamWare used a team incentive plan. What were your reactions to their plan? Perhaps the two most important issues from the employee's perspective are the nature of the team and one's reaction to teamwork. First, an effective team has the advantage of pooling skills. For example, if Ricardo had good sales skills but was weak in technical knowledge, being part of a team with people with strong technical knowledge would allow him to compensate for this weakness. If he worked on an ineffective team, however, his personal strengths might be obscured by other members' weaknesses. Second, some people don't like working on teams. If Ricardo prefers to work by himself, he may view the team as a hindrance. So, the success or failure of a team incentive plan will depend much on the functioning of the team and Ricardo's desire to work with a team.

Organization-Wide Incentive Plans: Advantages and Disadvantages

Organization-wide incentive plans have several advantages over the plans that have been reviewed so far. As shown in Table 9.4, a major advantage is that by basing the payout on organization performance, employees will more closely

Box 9.5 Team Incentive Programs That Work

Many freight and shipping companies that had previously held comfortable and profitable market positions were badly shaken when the federal government largely deregulated the industry in the 1980s. In response to the upheaval, Viking Freight designed and implemented an incentive program that emphasizes team performance. Toward that end, each work group within a terminal location has its own objectives, which vary according to the nature of the work. Objectives are determined for each work group by an executive committee and an engineering group. All of the employees, except for some clerical and secretarial staff, have work group goals. The precise objectives take into consideration the individuals in the group, as well as the market conditions of the particular terminal. The payout period is four weeks, so at the end of each four-week period, a determination is made as to whether the work groups' goals were met.

If the work group meets its goals, the employees are eligible for a bonus, the size of which depends on the terminal's performance. The terminal's performance is, in turn, based on four criteria: the amount of revenue earned, the percent of performance achieved, on-time service (at least 98 percent of the shipments must be on time), and the claims ratio (the cost of damaged or lost freight must be below a certain level). These criteria are entered into an objective formula to calculate the bonus.

Assuming that both the work group and the company as a whole meet their objectives, employees receive a payout based on their salaries. The maximum amount of payout that employees can earn is a function of the job. For example, hourly employees can receive bonuses as high as 7.5 percent of their pay, while the terminal manager may earn a bonus worth up to 20 percent of his or her pay. These percentages were based on the impact top management felt each job has on the company's success.

Top management has instituted several practices to maintain the motivational value of the program. One such practice is the way in which the payout is distributed. The payout is presented at a meeting, which is led by top management. The meeting begins with a review of the company's performance over the last four weeks and provides an opportunity for employees to raise any concerns or problems. The payout, which is separate from the regular paycheck, is handed out at the end of the meeting. At the same time, a chart containing information on the base pay, the payout level, and employees' total compensation is displayed. A second practice involves the weekly posting of the performance of each terminal, so that all employees can see how well they are doing. This, too, reinforces the importance of the objectives.

Konica U.S.A. developed a simpler plan for its sales force. Salespeople were placed into teams of 10 to 15 members, for the purpose of generating new accounts. If every member of the team developed 20 new accounts, each person in the team would receive a $1,000 bonus. The team with the highest sales volume would be eligible for a cruise. Star I.T., an IBM manufacturing facility, uses a similar approach to motivate quality-improvement projects. Employees are given $50 for each quality improvement team they participate in (they may participate in no more than eight teams each year). At the end of each year, the three best quality improvement projects are selected, and the team that developed the project is given $15,000 to divide among its members.

Sources: Adapted from T. Stambaugh, "An Incentive Pay Success Story," *Personnel Journal* 71 (1992), 48–54; R. Eisman, "Strength in Numbers," *Incentive,* 167, (1993), 53–55; and R. Sisco, "Put Your Money Where Your Teams Are," *Training* 29, (1992), 41–45.

identify with the organization. Moreover, this type of plan encourages cooperation throughout the organization, not just at a team or department level. A third advantage is that, like the individual incentive or team incentive approach, an objective formula will be used, so that determining whether or not the goals have been met will be relatively simple.

On the negative side, organization-wide plans are quite susceptible to social loafing. Compared with the team incentive approach, employees are likely to feel

Table 9.4 **Advantages and Disadvantages of an Organization-Wide Incentive Plan**

Advantages	Disadvantages
1. Encourages identification with the organization	1. Encourages social loafing
2. Increases cooperation throughout the organization	2. May not be very motivating
3. Is objective	3. Equity concerns when targets not met
	4. The formula may be difficult to understand

even less responsible for and in control of success. Also, as described earlier, the payout from a profit-sharing plan is frequently issued on an annual basis, and some or even all of the payout may be put into a retirement fund. The motivational value of such plans is therefore likely to be lower than it is for the individual or team incentive plan. Another problem is that equity or fairness issues are likely to be raised when an organization does not meet its goals. For example, when Du Pont's fibers division adopted a variable pay plan in the late 1980s in which 6 percent of employee pay was put "at risk," depending on the division's profits, many of the employees worried about whether the profit target would be manipulated by top management. As one employee stated it, "There are so many loopholes for management, how do we know if we've reached our goal?"[28] Finally, in a related vein, the formulas for these plans may be complex and difficult for employees to understand. As a consequence, they may believe the P-f-P is simply a management plan to take advantage of the employees. Many companies, such as General Electric, do in fact use a variety of accounting tactics to avoid swings in year-to-year profitability.[29]

Kinds of Organization-Wide Incentive Plans

Recall that there are two kinds of organization-wide incentive plans: cost savings and profit-sharing. Because they are rather different in the way they operate, each will be discussed separately.

Cost savings. Cost-savings or gain-sharing plans emphasize improving productivity by decreasing costs. Cost-savings plans work best in small organizations, where there is a great deal of trust between the workers and management, and where the market and product are quite stable and sales are good. Such plans will be less successful when the company manufactures a new product, because there are likely to be major fluctuations in sales.[30] There are three basic types of cost savings plans: the Scanlon plan, the Rucker plan, and Improshare.

Scanlon plan
Relies on a formula that contains two factors: a monetary index of output, reflecting how much was produced, and a measure of input or what it might cost the company to produce this output. The goal of the plan is to lower the input relative to output.

Scanlon plan. The Scanlon plan is named after the person who popularized this approach, Joseph Scanlon. Scanlon initiated this plan during the 1930s when his steel mill was on the verge of going out of business. As the union leader, he was able to convince workers in the plant to refrain from demanding wage increases, while persuading management to agree to increase pay when productivity improved. As a result of this agreement, the company's business improved, and ultimately the workers prospered.[31]

The Scanlon plan relies on a formula that contains two factors: a monetary index of output, reflecting how much was produced, and a measure of input, or what it cost the company to produce this output (such as labor costs). The goal of the plan is to lower the input relative to output. In other words, the lower costs are, the higher the productivity level will be. The assumption is that the workers have the capacity to lower the cost of labor.[32] Under the Scanlon plan, workers can lower the cost of labor by making money-saving suggestions. In one facility that implemented a Scanlon plan, suggestions in the first year of the plan fell into four categories: (1) those focusing on ways to improve quantity, (2) those focusing on ways to improve quality, (3) those focusing on ways to reduce costs, and (4) those focusing on nonproductivity related problems, such as management complaints.[33]

Table 9.5 contains an example of how a payout is derived in a typical Scanlon plan. Steps 1 through 4 show how output is calculated. Note that sales dollars are not the only factor included in the total output figure. Such things as discounts are factored in as well (Step 2). Step 6 indicates the allowed payroll costs, as determined when the plan was designed. As shown in Table 9.5, the formula stipulated that costs should not exceed 20 percent of the output. Given the output was valued at $1,200,000, 20 percent of this figure, or $240,000, is the expected or allowed cost of labor. The payout will be the difference between the actual cost and the allowed cost, after various adjustments are made. Step 7 indicates that the actual cost of labor in this time period was $210,000, which is $30,000 less than the allowable amount. The bonus pool, then, is $30,000 (Step 8). The next few steps involve adjustments to this figure. In this example, the company takes a 25 percent share of the bonus pool (Step 9), leaving $22,500. A small portion of this remaining pool is then set aside for periods of low production (Step 10). The remaining portion, $16,875 is divided among the employees.[34]

Rucker plan. A variant to the Scanlon plan, the Rucker plan (named after the person who developed it, Allan Rucker), replaces sales as the measure of output with something called "value added." Value added is simply the sales value of production, after subtracting nonlabor costs (materials, supplies, electricity, and so on). In most other ways, the Rucker plan is quite similar to the Scanlon plan. The major advantage of the Rucker plan is that it takes into account inflation increases in nonlabor costs. On the negative side, because nonlabor costs are factored out, employees can only make productivity improvements by reducing direct labor costs.

Rucker plan
A variant to the Scanlon plan, this plan replaces sales as the measure of output with something called "value added," which is the sales value of production after subtracting nonlabor costs.

Table 9.5 **Sample Scanlon Plan Formula**

1. Quarterly sales	$1,100,000
2. Minus sales returns, discounts, etc.	25,000
3. Net sales	$1,075,000
4. Add increased inventory	125,000
5. Total output	$1,200,000
6. Allowed payroll costs (20 percent of output)	240,000
7. Actual payroll costs	210,000
8. Bonus pool	30,000
9. Company share (25 percent)	7,500
Subtotal	22,500
10. Reserve for deficit quarters (25 percent)	5,625
11. Employee share to be distributed (75 percent)	16,875
(See text for explanation.)	

In addition, the formula is even more difficult to communicate to employees than the Scanlon plan! The Rucker plan, then, probably is most effective when inflationary pressures pose a problem.[35]

Improshare
Stands for "improved productivity through sharing," and focuses on the number of hours of work. Improshare also involves a formula that compares input to output, where input is the number of hours that it should take to complete the work compared with the number of hours it actually took to do the work.

Improshare. Improshare, which stands for "improved productivity through sharing," was created by Mitchell Fein in the early 1970s. Unlike the Scanlon or Rucker plans, Improshare focuses on the number of hours of work. The Improshare, like the Scanlon and Rucker plans, also involves a formula that compares input to output. Under the Improshare approach, though, input is the number of hours that it should take to complete the work compared with the number of hours it actually took to do the work. If, for example, management estimated it would take 240 hours to complete a production run, yet it only took 160 hours, employees would be accorded a predetermined bonus for the number of hours saved.

Proponents of Improshare point to a number of potential advantages of this approach over the Scanlon and Rucker plans. In particular, Improshare has greater flexibility and is easier to implement. In terms of disadvantages, however, Improshare tends to emphasize quantity over quality and excludes the possibility of producing savings from anything other than number of hours worked.[36]

In sum, cost-savings plans can be very effective motivators. Although most of the applications of these programs have been in manufacturing facilities, they are equally applicable in the service sector, including hospitals, libraries, and consulting firms. Which of the approaches is best will depend on a number of considerations, such as the degree to which employee involvement is desired and the importance of product quality.[37]

Finally, this is an appropriate point to mention that while these plans have the aura of objectivity and precision, numerous judgment calls must be made in the development stages. Ultimately, then, even the cost-savings plans are affected by subjectivity.

Profit Sharing. Many large, well-known organizations either currently use or have used profit-sharing plans in the past, including General Motors, Monsanto, Ford, Hewlett-Packard, to name just a few.[38] Essentially, profit sharing provides a payout to employees when the company, plant, or unit reaches a certain financial target. Depending on the nature of the job and the company, a profit-sharing plan may be quite lucrative. For example, Figure 9.2 illustrates the profit-sharing plan for Deryck Maughan, chairman of Salomon Brothers, the investment banking firm. As you can see, the plan resembles a bingo card. If the company does extremely well, Maughan receives a bonus of up to $24,000,000 (his base pay is $1,000,000)! According to the company, it would take a "very extraordinary" performance for Maughan to earn that bonus. Most profit-sharing plans are not quite so rewarding.[39] Consider Colorado Memory Systems (CMS), a computer component manufacturer that was purchased by Hewlett-Packard in late 1992. After the purchase, employees at CMS expressed concern that their individual performance would go unrewarded now that they were owned by a giant. In addition, employees of Colorado Memory Systems were paid much less than their counterparts at H-P. To deal with these problems, the company began a profit-sharing plan, which put 10 percent of the employees' pay "at risk." If profits were high, employees would get as much as 20 percent of their pay back. If profits were only satisfactory, they would get the full 10 percent back.[40]

There is little hard scientific evidence regarding the effectiveness of profit-sharing plans. However, the available studies do suggest that profit sharing on

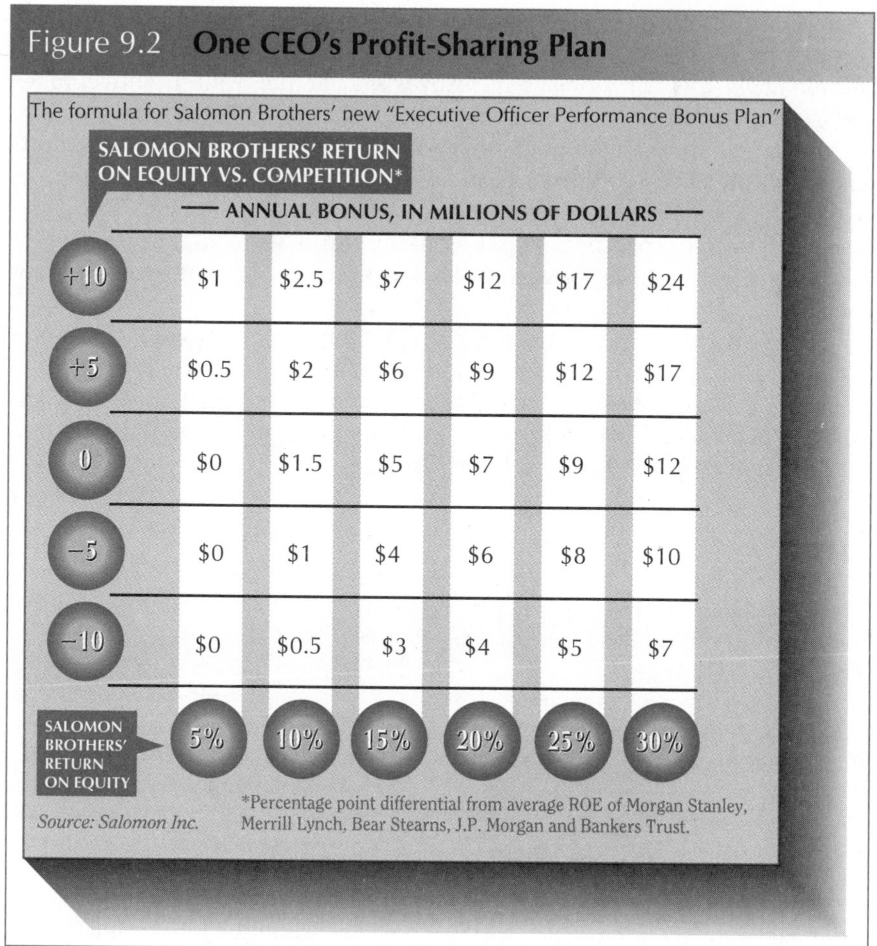

Figure 9.2 **One CEO's Profit-Sharing Plan**

The formula for Salomon Brothers' new "Executive Officer Performance Bonus Plan"

SALOMON BROTHERS' RETURN ON EQUITY VS. COMPETITION*

ANNUAL BONUS, IN MILLIONS OF DOLLARS

SALOMON BROTHERS' RETURN ON EQUITY VS. COMPETITION*	5%	10%	15%	20%	25%	30%
+10	$1	$2.5	$7	$12	$17	$24
+5	$0.5	$2	$6	$9	$12	$17
0	$0	$1.5	$5	$7	$9	$12
−5	$0	$1	$4	$6	$8	$10
−10	$0	$0.5	$3	$4	$5	$7

SALOMON BROTHERS' RETURN ON EQUITY (columns: 5%–30%)

*Percentage point differential from average ROE of Morgan Stanley, Merrill Lynch, Bear Stearns, J.P. Morgan and Bankers Trust.

Source: Salomon Inc.

Source: From M. Siconolfi, "Salomon's Chief Stands to Hit the Jackpot," *The Wall Street Journal,* May 5, 1994, C1.

average increases productivity 7 percent. If that figure seems rather low to you, consider the following points:[41]

1. In many profit-sharing plans, anywhere from some to all of the payout goes into a retirement fund, rather than into the employees' paycheck. Would you be highly motivated if the payout went into a fund you could not utilize until you retired, quit the company, or were disabled?
2. In many cases, employees feel little or no control or influence over the objectives. If, for example, you were a customer service employee in a company with 5,000 employees, you may feel, quite correctly, that your efforts have only the smallest influence on the company's profits for that year.
3. Remember that a distinguishing characteristic of these plans is that payouts are distributed only once each year. There is a considerable time lag, therefore, between each payout, which serves to reduce motivation.

Now that you have read about the general advantages and disadvantages of organization-wide incentive programs, it is time to consider the advantages and disadvantages from an employee perspective. Recall that in the opening case of this chapter, Corporate Solutions had a profit-sharing plan. What would you tell Ricardo about this type of plan? In many ways, like the team incentive, much will depend on the effectiveness of the other employees. In a very large organization, particularly for employees other than the top executives, Ricardo's efforts will have little effect. If Ricardo is an extremely hard-working and highly successful individual, he may become quite frustrated working for such an organization. On the other hand, the pressures of this organization may be less, and he may enjoy the camaraderie and organizational cooperation that such programs encourage.

Not surprisingly then, many organizations combine the strengths of two or three approaches to eliminate the weaknesses inherent in any one P-f-P plan. To return to our opening case, none of the four pay plans is clearly superior to the others. Much will depend on the nature of the organization, and Ricardo's own personal preferences, as to which is the best plan.

Box 9.6 Meet the Grandparent of Pay-for-Performance Plans and One of the Grandchildren

Tales from the Trenches

How would you respond to a job offer from a company where 20 percent of the employees quit within two months, employees pay for their own hospitalization insurance, there are no paid holidays or sick days, you must accept a job reassignment, and overtime is mandatory? Even if you are an executive, you must compete for the same parking spaces and eat in the same dining room as everyone else. No way you would take such a job? Then you may be surprised to hear that this company receives more than 10,000 unsolicited applications annually, and the employee turnover rate is less than 3 percent for employees who have passed probation. Why would so many people be interested in working for this company? Consider the following. The company has not had a layoff due to a business slowdown in 45 years. And even though the company does not provide any paid holidays or sick days, the average total compensation for production workers in 1992 was $45,000. By now you probably want to know the name of this company and the type of business it is in.

Lincoln Electric Company is headquartered in Cleveland, Ohio. It manufactures welding machines and motors. Although chances are you have never heard of this company before, it has the most well-known pay-for-performance plan in existence, and probably the longest running. That is why it is referred to here as the grandparent of P-f-P plans.

In practice, the plan is really quite simple. All production workers are paid on an individual incentive plan; there is no base wage for these employees. Because Lincoln Electric makes many parts for many different products, there are 70,000 piece rate plans. Although management makes changes in the piece rate as production methods are modified, workers have the right to question the alterations. Many of the piece rates have stayed the same for years (to maintain pace with inflation, a cost of living index is used to make annual adjustments). In addition to the piece rate, production workers are eligible for an annual bonus, which is a function of a merit rating and company profits. The merit rating is determined by the worker's output (assessed by the production department), a measure of quality (evaluated by the quality-assurance department), dependability (based on absenteeism, tardiness, and other criteria), and personal characteristics (such as attitude, cooperation, and so forth). The merit rating system is designed so that each department is allocated 100 points per

(continued on following page)

Sources: Adapted from C. Wiley, "Incentive Plan Pushes Production," *Personnel Journal,* 72 (1993), 86–91; and S. Tully, "Your Paycheck Gets Exciting," *Fortune,* November 1, 1993 83–98.

Box 9.6 Meet the Grandparent of Pay-for-Performance Plans and One of the Grandchildren

(continued from previous page)

employee; if one employee receives 120 points, other employees must receive less than 100 points. Once the available bonus pool is determined, a formula is used to calculate the amount of money given to each worker. In addition, workers participate in an employee stock-ownership plan.

Is pay for performance working at Lincoln Electric? By all measures, it is extremely successful, a testimony to the motivational properties of a carefully designed and implemented pay program that has stood the test of time.

Now meet one of the grandchildren, AT&T, which has recently implemented a P-f-P plan that will cover more than 100,000 employees. AT&T's plan, which began in 1986, was designed to reduce base pay while increasing the pay-for-performance portion of paychecks. For the first few years of the plan, AT&T simply reduced the magnitude of pay raises and increased the size of bonuses. Most recently, however, the company has designed a plan for executive, managerial, and professional employees that is somewhat similar to the one at Lincoln Electric. The new plan will reward individuals with a yearly bonus. The size of the bonus will depend on the individual or his or her work group's performance, the individual's unit performance, and, most importantly, the company's performance as a whole. The company's performance as a whole is calculated using a formula called economic value added (EVA), which is a function of net operating profits after such things as capital have been subtracted.

Tales from the Trenches

The individual portion of the bonus depends on the employee's performance rating, the company's success as measured by EVA, and the size of the individual's salary. The company expects to give as many as 15 percent of all managers no individual bonus at all, in order to encourage improvement. The second component is based on unit (for example, the credit card division) performance. The company is divided into about 35 units, and each is given its own EVA goal. The third component is based strictly on the company's overall EVA performance. If the company matches its target EVA, all managers will receive an additional 7.3 percent of their salaries; if the EVA is far exceeded, managers may receive as much as 11 percent above their base salaries.

In light of the fact that each of the P-f-P plans reviewed earlier have weaknesses, it is not surprising that many companies are using a combination of plans to fully motivate their employees.

Conclusion

Pay-for-performance plans are an important motivational tool for organizations. As such, they play an important role in the human resources area. Although merit pay plans are among the most common P-f-P approaches, they have a number of significant weaknesses, which in turn weaken their motivational value. Individual incentive programs, perhaps the most motivating, have several serious disadvantages, particularly in light of today's emphasis on teams and quality. Accordingly, more companies have designed and implemented team incentives and organization-wide incentive plans. Although these plans are not perfect either, in tandem with other rewards, they can clearly improve organizational performance.

Applying Core Concepts

1. Think about your current job (or a previous job). Does the company use a pay-for-performance plan? Why or why not? Would it be helpful for the organization if it did use a pay-for-performance plan? Why?

2. Which kind of pay-for-performance plan do you think universities and colleges should use for faculty? Explain your answer.
3. If you were Ricardo in the opening case of this chapter, which company would you choose to work for? Why?
4. Think of a job for which a pay-for-performance plan probably would *not* work. Explain why it would not work. On what other basis should pay differences occur in this job (for example, seniority)?
5. As a manager of a staff of customer service representatives in a service business, what type of pay-for-performance plan do you think would work best? What about for automobile mechanics at a car dealership?

Key Terms

- Merit pay
- Individual incentive
- Team incentive
- Organization-wide incentive
- Profit-sharing plan
- Cost savings (gain-sharing) plan
- Social loafing
- Scanlon plan
- Rucker plan
- Improshare

Chapter 9: Experiential Exercise

Pay for Performance

Your task is to complete the performance appraisal form and make a salary increase recommendation for both of the employees described below. Also, make recommendations as to how you would change the rating form for next time you need to make salary increase recommendations. Be prepared to explain your reasoning.
Here are several things you should know about Mary Wilson, Jack Smith, and the merit raise program:

1. They have both worked for the company for 3 years.
2. They have roughly the same experience and education; although they are both administrative assistants, they have somewhat different responsibilities.
3. They are paid the same ($29,000), and this is average compared to other administrative assistants in the company.
4. They could earn up to $32,000 in their present pay grade.
5. You have been allocated $2,900 (5 percent) additional dollars to give them in a merit raise; the employees know the average raise should be 5 percent.
6. You do not have to spend the entire $2,900, but if you don't, you will have to explain to your boss why you did not spend it.
7. They have had average raises in the three years they have been here.
8. The overall rating determines their raise—*failed to meet standards* will give them a 0 percent raise, *some improvement* a 2 percent raise, *fully met standards* a 4–5 percent raise, *consistently exceeded standards* a 6 percent raise, and *significantly exceeded standards* an 8 percent raise. Of course, because of the size of the raise pool, if you give one of the employees an 8 percent raise, you can't give 6 percent to the other employee.
9. Finally, assume the employee will see the form when you have completed it.

Jack Smith

Jack Smith has worked as an administrative assistant for several years under your direction. He is responsible for scheduling meetings, filing correspondence, responding to customer inquiries, and completing reports. On the negative side, he has had some disagreements with customers. In one situation, he became noticeably irate over the phone with a customer, and ended up slamming the phone down. On another occasion, a customer demanded to speak with Jack's supervisor. When you got on the phone, the customer said that Jack had tried to cut her call off, and refused to answer some of

Chapter 9: Experiential Exercise *(continued)*

her questions. When you asked Jack about the incident, he said that he was very busy that day, and was rushing to go to a meeting. Another shortcoming appears to be in the filing correspondence area. Jack seems to make more mistakes than other administrative assistants. On about three occasions, a file was totally misplaced in the drawers, and it took Jack several hours to locate it. On the positive side, Jack has come up with several creative ideas for the reports. One of the most innovative contributions he made was the computerization of the reports, which saves the company hundreds of hours yearly. He has also developed a customer satisfaction survey, which is now used by several other departments. He developed these ideas on his own, although he sought your approval when he completed them. In other areas, Jack seems to be about average, and there have been no complaints about his performance from other employees. Jack seems to really like his job, and has told you that he has no interest in moving to other jobs or other departments. As he said last year, "I really like working here, I do a good job, and I have zero interest in moving elsewhere."

Mary Wilson

Mary's responsibilities include typing papers and reports. She is also responsible for handling customer inquiries and serving as a coordinator between different departments. Mary is a very conscientious, hard-working employee who puts a great deal of effort into her job (she frequently takes a short lunch, sitting at her desk). She is extremely pleasant with everyone, offers to help people when they are too busy, and is a great writer. She even volunteered to help write the departmental newsletter, although that is not part of her job! She is now the editor, and sometimes stays late to finish it. She has a great deal of experience with several different companies, and is familiar with just about every work processing package (e.g., Word, WordPerfect, WordStar, Wordiest). She almost never makes a mistake, and proofreads her typing carefully. On the negative side, she was late in completing three important projects this year, and on at least ten different occasions, she asked for an extension of time on an assignment (which you reluctantly agreed to provide). At times, she is unable to return a customer's call until two days later, even though your organization has a policy of returning phone calls within twenty-four hours. Finally, she will sometimes take a half hour or more to explain something to a coworker, which would take anyone else five minutes. Group meetings also seem to take about twenty percent longer than normal when she attends. In terms of future plans, Mary has told you that she really would like to become a supervisor, and help run another department.

The Rating Form

Employee's Name:

Use the following scale for making your ratings:
1-*failed to meet standards*
2-*some improvement*
3-*fully met standards*
4-*consistently exceeded standards*
5-*significantly exceeded standards*

1. Quantity of Performance Justification for rating:	1	2	3	4	5
2. Quality of Performance Justification for rating:	1	2	3	4	5
3. Customer Service Justification for rating:	1	2	3	4	5

Chapter 9: Experiential Exercise *(continued)*

The Rating Form, cont'd

4. Work Effort Justification for rating:	1	2	3	4	5
5. Overall Rating: Justification for rating:	1	2	3	4	5

Chapter 9 References

1. M. Beer, P. Spector, P. Lawrence, D.Q. Mills, and R. Walton, *Managing Human Assets* (New York: The Free Press, 1984).
2. M. Weitzman and D. Kruse, "Profit Sharing and Productivity," in *Paying for Productivity,* ed. A. S. Binder (Washington: The Brookings Institute, 1990).
3. L. Hatcher and T. Ross, "From Individual Incentives to an Organization-Wide Gain-Sharing Plan: Effects on Team-Work and Product Quality," *Journal of Organizational Behavior* 12 (1991), 169–83.
4. L. Dyer, D. Schwab, and R. Theriault, "Managerial Perceptions Regarding Salary Increase Criteria," *Personnel Psychology* 29 (1976), 233–42.
5. B. Gerhart and G. Milkovich, "Employee Compensation: Research and Practice," in *Handbook of Industrial and Organizational Psychology,* vol. 3, ed. M.D. Dunnette and L.M. Hough (Palto Alto, CA: Consulting Psychologists Press, 1992).
6. R. Heneman, "Merit Pay Research," in *Research in Personnel/Human Resource Management,* ed. G. Ferris and K. Rowland (Greenwich, CT: JAI Press, 1990).
7. Gerhart and Milkovich, "Employee Compensation."
8. K. Teel, "Are Merit Raises Really Based on Merit?" *Personnel Journal* March, (1986), 88–95.
9. Gerhart and Milkovich, "Employee Compensation."
10. Heneman, "Merit Pay Research."
11. D. Scott, F. Hills, S. Markham, and M. Vest, *Evaluating a Pay-for-Performance Program at a Transit Authority.* Paper presented at the National Academy of Management meetings, New Orleans, 1987.
12. Heneman, "Merit Pay Research."
13. Ibid.
14. S. Markham, "Pay-for-Performance Dilemma Revisited: Empirical Example of the Importance of Group Effects." *Journal of Applied Psychology,* 73 (1988), 172–80.
15. Heneman, "Merit Pay Research."
16. K. Bartol and D. Martin, "Effects of Dependence, Dependency Threats, and Pay Secrecy on Managerial Pay Allocations," *Journal of Applied Psychology,* 74 (1989), 105–13.
17. K. Bartol and D. Martin, "When Politics Pays: Factors Influencing Managerial Compensation Decisions," *Personnel Psychology* 43 (1990), 599–614.
18. Heneman, "Merit Pay Research."

19. C. Carey, "Motivation Can Be Managerial Dilemma," *St. Louis Post-Dispatch,* September 7, 1992, 11BP.
20. G. Milkovich and A. Wigdor, *Pay for Performance: Evaluating Performance Appraisal and Merit Pay* (Washington: National Academy Press, 1991).
21. B. MacLean, "Value Added Pay Beats Traditional Merit Programs," *Personnel Journal* 69 (1992), 46–52.
22. Milkovich and Wigdor, "Pay for Performance."
23. F. Hills, *Compensation Decision Making* (Fort Worth, TX: Dryden, 1987).
24. J. Rigdon, "More Firms Try to Reward Good Service, but Incentives May Backfire in Long Run," *The Wall Street Journal,* December 5, 1990, B1, B7.
25. Milkovich and Wigdor, "Pay for Performance."
26. B. Graham-Moore and T. Ross, "Introduction to PG: A Theoretical Model," in *Productivity Gainsharing,* ed. B. Graham-Moore and T. Ross (Englewood Cliffs, NJ: Prentice-Hall, 1983).
27. S. Tully, "Your Paycheck Gets Exciting," *Fortune,* November 1, 1993, 83–98.
28. L. Hays, "All Eyes on Du Pont's Incentive Pay Plan," *The Wall Street Journal,* December 5, 1988, B1.
29. R. Smith, S. Lipin and A.K. Naj, "Managing Profits," *The Wall Street Journal,* November 3, 1994, A1, A11.
30. B. Graham-Moore, "The Literature of PG," in *Productivity Gainsharing,* ed. B. Graham-Moore and T. Ross (Englewood Cliffs, NJ: Prentice-Hall, 1983).
31. C. Frost, R. Wakeley, and R. Ruh, *The Scanlon Plan for Organizational Development: Identity, Participation, and Equity* (East Lansing, MI: Michigan State University Press, 1974).
32. M. Bazerman and B. Graham-Moore, "PG Formulas: Developing a Reward Structure to Achieve Organizational Goals," in *Productivity Gainsharing,* ed. B. Graham-Moore and T. Ross (Englewood Cliffs, NJ: Prentice-Hall, 1983).
33. B. Graham-Moore, "Ten Years of Experience with the Scanlon Plan: DeSoto Revisited," in *Productivity Gainsharing,* ed. B. Graham-Moore and T. Ross (Englewood Cliffs, NJ: Prentice-Hall, 1983).
34. Bazerman and Graham-Moore, "PG Formulas."
35. Graham-Moore, "The Literature of PG," and Bazerman and Graham-Moore, "PG Formulas."
36. Ibid.
37. W. Hauck and T. Ross, "Is PG Applicable to Service Sector Firms?" in *Productivity Gainsharing,* ed. B. Graham-Moore and T. Ross (Englewood Cliffs, NJ: Prentice-Hall, 1983).
38. Gerhart and Milkovich, "Employee Compensation."
39. M. Siconolfi, "Salomon's Chief Stands to Hit the Jackpot," *The Wall Street Journal,* May 5, 1994, C1, C19.
40. D. Hogarty, "New Ways to Pay," *Management Review* 83 (1994), 34–36.
41. Gerhart and Milkovich, "Employee Compensation."

chapter 10 Employee Benefits

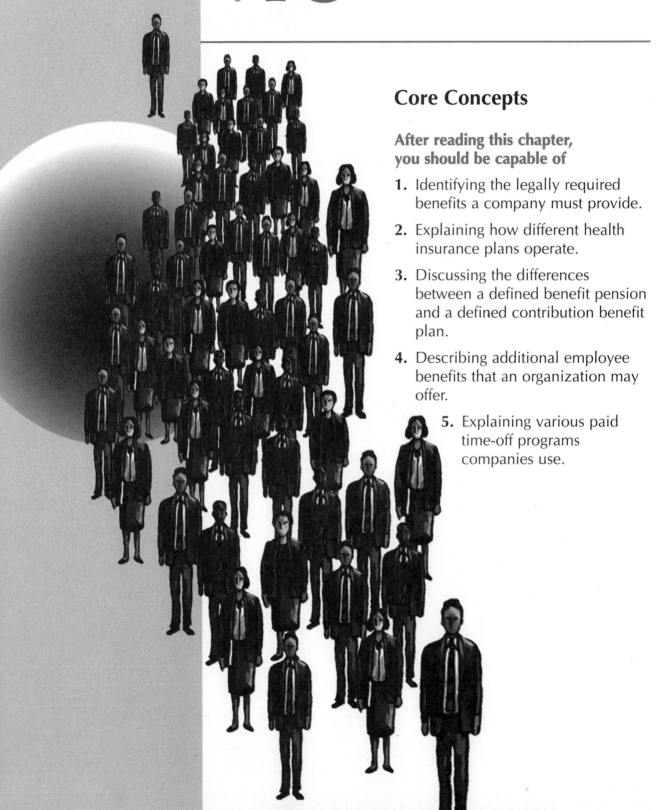

Core Concepts

After reading this chapter, you should be capable of

1. Identifying the legally required benefits a company must provide.
2. Explaining how different health insurance plans operate.
3. Discussing the differences between a defined benefit pension and a defined contribution benefit plan.
4. Describing additional employee benefits that an organization may offer.
5. Explaining various paid time-off programs companies use.

Opening Case

Imagine you have job offers from three different companies. All three jobs seem identical in terms of the type of work, the opportunities for advancement, and the boss who would be supervising you. The pay is identical for two of the companies (NewForm and Tradition); however, the third company (FreeStyle) made you a job offer for $2,000 more per year than both NewForm and Tradition. The only difference that you can see between NewForm and Tradition is the nature of the benefit programs offered by each company. NewForm offers a cafeteria benefits program, which as the human resources manager explained it, may even provide you with additional money or vacation time. That sounds almost too good to be true. NewForm also offers a 401(k) retirement program, which allows you to set aside some of your salary into a retirement fund. The human resources manager smiled when she described the 401(k) plan to you and then added, "You get to pretend you are in Las Vegas, because employees are able to invest this money as they choose. Options include various stock funds, bonds, money market funds, as well as other alternatives. In fact," she added with a laugh, "some employees have even asked whether they can use the funds for state lottery tickets or poker tables. We also match 50 cents for each dollar you set aside, up to 2 percent of your salary."

Tradition, on the other hand, seems to offer a more standard benefits program. The personnel assistant emphasized its advantages: "We offer the alternative of two different health maintenance organizations (HMOs), and we have a preferred-provider organization (PPO) option as well. We also offer flexible spending accounts." You noticed that Tradition provides a retirement program, which was called a "defined benefit" program. This program seemed different from the one offered by NewForm, but you are not quite sure how it works.

Finally, FreeStyle offers no benefits as far as you can tell. There is no health insurance program and no retirement program. You wonder whether this is even legal—isn't every company required to offer a health insurance program? But a salary that is $2,000 higher than the other two companies sounds appealing. What should you do?

This chapter explains what different types of employee benefits are, how they work, why companies provide certain kinds of benefits, and what some of the implications of these different benefits are for you as an employee. As you will see, employee benefit regulations and programs are continuously changing. To make the most out of your employment situation, you will need to become knowledgeable about your benefits program. Whether you are choosing among different job offers, changing your family status (for example, getting married, becoming divorced, or having a child), preparing for retirement, or being laid off from work, it is important to fully understand your rights, privileges, and requirements as they pertain to benefits. This chapter is divided into four sections: (1) legally required payments (such as social security), (2) pension and health insurance plans, (3) miscellaneous benefits (such as tuition reimbursement and child care), and (4) pay for time not worked (such as vacation).

The chapter focuses on how benefits affect you as an employee. Although you may not be aware of how much your benefits are worth, businesses are becoming increasingly aware of their costs associated with benefits. A 1990 U.S. Chamber of Commerce survey found that on average, benefits account for 38 percent of private industry payroll costs.[1] As you can see in Figure 10.1, the four most expensive benefits were: legally required benefits, medical care, paid time off, and pensions. It is no wonder that companies nowadays are carefully examining and introducing many changes in their benefits program. It is therefore increasingly important for employees to understand how their benefits work.

Figure 10.1 **Percentage of Payroll Costs Associated with Different Benefits**

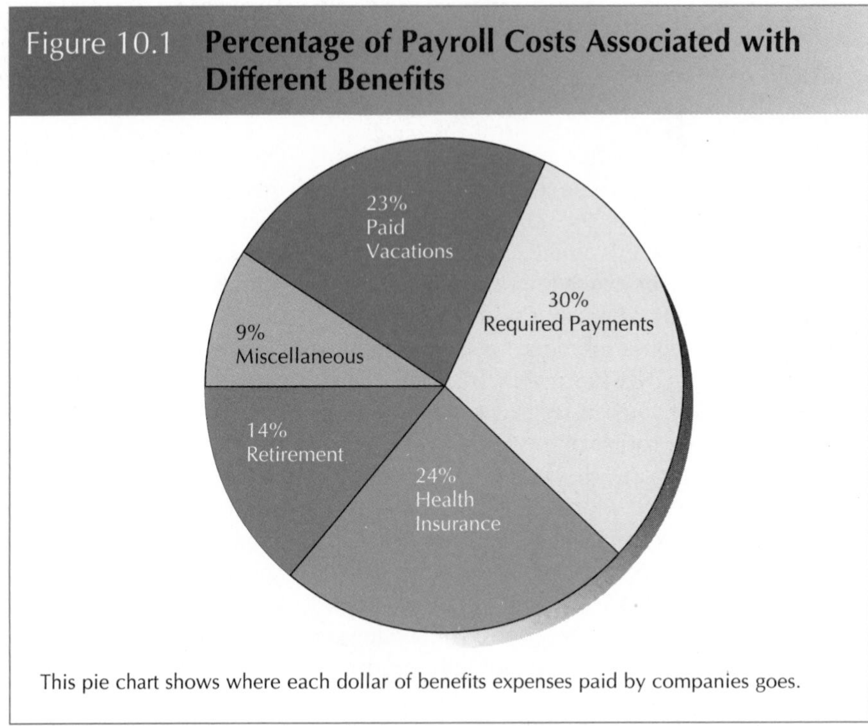

This pie chart shows where each dollar of benefits expenses paid by companies goes.

Legally Required Benefits

You may be surprised to learn that only a few benefits are required by law. Most of the benefits provided by private companies are optional. You may even question whether some of the legally required benefits are really "benefits" at all. The three legally required benefits are the following:[2]

1. Social Security/Medicare.
2. Unemployment compensation.
3. Workers' compensation.

Next, you will learn about each of these three benefits in greater detail, and what they provide for employees.

Social Security/Medicare

Social Security/ Medicare
Two government programs that receive funding from employees and their companies, which are used for retirement, disability, survivor benefits, and health care expenses.

The basis for the Social Security/Medicare law is the Social Security Act of 1935. If you work as an employee for a company, you may find that there are two entries in your pay stub labeled "FICA," which stands for the Federal Insurance Contribution Act. The funds received from this act are used for two purposes: Social Security payments and Medicare payments. In 1995, employees paid 6.2 percent of up to $61,200 of their earnings to the Social Security fund, and 1.45 percent of their earnings to the Medicare fund. You may now be wondering, "If this is considered a legally required company benefit, why will money be deducted from my paycheck for it?" This is considered a company-sponsored benefit because the company matches your payments; in other words, the company pays an additional 6.2 percent of up to $61,200 of your earnings into the Social Security fund and an additional 1.45 percent of your earnings into a Medicare fund. You are probably now thinking, "So, what benefit do I receive from all this?" First, if your company was not paying the matching amount (for example, if you were self-employed or serving as a consultant to the company), *you* would be paying the additional amount. In other words, if you were self-employed, you would be paying the full amount (12.4 percent and 2.9 percent of the salary stated earlier). Second, the Social Security and Medicare funds are used for four purposes that you may not be eligible for now, but probably will be eligible for one day:[3]

1. Retirement Income. When you retire, you will be eligible for monthly payments for the rest of your life. The size of the payments will depend on how much money you earned during your career. A common rule of thumb is that Social Security payments will replace approximately 30 percent of your final-year earnings. The maximum monthly payment for a worker retiring at age 65 in 1993 was $1,128. Social Security payments, therefore, may comprise a substantial part of your income when you retire.
2. Disability Income. If you become completely disabled and unable to work, you may be eligible for monthly Social Security payments.
3. Survivor Benefits. Depending on the age and status of your spouse and children, they may be eligible for certain Social Security benefits if you die.
4. Health-Care Expenses. If you are at least 65 or older or are receiving Social Security disability payments for 24 months, you will be eligible for Medicare coverage. Medicare coverage pays for such needs as hospital stays.[4]

Disability income
If an employee were to become completely disabled and unable to work, social security would provide monthly payments.

Survivor benefits
Depending on the age and status of an employee's spouse and children, they may be eligible for monthly social security benefits if the employee dies.

Unemployment Compensation

Unemployment compensation provides payments to an employee who is terminated. Although it may seem odd that you would receive this legally required benefit only if you are no longer working for the company, in today's workplace, layoffs are rather common. So it pays to be aware of the regulations affecting unemployment compensation. This benefit was initially established by the Social Security Act of 1935, but each state administers its own program. Accordingly, the amount of money an individual is eligible for differs from state to state. In Missouri, for example, the maximum weekly amount an individual would receive is about $170; in New Jersey, the maximum one could receive is about $300, which is about the highest in the nation.[5]

Unemployment compensation
Provides payments to an employee who is terminated by such means as a layoff (not for being fired or quitting).

Because the purpose of unemployment compensation is to provide financial support for employees who have been laid off due to a poor economy or stagnant business conditions, a company has the right to deny unemployment compensation to an employee who was terminated for other reasons. Accordingly, employees who were terminated for poor performance, voluntarily quit, or became unemployed because of a labor dispute may not be eligible for unemployment compensation. Most states provide for unemployment benefits for up to 26 weeks; in some states, however, unemployment benefits may continue even longer. Unemployment compensation is not intended to provide a paid vacation for recipients—those receiving unemployment compensation must register for work at the state employment office, prove their availability for work, and be actively seeking employment. Further, recipients must not refuse an offer of suitable work without good reason.

Finally, in addition to government-mandated programs, some companies offer a program called supplemental unemployment benefits (SUB), which provides additional payments to workers who are on a temporary layoff. A SUB program is often part of a union contract.

Workers' Compensation

Workers' compensation A benefit that provides income and payments for workers injured, disabled, or killed on the job.

Workers' compensation is a benefit that provides income and payments for workers who are injured, disabled, or killed on the job. Because such programs are administered entirely by the state, without any federal involvement, they differ greatly from state to state. In all states, however, workers' compensation is designed to provide income to workers in the case of total or partial disability (or, in the case of death, to provide income to their survivors), coverage for medical expenses (such as hospitalization), and coverage for rehabilitation costs (such as occupational therapy).

When most people think of workers' compensation, they consider the traditional cases in which a construction or production worker is injured while working. However, there have been a number of interesting cases involving different kinds of situations for which employees have received workers' compensation. For example, would an employee who is injured at the company picnic during a relay race be eligible for workers' compensation? In some cases, the company may in fact be required to make workers' compensation payments. In the past few years, there have also been large numbers of workers' compensation claims regarding mental distress produced by work-related problems. Depending on the state in which you work, if you can demonstrate that you were unable to work because of mental distress caused by the job, you may be eligible for workers' compensation.[6]

It may come as a surprise to you that Social Security/Medicare, unemployment compensation, and workers' compensation are the only benefits a company is legally required to offer. There are, however, trends suggesting that over the next few years, your company will be required to provide more benefits. First, the Family and Medical Leave Act requires most companies to provide unpaid leave of up to 12 weeks to employees needing time off for family (such as to care for a newborn child) or medical purposes (for example, the employee is experiencing health problems). This law will be described in greater detail under the section titled "Miscellaneous Employee Benefits." Additional federal laws of this nature may be passed in the future. Second, many states have already begun to require certain additional benefits. For example, some states (California, for one) require companies to provide short-term disability coverage. Thus, while relatively few benefits are required today, the list may be longer in the future.

Returning to the three companies described in the beginning of this chapter, do not assume that FreeStyle will provide even these required benefits. The reason is that if you are hired as an independent contractor or consultant, the company will not have to provide even the required benefits. Therefore, you should check to see exactly what your employment status would be if you were hired by FreeStyle. Otherwise, you might have to pay the FICA taxes on your own. Next, two commonly offered, but not legally required, benefits will be discussed in greater detail: pension and health insurance plans.

As you will see, pension and health insurance programs can be quite valuable to you as an employee.

Pension and Health Insurance Programs

Pension Plans

Recall that one purpose of the Social Security Act of 1935 was to provide retirement funds for workers. You may therefore wonder why an additional, optional pension program is even necessary or important to you. The answer is that Social Security is designed to replace only about 30 percent of the final income of the average worker; if you are able to reduce your expenses dramatically when you retire, this may be sufficient. If, however, you intend to continue living the type of lifestyle that you had while you worked, you will need to substantially supplement any Social Security payments you receive.[7] Participation in a company-sponsored pension program may therefore be of great value. It may come as a surprise to you, then, that only 81 percent of employees in medium and large firms are covered by some type of company-sponsored retirement program, and even fewer (only 42 percent) of employees in small firms (companies with fewer than 100 employees) are covered by a retirement program.[8]

There are several different kinds of company-sponsored pension programs, but they may be divided into two types: defined benefit and defined contribution. Defined benefit pension plans are becoming less prevalent in business and industry than they once were. Defined contribution plans require you to play a much greater role in the management of pension funds, and therefore it is important that you thoroughly understand how this type of plan works.[9]

Defined Benefit Pension Programs

A defined benefit pension program is described in terms of what the employee will receive upon retirement. In other words, the plan relies on a *formula,* which determines exactly what this retirement income will be. As shown in Figure 10.2, 63 percent of employees working for medium and large companies are covered by this type of plan, while only 20 percent of employees in small companies (with fewer than 100 employees) are covered by this type of plan.[10] Although different formulas are used, one of the most common is the "percentage of earnings per year of service" formula. This formula is also regarded as among the fairest. It has three components to it, which generally are multiplied together to give an annual sum of money upon retirement. The three components are: (1) an index of yearly earnings or salary, often the average of one's salary for the last five years of employment; (2) years of service, or the number of years an employee has worked for the company; and (3) a constant, to reflect a percentage of salary. The typical constant is 1.5 percent. An example of such a formula is provided in Table 10.1.

Defined benefit pension program
Described in terms of what the employee will receive upon retirement, the plan relies on a formula that determines exactly what the employee will receive upon retirement.

There is one very important issue related to a defined benefit pension. As presented here, there is no automatic change in the formula once an employee has retired. Therefore, a retiree would not necessarily receive any increase in the amount of money over the years. As a result of inflation, the buying power of a retirement check is likely to diminish over time. Even at a relatively low rate of inflation, say 4 percent, one dollar would be worth only 69 cents after ten years. It is, therefore, important to find out whether the pension plan provides an adjustment for cost of living. For example, the University of Missouri–St. Louis offers its

Figure 10.2 **Percentages of Employees Receiving Different Pension Plans**

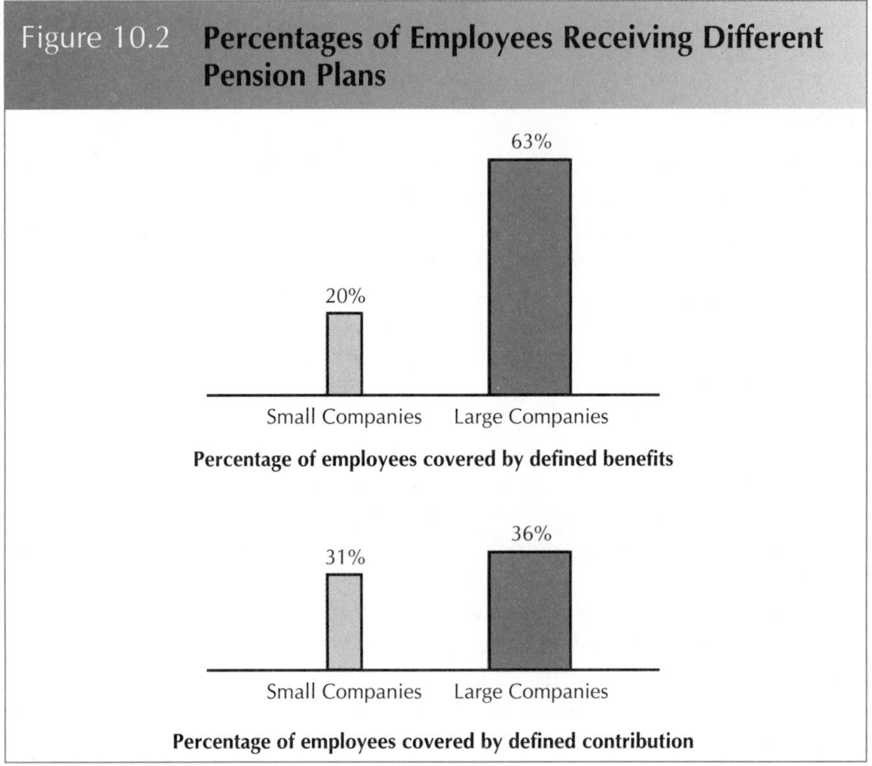

Table 10.1 **Typical Defined Benefit Formula**

Example of a Defined Benefit Pension Formula

Annual yearly retirement pay = (a) final yearly salary × (b) years of service × (c) .015

Based on this formula, an employee who made $40,000 in his or her last year of employment and had worked with the company for 40 years would receive an annual yearly retirement check of $24,000. This would not include any Social Security payments to which the employee was entitled.

retirees the option of having an automatic, annual increase of either 2 percent or 4 percent, in exchange for a reduced annual retirement check.

The defined benefit pension plan has several possible advantages for the employee. First, it provides a guaranteed portion of money to an employee upon retirement. No matter what happens, the employee is assured at least some portion of money (the effect of a company declaring bankruptcy will be discussed later). A second advantage of the defined pension plan is that for plans with formulas that take into account years of service, long-term employees will be rewarded more than short-term employees. As shown in Table 10.2, all other things being equal, the employee who stays with the same company for his or her entire career would receive a larger annual pension payment than an employee who works for four

Table 10.2 **Effects of Seniority on Employee Pensions**

Comparison of pension benefits under a defined benefit program for a worker who stayed with one company for her entire career compared to a worker who worked for four different companies.

Using the formula in Table 10.1, assume Jean has worked for the same company, and Sam has worked for four different companies (salaries and pension formulas are assumed to be the same for both employees).

	Jean	**Sam**
Years		
1–10		Company A: $20,000 × 10 × .015 = $3,000
11–20		Company B: $30,000 × 10 × .015 = $4,500
21–30		Company C: $40,000 × 10 × .015 = $6,000
31–40	$50,000 × 40 × .015 = $30,000	Company D: $50,000 × 10 × .015 = $7,500
	Total annual check: $30,000	Total annual check: $21,000

Note that Jean receives a higher annual retirement check because the defined benefit formula rewards long-term seniority. Sam receives $9,000 less each year of retirement than Jean, which can be a considerable difference.

different companies in his or her career. Finally, the employee in a defined benefit plan has little or no risk involved. It is the company's responsibility to make sure that the plan has enough money (or, in technical terms, is properly funded) to pay retirees.[11]

Defined Contribution Pension Programs

In a defined contribution pension program, each participating employee has an individual fund into which contributions may be made by the company, the employee, or both, depending on the specific plan. This type of plan describes *how* contributions are made, not how much the employee will get upon retirement. A defined contribution plan, therefore, provides no promises as to how much money an employee will get when he or she retires. As shown in Figure 10.2, 36 percent of employees in medium and large companies are covered by this kind of pension plan, while 31 percent of employees in small (fewer than 100 employees) companies are covered by this type of plan.[12]

Defined contribution pension program
In this program, each participating employee has an individual fund into which contributions may be made by the company, the employee, or both, depending on the specific type of plan.

There are several other common features of a defined contribution pension program. One distinct feature is that, in most cases, employees have a choice of where to invest their retirement fund. Most companies, for example, offer mutual funds, company stock, bonds, and similar investment vehicles. One type of fund that is quite popular with employees is the guaranteed investment contract, or GIC. GICs are similar to bank-sponsored accounts, such as money markets, with one major difference: GICs are usually held by insurance companies. Given that some insurance companies have recently had financial difficulties, GICs are probably a riskier investment than the name suggests.[13] As described in Box 10.1, most employees are far too conservative in their investment strategies and tend to place most of their funds into relatively secure, but poorly paying investments.

Guaranteed investment contract
A type of fund offered by most companies that is similar to bank-sponsored accounts, guaranteed investment contracts have one major difference: GICs are usually held by insurance companies.

A second feature of most defined contribution pension plans is the option to use the funds for various purposes. Specifically, most of these plans allow the employee to withdraw the monies when he or she leaves the company. Unless the employee is very careful, however, not only will he or she have to pay income tax, but there may be additional monetary penalties as well. Similarly, some defined contribution plans permit the employee to borrow from the fund for such purposes as making a down payment on a home. Thus, in many ways, the defined contribution plan permits greater flexibility for the employee than does the defined benefit program.

There are several different types of defined contribution programs. Only a few will be described here.

401(k)
A type of savings program that has become quite popular since its introduction in 1981. The 401(k) program permits employees to place about $9,000 each year into a retirement fund tax-free until it is withdrawn.

401(k). A **401(k)** is a savings program that has become quite popular since its introduction in 1981. A recent survey showed that more than 95 percent of very large companies offered this type of pension plan. The 401(k) program permits employees to place about $9,000 each year into a retirement fund. This money is not taxed. Moreover, most companies will match the employees' contributions; a typical match is that the company adds 50 cents to the fund for each $1 that the employee sets aside, up to 2 percent of the employee's salary. Hence, if an employee was earning $30,000 and puts aside $600, the company would add another $300 to the fund, resulting in a total tax-free accumulation of $900 for the year.[14]

Despite the large number of companies offering a 401(k) plan, it is estimated that only 57 percent of eligible employees actually participate. The value of participating early in your career can be shown with the following figures. If you begin putting away $2,000 each year at age 21 and continue until age 64, you will have more than $1 million by age 65 (assuming an annual rate of return of 9 percent). In comparison, if you waited until you were 40 years old, you would have less than $200,000 by age 65.[15]

Although many large companies offer a 401(k), Household International has one of the best plans. This company matches 100 percent of employees' contribution for up to 6 percent of the employee's salary. Although not quite as lucrative,

Box 10.1 Issues in Pension Funds

Tales from the Trenches

Although 401(k)s can be an excellent way to save for retirement, employees tend to invest their funds poorly. A recent survey shows that most participating employees invest either in their company stock or guaranteed investment contracts (GICs). In many cases, these are not the best investments. Ford Motor employees, for example, allocated 50 percent of their 401(k) funds in Ford Motor common stock—but over a three-year period, the stock actually *declined* 12 percent. Another 24 percent of 401(k) funds were invested in GICs, which produced a three-year annual growth rate of only 9 percent, compared to a growth rate of more than 16 percent for a general stock fund. Similar trends occurred at IBM. Fifty-three percent of employee 401(k) funds were invested in GICs, which produced a growth rate of only 8.8 percent. Only 4 percent of the funds were invested in the option with the highest return rate (a small company stock fund), which produced a growth rate of 37 percent. These investment strategies are quite typical. A recent survey found that 31 percent of 401(k) funds were invested in GICs and 30 percent were invested in company stock. The lesson is this: invest wisely.

Source: Adapted from T. Pare, "Is Your 401(k) Plan Good Enough?" *Fortune*, December 28, 1992. 78–83.

Ford Motor Company matches 50 cents for each dollar contributed by employees for up to 5 percent of salary. Finally, General Electric matches 50 cents for every dollar contributed by employees for up to 6 percent of salary. The percentage of salary moves up to 7 percent after the employee contributes for three years.[16]

Deferred Profit Sharing. In another kind of defined contribution plan, known as **deferred profit sharing**, the contributions are made only by the employer and are determined by the profitability of the company. Only about 10 percent of employees in the United States are eligible to participate in this type of plan. There are two basic approaches that a company can use for determining the contributions. One approach is to have a predetermined formula. Just over half (60 percent) of employees who participate in such a plan have this kind of formula. The second approach is to have no preset formula; contributions are determined by the board of directors each year (40 percent of employees who participate in deferred profit sharing have this kind of approach). Among other reasons, the second approach permits much greater flexibility for the company. From the company's standpoint, the deferred profit-sharing plan makes good business sense—if a company is doing poorly, it may have a difficult time paying for employee benefits. Furthermore, it may motivate employees to work harder. From an employee's or applicant's perspective, however, this means a poorly performing company may provide little or no pension contribution.[17]

Deferred profit sharing The retirement fund contributions are usually made only by the employer and are determined by the profitability of the company.

Employee Stock Ownership Plans. Employee Stock Ownership Plans, or ESOPs as they are commonly called, became popular during the 1970s and 1980s. The two major reasons for companies instituting this type of plan are tax advantages and the potential to increase employee motivation. Approximately 10 million employees in the United States are covered by ESOPs. Very briefly, the ESOP provides employees with company stock while at the same time allowing the company to borrow money from a bank at a reduced tax rate. Because contributions to the employees' funds are in the form of company stock, employees should be motivated to work hard in order to increase the value of the company stock and therefore the value of their retirement fund. The principal disadvantage of this retirement program is that employees' retirement funds are directly tied to the stock value of the company. At one brokerage firm, Thomson McKinnon, employees owned about 75 percent of the company's stock, which was valued at $140 million in 1986. As a result of the stock market crash in 1987, the value of Thomson's stock fell in value, and in mid-1989, employees were sent a letter telling them it was possible that their ESOP funds would have no value whatsoever in the future.[18]

Employee stock ownership plan (ESOP) The ESOP provides employees with company stock while at the same time allowing the company to borrow money from a bank at a reduced tax rate.

What are the basic advantages of a defined contribution program for employees? In general, such programs tend to benefit younger employees, who are more likely to leave companies after a short tenure. Also, for the employee who invests funds wisely, the defined contribution retirement program may be quite rewarding. Finally, you may be able to borrow from your fund at a low interest rate or even withdraw money under certain circumstances. On the negative side, depending on the type of plan, poor business conditions or a weak economy may lower the amount of money your company contributes. Similarly, poor investment choices can have a devastating effect on your retirement funds. From the company's perspective, there are fewer government requirements, and perhaps most importantly, no promises are made about the future, which in turn reduces the company's obligations. For organizations, then, a defined contribution plan is generally superior.

ERISA

Employee Retirement Income Security Act (ERISA)
An act instituted in 1974 to eliminate pension mismanagement and abuse.

Aside from the many tax laws that pertain to pension plans, there is one major federal law that governs pension plans: ERISA. Enacted in 1974, ERISA stands for the Employee Retirement Income Security Act, and was instituted to eliminate pension mismanagement and abuse. Although intended as a reform act, some pension practitioners felt it would impose many costly and confusing regulations and joked that ERISA stood for "Everything Ridiculous Invented Since Adam!" While some of the regulations established by ERISA have no visible effect on you as an employee, all of the provisions are very important for organizations to follow. ERISA contains six basic provisions:[19]

1. Reporting and disclosure rules.
2. Fiduciary standards.
3. Funding rules.
4. Plan participation rules.
5. Vesting standards.
6. Plan termination insurance.

Each of these provisions will now be briefly explained.

Summary plan description
A certain type of report that details the fiscal health and outlines the company's pension plan and that must be available to all new participants.

Reporting and Disclosure Rules. Under ERISA, companies are required to provide reports on the fiscal health of the pension plan to a variety of parties, including the participating employees. One of these reports is the Summary Plan Description, which outlines the company's pension plan. This must be provided to all new participants. Employees who are concerned about the financial health of the pension plan should ask for a copy of Form 5500, which the company must provide on written request. Finally, each employee must receive a summary annual report of the pension plan, which describes what he or she would receive upon retirement at age 65.[20]

Fiduciary
A person to whom property or power is entrusted for the benefit of another, such as a person who has authority over the pension plan management, assets, or administration.

Fiduciary Standards. A fiduciary is a person to whom property or power is entrusted for the benefit of another. In the present context, a fiduciary is any person who has authority over the pension plan management, assets, or administration. Typically, a company will have an employee who helps administer or invest the pension funds, who in turn is a fiduciary. ERISA established a number of responsibilities and legal requirements for such an individual, including the requirement to diversify pension plan investments to minimize risk of large losses, to act with proper skill, and to operate solely in the interest of the plan participants.[21]

Funding rules
Requires the pension plan to have sufficient funds so that promised benefits will be available to employees when they retire.

Funding Rules Simply stated, funding rules require the pension plan to have sufficient funds so that promised benefits will be available to employees when they retire. The use of the term "promised benefits" is quite deliberate here. Recall that defined contribution programs make no promises as to how much money you will have at the time of retirement. Therefore, there are no funding regulations for such plans. This is one ERISA regulation that does *not* pertain to defined contribution programs.

Plan Participation Rules. Initially, companies had tremendous latitude as to when a new employee would become eligible to participate in the pension plan. ERISA established the maximum time a new employee had to wait. That is, once an employee reaches age 21 and completes one year of service, he or she must be allowed to participate within six months. A year of service is defined by the law to mean 1,000 hours or more of work during a 12-month period. Thus, part-time employees might not become eligible for the pension plan.[22]

Vesting
Refers to the rights an employee has to the pension benefits if employment is terminated prior to retirement.

Vesting Standards. Vesting refers to the rights an employee has to his or her pension benefits if employment is terminated prior to retirement. In other words, if an employee leaves the company prior to a certain time period, he or she may automatically lose some or all of the pension funds. This regulation is important to understand, because it could lead to a significant loss of pension funds. The vesting rules provide the standards by which a participating employee must gain the rights to his or her pension funds. The Tax Reform Act of 1986 stipulates that a company may use *either* of the following:[23]

A. An employee will be fully vested in five years of service.
B. An employee will be vested 20 percent in the first three years of service and 20 percent for each following year (this means the employee is fully vested in seven years).

Regardless of which of these plans is used, an employee must become fully vested when he or she reaches normal retirement age. Knowing the vesting rules is important for you, as an employee, because leaving a company before being fully vested means you would forfeit some or all of your pension funds. For example, if your company used plan A, and you left the organization four years after you began, you would never receive any company-provided pension funds. If your company used plan B, and you left the organization after six years, you would receive only 80 percent of the pension funds you were eligible for. If you were to quit or were terminated from several companies over a period of a number of years, you may lose out on large sums of pension money.

Plan Termination Insurance. Similar to the stock market crash of 1929 when numerous banks failed, leaving depositors penniless, companies would sometimes go bankrupt, leaving pensioners with little or no company-sponsored pension. One such case was the Studebaker plant in South Bend, Indiana, which closed in 1963. Because of severe underfunding, a typical 40-year-old worker with 20 years of service received a lump-sum payment of only $350 instead of a lifetime monthly pension check. This and similar cases resulted in the establishment of the Pension Benefit Guaranty Corporation (PBGC). The PBGC serves as an insurance program whereby pension plan participants are guaranteed at least some benefits, even if the fund is terminated before being fully funded. The employer pays a premium to participate in this program; currently the rate is $19 per participating employees (the rate may go as high as $72 for underfunded programs). While this program serves to guarantee a basic pension, the maximum monthly payment a participant may get is $2,250 per month. For highly paid participants, this may be far less than they would otherwise receive. Does participation in the PBGC apply to all pension programs? The answer is no. Only companies providing a defined benefit pension program participate, because defined contribution programs make no promises as to what participants will end up with.[24]

Pension Benefit Guaranty Corporation
Serves as an insurance program whereby pension plan participants are guaranteed at least some benefits even if the fund is depleted.

In addition to ERISA, there are other laws that affect pension plans. The Civil Rights Act of 1964, for example, was used to sue the city of Los Angeles' Department of Water & Power on the grounds that it required women to make higher contributions to the pension plan. The department's argument was that because women on average live longer, they should be required to give larger contributions than men in order for both sexes to have the same payments upon retirement. The Supreme Court, however, ruled against the Department and argued that this method led women to be treated as a group, which in turn was discriminatory.

Finally, you should be aware that there are other pension programs, such as an individual retirement account (IRA), that employees can use as a tax-deferred retirement savings program. Some companies have also implemented a simplified employee pension (SEP) program, which requires very little paperwork and low administrative costs. Certain workers, such as employees in a public school system, may be eligible to participate in a 403(b) plan or tax-deferred annuity, which allows them to contribute money to a pension fund. A major advantage of all of these programs is that they enable you, as an employee, to lower your present taxes, while saving for retirement.

Returning to the three companies you read about in the beginning of this chapter, you probably realize that NewForm and Tradition have very different pension plans, with quite different implications. NewForm has a 401(k) plan, which, depending on how much money you are able to set aside, could be quite valuable. However, it will take discipline on your part to participate in the plan and set aside money for the 401(k). It would be useful to find out what investment options the plan offers. Tradition has a defined benefit plan. It would be very helpful to find out just what type of formula is used. Because Tradition has a defined benefit plan, it will require far less effort on your part to participate. Thus, each plan has its own strengths and weaknesses. Which plan do you prefer?

In closing, retirement may be the furthest thing from your mind. Nevertheless, without careful planning and consideration, you may find yourself with insufficient income when retirement does occur. Next, you will learn more about health insurance programs and some critical issues pertaining to them.

Health Insurance

Americans spend more than $800 billion per year on health care, which amounts to 14 percent of the gross domestic product. As you probably know, medical services are quite expensive. The national average charge for open-heart surgery, for example, is $7,280; and that figure is only for the physicians' charges—it does not include the hospital room and other service fees. The average annual cost per

Box 10.2 Having Health Insurance Pays

For a variety of reasons, many people do not have and cannot get health insurance. The results can be devastating. Arno Larsen retired early and was not able to purchase a policy from an insurance company. When he later needed two prostate operations, he had to pay the $6,500 fees out of his own savings. Gretchen van der Grinten was laid off from work. When her self-employed husband, Nick, needed kidney stone surgery, they did not have health insurance coverage. They cannot afford the $12,000 needed to pay for the surgery. Craig Miller, a maintenance mechanic at Southwestern Bell, is fortunate to have an exceptionally good health insurance program. His wife, Sandra, was hospitalized with dangerously high blood pressure while pregnant. She later gave birth to a premature baby, who spent nine weeks in the hospital. Subsequently, Sandra Miller had gallbladder surgery. The total costs to the Miller family? Zero. Having health insurance can pay; having *good* health insurance can really pay.

Source: Adapted from L. Smith, "A Cure for What Ails Medical Care," *Fortune,* July 1, 1991, 49.

employee for health insurance was $3,605 in 1991; in some organizations, the employee pays little or none of this cost. Only recently has the inflation rate for medical services come down to a point where it roughly matches the general rate of inflation. Do you know how much your employer pays for your medical insurance, or how much it would cost to obtain medical insurance on your own? You may be surprised to learn that if you had to purchase medical insurance on your own, you would probably pay three thousand dollars per year for even minimum coverage. In comparison, depending on the company you work for, you may pay little or nothing for health insurance. Most medium and large companies sponsor some form of health insurance. In fact, 92 percent of employees working in medium to large businesses are covered, but only 67 percent of employees in small businesses are covered. Furthermore, many part-time workers are not eligible to participate in a company's health insurance program.[25]

Health insurance plans typically cover a number of services, including hospital stays, physician treatment, mental and nervous disorders treatment, surgery, and in some cases, routine medical services (such as annual physical exams).

This section of the chapter describes different kinds of company-sponsored health insurance programs, along with several important regulations that you should be aware of. Before discussing the different types of programs, however, it is important to define several basic terms that are associated with health insurance programs. Because health insurance operates much like car or home insurance, you are likely to have heard of these terms before. *Premiums* are payments that you as an employee make for the insurance coverage; they are similar to the car insurance payments that you make on a regular basis to an insurance company. Unless your company pays for your entire health insurance program, money is likely to be automatically taken from your paycheck to pay health insurance premiums. The *deductible* refers to the amount of money you must pay before the insurance company reimburses you for expenses. For example, your health insurance plan may have a $250 deductible, which means that you will pay the first $250 on health insurance claims, after which the insurance company will begin to make payments. The copayment refers to the amount of money the employee must pay for the specific health service. For example, after the deductible has been paid, the health insurance program may pay only 80 percent of the costs; your copayment, then, would be 20 percent. Finally, maximum out-of-pocket annual payment refers to the most that an employee would have to pay for medical expenses in a single year.

Copayment
The amount of money the employee must pay for the specific health service.

Maximum out-of-pocket annual payment
The most that an employee would have to pay for medical expenses in a single year.

Kinds of Health Insurance Programs

There are several types of health insurance programs that a company may offer to employees. Fee for service, HMOs, PPOs, and POSs are among the most common. There are important differences between these plans, which you will read about in greater detail next.

Fee for Service. This is the traditional health insurance program. In a fee-for-service program, you (and/or your company) pay for each medical service provided to you. A typical fee-for-service program would permit the employee to use any medical professional or facility he or she wishes, would have a deductible (which, much like car insurance, might be higher or lower, depending on the size of the premium), and a copayment of 20 percent. Fee for service is currently the

Fee-for-service program
The traditional health-insurance program in which the employee and/or the employer pay for each medical service provided.

most commonly used health care plan, though this is changing rapidly. Like automobile insurance, your company may offer different levels of coverage. For example, in 1991, AT&T offered employees three levels of coverage, ranging from a plan with a $2,500 deductible, a copayment of 30 percent, and a maximum out-of-pocket annual payment of $3,000 to a plan with a deductible of $150 to $300, a copayment of 0 percent to 20 percent (depending on the treatment), and a maximum out-of-pocket annual payment of $1,000. The employee premiums would, of course, be highest for the latter plan.[26]

A few problems are associated with the traditional fee-for-service approach, particularly from the employer's point of view. First, there is little incentive for medical professionals and facilities to keep costs down. Because, in most cases you, the employee, pay a relatively small copayment, there is little pressure and even less opportunity for you to shop around for the least costly medical professional (have you ever asked a doctor how much he or she charges for a particular procedure?). Second, fee-for-service programs generate a great deal of paperwork and administrative work to keep track of the bills and reimbursements, which in turn creates additional expenses. Other programs, such as HMOs and PPOs, have been developed in response to these problems. These alternatives are discussed next.[27]

Health maintenance organization (HMO) A network of medical professionals and hospitals that provide health care for participants.

HMOs. Although the health maintenance organization, or **HMO**, has been in existence for more than 40 years, HMOs received their biggest boost with the passage of the HMO Act of 1973, which may require a company to offer an HMO. HMOs are rapidly gaining popularity, as this system uses a number of cost-saving techniques. Basically, an HMO is a network of medical professionals and hospitals

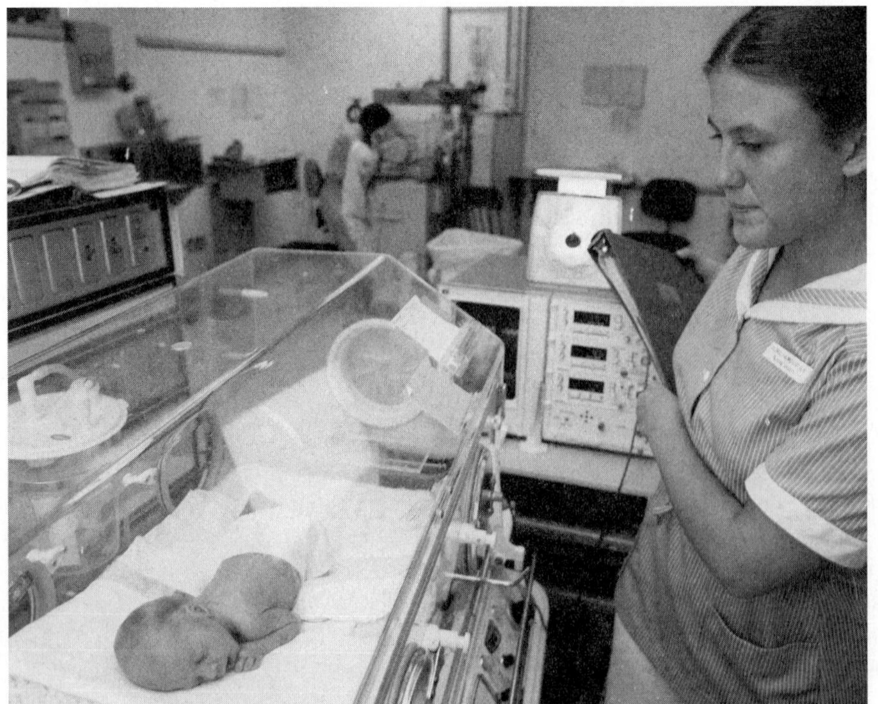

Health care options offered by many companies today include HMOs, PPOs, and PSOs, all presenting different insurance options to employees. Everything from having a baby to your annual physical exam should be carefully considered before choosing an insurance program for you and your family.

that provide health care for participants. If you enroll in an HMO, you are usually required to select a primary-care physician who works for the HMO. The **primary-care physician** decides what kind of treatment you need and will refer you (if necessary) to the appropriate specialist within the HMO. The basic advantages to employees who enroll in the HMO are as follows. Unlike traditional fee-for-service health insurance plans, HMO participants usually pay no deductible and little, if any, copayment (there may be a very small charge, such as $5, per office visit). If you use health care services with at least some regularity, HMOs may be less expensive for you than the fee-for-service plan. Second, HMOs often provide coverage for health expenses that are not covered by traditional fee-for-service plans, such as the annual physical exam. Finally, HMOs typically require employees to complete little or no paperwork.[28]

Primary-care physician
The physician chosen through an HMO that decides what kind of treatment is needed and provides referrals to the appropriate specialists within the HMO.

While the HMO offers several advantages to companies and to employees, there are some drawbacks, particularly from the employee viewpoint. First, most HMOs require the employee to use a medical professional that is part of the network; you would not be reimbursed if you used professionals or services outside of the network. Also, most HMOs require that you first seek treatment from the primary-care physician. Only if the primary-care physician cannot treat you will you be permitted to see a specialist. The degree to which this creates a problem may depend upon the number of specialists associated with the HMO and how important it is to you to be seen by a specialist. A recent survey indicated that 14 percent of HMO participants were dissatisfied with the choice of specialists made available to them. Second, the same survey found large differences in waiting time to obtain an appointment and to see the doctor. Nevertheless, respondents in HMOs were on average just as satisfied with their medical experiences as were respondents in other types of programs.[29]

PPOs. A preferred-provider organization or **PPO,** is simply a network of medical professionals and hospitals that have agreed to give discounted services. Unlike the HMO, participants may go to any medical professional or hospital they wish; participants merely pay less for PPO services than they do for non-PPO services. For example, you may have a copayment of only 10 percent for a PPO doctor, with a deductible of only $100. Conversely, you might have a copayment of 20 percent for a non-PPO doctor, with an annual deductible of $250. Compared to an HMO, then, participants have far greater choice with the PPO system. However, the PPO plan may cost you more than an HMO and companies find that this approach does little to cut expenses.[30]

Preferred-provider organization (PPO)
A network of medical professionals and hospitals that have agreed to give discounted services. Unlike the HMO, participants may go to any medical professional or hospital they wish.

Point-of-service (POS) plan
A plan that attempts to combine the advantages of the HMO with the advantages of the PPO.

POS. The **point-of-service plan,** or POS, attempts to combine the advantages of the HMO with the advantages of the PPO. Typically, the POS operates like the HMO in that you must first check with your primary-care physician. Only if the primary-care physician gives you a referral can you see a specialist. On the other hand, like the PPO, you can use any medical professional or service you would like. However, you will be reimbursed at different rates, depending on whether you use a professional associated with the POS (an **in-network** professional) or whether you use a professional not associated with the POS (an **out-of-network** professional). Obviously, the charge for seeing an in-network professional will be much lower. Thus, the POS tries to combine both the HMO and the PPO concepts to best serve the employees.[31]

In-network
A list of medical professionals that are associated with the plan (POS, HMO, or PPO).

Out-of-network
Any medical professional not associated with the plan (POS, HMO, or PPO). If an employee chooses a doctor that is out-of-network, the cost will be higher than using an in-network professional.

As you can see, there are a number of different kinds of insurance plans that your company may offer. Carefully examining the alternatives, in conjunction with your particular needs, will help you choose the best options. The next section explains some additional terms and conditions associated with health insurance plans.

Additional Terms Associated with Health Insurance Plans

Several important terms and conditions of health insurance plans are important to know. A complete understanding of these terms will help you, as an employee, make better decisions with regard to health care.

Preexisting condition An illness, injury, or pregnancy that an individual has prior to becoming covered by the health insurance plan.

Preexisting Condition. A very important term in the health insurance field is preexisting condition. A preexisting condition is generally defined as an illness, injury, or pregnancy that an individual has prior to becoming covered by the health insurance plan. Many health insurance plans will not cover charges related to a preexisting condition until a set time period has passed. For example, imagine you were receiving treatment for a heart condition. When you switch jobs, you may become covered by a new health insurance plan. Your new plan may have a preexisting condition clause that states that you must complete three months of coverage under the new company's insurance plan without receiving treatment for the condition, or you might have to complete twelve months of coverage. If you needed emergency treatment for your heart condition, for example, prior to three months being completed, your new insurance may not pay anything. Obviously, this could result in considerable expense to you. Although the preexisting condition concept may seem fairly straightforward, in fact it is quite complex. There are at least two ways to avoid problems with a preexisting condition clause. One, some health insurance plans do not contain such a clause; HMOs in particular often do not have a preexisting condition clause. So, check carefully to see if you are

Box 10.3 The Changing Rules for Retirees' Health Insurance

Tales from the Trenches

As a result of recent accounting rule changes, many companies are reducing or even eliminating their retirees' health insurance program. One company that is involved in a legal battle over retiree health benefits is John Morrell & Company, a meatpacker based in Sioux Falls, South Dakota. The legal battle began when the company sent a letter to their retirees in early 1992, indicating that the retirees would pay more for the cost of prescription drugs, have a higher premium, and face higher maximum annual out-of-pocket costs. According to the company, when combined with the federal Medicare program, retirees would still have a better benefits program than most companies provide. Somewhat surprisingly, the company, not the retirees, began the legal contest by suing the retirees in court. What was the purpose of the company's lawsuit? To have the judge declare that the company could alter the health benefits of retirees at any time. Although Medicare still covers many of the retirees' costs, changes in the company-sponsored health insurance program means higher costs to the retirees in such areas as prescription drugs. Previously, for example, the retirees paid a flat $2 for prescription drugs; under the new retiree health insurance policy, Gerrit Zwak (one of the retirees) will pay as much as 30 percent for his wife's heart drug, which costs $105 retail. The retirees' biggest concern is that next year, the company will reduce the health insurance plan even further.

Source: Adapted from R. Rose, "Chilly Sunset," *The Wall Street Journal,* February 2, 1993, A1, A6.

switching to a plan that has a preexisting condition clause. Second, as explained next, using the COBRA option may help protect you from a preexisting condition. In any case, read the clause carefully, and make sure you fully understand all of the implications.

COBRA. The term **COBRA** stands for something that has nothing to do with health insurance—instead it refers to the Consolidated Omnibus Budget Reconciliation Act. For our purposes, COBRA of 1985 requires companies with 20 or more employees to offer continued health insurance coverage to participants who would otherwise no longer be eligible to participate in the health insurance plan. Imagine, for example, you were terminated from a company or that you were covered under your father's or mother's health insurance plan, which you will no longer be eligible for now that you are graduating from college. For both of these situations, you or your parent should be able to continue your coverage for some period of time (the maximum amount of time you will be able to continue coverage depends on the situation). For example, if you were terminated, you would be able to continue coverage for up to 18 months. Of course, such continued coverage is not free; your company can require you to pay all of the costs, plus an additional 2 percent to cover administrative charges. Returning to preexisting conditions, use of COBRA would permit you to continue your previous health insurance until the preexisting condition clause expired. You should plan carefully to ensure that you are covered in case of expensive health care treatment. COBRA may be a useful option toward meeting this goal.[32]

COBRA
The Consolidated Omnibus Budget Reconciliation Act (COBRA) of 1985 requires companies with 20 or more employees to offer continued coverage of health insurance to participants who would otherwise no longer be eligible to participate in the health insurance plan.

Utilization Review. In an effort to reduce continuously growing costs of health care, many insurance companies are turning to use of the utilization review. The **utilization review** refers to a process by which medical services are analyzed and reviewed. The utilization review may require the use of second opinions (in which a second medical professional's opinion is required before a particular planned surgical procedure is performed), concurrent reviews (in which an independent medical professional monitors your hospital stay), and review of medical bills. Utilization reviews may prevent unnecessary surgeries and cut down on the length of time you spend in a hospital. At the same time, a utilization review may result in your hospital stay being shorter than you would like or additional expenses for you if the insurance company refuses to pay the entire bill. As a consumer, there is little you can do about utilization reviews. Be sure, however, that you learn what the requirements of your health insurance program are (for example, is a second opinion necessary in order to have a surgical procedure reimbursed?) and be sure to carefully review all documents concerning your health insurance. Ask your company benefits representative if you have any questions. There may also be an appeal process for you to request reconsideration if you feel you have been treated unfairly.[33]

Utilization review
A process by which medical services are analyzed and reviewed.

Flexible Spending Accounts. **Flexible spending accounts** (or FSAs, as they are sometimes referred to) allow an employee to pay for health care expenses or dependent care assistance expenses on a before-tax basis. A before-tax basis means that you, as an employee, would not pay any federal, state, or Social Security/Medicare taxes on that money. If you spend a fairly large sum of money on either health care or dependent care (such as payments to a day care center), you may find that an FSA will save you considerable money. The way the FSA works is that each year, your company (if it has set up an FSA program) will ask you how much money you wish to set aside for the health care and dependent care

Flexible spending account (FSA)
FSAs allow an employee to pay for health care expenses or dependent care assistance expenses on a before-tax basis.

assistance funds (there is, of course, a limit to how much you can set aside for each). The major potential disadvantage of the FSA system is that it is a "Use It Or Lose It" program; you forfeit any money you set aside that you do not use. A 1989 survey of medium and large companies showed that 23 percent of employees were eligible for participation in an FSA. Only 8 percent of employees in small companies were eligible.[34]

Returning to the three companies described in the opening case, it is beginning to look as though FreeStyle may not be quite the deal you might have at first thought. Even though the starting salary is $2,000 more than the other two companies, it is clear that health insurance alone might cost more than $2,000 each year. In comparing the other two companies, Tradition seems to have some of the features discussed, including the FSAs, HMO, and PPO options. NewForm, as you may recall, has a cafeteria benefits plan. You probably are wondering what that is; we will discuss it in the next section. For now, though, it would be useful to seek more information from NewForm to find out what type of health insurance options they offer. Likewise, it may be worth getting information from both companies as to the specific details of the health insurance plans and how much the premium is for each plan. Next, you will read about other benefits, such as unpaid leave, long-term disability insurance, and long-term care.

Miscellaneous Employee Benefits

In addition to health insurance and pension plans, many companies offer other types of benefits. As with health insurance, you may be able to purchase some of these additional benefits from an insurance company on your own, but your company may pay part or all of your premiums and obtain a better rate than you would on your own. It is important, therefore, to find out about these other benefits as well. This section of the chapter discusses unpaid leave, disability insurance, long-term care, and dental insurance, and briefly mentions a number of other benefits such as tuition reimbursement and child-care facilities. This section concludes with an explanation of a cafeteria benefits plan.

Family and Medical Leave

Family and Medical Leave Act (FMLA) Passed in 1993, this act requires companies that have at least 50 employees to grant an unpaid leave to employees who meet any of the following conditions: the employee has become responsible for a child; the employee is providing care for a child, parent, or spouse with a

As noted earlier, many companies are obliged by law to offer you unpaid leave. This law, referred to as the Family and Medical Leave Act (FMLA), was passed by Congress in 1993. Briefly, this law requires companies that have at least 50 employees to grant an unpaid leave to employees who meet any of the following conditions:[35]

1. The employee has become responsible for a child through birth, adoption, or foster care.
2. The employee is providing care for a child, parent, or spouse with a serious health condition.
3. The employee is experiencing a serious health condition, that leaves him or her unable to perform the job.

For any of these three conditions, the employee can elect to take up to 12 weeks of unpaid leave within a 12-month period. Under certain conditions, the employee can take intermittent leave; that is, the employee may be able to take the leave one day each week of the year.

Although the law does not require the company to pay the employee during the leave, the company must continue to include him or her under the health insurance plan. Upon return from the leave, the company must provide an equivalent job with the equivalent benefits, pay, and other terms and conditions of employment.

serious health condition; or the employee is experiencing a serious health condition that leaves him or her unable to perform the job.

Disability Insurance

Disability insurance provides income in case you become unable to work due to an accident or illness. You may ask, "Doesn't Social Security or workers' compensation cover this situation?" They may, but those mandatory programs typically pay a far lower percentage of one's salary; even though mandatory programs such as Social Security may provide some income, it may be too little to cover your living expenses. That is why it is important to have additional coverage through disability insurance.

Generally, disability insurance is divided into short-term disability (STD) insurance and long-term disability (LTD) insurance. As suggested by the names, STD covers short-term disabilities, usually for a period of six months or less. LTD refers to long-term disabilities, usually for periods of time greater than six months. LTD plans generally have a two-stage period. In the first stage, LTD benefits are paid to an employee who, due to the disability, is unable to perform his or her regular job. In the second stage, which typically occurs two or three years later, benefits may continue only if the individual is unable to perform any occupation for which the person is qualified for by training or experience. A 1989 survey of medium and large companies found that 45 percent of employees were eligible to participate in disability insurance, but only 20 percent of employees in small firms were eligible.[36]

Short-term disability (STD) insurance Insurance that covers short-term disabilities, usually for a period of six months or less.

Long-term disability (LTD) insurance Insurance that covers long-term disabilities, usually for periods of time greater than six months.

Because most people mistakenly assume they will never experience a disabling condition, LTD insurance is often ignored by employees. Indeed, one expert refers to disability coverage as the "Rodney Dangerfield of insurance," because it gets limited respect and little attention. It is probably a wise idea to at least consider the option of obtaining such insurance. A recent estimate indicates that a typical 40-year-old professional employee should pay roughly $39 per month in premiums for each $1,000 of monthly disability coverage. You should carefully review the terms and conditions of the disability insurance policy. For example, the ideal policy would continue paying until you are 65, when you would become eligible for Social Security payments; but many policies end after three to five years of disability. Another consideration is the renewability and cancellation clauses in the policy. The best policies guarantee you the right to continue coverage as long as you pay your premiums (thereby preventing the insurer from arbitrarily canceling your policy). Finally, just as with certain pension plans, inflation gradually reduces the value of a fixed disability income. The best policies offer some kind of adjustment for cost-of-living increases.[37]

Long-Term Care

Long-term care insurance is a program that pays for medical care at your home or in a nursing home. You are probably thinking, "Only the elderly need that kind of

Long-term care insurance
An insurance program that pays for medical care at home or in a nursing home.

care; I'm too young to worry about that." In reality, it is not just elderly people who sometimes require such care. Sometimes an injury (such as falling off your roof while fixing the TV antenna or cleaning gutters) may require that you spend some time at a long-term care facility (nursing home) or obtain medical care in your own home. In fact, millions of Americans will need a nursing home at least once during their lifetime. It is also worth noting that some long-term care insurance programs cover your parents, as well as you and your family. Therefore, you should at least consider obtaining long-term care insurance.[38]

Dental Insurance

Most large companies today sponsor dental insurance plans. These are similar in most ways to health insurance plans. Typically, preventive dental services (such as routine exams, cleaning, and standard X rays) are completely covered, while basic services (such as fillings) have a deductible and small copayment (perhaps 20 percent). Major services (for example, inlays) have a deductible and a much larger copayment (maybe 50 percent).

Additional Benefits

There are a great many other benefits that a company may provide or sponsor. Although not all of these can be described or even mentioned here, two are worth mentioning in somewhat greater detail: tuition reimbursement and child-care centers.

Tuition reimbursement
Tuition reimbursement programs vary in terms of the amount of reimbursement they provide, but they usually provide 75 to 100 percent reimbursement contingent on a passing grade.

Tuition Reimbursement. Tuition reimbursement is becoming a much sought-after benefit because many full-time employees are returning to (or beginning) college for further education. Although more than two-thirds of medium and large size companies offer some tuition aid, fewer than 10 percent of eligible employees usually participate. Tuition-aid programs vary in terms of the amount of reimbursement they provide. The norm today is for companies to provide anywhere between 75 percent to 100 percent reimbursement. Most companies require the employee to "successfully" complete the course (for example, obtain a passing grade); some companies reimburse the employee in proportion to the grade obtained (such as 100 percent reimbursement for an A, 75 percent reimbursement for a B and so on)—and you thought good grades never paid off! Many companies also subsidize related educational expenses, including textbooks, registration fees, and laboratory fees. A few companies will even reimburse for graduation fees, entrance exams, and similar costs.

Child Care. Today, a majority of women with children are working in the labor force. Working women with very young children often must find a full-time babysitter or arrange for some type of day care. Accordingly, an increasingly valuable benefit is some type of child-care support. The best, of course, is an on-site day care center. SAS, a computer software firm, is one of the few firms that provides free on-site day care. SAS provides this service to any employee with one or more years of service. What do you think the estimated yearly value of this benefit is? If you guessed about $4,200 you are right.[39] In fact, employees must pay taxes to the IRS as if they received this money from the company. As you can imagine, the day care center is quite popular. More than 300 children are enrolled, and there is a waiting list of 80 children. Other companies, such as America West (an airline), help subsidize the costs of the day care center.[40] From an employee perspective, there is at least one potential advantage of an on-site day care center: proximity to work. Not only does this mean that both the child and the employee commute back and forth to the same area, but the parent may be able to visit the child during lunch breaks. From a company's perspective, a company-sponsored day care center can be a considerable expense. In addition to obtaining qualified staff, the company will have to pay considerable liability insurance, facilities costs, and so forth.

Finally, some additional benefits that a company may offer include vision care, legal and financial advice, employee discounts on goods and services, and free or reduced costs for meals. Many companies offer additional benefits to top executives, including the use of a company car and membership in country clubs. One of the best companies for benefits is IBM, which provides home mortgage assistance, as well as up to $50,000 for the care of disabled children. The next section discusses one way to offer a wide choice of benefits to an employee, while allowing the company to control its costs: the cafeteria or flexible benefits plan.

Cafeteria Benefits

Perhaps the best way to understand a cafeteria benefits plan is to think of a lunch cafeteria, to which the customer pays a flat monthly fee. The menu consists of a choice of soup or salad, three different main courses, a soft drink or hot beverage (coffee, tea, or hot chocolate), and a dessert. If, however, the customer chooses to not select a dessert, he or she receives a refund of 50 cents each day. An advantage of this type of plan is that the cafeteria could add additional offerings, without incurring much, if any, additional cost. For example, in addition to choosing between soup and salad, the menu could be modified so that the customer could choose either soup, salad, or an appetizer. The cost to the company would remain the same, since the customer can only pick one of the three items. The assumption is that with greater choice, customers will be more satisfied with their selection and more able to meet their own needs. The logic of the cafeteria benefits plan is very much the same. Essentially, a cafeteria plan allows employees to have a choice between taxable (usually cash) and nontaxable elements of compensation (such as health insurance).[41]

Cafeteria benefits
A benefits plan that provides a choice between taxable (usually cash) and nontaxable elements of compensation (such as health insurance).

Why would companies develop a cafeteria benefits plan? First, as described in an earlier chapter, the characteristics of the workforce are changing. As one benefits expert remarked, "The 'prototypical employee' (a married male, age 35 to 45, two children preparing for college, with a heavily mortgaged home and two cars) for whom most group benefit programs were designed . . . [is] starting to become a demographic dinosaur." In other words, different employees need different benefits. Just as some people prefer salad over soup, or would rather forgo dessert, the single employee with no children, for example, may prefer more vacation time or simply cash, while the single-wage earner with several children may prefer greater health insurance coverage. Second, use of a cafeteria plan allows companies to add new options at little or no cost. Thus, a plan may provide 100 credits to each participant to spend on the benefits plan. Just as with the cafeteria lunch plan wherein selection of a new dish means the customer must forgo a different dish, the cafeteria benefits plan means the employee will need to forgo some amount of another benefit, or pay more, if he or she chooses a new offering. Finally, another reason companies may adopt a cafeteria plan is to reduce increasing costs. For example, Educational Testing Service, one of the original adopters, bases its contributions on the same percentage of salary as it did when it first introduced its cafeteria plan in the mid-1970s. United Hospitals, Inc. (UHI), is a company that successfully changed to a cafeteria benefits plan in the late 1980s. Not only was the company able to contain or even reduce the cost of health benefits, but employees in many cases were able to receive extra money. In some cases, employees took home as much as an additional $100 per month. Most of the employees pay no more than $20 per month for their benefits. A critical factor in the success of UHI's program was that employees were given much information about the plan, and it changed their approach to medical services.[42]

Add-on plan
A cafeteria plan in which all existing benefits are maintained and new ones added.

Modular plan
A cafeteria plan in which the employee is offered a choice of several benefit "packages" or modules.

There are several different types of cafeteria benefit plans. For example, the plan adopted by Educational Testing Service in the mid-1970s is referred to as an **add-on plan.** In this plan, all existing benefits are maintained. The benefit plan is supplemented by a number of additional, optional benefits. An example of a **modular plan** is illustrated in Table 10.3. In this type of cafeteria plan, the employee is offered a choice of several benefit "packages" or modules. An employee chooses one of the packages and cannot substitute. As you look at Table 10.3, observe that if the employee chooses Module B, he or she would get either $300 cash or $300 in a flexible spending account to be used for day care.

Table 10.3 **Example of a Modular Cafeteria Benefits Plan**

	Medical	Dental	Life	FSA/Cash
A	Comprehensive Plan: $200 deductible/person, then plan pays 90% of expenses and you pay 10%. Maximum you could pay—$1,000 excluding deductible.	100% preventive care 50% other care $1,000 lifetime max. for orthodontia. You pay for dependent dental coverage.	Company-paid: 2 × pay with $50K max. Employee-paid life: 1 ×, 2 × or 3 × Company-paid with $150K max. Employee-paid dependent life: Spouse—$10,000 Children—$5,000	Not available.
B	Comprehensive Plan: $300 deductible/person, then plan pays 80% of expenses and you pay 20%. Maximum you could pay—$1,000 excluding deductible.	100% preventive care 75% other care 60% orthodontia $1,500 lifetime max. for orthodontia. Company-paid dental coverage for employees and dependents.	Company-paid: 2 × pay with no max. Employee-paid life: 1 × or 2 × pay with no max. Employee-paid dependent life: Spouse—$10,000 Children—$5,000	$300 per year from company available for dependent day care or health care or as cash. Salary reduction: up to $5,000 for dependent day care.
C	Comprehensive Plan: $600 deductible/person, then plan pays 80% of expenses and you pay 20%. Maximum you could pay—$3,000 excluding deductible.	Not available.	Company-paid: $10,000 Employee-paid life: 1 × or 2 × pay with no max. Employee-paid dependent life: Spouse—$10,000 Children—$5,000	$800 per year from company available for dependent day care or health care or as cash. Salary reduction: up to $5,000 for dependent day care.

Adapted from McCaffery (1992).

What should you be careful about if you work for a company with flexible-cafeteria benefits? First, you should consider your choices very carefully. For example, although you may think you would rather have cash than participate in the LTD insurance plan, think twice. Second, pay careful attention to any changes that your company announces. Third, when you are completing your forms to select your choices, be sure you complete the forms accurately.[43]

Returning to the three companies described in the opening case, it would be helpful to carefully examine any additional benefits provided by each company. Depending on your own needs and interests, some of the additional benefits offered by one of the three companies may be particularly valuable. If, for example, you were planning to go to graduate school while working, a company offering total tuition reimbursement might provide tremendous savings over a company that does not offer this benefit. Conversely, if you had very young children and were part of a dual-career family, you may find that a company providing an on-site day care center would be valuable. Therefore, it is important that you thoroughly investigate *all* of the benefits that each company offers. However, before you make a definite choice based on current differences among the three companies, you should realize that companies have considerable latitude in changing or eliminating benefits; so if your choice of jobs varies on several factors (such as the opportunity for promotions, pay, type of work), do not let the benefits program be the only deciding factor.

Paid Time Off

Paid time off from work is the last benefits area that you will read about here. Compared to previous centuries, when employees often worked six or seven days every week, employees in the late 20th century work far fewer days. There are three categories of paid time off from work: vacation, holidays, and personal absences. Why companies provide these benefits, and some typical policies concerning them, are described in greater detail next.

Paid time off
Includes vacation, holidays, and personal absences.

Vacations

There are two basic reasons for companies to provide vacations to employees. First, it is widely recognized that employees need occasional breaks from the physical and mental demands of work. Second, it is widely believed that employees should be rewarded for staying with the company; most companies therefore offer longer vacation periods for more senior employees. Quaker Oats, for example, offers two weeks of vacation time to employees. After 25 years of service, Quaker Oats employees are entitled to five weeks of vacation. One of the most generous vacation policies is offered by Anheuser-Busch, where employees with 15 or more years of tenure receive ten weeks of vacation each year. Levi Strauss, however, has an even more unusual policy: employees may take every Friday afternoon off! That is equivalent to more than five weeks of vacation per year. In addition, employees are allowed up to seven additional weeks off after 20 years of service.[44]

Holidays

Most of us believe that certain days on the calendar are a time for family and friends to celebrate and spend time together. Companies have also recognized and accepted

Box 10.4 Extended Paid Time Off from Work

A small number of companies, particularly computer and high-tech companies, have begun to offer employees a kind of extended paid vacation, called a sabbatical (many universities offer a similar program for faculty members). Such companies may offer paid time away from work for up to one year; rather than a kind of vacation, though, the purpose of the sabbatical is usually to provide an opportunity for self-development. Sabbaticals are often highly valued benefits. For example, in the late 1970s, Tandem Computers surveyed its employees and found that sabbaticals were more highly desired than pensions. Less than 10 years later, almost one-quarter of Tandem's eligible workforce had participated in the sabbatical program.

On a somewhat smaller scale, Eastman Kodak provides up to one-week sabbaticals each year for community service. McDonald's provides paid eight-week sabbaticals every ten years for full-time employees. In 1982, Pace Harrington, the vice president of personnel, took his sabbatical to spend time with his family. As he explained, "Our employees work hard. We're a global company and we travel a lot. Our employees welcome the time simply to reflect on what they've accomplished and to prioritize their futures."

Sources: Adapted from C. Kleiman, "More Firms Add up Pluses of Sabbaticals," *Chicago Tribune,* December 6, 1992; and L. Lucian, "The Good News About Employee Benefits," *Money,* June 1992, 91–94.

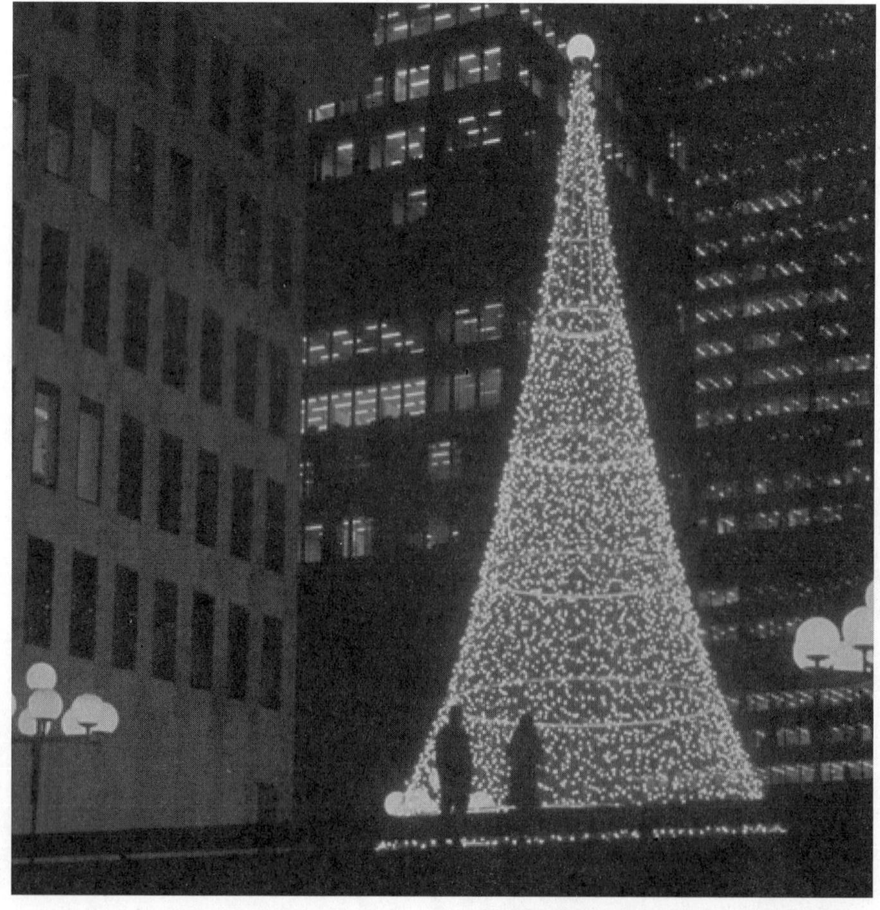

Image 72059, Series 72000 @ Corel Corporation

Christmas Day is just one of six holidays now recognized and paid for by nearly all companies in the United States. Holidays such as Christmas, New Year's, Memorial Day, Independence Day, Labor Day, and Thanksgiving are a time for family and friends to celebrate and spend time together.

this belief, and over the century, more and more days are being treated as paid holidays. Recent surveys show that companies provide an average of about nine paid holidays per year. Some companies give even more; Johnson & Johnson gives eleven paid holidays. The following six holidays are recognized and paid for by nearly all companies in the United States: New Year's Day, Memorial Day, Independence Day, Labor Day, Thanksgiving Day, and Christmas Day. Other days that may be included are Martin Luther King's Birthday, Presidents' Day, and Columbus Day.[45]

Personal Absences

Companies realize that on certain occasions, employees are unable to come to work for reasons beyond their control and therefore deserve to be paid despite their not being at work. Such reasons may include jury duty, family death, military duty, divorce hearings, and doctor visits. Rather than the employee simply not coming to work, companies offer personal absences as a way to have some advance notice (in the case of doctor visits, divorce hearings, or other appointments that can be anticipated) and still compensate employees. Many companies today provide two to five personal days per year and let the employee decide when such a day is needed. One should be careful not to use such days frivolously, though, as you may not have any remaining when you really need them.[47]

Personal absences Allowed on certain days in which the employee is unable to come to work for reasons beyond his or her control, such as jury duty, family death, military duty, divorce hearings, and doctor visits.

Most companies offer a fairly standard policy of paid time off from work. Some companies, such as the ones mentioned earlier, offer excellent vacation time. While it is useful to examine a potential employer's paid time off, you will probably find the policies to be quite similar from company to company.

Conclusion

Returning to the three companies discussed in the opening case, given what has been discussed here, which company do you think has the better benefits program? Do you think your answer will differ depending on your particular circumstances and needs? Employee benefits is a complicated area, but one that is critical for both companies and employees. Whether you are beginning your first full-time job, changing jobs, becoming unemployed, or changing your family status (such as having a child), it is imperative that you learn just what the implications are regarding your benefits.

Applying Core Concepts

1. Did you ever have a job in which the company did not provide Social Security/Medicare payments? Why didn't the company pay? Ask friends or relatives if they ever filed a workers' compensation claim. Ask them to tell you what the process was like.
2. What type of health insurance plan are you covered by now? How satisfied are you with the plan? If you currently have no such plan, discuss why not. What would you do if you had a serious medical problem needing professional help?
3. What type of pension plan do you think is best? What type of plan do you have now or do you expect to have soon?
4. Of the different additional benefits companies provide, which would you consider most valuable to you? Why?
5. Ask a few friends or relatives about the paid time off they have in their jobs. How do their plans compare to the ones you read about in this chapter?

Key Terms

- Social Security/Medicare
- Disability income
- Survivor benefits
- Unemployment compensation
- Workers' compensation
- Defined benefit pension program
- Defined contribution pension program
- Guaranteed investment contract
- 401(k)
- Deferred profit sharing
- Employee stock ownershp plan (ESOP)
- Employee Retirement Income Security Act (ERISA)
- Summary plan description
- Fiduciary
- Funding rules
- Vesting
- Pension Benefit Guaranty Corporation
- Copayment
- Maximum out-of-pocket annual payment
- Fee-for-service program
- Health maintenance organization (HMO)
- Primary-care physician
- Preferred-provider organization (PPO)
- Point-of-service (POS) plan
- In-network
- Out-of-network
- Preexisting condition
- COBRA
- Utilization review
- Flexible spending account (FSA)
- Family and Medical Leave Act (FMLA)
- Short-term disability (STD) insurance
- Long-term disability (LTD) insurance
- Long-term care insurance
- Tuition reimbursement
- Cafeteria benefits
- Add-on plan
- Modular plan
- Paid time off
- Personal absence

Chapter 10: Experiential Exercise

Choosing a Benefit Program at Emmett Press

"I want you to tell me the truth," said Mr. V. Emunah, owner and president of Emmett Press. Mr. Emunah, or just V, as he prefers to be called by his employees, recently called this meeting of his seventy-five employees to discuss his latest ideas. Emmett Press publishes mystery and science fiction books. Many of the employees have been with the company for more than twenty years, though in the last few years there has been much more turnover among the newer hires. Because the company is a specialty business and barely makes a profit, salaries are fairly low and the benefits program has been confined to those required by law. Today, however, as he has done for the last 50 years, Mr. Emunah is seeking a consensus as to what he considers an important human resources decision. Specifically, he has decided that he should implement some kind of benefit program.

After talking with his insurance company last month and reading an article in *Press Magazine* (the publishing company's professional magazine), Mr. Emunah decided that offering employees a benefit program would not only be good for tax purposes, but would provide employees with a valuable supplement to their compensation. However, he is not sure what type of benefit to offer. The three options are as follows:

1. A defined contribution pension plan;
2. A defined benefit pension plan;
3. A medical insurance program.

Mr. Emunah plans to spend approximately $2,000 per employee per year, regardless of which plan is chosen. As always, Mr. Emunah has called this meeting to discuss the options and have employees vote on which *one* they prefer. The procedure that is always followed is to have an initial vote by the employees, followed by each employee giving an explanation for his or her vote. After each employee expresses his or her current opinion, a final vote is taken and the majority wins.

Accordingly, you need to do the following:

1. Which of the three options described above would you vote for? Why?
2. Be prepared to convince others in your class as to why they should vote the way *you* did.

Chapter 10 References

1. R. McCaffery, *Employee Benefit Programs: A Total Compensation Perspective* (Boston: PWS-Kent, 1992).
2. Ibid.
3. U.S. Department of Health and Human Services, *Your Social Security Taxes . . . What They're Paying for, Where the Money Goes.* Social Security Administration, Publication No. 05-10010, January, 1995).
4. McCaffery, *Employee Benefit Programs.*
5. J. Hood and B. Hardy, *Workers' Compensation and Employee Protection Laws* (St. Paul, MN: West, 1984).
6. Ibid.
7. D. Kirkpatrick,. "Will You Be Able to Retire?" *Fortune,* July, 1989, 56–66.
8. U.S. Department of Labor, Bureau of Labor Statistics, *Employee Benefits in Medium and Large Firms* (Washington: U.S. Government Printing Office, 1990).
9. E.T. Allen, J. Melone, and J. VanDerhei, *Pension Planning.* (Homewood, IL: Irwin, 1988).
10. U.S. Department of Labor, *Employee Benefits.*
11. Congressional Research Service, *Retirement Income for an Aging Population* (Washington: Library of Congress, 1987).
12. U.S. Department of Labor, *Employee Benefits.*
13. T. Pare, "Is Your 401(k) Plan Good Enough?" *Fortune,* December 28, 1992, 78–83.
14. "Take Care of Your 401(k), and It'll Take Care of You," *St. Louis Post-Dispatch,* January 19, 1993, 12C.
15. J. Fierman, "How Secure Is Your Nest Egg?" *Fortune,* August 12, 1991, 50–54.
16. Pare, "Is Your 401(k) Plan Good Enough?"
17. U.S. Department of Labor, *Employee Benefits.*
18. W. Lambert, "ESOP at Thomson McKinnon Is Focus of Employees' Suit," *The Wall Street Journal,* September, 25, 1989, A7C.
19. McCaffery, *Employee Benefit Programs.*
20. C. Willis, "How to Protect Your Retirement Money," *Money,* November 1991, 90–95.
21. Allen et al., *Pension planning.*
22. McCaffery, *Employee Benefit Programs.*
23. Ibid.
24. Ibid.
25. E. Faltermayer, "Let's Really Cure the Health System," *Fortune,* March 23, 1992, 46–58.
26. L. Luciano, "Getting the Most from Your Company Benefits," *Money,* May 1991, 109–20.
27. "Wasted Health Care Dollars," *Consumer Reports,* July 1992, 435–448.
28. "Are HMOs the Answer?" *Consumer Reports,* August 1992, 519–27.
29. Ibid.
30. Ibid.
31. Ibid.
32. McCaffery, *Employee Benefit Programs.*
33. "Are HMOs the Answer?"
34. U.S. Department of Labor, *Employee Benefits.*
35. M. Rothstein, C. Craver, E. Schroeder, E. Shoben, and L. VanderVelde, *Employment Law* (St. Paul, MN: West, 1994).
36. McCaffery, *Employee Benefit Programs.*
37. M. Brown, "Disability Insurance Seldom Receives High Priority," *St. Louis Post-Dispatch,* June 15, 1992, 23BP.
38. McCaffery, *Employee Benefit Programs.*

39. Ibid.
40. L. Luciano, "The Good News About Employee Benefits," *Money,* June 1992, 90–112.
41. Woodford, K. "Child Care Soars at America West," *Personnel Journal,* December 1990, 46–47.
42. McCaffery, *Employee Benefit Programs.*
43. M. Markowich, "Flex Still Works," *Personnel Journal,* December, 1990, 62.
44. McCaffery, *Employee Benefit Programs.*
45. Luciano "The Good News."
46. McCaffery, *Employee Benefit Programs.*
47. Ibid.

part 4

Improving the Workplace

Chapter 11

Employee Training and Development

Chapter 12

Work Redesign for Productivity and Quality Improvement

Chapter 13

Safety and Health in the Workplace

chapter 11 Employee Training and Development

Core Concepts

After reading this chapter, you should be capable of

1. Identifying current trends in employee training and development.
2. Conducting a training needs analysis.
3. Describing different training techniques.
4. Discussing the advantages and disadvantages of different training techniques.
5. Applying basic learning principles in developing a training program.
6. Explaining how to examine training program success.

Opening Case

Sally Andrews has been working part-time for her present company, In-Sync Corporation, for one year now, and she will soon be moving to full-time status. As part of this arrangement, Sally will continue to work in her present position (as a customer service representative) for about 12 months. After this period of time, she will become the area supervisor. Yesterday, Sheila, the customer service area manager, called Sally back into her office to discuss the matter further.

"As you know," Sheila began, "In-Sync is going through a number of changes. One of the biggest adjustments involves our management style—we must become more participative, open, and, above all, capable of handling a racially and ethnically diverse workforce. Our supervisors can therefore no longer simply be promoted through the ranks. They must receive appropriate training and development so that they can deal with the many challenges and changes in this business."

Next, she talked about Sally's advancement into the supervisory position and the need for her to be properly prepared. Sheila concluded by saying, "It's imperative, then, that you receive training in certain key areas, such as conflict resolution, managing the diverse workforce, delegating work, and so forth. I want you to do two things in this regard. First, find out what key areas you need to know in order to become a highly effective supervisor. Second, once you have identified those areas, determine what kind of training program you would like to use."

After Sally discussed this assignment further with her manager, Sheila described a number of training methods Sally might use. "In the past, we have hired faculty from the college you are attending to conduct training for us. Or, you might use videotapes, which we could purchase from a training company. Yet another idea, which might work well and save money, would be for you to receive one-on-one instruction from Jean and Chris. Both of them have been supervisors for many years, and have an excellent reputation with the managers. They probably could provide some fine on-the-job training. Why don't you come back with a written proposal, indicating what training techniques you would like to use and how much they would cost."

That night, when Sally returned home from work, she began thinking about her area manager's assignment. How would she determine what supervisory skills she currently had and what supervisory skills she might need in the future? Moreover, once she determined the answer to this question, what training methods would work best for her? The more she thought about this second question, the more confusing it became. After all, there must be many colleges and universities that offer training programs and, based on the catalogs Sheila showed her, there are many videotapes to choose from. The idea of learning on the job from Chris and Jean sounds like a very inexpensive approach. Chris and Jean will be able to tell Sally what works at In-Sync and what does not work. On the other hand, both of them always seem to be busy. From what Sally has heard from other part-timers who work in their sections, Chris and Jean do not have the best reputation among their subordinates either. Despite these concerns, it seems as though on-the-job training might be the most practical, cost-effective way to learn needed supervisory skills.

This chapter explores more about training and development in the workplace. As you will see, training and development programs are quite important both to you as an employee and to organizations. You will learn how organizations determine training needs, the advantages and disadvantages of different training techniques, and how to increase the application of training to actual job situations. Finally, you will learn how to evaluate the success of a training program. First, however, we will discuss what training is, why it is important, and what organizations are doing in this regard.

What Is Training and Development and Why Is It Important?

Training and development
Planned efforts by organizations to increase employees' knowledge, skills, and abilities (KSAs).

Training and development may be defined as planned efforts by organizations to increase employees' knowledge, skills, and abilities (KSAs).[1] So why is training and development so important for both employees and organizations? There are several reasons:

1. Changes in the Workplace and the Workforce. As you have read in other chapters, both the workplace and the workforce are going through many changes. In terms of the workplace, the increased use of high technology (for example, computer-aided design, robotics, and electronic mail), the continuing shift from a manufacturing to a service economy, and the increasingly global business world necessitates ongoing employee training and development programs. In terms of the changing workforce, the increasing number of immigrants with limited educational background as well as continuing problems in the primary and secondary educational systems are forcing organizations to provide training and development programs, often for the purpose of improving basic writing and reading skills.[2]

2. Maintaining Competitiveness and Improving Productivity. Training and development is essential for maintaining global competitiveness. Japan and Germany, two of our toughest business competitors, have outstanding training and development programs, which helps them maintain high levels of productivity and flexibility.[3] From an organizational perspective, training and development programs can have a large payoff in terms of productivity improvement. Consider, for example, Will-Burt Company, a small manufacturing plant in Ohio. Several years ago, Will-Burt was on the brink of bankruptcy. Because the company was losing $700,000 annually due to defective products, the owner decided that only a major improvement in quality would enable the company to survive. After several other approaches failed, the owner turned to a training program, costing the company almost $200,000 the first year. What was the end result? After one year of training, the company's expenditures for defective products declined more than $500,000 annually.[4] Many other companies have experienced similar productivity gains from their training and development programs.
3. Regulatory Requirements. Various laws require companies to provide training. For example, the Occupational Safety and Health Act of 1970 (see Chapter 13) requires companies to provide training for a variety of purposes.[5] Certain industries, such as the nuclear waste industry, also require employees to receive training for a variety of purposes, especially safety-related issues.

In short, training and development is important for several reasons. Next, you will read about some current trends and practices in training and development.

Current Trends and Practices in Training and Development

Companies spend enormous amounts of money on employee training and development. Although estimates vary, $45 billion (or $400 per employee) is proba-

Box 11.1 Training and Development Programs: Their Impact on Your Pay

Even though company training and development programs may help your company, you might be wondering whether such programs are worth it for you as an employee. First, let's talk about how many employees participate in training programs. A survey conducted in 1991 found that 41 percent of all employees participated in some type of training program since starting work in their current job. More than 60 percent of college graduates reported participating in at least one training program. This reflects a significant increase from 1983, when only 35 percent of all workers reported some type of job-related training. Many employees, then, participate in training programs to improve their work skills.

Now, does participation in training affect your salary? This same survey examined average salaries earned by different groups of employees in 1991. To simplify matters, we will consider only college graduates. When college graduates whose job required special training were considered, those who took additional training to improve their skills made, on average, $2,000 more annually than those employees who did *not* take additional training. The gap was even larger for those college graduates whose job did not require special training. For those employees who did *not* take training to improve their skills, the average annual salary was approximately $31,000. For those employees who *did* take training to improve their skills, the average annual salary was about $35,000—a difference of $4,000. Clearly, company-sponsored training programs have a financial payoff for you.

Source: Adapted from A. Eck, "Job-related Education and Training: Their Impact on Earnings," *Monthly Labor Review,* October 1993, 21–38.

bly a reasonable estimate of the amount spent by U.S. companies on formal training annually! When informal, on-the-job training is included, the cost may be as much as $200 billion annually.[6] Although this might seem like a great deal of money, some experts have argued that companies do not spend enough money on employee training. First, the vast amount of this money is spent by a small number of very large companies, such as GTE, Xerox, Federal Express, and Boeing. Second, very few companies spend more than 2 percent of their payroll on training. Thus, the majority of companies, particularly small businesses, spend relatively little money on training and development.[7]

Table 11.1 reports the average number of hours spent training different groups of employees in 1993. As you can see, about three-fourths of companies  provide training to executives and middle managers, while about half provide training to customer-service employees. Only about one-third of companies provide training to production workers. Of the companies that provide training, most employees receive the equivalent of about four days of training per year.

Table 11.2 provides a summary of the most common areas of training provided by companies. The most popular categories, besides those to improve management and supervisory skills, include training to enhance computer skills, communication skills, and technical skills. Customer relations skills and clerical/secretarial skills training is also offered by many companies.

In terms of specific training topics, 70 percent or more of companies offer training in performance appraisal (75 percent), leadership (73 percent), interpersonal skills (71 percent), team building (71 percent), personal computer applications (71 percent), and the hiring process (70 percent). Many companies offer training in additional areas such as time management (67 percent), sexual

Table 11.1 **Types of Workers Receiving Training and Average Number of Hours**

Job Group	**Percentage of Companies Providing Training**	**Average Number of Hours Annually per Employee**
Professionals	70	36
First-line supervisors	66	36
Salespeople	41	33
Middle managers	76	33
Executives	74	32
Production workers	37	32
Customer-service representatives	52	29

Source: Adapted from P. Froiland, "Who's Getting Trained?" (p. 56), *Training,* October 1993.

Table 11.2 **Areas of Training Provided by Companies**

Type	**Percentage of Companies Providing**
Management skills	91
Basic computer skills	90
Communication skills	87
Supervisory skills	86
Technical skills	82
New methods/procedures	80
Executive development	77
Customer relations	76
Personal growth	73
Clerical/secretarial skills	73
Employee/labor relations	67
Sales skills	56
Remedial/basic education	48

Source: Adapted from P. Froiland, "Who's Getting Trained?" (p. 60), *Training,* October 1993.

harassment awareness (64 percent), stress management (60 percent), diversity (47 percent), and ethics (41 percent). Finally, about 20 percent of companies offer remedial education courses in the English language, basic mathematics, reading, and writing. This is particularly true for manufacturing firms (35 percent); remedial education programs are offered by far fewer health services (4 percent) and transportation/communications/utilities firms (6 percent).[8]

In addition to company-sponsored training programs, there are many government and union-sponsored training programs. Most states provide some kind of training program for workers. These programs primarily serve small manufacturing businesses. Most recently, some states have offered training grants, enabling each business to determine how to best provide the needed training. Many states contract with community colleges or vocational schools to provide training.

When an IBM plant in Colorado, for example, switched from manufacturing to software development, the Front Range Community College retrained more than half of the 2,000 employees.[9]

Unions are another source of training programs, generally through an apprenticeship system. Apprenticeship programs are particularly popular in mechanical and electrical trades, as well as other skilled crafts. Nevertheless, industry cost-cutting measures in the 1970s and 1980s reduced the number of apprenticeships in the United States, and only a small fraction of U.S. employees have worked as apprentices. In recent years, some unions have forged joint apprenticeship programs with management, such as the UAW-Chrysler National Training Center. In 1989, the five largest joint union-management training programs provided training for more than 700,000 workers.[10] If you want to learn more about apprenticeship programs, contact the U.S. Department of Labor at (202) 523-6666.

Now that you have a basic idea of the kinds of training and development activities that are being provided in the workplace, we will turn to the steps used to develop a training program. There are three basic steps in this process:

Box 11.2 **Training and Education Programs: An International Perspective**

How do you think the United States compares to other major industrial nations in terms of training and educating the workforce? Not surprisingly, the answer depends on which countries you choose for comparison. In general, though, U.S. primary and secondary education varies greatly in quality, as does vocational training. Company-sponsored training focuses on managers and technicians (though this is changing to some degree in recent years); the quality tends to vary widely.

The training and educational systems of our two major competitors, Germany and Japan, are far more consistent in quality and availability. Germany's major strength is that primary and secondary schooling is closely integrated with subsequent training programs, and in general educational programs have high quality. Vocational training is also very good; but what Germany is best known for is its outstanding apprenticeship program. In fact, more

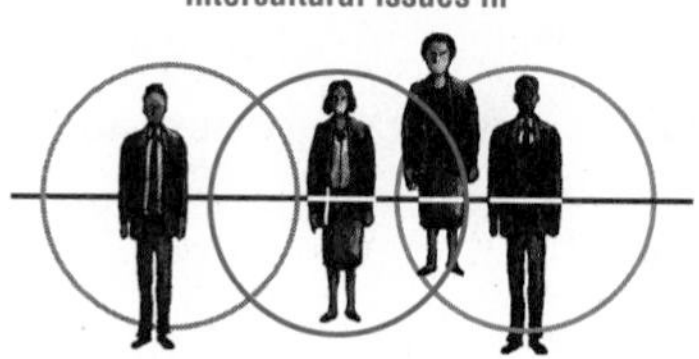

than half of the German workforce has completed an apprenticeship program. Many workers also participate in postapprenticeship programs, and businesses help sponsor a variety of high-quality training programs.

Although Japan's approach to education is somewhat different than Germany's, the result is much the same. Japan, as is widely known, boasts one of the best primary and secondary educational systems in the world. Once employed, Japanese workers receive extensive, ongoing, company-sponsored training. As one example, workers in Japanese automobile plants average almost 90 hours of training annually, while workers in the U.S. automobile plants average about 30 hours of training annually.

Our northern neighbor, Canada, has a training and education system quite similar to ours. Primary and secondary education varies greatly in terms of quality, as does the vocational education system. Companies provide relatively little training, by some estimates, about half as much as in the United States.

Korea's training and educational system has made great strides in the last few years. A strong primary and secondary school system has increased the quality of workers' basic skills, and vocational education has become remarkably strong in Korea. Nevertheless, company-sponsored training programs are scarce, and their quality is generally poor.

All in all, then, U.S. training and education programs could be improved. According to experts, the overall effectiveness of such efforts will greatly affect a country's ability to compete globally.

Source: Adapted from U.S. Congress, Office of Technology Assessment, *Worker Training: Competing in the New International Economy* (Washington: U.S. Government Printing Office, 1990), OTA-ITE-457.

1. Analyzing the organization's training needs and the objectives of the training program.
2. Deciding which training techniques and principles to use.
3. Evaluating the training program.

We turn now to the process of analyzing the organization's training needs and setting objectives for the training program. As you will see, training needs are determined by doing an analysis of the organization, the tasks/KSAs, and the employees.

Training Needs Analysis

Training needs analysis An assessment by the organization of what the training needs of its employees are.

A training needs analysis is used to answer the following three questions.[11]

1. What knowledge/skills/abilities (KSAs) do employees need?
2. Are some employees deficient in these KSAs?
3. Will training solve the deficiencies?[12]

A training needs analysis is a three-step process:

1. An organizational analysis.
2. A task/KSA analysis.
3. A person analysis.

We turn now to a more detailed discussion of each of these steps.

Step 1: Organizational Analysis

Organizational analysis The purpose of this analysis is to examine the organization, unit, or department and determine its basic business strategy, objectives, and goals.

The purpose of Step 1, the organizational analysis, is to examine the organization, unit, or department and determine its basic business strategy, objectives, and goals.[13] In today's constantly changing business environment, the organizational analysis may focus on the company's new business goals and challenges, and the implications for jobs.[14] One company conducting an organizational analysis, for example, found that recent changes in its business environment led to

1. Large contracts not being replaced.
2. Increased competition for old and new business.
3. More demands for customized products.
4. Greater emphasis on efficiency and cost reduction.
5. Increased emphasis on cooperation among companies.

Some of the key points to address in conducting an organization analysis, then, are the following:[15]

1. What are the organization's business strategies and objectives? Have these changed from the past?
2. How does the organization interface with the external environment? Is the external environment stable or turbulent?
3. Has the organization's culture, climate, and norms changed?
4. What are the implications of these answers for jobs in the organization?

As an example of an organizational analysis, consider Honeywell's plant in Ontario, Canada. In 1987, top executives of Honeywell Company decided to concentrate on a much smaller number of select products. As part of that strategy, each plant was to manufacture fewer products, and to achieve high quality and cost efficiencies for those products they did produce. Toward that end, Honeywell's Ontario plant embarked on a number of changes, including the adoption of a total quality management (TQM) program and the implementation of self-managed teams (see Chapter 12 for a description of TQM and self-managed teams). An analysis of these changes, and their implications for jobs, would constitute an organizational analysis.[16]

So far, we have described the organizational analysis from a company's perspective. But what about from your perspective as an employee? If you recall from Chapter 3, it was recommended that you, as an employee, think of yourself as a business. Put in this light, you should also do an organizational analysis, where the organization is you. What are your current business strategy and goals? How have these changed from the past? What is the nature of your external environment? For example, do you have a new supervisor? Do you have a new set of external customers? You should consider both short- and long-term perspectives. Also, do not focus solely on your present employer. Find out what other companies are seeking from their employees as well. Your present employer, for example, may not make much use of computer technology. But other employers may use computers to a far greater extent. It is important, then, to be familiar with trends in your industry, not just conditions in your current company.

In sum, an organizational analysis considers the broad perspective. Based on the findings from the organizational analysis, you are ready to go to the next step: a task/KSA analysis.

Step 2: Task/KSA Analysis

The second step, the task/KSA analysis, involves obtaining information from the organizational analysis to evaluate the tasks performed in each job and then determine the knowledge, skills, and abilities (KSAs) needed to perform these tasks effectively. Recall the previous example in which a company had found a number of changes in its business environment, including large contracts not being replaced, increased competition for old and new business, and increased demands for customized products. Based on those changes, the company determined that various work tasks had been modified or added, which meant greater need for KSAs such as effective communication, time management skills, and the ability to delegate work.

Task/KSA analysis Involves obtaining information from the organizational analysis to examine the tasks performed in each job and then determine the knowledge, skills, and abilities needed to perform these tasks effectively.

As a second example, recall the Honeywell Canada plant, which introduced TQM and a self-managed team approach. These changes, in turn, led to the identification of four new important job functions: achieving low cost, high product/process quality, on-time delivery, and team membership. These new job functions meant that certain additional tasks were added to each job, such as preparing an annual budget and developing and implementing cost-cutting ideas. Employees would now need various new KSAs, including basic reading skills and knowledge of accounting and financial principles, in order to succeed in their jobs.

In many ways, the task/KSA analysis is similar to doing a job analysis (see Chapter 5). Like a job analysis, one can use different procedures to conduct a task/KSA analysis. The following steps, however, are generally recommended for a task/KSA analysis.[17]

1. Develop a List of Task Statements. Using observation, interviews with workers and supervisors, and other techniques, develop a list of tasks performed in the relevant job(s).
2. Develop a List of Task Clusters. Once Step 1 is completed, categorize the tasks into a smaller number of task clusters. For example, a supervisory job might include four or five task statements pertaining to interacting with other departments. Interacting with other departments, then, might constitute one task cluster. Developing task clusters is particularly useful for organizing large numbers of tasks.
3. Develop a List of KSAs. Although there are several ways to obtain a list of KSAs, one of the more effective ways is to conduct focus panels with groups of supervisors and knowledgeable workers. The panels should be shown the task clusters, along with the task statements, and asked to generate KSAs that are needed to perform each task cluster successfully.
4. Assess the Importance of Tasks/KSAs. Now that both the relevant tasks and KSAs have been determined, it is necessary to focus on the *important* tasks and KSAs. This step establishes training priorities. Typically, a structured format is used. Both the task clusters and the KSAs are rated by supervisors and knowledgeable incumbents. Table 11.3 provides an example of a simple five-point rating scale that might be used for rating task importance.[18]

As before, we have emphasized the organization's perspective in conducting a task/KSA analysis. It is important, however, to apply this process to your own situation as an employee. That is, given the organizational analysis you conducted for your own career, what tasks are important for success? What new tasks do you anticipate will become important? For example, if increased computerization is occurring, you must consider how this will affect the tasks you perform now and in the future. What KSAs will you need to perform the new or revised tasks successfully? All of these considerations should be carefully examined.

In sum, the task/KSA analysis is a critical step in determining the likely content of a training program. Not only is this important from an organization's

Table 11.3 **A Rating Scale for Task Importance**

1 = Not important (improper task performance has no negative consequences)

2 = Slightly important (improper task performance can create some minor problems or negative consequences)

3 = Important (improper task performance can create significant problems or negative consequences)

4 = Very important (improper task performance can create serious consequences or problems, including extensive damage to equipment, serious injury to humans, or injury to the reputation of the company)

5 = Critical (improper task performance will create very serious consequence or problems, including major loss of equipment, possible death to humans, and major injury to the reputation of the company)

Source: Adapted from I. Goldstein, "Training in Work Organizations," in *Handbook of Industrial and Organizational Psychology,* (vol. 2), ed M. Dunnette and L. Hough (Palo Alto, CA: Consulting Psychologists Press, 1991), p. 535.

Box 11.3 Benefiting from Business Seminars: Tips for Participants

Many companies give their employees the opportunity to attend business seminars. Here are some suggestions for you, as a participant:

1. Plan Ahead. Learn what attire is appropriate for the seminar; you don't want to be too casual or too formal. Find out who will be presenting and what topics will be presented, and plan your schedule ahead of time. Write down specific questions that you have. Make sure that you assess ahead of time what you would like to learn from the seminar *and* what your supervisor and company would like you to learn from the seminar.

2. Network at the Seminar. A major reason, aside from the learning experience, for attending business seminars is to network and make contacts with other people in your field. You should probably bring business cards. If you get business cards from others, jot notes on the back of each one (for example, you might note that you promised to send some materials to the person).

3. Meet People before Each Session. If you arrive at a session before it begins, you may break the ice by asking people why they attended the seminar. If they are at the same session as you are, chances are they have the same interests as you do. Also, if possible, introduce yourself to the presenter. This may give you a chance to ask a question or two that might then be addressed in the session.

4. Bring Information Back to the Company. The best way to justify your attendance at the session is to return with information that you then share with your organization. Be sure to offer to make either an oral presentation or a written report about what you learned. This way, the company will be willing to send you again.

Source: Adapted from P. Lee, "Getting the Most Out of Conferences," *Training and Development,* May 1993, 10, 12.

perspective, but it is important from your perspective as an employee. We now discuss the third step in a training needs analysis, generally referred to as a person analysis.

Step 3: Person Analysis

The final step of a training needs analysis, the person analysis, addresses the question of whether certain employees are deficient in the important tasks/KSAs, and whether training would treat the deficiencies. There are several ways to determine employee deficiencies. One of the most popular ways is to examine measures of job performance. For example, any employee who received a less than satisfactory rating on any job dimension might be considered deficient in that area. This approach has several potential weaknesses. First, as discussed in Chapter 7, supervisor ratings are often subject to a variety of errors, including leniency. Some workers who are actually performing below average may be rated acceptable. Second, there may be KSAs that will be needed in the future but are not currently being used; there will be little or no information with regard to those KSAs.[19] Third, the intended purpose of the performance ratings may affect how they are made; ratings made for salary raise purposes may differ from ratings made for a training needs analysis.[20] One possible way to overcome some of these problems is to have employees complete self-ratings to establish their need for training on each of the KSAs.[21] However, employees may not be aware of or willing to admit a possible shortcoming.[22] Research indeed shows that there is little relationship between an employee's self-rating of training needs and the supervisor's rating of the employee's training needs.[23]

Person analysis Addresses the question of whether there are certain employees who are deficient in the important tasks/KSAs and whether training would address these deficiencies.

An alternative approach is to use proficiency tests or simulations. For example, rather than having the supervisor rate an employee's typing skills, the employee could be given a typing test. That way, an employee's KSAs can be measured in a far more objective fashion. Despite the potential advantages, this approach has several basic problems. First, proficiency tests may not completely reflect job performance. Second, for many areas (such as time management skills), proficiency tests may not exist. Third, the costs associated with proficiency testing may be quite high.[24]

Ultimately, there is no simple answer regarding the best way to conduct a person analysis. Ideally, you would use several approaches, perhaps a combination of self-ratings, supervisor ratings, and, where possible, proficiency tests to determine who needs training. You should also be aware that trainees who feel that the needs assessment was properly conducted will have a better reaction to the actual training program and will be more motivated to learn.[25]

Even though there may be employees who are deficient in certain KSAs, training is not necessarily the correct solution. For example, one company decided that a one-time incentive program would be far more effective in improving the employees' knowledge than would a training program. Employees ended up learning the material far better than they would have had the company sponsored a formal training program. It is important to realize that training programs are not a guaranteed cure-all for performance problems.[26] The solution to performance deficiencies may lie in improving the reward systems, selecting better employees, or purchasing better equipment. Figure 11.1 provides some suggestions as to when

Figure 11.1 Troubleshooting Performance Problems

A Guide for Troubleshooting Performance Problems

A. Is there a problem? ______

What do you observe that indicates there is a problem?

1. How long has this been a problem?
2. How general a problem is it?
   - Where does it occur
   - When does it occur?
   - How frequently does it occur?
   - Does it ever not occur in some locations or at some times?
3. How will you know when the problem is solved?
   - How will things look different?
   - What numbers will increase or decrease?

B. What is the problem? ______

1. Who is the performer in question?
2. What is the desired action?
3. What specifically does he perform incorrectly?
4. Does he ever perform correctly?
   If yes: When?
   If no: Has anyone ever performed correctly?
   When?
   Where?

C. Is the problem important? ______

What impact does the incorrect performance have on:

1. The product or service?
   Quality Cost Quantity
2. The company?
   Procedures Image
3. The performer or his department?
   Safety Ease of work
4. Other workers or departments?
   Safety Ease of work

Source: G. Rummler, "Human Performance Problems and Their Solutions," *Human Resource Management,* Winter 1972, 2–10.

Figure 11.1 **Troubleshooting Performance Problems *(continued)***

D. Where has the performance system broken down? ________________

Questions		**Action**
Does the performer:		
1. Know he is supposed to take the desired action? ■ How do you know?	If no:	Instruct him.
2. Know what the desired action is? ■ How do you know?	If no:	Instruct him.
3. Know when to take the desired action? ■ How do you know?	If no:	Instruct him.
4. Know how to take the desired action? ■ How do you know?	If no:	Instruct him.
5. Know the standard or level of performance expected? ■ Are there standards? ■ Does everybody agree on them? ■ Is anyone meeting them now?	If no standards: If standards:	Set them. Instruct in them.
6. Know whether he is taking the desired action or not? ■ How can he tell whether he is acting correctly?	If no:	Redesign job. Instruct in observing. Provide feedback.
7. Have adequate resources (e.g., time, equipment) to take the desired action?	If no:	Provide resources.
8. Receive negative consequences for taking the desired action? ■ Consider such sources of consequences as superiors, peers, subordinates, and the system.	If yes:	Remove negative consequences.
9. Receive no consequences for taking the desired action?	If yes:	Provide positive consequences.
10. Receive immediate, positive consequences for doing something other than the desired action? ■ Do "good" things happen to him if he doesn't do it?	If yes:	Remove positive consequences
Questions		**Action**
11. Receive no information on the consequences of taking the desired action? ■ Does he know it makes a difference to do it right?	If no:	Provide feedback.
12. Receive wrong information on the consequences of his actions? ■ Does information lead him to conclude he's doing okay when he is not?	If yes:	Correct feedback.
13. Receive information on consequences that is not sufficient for him to correct his performance (i.e., not clear, not specific, too late, too infrequent)? ■ Does he receive enough information to know how to correct?	If yes:	Provide better feedback.
14. Know how to interpret information in order to correct his performance? ■ Given good information, can he figure out how to change?		Instruct on how to interpret data.

a training program might be used to ameliorate a performance deficiency or when other supervisory responses are needed. It is critical that you determine the objectives of the training program before you proceed with the design of the program. The objectives that you specify for the training program may be less ambitious than you initially intended. Remember that training programs cannot address every problem.

In terms of your own person analysis, it is critical that you try to get as much feedback from other sources as possible. As described elsewhere in this book, mentors, peers, and your supervisor may be of help by giving you feedback. While it is often difficult to be self-critical, your ability to conduct an accurate self-analysis of your deficiencies may be one of the most important factors for a successful career. So take a hard look at yourself and think about where improvements or new KSAs are needed.

Recall that in the opening case of this chapter, Sally was asked to determine what knowledge, skills, and abilities she would need training for. A training needs analysis would be quite useful in this regard. For example, Sally could conduct interviews with In-Sync's top executives and managers to get their input about the business goals, strategies, and related changes, and how these would affect the job of an area supervisor. She could supplement this information by searching a library for newspaper and magazine articles on the impact of these changes on the supervisory job. Based on this information, Sally could then conduct a task/KSA analysis. Again, this information might be best obtained from top executives, human resource staff, and the area managers who have some ideas as to how the supervisor job will change. Finally, in terms of person analysis, the employee might be best off assuming that training in all key KSAs would be helpful. An additional advantage of going through a formal procedure of this nature is that the employee could demonstrate he or she took the assignment seriously and conducted a thor-

Box 11.4 Training and Development: The Motorola Approach

Tales from the Trenches

Some of the largest companies in the United States provide the best training programs around. Consider Motorola, which offers its employees a minimum of 40 hours of training annually. In fact, Motorola spends roughly 4 percent of its payroll on training, one of the highest percentages in the country. Motorola also created a training center, which it calls "Motorola University." Motorola University, headquartered in a suburb of Chicago, has 14 branches around the world and a budget of more than $100 million. Despite its large investment in training and development, Motorola intends to increase the amount of money devoted to this area.

First, the company plans to greatly increase the number of hours employees spend in training annually—perhaps to as much as 160 hours per year. Second, Motorola has worked actively with primary and secondary school districts to revise curricula, spending more than $1.5 million in this endeavor last year. For example, Motorola has helped redesign grading systems (for example, replacing grades with a three-level system—"change needed," "achieves standard," and "exceeds standard"). Another change championed by Motorola is to replace reading, writing, and arithmetic as separate subjects with more integrated approaches. For instance, rather than teaching arithmetic and physics as separate courses, high school teachers might address both topics under a course entitled "Newton's Laws." A third modification advocated by Motorola is more emphasis on cooperation in course work. For example, as part of the physical education course, students work on building human pyramids. To date, 32 school districts in Illinois have joined in partnership with Motorola to change their curriculum.

Despite Motorola's commitment to and financial investment in training and development, it is not without its critics. One criticism is that Motorola has done surprisingly little to scientifically document the cost-effectiveness of its training. A second criticism is that the formal, rigorous approach taken to training may hamper creativity. Third, some feel Motorola spends too much time on technical details and far too little time on current human issues, such as diversity training. Whether training at Motorola is modified to address these issues remains to be seen.

Source: Adapted from K. Kelly, "Motorola: Training for the Millennium," *Business Week,* March 28, 1994, 158–63.

ough investigation. In fact, it is possible that the organization would adopt the program for training other supervisors as well.

Now that you have learned how to go about determining which employees need training in what areas, we will turn to the techniques and principles used to provide the needed training. As you will see, many different training techniques and principles are available. We begin with a discussion of different training techniques, followed by a description of some basic principles of training.

Training Techniques and Principles

Figure 11.2 indicates the popularity of different training techniques used in industry. As you can see, videotapes, lectures, one-on-one instruction, and role plays are the four most popular methods. Techniques such as interactive video and multimedia are less commonly used, but they are rapidly gaining popularity. Because there are so many different methods, it is helpful to divide training techniques into two broad categories: on-the-job and off-the job approaches. On-the-job training is provided at the worksite. Off-the-job training is conducted away from the worksite. We begin first with a review of on-the-job methods, followed by a discussion of off-the-job approaches.

On-the-job training Involves training that is provided at the worksite.

Off-the-job training Involves training that is conducted away from the worksite.

On-the-Job Training Techniques

There are four basic kinds of on-the-job training:

1. One-on-one instruction.
2. Coaching.
3. Job rotation.
4. Apprenticeship/internship.

Each of these methods is described in greater detail next, along with their strengths and weaknesses.

One-on-One Instruction. As you can see in Figure 11.2, this is one of the most popular approaches to training and development. In one-on-one instruction, a person who serves as a trainer for the organization meets with the employee at the workplace (though perhaps in a separate area) and instructs the trainee (see Box 11.5 for a detailed description of how to give one-on-one instruction). Generally, the instructional method involves a description of the procedures, along with a visual demonstration by the instructor. Following this, the trainee practices, under the supervision of the trainer. Of course, various texts, videos, and other materials might be used to supplement this training method. It is important to point out that one-on-one instruction differs greatly from other, seemingly similar approaches, such as the SAWNOF ("Sit and Watch Nellie or Fred") approach. In the SAWNOF method, the employee is instructed to go sit and watch Nellie or Fred (usually, experienced workers). There are several major problems with the SAWNOF approach. First, while Nellie and Fred may be quite effective in their jobs, this does not necessarily mean they are effective trainers. In some cases, they may feel their own job is threatened, so Nellie and Fred may intentionally give wrong advice. Or, Nellie and Fred may be excellent trainers, but they may fear their own work will suffer if they spend too much time training other employees.

One-on-one instruction A person who serves as a trainer for the organization meets with the employee at the workplace and instructs the trainee.

SAWNOF approach The "Sit And Watch Nellie Or Fred" method of training, in which the employee is instructed to sit and watch Nellie or Fred (usually, experienced workers).

Figure 11.2 **Popularity of Different Training Techniques in Business**

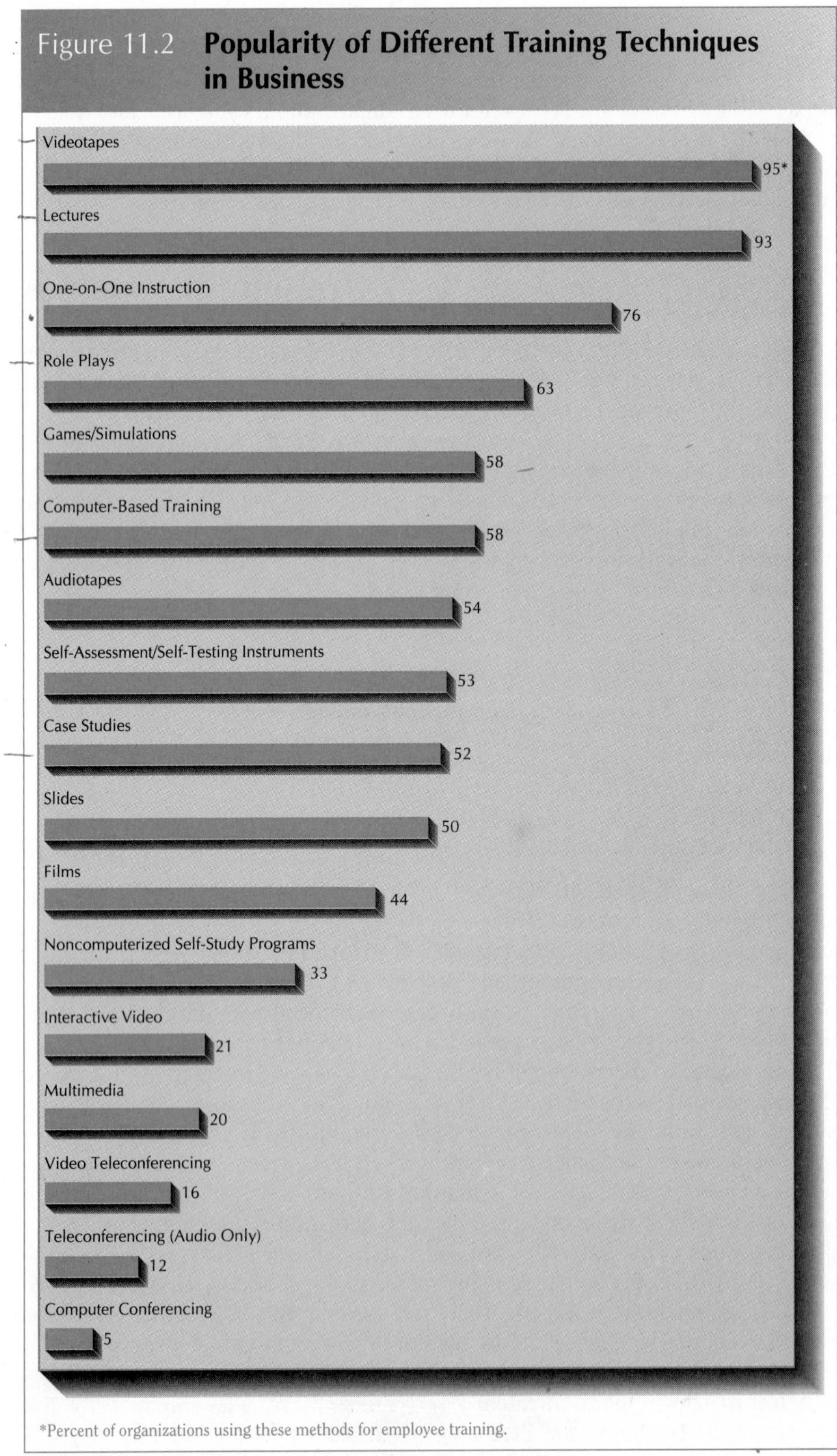

*Percent of organizations using these methods for employee training.

Source: P. Froiland, "Who's Getting Trained?" (p. 57), *Training,* October 1993.

Finally, the SAWNOF approach is generally informal and unplanned, so Nellie and Fred spend little or no time designing the training program. For these reasons, the SAWNOF approach often is ineffective.[27] Recall in the opening case of this chapter that the employee considered using two supervisors for one-on-one instruction. Do you think this would be appropriate? Particularly in light of the changing nature of the supervisory job, Sally should be wary of receiving one-on-one instruction from long-term supervisors, whose perspective and approach may reflect ineffective methods. One-on-one instruction therefore may not be useful in the In-Sync situation.

An effective one-on-one instruction program has several positive benefits, including cost-effectiveness, because workers are learning while they are producing and there is little need for expensive facilities or equipment. Another advantage is that the training is directly job related, because actual equipment is used to learn and practice. Third, the trainees will get immediate feedback on their performance.[28] Fourth, this training method is flexible—as the equipment or job changes, modifications are easily made in the training.[29]

In terms of disadvantages, one-on-one instruction has two basic problems. First, in many companies, one-on-one instruction is not carefully designed or systematically delivered. In other words, in many companies, it takes on more of the characteristics of the SAWNOF approach than the one-on-one instruction method. Second, one-on-one instruction generally works best for jobs or tasks that are fairly simple, routine, and motor oriented. For example, operating simple machinery, filing correspondence, and simple cleaning tasks may be well suited to one-on-one instruction. Other tasks, such as writing computer programs and piloting an airplane are probably not well served by this method. Third, there may be no one in the organization that is knowledgeable enough to train others. For example, a company that wishes to train employees in the use of computer-automated design (CAD) will not be able to use this method if no one in the organization is knowledgeable in this area.[30]

Coaching
Informal, unplanned training and development activities provided by supervisors and peers.

Coaching. Although different people use the term coaching to mean different things, coaching is defined here as informal, unplanned training and development activities provided by supervisors and peers. While coaching may provide valuable help for employees, it should be viewed strictly as a supplement to, rather than a substitute for, formal training and development programs.[31] There are many occasions for which the coaching method is most usefully applied:

1. When an employee demonstrates a new skill or ability.
2. When an employee expresses interest in a different job within the organization.
3. When an employee seeks feedback.
4. When an employee is expressing low morale, violating company policies or practices, or having performance problems.
5. When an employee needs help with a new skill following a formal training program.

In the right situations, then, coaching can be an effective supplement to formal training methods. When used by itself, however, coaching is likely to be inadequate.

Job rotation
A formal, planned program involving the assignment of trainees to varying jobs in different parts of the organization.

Job Rotation. Job rotation is a formal, planned program that involves assigning trainees to various jobs in different parts of the organization. Eli Lilly, the pharmaceutical company headquartered in Indiana, has one of the most well-known

Box 11.5 A Mini-Guide to Providing One-on-One Instruction

Have you been asked to serve as a trainer to provide one-on-one instruction? If so, here are some helpful suggestions for conducting the training session. First, get ready for instruction by doing the following:

1. Make a timetable indicating how long the instruction will last. Determine how long it should take the trainee to acquire each skill.
2. Break down the job into simple steps. Be sure to determine the key steps for each task.
3. Assemble all materials, including equipment and supplies, and be sure that everything is in proper order.

Now that you are prepared, here are some simple steps you can use in conducting the training:

1. Introduce Your Training Program. Be sure to put the worker at ease, determine what he or she knows about the task, and encourage the worker's participation.
2. Present the Task. A common approach is to begin by explaining what the machine, equipment, or task is, along with its related processes and operations. Then slowly demonstrate operation of the task or machine while giving a step-by-step description of what is happening. Ask questions to determine if the trainee is understanding. Next, repeat the demonstration, skipping the description.
3. Have the Trainee Try the Task. The trainee should continue to perform the task, while you observe. Correct any mistakes along the way, and return to Step 2 (presenting the task) as needed. Have the trainee repeat the task until it is completed without any mistakes. Be sure the trainee can perform the task successfully.
4. Monitor the Worker While He or She Performs the Task Independently. You should encourage the trainee to continue to ask questions. At first, you should check the worker's performance carefully. Once the employee's performance has been adequate for a while, you should decrease your monitoring.

Source: Adapted from K. Wexley and G. Latham, *Developing and Training Human Resources in Organizations,* (Glenview, IL: Scott, Foresman, 1981).

job rotation programs. The purpose of job rotation is to provide trainees with a larger organizational perspective and a greater understanding of different functional areas, as well as a better sense of their own career objectives and interests.[32] Not surprisingly, employees in a job rotation program tend to be in the early phase of their careers and are usually top performers.[33]

In terms of advantages, job rotation appears to improve the participants' job skills, increase job satisfaction, and provide valuable opportunities for networking within the organization. From a personal perspective, employees who participate in job rotations experience faster promotions and higher salaries than employees who do not participate. In terms of disadvantages, job rotations may create an increased workload for the participants due to the constant job change. Job rotation may also cause dissatisfaction in those employees who did not participate in the program. Whether this is due to their increased workload or due to resentment for not participating is unclear.[34]

Apprenticeship
A formal program involving a combination of classroom instruction and hands-on practice and training, primarily in the skilled crafts such as carpentry.

Internship
A program providing work experience to students prior to their graduation from an academic program.

Apprenticeship/Internship. An apprenticeship is a formal program involving a combination of classroom instruction and hands-on practice and training, primarily in the skilled crafts (such as carpentry). An apprenticeship, then, includes more than just on-the-job training.[35] Although internships are included here with apprenticeships, they are rather different: an internship is a program that provides work experience to students prior to graduation from an academic program. Typically, internships are completed by students in business, law, and the health professions. Therefore, an apprenticeship constitutes a complete program, while an internship is merely one part of a larger educational program.

In terms of the effectiveness of apprenticeships, most workers who have passed them are satisfied with their training and tend to earn significantly higher wages than employees who did not have an apprenticeship. There are some disadvantages to an apprenticeship program, however. First, there is a high dropout rate among trainees; it is estimated that fewer than 50 percent actually complete the apprenticeship. A second disadvantage of the apprenticeship program is the high cost.[36] As noted in the introduction, the number of employees undertaking an apprenticeship has fallen over the years in the United States, which has led to shortages of qualified applicants in the skilled crafts.

Because internships are far less formalized than apprenticeships, there is less known about them. Research does, however, indicate that students who have been through an internship experience have several advantages over students who have not had one, including superior performance ratings in subsequent jobs, higher starting salaries, and greater satisfaction with their jobs. Students with internships characterized by much freedom to make decisions tend to be more successful in making the transition from school to work. As a student, then, an internship provides a number of advantages, and organizations find that an internship program is helpful in training future employees.[37]

In sum, there are a number of on-the-job training techniques that might be used by an organization. Returning to the opening case of this chapter, because of the need to learn KSAs that other employees may not know either, the employee might be best off by using some type of off-the-job training program. These techniques are described next in greater detail.

Off-the-Job Training Techniques

This section provides a brief description of some of the most popular off-the-job training techniques, followed by a discussion of their advantages and disadvantages. We begin first with the lecture method, followed by videotape, computer-based training, equipment simulators, and conclude with some additional approaches.

Lecture. When you think of off-the-job training, does the term "lecture" immediately come to mind? As the term is used here, **lecture training** involves an instructor verbally presenting material to a group of trainees. The expert may encourage discussion and questions, but the majority of the information is delivered through one-way communication. There is little, if any, time set aside to practice skills. As shown in Figure 11.2, lectures are the second most commonly used training techniques. Only videotapes are more popular.

Lecture training
Involves an instructor verbally presenting material to a group of trainees.

If you were asked to describe the strengths and weaknesses of the lecture technique, you would probably have no trouble thinking of some weaknesses of this method. But what about the advantages of the lecture? First, the lecture method is quite effective for providing basic information (such as features of a new product or changes in a company's benefit program).[38] A second advantage is that it is a familiar training method; trainees will not be uncomfortable or intimidated by this method. Third, it is adaptable to nearly any topic. Fourth, a highly skilled lecturer can provide excellent training.[39]

Of course, the lecture method has numerous disadvantages. First, while a highly skilled lecturer can use this technique effectively, you have probably had

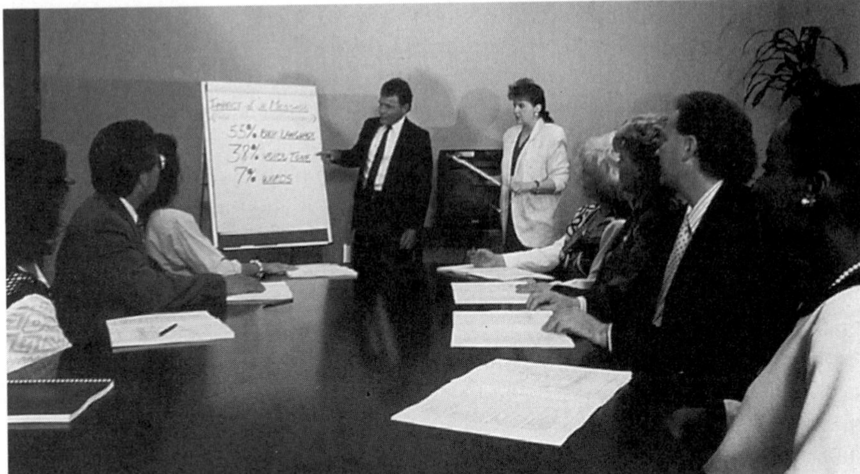

Although lecturing is one-way communication, managers find it an effective method of providing basic information because of its familiarity to employees and its adaptability to any topic.

one or two college instructors who talked in a monotone and presented the material in an extremely dull fashion. Some trainers are not effective lecturers, and as a result, participants become quickly bored.[40] Second, a lecture proceeds at a single speed; differences in the trainees' ability to comprehend are ignored. Third, scheduling all trainees to be present at the same time can be quite difficult, if not impossible. Fourth, the costs can be quite high—trainers can cost hundreds of dollars an hour, and trainees must miss work. Fifth, the lecture method is quite ineffective in some areas, such as for improving interpersonal skills.[41]

As with other techniques, the lecture method has both advantages and disadvantages. Next, you will read about the most popular training method, the videotape.

Videotape training
A videotape is used to present material to a group of trainees; it is the most popular training technique today.

Videotape. As shown in Figure 11.2, videotape training is the most popular training technique used today. There are many mail-order companies that market and sell training videotapes on every conceivable topic, including managing diversity, customer relations, communication skills, to name just a few. Some organizations prefer to create their own videotapes, tailored to specific needs and approaches.

Videotapes have several basic advantages. First, visually presented information is generally interesting and motivating to viewers. Second, videotapes allow for a wide range of content, such as experts demonstrating complex skills and behaviors. Videotapes are useful for showing skills and behaviors that might be difficult or impossible to observe otherwise (such as extinguishing fires). Third, because individuals can use the videotapes when they desire, they offer the capacity for self-pacing.[42] Fourth, scheduling is flexible, because the videotapes may be viewed privately or in small groups. Fifth, the costs may be quite reasonable, particularly since most of the expense is in development and a videotape can be reused. Commercially available videotapes may cost as little as a few hundred dollars.[43]

In terms of disadvantages, there is little scientific evidence that videotapes actually are more effective than any other technique, including lectures. Moreover, just as movies can be boring, videotapes can be quite boring too. Second, like the lecture, trainees are generally passive observers. In fact, there is even less opportunity to interact with the trainer. Further, like the lecture, the videotape method involves one-way communication, with no opportunity for questions. Finally, for companies wishing to create their own videotapes, development costs can add up to hundreds of thousands of dollars.[44]

In sum, despite what you might think, videotapes are not necessarily any better as a training technique than a lecture. Much will depend on how well designed the videotape is—some are excellent, others are quite ineffective for training purposes.

Computer-Based Training. Just as computers have had a major impact on business and life in general, computers have had a major impact on training. Recent advances in multimedia presentation have greatly enhanced the capabilities of **computer-based training.** Consider, for example, Toronto Dominion Bank, and how its 1,200 employees were trained in the past for customer service. The 1983 training program required one and one-half years to develop and five years to train all of the employees. By the time the training program ended in 1990, the bank's approach to customer service had radically changed. Why did it take so long for the employees to complete the training? The program had a traditional, classroom-based approach, and the company's facilities are spread across the country. Now the bank's training program is computer based, which offers many advantages. First, all employees are able to train at the same time, so there will no longer be a five-year gap between the first employee and the last employee being trained. Second, although development costs will be high, costs of conducting the training will be much lower, because employees can receive the software through the mail and complete the training without leaving their offices. Third, employees can learn at their own pace, when they have the time. Fourth, employees can learn on a need-to-know basis (such as before they begin a new assignment), rather than when the instructors are ready. Fifth, because the program includes a

Computer-based training
Computers are used to present material to trainees; either on a need-to-know basis, at their own pace, or in their own offices.

Computer-based training has a major impact on businesses and organizations. Employers can now use multimedia presentations to train employees, and the flexibility allows for different learning levels, time schedules, and provides a great deal of feedback to the trainees.

computer-administered test, an employee's understanding of the material can be easily evaluated, unlike in the classroom, where it is far more difficult to assess what an employee has learned.[45]

Because of its flexibility, computer-based training can be used to teach a wide variety of skills. For example, Anheuser-Busch uses a computer-based training program to train production workers on how to operate beer can packaging equipment. Burlington Northern Railroad uses computer-based training to teach crews railroad operation regulations. These are just a few examples of companies employing computer-based training on a large-scale basis.[46]

As you may surmise from the previous examples, computer-based training offers many advantages. First, it allows for a great deal of interaction for the trainees, and the use of multiple media (visuals, sound, and text) helps to reduce boredom. Second, computer-based training allows for highly flexible scheduling; all that one needs besides the program is a computer with the appropriate hardware. Third, this technique can be used for teaching many different KSAs. Fourth, computer-based training allows trainees to proceed at their own pace. Fifth, computer-based training provides a great deal of feedback and can be adapted to meet the specific needs of different trainees.

Computer-based training also has disadvantages. Probably the most significant disadvantage is the potential cost associated with this technique. Developing the materials can be very expensive, particularly when interactive opportunities are included. On the other hand, commercially available packages may be relatively inexpensive. A company deciding whether to use computer-based training will certainly need to examine its cost-effectiveness when compared to other techniques. When all factors are considered (training facilities, travel expenses, and so on), computer-based training may be more cost-effective than many other methods, particularly for large organizations.

A second disadvantage of this training method is that some individuals are intimidated by and are uncomfortable with computers. Given, however, the proliferation of computers in the workplace, more and more employees will be required to use them anyhow. In the near future, almost every job will involve computers to some extent.[47] Moreover, the organization can reduce the fear of computers by emphasizing the advantages of computer-based training.[48]

Finally, there is little indication that trainees actually learn more from computer-based training than they do using other techniques. In terms of speed, however, research indicates that computer-based training results in faster learning time than a traditional lecture approach.[49] In sum, computer-based training has become an extremely important technique. Its use is likely to become even more widespread in the future.

Equipment simulators
Used for jobs or tasks where improper use of actual equipment would pose a danger to the trainee (or others) or where the risk of substantial financial loss exists.

Equipment Simulators. You probably have either heard of or actually used an equipment simulator at one time or another. **Equipment simulators** are most frequently used for jobs or tasks where the use of actual equipment would pose a danger to the trainee (or others) or the risk of substantial financial loss exists. Air crews, naval officers, and space shuttle crews usually receive extensive training using this technique. Your author used a car simulator as part of his high school driver's education course.[50]

There are several basic advantages to equipment simulators. First, it may be the only safe way to train. Second, this technique requires a great deal of interaction with the equipment; third, the skills learned in training should be readily transferable to the workplace. The basic disadvantage of equipment simulators is the high cost associated with them, particularly in the development phase. Nonetheless, compared with the safety risks and possible financial loss of using the actual equipment, an equipment simulator may seem like a real bargain.[51]

Additional Tools: Role Plays and Cases. In addition to the techniques described so far, there are several other commonly used training tools, such as role plays and cases. These often serve as an adjunct to a lecture or videotape.

Role plays require the trainee to act out an assigned role in a hypothetical situation. In many instances, the trainee is given feedback regarding his or her performance. The basic advantage of a role play is that it enables trainees to practice new behaviors in a safe environment. The primary disadvantage of this technique is that many trainees are uncomfortable doing role plays.[52]

Role plays
A technique whereby trainees act out an assigned role in a hypothetical situation.

As part of a course in the business school, you may have used a case. Cases involve written descriptions of an organizational situation. Trainees must analyze the information and make a decision as to what they would do in the situation. A human resources case, for example, might describe an organization choosing between different kinds of pay-for-performance plans. The primary advantage of a case is that it provides a context for applying basic principles that might have been covered in a lecture or videotape. It also may offer an opportunity for interaction between the trainees and the trainer. The basic disadvantage of the case method is that a trainer who is not skilled in this technique can undermine its usefulness. Also, the case method may have little or nothing in common with the trainees' workplace, which may limit its effectiveness. To avoid this problem, it is recommended that the case be as similar as possible to the trainees' organization and that the trainees be encouraged to discuss its application to their own workplace.[53]

Cases
Involves a written description of an organizational situation.

Now that you have read about many different training techniques, you will learn about basic principles that facilitate learning.

Principles of Learning: General Guidelines

Over the years, experts have identified some basic principles that are important in designing a training program. Some of the more important ones are described next.[54]

Provide for Active Practice. Trainees must be provided an opportunity to practice and utilize the concepts being covered in the training program. For example, in the opening case, Sally must have an opportunity to practice the new skills and abilities in order for her to learn them properly.

Choose between Massed versus Distributed Learning Sessions. A major question in designing and conducting a training program is whether to use massed training (conducted in a compacted timetable, such as in a lengthy two-day program) or distributed training sessions (conducted over a longer period of time, such as one hour per week for sixteen weeks). It is generally believed that conducting too much training in too short a time period leads to less learning than occurs when the training program is spread out. However, time constraints may require that the training be completed in a very short time frame.

Massed training
A training session that is conducted in a compacted timetable, such as in a lengthy two-day program.

Distributed training
A training session that is conducted over a longer period of time, such as one hour per week for 16 weeks.

Provide Feedback to Trainees. Helpful feedback is important in training for several reasons. First, feedback helps trainees to correct mistakes. Second, feedback makes the learning more interesting for trainees. Third, having feedback enables trainees to set goals for improving their performance. As a trainer, though, be very careful about wording your feedback so that it is perceived as positive and helpful. Trainees tend to shun feedback that criticizes them. Above all, maintain a positive atmosphere. Too much criticism will turn your audience against you.

Transfer of training The principle that employees transfer the KSAs learned in the training period onto their jobs.

Maximize Application of Training to the Job. One of the biggest problems associated with training programs is the lack of a transfer of training. In other words, many trainees, even if they have effectively learned the KSAs in the training program, refrain from using them on the job. Although U.S. companies spend billions of dollars on training, it has been estimated that only a small portion of the KSAs learned in programs are actually used on the job.[55] Why does transfer so frequently fail to take place? There are three key factors:[56]

1. Lack of support for use of the new KSAs on the job.
2. Trainees are uncomfortable with using new KSAs.
3. Trainees perceive the training program to be impractical or irrelevant.

Now that you know some of the primary causes of the problem, let us review some techniques for increasing the transfer of training. What follows are some suggestions that can be used before, during, and after the training program, regardless of whether you are the trainer or trainee.[57]

1. Participants Should Be Actively Involved in Planning the Training Program. Even if you, as an employee, are not invited to participate in the planning, you should ask to be involved. A nonthreatening way to do this is to say something like, "I've heard that the human resources department is planning a training program, and I have some suggestions I would like to share."

2. Develop a Written Contract Between Trainees and Their Supervisors. The contract will stipulate what the employee will bring back from the training program (for example, it might specify that the employees create action plans with their supervisors and coworkers and review training highlights with them) and what the supervisor agrees to do in return (such as minimizing interruptions to the training program, providing encouragement and support for the new KSAs, or meeting with the trainee to discuss the program). This way, both trainees and their supervisors explicitly agree to work together to maximize training transfer. This is probably an excellent idea for Sally, the employee in the opening case, to ensure that new supervisory approaches are not discouraged.

3. Use Realistic Work-Related Situations. It is critical for the training to demonstrate, illustrate, and explain the KSAs in the most realistic, work-related situations as possible. The trainer should choose films, exercises, role plays, and other techniques with this in mind. Another way to do this is to have the trainees generate work situations where they can apply the principles and KSAs being taught.

4. Facilitate Trainee Participation. As a general rule, people learn more when they actively participate in the training process. In fact, the most interesting aspects of the training program are often the discussion and interaction between trainees. As a trainee, if you wonder how the concepts being taught apply to your job, ask. Don't be embarrassed.

5. Arrange Refresher Sessions. Employees may forget or experience difficulty using the KSAs. One way to reduce such problems is to plan a refresher session a

few months after the training program is over. This might also offer trainees an opportunity to recommend changes for the next time the program is conducted.

6. Support Training. Trainers can be actively involved in supporting the training after the program is over. As a trainer, the author has begun the practice of providing a telephone number to participants and encouraging them to contact him. The trainer can be helpful after the session in giving suggestions, especially if the participant experiences problems in using the KSAs.

Returning to the opening case, recall that Sally needed to recommend training techniques. Based on what you read in this section, do you have any suggestions as to which techniques would be best for her? One possibility would be to take some training programs offered by a local university, community college, or consulting firm that addresses the necessary skills, such as communication, delegation, and so forth. These programs might be particularly helpful because they typically have a live trainer who can provide feedback. Videotapes might be useful as well, but only if they provide practice and offer feedback. Lectures alone, without opportunity to practice, would probably be of little value. Computer-based training programs may also be available for purchase. *Training Magazine* publishes a catalog of various training products called "Expo-Lit," which are useful sources of information (call 1-800-328-4329 for information). Finally, as you can see from the learning principles, not only are the training techniques important, but how the training is conducted is just as significant.

Evaluating Training Program Success

The final step in conducting a training program is to evaluate its success. We first discuss why program evaluation is important, followed by a review of different measures of success.

Why Training Program Evaluation Is Important You might be wondering why you should evaluate the success of a training program. After all, if it seemed to go well, why bother? There are four basic reasons why you should assess the program's success:

1. Justifying Expenses. Because any human resources program takes money and time, it is important to justify the expense, particularly given today's emphasis on cost cutting and accountability. Failure to prove the cost-effectiveness of a program can come back to haunt even the best-run program; for example, the Michigan Public Service Commission recently prohibited the gas company from increasing customer charges to pay for a training program addressing quality and corporate culture. The Public Service Commission reasoned that the company had failed to show that the program would save money or improve service.[58] In addition, demonstrating the cost-effectiveness of your training program will enhance your own credibility.

2. Making Decisions about Future Programs. Once you have run a program, your company might question whether the program should be repeated, changed, or discontinued. By evaluating its success, a much more informed choice can be made.[59]

3. Making Decisions about Individual Trainees. Depending on the purpose, trainees may need to pass the program in order to be certified or qualified for a particular task or job. In many cases, passing the program will involve more than simply attending all sessions. The trainee may need to have a certain grade or score on some type of test. Formal evaluation of each participant's performance may therefore be necessary.[60]

4. Reducing Professional Liability. If you design or deliver a training program, you or your organization might be held legally responsible if a trainee subsequently becomes injured or killed in the course of performing the task or job. Thus, it is important to evaluate a training program to ensure that it can be defended against legal charges.[61]

Now that you know why evaluating a training program is important, we will discuss how to measure success. As you will see, success can be evaluated several different ways.

Defining Training Program Success

There are four basic measures of training program success:[62]

1. Trainee reactions.
2. The amount of learning that took place.
3. Behavioral change on the job.
4. Concrete results.

Each of these measures will be discussed in greater detail next.

Trainee reactions
An important index of program success, trainees are asked to record their reactions by means of a survey or questionnaire at the end of the training session.

Trainee Reactions. The simplest way to measure success is to examine trainee reactions to the training program. Figure 11.3 is an example of a questionnaire from a supervisory training workshop that is used to assess trainee reactions. There are several reasons why trainee reactions should be formally documented (perhaps with a questionnaire at the end of the training program). First, they can be used as evidence of the popularity of the training if the value of the program is challenged by other parties. Second, trainee reactions can be used to identify where changes should be made for future programs. Third, eliciting reactions enables the trainees to feel they have input into the training program.[63]

Although trainee reactions are an important index of program success, they have several limitations. Most importantly, just because trainees enjoyed a training program does not necessarily mean they learned anything. Other indicators of the success of the program are therefore important.

Amount of learning
Refers to the knowledge, skills, and abilities that trainees acquired from the program; the amount of learning is measured in the context of the training program, not on the job.

Amount of Learning. Amount of learning refers to the knowledge, skills, and abilities that the trainees acquired from the program. The amount of learning is measured in the context of the training program, not on the job. There are different ways of assessing the amount of learning, depending on the nature of the KSAs being taught and the training technique used. Many of the computer-based methods described earlier, for example, include a means of assessing the amount of learning. Other means of measuring how much the trainees learned include written tests and role-play exercises, which may then be evaluated by independent judges.[64]

While the amount of learning may be an important index of a program's success, particularly when trainees must pass the course to perform a certain task or

Figure 11.3 **A Questionnaire to Assess Trainee Reactions**

PROGRAM LEADER EVALUATION FORM
Supervisory Certificate Training Program

Program/Topic	**Employee Staffing, Parts I & II**		
Leader(s)	**Michael Harris**	**Date(s)**	**March 6–13, 1995**

1. Was the topic pertinent to your needs and interests?

☐ Very much so ☐ To some extent ☐ No

2. Ratio of lecture to discussion.

☐ Too much lecture ☐ O.K. ☐ Too much discussion

3. Please rate the instructor by checking the appropriate box below:

	Excellent	Very Good	Good	Fair	Poor
A. How well did the instructor state objectives?					
B. How well did the instructor keep the session alive and interesting?					
C. How well did the instructor use audio/visual materials?					
D. How helpful were the handout materials?					
E. How well did the instructor summarize during the session?					
F. How well did the instructor maintain a friendly and helpful manner?					
G. To what extent did the instructor involve the group?					
H. How was the summary at the close of the session?					

What is your overall rating of the instructor?

☐ Excellent ☐ Very Good ☐ Good ☐ Fair ☐ Poor

Source: The University of Missouri-St. Louis Continuing Education.

job, its major limitation is that it only assesses success within the training context. Whether the trainees actually use the KSAs on the job is a separate issue, which is addressed by behavioral change.

Behavioral Change. This aspect of program success refers to the degree to which the trainees' behavior *on the job* has been affected by the training program. Generally, you can assess behavioral changes by measuring trainees' performance on the relevant tasks. While this approach to measuring program success addresses whether the training has actually affected the way the job is done, it is often difficult to gather this information. Most important, however, is whether the training program affects the bottom line. This is the focus of the fourth measure: concrete results.

Behavioral change
This aspect of program success refers to the degree to which the trainees' behavior on the job has been affected by the training program.

Concrete results Address training program success in terms of the bottom-line outcomes, such as increased productivity, reduced accident rate, or whatever the objectives of the training program were.

Concrete Results. Concrete results address training program success in terms of the bottom-line outcomes such as increased productivity, reduced accident rate, or whatever the objectives of the training program are. Although this constitutes the best way to prove training program success, it can be difficult to assess accurately. As an example, consider a training program designed to improve the presentation skills of sales employees. Even though sales revenue may have increased after the program, it may not be entirely clear why sales revenues increased. Is it due to an improved economy, increased advertising, or some other factor? NCR, the computer and teller machine manufacturer, attempts to evaluate its training programs based on concrete results. A training course in new technical approaches for field engineers was able to cut the average number of hours for a service call in half—a clear savings in monetary terms.[65]

To do a completely scientific evaluation of a training program, you should be careful to address alternative explanations for any improvements. For example, as mentioned earlier, if you simply measure sales revenues for a group of trainees before the training and compare their sales revenues after the training, any increase may merely be due to general economic improvement rather than to the training. To avoid this type of problem, you should gather information on two groups of salespeople: one group that received the training and a second group that did not receive the training. If the training was effective, the group that received the training should have a larger increase in sales than the group that did not receive training. You should also use statistical analysis to show that the gains are statistically significant and are not simply due to chance improvement.

Conclusion

As a way of summarizing the information in this chapter by applying the material to an actual situation, assume that your boss has asked you to design and conduct a training program for your department (if you are not currently working, think about how you would do this for a department you used to work for or for a friend's department). You have three months to design and conduct the program. Here are a set of recommended steps you might use for this assignment. For each of the steps, consider what you would do.[66]

1. Conduct a Training Needs Analysis. Determine who needs training in which areas. Given what you read in this chapter, how would you go about this task? What would you do to increase employee acceptance of your training program?

2. Choose the Appropriate Training Techniques and Principles. Many different training techniques, along with their advantages and disadvantages, were described in this chapter. Which would you use for your training program. Why?

3. Discuss the Program with Supervisors, and Other Relevant Parties. If your training is to succeed, you will need relevant parties to accept and endorse the program. Failure to do so may doom even the best training programs. Identify the relevant parties in your department that should be consulted.

4. Release Course Objectives to Trainees before the Program. Don't forget that the trainees need to accept the program and must be motivated if they are to learn. What can you do to encourage the trainees to accept the program?

5. Use Action Plans at the End of Each Training Course. At the end of a training program, have the trainees write down the four or five basic points they learned. That way, they can show (both themselves and their supervisors) what they accomplished.

6. Encourage Participation throughout the Training Sessions. Trainees learn best when they actively participate in the program. What types of training techniques described in this chapter can you include that will be helpful in this regard?

7. Spread Out the Training Program. In most cases, a five-part training program is best spread out over several weeks, rather than being delivered all at once. By spreading out the program, you can review previous lessons, reduce disruptions to work, and provide time for trainees to try out what they have learned. How would you most effectively spread out the training?

8. Encourage the Application of Training. Depending on the training area, it may be critical that you take steps to encourage trainees to use the knowledge, skills, and abilities that you developed the training program to enhance. What would you do in this regard?

9. Evaluate the Results. You read about several ways to evaluate the cost benefits of training programs. Which would you use in your department? Why? Do not underplay the importance of this step; it will increase your credibility if you can demonstrate the success of the training program.

10. Establish a Long-Term Training and Development Program. Although you had only limited time to design and run the program, it is important to establish a long-term plan for training and development. With a long-term perspective in mind, what would you do differently?

Applying Core Concepts

1. If your supervisor (or a friend's supervisor if you are not currently working) asked you to conduct a training needs analysis, how would you go about this assignment?
2. Assume you were asked to develop a training program to improve customer sales skills. What training techniques would you use? Why?
3. Apply the learning principles to help Sally Andrews develop a training program for all of the supervisors at In-Sync.
4. If Sally Andrews implemented a training program for all of the supervisors at In-Sync, what would you suggest she do to demonstrate that the program was successful?

Key Terms

- Training and development
- Training needs analysis
- Organizational analysis
- Task/KSA analysis
- Person analysis
- On-the-job training
- Off-the-job training
- One-on-one instruction
- SAWNOF approach
- Coaching
- Job rotation
- Apprenticeship
- Internship
- Lecture training
- Videotape training
- Computer-based training
- Equipment simulators
- Role plays
- Case
- Massed training
- Distributed training
- Transfer of training
- Trainee reactions
- Amount of learning
- Behavioral change
- Concrete results

Chapter 11: Experiential Exercise

Training at Central Collection Agency

Central Collection Agency (CCA) is a collection agency. In this capacity, businesses pay CCA to collect overdue payments from consumers. Including all managers, supervisors, and collection agents, CCA employs about 500 workers (thirty are supervisors). The job of a collection agent is rather stressful as consumers who are contacted by CCA are under great stress and will do anything to avoid payment. Collection agents may even be threatened with physical violence. There are also many legal regulations that restrict what the collection agent may do and say. Coupled with the fact that the pay for collection agents is low and the turnover is high, a supervisor must be effective in hiring, training, supervising, and monitoring his or her subordinates.

When CCA first started twenty years ago, the company created a separate training department composed of three people. One person was a training specialist, who had a B.A. in education. The other two members of the department were former collection agency supervisors, who had years of experience managing collection agents. However, because of a low turnover rate among supervisors, the supervisory staff became increasingly skilled in managing the collection agents and there was less and less need for the training and development department to conduct sessions for the collection agents. As a result, the need for training declined to a point where a separate department was no longer needed. When a new CEO was hired three years ago, he eliminated the training department and contracted with Impact Trainers, a local training firm, to conduct any necessary training for the supervisors. All training of collection agents remains the responsibility of the supervisors.

Over the last three years, however, CCA has hired twenty new supervisors. Most of the new supervisors were hired from other agencies, but about five were collection agents who were promoted. Because of the large number of new supervisors, Impact Trainers has conducted three programs in the last two years.

Impact Trainers' Program Impact Trainers' supervisory program contains the following six modules, which are delivered over a five-day period:

- Collection Agencies and the Law
- Coaching and Training Subordinates
- Giving Performance Feedback
- How to Hire Effectively
- Communication Skills
- Telephone Courtesy

Impact Trainers uses a variety of materials and techniques in the program, including role plays, cases, short lectures, and films. At the end of each program, Impact Trainers also collects evaluations from the trainees. According to the owner of Impact Trainers, two key questions are: "Overall, how useful will the program be in your job?" and "Overall, how much did you learn from this program?" The average rating on each question was over 8 on a 9-point scale, which is extremely high for a training program. Some of the written comments by the supervisors included "Excellent training—wish I had gone through the program years ago" and "Worth every minute of the time." Not a single negative comment has appeared yet.

The Problem The problem that has come to the CEO's attention is that the new supervisors appear to be having difficulty in managing their collection agents. While it was first thought to merely be the result of hiring relatively large numbers of new supervisors three years ago, things appear only to have worsened in the last year. The turnover rate among collection agents is much higher than it was four years ago; their record of receiving payment within thirty days has declined noticeably over the last three years; and the number of complaints filed by consumers has increased dramatically. The feeling by the CEO and the top executives is that the training program is not effective. However, they do *not* want to reinstitute a training department. They would like you to do two things:

1. Why do you think the training is not effective? Are there other explanations, besides the training program, for the problems described here? Because the CEO likes concrete evidence for any recommendations, be sure to consider how you could document your conclusions.
2. What would you do to ensure that the training is more effective? Remember, you cannot reinstate a training department and the CEO is very unlikely to approve expensive changes.

Chapter 11 References

1. K. Wexley and G. Lantham, *Developing and Training Human Resources in Organizations* (Glenview, IL: Scott, Foresman, 1981).
2. I. Goldstein, "Critical Training Issues: Past, Present, and Future," in *Training and Development in Organizations,* I. Goldstein and Associates (San Francisco: Jossey Bass, 1989).
3. U.S. Congress, Office of Technology Assessment, *Worker Training: Competing in the New International Economy* (Washington: U.S. Government Printing Office, 1990), OTA-ITE-457.
4. D. Hogarty, "A Little Education Goes a Long Way," *Management Review,* June 1993, 24–28.
5. B. Mintz, *OSHA: History, Law, and Policy* (Washington: Bureau of National Affairs, 1984).
6. U.S. Congress, *Worker Training.*
7. G. Kimmerling, "Gathering Best Practices," *Training and Development,* September 1993, 28–36.
8. P. Froiland, "Who's Getting Trained?" *Training,* October 1993, 53–64.
9. U.S. Congress, *Worker Training.*
10. Ibid.
11. Wexley and Latham, *Developing and Training.*
12. Ibid.
13. Ibid.
14. M. Berger, "A Market-Led Training Needs Analysis," *Industrial and Commercial Training* 25, no. 1, (1993) 27–30.
15. Ibid.
16. N. Nopper "Reinventing the Factory with Lifelong Learning," *Training* May (1993), 55–58.
17. I. Goldstein, "Training in Work Organizations," in *Handbook of Industrial and Organizational Psychology,* vol. 2, ed. M. Dunnette and L. Hough. (Palo Alto, CA: Consulting Psychologists Press, 1991).
18. Ibid.
19. Wexley and Latham, *Developing and Training.*
20. M. Harris, D. Smith, and D. Champagne, "A Field Study of Performance Appraisal Purpose: Research versus Administrative-Based Ratings," *Personnel Psychology* 48 (1995), 151–160.
21. J.K. Ford, and R. Noe, "Self-Assessed Training Needs: The Effects of Attitude Toward Training, Marginal Level, and Function," *Personnel Psychology* 40 (1987), 39–53.
22. M. Harris, and J. Schaubroeck, "A Meta-Analysis of Self-Supervisor, Self-Peer, and Peer-Supervisor Ratings," *Personnel Psychology* 41 (1988), 43–62.
23. J. McEnery and J. McEnery, "Self-Rating in Management Training Needs Assessment: A Neglected Opportunity," *Journal of Occupational Psychology* 60 (1987) 49–60.
24. Wexley and Latham, *Developing and Training.*
25. R. Noe and N. Schmitt, "The Influence of Trainee Attitudes on Training Effectiveness: Test of a Model," *Personnel Psychology* 39 (1986), 497–523.
26. P. Thayer and W. McGhee, "On the Effectiveness of Not Holding a Formal Training Course," *Personnel Psychology,* 30 (1977), 455–56.
27. L. Rae, "Training 101: Choose Your Method," *Training & Development,* April 1994, 19–25.
28. Wexley and Latham, *Developing and Training.*
29. S. Gordon, *Systematic Training Program Design* (Englewood Cliffs, NJ: PTR Prentice-Hall, 1994).
30. Ibid.

31. B. Kaye, "Career Development—Anytime, Anyplace," *Training and Development,* December 1993, 46–49.
32. Wexley and Latham, *Developing and Training.*
33. M. Campion, L. Cheraskin, and M. Stevens, "Career-Related Antecedents and Outcomes of Job Rotation," *Academy of Management Journal* 37 (1994), 1518–42.
34. Ibid.
35. U.S. Congress, *Worker Training.*
36. Ibid.
37. M.S. Taylor, "Effects of College Internships on Individual Participants," *Journal of Applied Psychology* 73 (1988), 393–401.
38. Wexley and Latham, *Developing and Training.*
39. U.S. Congress, *Worker Training.*
40. Ibid.
41. Wexley and Latham, *Developing and Training.*
42. Gordon, *Systematic Training.*
43. U.S. Congress, *Worker Training.*
44. Gordon, *Systematic Training.*
45. T. Falconer, "No More Pencils, No More Books," *Canadian Banker* 101, March/April 1994, 21–25.
46. U.S. Congress, *Worker Training.*
47. Ibid.
48. J. Martocchio, "Microcomputer Usage as an Opportunity: The Influence of Context in Employee Training," *Personnel Psychology* 45 (1992), 529–52.
49. D. Dossett and P. Hulvershorn, "Increasing Technical Training Efficiency: Peer Training via Computer-Assisted Instruction," *Journal of Applied Psychology* 68 (1983), 552–58.
50. Wexley and Latham, *Developing and Training.*
51. U.S. Congress, *Worker Training.*
52. D. Swink, "Role-Play Your Way to Learning," *Training and Development,* May 1993, 91–97.
53. Wexley and Latham, *Developing and Training.*
54. Ibid.
55. T. Baldwin and J.K. Ford, "Transfer of Training: A Review and Directions for Future Research," *Personnel Psychology* 41 (1988) 63–105.
56. M. Broad and J. Newstrom, *Transfer of Training* (Reading, MA: Addison-Wesley, 1992),
57. Ibid.
58. "Michigan Disallows Corporate Culture Program," *Fortnightly* 131 (1993), 45.
59. P. Sackett and E. Mullen, "Beyond Formal Experimental Design: Towards an Expanded View of the Training Evaluation Process," *Personnel Psychology* 46 (1993), 613–27.
60. Ibid.
61. Gordon, *Systematic Training.*
62. G. Alliger and E. Janak, "Kirkpatrick's Levels of Training Criteria: Thirty Years Later," *Personnel Psychology* 42 (1989), 331–42.
63. Wexley and Latham, *Developing and Training.*
64. W. Hicks and R. Klimoski, "Entry into Training Programs and Its Effects on Training Outcomes: A Field Experiment," *Academy of Management Journal* 30 (1987), 542–52.
65. B. Filipczak, "The Business of Training at NCR," *Training,* February 1992, 55–60.
66. "12 Steps to Better Training," *Training,* June 1993, 14–15+ .

Work Redesign for Productivity and Quality Improvement

chapter 12

Core Concepts

After reading this chapter, you should be capable of

1. Explaining what the classical (scientific management) approach to work design is.
2. Explaining the alternative approaches to classical work design, including job enlargement, job enrichment, quality circles, team concept, total quality management, and reengineering.
3. Describing the advantages and disadvantages of different work design approaches.
4. Identifying the role of the human resource function in work redesign.
5. Outlining the factors in deciding whether work redesign is the solution to an organization's problems.

Opening Case

Fiona has worked for several years now as an order processor in the customer service department of Myra's Mystery, a large mail-order company specializing in lingerie and sleepwear. Her responsibilities include opening customer mail-in orders and entering the orders into a computer terminal. Once the order is entered, the billing department must review the payment method and approve shipment. Approved orders are filled in the warehouse area by an employee who retrieves the items from shelves. The order is then given to another employee in the packaging area, who packs the materials into the appropriate container. Every hour or so, another employee collects the packages and brings them to the mailroom, where the necessary postage is added. The packages are then taken to United Parcel Service or the U.S. Post Office for shipment.

Over the years, Fiona has observed several problems with the way orders are processed. One problem is that it takes quite a lot of time between when she enters the order into the computer and the actual mailing of the order. A second problem is that mistakes seem rather frequent. Sometimes she enters the wrong items into the computer (usually when the customer wrote an illegible number), other times warehouse personnel pack the wrong items. A third problem is that many questions come up that the company regulations stipulate a supervisor must answer. For example, Fiona is required to ask her supervisor how to handle an order that is missing payment. Although she knows the right answer (always call the customer), the company requires order processors to have the supervisor sign a form to allow them to proceed. This of course slows down the speed with which the order can be filled.

When Fiona began working this job, business was booming. Thirty new order processors were hired the same month she was hired. But since that time, orders have slowed down somewhat. This is probably due to increased competition from other companies as well as a slump in the general economy. Just yesterday, top management announced there would be a major restructuring of the company's operations. When Fiona asked her supervisor about this, he answered, "The company is probably going to reengineer. Who knows what will happen then!" Before Fiona had the chance to ask her supervisor what "reengineer" meant, he had to go to a meeting, which lasted the rest of the day.

Fiona is particularly concerned about how reengineering, or whatever changes will be made, will affect her future in the company. One of her friends worked for a company that implemented work teams. As a result, her friend's job changed dramatically. In addition, far fewer supervisor or managerial positions remained, and opportunities for advancement were reduced. Fiona wonders whether layoffs will take place at Myra's Mystery, and how any changes will affect her job.

This chapter discusses the design of jobs and work. In the last few years, many companies have changed the design of their jobs, for several reasons. First, many companies have used job and work design changes as a means of increasing productivity and improving quality. Second, the nature of work itself has changed in many ways. Consider, as an example, the increasingly widespread use of personal computers (PCs), which has changed the speed and ease with which information can be obtained. In turn, PCs have led to the elimination of certain traditional tasks (such as completing paper reports) and the addition of new tasks (for example, performing statistical analyses) for many employees. Third, more people today are likely to seek interesting and challenging work. Many employees become quickly bored performing the same task over and over.

The remainder of this chapter will discuss ways to design jobs and work. First, you will read about the classical approach to work design, often referred to as scientific management. Following that section, you will read about a variety of alternative approaches, including job enrichment, the team concept, total quality management, and reengineering. You will see that there is no one best approach to work design. Rather, each method has its own potential strengths and weaknesses.

Work Design: Classical Approach

The classical approach to job design, often referred to as scientific management, is associated with names you may have heard before in other management courses, such as Frederick Taylor and Henri Fayol, both of whom lived in the beginning of this century. Although the term scientific management often has a negative connotation attached to it, many organizations base their work design on this approach. The classical approach to work design rests on several basic principles listed in Table 12.1. A good example of an organization that uses the classical approach would be a large automobile manufacturer, such as General Motors, particularly as it existed 10 or 15 years ago. Cars would be produced using a traditional assembly line, in which each worker is assigned one or two very simple tasks to perform over and over again. For example, one worker might be assigned the task of affixing the side mirrors, another worker might be assigned the task of affixing the rearview mirror, and yet a third worker might be responsible for attaching the side mirror sticker (one that reads "Images are closer than they appear in the mirror"). The speed or pace of the assembly line, as well as the equipment, layout, and other decisions, would be determined by employees other than the production workers themselves, generally by industrial engineers. There would be little or no need for the workers to interact with one another. Turning to the opening case, it should not surprise you that the jobs at Myra's Mystery are based on the classic work design approach. In particular, each job appears quite simple and specialized. Although there was no description of the work techniques, it is likely that the pace, methods, and other aspects are determined by someone other than the employees who perform the work.[1]

Scientific management The classical approach to job design, which concentrates on such principles as specialization and simplification, repetitiveness, mechanical pacing, limited interpersonal interaction, and predetermined work techniques

Although the classical approach began to wane in popularity by the 1940s, it is still widely used, albeit in a somewhat modified fashion, by many companies. The primary advantage of this approach is that it is highly efficient, especially for simple production jobs, with high quantity output.[2] A second advantage is that classical work design makes it easy to replace workers who leave, because each job is very simple and easy to learn. There are two primary disadvantages to the classical work design. First, many workers react negatively to this kind of work; boredom and dissatisfaction are common reactions. Unless these kinds of reactions are held in check, productivity can ultimately suffer. Second, the classical work design provides little opportunity for innovation by the employees. As a result of these

Table 12.1 **Selected Principles of Classical Job Design**

1. *Specialization and Simplification.* Each job consists of a few, very simple sets of tasks.
2. *Repetitiveness.* Each job involves repeating the same tasks over and over again.
3. *Mechanical Pacing.* Employees work at a speed determined by engineers, who focus on the nature of the product, rather than the employees' natural rhythm or pace.
4. *Limited Interpersonal Interaction.* There is limited need for job-related interaction between employees.
5. *Predetermined Work Techniques.* Staff specialists determine what tools to use, how to use them, and other work technique decisions; employees have little or no influence over these decisions.

Source: Adapted from R. Griffin, *Task Design: An Integrative Approach* (Glenview, IL: Scott, Foresman, 1982).

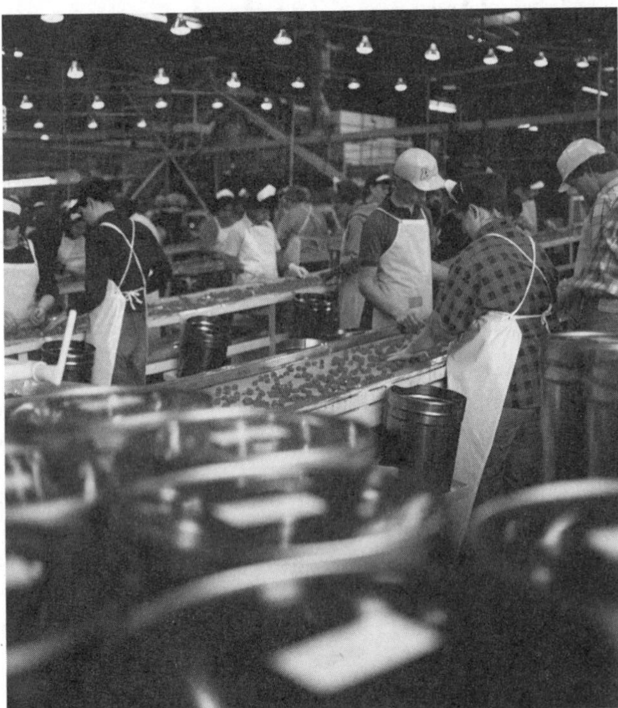

The traditional assembly line is the classical approach to job design, and is the method used in which each worker is assigned one or two very simple tasks to perform over and over again. This highly efficient method of production is still used widely by such companies as General Motors, although in a somewhat modified fashion today.

Box 12.1 Classical Job Design and United Parcel Service

Perhaps the most successful organization in the United States using classical job design is United Parcel Service (UPS). Best known for their boxy brown trucks, UPS is the largest transportation company in the United States. UPS is based on the classical job design model and, in fact, employs more than 3,000 industrial engineers to ensure maximum efficiency. As stipulated by the classical approach, extensive, detailed regulations exist to ensure maximum efficiency. For example, delivery personnel must walk at a specific pace (three feet per second) and pick up and deliver a predetermined number of packages (on average, 400 per day). In return, employees (who are unionized) are well paid; delivery personnel earn between $40,000 to $50,000 annually, making them among the highest paid truck drivers in the United States. As a result of increased competition, however, UPS has been forced to implement several changes in its service. First, UPS has expanded its guaranteed 10:30 A.M. delivery time to most of the country. Second, UPS has started a package tracing system, so that the location of each package can be readily determined as it moves from one point to the next. Third, the company has increased the number of services and products it offers customers. All of these changes have begun to adversely affect the delivery personnel, who complain about conflicts between achieving high-quality customer service, meeting deadlines, and following safety rules. The company has responded by hiring better skilled, often college-educated, workers. But this may have only added to the problems, as higher-educated workers may be less content with this highly structured job. In light of the increasing competition from other companies, though, more changes in UPS may be coming soon. One interesting question, as you read further in this chapter, is whether a different job design would be more effective in adapting to current and future changes at UPS.

Source: Adapted from R. Frank, "Driving Harder," *The Wall Street Journal,* May 23, 1994, A1, A5.

disadvantages, several alternatives to the classical work design approach have been introduced over the last 40 years. You will now read about these in greater detail.[3]

Alternatives to Classical Work Design: An Overview

A number of alternatives to classical work design are available to organizations. We will discuss the following: job enlargement, job enrichment, quality circles, total quality management, the work team, and reengineering. Although these programs differ from one another in a number of ways, they can be compared and contrasted with regard to three important factors:

1. Degree of overall impact;
2. Degree of employee empowerment;
3. Linkage to technology.

Degree of overall impact refers to how far reaching their effects are on overall organizational practices, policies, and norms. As you can see in Table 12.2, some work designs have little overall impact (for instance, quality circles), while other approaches produce much greater overall impact (such as reengineering). Employee empowerment refers to how much decision-making power and authority employees at the lowest level of the organization acquire as a result of the program. Some programs provide little empowerment (such as job enlargement), while others produce high levels of empowerment (for example, work team). Finally, the link to technology category refers to the degree of impact the design has on workplace technology (that is, the processes, equipment, and methods of performing the work). Programs that have a high link to technology (such as reengineering) are likely to require major changes in the technology. For programs with little linkage (such as job enlargement), technology is unlikely to be affected by the program.

Employee empowerment
Refers to how much decision-making power and authority employees at the lowest level of the organization acquire as a result of the work design available to organizations.

Early Approaches to Alternative Work Design: Job Enlargement and Job Enrichment

Job enlargement and job enrichment were among the earliest alternatives proposed to the classical work design. Recall the two basic disadvantages mentioned

Table 12.2: **Characteristics of Work Design Programs**

Program	Impact	Empowerment	Link to Technology
Job enlargement	Low	Low	Low
Job enrichment	Modest	Modest	Modest
Quality circles	Low	Low	Modest
Work teams	High	High	High
TQM	Modest-High	Low-High	Modest-High
Reengineering	Very High	Modest-High	Very High

regarding the classical work design, namely, negative worker reactions and lack of worker innovation. Both job enlargement and job enrichment attempt to overcome the disadvantages of the classical work design by increasing the scope of an employee's job.

Job Enlargement

Job enlargement
Involves increasing the number of tasks performed by each employee and having jobs that are somewhat less specialized

Job enlargement was an approach developed in the 1950s. As suggested by the term, job enlargement involves increasing the number of tasks performed by each employee.[4] Figure 12.1 demonstrates how this works. Using the previous example of an automobile production line, rather than having one worker affixing the side mirror and another worker attaching the rearview mirror, one worker might be assigned the task of attaching both side and rearview mirrors. In essence, then, job enlargement differs from the classical approach of job design in one way: jobs are somewhat less specialized. Rather than only doing one simple task, the workers

Figure 12.1 **Classical Work Design versus Job Enlargement**

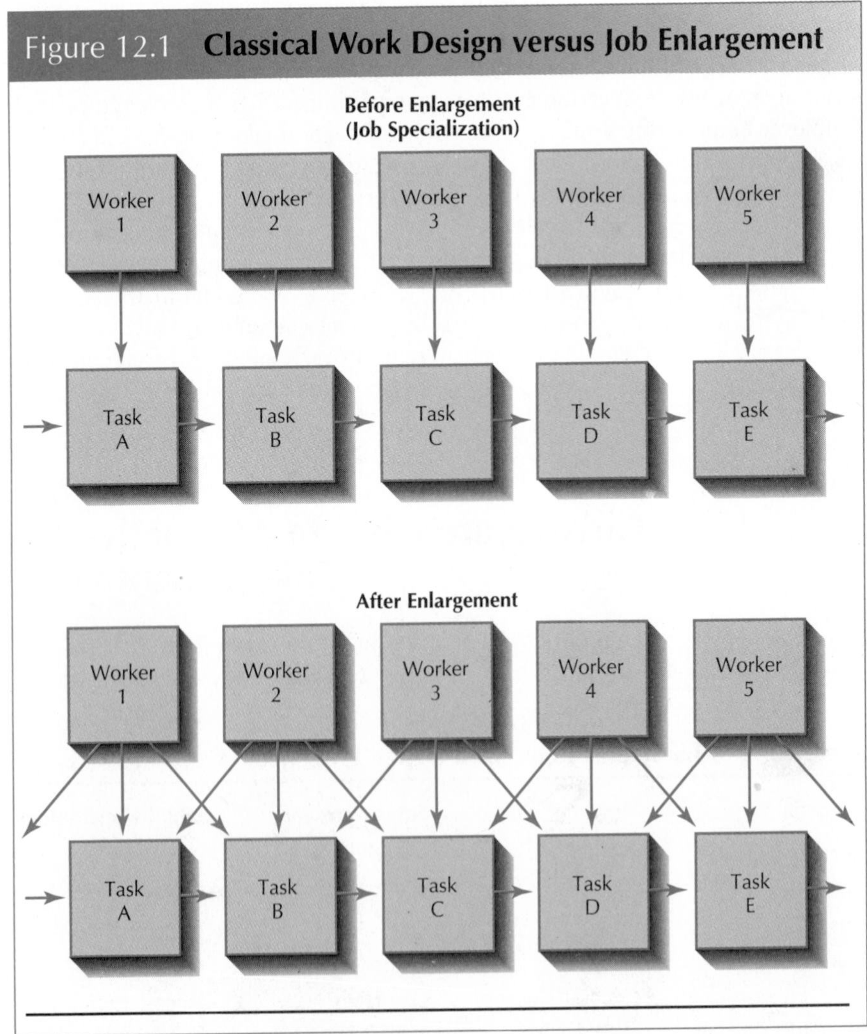

Source: R. Griffin, *Task Design: An Integrative Approach* (Glenview, IL: Scott, Foresman, 1982).

may perform three or four simple tasks. Returning to the opening case, the company might implement job enlargement by increasing the number of responsibilities assigned to the workers. Rather than having one employee retrieve the necessary items from the shelves and a different employee packaging the items, for example, the company might have the same employee do both tasks.

Although there is evidence that job enlargement can somewhat improve worker satisfaction, and productivity may increase, this approach did not become a popular workplace trend. There are probably two reasons for this:[5]

1. Job enlargement only results in small improvements, since workers merely have more assigned tasks.
2. Some view job enlargement as a ruse by management to increase productivity of workers, while cutting back on the number of employees.

Although job enlargement as a specific approach is rarely used in industry today, it did increase awareness of the danger of work oversimplification. As such, job enlargement constitutes an important step in work design.

Job Enrichment

Job enrichment Increasing job satisfaction by using such intrinsic factors as achievement, recognition, and the work itself of enforcing extrinsic factors such as company policy and supervision.

The job enrichment approach was popularized in the 1960s and 1970s by two separate proponents. One proponent, Frederick Herzberg, developed the job enrichment notion as a result of a study of accountants and engineers conducted in the late 1950s. In this study, Herzberg asked participants to describe a work situation where they felt exceptionally satisfied or exceptionally dissatisfied with their work. Herzberg and his colleagues then sorted the responses into broad categories, such as those involving the work itself, those involving supervisors, and so forth. Herzberg found that the majority of satisfying situations involved intrinsic factors, such as achievement, recognition, and the work itself. He concluded that intrinsic factors therefore increase job satisfaction. On the other hand, Herzberg found that extrinsic factors, such as company policy and supervision, were associated primarily with dissatisfying situations. Herzberg interpreted this to mean that extrinsic factors primarily cause dissatisfaction, but contribute little or nothing to satisfaction.[6] The implication of this theory, known as the two-factor theory, is that motivation can be improved by increasing the intrinsic satisfaction associated with the job. Rather than merely adding additional tasks, as suggested by job enlargement, Herzberg advocated adding tasks that involve greater recognition, responsibility, and growth opportunities.[7]

In the 1970s, Richard Hackman and Greg Oldham jointly developed the job characteristics model, which in many ways is similar to the two-factor theory. According to Hackman and Oldham, five characteristics of a job (skill variety, task identity, task significance, autonomy, and feedback) affect key psychological states, (meaningfulness of work, responsibility for work, and knowledge of results), which in turn affect internal work motivation, satisfaction, and work effectiveness. To increase work motivation, jobs must be designed to incorporate high levels of the five job characteristics.[8]

Job enrichment has four major features:

1. Each employee is made responsible for a complete unit of work.
2. Each employee is accountable to the customer.
3. The work should be designed to provide feedback to the employee.

4. Employees should have greater opportunities to make decisions regarding their work.

If you compare these points to those outlined in Table 12.1, which contains the principles of classical job design, you will note several significant differences between the two approaches. As an illustration of how job enrichment principles might be used to design a job, consider Myra's Mystery, the company described in the opening case. A job enrichment approach would require that the same employee complete as much of the entire order as possible. The employee who opens the order, for example, might proceed to retrieve the necessary goods from the shelves and package the materials. This employee might also include in the package a card with his or her name, so that the consumer could directly contact him or her regarding any problems, thereby increasing accountability to the customer. And, rather than asking the supervisor what to do for every special situation, the employees might be trained to deal with many of the common problems.

The job enrichment approach to work design has, like all of the work design programs, both advantages and disadvantages. One advantage is that research has shown the method to be effective in improving worker attitudes (such as job satisfaction) as well as worker productivity.[9] Additionally, as indicated in Table 12.2, job enrichment is less disruptive than other work redesign approaches. Such programs, then, may be easier to implement successfully than some others. In terms of disadvantages, however, job enrichment programs lead to relatively modest productivity improvements. Yet, at the same time, job enrichment can still create upheaval. For example, when employees become more empowered, there may be less need for supervisors. Consequently, supervisors may be laid off or forced to move to different (perhaps lower paying) jobs. The costs of the program, then, may outweigh the benefits.[10]

Quality Circles

Quality circle
Originating in Japan in the early 1960s, the quality circle usually has between 3 and 15 members who meet on a regular basis, and their purpose is to identify, discuss, and solve production or business-related problems within the members' work area.

Although quality circles are less an approach to work design than an addition to the existing organizational structure, we will discuss them here. First initiated in Japan in the early 1960s, quality circles did not debut in the United States until 1974. A quality circle typically has the following characteristics:

1. There are between 3 and 15 members, who participate voluntarily.
2. Meetings take place on a regular basis, usually for an hour per week.
3. Their purpose is to identify, discuss, and solve production or business-related problems within the members' work area.

In most quality circles, the group chooses the problems to examine. As a rule of thumb, the group will generate a list of 50 problems, and solve from 2 to 4 problems per year.[11] Generally, quality circles do not consider human resource and management issues (such as pay or supervision).

Advantages and Disadvantages of Quality Circles

Quality circles grew rapidly in popularity during the late 1970s, but began to wane almost as quickly by the mid-1980s. Currently, slightly more than half of the Fortune 1,000 companies use quality circles.[12] There are both advantages and disadvantages to quality circles. Because they have only a small overall impact, quality circles are easier to implement in organizations than most other work redesign programs. Moreover, they appear to be useful in solving minor productivity problems.[13] Quality circles also have a number of disadvantages. First, they tend to die within one and a half years of implementation.[14] A major difficulty in maintaining quality circles is that companies do not provide significant rewards (such as pay raises) for participation. Also, because most quality circles do not permit discussion of human resource and management issues (such as supervision), employees may become frustrated. A "honeymoon" effect is therefore quite common with quality circles: initially, employee attitudes significantly improve and many suggestions for improvements are offered. After one or two years, however, the romance is over, and attitudes and suggestions decline. Thus, the value of a quality circle program tends to be rather short term.[15] A final disadvantage is recent legal rulings, which indicate that quality circle programs may constitute an illegally formed union. In the future, then, there may be legal restrictions on their usage.[16]

Because of these disadvantages, some experts feel that the major value of quality circles is that they may serve as a transition step in changing over to the work team approach. This approach is described in greater detail next.

Work Team

Work team
The typical work team consists of between 3 and 30 employees, with one person assigned as the team leader; the team may have anywhere from some control to complete control over the project or problem.

The work team approach gained popularity in the United States during the mid-1980s and continues to be popular in the 1990s. A recent survey indicated that about 50 percent of Fortune 1,000 companies expect to make more use of teams in the near future.[17] As shown in Table 12.3, there are several different kinds of teams. For present purposes, however, we will focus on only one kind of team: the work team. The typical work team consists of from 3 to 30 employees, with one person assigned as the team leader. The team may have anywhere from some control over decisions that affect it to virtually complete control over decisions that affect it. A team with limited control over decisions may, for example, have the authority to make staff scheduling and assignment decisions. Any other decision (for example, hiring) must be made by the manager. At the other end of the spectrum, a self-managed or autonomous work team has control over such things as who gets hired, who gets promoted, and who gets terminated, as well as staff scheduling and assignments. The function of the team leader in a self-managed work team

Table 12.3: **Kinds of Teams**

Name	Definition
1. Problem-solving team	Group of knowledge workers gathered temporarily to solve a specific problem
2. Management team	Group of managers from variety of functions that coordinates work teams
3. Virtual team	Group of workers who are linked by computer
4. Work team	Group of workers who function on a permanent team to perform basic tasks

Source: Adapted from B. Dumaine, "The Trouble with Teams," *Fortune,* September 5, 1994, 86–92.

Box 12.2: So You Want to Be a Team Leader?

Now that you have read about work teams and found that many companies are either considering their use or actually using them, you may be thinking that you would like to be a team leader. To begin with, you should realize that the tasks of a team leader in a self-managed work team are considerably different from the tasks performed by the traditional supervisor. Therefore, your motivations for being a team leader are likely to differ, as are the abilities and experiences that will be required. Let's look first at the motivations you think a traditional supervisor or manager might need to succeed. What would you guess? If you said things like the need to be in control, the need for prestige, the need for respect, and the need for power you are on the right track. Now, if you have been carefully reading, what might you guess are some of the motivations a team leader should have? If you said things like the need for helping others make decisions, the need for seeing people challenge themselves, and the need for helping others learn, you are correct. If you want to be a team leader, then, you should think more carefully about what motivates you and where your interests and strengths lie.

Now let's consider the tasks performed by a typical team leader:

1. Coaching and training of team members.
2. Team building (such as facilitating team decision making and mediating conflicts within the team).
3. Serving as liaison with other teams, departments, and units.
4. Traditional supervisory activities (scheduling, disciplining, and so forth).

Typically, the first three tasks take considerably more time than the fourth, since the team often has taken over many of the activities traditionally performed by the supervisor. The reverse is true for the traditional supervisor, who probably spends relatively less time on the first three tasks. Which mix of the above listed tasks would you like most?

Now that you know what the team leader does, what should you do if you are appointed a team leader for a newly formed team? Here are some suggestions:

1. Establish and Communicate Clear Objectives for the Team. Make sure you emphasize the urgency and importance of these objectives. Remember, if your organization has recently implemented teams, employees will have many questions and concerns about what it is they should be doing now.

2. Carefully Plan and Guide Initial Meetings and Activities of the Team. Decisions, events, and behaviors early on in the life of the team often set the tone and determine the suc-

(continued on following page)

Source: Adopted from J. Katzenbach and D. Smith, *The Wisdom of Teams* (Boston: Harvard Business School Press, 1993); and R. Wellins, W. Byham, and J. Wilson, *Empowered Teams* (San Francisco: Jossey-Bass, 1993).

differs significantly from that of the traditional supervisor (see Box 12.2 for further discussion of the differences).[18]

Advantages and Disadvantages of the Work Team

In terms of the advantages of the work team, companies have demonstrated phenomenal increases in productivity. Federal Express, for example, reported a 40 percent increase in productivity after adoption of work teams. Another potential advantage is the increased innovation that follows. Two work teams at Boeing, the giant aerospace company, for instance, discovered a blueprint plan conflict in where to place the passenger oxygen and fresh-air nozzles (both teams had placed their component in the same place). Within hours of the discovery, a solution had been worked out (a special clamp was designed to hold both). Without the teams, the problem may not have ever been discovered until production began.[19]

Box 12.2: So You Want to Be a Team Leader?

(continued from previous page)

cess or failure of the team. Early mistakes can cause irreparable damage. But be sure not to adopt the role of the traditional supervisor by dominating the meetings. Your goal as a team leader is to facilitate the decisions, not make the decisions.

3. Facilitate Early Development of Rules, Responsibilities, and Norms. Norms, or unwritten rules, develop quite quickly in any social context. It is important, therefore, that you as a team leader facilitate the establishment of those norms early on. One important norm, for example, concerns how conflict will be handled by the team. If you convey the message, either intentionally or unintentionally, that conflict is avoided, subsequent disagreements may be ignored, even when they need to be addressed by the team.

4. Encourage the Team to Interact a Great Deal. It is important for the team members to get to know one another quickly and to form team cohesiveness as early as possible. Having the team interact together at work, after work hours, and on the weekend is important.

5. Utilize Positive Reinforcement. It is critical for the team leader to establish a norm of frequent positive feedback, particularly in the beginning when the team is starting off. Remember, positive reinforcement is much more than just money; it includes verbal praise, written commendations, free movie tickets, and many other things. Be particularly willing to reward members who enhance group functioning. For example, the team member who helps coach another employee must be rewarded for this effort.

The following suggestions apply to the team leader of a more mature, established team:

1. Establish Yourself as a Source of Inspiration for the Team. You must encourage the team, as well as individuals, when there are problems and challenges. You must also motivate the team to work to its fullest capacity. Think of a cheerleader; that is a critical role as a team leader.

2. Effectively Represent the Team to Other Parties. A major component of the team leader's role will involve interactions with other teams, departments, and managers. You will serve as an important filter of information spreading from the team to other units, as well as a critical interface for information coming from other units to the team. The more effective you are in these roles, the more effective your team will be.

3. Develop Your Team Members. One of the most important roles played by the team leader is that of a coach. By providing opportunities for team members to learn new skills and participate in appropriate training programs and related activities, you will be seen as a more effective team leader.

While the work team can produce major boosts in productivity, it is not without its disadvantages. The primary disadvantage of this technique is that it takes a great deal of time and effort to implement properly. For example, a reopened Owens-Corning Fiberglas plant using autonomous work teams experienced many production problems early on. As a result, employees were required to work overtime, and their shifts were constantly changing. Another result was that employee training lagged far behind. [20] A second primary disadvantage is that work teams will not work in all situations. Can you think of any jobs like this? One example would be cross-country truck drivers. Work teams would probably not be helpful there because the job involves a solo effort. There are certainly jobs and situations in which the work team will simply take more time and effort than it is worth.[21]

We turn now to a work design approach that was popularized in the United States in the mid-1980s and that continues to have a major influence over organizations: total quality management.

Box 12.3 The Work Team Can Be Used in Small Businesses, Too

Tales from the Trenches

Because most of the attention has been on the work team as implemented in Fortune 500 companies, you may conclude that this work design approach will not be useful in small businesses. Indeed, some small business owners believe the work team increases red tape, or that it takes too much time and effort to implement. But, the work team also can be effective in a small business, as demonstrated by its success at Published Image, a newsletter publisher with only 26 employees.

Eric Gershman founded the business in 1988, for the purpose of printing mutual-fund publications. Although the company was doing more than a half-million dollars in sales by 1991, it was teetering on the brink of disaster. Customer complaints were extremely high (one-third of the clients were lost annually), quality was terrible, and one out of two employees quit each year. To save the company, Eric Gershman radically changed the work design. Prior to the change, Published Image was organized like most other printing companies, with separate departments for sales, production, and editing. Now, the company has four independent teams. Each team has a staff of salespeople, editors, and production personnel and is responsible for its own clients. Each team member is also cross-trained, so that anyone can do any job. This is particularly helpful for meeting deadlines, when everyone has to pitch in to do the same thing. For example, Shelley Danse, an account executive, also does proofreading and layout when needed. Another advantage of the cross-training is that employees have a better understanding of the big picture and take much greater responsibility for success of the organization. Customers have also responded positively. Peter Herlihy, vice president of mutual-fund marketing at Fleet Financial Group, noted that because all team members know what is going on, any employee can answer customer questions. Team members participate heavily in decision making. Among other things, they decide their work schedules and prepare budgets. To support the concept, bonuses are based on team success (the timeliness and accuracy of work). Depending on the team's score, members may earn as much as 15 percent above and beyond their salaries. The effect of the work team has been astounding. Revenues increased to $4 million by 1993, the loss of customers slowed to under 5 percent annually, and employee turnover virtually ceased. As Eric Gershman summarized the results, "my job is basically to eliminate my job." The work team, then, can be useful even in small businesses.

Source: Adapted from M. Selz, "Testing Self-Managed Teams, Entrepreneur Hopes to Lose Job," *The Wall Street Journal,* January 11, 1994, B1, B2.

Total Quality Management

Total quality management TQM emphasizes a business objective (quality) and articulates various policies, practices, and management philosophies to support that objective and to enhance product or service quality.

Total quality management, or TQM as it is popularly referred to, was introduced in the United States in the mid-1980s. Originally adopted by Japan in the 1950s, the establishment of the Malcolm Baldrige National Quality Award has solidified TQM's presence in the U.S. business world. In a nutshell, TQM emphasizes a business objective (quality), and it articulates various policies, practices, and management philosophies to support that objective. Because of the importance of TQM today, you will next learn in greater detail what TQM is, along with its common features and characteristics.

What Is TQM?

As suggested by the name, the goal of total quality management is to enhance product or service quality. In the quest for high quality, management's role is to design and implement systems that will facilitate quality enhancements. The role

Work teams are popular and widely used, as in this Honda automobile manufacturing plant. Each team member is responsible for his or her task as well as the overall quality of the product. In fact, Honda provides many formal training classes for its employees.

Photo Courtesy of Honda, Marysville, Ohio

of employees is to make decisions, build customer relationships, and improve quality in all processes. TQM, then, introduces a number of work design changes. Perhaps most importantly, however, TQM involves several significant changes in our assumptions about work. Some of the more interesting principles are discussed next.[22]

TQM Principles

Although there are several different approaches to TQM, we will focus on the principles developed by W. Edwards Deming. Some of the highlights of Deming's philosophy are presented in Table 12.4.[23]

As you look at Table 12.4, the first four principles should fit well with material that you have read in this or in other chapters. Certainly, an emphasis on

Table 12.4: **Selected Highlights of Deming's TQM Principles**

1. Constantly improve production and service systems by increasing quality and productivity, thereby reducing costs.
2. The purpose of supervision is to help people and technology to work better.
3. Eliminate departmental barriers, and emphasize teams representing different areas.
4. Implement ongoing training and education programs.
5. Increase consistency in production.
6. The majority of quality and productivity problems lie with the technology, not the employees.
7. Eliminate work standards, quotas, and quantitative objectives in the production and service areas. Eliminate performance ratings.

Source: Based on R. Schuler and D. Harris, "Deming Quality Improvement: Implications for Human Resource Management as Illustrated in a Small Company," *Human Resource Planning* 14 (1991), 191–207.

teams, as suggested in the third principle, would be consistent with concepts described earlier. The last three principles listed in Table 12.4, however, may seem rather puzzling. In fact, the seventh principle, the elimination of quotas and quantitative objectives, may appear completely contrary to what you have read elsewhere in this book.[24]

To understand the fifth principle in Table 12.4 (increase consistency in production), consider the following example. Suppose you were trying to buy a car and were considering the Sphinx, manufactured by Giza Motor. After reading *Consumer Reports* and other magazines, you identify a concern with the quality of the car. The concern is that the quality of the Sphinx varies considerably; some of these cars have very shoddy quality, others have outstanding quality. Would you be willing to buy a Sphinx? You would probably say no, primarily because you would be worried about getting a lemon. Deming's TQM approach would be to eliminate the variation as much as possible. In the end, the Sphinx may have just average quality (though the company would continue to try to improve quality), but at least you as a customer would know what to expect. This is one reason Deming's principles emphasize the need for consistency in production.

The sixth principle may also seem somewhat surprising in that it shifts blame for work-related problems from the workers to the machinery and equipment. This principle stems from Deming's experience in the manufacturing arena, where he found that many problems were due to the machinery or equipment, not the employees. Whether, in fact, equipment is the most common source of productivity problems is still questionable.

What do you think accounts for the seventh principle in Table 12.4, namely, that companies should avoid use of objective quotas and individual performance ratings? According to Deming, it is most important that companies achieve consistency in production and service. Using individually based performance ratings encourages less consistency. Perhaps even more importantly, though, Deming argues that it is technological differences, not human differences, that account for differential performance by different employees. Using a performance evaluation system that assumes some employees are more productive than others is therefore inappropriate, according to Deming. Further, emphasis on individual performance may hamper quality improvement efforts.

Continuous improvement
Emphasizes ongoing efforts to improve productivity and quality.

One of the most important TQM practices is continuous improvement, which emphasizes ongoing efforts to improve productivity and quality. Only by stressing the continuous nature of quality improvement will organizations be able to make major improvements. Box 12.4 provides an actual example of how Deming's principles facilitated quality improvement efforts in one organization.

Advantages and Disadvantages of TQM

In terms of basic advantages of TQM, a focus on quality is certainly important in many organizations. TQM can be credited with helping U.S. manufacturers greatly improve quality, an area that had previously been quite problematic. Thus, for a company concerned about quality, a TQM program may be quite helpful. TQM is particularly appropriate when the company is basically sound but wishes to introduce change, albeit in a gradual way.[25]

With regard to disadvantages, TQM certainly does not guarantee organizational success. As an example, The Wallace Company won the 1990 Malcolm

Box 12.4: **The TQM Experience at Ensoniq**

Ensoniq, a relatively small company that manufactures professional-quality electronic musical instruments, implemented TQM practices several years ago. Although the company was slightly profitable with revenues of $25 million, the business was under pressure from international competition to improve quality. Top management felt, therefore, that implementation of TQM was vital for the continued success of the business. After attending a seminar on TQM, touring a Harley-Davidson plant using TQM, and reading several books, the president of Ensoniq began the process of implementing TQM. One goal of the program was to improve production consistency. For example, the soldering machine is a critical piece of equipment in this industry. For years, the company had been unable to get the machine to function at an acceptable error rate (the machine was creating an error rate between 1,500 to 3,500 errors per million parts). Using TQM techniques, the company conducted a series of experimental adjustments to the machine, and by tracking their effects on error rate, Ensoniq was able to vastly improve the quality. Design engineers participated in the next wave of experiments, thereby further improving the error rate. It should be pointed out that if the workers had been paid on an individual incentive system, they may have been reluctant to spend time improving the error rate of the machine, as this would have taken time away from their opportunity to earn more money. (Do you see, then, why the seventh principle in Table 12.4 makes sense?) In terms of human resource practices, Ensoniq made numerous changes. For example, the company eliminated pay for performance of any kind and instituted pay for hourly employees based on seniority, job grade, and the labor market. There are few grades, and most employees reach the top grade of the grade system quite quickly. In accord with the fourth principle in Table 12.4, Ensoniq implemented extensive training programs. Employees average well over 100 hours of training annually, compared with less than 30 hours that production workers at other companies receive. The results of the TQM program appear to be paying off. Since implementation, product returns have dropped by more than 50 percent, market share has increased, and productivity has improved more than 30 percent. Turnover has also decreased, as have the number of employee complaints.

Source: Adapted from R. Schuler and D. Harris, "Deming Quality Improvement: Implications for Human Resource Management as Illustrated in a Small Company," *Human Resource Planning* 14 (1991), 191–207.

Baldrige National Quality Award on the basis of its TQM program. In early 1992, this same company filed for bankruptcy under Chapter 11.[26] A TQM program often results in the creation of many committees, programs, and policies with unknown goals and purposes.[27] Florida Power & Light found that the application of TQM principles stifled innovation and created a new bureaucracy. One quality improvement team went through an entire seven-step process to determine where to relocate a water cooler![28]

Despite the potential gains from a TQM program, some experts have felt that a more radical approach to work redesign is sometimes needed. As you will see next, reengineering is a work design program that might incorporate many of the possibilities that have been mentioned in this chapter so far, while fundamentally redesigning the entire organization.

Reengineering

Reengineering is the work design approach of the 1990s. The basic principles of this approach were first described in a book entitled *Reengineering the Corporation: A Manifesto for Business Revolution,* published in 1993 by Michael Hammer and James Champy.[29] Unlike most of the other work design approaches described here, reengineering offers little in the way of specific guidelines as to how to design work. Rather, reengineering is defined as a radical redesign of business processes, procedures, and structures.[30] The best way to understand reeingineering, then, is to imagine someone said to you, "If you could be anything or any person in the world what or who would you want to be? Write a description on this piece of paper." By the same token, reeningeering involves the company asking itself, "If we could start all over again, how would the company's business processes look?" (Business processes refer to the activities that support valued customer outcomes, such as order fulfillment.) Once this vision is determined, the company begins to redesign itself. In some reengineering programs, organizations have involved customers throughout all stages.

Functional arrangement The traditional arrangement of organizational structure that is organized by departments and work is organized by task and job similarity.

Process arrangement The arrangement of an organization that is organized by activities that provide value to the customer.

Although not required, many reengineering efforts involve changing the organizational structure from a functional arrangement to a process arrangement. The difference between the two types of work arrangements is illustrated in Figure 12.2. As shown in Figure 12.2, the functional, or traditional, arrangement is structured along departments such as finance and marketing. Work is organized by task and job similarity. The process arrangement, on the other hand, is organized by activities that provide value to the customer. As shown in Figure 12.2, order fulfillment is one business process, which includes receiving, processing, and shipping of customer orders. Under the functional arrangement, separate departments would be created for receiving, processing, and shipping orders.[31]

Because reengineering does not contain any specific guidelines that must be followed, a variety of changes may be implemented as part of this program. In many cases, work teams will be introduced and the number of supervisors reduced. TQM practices may be adopted. Reengineering is considered particularly appropriate for large, established organizations that are facing strong competition.[32]

Figure 12.2 **Functional versus Process Arrangement**

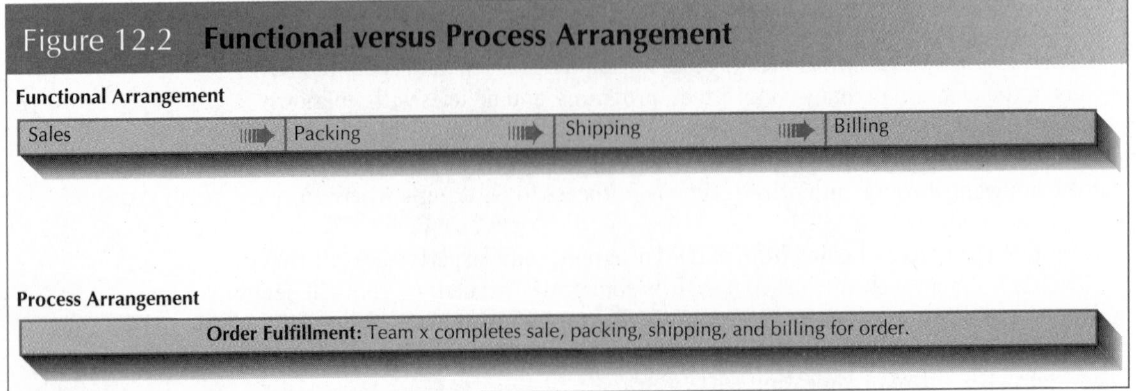

In short, as shown in Table 12.2, of all the work design programs, reengineering has the greatest amount of overall impact on the organization. As such, reengineering has the possibility of creating much improvement in the organization.

Common Pitfalls in Reengineering

Not all reengineering efforts are successful. Organizations can fall into a number of common pitfalls:[33]

1. Adjusting, Rather than Changing. IBM Credit Corporation is one of the most widely known examples of an organization that underwent reengineering. When it first began this endeavor, however, IBM Credit attempted to change its credit processing operation merely by automating. Because no other changes were made in the system, however, significant improvements did not materialize. Only when the entire credit processing operation was completely overhauled did productivity dramatically improve (for example, credit processing was reduced from one week to four hours without an increase in the number of employees).

2. Trying to Reengineer without Violating Norms. In the process of making radical change by restructuring organizations through reengineering, employees are likely to get offended, "sacred cows" are likely to get trampled on, and some employees' jobs may change or even be eliminated. All of these changes are likely to occur, and they are necessary to the successful reengineering of the organization. In many cases, failure to incorporate such changes has doomed the entire effort.

3. Failing to Devote Sufficient Time, Energy, and Resources. Reengineering is a very time-consuming and expensive procedure. Consider, for example, the experience of AT&T Global Business Communication Systems. This organization, which has annual sales of more than $3 billion, spent two years in the reengineering process. As part of that effort, hundreds of job descriptions were rewrittten, new reward systems were developed, the computer system was modified, and changes were made in all areas of the company, including manufacturing, shipping, and billing. Most companies use consultants to help with the reengineering as well, which can result in charges of as much as $250,000 each month. It is recommended that between 20 percent to 50 percent of the CEO's time be devoted to the reengineering process. Given this, most experts suggest that reengineering not even be attempted unless the organization is willing to put forth all of the necessary effort and resources that must be go into reengineering.

4. Ignoring the Need for Acceptance by Those Affected. While reengineering is likely to offend some employees, there must be a critical mass of employees who understand, accept, and support the resulting changes. For example, in redesigning its accounts payable department, Ford Motor Company had to modify the attitudes and behavior of the employees involved in this operation. Previously, these employees maintained an adversarial relationship with the vendors; under the new structure, employees had to demonstrate a cooperative relationship with the vendors. In a similar vein, many of the assumptions and

procedures for reengineering may run counter to company practices and procedures. For example, an organization that values consensus may have difficulty accepting changes some employees oppose.

Advantages and Disadvantages of Reengineering

Although it is a relatively new work design approach, reengineering appears to have several advantages and disadvantages. In terms of its effectiveness, reengineering is a very powerful weapon, capable of vastly improving the organization. By the same token, however, reengineering can cause a great deal of upheaval and strife. Even the proponents of reengineering estimate that the technique fails to achieve expected goals in at least 50 percent of cases.[34] In some instances, an organization may proceed with a reengineering process because it is the latest trend and not because the changes will be useful. For example, Greyhound Bus recently implemented an automatic reservation system, even though it had serious problems yet to be ironed out. One reason for its implementation, despite the many problems that existed, was the fact that it was part of a reengineering program.[35]

If reengineering is effective, a major advantage is that it will have a widespread impact. Unlike other organizational change efforts that often neglect to consider the implications for other aspects of the organization, reengineering emphasizes the need to modify the entire unit or organization. In turn, this may reduce subsequent problems that result from failure to consider the ramifications of any change program.

At the same time, as suggested earlier, reengineering so far has not produced specific steps or procedures. It may be that some approaches to reengineering are much more successful than others. Until a more systematic treatment of the technique is provided, little will be known as to the best way to go about (and the problems to avoid in) a reengineering effort. Finally, reengineering may simply be a fad, and like Hoola hoops and mood rings, it may soon disappear from the scene.

In sum, there are many different approaches to work design. Some are likely to have a greater impact on organizations than others. Next, you will read about the role of the human resource function in a work redesign program, followed by a discussion of some issues organizations must consider before undertaking a work redesign program.

The Role of the Human Resource Function in Work Redesign Programs

The human resource function plays a critical role in any work redesign program. The specific areas include the following:[36]

1. Helping Choose and Train Members of the Task Force. In many companies, the human resources department helps determine *how* members are chosen for the task force that will lead the work redesign. In some cases, the human resources department is also instrumental in deciding *which* employees are appointed. Depending on the specific program, the task forces members may need training to perform their roles successfully. Reengineering programs often require that members go through extensive training programs, which may

take as long as six weeks. Although outside trainers may conduct much of the training, human resource staff should be able to do some as well.

2. Revise Job Descriptions. Many of the work design programs described here dramatically change the nature of jobs, necessitating revision of the job descriptions. In some cases, such as reengineering, where the organization's structure may radically change, the nature of the job descriptions themselves may change. Because the nature of the work has been completely reconsidered, the format and orientation of the job descriptions may need to be completely changed.
3. Modify Reward Systems. Because work redesign programs often change the way in which people work, as well as their work objectives, modifications are often required in the reward systems. As one example, TQM shifts the focus from quantity to customer satisfaction. Pay-for-performance plans must change accordingly. In the work team approach, pay-for-performance plans must change to reward team, as compared with individual, performance. Failure to make such changes may have a negative effect on the success of the work redesign program.
4. Implement and Conduct Training. Virtually every work redesign program requires that employees learn some new skills or approaches to work. In some cases, job training will be extensive. One company provided the equivalent of 20 full days of training to leaders of the newly formed teams. A major purpose of this training was to change the employees' emphasis on meeting some internal standard to satisfying the customer. In some cases, then, the training is less focused on specific skills and more focused on work orientation.
5. Help Facilitate Change Resulting from the Program. Changing the organization in order to implement the new program may be quite difficult. It is here, however, that human resources play the greatest role. In order to facilitate the change resulting from reengineering, one organization held a Friday good-bye party for the work design that was to be replaced. Employees talked about the "good old days," photos were displayed, and a farewell speech was given by one of the presidents. A symbolic wall representing the old work system was even destroyed. On Monday, when employees returned to work, a wall symbolic of the new organization had been created. In terms of more mundane activities, human resources can a play a critical role in communicating about the changes through newsletters, videotapes, and group meetings.

Is Work Redesign the Answer?

Now that you have read about various work design programs and the role played by the human resource function in a redesign effort, you may be wondering whether work redesign can solve all of your organization's problems. The answer is, of course, that work redesign is not always the solution to problems within your organization. Before you recommend such a program, consider the following points.[37]

1. Is There Sufficient Reason to Believe that the Work Design Program Will Accomplish Its Objectives? A top executive or manager may sometimes suggest

implementation of a work redesign program simply because he or she attended a seminar or read an article, without consideration of the appropriateness of this change. This is particularly problematic with a fad, as many companies feel compelled to keep up with the "corporate Joneses." Obviously, this is not a good reason for implementing a work design program. Existing problems may be better solved through other means, such as fixing faulty equipment, improving supervision, or providing increased technical training. If the actual sources of problems lie in some of these areas, work design programs may merely create more problems than solutions.

2. Will Employees Be Able to Adapt? Even if a work design program appears appropriate, the organization must consider employees' readiness for change. Employees may not be ready for change for several reasons. First, employees may not have the skills and abilities necessary to perform the new tasks. To deal with this issue, the organization must provide extensive training for employees. But not all employees will be able to learn the new skills. One organization, for example, found that 5 percent of the employees could not perform the newly designed jobs, even with the appropriate training. The organization must decide what to do with those employees.

   Not all employees desire work involving greater autonomy and control that characterizes many of the work redesign programs. Some employees actually prefer simple, routine work, and they will be unhappy having to make many of the decisions traditionally made by the supervisor. You will need to consider, then, whether the employees will be less satisfied and motivated in their newly designed jobs.

   Finally, it is important to consider whether middle-level managers and supervisors can adapt to the new system. In many cases, it is these employees who are most resistant to change, because in many cases they will lose their authority and control, if not their jobs. Many supervisors and managers have trouble adjusting to the new and quite different tasks and responsibilities that come with the work team, TQM, and reengineering.

3. Are Organizational Practices, Policies, and Culture Compatible with the Program? Even if employees have the requisite skills and interest, organizational practices, policies, and culture may create barriers to work redesign. Existing technology may hamper or even preclude programs such as the work team. Consider, for example, an automobile assembly line, where units move down the assembly line at a preestablished pace. It may not be possible to introduce the work team design without costly changes to existing technology. A Volvo automobile assembly plant in Sweden, reported that implementation of an assembly line designed for job enrichment resulted in a 10 percent higher cost than an assembly line designed for the classical approach. And, recently, several such Volvo plants were closed owing to their low productivity. Human resource practices may also impede work redesign programs. For example, job enrichment may necessitate higher salaries, which in turn may increase labor costs. Particularly in a union environment, where such things as job descriptions are determined through contract negotiation, any work redesign program may create conflict and tension. Finally, various organizational control systems may be dramatically affected by work redesign. Consider, for example, the accounting system that existed in the purchasing department of one large

organization. In order to maintain close financial controls, employees were greatly limited in their interactions with vendors. The purpose of these regulations was to reduce opportunities for theft and other dishonest behavior. Introduction of work redesign programs may have interfered with these controls. In short, it is important to think carefully before recommending a work redesign program. Although these techniques can improve productivity as well as employee satisfaction and morale, there is no guarantee they will work.

Conclusion

We have discussed many different work design systems, ranging from the classical approach to the reengineering approach. As you read, there is no one best approach to work design. Each of the approaches has both advantages and disadvantages. Some of the approaches involve few changes in existing norms, technology, and human resource practices, while other approaches require significant modifications in these areas. Before an organization embarks on a redesign program, it must consider whether this is the most appropriate improvement technique, whether employees can adapt, and whether the organizational practices, policies, and culture are compatible with the intended work redesign. If the answer is no to any of these issues, caution is recommended. Finally, while some of these work redesign programs may be fads, they have left their mark on workplace practices for many years to come.

Applying Core Concepts

1. Think of a job you have had, or ask a friend to describe a job he or she has had. What type of work design did this job have?
2. Review the job and organization described in the opening case. How appropriate would each of the following work redesign approaches have been: job enlargement, job enrichment, quality circles, team concept, total quality management, and reengineering? If you were the manager in charge, which work redesign program would you have chosen? Why?
3. Describe some of the responsibilities and tasks for the human resource function in the opening case if Myra's Mystery decides to implement a total quality management program.
4. Do you think a work redesign approach would have solved the problems described in the opening case? Why or why not?
5. How do you think a work team approach would affect your job if you were Fiona's supervisor at Myra's Mystery? What would you do as the supervisor to adjust to these changes?

Key Terms

- Scientific management
- Employee empowerment
- Job enlargement
- Job enrichment
- Quality circle
- Work team
- Total quality management (TQM)
- Continuous improvement
- Functional arrangement
- Process arrangement

Chapter 12: Experiential Exercise

G.G. Games (GGG) is a toy manufacturer that has been in business for ninety-five years. It is known for high quality, innovative board games that are sold primarily for age groups ten years and up, including adults. Some of the more popular games produced by GGG (of which you may not be familiar), include King Tut's Tomb, Squeeze Play, and Shuckle-Mania. GGG is composed of the traditional functional areas, including marketing, sales, manufacturing, human resources, and accounting, as well as product development. The issue that you are addressing is the product development group, which is responsible for design of new games. Product development is critical for GGG because consumers are always seeking new games to purchase. In fact, new products create almost one-fourth of GGG's sales in any given year.

The product development group at GGG has traditionally been quite different from the other areas in many ways. The product development group is composed of twenty-five employees, including a vice president, two managers, two administrative assistants, and twenty "creative types" (included in the creative types are four design artists). Unlike other professional employees, who typically come to work in business attire, the product development employees make a point of only working in casual clothing (typically, jeans and a T-shirt). Second, the product development group works with a minimal amount of interaction with other employees. In fact, their office is located quite some distance from the two GGG factories and the corporate office. Third, this group works in almost complete secrecy; only the CEO and President of GGG are allowed to attend its meetings. As a result of the secrecy, the product development group has been nicknamed the PIA (product development intelligence agency), after the CIA. Fourth, the product development group members never attend company functions, including the annual picnic. Fifth, the product development group makes a point of ignoring any feedback or suggestions from other employees. In fact, this has recently led to problems with quality, because the design of one of the games was so intricate, that production made the pieces with numerous errors. As a result, most employees avoid the product development employees, and consider them to be arrogant snobs. The President and CEO, however, have a strong background in product development and view this group as extremely important to the success of GGG. Of course, the product development employees recognize this special relationship and work hard to maintain the good-will of the President and CEO.

The product development group operates in the following way. Group members are responsible for different types of games (for example, educational, specialized, adult). Using a variety of sources, members continuously research and investigate new ideas. Once a month, the entire group meets to discuss new ideas. Decisions are made about the most promising ideas, and small committees are formed to develop the ideas further. The committees' ideas are then reviewed, and further decisions are made. Ultimately, the project group develops a lengthy proposal, including sample pieces, which is approved by the vice president of product development. This vice president must then present the ideas to the CEO and other top executives of the company, who must ultimately approve a project. From there, the project is taken to marketing and production, who offer new suggestions, and sometimes require major modifications that consume considerable time. Before production, the CEO must make final approval.

Last week, the President of GGG suggested that changes must be made in how the product development group operates. One of the reasons for this change, she noted, is that other companies are significantly decreasing the lag time between design and production. GGG's lag time apparently is one of the longest in the business now. A second problem is that recent new products have created problems at the production stage. This in turn has led to further delays and in some cases, defective products.

You should take the role of the vice president of human resources, and discuss how you will restructure the product development group to address the two problems mentioned above. Be sure to indicate what problems your proposal may encounter and how you will address those problems. Be sure to incorporate issues and solutions from this chapter as well as other chapters in this book (for example, pay for performance, performance management).

Chapter 12 References

1. R. Griffin, *Task Design: An Integrative Approach* (Glenview, IL: Scott, Foresman, 1982).
2. M. Williams, "Back to the Past," *The Wall Street Journal,* October 24, 1994, A1, A4.
3. Griffin, *Task Design.*
4. M. Campion and C. McClelland, "Follow-up and Extension of the Interdisciplinary Costs and Benefits of Enlarged Jobs," *Journal of Applied Psychology,* 78 (1993), 339–51.
5. Griffin, *Task Design.*
6. J. Campbell and R. Pritchard, "Motivation Theory in Industrial and Organizational Psychology," in *Handbook of Industrial and Organizational Psychology,* ed. M. Dunnette (Chicago: Rand McNally, 1976).
7. Griffin, *Task Design.*
8. J.R. Hackman and G.R. Oldham, *Work Redesign* (Reading, MA: Addison-Wesley, 1980).
9. R. Guzzo, R. Jette, and R. Katzell. "Effects of Psychologically Based Intervention Programs on Worker Productivity: A Meta-analysis," *Personnel Psychology,* 38 (1985), 275–91.
10. D. Katz and R. Kahn, *The Social Psychology of Organizations* (New York: Wiley, 1978).
11. W. Mohr and H. Mohr, *Quality Circles* (Reading, MA: Addison-Wesley, 1983).
12. B. Dumaine, "The Trouble with Teams," *Fortune,* September 5, 1994, 86–92.
13. Ibid.
14. R. Guzzo and G. Shea, "Group Performance and Intergroup Relations in Organizations," in *Handbook of Industrial and Organizational Psychology,* vol. 3, ed. M. Dunnette and L. Hough (Palo Alto, CA: Consulting Psychologists Press, 1992).
15. R. Griffin, "Consequences of Quality Circles in an Industrial Setting: A Longitudinal Assessment," *Academy of Management Journal* 31 (1988), 338–58.
16. J. Case, "When Teamwork Is Un-American," *Inc.* November 1993, 29–30.
17. Dumaine, "The Trouble with Teams."
18. B. Dumaine, "Who Needs a Boss?" *Fortune,* May 7, 1990, 52–60.
19. Dumaine, "The Trouble with Teams."
20. F. Bleakley, "How an Outdated Plant Was Made New." *The Wall Street Journal,* October 21, 1994, B1, B11.
21. Dumaine, "The Trouble with Teams."
22. B. Spencer, "Models of Organization and Total Quality Management: A Comparison and Critical Evaluation," *Academy of Management Review* 19 (1994), 446–71; and H. Costin, *Management Development and Training: A TQM Approach* (Fort Worth, TX: The Dryden Press, 1996).
23. R. Schuler and D. Harris, "Deming Quality Improvement: Implications for Human Resource Management as Illustrated in a Small Company," *Human Resource Planning* 14 (1991), 191–207.
24. G. Dobbins, R. Cardy, and K. Carson, "Examining Fundamental Assumptions: A Contrast of Person and System Approaches to Human Resource Management," in *Research in Personnel/Human Resource Management,* ed. G. Ferris and K. Rowland (Greenwich, CT: JAI Press, 1991).
25. R. Krishnan, A. Shani, R. Grant, and R. Baer, "In Search of Quality Improvement: Problems of Design and Implementation," *Academy of Management Executive* 7 (1993), 7–20.
26. R. Hill, "When the Going Gets Rough: A Baldrige Award Winner on the Line," *Academy of Management Executive* 7 (1993), 75–79.

27. R. Chang, "TQM Goes Nowhere," *Training & Development* 47 (1993), 22–29; and J. Dean and D. Bowen, "Management Theory and Total Quality: Improving Research and Practice through Theory Development," *Academy of Management Review* 19 (1994), 392–418.
28. W. Lee, "Deming's Not for Us," *The Wall Street Journal,* January 31, 1994, A12.
29. "The Promise of Reengineering," *Fortune,* May 3, 1994, 94–97.
30. S. Greengard, "Reengineering: Out of the Rubble," *Personnel Journal,* 72 (1993), 48A–48O.
31. M. Hammer and J. Champy, *Reengineering the Corporation: A Manifesto for Business Revolution* (New York: HarperCollins, 1993).
32. T. Steward, "Reengineering: The Hot New Managing Tool," *Fortune,* August 23, 1994, 41–48.
33. Hammer and Champy, *Reengineering the Corporation.*
34. Ibid.
35. R. Tomsho "How Greyhound Lines Re-Engineered Itself Right Into a Deep Hole," *The Wall Street Journal,* October 20, A1, A6.
36. Greengard, "Reengineering: Out of the Rubble."
37. J.D. Osburn, L. Morgan, and E. Musselwhite, with C. Perrin, *Self-Directed Work Teams: The New American Challenge* (Homewood, IL: Irwin, 1990); and Hackman and Oldham, *Work Redesign.*

Safety and Health

chapter 13

Core Concepts

After reading this chapter, you should be capable of

1. Understanding the Occupational Safety and Health Act and what it covers.
2. Explaining the four approaches companies have used to reduce workplace accidents.
3. Discussing current safety and health issues in the workplace.
4. Offering suggestions as to how organizations can improve safety and health in the workplace.

Opening Case

Poultry plants constitute one of the fastest growing industries in the United States today, employing more than 200,000 workers nationwide. In some small towns, the poultry plant is one of the few employers offering full-time jobs that pay above minimum wage. Although they offer many job opportunities, critics feel that poultry plants take advantage of workers and contain dangerous, demeaning work. The typical poultry plant hires workers to perform a variety of tasks, ranging from preparing the birds for slaughter to removing the feathers to packing the processed parts into cardboard containers for shipment. All of these tasks have their own unique dangers and difficulties. For example, after the birds are slaughtered and plucked, mostly by machines, workers must remove the poultry's limbs and organs. In many plants, however, the workers are closely grouped together and work with sharp knives and tools. The opportunity for accidental cuts is always present. Packing the poultry presents different problems for workers. At one plant, workers must lift at least 12 five-pound boxes per minute and place them into a larger container. This means that each worker must lift 3,600 pounds per hour each workday. Other conditions in a typical poultry plant that all workers face include cold temperatures throughout most of the plant, slippery floors, poor sanitary conditions, and extremely fast-paced work. Critics also charge that workers have little or no freedom in most poultry plants. A commonly cited problem is that workers are required to ask supervisors for permission to use the restroom. Without permission, a worker who leaves to use the bathroom can be terminated. Industry spokespeople defend the conditions by acknowledging that the work is dirty and demanding. In light of the nature of the job, they maintain that they are doing everything they can do to ensure safety and health standards. Most of the workers who are employed at these plants have little formal education, and the plants have very high turnover rates. A growing number of poultry plant workers are illegal immigrants and worry about being caught.[1]

Do you wonder whether there are laws protecting workers from safety hazards such as those that seem to exist in poultry plants? Might there be things companies can do to decrease the number of accidents?

This chapter addresses safety and health issues as they may affect workers' physical and mental well-being in the workplace. As you will learn, companies are legally required to protect workers from many safety and health hazards in the workplace. Some companies have gone beyond legal requirements and provide additional programs and practices to improve employee safety and health on the job. These, and related issues, are addressed in this chapter. First, you will read about the laws that govern safety and health in the workplace, followed by a discussion of organizational programs for reducing workplace accidents. The third section of this chapter addresses current issues in workplace safety and health, including violence, lower back pain ailments, drug and alcohol use, psychological stress, and indoor pollution.

The Law and Workplace Safety and Health

Occupational Safety and Health Act of 1970: An Introduction

Occupational Safety and Health Act of 1970 Passed by Congress in 1970, the purpose of this law was to reduce the high rate of workplace

Congress passed the Occupational Safety and Health (OSH) Act of 1970 after a great deal of deliberation and discussion. The basic purpose of this law was to reduce the high rate of workplace accidents, injuries, and deaths in the United States. At the time the OSH Act was passed, it was estimated that more than 2 million workers became disabled from workplace accidents in the United States annually, and almost 15,000 U.S. employees died from work-related accidents each year. In addition, it was estimated that workplace accidents and safety hazards resulted in billions of dollars lost in medical costs, time off from work, and related expenses.[2]

accidents, injuries, and deaths in the United States.f

While the OSH Act is quite complex, it contains four basic provisions:

1. The duty to maintain a workplace that is safe and healthful for employees.
2. The duty to comply with specific standards.
3. Record-keeping and reporting obligations.
4. A mandate for various regulatory agencies.

Each of these provisions, along with their implications for you as an employee, is discussed next.

Maintaining a Safe and Healthful Workplace: Your Employer's Basic Obligation

The OSH Act basically requires your employer to do the following.[3]

1. Comply with basic safety regulations.
2. Eliminate hazards to safety and health.

The OSH Act covers most private-sector businesses in the United States, including all 50 states as well as the District of Columbia, Puerto Rico, and U.S. territories. Unlike many of the employment discrimination laws that you read about in other chapters, this act is not affected by the size of the company. Even a company with two employees is covered by the OSH Act.[4] The only organizations excluded from OSH Act coverage are as follows:[5]

1. Self-employed workers.
2. Farms that employ only immediate members of the farmer's family.
3. Businesses which are covered by other federal agencies' health and safety rules.
4. Federal, state, and local government employees.

Clearly, then, nearly all private-sector employees are covered by the OSH Act. Government employees are not covered.

Several entities were created to administer and oversee the OSH Act. The Occupational Safety and Health Administration (or, as it is typically referred to, **OSHA**) is the major agency (actually it is a branch of the U.S. Department of Labor). OSHA has four major responsibilities:[6]

1. Establishing safety standards.
2. Permitting variances, or exceptions, to those standards.
3. Inspecting workplaces.
4. Issuing citations, indicating a violation of OSH Act regulations.

Two other relevant entities are the Occupational Safety and Health Review Commission (OSHRC) and the National Institute for Occupational Safety and Health (NIOSH). The purpose of the OSHRC is to review appeals from companies that have been issued a citation by OSH. NIOSH provides research and training support for OSHA. The research performed by NIOSH focuses on developing new safety and health standards; the training is for OSHA inspectors and other staff involved with OSH Act enforcement.

Occupational Safety and Health Administration (OSHA)
The major agency created to administer and oversee the OSH Act, including establishing safety standards, permitting variances (or exceptions) to those standards, conducting inspections of workplaces, and issuing citations to indicate a violation of OSH Act regulations.

Occupational Safety and Health Review Commission
The purpose of the OSHRC is to review appeals from companies that have been issued a citation by OSHA.

National Institute for Occupational Safety and Health
NIOSH provides research and training support for OSHA. The research focuses on developing new safety and health standards; the training is for OSHA inspectors and other staff involved with OSH Act enforcement.

Depending on the nature of the business, your employer must follow either the guidelines that have been developed for the industry or the OSH Act's General Duty Clause, which requires compliance with basic standards and makes the employer responsible for providing a workplace that is free from recognized safety and health hazards.[7]

Complying with Specific Standards

General Duty Clause OSHA guidelines that require compliance with basic standards, as well as the responsibility of providing a workplace that is free from recognized safety and health hazards.

For some industries, and for many types of materials, standards for safe use have been developed. One industry for which there are specific standards is the construction industry. Many materials are also covered by standards for safe use issued by OSHA, including electrical systems, asbestos, lead, and blood-borne pathogens. Each of these standards is described in documents available from the Government Printing Office, located in Washington, D.C. These documents are lengthy and difficult to understand, yet knowing what these documents contain is critical for avoiding OSHA citations. Organizations such as the National Safety Council offer workshops in understanding these laws.[8]

Box 13.1 Workplace Facilities: Your Rights as an Employee

Your Turn

The OSH Act provides a number of basic laws with regard to a workplace facility. Failure to follow these regulations may be a violation of the OSH Act. The following is only a partial list of an employer's obligations. Does your current employer provide all of the features?

1. **Cleanliness.** The workplace must be kept clean and neat as permitted by the nature of the work (a poultry plant cannot be expected to be kept as clean as a clothing store). Restrooms and water fountains should be cleaned regularly. Does your company appear to meet this standard?
2. **Toilets.** The company must provide separate toilets for men and women, unless the toilet can be locked from inside and used only by one person at a time. There is a formula for the number of toilets that must be provided, which depends on the number of employees. Both hot and cold water must be available in the restroom. Does your current employer provide these things?
3. **Temperature.** Comfortable temperatures must be maintained in the facility, though the act does not define precisely what that temperature is. It is understood to be a temperature that would not adversely affect workers' health or safety. Recall in the opening case that poultry plants are generally cold environments; however, they appear to meet legal regulations in this regard.
4. **Noise.** There are certain noise levels that may not be exceeded. Employees must be provided with protective equipment and occasionally tested for hearing impairment when noise levels exceed 85 decibels for more than eight hours.
5. **First Aid.** At a minimum, first aid equipment must be available at the facility. Moreover, medical care must be available within a reasonable distance of the workplace, or there must be someone at the facility trained in first aid, or a doctor must be available when needed.
6. **Fire Equipment.** In addition to having an emergency fire prevention plan, the company must have an evacuation plan, an alarm system, and appropriate types of fire extinguishers.
7. **Food Service.** Food service areas must be hygienic; food must be unspoiled and properly prepared and stored.

These are just some of the general workplace regulations required under the OSH Act.

Source: Adapted from L. Joel, *Every Employee's Guide to the Law* (New York: Pantheon, 1993).

Recall the opening case involving a poultry plant. Do you think that OSHA has developed specific standards for this industry? If you answered no, you are right. Critics maintain that standards for the poultry industry should be developed. But poultry plants still have to obey rules specific to the equipment. For example, one plant was fined for having an exposed piece of equipment that caused serious injury to a worker's legs. Other plants have been fined for failure to provide proper fire safety, as well as other violations. Some critics maintain that poultry plants would be much safer if industry-specific standards were developed.[9]

A related regulation, the Hazard Communication Standard of 1985, covers all hazardous chemicals. As of 1987, companies covered by the OSH Act must meet the requirements of the Hazard Communication Standard. Specific details of this law are discussed in the next section.

Hazard Communication Standard of 1985
A regulation that covers all hazardous chemicals. As of 1987, companies covered by the OSH Act must meet the requirements of the Hazard Communication Standard.

Record-Keeping and Reporting Obligations

As with most laws, the OSH Act requires extensive record keeping and reporting. The basic record-keeping and reporting obligations are as follows:[10]

1. A listing of work-related injuries and illnesses (OSHA form No. 200).
2. Records of work-related injuries and illnesses (OSHA form No. 101).
3. Various right-to-know information.
4. Other items.

OSHA Form No. 200
This form must be used by most employers with more than ten workers. This form records information about workers who are injured or become ill as a result of the job and if the injury or illness resulted in death, days off from work, transfer, termination, medical treatment, unconsciousness, or work/motion restrictions.

OSHA Form No. 200. This form, which is shown in Figure 13.1, must be used by most employers with more than ten workers (certain industries, such as retailers, are not required to keep these forms). The company must complete this form by recording information about workers who are injured or become ill as a result of the job and if the injury or illness resulted in death, days off from work, transfer, termination, medical treatment, unconsciousness, or work/motion restrictions. This information must be summarized and posted by February 1 of each year. Employees, former employees, and OSHA officials must also be allowed access to the form.

OSHA Form No. 101. Employers who use Form No. 200 must also complete this form. This form requires detailed information about work-related injuries and illnesses, including the circumstances of the incident, a description of the injury or illness, and the name of the doctor and hospital that provided treatment.

OSHA Form No. 101
Employees who use Form No. 200 must also complete this form, which requires detailed information about work-related injuries and illnesses, including the circumstances of the incident, a description of the injury or illness, and the name of the doctor and hospital that provided treatment.

Various Right-to-Know Information. There are many other important laws and regulations that give you, the employee, the right to be notified of possible safety and health issues. One of the most important of these, the Hazard Communication Standard of 1985, requires companies to provide their employees with information concerning hazardous chemicals. The law requires companies to provide this information through several means:

- Material safety data sheets, which are developed by the manufacturers of the chemicals. These forms describe the properties of the chemicals, indicate the proper means of using them, and offer medical advice if workers are exposed to the chemicals;
- Employee training on how to interpret the material safety sheets, how to identify when the chemical is being improperly stored or exposed, and related safety measures.
- Proper labeling of the chemicals.

Figure 13.1 OSHA 200 Log

Bureau of Labor Statistics
Log and Summary of Occupational
Injuries and Illnesses

NOTE: This form is required by Public Law 91-596 and must be kept in the establishment for *5 years.* Failure to maintain and post can result in the issuance of citations and assessment of penalties. *(See posting requirements on the other side of form.)*

RECORDABLE CASES: You are required to record information about every occupational death; every nonfatal occupational illness; and those nonfatal occupational injuries which involve one or more of the following: loss of consciousness, restriction of work or motion, transfer to another job, or medical treatment (other than first aid). *(See definitions on the other side of form.)*

Case or File Number	Date of Injury or Onset of Illness	Employee's Name	Occupation	Department	Description of injury or illness
Enter a nondupli-cating number which will facilitate com-parisons with supple-mentary records.	Enter Mo./day.	Enter first name or initial, middle initial, last name.	Enter regular job title, not activity employee was per-forming when injured or at onset of illness. In the absence of a formal title, enter a brief description of the employee's duties.	Enter department in which the employee is regularly employed or a description of normal workplace to which employee is assigned, even though temporarily working in another depart-ment at the time of injury or illness.	Enter a brief description of the injury or illness and indicate the part or parts of body affected. Typical entries for this column might be Amputation of 1st joint right forefinger. Strain of lower back; Contact dermatitis on both hands. Electrocution—body
(A)	(B)	(C)	(D)	(E)	(F)
					PREVIOUS PAGE TOTALS →
					TOTALS (instructions on other side of form.) →

OSHA NO. 200

FOLD

Source: S. Kahn, B. Brown, and M. Lanzarone, *Legal Guide to Human Resources* (Boston: Warren, Gorham, and Lamont, 1995).

Figure 13.1 OSHA 200 Log *(continued)*

U.S. Department of Labor

For Calendar Year 19 ____ Page ___ of ___

Company Name

Establishment Name

Establishment Address

Form Approved
O.M.B. No. 1220-0029

Extent of and Outcome of INJURY						Type, Extent of, and Outcome of ILLNESS												
Fatalities	Nonfatal injuries					Type of Illness							Fatalities	Nonfatal Illnesses				
Injury Related	Injuries With Lost Workdays				Injuries Without Lost Workdays	CHECK Only One Column for Each Illness *(See other side of form for terminations or permanent transfer.)*							Illness Related	Illnesses With Lost Workdays				Illnesses Without Lost Workdays
Enter DATE of death Mo./day/yr.	Enter a CHECK if injury involves days away from work, or days of restricted work activity, or both.	Enter a CHECK if injury involves days away from work.	Enter number of DAYS *away from work.*	Enter number of DAYS of *restricted work activity.*	Enter a CHECK if no entry was made in columns 1 or 2 but the injury is recordable as defined above.	Occupational skin diseases or disorders	Dust diseases of the lungs	Respiratory conditions due to toxic agents	Poisoning (systemic effects of toxic materials)	Disorders due to physical agents	Disorders associated with repeated trauma	All other occupational illnesses	Enter DATE of death. Mo./day/yr.	Enter a CHECK if Illness involves days away from work, or days of restricted work activity, or both.	Enter a CHECK if Illness involves days away from work.	Enter number of DAYS *away from work.*	Enter number of DAYS of *restricted work activity.*	Enter a CHECK if no entry was made in columns 8 or 9.
						(7)												
(1)	(2)	(3)	(4)	(5)	(6)	(a)	(b)	(c)	(d)	(e)	(f)	(g)	(8)	(9)	(10)	(11)	(12)	(13)

Certification of Annual Summary Totals By ____________ Title ____________ Date ____________

FOLD

OSHA NO. 200

POST ONLY THIS PORTION OF THE LAST PAGE NO LATER THAN FEBRUARY 1.

This standard also requires that the employer develop a plan describing how these activities will be conducted.

In addition to the Hazard Communication Standard, your employer has other obligations to inform you of hazardous and toxic chemicals that are used or produced at the facility. For example, your employer must provide relevant information about health and safety hazards within a month after your employment starts or you are transferred to a different job that involves exposure to additional substances. Your employer must also provide such information if you request it in writing.

Despite all of these obligations, many companies neglect to provide information. Poultry plants, like those described in the opening case, for example, have been accused of providing workers with little more than a brief lecture on hazardous chemicals and the problems they might cause.

Other Items. Your employer also is obligated to post copies of any citations issued by OSHA, as well as a copy of the OSHA Job Poster illustrated in Figure 13.2.

Figure 13.2 OSHA Job Poster
Job Safety & Health Protection

The Occupational Safety and Health Act of 1970 provides job safety and health protection for workers by promoting safe and healthful working conditions throughout the Nation. Provisions of the Act include the following:

Employers

All employers must furnish to employees employment and a place of employment free from recognized hazards that are causing or are likely to cause death or serious harm to employees. Employers must comply with occupational safety and health standards issues under the Act.

Employees

Employees must comply with all occupational safety and health standards, rules, regulations and orders issued under the Act that apply to their own actions and conduct on the job.

The Occupational Safety and Health Administration (OSHA) of the U.S. Department of Labor has the primary responsibility for administering the Act. OSHA issues occupational safety and health standards, and its Compliance Safety and Health Officers conduct jobsite inspections to help ensure compliance with the Act.

Inspection

The Act requires that a representative of the employer and a representative authorized by the employees be given an opportunity to accompany the OSHA Inspector for the purpose of aiding the inspection.

Where there is no authorized employee representative, the OSHA Compliance Officer must consult with a reasonable number of employees concerning safety and health conditions in the workplace.

Complaint

Employees or their representatives have the right to file a complaint with the nearest OSHA office requesting an inspection if they believe unsafe or unhealthful conditions exist in their workplace. OSHA will withhold, on request, names of employees complaining.

The Act provides that employees may not be discharged or discriminated against in any way for filing safety and health complaints or for otherwise exercising their rights under the Act.

Employees who believe they have been discriminated against may file a complaint with their nearest OSHA office within 30 days of the alleged discriminatory action.

Citation

If upon inspection OSHA believes an employer has violated the Act, a citation alleging such violations will be issued to the employer. Each citation will specify a time period within which the alleged violation must be corrected.

The OSHA citation must be prominently displayed at or near the place of alleged violation for three days, or until it is corrected, whichever is later, to warn employees of dangers that may exist there.

Proposed Penalty

The Act provides for mandatory civil penalties against employers of up to $7,000 for each serious violation and for optional penalties of up to $7,000 for each nonserious violation. Penalties of up to $7,000 per day may be proposed for failure to correct violations within the proposed time period and for each day the violation continues beyond the prescribed abatement date. Also, any employer who willfully or repeatedly violates the Act may be assessed penalties of up to $70,000 for each such violation. A minimum penalty of $5,000 may be imposed for each willful violation. A violation of posting requirements can bring a penalty of up to $7,000.

There are also provisions for criminal penalties. Any willful violation resulting in the death of any employee, upon conviction, is punishable by a fine of up to $250,000 (or $500,000 if the employer is a corporation), or by imprisonment for up to six months, or both. A second conviction of an employer doubles the possible term of imprisonment. Falsifying records, reports, or applications is punishable by a fine of $10,000 or up to six months in jail or both.

Voluntary Activity

While providing penalties for violations, the Act also encourages efforts by labor and management, before an OSHA Inspection, to reduce workplace hazards voluntarily and to develop and improve safety and health programs in all workplaces and industries. OSHA's Voluntary Protection Programs recognize outstanding efforts of this nature.

OSHA has published Safety and Health Program Management Guidelines to assist employers in establishing or perfecting programs to prevent or control employee exposure to workplace hazards. There are many public and private organizations that can provide information and assistance in this effort, if requested. Also, your local OSHA office can provide considerable help and advice on solving safety and health problems or can refer you to other sources for help such as training.

Consultation

Free assistance in identifying and correcting hazards and in improving safety and health management is available to employers, without citation or penalty, through OSHA-supported programs

Figure 13.2 OSHA Job Poster *(continued)* Job Safety & Health Protection *(continued)*

in each State. These programs are usually administered by the State Labor or Health department or a State University.

Posting Instructions

Employers in States operating OSHA approved State Plans should obtain and post the State's equivalent poster.

More Information

Additional information and copies of the Act, specific OSHA safety and health standards, and other applicable regulations may be obtained from your employer or from the nearest OSHA Regional Office in the following locations:		
	Atlanta, GA	(404) 347-3573
	Boston, MA	(617) 565-7164
	Chicago, IL	(312) 353-2220
	Dallas, TX	(214) 767-4731
	Denver, CO	(303) 844-3061
	Kansas City, MO	(816) 426-5861
	New York, NY	(212) 337-2378
	Philadelphia, PA	(215) 596-1201
	San Francisco, CA	(415) 744-6670
	Seattle, WA	(206) 442-5930

Under Provisions of Title 29, Code of Federal Regulations, Part 1903.2(a)(1) employers must post this notice (or facsimile) in a conspicuous place where notices to employees are customarily posted.

Lynn Martin

Lynn Martin, Secretary of Labor

U.S. Department of Labor

Occupational Safety and Health Administration

Washington, DC
1991 (Reprinted)
OSHA 2203

Box 13.2: Are You More Likely to Get Hurt at a Small Company or a Big Company?

Obviously, a production factory is going to have more accidents than a securities firm. But what about small companies compared to large companies? Does the company's size affect the number of accidents that occur? The answer appears to be yes. Smaller companies appear to have a much higher accident rate than bigger companies. From 1988 to 1992, more than 4,000 workers died at companies with fewer than 20 employees. During the same period of time, only 127 employees died at companies with more than 2,500 workers. Taking into account the differential size of the workforce, there were 1.97 deaths per thousand workers at small companies and .004 deaths per thousand workers at large companies. Why the great difference in the number of job-related deaths in small as compared to large companies? There are a number of explanations. First, small businesses generally have fewer resources to deal with safety issues. One person may be responsible for human resources, safety, and general administration issues in a small company. In a large firm, several staff members may specialize in the safety area. Small companies also face greater business competition. Renaissance Metals, for example, a small metal refinishing company, routinely violates OSHA rules by failing to remove elevator doors. But removing the doors would cost the company anywhere between $300 and $1,600, when the company only charges $500 for the entire job. As the owner explained, being required to remove the doors would mean other companies who did not remove the doors would simply get the business instead. Many small businesses only survive because they keep their costs down, which may include neglecting certain safety standards.

Another factor that accounts for the higher death rate at small companies is the limited attention OSHA gives to these businesses. Because certain small, low-hazard industries are exempt from some OSH Act regulations, and OSHA does not monitor smaller companies nearly as closely as it does larger ones, small companies are under less pressure to have effective safety programs and practices. For example, after 56-year-old Ulysses Griffin died from severe silicosis (a disease of the lungs), it was found that the firm he worked for, Commercial Steel Treating Company, had failed to provide workers with proper information and equipment for the handling of silica dust.

The bottom line is that the risks of job-related accidents, illnesses, and death are higher at a small company than they are at a large company. The onus may be on you, the employee, to ensure that your company is complying with the relevant OSH Act laws.

Source: Adapted from B. Marsh, "Workers at Risk," *The Wall Street Journal,* February 3, 1994, A1, A5.

Mandate for Regulatory Agencies: OSHA's Activities

In addition to establishing safety standards, OSHA has two key enforcement responsibilities:[11]

1. Inspections.
2. Establishment of variances.

The Inspection. To enforce the OSH Act, OSHA relies heavily on the inspection of workplaces. An inspection is ordinarily not conducted unless it is chosen through random selection or an employee complaint. Unlike other agencies that must notify a business before they can inspect it, OSHA generally does not give any forewarning of an inspection. Rather, the OSHA inspector will simply arrive at the facility and request admission. After explaining why the facility was chosen, the purpose of the inspection, the standards likely to apply, and other relevant information, the inspector will conduct an initial exploration. Among the items the inspector will examine are OSHA Form No. 200, evidence regarding implementation of the Hazard Communication Standard program, and other safety and health practices. Generally, if the company's employee lost-workday rate seems to be below average and no employee complaints have been filed, a limited inspection will be conducted.

After the inspection, the area director of the OSHA office will determine what, if any, citations should be issued to the company. Any proposed citations must be provided to the company in writing. The company has a variety of opportunities to reduce or even eliminate the citations, through negotiation with OSHA, appeal to OSHRC, or ultimately suing through the federal court of appeals.

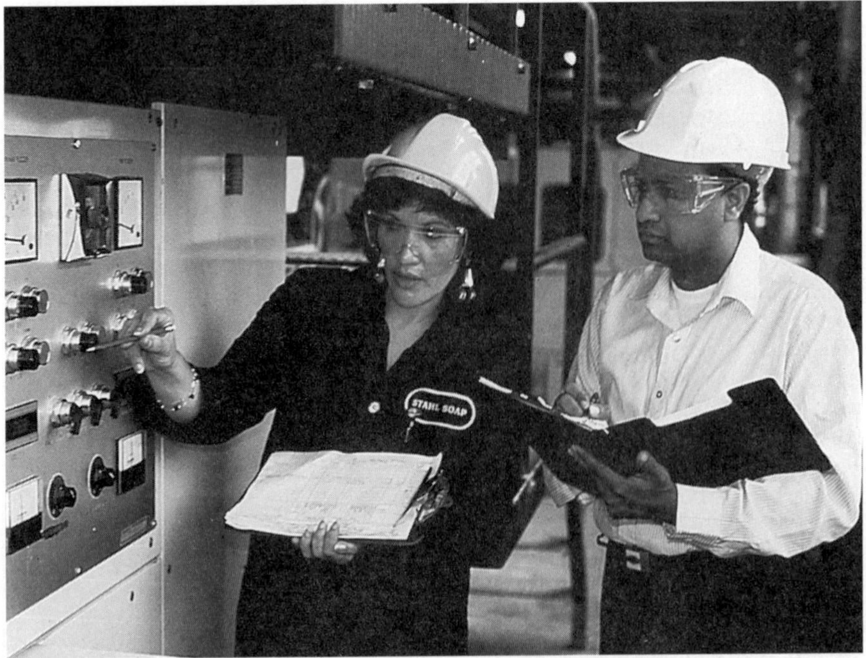

Workplace inspections are required by regulatory agencies such as OSHA, and are usually done on a random basis or because of an employee complaint. Inspectors will see to it that safety measures are enforced, all equipment is operational and safe, and that employees are taking adequate precautions while working with heavy machinery, dangerous chemicals, or any other hazardous substances.

Box 13.3: What Can You Do If Your Company Is Violating the OSH Act?

You might now be wondering what you can do if you think your employer is violating the Occupational Safety and Health Act. Under the law, you as an employee have the right to file a complaint with the local office (some states, such as Indiana, have federally accepted occupational safety and health programs) or the OSHA office in your area (or, for general information, call 1-800-392-7743).

In order to file a complaint, you will need to complete a standard form indicating the nature of the hazard(s), the number of employees exposed to or threatened by the hazard(s), and your name and address. Although you may indicate on the form that you wish your identity to be kept confidential, your employer may be able to figure out who filed the complaint. There is protection against retaliation for filing a complaint under the OSH Act; but don't count on it always helping you. To investigate your complaints, OSHA may conduct an inspection of the facility.

If OSHA issues a citation or determination of wrongdoing, your company may be assessed a financial penalty, which can range from as little as $7,000 per violation to as much as $70,000 per violation.

Filing a complaint may sound fine if you have the luxury of avoiding the hazard, but what if your supervisor assigns you to perform a task that you think is dangerous? For example, what if you are instructed to stand on an office chair to paint the ceiling (the OSH Act, incidentally, has regulations applicable to ladders)? What if your supervisor says "Do it or I'll fire you now?" The OSH Act does provide protection for you in this case, and you do not have to perform an unsafe task. But before you simply say "No, I won't!" and walk away, you should consider the following:

1. Does the unsafe condition that you are concerned about create a substantial risk of serious illness or physical harm? If the answer is no, then you should do the work. If the answer is yes, OSHA will probably support your refusal to perform.
2. Has the employer really violated OSH Act regulations? There are dangerous jobs in this world. The question is whether the employer has followed the relevant standards or guidelines. The poultry plants described in the opening case may not be in violation of OSHA rules—some jobs are just plain dirty and dangerous. If the company has not violated the regulations, OSHA will not get your job back for you. Just because a certain task seems dirty or unsafe does not mean you have the legal right to refuse to do it. On the other hand, you do have the right to quit and find a different job.
3. In addition, you should consider how urgent the situation is (for example, do you have time to file an OSHA complaint before you are supposed to perform the task), and try asking your supervisor to fix the situation first (for example, tell the supervisor you would like to obtain a proper ladder for this task). Otherwise, be ready to look for another job.

Source: Adapted from L. Joel, *Every Employee's Guide to the Law* (New York: Pantheon, 1993).

Variances. In certain cases, an employer may request either a temporary or permanent exception to an OSHA standard. For example, a company may wish to experiment with a new cover on a power machine and, for that reason, seeks permission to deviate from the standards. Toward that end, the company would seek an **OSHA variance.** OSHA would inspect and possibly hold a hearing on the proposed deviation. If OSHA agrees to the modification, a variance would be granted, thus permitting this deviation.

OSHA Variance
In certain cases, an employer may request either a temporary or permanent exception to an OSHA standard and must seek a variance. OSHA would inspect and possibly hold a hearing on the proposed deviation. If OSHA agrees to the modification, a variance would be granted, thus permitting this deviation.

In sum, there are myriad laws promoting safety and health in the workplace. In addition to the legal requirements, the financial costs associated with injury, illness, and deaths, as well as the moral and ethical implications, have led companies to develop a variety of programs and policies to lower the rate of workplace accidents. Some of these practices are discussed next.

Company Efforts to Reduce Workplace Accidents

Companies' efforts to reduce workplace accidents may be organized into four categories:

1. Empowering employees.
2. Rewarding employees.
3. Training employees.
4. Testing employees.

Empowering Employees

In keeping with current trends in employee empowerment (see Chapter 12), many companies are granting employees the authority to improve safety in the workplace. State Fair Food's, a division of Sara Lee Corporation, instituted employee safety teams in its burrito and corn dog manufacturing plant. The teams have permission to correct safety problems immediately, without obtaining approval from management. The teams found that the major contributors to workplace accidents were relatively minor items, such as slippery floors and poor lighting. Within two years of implementation, almost 70 percent of the employees had participated on a safety team. Norfolk Southern Railroad implemented a similar program. In addition, the company moved more than half of its corporate safety employees to the operating divisions so that they could work more closely with the safety teams. As a result of this as well as other changes, Norfolk reduced the number of injuries on the job from 6.06 injuries to 2.0 injuries per 200,000 person hours worked.[12] At Sonoco Products Paper Division, production employees have both the authority and obligation to stop a machine from operating if they determine work conditions are unsafe.[13]

Rewarding Employees

Companies use a variety of rewards to improve employee safety. Landstar Systems, a trucking firm based in Connecticut, began to reward for safety results throughout the company. At the highest levels, managers and executives are evaluated on safety during their yearly performance review. The drivers, who are independent owner-operators, are eligible for a number of rewards. First, an annual reward called the President's Safety Award is given to safe drivers. Second, drivers who have excellent safety records (including no moving violations) and are top revenue producers are eligible for a major reward program that can lead to savings bonds and sea cruises. State Fair Foods also uses monetary compensation to reward employees who do not have accidents, and the company maintains a trophy room for displaying the safety awards the company wins.[14]

Another way to reward safety behavior is to use intrinsic approaches. One method is to graph safety behaviors and post the results in a visible spot. Workers can then help establish a goal for improvement following training or some other kind of intervention. Subsequent to the intervention, safety behavior can be graphed so that workers can see the improvements.[15]

The use of rewards is clearly one way to reduce accidents. But can you see any potential problems with rewarding employees? One problem is that employees and companies may neglect to report injuries and accidents. In turn, this can lead to penalties by OSHA or, from an employee perspective, greater safety and health problems.[16]

Training Employees

In addition to training requirements mandated by the OSH Act, many companies have developed and implemented additional safety training programs. Landstar Systems conducts employee safety training as part of its orientation program for new hires. This day-and-a-half session emphasizes the role that all workers have in safety, and the loss associated with even one accident. At Sonoco Products, new hires at the cylinder mill and corrugating department go through four days of classroom training in safety principles, followed by on-the-job training. Before beginning to work independently, each new hire must work for one week as an apprentice with a more experienced employee.[17]

Companies also train current employees. Sonoco employees participate in a safety program that emphasizes awareness of safety problems created by other workers. But as described in Chapter 11, traditional training programs may fail to change on-the-job behavior. So Occidental Chemical adopted a different approach, called the Safety Congress. The purpose of the Safety Congress was to increase employee commitment to and involvement in safety programs. Toward that end, the Safety Congress comprised both management and production employees, who made presentations about safety and discussed the implications for the company. What both parties learned was that safety practices varied a great deal from plant to plant, and that employees often received mixed messages about the relative importance of safety and production goals. As a result of the Safety Congress, employees came away with much greater commitment and involvement in safety programs.[18]

Testing Employees

Various selection procedures have been used to screen out applicants who pose a safety risk. The two most common approaches are drug and personality tests. (Because drug testing was discussed in Chapter 5, we will only discuss personality tests here.) In terms of personality tests, there is some evidence that certain measures can successfully predict accidents. The Safety Locus of Control Scale, for example, has been examined in several studies, using bus drivers, hotel employees, and grocery store workers. In each case, the Safety Locus of Control Scale was found to be a useful predictor of job-related accidents.[19] Other studies have shown that measures of distractibility and social maladjustment are useful predictors of accidents.[20]

In sum, a variety of programs and practices are available to help companies reduce accidents. By combining a number of these approaches, companies will be able to significantly reduce accidents. We turn now to a discussion of some current safety and health issues in the workplace and discuss programs and practices that companies are using to deal with them.

Current Safety and Health Issues in the Workplace

In this section, you will read about issues such as violence in the workplace, lower back pain, cumulative trauma disorders, drug and alcohol abuse, psychological stress, and indoor air pollution. Regardless of the nature of your job, you may be vulnerable to one or more of these problems. We begin first with a discussion of workplace violence.

Box 13.4: **Profile of a Workplace Killer**

Wondering whether a coworker of yours may go on a shooting rampage? Experts have developed a list of characteristics that typifies many employees who commit violence in the workplace. Some of the key characteristics of a perpetrator of workplace violence include the following:

- Generally male, in his 30s or 40s.
- Expects to lose his job or has lost his job.
- Has a history of conflicts with other people at work.
- Tends to stay by himself.
- Has trouble accepting authority.
- Tends to blame problems on other people.
- Has threatened other people at work.
- Is extremely interested in guns.

Many people may fit this profile; it does not mean they are going to commit violence at work. Other experts say that certain work environments predispose employees to violence. Some of the characteristics of violence-prone organizations include the following:

- There is much labor-management friction.
- Many grievances are filed by employees.
- Injury claims, particularly psychologically based, are common.
- Employees are overworked.
- Employees experience much stress.
- An authoritarian management style is used.

Source: Adapted from H. Bensimon, "Violence in the Workplace," *Training & Development,* January 1994, 26–32.

Workplace Violence

Almost everyone has heard of incidents where a current or former employee went on a rampage, wounding or killing other workers. More than one thousand people were murdered at work in the United States during 1992, a 30 percent increase from the 1980s. Some of the most well-known incidents involve post office workers, such as the postal carrier who shot 14 people in 1986. Homicide is now the second largest cause of death at work. Only transportation accidents are responsible for more deaths. These statistics have clearly frightened both employees and employers, and companies have initiated a variety of programs and policies to alleviate the problem.[21]

More Careful Preemployment Screening. Some companies ask applicants for information about prior criminal convictions. But applicants may lie, and not all violent people have prior convictions. Other companies have turned to paper-and-pencil tests to try to screen out potentially violent workers. This may work to some degree with new applicants, but for an organization like the U.S. Post Office, with more than 700,000 current employees, this is not a tenable solution.[22]

Conflict Resolution Programs. Given that many cases of violence are caused by prior disagreements between coworkers, some companies are developing conflict resolution programs to defuse the problem. The U.S. Post Office, for example, has established a team of workers whose responsibility will be to solve workplace conflicts. While this tactic may have some promise, violence-prone employees may be no more satisfied with this program's outcome than with the other events or decisions that upset them.

Anonymous Reporting Systems. Some companies are establishing anonymous reporting systems so that coworkers can provide information to the proper authorities without their identity being revealed. The U.S. Postal Service, for example, instituted this kind of system, and received 10,000 phone calls. In response, postal inspectors spent 100,000 hours investigating tips. Of course, many of these calls will prove to be meaningless.

Increased Security Measures. One of the most important steps that a company can take to reduce workplace violence is to improve its security measures. One law firm, after an unhappy client shot eight workers, keeps its doors locked and provides an emergency alarm for the receptionist. You are probably familiar with the combination lock used by most airports on entrances to airplanes, which was implemented after similar incidents.

Despite the alarm over workplace violence, some experts maintain the threat is greatly exaggerated. Statistics show that in 1993, only 59 employees were killed by current or former coworkers. Given that there are 120 million workers in the United States, the odds of being killed by a coworker are 1 in 2.1 million, so you are much more likely to be struck by lightning (where the odds are 1 in 600,000 of dying). Other studies have added to the confusion by reporting different statistics. A 1994 study conducted by the Justice Department, for example, reported that one million employees are victims to nonfatal workplace violence each year. This study has been criticized on two grounds, however. First, a large number of the violent acts occurred in areas other than the actual facility, including in garages and on public property. Second, the survey included attacks on police, security guards, and convenience-store workers, occupations which are prone to violence. Research reported by Northwestern National Life also indicated high levels of workplace violence—as many as 25 percent of workers were allegedly harassed, threatened, or physically attacked during a 12-month period. But the study had a relatively low response rate (perhaps as low as 29 percent), so it is quite possible that many of the nonrespondents had not been victims of such behavior.[23]

In sum, workplace violence is certainly a safety issue that should concern both companies and employees. Whether it is an epidemic, however, is not quite clear.

Lower Back Pain

Lower back pain and associated disabilities constitutes one of the largest sources of days missed from work and is a major contributor to an organization's workers' compensation costs. As shown in Box 13.5, "Some Common Causes of Lower Back Pain," a number of physical features on jobs appear to increase the likelihood that an employee will experience lower back pain. The workers most likely to experience lower back pain are trash collectors, nurses and nurse's aides, truck drivers, heavy equipment operators, mechanics, maintenance workers, manual laborers, warehouse workers, protective service employees (such as police officers), and typists. Based on Box 13.5, can you explain why these jobs would be particularly susceptible to lower back pain? The answer is that all of these jobs involve either lifting (for instance, nurses), pushing or pulling (such as warehouse workers), carrying (manual laborers, for example), or body vibration (such as truck drivers). Finally, if you are between the ages of 35 and 45, you are in the age group most likely to experience lower back pain because the effects of aging are most dramatic at this age. Workers younger than 35 who report lower back pain are most likely to develop the symptoms as a result of inexperience with the aggravating tasks.[24]

Box 13.5 Some Common Causes of Lower Back Pain

1. **Lifting Objects That Weigh between 25 and 35 Pounds.** These are the objects that are most likely to cause lower back pain. Objects that are lighter are easier to lift and therefore cause less strain. Workers are more careful in lifting objects that are heavier than 35 pounds; objects that are much heavier than 35 pounds usually require a mechanical aid or assistance from a second person. How often do you lift objects that weigh between 25 and 35 pounds in your job?
2. **Pushing and Pulling Objects.** If you spend much time at work pushing and pulling heavy objects, you are more likely to experience lower back pain. How often do you perform such tasks in your job?
3. **Carrying Heavy Items.** This category poses similar risks as those caused by lifting, but with an added element of risk because carrying items may create sudden and severe strains to the back. Two activities are particularly prone to create lower back pain: shifts in weight as the object is moved and slips in the employee's hands or feet. How often do you carry heavy items in your job?
4. **Prolonged Periods of Sitting.** If you work in a sedentary office job, you may spend little or no time lifting, pushing, pulling, or carrying objects. You are, however, not immune from lower back pain as workers who sit for long periods of time, especially in cramped positions or at desks or tables that are not at proper heights, may experience occasional symptoms.
5. **Body Vibration.** Jobs that involve continuous vibration, such as heavy truck drivers and operators of heavy construction equipment, are susceptible to lower back pain. While standards for what constitutes unsafe amounts of vibration exist, they are not legally binding on companies, and many jobs exceed the standards. Does your job involve much body vibration?

Source: Adapted from J. Hollenbeck, D. Ilgen, and S. Crampton, "Lower Back Disability in Occupational Settings: A Review of the Literature from a Human Resource Management View," *Personnel Psychology* 45 (1992), 247–78.

Company Programs to Reduce Lower Back Pain Problems. Companies have emphasized two basic strategies for reducing lower back pain problems: selection/placement and training.[25]

- **Careful Selection.** Many companies screen applicants for future or current lower back disability. Medical examinations are the most common approach; frequently, a spinal X ray is used as part of the examination. While you might think an examination by a medical professional would effectively screen out employees with current or future lower back pain, research indicates that medical examinations and spinal X rays are actually not very accurate predictors of such problems. A physical fitness or physical strength test is the second most common procedure for future or current lower back pain disability. Such tests appear to be far more promising than the medical examination, but more research is needed. Finally, a relatively new approach to selection/placement is the use of computerized movement analyzers, which record a person's movement and strength from a variety of positions. Use of these machines is far too recent to objectively analyze their effectiveness. Finally, in light of the Americans with Disabilities Act of 1990, attempts to select workers on the basis of lower back pain disability may be considered discriminatory.
- **Training Programs.** Many companies offer training as an approach for reducing lower back pain. Table 13.1 provides an outline of a typical lower back pain training program. As you can see, the typical training program addresses several basic areas that have been shown to be helpful in reduc-

Table 13.1: **A Typical Lower Back Pain Training Program**

Work-Site Assessment

I. Review your job for risk factors, lifting techniques, safety equipment, etc.
II. Take slides of employees at work
III. Review injury records

On-Site Education

I. Introduction
  A. Present facts regarding back injury
  B. Overview of general causes of back injury
  C. Outline goals of the session
II. Anatomy
  A. Overview of vertebrae, ligaments, muscles, discs, joints, and nerves
III. Causes of Back Injuries
  A. Poor posture
  B. Forward bending
  C. Decreased flexibility
  D. Poor physical fitness
  E. Accidents
  F. Poor work habits: Proper/improper standing, sitting, lying, lifting
IV. Basic Body Mechanics
  A. Principles of lifting
  B. Proper sitting, sleeping, standing, driving positions
V. Health Education
  A. Aerobics
  B. Flexibility & exercises
  C. Strength & exercises
  D. Home program: Daily living and household activities (e.g., getting out of bed, dressing, tooth brushing, vacuuming, dishes, shopping, cooking, etc.)
  E. Nutrition
  F. Weight control
  G. Stress management
  H. Relaxation techniques
VI. First Aid
  A. What to do for a new injury
VII. Summary
  A. Summarize anatomy, posture, body mechanics, exercise program
  B. Provide written materials on all topics and exercises presented
  C. Life back care: Practical application of methods
  D. Peer pressure/team effort

On-Site Followup

I. Monitor safety/injury records
II. Review injured employees' records
III. Make further recommendations if needed

Source: J. Hollenbeck, D. Ilgen, and S. Crampton, "Lower Back Pain Disability in Occupational Settings: A Review of the Literature from a Human Resource Management View;" *Personnel Psychology* 45 (1992), 247–78.

ing problems, including awareness of the causes of lower back pain, recommendations for proper lifting and sitting techniques, and suggestions for basic exercises and health care.

In sum, lower back pain and related disabilities are a problem both for the company and the employee who suffers from them. If you have a job that involves some or all of the activities listed in Box 13.5, you should consult your physician for suggestions (for example, exercises) to avoid future problems.

Cumulative Trauma Disorders

Have you ever worked in a job where you experienced aches in your wrist, shoulder, or arms? In the 1980s, this was frequently identified as carpal tunnel syndrome. Repetitive stress injury was first identified in the 1990s. Together, these ailments are frequently referred to as cumulative trauma disorders (CTDs). First, let's discuss some popular myths about these ailments, then we will examine what the legal requirements are in this regard.[26]

Cumulative Trauma Disorders (CTDs)
Trauma to the wrist, shoulder, or arms, such as repetitive stress injury and carpal tunnel syndrome.

Repetitive Stress Injury
First identified in the 1990s, this injury is a form of muscle strain, usually not crippling.

Carpal Tunnel Syndrome
First identified in the 1980s, this injury involves pressure on the median nerve, which is located in the wrist, and often requires surgery.

Popular Myths about CTDs. There is a great deal of mistaken information about CTDs. What follows next is a list of some of the most common myths about this ailment, along with the facts about each. You will see that relatively little is known about these problems.

1. **Myth:** Repetitive stress injury is another name for carpal tunnel syndrome. **Fact:** These are quite different ailments. Repetitive stress is usually a form of muscle strain, generally not crippling. Carpal tunnel syndrome involves pressure on the median nerve, which is located in your wrist. It often requires surgery. While these are often lumped together as CTDs, they are really different ailments.
2. **Myth:** Repetitive stress primarily affects workers who use keyboards (such as secretaries). **Fact:** Keyboard users account for only 12 percent of reported cases. As shown in Figure 13.3, the occupations most affected by repetitive stress injuries include meatpackers, automobile manufacturers, and poultry processors.
3. **Myth:** Preventing CTDs involves simple alterations of work tasks and work conditions (such as the position of one's chair). **Fact:** Relatively little is really known about how to prevent CTDs. Some research indicates that remedies such as wrist rests on the keyboard exacerbate, rather than alleviate, the problem.
4. **Myth:** CTDs are by-products of the modern workplace. **Fact:** There is ample evidence that CTDs occurred several centuries prior to our time. Modern-day technology has not created this problem.

Now that you know something about the facts regarding CTDs, you may wonder why this ailment is causing so much commotion in the workplace. The answer is that there is much legal action going on regarding CTDs. Both sufferers of the symptom and OSHA have become involved in legal action.

Legal Action Regarding CTDs. CTDs present an important issue in the workplace because a number of lawsuits have been filed by workers who charge that improper equipment has caused them to suffer. The defendants, who include IBM, AT&T, and Eastman Kodak, make keyboards, cash registers, and grocery store scanners. In fact, more than 3,000 lawsuits have been filed against such companies. Millions, if not billions, of dollars are at stake. One of the major problems is that there is practically no research regarding CTDs, so there is little scientific proof one way or the other regarding the causes of CTDs. The only significant court ruling to date took place in England, where a judge ruled against a plaintiff

Figure 13.3 Repetitive Stress Injuries by Year and Occupation

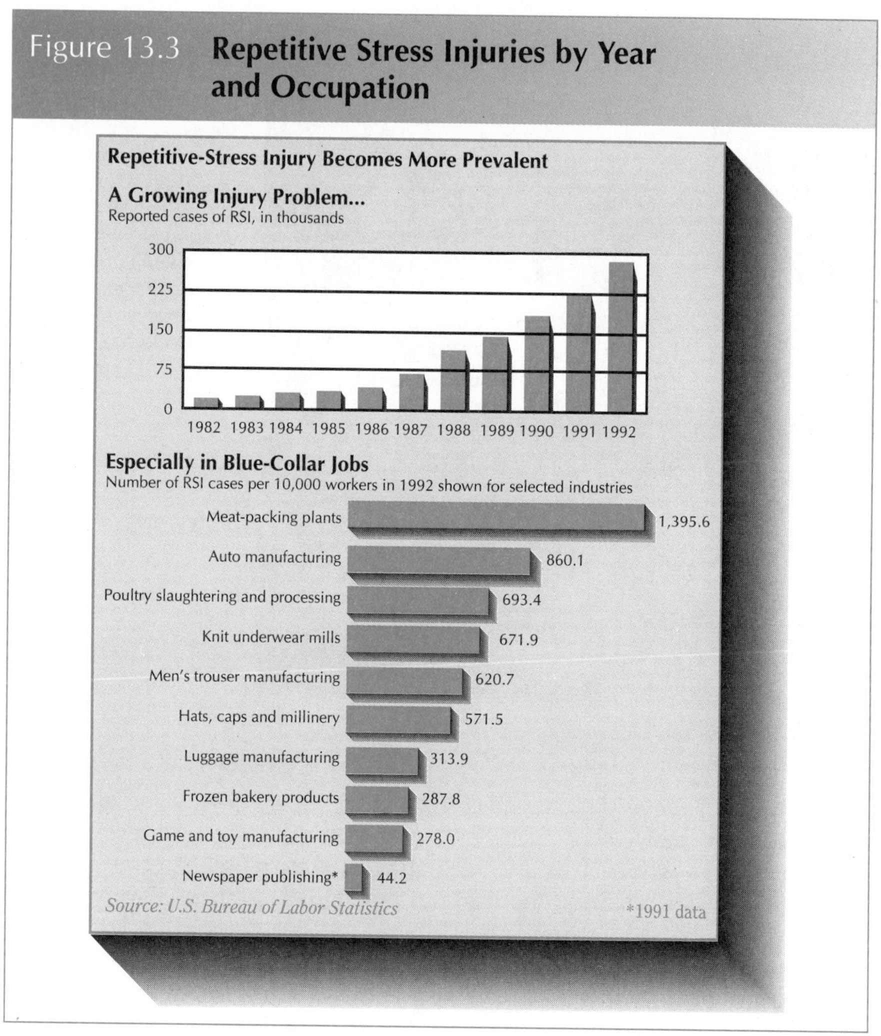

Source: E. Felsenthal, "Out of Hand," *The Wall Street Journal,* July 14, 1994, A4.

who worked on a computer to edit a newspaper. In dismissing the claim, the judge noted that cumulative trauma disorder was an unknown concept and did not have any medical status.[27]

In a carefully watched case that began in 1988, OSHA conducted an investigation of a Pepperidge Farm plant that produced the Milano cookie. OSHA found that 69 employees who worked on putting the tops on this cookie suffered from a variety of cumulative trauma disorder ailments and levied a $1.4 million fine against the plant.[28] Pepperidge Farm fought this judgment in court, and the judge reduced the penalty to less than $300,000. The major reason for reducing the fine was that OSHA did not prove that there was a reasonable procedure for reducing the hazard. That is, the court felt that there was no known cure or procedure for reducing the problem.[29] As a result, OSHA recently released proposed standards for CTDs and related syndromes. The standards would require such things as the

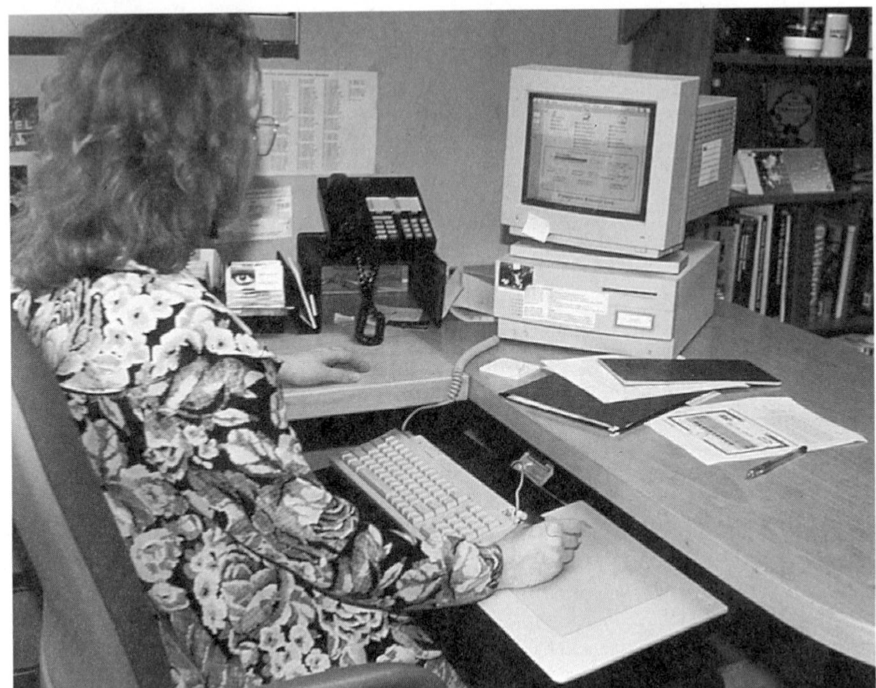

Alternatives exist to the traditional office equipment that has been linked to repetitive stress injuries. Human resource departments now provide employees with ergonomic office equipment such as this special pen and mouse pad to alleviate stress on the wrist that can be caused by the traditional keyboard.

company paying for vision tests and corrective lens for employees who spend more than four hours daily using video-display monitors. The standards also include a list of high-risk tasks, such as use of vibrating tools for more than two hours at a time and activities requiring the identical motion being repeated every few seconds for more than two hours.[30]

Cumulative trauma disorder is an important topic today, and there will certainly be changes in the workplace as more becomes known about this problem. If you work in a job that involves a combination of the following—rapid and repetitive motion, awkward positions, powerful limb movements, strong vibrations, and little control over the pace of work—you may be susceptible to CTDs.[31]

Drug and Alcohol Use

Employee Assistance Program
An organization-sponsored program that helps identify workers in need of counseling, motivates them to obtain the needed counseling, and provides the proper counseling sources.

Anywhere from 5 percent to 10 percent of employees report using drugs either at work or off the job. The cost to business and industry of drug and alcohol use is somewhere in the billions of dollars, due to decreased productivity, higher absenteeism, and increased medical bills. In addition, drug and alcohol use has been tied to many accidents, particularly in the transportation and construction industry. As a result, certain industries and many companies have adopted programs to alleviate drug and alcohol-related problems. Companies have emphasized two solutions: employee testing and employee assistance programs (EAPs).[32] Because employee testing was addressed in Chapter 5, however, only EAPs will be discussed next.

An EAP is an organization-sponsored program that helps identify workers in need of counseling, motivates them to obtain the needed counseling, and provides the proper counseling sources.[33] While many EAPs were initially established to help with drug- and alcohol-related problems, they are now used to help with any type of psychological problem (for example, depression) that an employee is experiencing. Although most programs allow employees to self-refer, in many cases it is the supervisor who prompts the employee to seek treatment from the EAP. Toward that end, many companies train managers to use a procedure known as constructive confrontation. Constructive confrontation involves four basic steps:[34]

Constructive Confrontation
Useful in helping supervisors prompt employees to seek treatment from the EAP, constructive confrontation involves four steps: (1) the supervisor confronts the employee with evidence of unsatisfactory performance; (2) the supervisor provides coaching to improve the employee's performance; (3) at the same time, the supervisor encourages the employee to contact the EAP; and (4) the supervisor continues to inform the employee of the consequences of continued unsatisfactory performance.

1. The supervisor confronts the employee with evidence of unsatisfactory performance.
2. The supervisor provides coaching to improve the employee's performance.
3. At the same time, the supervisor encourages the employee to contact the EAP.
4. The supervisor continues to inform the employee of the consequences of continued unsatisfactory performance.

While many companies use EAPs, some have questioned their effectiveness, as well as their basic features. Whether constructive confrontation, for example, is truly the best strategy has yet to be demonstrated. Nevertheless, many companies have found EAPs to be a cost-effective alternative to other treatment sources that employees might use. In addition, some companies believe that presence of an EAP promotes positive employee relations.[35]

Companies will continue to be concerned with employee drug and alcohol use. Although many organizations use drug testing and EAPs, the problems associated with these substances are unlikely to go away anytime soon.

Psychological Stress

Simply reading the word *stress* may cause your palms to get clammy, your heartbeat to increase, and your breathing to become more rapid. Whether you are only attending school, or attending school while working part time or full time, you will sometimes experience stress. Psychological stress has been linked to numerous problems, including greater susceptibility to the common cold, ulcers, colitis, and numerous other ailments. Hospital employees' stress levels have been linked to higher rates of malpractice lawsuits and medication errors.[36] In some cases, work-related stress may result in workers' compensation payments to employees, amounting to hundreds and thousands of dollars in additional costs to the company. Psychological stress, then, can be a major expense for organizations. The remainder of this section addresses the causes of stress and what companies can do to reduce stress-related problems.

What Causes Stress? While there have been many explanations for what causes psychological stress at work, the demand-control model is among the most popular.[37] According to the demand-control model of stress, two factors determine the amount of stress you, as an employee, will experience. One factor is job demands. Job demands include the degree to which you must work quickly with great concentration, have more to do than you are capable of completing in the allocated time (often referred to as role overload), or have conflicting requirements (such as two bosses with different standards). There are other sources of job demands as well, such as role ambiguity (being unsure of what the expectations or goals of your job are), the lack of feedback regarding your job performance, and the fear of job loss.[38] Job demands are the psychological perception that you have of the job;

Demand-Control Model of Stress
The theory that states that an employee will experience the most stress when the job has high demands and little control.

a physically demanding job, for example, is not perceived as demanding if you are physically fit.

The second factor is control, specifically the amount of control that you have in the job with regard to making decisions and using different skills. A worker in a traditional assembly line that is based on scientific management principles engages in little or no decision making. In addition, because the worker performs one or two simple tasks over and over again, the worker has little or no skill variety. A worker in this type of position would have low control.

According to the demand-control theory, an employee will experience the most stress when the job has high demands and little control. As an analogy, how would you feel if you were driving a car at 80 miles per hour (high demand)? Your stress level would undoubtedly depend on how well you controlled the vehicle (e.g., you had a firm grip on the steering wheel and the pavement was ice-free). You would probably not mind being in a speeding vehicle, as long as you had control. But how would you feel if you did not have control over the car? What if the road was icy? In that case, you would probably experience a great deal of stress![39]

Based on the demand-control model, some jobs have been found to elicit far greater stress than other jobs. Figure 13.4 provides some average ratings for different jobs on the demand-control dimensions. The jobs that are rated highest on stress include telephone operator, waitress, and garment stitcher.

We have emphasized stressors that are created at work. In today's world, however, especially given the number of dual-career families, many employees experience stress emanating from conflicts between work and non-work sources. Stress may arise, for instance, when an employee wants to attend his child's birthday party but is unable to because his supervisor requires him to work overtime. In addition, workers often suffer at work from stress emanating from their personal life, including financial difficulties, marital problems, and life changes.[40]

Now that you know what the causes of stress are, you will read about two kinds of programs companies use to reduce stress.

Stress Management Training. Several programs and practices are available to help organizations reduce stress in the workplace. One approach is to provide stress management workshops, in which employees receive training in how to deal with stress. Table 13.2 provides a sample program for this kind of workshop. As you can see, the emphasis in this stress management workshop is on strategies that an employee can use to reduce stress. The stress management workshop approach emphasizes the treatment of the demand aspect of stress.[41] Stress management programs differ from one another in terms of their focus—some emphasize relaxation techniques (such as meditation), others focus on practical skills (such as time management) to reduce stress, while other workshops use a combination of these techniques.[42]

Other stress reduction efforts focus on changing the organization, particularly by increasing employee control. As you read in Chapter 12, many companies are empowering workers to make decisions while increasing skill variety. A side benefit of such programs is that they may lower stress levels in the workplace.[43]

Wellness Programs
Some organizations have implemented work-site wellness programs to improve the overall physical and mental health of their workforce. They typically involve a series of educational and behavioral change courses designed to encourage smoking cessation, proper diet and nutrition, and improved physical fitness.

Wellness Programs. Although not designed solely to alleviate stress, many organizations have implemented work-site wellness programs to improve the overall physical and mental health of their workforce. Such programs are relatively new; however about 75 percent of large companies now offer some type of wellness program.[44]

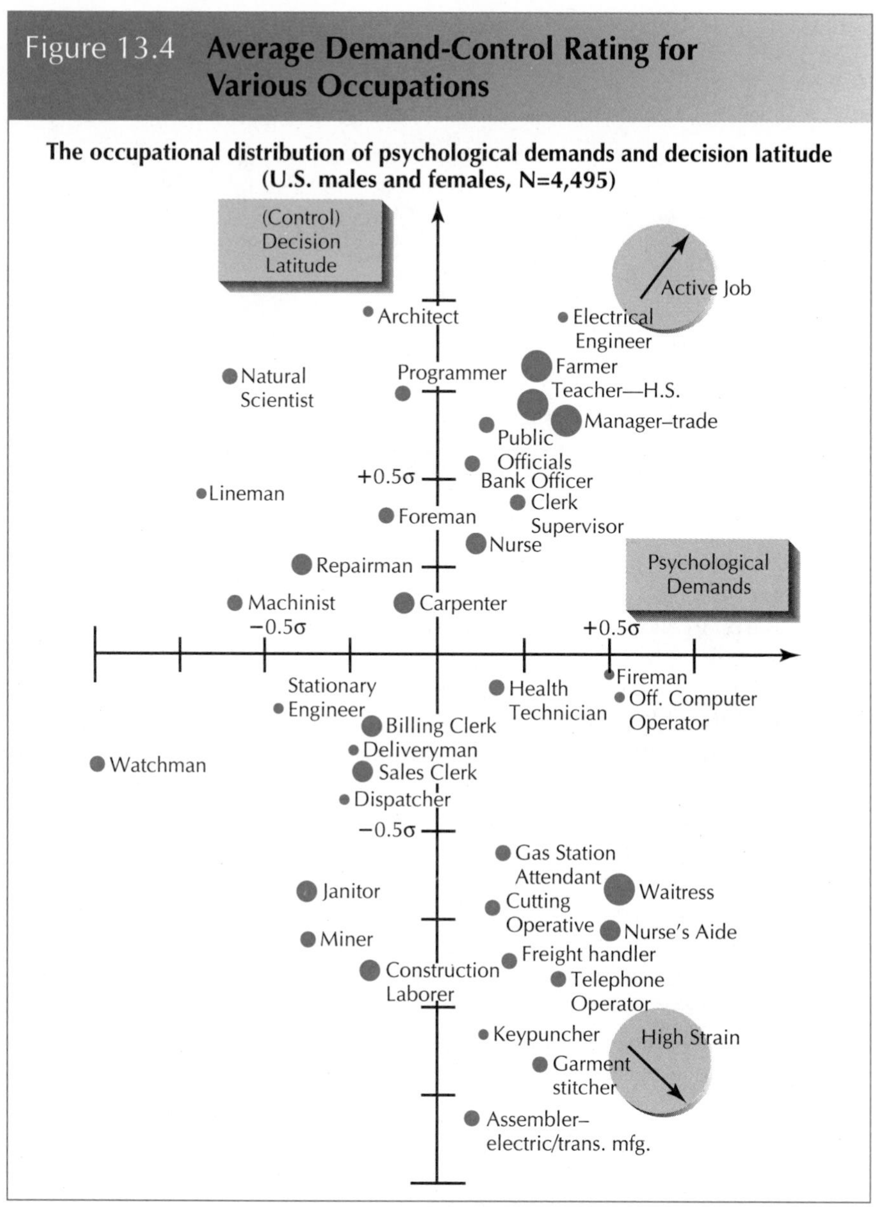

Figure 13.4 Average Demand-Control Rating for Various Occupations

Source: R. Karasek and T. Theorell, *Healthy Work: Stress, Productivity, and the Reconstruction of Working Life* (New York: Basic Books, 1990).

Wellness programs typically involve a series of educational and behavioral change courses designed to encourage smoking cessation, proper diet and nutrition, and improved physical fitness. Northern Telecom, for example, recently implemented a wellness program that includes a low-cost fitness center, weight management classes, and a long list of physical education courses, including martial arts. Employees pay a nominal fee of \$10 per month (\$15 for the family) to attend programs. Seventy percent of the employees now participate. Nike, the sports

Table 13.2 **A Sample of a Daylong Stress Management Workshop**

1. What is stress?
2. How much stress do you experience?
3. How does stress affect you?
4. What causes stress?
5. Why do different people experience stress differently?
6. Coping with stress.
   - Learning to relax
   - Exercising
   - Eating right
   - Confronting stress
7. Designing a stress reduction program.

Source: Adapted from M. Matteson and J. Ivancevich, *Controlling Work Stress* (San Francisco: Jossey-Bass, 1987).

equipment company, boasts one of the best fitness centers in the country. The fitness center includes weights and two aerobic studios, as well as tennis and basketball courts. In addition, there are volleyball courts, a five-mile running track, and a large lake on the premises.[45]

Despite the popularity of wellness programs, there has been little rigorous examination of their effectiveness. Many companies, however, report high employee enthusiasm and satisfaction with such programs. Northern Telecom, for example, found that 91 percent of the employees agreed that the program improved the quality of their worklife and reduced stress.[46] One of the most carefully conducted studies of wellness programs reported an average cost per employee of between $17 and $39 annually. The cost of the programs, then, was relatively low. In terms of risk prevention (such as a reduction in high blood pressure), the nature of the wellness program had a major effect. Yet, programs that only provided courses or a fitness facility had a negligible effect on risk prevention. Significant improvements were reported only if the program featured an administrator who contacted employees at risk and provided encouragement to them. Thus, the mere presence of a fitness center appears not to be enough; someone must prompt the employees to participate.[47]

In sum, psychological stress is a common problem in the workplace. Although many companies have programs to alleviate stress, much of the responsibility is on the employee to learn how to cope. Although this is easier said than done, my advice to you is as follows:

1. Only worry about the important stuff.
2. Nothing at work is that important.
3. Find enjoyable things to do, such as reading and walking, that will enable you to relax.

Indoor Air Pollution

If you primarily work indoors, you may be exposed to a number of airborne health hazards. We will discuss two of the more commonly considered ones: sick building syndrome and tobacco smoke.

Sick Building Syndrome
Caused by either bacteria/fungi contamination of the heating/cooling ducts or vehicle fumes from outside air, the symptoms include skin and mucous membrane irritations, headaches, and fatigue, which are thought to be caused by working in a modern office building.

Sick Building Syndrome. According to the World Health Organization, you have sick building syndrome if the following apply:

1. You have an abundance of skin and mucous membrane irritations.
2. You experience ailments such as headaches and fatigue.
3. You work in a modern office building.

Have you ever experienced such symptoms? It is generally assumed that sick building syndrome is caused by either bacteria or fungi contamination of the heating or cooling ducts or by vehicle fumes from outside air. However, two studies that were published in the early 1990s have cast doubt on the authenticity of sick building syndrome. In these two studies, ventilation levels were increased, yet no reduction in sick building syndrome was reported. On the basis of these studies, some experts have concluded that there is no evidence for such a syndrome.[48] Whether scientists will find evidence for this ailment in the future is unclear. If you feel you are suffering from this syndrome, try to eliminate sources of fumes and obtain more fresh air, by opening any windows or simply going outside more frequently.

Tobacco Smoke. Smoke from cigarettes, cigars, and pipes may create health problems for both smokers and nonsmokers. The following facts are widely accepted.[49]

1. Tobacco causes more deaths than alcohol, drugs, car crashes, and AIDs combined.
2. Tobacco causes one out of every six deaths nationwide.
3. Almost 400,000 Americans die each year due to cigarette smoking.

While the risks to smokers have been known for quite some time, the effects on nonsmokers from secondhand smoke have only recently become known. Although some controversy remains as to the danger of secondhand smoke, most experts agree that the risk of lung cancer is increased by exposure, if only by a small amount.[50] In the last few years, many employers have begun to actively combat smoking. There are several reasons why organizations seek to reduce or eliminate smoking among employees. First, smokers tend to have higher health insurance claims than nonsmokers. Second, smoking may be a safety hazard on the job. Third, in some states, employees can receive workers' compensation for smoke-related illnesses. Fourth, OSHA has proposed regulations to cover indoor air quality and smoke, and other regulations exist that prohibit smoking.[51] Organizations use a variety of policies to reduce smoking as follows:

1. **Refusing to Hire Smokers.** A few companies, such as Lockheed Aeronautical and Turner Broadcasting System, officially refuse to hire applicants who smoke. Note that in some states, such as Missouri, an employer cannot discriminate on the basis of an applicant's smoking habits. In these states, it is illegal to refuse to hire or terminate employees merely because of their tobacco use away from work.[52]

2. **Restricting Smoking at the Worksite.** The most common organizational strategy to reduce employee smoking is to restrict smoking at work. For example, Capital Blue Cross, located in Harrisburg, Pennsylvania, introduced restricted smoking areas in 1988 wherein employees were only permitted to smoke in certain areas of the employee lounge. By 1991, management decided to limit smoking only to a covered patio area. The policy was modified again in 1992 to

permit smoking only in certain areas at certain times. Some companies have gone a step further and banned smoking altogether at the workplace. The Bank of Santa Clara in California is one such example. Despite the fact that the president of the bank is a smoker, this bank recently banned smoking in its building. Why? The city of Santa Clara recently passed a law outlawing smoking in the workplace—penalties may include fines and even imprisonment.[53]

3. **Imposing Penalties on Smokers.** Some companies penalize smokers by adding a surcharge to their health care costs. Texas Instruments charges an additional $10 per month to employees for each covered family member who smokes, up to $30 extra per month. According to company officials, this surcharge does not even come close to the extra costs of medical care for the company.[54]

In short, companies are actively involved in reducing smoking. Given that many Americans favor smoking bans, such programs are likely to be accepted by most employees. Organizations concerned about negative reactions on the part of employees should thoroughly explain the reasons for the policies, focusing on concern for employees' health and well-being, rather than on the company's financial gain.[55] Finally, despite the many reasons to restrict smoking, 30 states have laws protecting smoking rights, and right-to-privacy laws may offer some protection to smokers as well.

Conclusion

Safety and health in the workplace is an important concern for both companies and employees. There are many laws that govern safety and health in the workplace, and it is important for companies to know and follow these laws to avoid legal problems. Through the use of employee empowerment, training programs, reward systems, and the careful selection of employees, companies should be able to reduce their accident rates. Several current safety and health issues were also discussed in this chapter. For employees, it is important that you encourage your employer to develop and implement safety and health programs to address such things as workplace violence, lower back pain, and alcohol and drug use. By providing effective programs to address these issues, your employer will reduce expenses and have a more productive workforce. You, in turn, will experience improved health and safety.

Applying Core Concepts

1. Does the Occupational Safety and Health Act apply to your current job? Why or why not? If the act does *not* cover your job do you think it should? What tools, pieces of equipment, machinery, or equipment are affected by this law?
2. As noted in the chapter, OSH standards specific to poultry plants do not exist. Should specific standards be developed? Why or why not?
3. If poultry plants wanted to improve safety in the plants, which of the four approaches described in this chapter do you think would work best? Why?
4. Which of the current safety and health issues in the workplace concern you most in your current job or future career plans? What has your company done to address these concerns? What do you expect your company to do in the future to address these issues?

Key Terms

- Occupational Safety and Health Act of 1970
- Occupational Safety and Health Administration (OSHA)
- Occupational Safety and Health Review Commission
- National Institute for Occupational Safety and Health
- General Duty Clause
- Hazard Communication Standard of 1985
- OSHA form No. 200
- OSHA form No. 101
- OSHA variance
- Cumulative Trauma Disorder (CTD)
- Repetitive Stress Injury
- Carpal Tunnel Syndrome
- Employee Assistance Program
- Constructive Confrontation
- Demand-Control Model of Stress
- Wellness Programs
- Sick Building Syndrome

Chapter 13: Experiential Exercise

Trouble Waiting to Happen

Jane Hoops works for Carter Cardboard. Her job involves operating a large cutting machine. Carter Cardboard produces custom-ordered cardboard pieces, that are purchased by other companies for use in a wide variety of products, including suitcases, briefcases, and purses. Carter Cardboard purchases the raw material from paper companies and then cuts the cardboard to the desired shape and size. Carter Cardboard is a small company, employing about thirty workers. Most of the workers are immigrants to the U.S., have been with the company for 10–15 years, and would have a difficult time finding jobs elsewhere. Jane is one of the newer employees. Although the wages are low, she manages to pay all of her bills (though she has practically no money in savings). Perhaps the best feature of the job is that it offers a good pension plan and excellent medical coverage. These aspects are particularly important because Jane is a single mother, who is raising two young children.

Since she has begun working at the company, Jane has observed the company become increasingly unconcerned about work conditions. In particular, the cleanliness and safety of the facility has worsened substantially since Jane began working at Carter Cardboard. It is quite common to find scraps of material on the floor. This is particularly problematic at the beginning of the month, when a large order of vinyl-coated material is usually cut, because these materials are particularly slippery. Although she has never fallen at work, Jane has slipped several times.

In addition to finding scraps on the floor, Jane feels several of the cutting machines do not have the required safety features (such as covers). When she complained to Ronnie, the supervisor, about this hazard, he answered: "These machines may not have the Federally required covers—but you know that many government rules are ridiculous. Don't you usually drive over the posted speed limits on the highways? Besides, no one has ever gotten hurt on our machines." The second time she asked him what he was going to do about the problem, he snapped back: "If you don't like the work conditions, why don't you just quit? There are plenty of people who would be happy to get your job."

Most recently, Jane has found a number of instances where the electrical wiring seemed loose or thinly worn. When she mentioned this fact to the owner (who occasionally walks through the manufacturing area), he said: "Well, I'd like to rewire this entire building but I'm afraid we just don't make enough money in this business to pay for rewiring. In fact, we actually lost money last year, and I worry that a major expense like this could close the business down."

One week ago, Jane's best friend at work, Nashina, received a mild electrical shock when she accidentally brushed against some electrical wiring. Jane cannot take this any longer. She knows that the company violates many OSHA rules, but she doesn't want to lose her job either. Although she has applied for other jobs in the last year, she has not received any job offers. What do you recommend that she do?

Chapter 13 References

1. T. Horwitz, "9 to Nowhere," *The Wall Street Journal,* December 1, 1994, A1, A8.
2. B. Mintz, *OSHA: History, Law, and Policy* (Washington: Bureau of National Affairs, 1984).
3. J. Ledvinka and V. Scarpello, *Federal Regulation of Personnel and Human Resource Management* (Boston: PWS-Kent, 1991).
4. M. Rothstein, C. Craver, E. Schroeder, E. Shoben, and L. Vander Velde, *Employment Law* (St. Paul, MN: West, 1994).
5. N. Tompkins, *A Manager's Guide to OSHA* (Menlo Park, CA: Crisp Publications, 1993).
6. Ledvinka and Scarpello, *Federal Regulation.*
7. Tompkins, *A Manager's Guide to OSHA.*
8. P. Sunstrom, "Become the Company's OSHA Oracle," *Security Management,* March 1994, 24–32.
9. Horwitz, "9 to Nowhere."
10. L. Joel, III, *Every Employee's Guide to the Law* (New York: Pantheon Books, 1993).
11. Tompkins, *A Manager's Guide to OSHA.*
12. M. Verespej, "Better Safety Through Empowerment," *Industry Week,* November 15, 1993, 56–68.
13. J. Lee, "Sonoco Stresses Employee Involvement to Alter Company's Safety Performance," *Pulp & Paper,* March 1992, 198–200.
14. Verespej, "Better Safety."
15. T. Krause, "A Behavior-Based Safety Management Process," in *Applying Psychology in Business,* ed. J. Jones, B. Steffy, and D. Bray (Lexington, MA: Lexington Books, 1991).
16. Horwitz, "9 to Nowhere."
17. Lee, "Sonoco Stresses Employee Involvement."
18. S. Smith, "Occidental Chemical: Making Changes for the Better," *Occupational Hazards,* May 1992, 65–68.
19. J. Jones and L. Wuebker, "Accident Prevention through Personnel Selection," *Journal of Business and Psychology* 3 (1988), 187–98.
20. C. Hansen, "A Causal Model of the Relationship among Accidents, Biodata, Personality, and Cognitive Factors," *Journal of Applied Psychology* 74 (1989), 81–90.
21. J. Rigdon, "Companies See More Workplace Violence," *The Wall Street Journal,* April 12, 1994, B1, B6.
22. H. Bensimon, "Violence in the Workplace," *Training and Development,* January 1994, 26–32.
23. E. Larson, "Trigger Happy," *The Wall Street Journal,* October 13, 1994, A1, A11.
24. J. Hollenbeck, D. Ilgen, and S. Crampton, "Lower Back Pain Disability in Occupational Settings: A Review of the Literature from a Human Resource Management View," *Personnel Psychology* 45 (1992), 247–78.
25. Ibid.
26. E. Felsenthal, "Out of Hand," *The Wall Street Journal,* July 14, 1994, A1, A7.
27. N. Taslitz, "OSHA, ADA, and the Litigation of CTDs," *Managing Office Technology,* March 1994, 39–46.
28. Felsenthal, "Out of Hand."
29. Taslitz, "OSHA, ADA."
30. E. Felsenthal, "Guide on Repetitive Stress Injuries Fails to Provide Specific Solutions," *The Wall Street Journal,* July 19, 1994, B8.
31. Horwitz, "9 to Nowhere."
32. M. Harris and L. Heft, "Alcohol and Drug Use in the Workplace: Issues, Controversies and Directions for Future Research," *Journal of Management* 18 (1992), 239–66.

33. W. Sonnenstuhl and H. Trice, *Strategies for Employee Assistance Programs: The Crucial Balance* (Ithaca, NY: ILR Press, 1986).
34. Ibid.
35. F. Luthans and R. Waldersee, "What Do We Really Know about EAPs?" *Human Resource Management* 28 (1989), 385–401.
36. J. Jones, B. Barge, B. Steffy, L. Fay, L. Kunz and L. Wuebker, "Stress and Medical Malpractice: Organizational Risk Assessment and Intervention," *Journal of Applied Psychology* 73 (1988), 727–35.
37. R. Karasek, "Job Demands, Job Decision, Latitude, and Mental Strain: Implications for Job Redesign," *Administrative Science Quarterly* 24 (1979), 285–306.
38. M. Matteson and J. Ivancevich, *Controlling Work Stress* (San Francisco: Jossey Bass, 1987).
39. R. Karasek and T. Theorell, *Healthy Work: Stress, Productivity, and the Reconstruction of Working Life* (New York: Basic Books, 1990).
40. M. Frone, M. Russell, and M.L. Cooper, "Antecedents and Outcomes of Work-Family Conflict: Testing a Model of the Work-Family Interface," *Journal of Applied Psychology* 77 (1992), 65–78.
41. Matteson and Ivancevich, *Controlling Work Stress.*
42. R. Kahn and P. Byosiere, "Stress in Organizations," in *Handbook of Industrial and Organizational Psychology,* vol. 3, ed. M. Dunnette and L. Hough (Palo Alto, CA: Consulting Psychologists Press, 1992).
43. L. Levi, *Preventing Work Stress* (Reading, MA: Addison-Wesley, 1981).
44. J. Mason, "The Cost of Wellness," *Management Review,* July 1994, 29–32.
45. J. Bers, "Rising Health Costs Put FM & Wellness in the Spotlight," *Facilities Design and Management,* May 1994, 68–71.
46. Mason, "The Cost of Wellness."
47. J. Erfurt, A. Foote, and M. Heirich, "The Cost-Effectiveness of Worksite Wellness Programs for Hypertension Control, Weight Loss, Smoking Cessation, and Exercise," *Personnel Psychology* 45 (1992), 5–27.
48. S. Hughes and B. Holt, "Is Sick Building Syndrome for Real?" *Journal of Property Management,* July/August 1994, 32–34.
49. R. Ramsey, "It's Time to Settle the Smoking Issue Once and for All," *Supervision,* November 1994, 14–23.
50. "Secondhand Smoke: Is It a Hazard?" *Consumer Reports,* January 1995, 27–33.
51. R. Yandrick, "More Employers Prohibit Smoking," *HRMagazine,* July 1994, 68–71.
52. Ibid.
53. S. Cocheo, "Smokers: Step Outside to Read This," *ABA Banking Journal,* October 1994, 127, 128.
54. Yandrick, "More Employers Prohibit Smoking."
55. J. Greenberg, "Using Socially Fair Treatment to Promote Acceptance of a Work Site Smoking Ban," *Journal of Applied Psychology* 79 (1994), 288–97.

part 5

Maintaining Effective Employee-Employer Relationships

chapter 14 Unions: The Organizing Process

Core Concepts

After reading this chapter, you should be capable of

1. Applying the basic laws governing the relationship between unions, employees, and management.
2. Explaining why workers might wish to have a union represent them.
3. Understanding the basic steps in a union campaign.
4. Discussing the issues and laws that apply in a union campaign.

Opening Case

Rachel has worked for several years at EZ-Rest, a company that manufactures office chairs. Tomorrow a critical vote will take place. At issue is whether the workers at EZ-Rest will be represented by a union. As she thinks about how to vote, Rachel knows it will not be an easy decision. A great deal has happened within the company in the last year and a half, and both the union and management have campaigned hard. No matter how the election goes tomorrow, things are going to be quite different.

As Rachel thinks back to the first day she worked at the company, changes have already been quite dramatic. The firm was then owned and managed by the grandson and granddaughter of the founder, who started the company in 1903. In fact, it was the grandson and granddaughter who had interviewed and subsequently offered her the job. The business was rather small, with only about 200 full-time workers. Work hours were not rigidly set: employees sometimes came in an hour early and then left an hour early, and they could take lunch whenever they wanted. People stopped to chat with one another occasionally, and sometimes the owners even joined in. Dress was casual, and laughter could often be heard in the office area. Once a month, there was a company picnic, and the owners contributed all of the drinks, hotdogs, buns, and potato chips. During the entire first six months Rachel worked there, not a single person was fired. But at the end of her first six months at EZ-Rest, the grandson and granddaughter sold the business to someone else, and the atmosphere changed almost overnight.

The new owner, Mr. Payne, had a completely different view of business. First, he fired the two top managers, who had worked for the company for 20 years, and replaced them with his own son and daughter. Neither the son nor daughter had ever managed other employees. Both had recently graduated from college (although nobody knew what their majors were). Next, the new owner hired a consultant to review the business and make recommendations for changes. Based on the consultant's report, the business was moved to an older building in a different location, which didn't even have a lunchroom or lounge area. The new location was also much more difficult to get to, as no public transportation was nearby. Another change that the consultant brought about was a new employee handbook, which, among other things, contained a dress code (no more jeans, T-shirts, or casual footwear allowed) and included a provision stating that employment could be terminated at any time for any reason at all.

But the two final blows came when the new owner announced that every employee's pay would be reduced by 10 percent, and then terminated 15 people as part of a "cost cutting program." The next day, Joe and Mary, the two most senior employees, went around the office asking people to stay after work for a meeting at Xanadu's (the local eatery). At that meeting, for which nearly everyone showed up, Joe and Mary explained that they had been in contact with a union for the purposes of becoming organized. They went on to explain the advantages of being unionized, as well as the stages in a union campaign.

Little did Rachel know how stressful the workplace would become. One year after the meeting at Xanadu's, a union election was scheduled. Management hired a consultant to help fight the union. Both the union and management held meetings, and management passed around flyers detailing stories of union corruption. In the meetings, the owner talked about the number of businesses that were closed when they became unionized. When asked if the same would happen to this business, he simply smiled and said, "Who knows? I certainly wouldn't exclude it from the realm of possibilities."

As she thinks about these matters, Rachel really wonders whether she should vote for the union or not. As the union representatives tell it, only under the union will she have job security, reasonable wages and benefits, and a secure future. Yet according to management, having a union will create nothing but problems, and a good chance of having no job. How should she vote in the election tomorrow? As you will see in this chapter as well as the next, unions play an important role in human resources. Regardless of whether the company you work for is unionized, or is trying to avoid becoming unionized, a union is an important force to reckon with. In this chapter, you will learn why employees might wish to unionize and how union campaigns work. You will also read a brief history of unions and learn about the various laws that govern the relationship between unions, management, and employees. We begin, however, with a discussion of what exactly a union is and what role is performed for employees who are represented by the union.

What Is a Union?

Union
An organization of workers whose purpose is to represent the employees in their dealings with management.

According to the dictionary definition, a union is simply an organization of workers. (Chapter 15 will describe the structure of a union, as well as some of the important positions within a union, in greater detail.) The primary purpose of a union is to represent the employees in their dealings with management. A union fulfills this function through three mechanisms:

1. The union is responsible for negotiating a contract with management that covers the terms and conditions of employment, including pay, benefits, work hours, and job assignments.
2. The union is responsible for overseeing the provisions and rules of the contract.
3. The union is responsible for representing employees in grievances or complaints filed against the company.

We will discuss each of these mechanisms in greater detail in Chapter 15. For now, it should be clear that through these mechanisms, the union has a significant influence on human resources within an organization. Let us turn next to a brief history of unions in the United States, which will give you a greater understanding of the relationship between management and unions. Because of the important role laws played in the history of unions, they will be discussed in this section as well.

Unions in the United States: A Brief History[1]

In the Beginning

If there is one word to summarize the history of unions in the United States, the word would be "conflict." Organized unions in the United States did not appear until the early 1800s. Prior to this time, the labor market was such that there was really no need for a union. A shortage of people in early colonial America, as well as a surplus of cheap land in the country, provided many opportunities for employees who were dissatisfied with their jobs. But as business conditions began to change in the 19th century, unions representing skilled trades, such as carpenters and tailors, appeared. Management used two tactics to fight these early unions. One tactic was to form employer organizations, which pooled their resources to resist such things as wage increases. A second approach was to fight unions through the courts, by arguing that labor unions comprised an illegal conspiracy to restrain trade. To management's delight, the courts largely accepted this argument, and beginning in 1806, numerous courts ruled that union activities, such as strikes, were illegal. Not until 1842 did the courts begin to recognize that a union strike could, under some circumstances, be legal.

For the most part, though, U.S. unions enjoyed a feast or famine kind of existence during the 19th century. When the economy was doing well and the unemployment rate was low, unions fared well. In periods when the economy worsened and the unemployment rate increased (such as during the 1840s, when large numbers of immigrants arrived from Europe), union strength declined. For example, in 1836, 300,000 workers belonged to a union, representing more than 6 percent of the workforce. By the mid-1870s, on the other hand, only 50,000 employees were union members.

The late 1800s marked the earliest attempts to form a large, national union. The first such attempt, the Noble and Holy Order of the Knights of Labor, was founded by tailors who sought to organize a wide range of workers. The Knights' membership grew rapidly, from 9,000 in 1878 to 700,000 in 1886, following a highly successful strike against Wabash Railroad in 1885. But rapid growth in membership created numerous problems, resulting in the subsequent decline and extinction of the Knights by 1900. As the Knights' strength began to decline, however, a new union would take its place: the American Federation of Labor, better known by its acronym, the AFL.

The Rise of the AFL

The American Federation of Labor, founded in 1881, was highly influenced by one of its earliest presidents, Samuel Gompers. A highly pragmatic and skilled leader, Gompers adopted several principles that ensured the success of the new organization. One major principle was that individual unions within the AFL umbrella would remain autonomous; essentially, the AFL practiced organizational decentralization. Another key principle was that the AFL, unlike many predecessors, espoused no particular political or ideological position. Rather, the AFL emphasized job-related goals, such as wage increases, that virtually everyone could accept. These and other principles ensured much greater internal cohesiveness than earlier labor organizations, such as the Knights of Labor, had experienced. As a result of the success of the AFL, the number of unionized employees grew from about 500,000 in 1897 to more than 2 million by 1904, an unparalleled growth rate in the history of unions.

The fast rise in unionization did not go unchallenged. Management fought back using a variety of tactics, including discharging workers with union sympathies and using military forces to end strikes. Such tactics often ended in violence. In one of the most publicized events, eleven children and two women died when their tent site was burned to the ground by the militia. Businesses also successfully sought support from the court system, which frequently ruled against union activities and in favor of management.

World War I and Its Aftermath

The growth of the AFL continued through World War I. Its success was aided by support from the president of the United States in exchange for Gompers' promise not to strike and interfere with the war effort. But once again, union growth reached a halt during the 1920s. Among the reasons were Samuel Gompers' death, the courts' continued antagonism toward unions, and a major campaign by management to defeat unions. By 1929, fewer than 3 million workers were unionized.

The Depression Years and the Wagner Act

Wagner Act (National Labor Relations Act) Passed in 1935, this law gives workers the right to organize and participate in union activities, prohibits various management tactics that would discourage unions, outlaws company-sponsored unions, and forbids the company from discriminating against employees for participating in union activities.

While the depression years led to major job losses in the United States, President Roosevelt and his New Deal policies marked the beginning of a major shift in public policy toward unions. In 1935, Congress passed a law known as the Wagner Act (after the senator who drafted it), or, more formally, the National Labor Relations Act (NLRA). As you can see from Table 14.1, the Wagner Act is very much a pro-union law. Among other provisions, this law gives workers the right to organize and participate in union activities, prohibits various management tactics that would discourage unions, outlaws company-sponsored unions, and forbids the company from discriminating against employees for participating in union activities. The NLRA also established the union election process, as well as the National Labor Relations Board (NLRB), which is responsible for administering and interpreting the act.[2]

World War II and the Taft-Hartley Act

National Labor Relations Board (NLRB) Established by the Wagner Act, this board is responsible for administering and interpreting the act and related laws.

Taft-Hartley Act (Labor-Management Relations Act) Passed in 1947, this act was a pro-management law designed to protect employers from unfair union practices.

The years following passage of the NLRA were generally good ones for the union movement. Despite internal bickering and formation of a new union federation called the Committee for Industrial Organization (CIO), which competed with the AFL, the number of unionized employees swelled. By the end of 1941, more than 10 million employees were union members, an increase of more than 7 million in just three years. During World War II, unions continued to grow in terms of membership. As a result, unions became more active in politics, and after World War II they increasingly turned to strikes and work stoppages to achieve their goals. But this turn of events led to public sentiment for curbing union power. In 1947, the Taft-Hartley Act (named after the congressmen who sponsored the bill) or, more formally, the Labor-Management Relations Act, was passed. This act was a pro-management law designed to protect employers from unfair union practices. As you can see from Table 14.2, the Taft-Hartley Act gives companies a number of basic rights in their dealings with the union.[3]

Post World War II and the Landrum-Griffin Act

The percentage of the private-sector workforce that was unionized peaked in the mid-1950s, when approximately one out of every three workers belonged to a union. Although the 1950s in many ways was a good time for unions (for instance, the AFL and CIO merged to form the AFL-CIO, which increased their strength), several events occurred that would be detrimental for unions. First, unions received a great deal of negative publicity during this time regarding possible corruption. Second, internal conflicts among unions continued, leading to, among other events, the expulsion of the International Brotherhood of Teamsters from the AFL-CIO. Third, Congress passed legislation that further restricted unions. In particular, the Landrum-Griffin Act (or, more formally, the Labor-Management Reporting and Disclosure Act) was passed by Congress in 1959. While the first two major laws (the Wagner Act and the Taft-Hartley Act) protected unions and com-

Table 14.1 **The National Labor Relations Act: A Pro-Union Law**

The NLRA protects you, as a union member, union organizer, or employee in the following ways:

1. It prohibits the company from firing you because you engage in union activities or are a member of the union.
2. It prohibits the company from refusing to hire you because you belong to a union.
3. It prohibits the company from denying you the opportunity to form a union.
4. It prohibits company-sponsored unions.
5. It prohibits the company from threatening you with regard to union activities or union representation.
6. It prohibits the company from banning you from discussing the union during work breaks.
7. It prohibits the company from discriminating against the union with regard to room usage and similar privileges.
8. It provides for numerous other requirements, such as good faith bargaining by both management and the union in establishing a contract.

Table 14.2 **The Taft-Hartley Act: A Pro-Management Law**

The Taft-Hartley Act protects companies from a variety of union practices. Included among the provisions are the following:

1. It prohibits the union from requiring employees to be a member of the union in order to be hired (in other words, a closed shop is illegal).
2. It bans featherbedding, in which companies pay employees who are not actually working.
3. It allows management to discuss the ramifications of unionization with employees.
4. It prohibits unions from refusing to bargain with the company.
5. It prohibits unions from charging excessive dues.
6. It permits the president of the United States to halt a strike if public health or safety are threatened.

panies, respectively, the major purpose of the Landrum-Griffin Act was to protect employees from unions. The Landrum-Griffin Act provides the following rights for employees.[4]

Landrum-Griffin Act (Labor-Management Reporting and Disclosure Act)
Passed in 1959, this act's major purpose was to protect employees from unions.

1. The right to equal treatment by the union.
2. The right to free speech and assembly.
3. The right to fair discipline hearings.
4. The right to fair union elections.
5. The right to fair representation.
6. The right to sue the union.

Some of the specific details of your rights as an employee under this act are provided in Table 14.3.[5]

Recent Union Trends

The mid-1950s marked the beginning of a decline that continues even today both in the number of unionized private-sector employees, as well as in the influence

Table 14.3 **Landrum-Griffin Act: A Pro-Employee Law**

The Landrum-Griffin Act mandates a number of employee rights in terms of the way the union deals with them. These include the following:

1. As part of the right to free speech and assembly, you have the right to speak out during meetings, as well as the right to publicly criticize a union leader.
2. You have the right to vote for local union representatives, and a secret ballot must be used.
3. Even if you refuse to join the union that represents your work group, the union must treat you equally.
4. The union has an obligation to do its best to represent you in such things as arbitration hearings; if it fails to do so, you may sue the union, for a kind of malpractice.
5. While the union has the right to discipline you under certain circumstances, you have the right to a fair hearing, including sufficient time to prepare for the hearing, a written copy of the charges, and access to a lawyer if the union is using one.

Box 14.1 The History of Unions: An International Perspective

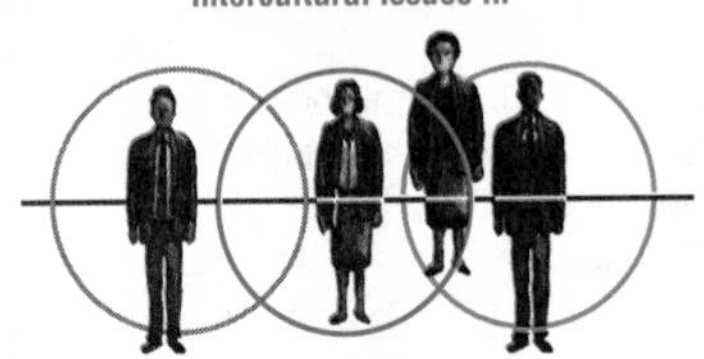

While the history of unions in the United States is characterized by conflict with management, that is by no means a typical pattern in the rest of the world. As an example, if you visited West Germany, you would find that the term "codetermination" is used to describe union-management relations in some of the largest industries. The concept of codetermination is, in fact, required by various laws, such as the Codetermination Law of 1951, which requires coal, iron, and steel companies to fill half of the seats on the supervisory board (contrary to the name, this board is comparable to a board of directors in the United States) with employee representatives. Work councils also have the right to participate in certain major management decisions. Another feature of codetermination is the position of labor director, who is chosen by the supervisory board from a slate of union leaders. The labor director is actively involved in general management activities, and this individual must be a member of the executive committee. New laws passed since the Codetermination Law of 1951 have extended codetermination to other industries in West Germany as well.

Japan has also experienced a much more cooperative relationship between unions and management than the United States has. Perhaps in keeping with the cultural emphasis on cooperation and group harmony, post World War II union growth was strongly encouraged by Japanese corporate leaders. In contrast to the United States, where management typically resisted unions, unions in Japan enjoyed positive relations with management. In fact, management often openly directed pro-company employees to join in union activities, if only to help moderate the unions. Despite strong management support, unions at various times have taken strong stands against the company. Initially, management responded by forming a second union in hopes of destroying the original union. When that strategy failed to work, management turned to a more participatory model and actively sought suggestions from the union to avoid problems. In fact, company executives and union leaders typically maintain cordial relations, often socializing together.

Source: Adapted from C. Kerr and P. Staudohar, *Industrial Relations in a New Age.* (San Francisco: Jossey-Bass, 1986).

Figure 14.1 Percentage of Unionized Employees

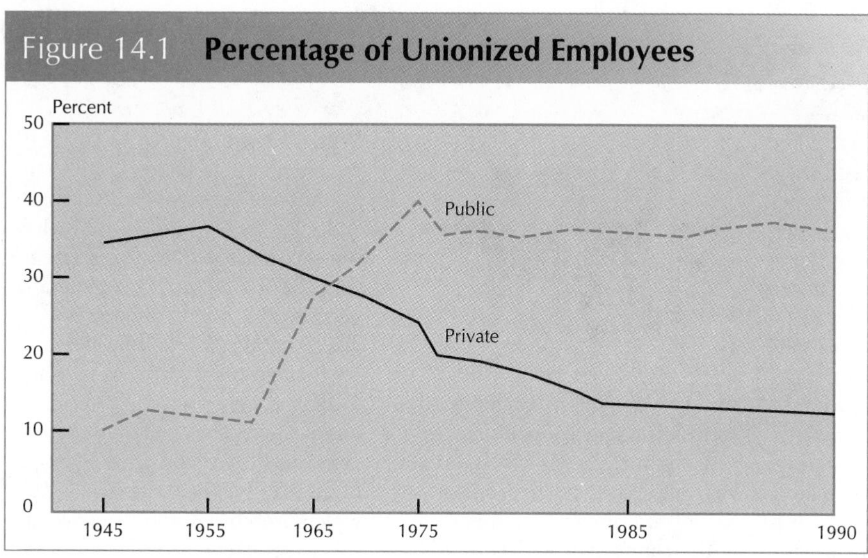

Private is union members as a percentage of all private, nonagricultural wage and salary workers. *Public* is union members as a percentage of total public-sector employment. The increase in public unionization between 1960 and 1970 reflects in part the recategorization of employee associations as unions.
Source: R. Edwards, *Rights At Work* (Washington: The Brookings Institute, p. 85, 1993).

of unions in the workplace and on the political scene. As shown in Figure 14.1, there has been a fairly steady decline in the percentage of unionized employees in the private sector. Although many reasons have been offered as to why union strength has declined, four reasons stand out:

1. Unions appear to have put fewer resources into attracting new members in the last few decades; this may be changing, however (see Box 14.2, "Applying Pressure Where It Counts").
2. Recent legal decisions have generally sided with management and, in turn, have weakened union power.
3. Companies have stepped up their campaigns to keep out unions.
4. Workers are increasingly critical of unions and less likely to see unions as helpful, especially in light of new civil rights and privacy laws.[6]

At present it seems that the number of unionized workers is continuing to decline. In 1994, only 11 percent of private-sector employees were unionized, and some estimate that only 7 percent of private-sector employees will be union members by the year 2001. In comparison, recall that about 33 percent of private-sector employees were union members in the mid-1950s. Whether unions will ever flourish again remains a major question.[7]

In sum, unions in the United States have had a history of resurgence, followed by decline, only to become revived. Over the years Congress has passed three major laws affecting unions. An easy way to remember the order of these laws is to keep in mind that they occur in the reverse alphabetical order: the oldest law is the Wagner Act, followed by the Taft-Hartley Act, and then the most recent one, the Landrum-Griffin Act. If you think about it for a while, the focus of each of these laws

Box 14.2 Applying Pressure Where It Counts: One Union's Tactics to Gain More Members

Tales from the Trenches

One union that has used some unorthodox tactics to gain new members is the Service Employees International Union (SEIU), which represents many janitorial workers. In their effort to gain new members, the SEIU has begun to embarrass the customers of various janitorial service companies. Consider, for example, the SEIU's recent action at the Old Ebbitt Grill, located across from the White House, in Washington, D.C. Long known as a restaurant for politicians and other important people, union representatives recently entered Old Ebbitt Grill and began shaking soda cans filled with ball bearings, while shouting "Justice for Janitors!" Why target this restaurant when it doesn't even employ any janitors? The answer is that it is located in a building that contracts nonunion janitors. This is just one incident in which a union has annoyed not the company it wishes to unionize, but a customer of the company it wishes to unionize. Apple Computer went through a similar experience. The actual target of the campaign was Shine Building Maintenance, Inc., which provided janitorial service for Apple Computer. But SEIU harassed Apple Computer and, in particular, John Sculley, then Apple's CEO. SEIU members would follow Sculley to symphonies, company exhibitions, and even to his home. After a few years, Shine's workers were unionized. SEIU's tactics have generally been successful, as judged by the additional 30,000 janitors it represents since 1986. At the same time, SEIU has suffered some defeats. As one example, an Atlanta-based company sued the union for a violation of the National Labor Relations Act, which prohibits secondary boycotts (picketing of companies not directly involved in the dispute). SEIU decided to settle the suit out of court and ultimately stopped its entire union drive in Atlanta. Overall, though, these aggressive tactics seem to be paying off. Do you think such tactics are fair?

Source: Adapted from M. Ybarra, "Waxing Dramatic," *The Wall Street Journal,* March 21, 1994, A1, A9.

makes a great deal of sense. The Wagner Act is pro-union, which is understandable because before its passage union activity was often deemed illegal. The Taft-Hartley Act, on the other hand, attempted to rectify a perceived imbalance that favored unions. This law, then, limits or prohibits certain union activities and practices. Finally, the Landrum-Griffin Act recognizes the rights of the individual employees, which may have gotten lost in the contest between union and management. Next, you will read a brief history of unions in the public sector or government.

History of Unions in the Public Sector[8]

The union experience in the public sector or government, differs in several ways from that in the private sector. The laws represent one major difference. Public-sector employees wishing to form unions faced a major legal barrier for many years because they were exempt from coverage under the NLRA, which provided only private-sector employees with the right to unionize. Not only did public-sector employees not have the right to unionize, but under certain amendments to the NLRA, federal employees who went on strike could be discharged and barred from reemployment for three years. Similar laws and judicial decisions in other states, such as the Condon-Wadlin Act in New York (which required discharge for strikes by state employees and a ban on salary increases for that unit for three years), maintained this restriction for other public-sector employees. Only among postal workers were unions popular, as various laws passed in the early part of the 20th century provided limited support for unions in this arena.

In 1962, President John F. Kennedy wrote Executive Order 10988, laying the groundwork for a series of laws that greatly increased the rights of public-sector employees to unionize. In 1970, the Postal Reorganization Act mandated that postal workers be covered by the private-sector union laws. Other federal employees were granted extensive unionization rights through the Civil Service Reform Act of 1978. Table 14.4 summarizes some of the key points regarding unionization rights mandated by these two laws.

Table 14.4 **Federal Employees' Unionization Rights under the Civil Service Reform Act and the Postal Reorganization Act**

Topic	Civil Service Reform Act (1978)	Postal Reorganization Act (1970)
Overall administration	Federal Labor Relations Authority	National Labor Relations Board
Basic employee rights	Form, join, and assist unions (or refrain) free from interference, restraint, or coercion	Same (Labor Management Relations Act)
Unfair labor practices	Several, with the most important concerned with organizing and good faith bargaining.	Similar.
Collective bargaining	Good faith bargaining required on personnel policy, practices, and working conditions, with many provisions and exceptions	Good faith bargaining on wages, hours, and terms and conditions of employment; very few topics unlawful.
Resolution of contract disputes	Mediation, fact-finding, and whatever action deemed necessary by the Federal Service Impasses Panel to settle the dispute	Mediation, fact-finding, and binding arbitration

Source: C.J. Coleman, *Managing Labor Relations in the Public Sector* (San Francisco: Jossey-Bass, 1991).

Box 14.3 Health Care Industry: A Hot Bed of Union Activity

Tales from the Trenches

While unions seem stymied in many industries, union campaigns have been fairly successful in the health care industry, particularly in hospitals and nursing homes. In the last five years, the number of union elections in this industry has risen dramatically. And compared to most other industries, unions have been fairly successful in elections here, winning between 53 to 58 percent of the time, depending on the specific year being examined.

Why have unions been targeting, and winning, elections in this industry? Experts point to the dramatic cost-cutting going on in the health care field, which has led to salary reductions, closures, layoffs, and the use of lower-skilled workers to do tasks traditionally performed by higher-paid employees. A good example is Crouse Irving Memorial Hospital, located in Syracuse, New York. In the first election, the union lost by a wide margin. After nurses were given a 6 percent pay cut, the union conducted a new campaign, and this time it won.

Another reason for the increased success of unions here is a small, but significant, change in the law. The change involves a 1991 Supreme Court decision that hospital workers may be divided into eight categories (registered nurses, clerical employees, etc.), where previously these workers were lumped into a fewer number of categories, making elections more difficult for unions to win. Finally, while many traditional unionized industries have had declining numbers of workers to unionize, the health care industry has added many workers over the last few years. This industry, therefore, has been a rich source for union organizers.

Sources: Adapted from R. Tomsho, "Mounting Sense of Job Malaise Prompts More Health-Care Workers to Join Unions," *The Wall Street Journal*, June 9, 1994, B1; and S. Deshpande and D. Flanagan, "Determinants of Union Victory in the Health Care Sector," *Health Care Management Review*, Summer, 1994, 64–69.

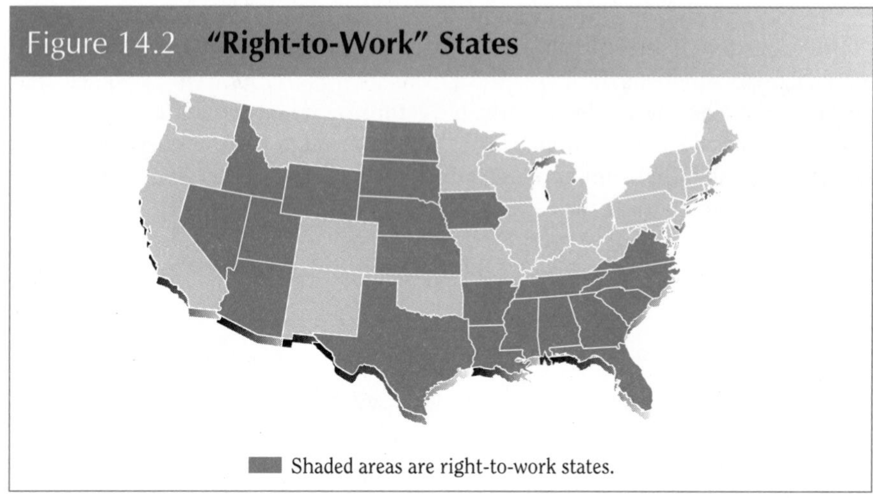
Shaded areas are right-to-work states.

Figure 14.2 "Right-to-Work" States

Source: D. McWhirter, *Your Rights at Work* (New York: Wiley, p. 202, 1993).

Box 14.4 What Type of Shop Do You Work In?

Your Turn

If you have ever worked in a unionized company, you probably have heard the term "union shop" or "agency shop." You may even have heard an older union member discussing the term "closed shop." What do these terms mean? These terms refer to various conditions that an employee must meet in order to be hired and remain employed if his or her job is represented by a union.

A *closed shop* is a union-management agreement that only union members will be hired. If you were applying for a job in a closed shop, you would have to be a union member *before* you could be hired. This type of arrangement was permitted under the law until 1947, when the closed shop was prohibited under the Taft-Hartley Act.

Although the Taft-Hartley Act prohibits the closed shop, the union shop was permitted under this law. In a *union shop,* applicants who are hired are required to join the union within a certain period of time. A Supreme Court decision, however, ruled that no law can force an individual to join an organization against his or her will. According to the Supreme Court, what Congress must have really meant to do was to allow an agreement requiring covered individuals to pay dues or an agency shop. Thus, while an agency shop is permitted by law, employees can only be required to pay union dues—they cannot be required to join the union. Now, you may wonder what the difference between paying union dues and joining the union means in practical terms. The primary difference is that some portion of union dues goes toward supporting various political causes, so if you are not a member of the union, you are eligible for a refund of that portion of the dues.

Finally, you may have heard the expression "right-to-work state." In a *right-to-work state,* such as Georgia, even an agency shop is prohibited by the law. The Taft-Hartley Act permits states to decide whether they will be a right-to-work state. To date, 21 states have right-to-work laws. In these states, it is not possible to force employees of a unionized company to pay dues, let alone join the union. As you can see from Figure 14.2, most of these states are in the southern or western part of the United States.

Legislation granting unionization rights for state and local government employees began in the 1960s. Because these laws are decided by each state, however, they vary greatly. Thus, while 28 states have incorporated comprehensive laws similar to private-sector regulations, other states have either no laws (as is the case in Louisiana and South Carolina, for example) or have laws covering only some public employees. For example, Indiana permits collective bargaining only for teachers. Missouri permits collective bargaining for all public employees *except* certain law enforcement employees, civilian National Guard employees, and teachers. Moreover, Missouri's law permits only limited negotiation rights.

As a result of favorable laws passed in the early 1960s, public-sector unions grew rapidly during this time period. In the years between 1962 and 1982, for example, the number of unionized workers in the public sector more than doubled. The most dramatic growth occurred for state and local employees. The percentage of these workers who belonged to a union increased by almost 300 percent, far exceeding the union growth for federal employees, which increased by 60 percent.

Now that you have read about the history of unions, you may wonder why an employee or group of employees would want a union to represent them. We will discuss that topic next.

Why Workers Join Unions

Workers' interest in and willingness to vote for union representation is a function of three key factors:

1. Job dissatisfaction.
2. Lack of control.
3. Positive attitudes toward and perceptions of unions.

A good way to remember these factors is to use the acronym SLAP, which stands for (dis)*S*atisfaction, *L*ack of control, *A*ttitudes toward and *P*erceptions of unions. Each of these factors is described in greater detail next.[9]

Job Dissatisfaction

Job dissatisfaction is the basic factor that encourages employees to consider unionization. Although many issues may contribute to job dissatisfaction, several stand out in explaining why employees may join a union:

1. Wages and benefits.
2. Job security.
3. Safety.
4. Promotions.
5. Supervisors.

The first four issues probably will not surprise you. Unions generally negotiate higher wages and benefits for the employees. Historically, unions have helped employees to maintain job security by specifying the terms and conditions under which layoffs can occur. In many cases, the union also provides substantial

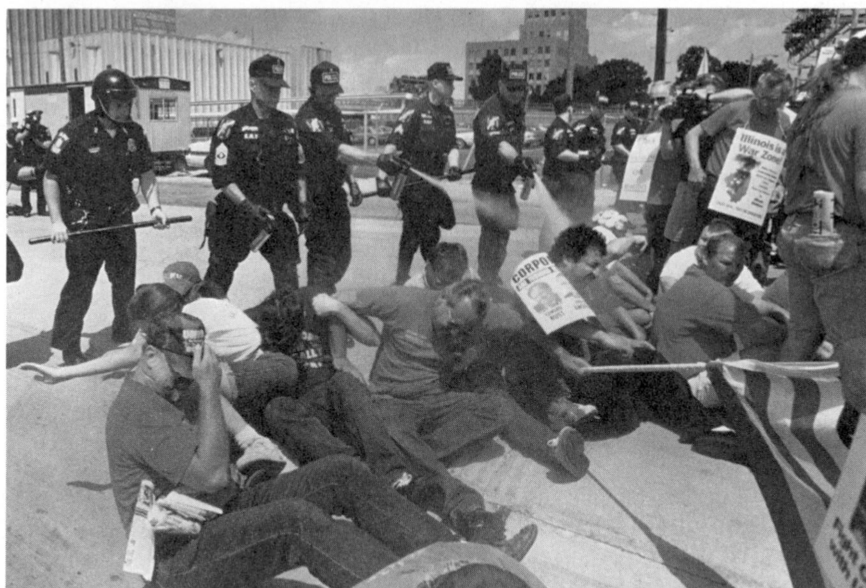

Union strikes can sometimes turn violent when union and management clash over personnel issues. Staley workers and their supporters are shown here being sprayed with pepper gas by police in the city of Decatur, Illinois, in June of 1994.

financial aid to workers who have lost their jobs. Unions also help to improve unsafe conditions in the plant. In terms of promotions, if you have ever been passed by for advancement, you were likely to have questioned the fairness of the decision. Unions offer procedures to make promotion decisions more objective; typically, promotions in a unionized facility will be heavily based on seniority. But what about satisfaction with supervisors? Ineffective supervisors are often a major source of problems, because they may show favoritism, make arbitrary pay decisions, and engage in similar behaviors. The union offers to reduce the power of the supervisor and restore the balance of control to the workers by requiring the supervisor to make personnel decisions on the basis of much more objective criteria, such as seniority. The union also provides a mechanism for the employees to challenge supervisory decisions (such as a formal grievance procedure). Hence, wages, benefits, job security, safety, promotions, and poor supervision are areas that the union usually addresses. On the other hand, dissatisfaction with the kind of work that you do is *unlikely* to influence your interest in joining a union. Can you think of why this might be? One answer is that the union will have little or no effect on the kind of work that you do. If anything, in fact, unions may prefer that workers do very simple, routine work. If you like much more variety in your work, you may find a union problematic.[10]

Returning to the opening case, the employees of EZ-Rest were considering voting for union representation. Do you recall some of the factors that seemed to lead up to this situation? Two major factors seemed most pertinent: the pay cut and the terminations of several employees. If you were an employee, how would you feel about your pay and job security at EZ-Rest? Given these considerations, it is not surprising that the employees sought union representation.

Lack of Control

If the expression "the grass is always greener on the other side" is at all true, few workers are satisfied. It is not surprising, then, that only 25 percent of workers today consider themselves extremely satisfied (compared with 40 percent in 1973).[11] So, why aren't unions much more popular? The answer lies, in part, with the control issue. Have you, for example, ever been very dissatisfied with your pay, benefits, and other aspects of a job? Did you think about joining a union? If you said no, why didn't you think of joining a union? Was it because you chose to change jobs instead? Or did you try to improve matters by complaining or threatening to sue the company for discrimination? There are several alternatives one might try to eliminate employee dissatisfaction besides forming a union.[12] But some workers lack the control to change jobs, complain, or threaten to sue. The job market for their occupation may be very limited, and they may not have the resources to pursue a lawsuit. They may have tried complaining to management, only to have been ignored or perhaps told to leave if they were unhappy. Employees who lack control over the situation are more likely to seek union representation as a means of improving their job satisfaction than are employees who have control and can find another job or change the situation.[13]

What about EZ-Rest, the company in the opening case of this chapter that was in the midst of a union campaign? Do you think the employees had much control over things there? It would appear that the new owner made a number of major changes without the input of the employees. That is probably one reason employees felt little or no control in the situation. Recall also that the two most senior employees, Joe and Mary, contacted the union. Because they were the most senior employees, they were probably also the oldest and would likely face the most difficult time obtaining a new job. If the employees at EZ-Rest did indeed feel they had little control over the situation, they would probably be interested in having a union represent them.

Positive Attitudes Toward and Perceptions of Unions

This factor has two separate components, both of which are important. To illustrate the attitude part, play the word association game for a moment. When you think of the word "union," what is the first thought that comes to mind? Some people will immediately think of words such as "helpful," "fair," and other positive adjectives. Other people will respond with words such as "corrupt," "strikes," and "unfair." The words you associate with unions often depend on your background and experience. In general, some people have favorable attitudes toward unions and will be more likely to vote for union representation, others have negative attitudes toward unions and would be less likely to vote for union representation. Table 14.5 contains a set of items that measure your attitudes about unions in general. As you can see, this attitude is affected by such issues as your perceptions of union corruption, the degree to which you believe unions are helpful, and the amount of power you think they have.[14]

The second component, perceptions, refers to specific beliefs regarding the ability of the union at issue to help the employees. If workers believe that the union in question can improve the workplace features that employees are dissatisfied with, such as pay, job security, and treatment by supervisors, they will be more likely to vote in favor of and join the union. Research shows that when it

Table 14.5 **Assessing Your Attitudes Toward Unions**

For each of the statements below, mark a "1" if you agree and a "0" if you disagree.

1. Unions are often corrupt. ______
2. Unions cause more trouble than they are worth. ______
3. Unions are unnecessary in today's world. ______
4. Unions have far too much power. ______
5. Unions are more concerned about their own agenda than about the workers they represent. ______

Add up the scores on the questions. If your total score is 1 or less, you are relatively likely to support unionization. If your total score is 2 or 3 you are relatively unlikely to support unionization. If your total score is 4 or 5, you are likely to oppose a union no matter how dissatisfied you are.

comes to voting in an actual election, it is the perceptions or specific beliefs about the union that are the most important.[15]

At EZ-Rest, the union probably had a distinct advantage in that the new owner of the company had made several significant changes that adversely affected the employees. As such, the workers' perceptions of the union were probably much more positive than if the new owner had made none of those changes.

In sum, employees will be more likely to vote for a union when they are dissatisfied with such factors as pay, benefits, and job security; when they believe they lack control and therefore have no other means of dealing with the dissatisfying situation, and when they have favorable attitudes toward union and believe the union in question will improve things. Now that you have read about why workers may wish to have a union, you will read about why managers generally dislike unions, followed by a discussion of the process that companies go through in becoming unionized.

Managers' Attitudes Toward Unions

Besides historical factors, there are other reasons why an adversarial relationship exists between management and unions. A primary reason why managers resist unions is because of the restrictions the unions place on managerial discretion and decision making. In essence, the presence of a union means that management can no longer choose to do merely what is in its best interests. The existence of a written contract, which specifies how promotions will be made, how layoffs will be decided, and so forth, largely ties management's hands. Relatedly, if an employee feels his or her treatment has violated the terms of the contract, the employee will have an opportunity to overturn the decision. Many managers feel unions therefore endanger the profitability of the firm. Because this is a widespread perception, a great deal of research has been conducted to examine the effect of unions on various important business and human resource outcomes.

A summary of these findings indicates the following:

1. Employees who work at unionized companies on average are paid 10 percent more than employees who work at nonunionized companies.[16]

2. Unionized firms tend to be somewhat less profitable than nonunionized firms.[17]
3. Unionized firms are no more likely to have layoffs, closures, or bankruptcy than are nonunionized firms.[18]

In sum, while presence of a union will certainly reduce managerial discretion and control, and often raise wages while lowering profits, unions do not seem to increase the likelihood of job loss or bankruptcy. However, the negative effects of unionization are sufficient reason for most companies to fight to keep unions out.

How Companies Become Unionized: The Union Election

In many ways, a union election is similar to a political election. The union in the EZ-Rest company in the opening case would have gone through a number of specific steps before reaching election day.[19]

Union Election
The process used to establish a union within an organization. The union election begins by contact between the workers and the union, next at least 30 percent of the relevant employees must sign authorization cards, then the group may petition the NLRB for permission to hold an election.

Step 1: Initiation of Contact

The union election begins by contact between the workers and the union. The contact may be initiated by either party; the union may contact the employees or the employees may contact the union. In the opening case, Joe and Mary contacted the union first.

Step 2: Authorization Cards

Regardless of how the contact is initiated, the second step of the process requires that at least 30 percent of the relevant employees sign authorization cards. If you examine Figure 14.3, you will see what an authorization card looks like. This step

Authorization Card
The equivalent of obtaining sufficient numbers of signatures of eligible voters for a political candidate to appear on the ballot, at least 30 percent of the relevant employees must sign these cards.

Figure 14.3 Authorization Card

UNITED GLASS AND CERAMIC WORKERS
OF NORTH AMERICA, AFL-CIO, CLC

OFFICIAL MEMBERSHIP APPLICATION AND AUTHORIZATION

I hereby apply for membership in the United Glass and Ceramic Workers of North America, AFL-CIO, CLC. I hereby designate and authorize the United Glass and Ceramic Workers of North America, AFL-CIO, CLC, as my collective bargaining representative in all matters pertaining to wages, rates of pay and other conditions of employment. I also authorize the United Glass and Ceramic Workers of North America, AFL-CIO, CLC, to request recognition from my employer as my bargaining agent.

SIGNATURE OF APPLICANT ____________________
EMPLOYED BY ____________________
APPLICATION RECEIVED BY ____________________
DATE ____________________

Source: G. Dessler, *Personnel/Human Resource Management* (Englewood Cliffs, NJ: Prentice Hall, 1991).

may be compared to the process of obtaining sufficient numbers of signatures of eligible voters for a political candidate to appear on the ballot. In the present case, at least 30 percent of the eligible "voters," or employees, must sign the authorizations cards for the campaigns to proceed to Step 3. Failure to obtain signatures from at least 30 percent of the eligible employees means that the campaign is over. Once the union believes it has at least 30 percent of the necessary signatures, it may petition the National Labor Relations Board (NLRB) for permission to hold an election. Although this step was not mentioned in the EZ-Rest case, it is necessary in order to hold the actual election.

While signing an authorization card does not require that the employee vote in favor of the union in the actual election, you should be aware that the company may consent to recognize the union even without an election if more than 50 percent of the employees signed the authorization cards. Signing an authorization card, then, is vital for the union campaign to continue.

Step 3: Petitioning the NLRB

Bargaining Unit
Refers to the employees who will be voting in the election; if the union wins, these are the employees the union will represent.

Once the NLRB receives the petition, it must determine what the appropriate bargaining unit should be. The bargaining unit refers to the employees who will be voting in the election, and if the union wins, these are the employees who will be represented by the union. The NLRB determines the bargaining unit on the basis of such factors as the similarity of employees with regard to their pay, benefits, type of work performed, physical proximity, organization structure, and so forth. The aim is to establish a bargaining unit in which covered employees share common interests and goals. In addition to determining the appropriate bargaining unit, the NLRB must decide whether an election can be held. Several factors may prohibit an election from being held. These include the following:[20]

1. A union election was held within the last 12 months.
2. The employees of the bargaining unit are already covered by another union.
3. The union has engaged in unfair practices, such as coercing employees to sign authorization cards.

Step 4: The Campaign

Assuming the NLRB authorizes an election, the next step is for both the union and management to present their arguments to the workers. Because of the company's easy access to employees, legal requirements stipulate that management must refrain from a number of activities. An easy way to remember the forbidden activities is to think of them as a "no SPITting" rule. Specifically, management may not do any of the following:[21]

No SPITting Rule
The legal requirements that stipulate what management cannot do to employees who are unionizing: spy on union activities, promise changes in personnel practices, interrogate employees, or threaten employees.

1. *S*py on union activities.
2. *P*romise changes in personnel practices.
3. *I*nterrogate employees.
4. *T*hreaten employees.

Examples of each of these categories are provided in Table 14.6, along with alternative actions that are allowed by the law. As you might guess, there are many ambiguous situations related to these laws. For example, consider the issues of

Table 14.6 **No SPITting: Dos and Don'ts for Management During the Representation Campaign**

Don't	Do
1. Spy on employees by attending union meetings; listen to phone conversations about unions.	1. Allow employees to tell you what happened in meetings.
2. Interrogate employees; have private meetings with individual employees, where you ask about the union; ask in face-to-face meetings with employees about their feelings for the union.	2. Meet with employees in groups to discuss issues; have anonymous surveys publicly completed by employees.
3. Promise specific changes; add new benefits; promotions, etc.	3. Ask employees to give the company a chance to make changes.
4. Threaten employees, say that the facility will close, jobs will be eliminated, or the union will go on strike.	4. Say the facility might close, unions sometimes strike, jobs might be lost.

threats. Do you see the distinction between saying "this facility ***will*** close if the union wins" and saying "some facilities close when a union wins?" According to labor laws, the first statement is an illegal threat; the second is permissible because it is only a statement of fact. From an employee's perspective, however, the implications of these two statements may be the same.

To return to the opening case, you may remember that the new owner talked about companies that closed when they became unionized. That would probably be legal, because he did not say that the same would happen to this company. And when he was asked if that would happen to EZ-Rest, he answered, "Who knows?" So, it is likely that his comments would be considered facts, rather than threats. Do you think his comments sounded threatening? Even though you may interpret them that way, as long as he sticks to the facts (for example, it is true that some companies close after becoming unionized), his comments are permissible under the law.

The ultimate punishment that can be leveled against the company for violation of campaign laws is automatic recognition of the union. A company that violates too many of these regulations runs the risk of losing by default.

Because the union campaign is similar to a political campaign between two or more rival candidates, it should not surprise you that union campaigns have certain common themes. Some of the most common themes or campaign issues that management uses include the following:[22]

1. Things are not so bad.
2. Management provides a number of rewards, which might disappear with unionization.
3. A union cannot guarantee anything.
4. A strike may occur; if so, everyone will lose.
5. Union representatives are outsiders; they don't really care about employees.
6. Give management a chance to improve things.

Union supporters often use T-shirts, caps, placards, buttons, bumper stickers, posters and the like to urge members to "vote union."

Thus, most of the issues raised by management revolve around two broad factors:

1. Things currently are not so bad.
2. The union will only make matters worse.

Four common union themes are the following:

1. Things may improve, but only because management feels challenged by the union.
2. Management is trying to frighten employees by threatening them.
3. The union is the employees; employees decide whether to strike.
4. Unions are good (unions may use quotes from appropriate respected public figures to support this assertion).[23]

Because management is in a defensive position in many union campaigns, the union often has the opportunity to go on the offensive and criticize many management actions.

In addition to these basic themes, both the union and management use a variety of specific tactics and techniques during the campaign. Some of the more common management tactics are to do the following:

1. Hire a labor lawyer.
2. Hire a consultant.
3. Fire employees who actively support the union.
4. Spread rumors about job loss or the facility closing.
5. Delay the election date.
6. Give new benefits.[24]

Do any of these tactics surprise you? You might wonder whether some of them, such as firing union supporters, are legal given what you read earlier in this chapter. In fact, several of these tactics, such as firing union supporters, are illegal under the National Labor Relations Act, which bans discrimination on the basis of union affiliation or activity. So why do companies often engage in such behaviors? Many companies believe that this is a useful way to intimidate workers so that they will vote against union representation. Careful research shows, however, that using illegal tactics is not always beneficial for the company. While spreading rumors about possible plant closure, for example, does appear to discourage workers from voting for the union, delaying the election may actually backfire and appears generally to encourage workers to vote in favor of the union. Some frequently used tactics, then, appear to arouse more, rather than less, sympathy for the union.[25]

On the other hand, there is evidence that consultants and supervisors play a positive role in defeating the union. Consultants specializing in union campaigns, used in nearly 50 percent of union campaigns, appear to be a significant factor in defeating the union. Supervisors, perhaps because of their close relationship with the "voters," also appear to have a major effect on whether the union wins. If supervisors argue against the union, the union is likely to lose the election.[26]

There are also a number of commonly used union tactics. Some of the most popular union tactics are the following:[27]

1. Mailing letters to employees describing the union and its benefits.
2. Holding meetings with employees.
3. Confronting the company.
4. Coordinating resources with other unions.
5. Working with community leaders to support unionization.

Compared with management tactics, which union tactics are most effective remains somewhat unclear. Much more depends on how the union communicates with the employees and the content of the communication, rather than the particular tactics used by the union. Most importantly, the union must develop a close, personal relationship with the employees. As an analogy to the political process, voters are often swayed by that intangible factor referred to as "charisma" as much as they are affected by the specific issues, such as crime and taxes.[28]

Step 5: Election Results

In order to win the election, the union must receive a simple majority (50 percent + 1) of the votes cast. It is also possible that the election will involve several unions wishing to represent the employees. If there is no simple majority, a runoff election is held between the two choices receiving the highest number of votes (this may include the "no union" option).

How have unions fared in elections over the years? If you remember the history of unions described earlier, it will not surprise you that unions have experienced more election losses than victories over the last few decades. In terms of the overall vote, while around 75 percent of workers would vote for a union in 1950, this number shrank to only 49 percent by 1989. Not surprisingly, then, the number of campaigns won by unions has declined from about 76 percent in the early 1950s to fewer than 50 percent by 1993. Thus, unions have experienced increasing difficulty in expanding their base of employees.[29] The only area in which unions have significantly increased in size is in the public sector or government offices, but even that trend has slowed during the past two decades.

Conclusion

The history of unions in the United States is a long, often bitter story of two competing interest groups. In the last 40 years, however, management has increasingly held the upper hand over unions. The major exception has been the growth of unions in the public sector, but even that trend has slowed lately. Many laws now govern the relationship between unions, management, and employees, such as the Wagner Act, the Taft-Hartley Act, and the Landrum-Griffin Act. Workers may wish to have union representation for several basic reasons. As you also read, the union campaign has several distinct steps. The union campaign also has numerous laws governing what can be said and done, particularly by management. As you will see in the next chapter, once a union wins the election, the order of business becomes that of negotiating a contract and making sure that it is properly followed.

Applying Core Concepts

1. Imagine the following situation. Chris Matthews, the owner of a manufacturing business, finds out that a local union has contacted the employees at the plant. In response, Chris posts the following memo: "I recently learned that a union has contacted you regarding possible representation. I can tell you now that I oppose any union, and if somehow the union won an election, I would refuse to negotiate a contract. I will immediately shut down the facility as well. Moreover, if I find out that any of you participate in any way with the union, I will immediately fire you." Is this memo legal? What laws have been violated?
2. Given what you read about EZ-Rest in the opening case, what might the new owner have done differently so that the workers did not become interested in unionization? What actions could he have taken during the campaign that were legal?
3. Explain why a union campaign is similar to a political campaign.
4. Considering laws you read about in earlier chapters, such as various Civil Rights Acts, explain why workers may see unions as less helpful today than they were in the past.
5. How do you feel about unions? What factors (such as your work experience) do you think explain your feelings toward unions?

Key Terms

- Union
- Wagner Act (National Labor Relations Act)
- National Labor Relations Board
- Taft-Hartley Act (Labor-Management Relations Act)
- Landrum-Griffin Act (Labor-Management Reporting and Disclosure Act)
- Union election
- Authorization card
- Bargaining unit
- No SPITting rule

Chapter 14: Experiential Exercise

Union Organizing at SGA Industries

Introduction President White sat in his office at SGA Industries thinking about the union election taking place down at the plant auditorium. He felt that the company had waged a successful campaign to persuade workers that their best interests would be served only if the company remained union free. As he awaited the election results, his mind began to wander back to the events leading up to today's election.

Background SGA Industries is best known as the world's largest producer of women's hosiery and employs approximately 6,500 people in ten plants in five communities in Georgia and South Carolina. The company's headquarters is located in Anderson, Georgia. The company's sales subsidiary, SGA Inc., has 12 offices in major market areas throughout the United States and sells its products directly to distributors around the world. The company's strategy of strong identification with the customer has made the SGA name one of the most recognized in the entire hosiery industry.

SGA was founded in 1907 by Sam Gerome Anderson. Anderson built the company and the community was named after him in 1910. Ever since, the fortunes of Anderson residents have been interwoven with those of SGA. Over the years the company supported the community; donating land and money for churches, schools, and hospitals and providing jobs for nearly a third of the town's residents. As the years passed, further expansion and product diversification occurred, and the company gained a reputation as an industry leader in the design, production, and marketing of women's and men's hose and undergarments.

After the death of the last family member, Alexandra Anderson, SGA was managed by four chief executive officers in less than a dozen years before the company was purchased for $250 million by Jack Phillips. The new owner was a well-known Atlanta entrepreneur and business leader. Soon after the purchase, Phillips appointed Ted White as President of SGA.

Labor–Management Relations Over the years SGA enjoyed a reputation as a steady job provider in an unstable industry. The company provided for its workers and treated them like family members. Many believe that the company's generosity to its employees and the town of Anderson helped to defeat an earlier union organizing drive by the Textile Workers of America by a vote of 3,937 to 1,782. At the time of the vote, the Chairman called it "an expression of confidence by employees." The SGA vote was viewed as a severe blow to union organizing efforts in the South.

When Phillips purchased SGA, he announced that his major goals would be to improve the community and to improve the quality of life for SGA employees and their families. Phillips invested over $100 million to reach these goals. The total included funds for pay increases, new job benefits, capital improvements, including the use of robots, community improvements, and other contributions. These improvements were also accompanied by a shift in management philosophy. The theme of the new management approach was self-sufficiency, and it signaled an end to the benevolent paternalism that had so long characterized employee relations at SGA. Greater emphasis was placed on employee performance and productivity.

During the mid-eighties, the entire hosiery industry experienced major problems. Growing foreign competition and imports had a negative impact on domestic hosiery manufacturers. Many manufacturers attempted to reverse the impact by intensive capital investments in new technology, reorganization and downsizing of plants, and by instituting programs to improve employee productivity and efficiency. SGA was not spared from this competition. Its international sales fell dramatically from $26 million to $10 million. Faced with increasing imports and weak consumer sales, the company was forced to lay off 1,500 employees, reduce pay scales, and to rescind many of the perks that the workers had enjoyed under the Anderson family. Many of these changes drew worker protests and created a good deal of tension between workers and management.

Wages in the industry had been rising steadily but were still lower than wages in the manufacturing sector in general. On a regional basis, the differential was still quite wide, with a study showing that wages ranged from $5.56 per hour in South Carolina to $8.90 in Michigan. In addition, as technology advanced, more skilled operatives were required, thus increasing the cost of turnover to companies. Employers in the industry also were becoming increasingly more dependent on women and

Contributed by Gerald E. Calvasina, The University of North Carolina at Charlotte.
Source: S. Nkomo, M. Fottler, R. Mcafee (1996). *Applications in Human Resource Management.* Cincinnati, OH: South-Western.

minorities for employees. At SGA 40 percent of the employees were women and 35 percent of the total work force were minorities. Minorities and women made up less than 2 percent of the management staff.

The Election Campaign Despite its earlier defeat, the Amalgamated Clothing and Textile Workers Union (ACTWU) was back in Anderson, armed and ready for an organizing effort that would divert the attention of SGA management for several long and tense months.

While many employers learn of union organizing efforts by their employees only after the National Labor Relations Board informs them, the ACTWU's efforts to organize SGA employees were clearly out in the open a full nine months before the election. With a union office in downtown Anderson and a healthy budget, the ACTWU, led by Chris Balog, engaged in one of the most sophisticated union organizing efforts ever seen in the area. Using computerized direct mailing to stay in touch with workers and extensive radio and television advertising, the union effort at SGA attracted wide attention. Many observers felt that the outcome of ACTWU's drive would have significant implications for the ability of labor unions to make inroads into traditionally nonunion regions of the country.

Union's Campaign The campaign issues developed and communicated to workers were for the most part predictable. Job security was brought to the front early and was easily introduced to the campaign in the wake of over 1,500 layoffs and selective plant closings by SGA management. In addition, in attempting to become more competitive in the face of increasing foreign competition, increased workloads and reduced wage rates were key issues raised by the union. The union repeatedly accused Phillips of engaging in unfair labor practices by threatening to sell or close the company if the union were to win bargaining rights for SGA workers. To a certain extent, the union did expand on the traditional wages, hours, and working conditions issues typically raised in organizing efforts. As the campaign progressed, Phillips became a focal point of union rhetoric, and the union attempted to portray Phillips as a greedy and ruthless city slicker from Atlanta who was not interested in the long-term survival of SGA and its employees.

Management's Campaign While Phillips became a focal point of union criticism as the campaign wore on, his role in management's response to the organizing effort was critical throughout the months preceding the election. With President White leading the anti-union campaign, backed by a sophisticated strategy developed by an Atlanta law firm, specializing in anti-union campaigns, SGA was able to quickly respond to every issued raised by the union.

The SGA strategy to defeat the union organizing effort included extensive meetings with community, business, and religious leaders in an attempt to influence workers' views about the union. Extensive use of anti-union films were required viewing for workers on company time. Letters sent to workers' homes by President White and Phillips emphasized the need for team spirit, not only to keep the union out, but to overcome the threat created by hosiery imports. President White put it this way: "We intend to do everything that is proper and legal in this campaign to defeat the union. This is essential if we are to remain competitive in the hosiery business. Every day we are facing more and more foreign competition. Not only do our workers understand this, but I think the public does also. We have been able to communicate with our workers in the past, and we don't need a third party voice. We all must work together as a team. The only way SGA can beat the encroaching foreign competition is to streamline and consolidate our operations."

White and Phillips made repeated visits to plants to shake hands and listen to workers' concerns. The weekly employee newsletter was filled with anti-union letters written by workers and community members. Late in the campaign a letter was sent to SGA workers from Jack Phillips explaining why they should vote against the union (see Exhibit A). In response to the union claim that Phillips was attempting to sell the company, Phillips also told the workers that "SGA is not for sale, but if I determine that the company cannot operate competitively, I can and I will cease to operate SGA. This is entirely up to me and nobody can stop me—including this union."

Employees' Views The employees were divided over the union organizing campaign. Several employees formed an Anti-Union Committee which organized an SGA Loyalty Day. A statement by Terry Floyd, a shift leader, summed up the view expressed by some employees: "We, as employees of SGA, do not feel that it is in the best interest of our company and its employees to be represented by ACTWU. Many generations of the same families have worked at this plant; part of our strength is family heritage. I'm afraid a union will destroy that strength. We feel that a union is not needed and that we can work with management as a team." At one rally sponsored by the Anti-Union Committee, "No Union" badges, "Be Wise–Don't Unionize" T-shirts, and "Vote No" hats were worn by several hundred employees.

Other workers expressed support for the union. One worker stated, "We need a union for protection. At

Exhibit A Letter to SGA Employees

TO ALL SGA EMPLOYEES:

It is only fair for you to know SGA's policy on unions. Our policy is quite simple. We are absolutely opposed to a union at any of our plants. We intend to use every legal and proper means to stay non-union.

As you know, the hosiery industry has been under great pressure and competition from foreign firms. Sales in the industry have dwindled over the past few years and we are in a poor profit position. Our government has done little to protect your jobs and stop the imports from eroding our sales. Only you and I can save this company and your jobs.

Our whole industry has been forced to modernize our production process to make it more efficient. In fact you know that many firms have merged together to strengthen their market position. Our company, too, will have to explore the possible advantages of pooling resources and products. In the long run such strategy can only benefit employees and management alike. I know bringing in the ACTWU at this time will only drive up our operating expenses and jeopardize our chances of making such arrangements. Only management has the right to decide how to operate this company. If we find we cannot operate this company profitably, we may be forced to consider other options.

We are convinced that unions have the tendency to create an adversarial relationship between employees and management. Cooperation and teamwork cannot exist in such a hostile environment. It is only through cooperation and teamwork that we will get through the crisis.

No SGA employee is ever going to need a union to keep her job. We know that ACTWU cannot help this company or you and will probably cause us to lose even more of our market and threaten your job security. I urge you—do not vote for the union. Let's all pull together and remember the goodwill of the Anderson family and how it has stood behind you all of these years.

Sincerely,

Jack Phillips

Jack Phillips
Chief Executive Officer

least it would give us a voice. Supervisors can be too arbitrary." Others pointed to pay increases and bonuses for top management in the wake of wage cuts and layoffs for plant workers. Many older employees, who remembered the generosity of the Anderson family, also expressed bitterness toward SGA and worried about their pensions.

Questions

1. What was the impetus for the union organizing effort at SGA Industries?
2. Discuss SGA's strategy in managing the representation campaign.
3. Discuss any potential unfair labor practice charges SGA management might face as a result of their campaign strategy.

Chapter 14 References

1. A. Sloane and F. Witney, *Labor Relations* (Englewood Cliffs, NJ: Prentice-Hall: 1977).
2. D. Leslie, *Labor Law in a Nutshell* (St. Paul, MN: West, 1986).
3. D. McWhirter, *Your Rights at Work* (New York: John Wiley, 1993).
4. Ibid.
5. Ibid.
6. R. Edwards, *Rights at Work* (Washington: The Brookings Institute, 1993).
7. Labor Letter, *The Wall Street Journal,* August 30, 1994, A1.
8. C.J. Coleman, *Managing Labor Relations in the Public Sector* (San Francisco: Jossey-Bass, 1990).
9. J. Brett, "Why Employees Want Unions," *Organizational Dynamics* Spring, (1980), 47–59.
10. R. Dunham, and F. Smith, *Organizational Surveys* (Glenview, IL: Scott, Foresman, 1979).
11. "Work Week," *The Wall Street Journal,* November 29, 1994, A1.
12. C. Rusbult, D. Farrell, G. Rogers, and A. Mainous, "Impact of Exchange Variables on Exit, Voice, Loyalty, and Neglect: An Integrating Model of Responses to Declining Job Satisfaction," *Academy of Management Journal* 31 (1988), 599–627.
13. S. Youngblood, A. DeNisi, J. Molleston, and W. Mobley, "The Impact of Work Environment, Instrumentality Beliefs, Perceived Labor Union Image, and Subjective Norms on Union Voting Intentions," *Academy of Management Journal* 27 (1984), 576–90.
14. M. Zalesny, "Comparison of Economic and Noneconomic Factors in Predicting Faculty Vote Preference in a Union Representation Election," *Journal of Applied Psychology* 70 (1985), 243–56.
15. S. Deshpande and J. Fiorito, "Specific and General Beliefs in Union Voting Models," *Academy of Management Journal* 32 (1989), 883–97.
16. S. Jarrell and T. Stanley, "A Meta-Analysis of the Union-Nonunion Wage Gap," *Industrial and Labor Relations Review* 44 (1990), 54–67.
17. Labor Letter, *The Wall Street Journal,* August 23, 1994, A1.
18. Ibid.
19. H. Cheeseman, *Business Law: The Legal, Ethical, and International Environment* (Englewood Cliffs, NJ: Prentice-Hall, 1992).
20. S. Kahn, B. Brown and M. Lanzarone, *Legal Guide to Human Resources* (Boston: Warren, Gorham, & Lamont, 1995).
21. Ibid.
22. J. Getman, "Ruminations on Union Organizing in the Private Sector," in *Human Resources Management: Readings,* ed. F. Foulkes (Englewood Cliffs, NJ: Prentice-Hall, 1989).
23. Ibid.
24. R. Peterson, T. Lee, and B. Finnegan, "Strategies and Tactics in Union Organizing Campaigns," *Industrial Relations* 31 (1992), 370–81.
25. R. Freeman and M. Kleiner, "Employer Behavior in the Face of Union Organizing Drives," *Industrial and Labor Relations Review* 43 (1990), 351–65.
26. Ibid.
27. Peterson, Lee, & Finnegan, "Strategies and Tactics."
28. Getman, "Ruminations on Union Organizing."
29. Edwards, *Rights at Work.*

Unions: Negotiating and Administering an Agreement

chapter 15

Core Concepts

After reading this chapter, you should be capable of

1. Explaining the structure of a union.
2. Discussing the steps in contract negotiations.
3. Describing the steps in a typical grievance procedure.
4. Defining a union decertification election.
5. Providing suggestions for improving management-union relationships.

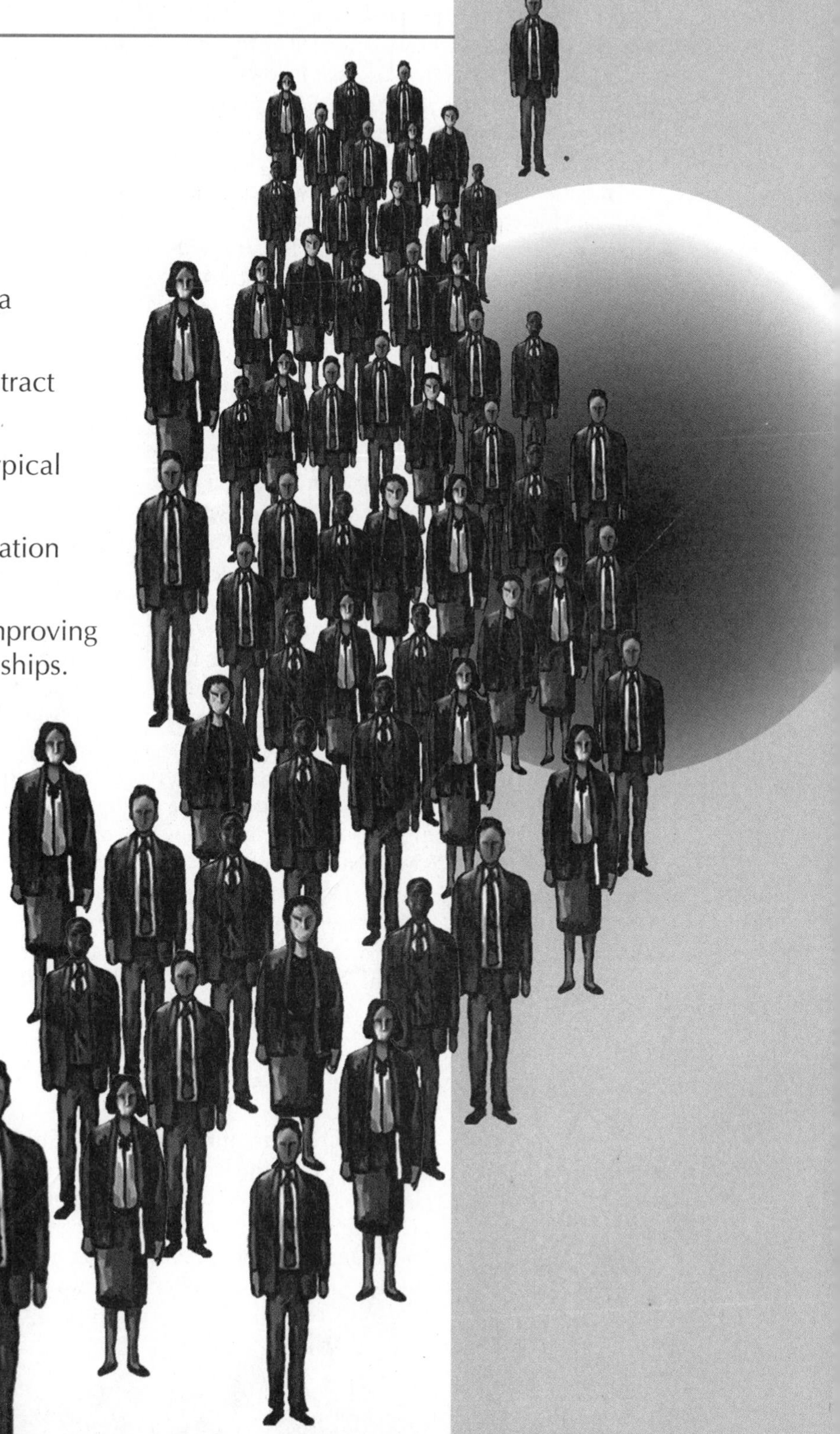

Opening Case

Phyliss Martin, a maintenance worker at Wilson Ship Builders, was recently terminated by the company. A brief history of her case is as follows. About one year ago, a random drug test revealed that Phyliss recently had used marijuana. For this, she was suspended without pay for one week. About one month later, Phyliss was arrested near her home and indicted for drug possession with the intent to distribute illegal substances. Because Wilson Ship Builders is the major employer located in a small town, her arrest was reported on the front page of the newspaper as well as on the 10 o'clock news. The company terminated her on the grounds that she violated its policy prohibiting employees from using illegal drugs while on company grounds or on company business, and that illegal drugs are grounds for dismissal even if used off the company grounds if they have a negative effect on performance or the safety of the employee or other employees. In addition, conviction for a felony crime was grounds for immediate dismissal. Because Phyliss is a union worker, however, she is covered by a contract that gives her the right to file a grievance, or to seek reconsideration of this decision. In fact, she may be able to seek reconsideration through an impartial third party, typically referred to as an arbitrator. The arbitrator, if her grievance goes that far, will attempt to determine whether in fact the company's decision has been fair, in light of the terms and conditions of the bargaining agreement.

Given what you have read about Phyliss Martin's case, do you think that the decision to terminate her was fair in light of the bargaining agreement? What would you have ruled if you were the arbitrator? In an actual case very similar to the one described here, the arbitrator decided that the company had indeed been wrong in discharging Phyliss. His reasoning was that the company had no proof that she was under the influence of drugs when she was arrested. Moreover, the contract only permitted termination when the employee is *convicted* of a felony crime. At the time of the termination, Phyliss had been arrested and indicted, but had not yet been found guilty.

Regardless of whether you agree or disagree with the arbitrator's decision, it should be clear to you through this example that employees covered by a union contract may have considerable protection from management decisions. Indeed, as identified in the previous chapter, a major function of the union is to administer the contract and represent the employees in disputing management decisions. As in the situation experienced by Phyliss Martin, the protection afforded by the union can be considerable.

This chapter discusses in greater detail the key functions performed by a union in a covered facility. As you will see, the union must first negotiate a collective bargaining agreement (or, in the case of a facility in which the contract will expire, the union must renegotiate a new contract). Once a contract is negotiated and approved by the relevant parties, the union's task is to administer the contract and represent the employees in the grievance process. In addition, you will read about some suggestions that might help management to maintain effective relationships with the union.

Union Structure: Who's Who in the Union

Union structure
Labor unions have three major levels in their structure: the local unions form the first layer; national and

Labor unions have three major levels in their organizational structure.[1] As shown in Figure 15.1, the local unions form the first layer in the union structure. Each local union represents a group of employees working in one area for the company. The local union is responsible for negotiating the contract, administering the contract, and organizing nonunionized workers. As a member of a union, you are likely to interact most often with two people in the local union: the business rep-

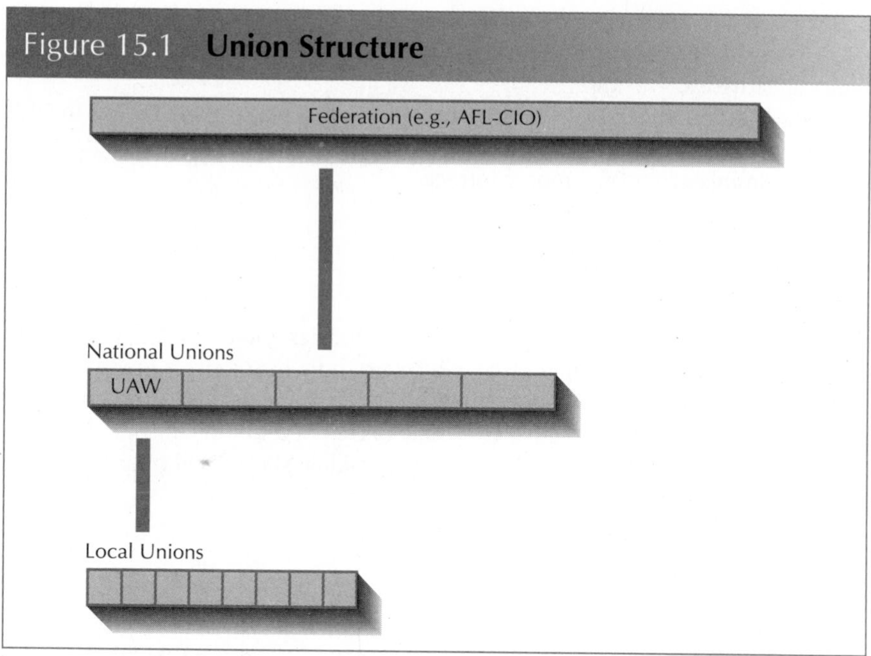

Figure 15.1 Union Structure

resentative and the union steward. As suggested by the term, the business representative plays a key role in the success of the local union. Usually a full-time job, the business representative has the primary responsibility for representing the union in contract negotiations. He or she will also represent the union at certain stages in the grievance process and has a major responsibility for collecting union dues, paying union bills, and interacting with the national union. The union steward plays a key role in day-to-day relationships with management. Typically, the union steward holds a regular job within the company and performs the union-related work on a part-time basis. Most grievances begin with the union steward. Both the business representative and the union steward, then, play an important role in the local union.

National and international unions form the next level in the structure. As shown in Figure 15.1, they are composed of local unions. Presently, there are nearly 200 national unions in the United States. Their rules and regulations stipulate the conditions under which the local unions operate. The national union generally has extensive power over the local union, including the right to approve any contracts, strike decisions, and so forth. The national union also plays a major role in formulating policies, such as collective bargaining goals. The local union pays dues to the national union. In return, the national union provides a variety of support activities to the local unions, including legal assistance, financial assistance during strikes, and various educational services. The national unions are operated by officers who are elected by delegates from the local unions.

Federations represent the top of the union structure. As discussed in Chapter 14, the American Federation of Labor and Congress of Industrial Organizations (AFL-CIO) is an example of a very large, powerful federation. More than 100 national unions belong to the AFL-CIO. This federation is governed by an executive

international unions form the next level; and federations represent the top of the union structure.

Business representative
The business representative's primary responsibility is to represent the union in contract negotiations, and also is responsible for collecting union dues, paying union bills, and communicating with the national union.

Union steward
The union steward plays a key role in day-to-day relationships with management, usually performing the union-related work on a part-time basis.

council and delegates from the national unions. The federation provides numerous services to the national unions that belong to it, and it frequently engages in political activities.

Now that you understand the structure of a union, you will read about the two primary tasks performed by the union for its bargaining unit employees: negotiating and administering the union contract.

Negotiating the Union Contract

The purpose of the union contract is to establish rules and regulations, agreed to by both union and management, that will govern human resources practices (promotions, pay, benefits, job assignments, and so forth) for the bargaining unit employees. As you can see in Figure 15.2, negotiation of a union contract generally involves four steps: preparation, initial stages, middle stages, and final stages. We will consider each step in greater detail.[2]

Preparation for Negotiations

Unlike earlier years, when contract negotiations were often characterized by shouting, threatening, and other aggressive behaviors, contract negotiations today are far more frequently the product of thorough preparation. This is because most union contracts must be negotiated every few years, so treachery or overt manipulation on the part of one side is likely to backfire the next time around. Preparation for the negotiation requires that both parties determine their basic objectives and obtain and analyze information on each of the bargaining issues. For example, in preparing for its 1994 through 1997 collective bargaining objectives, the United Rubber Workers union decided on four basic goals:

1. Increasing wages and obtaining cost-of-living adjustments.
2. Improving job security.
3. Providing further training and career development programs.
4. Improving pension programs.[3]

Let us consider one bargaining issue in greater detail and see what kinds of information will be collected in preparing for the negotiations. Specifically, we will consider the kind of information that will be obtained for determining the appropriate wage.

Determining Appropriate Wage. Three factors are generally considered in determining the appropriate wage:

1. The wage paid by other comparable companies.
2. The company's ability to pay.
3. The cost of living.

The first factor, often referred to as the comparative norm, is the wage paid by other companies. While this may sound fairly simple in principle, in practice, the comparative norm is much more complex. For example, what are "other comparable companies"? Are they all companies in the same industry (such as all automobile manufacturing firms), regardless of size and profitability? Second, the company negotiating the contract may actually be part of several industries, not

Figure 15.2 **Steps in Negotiating a Union Contract**

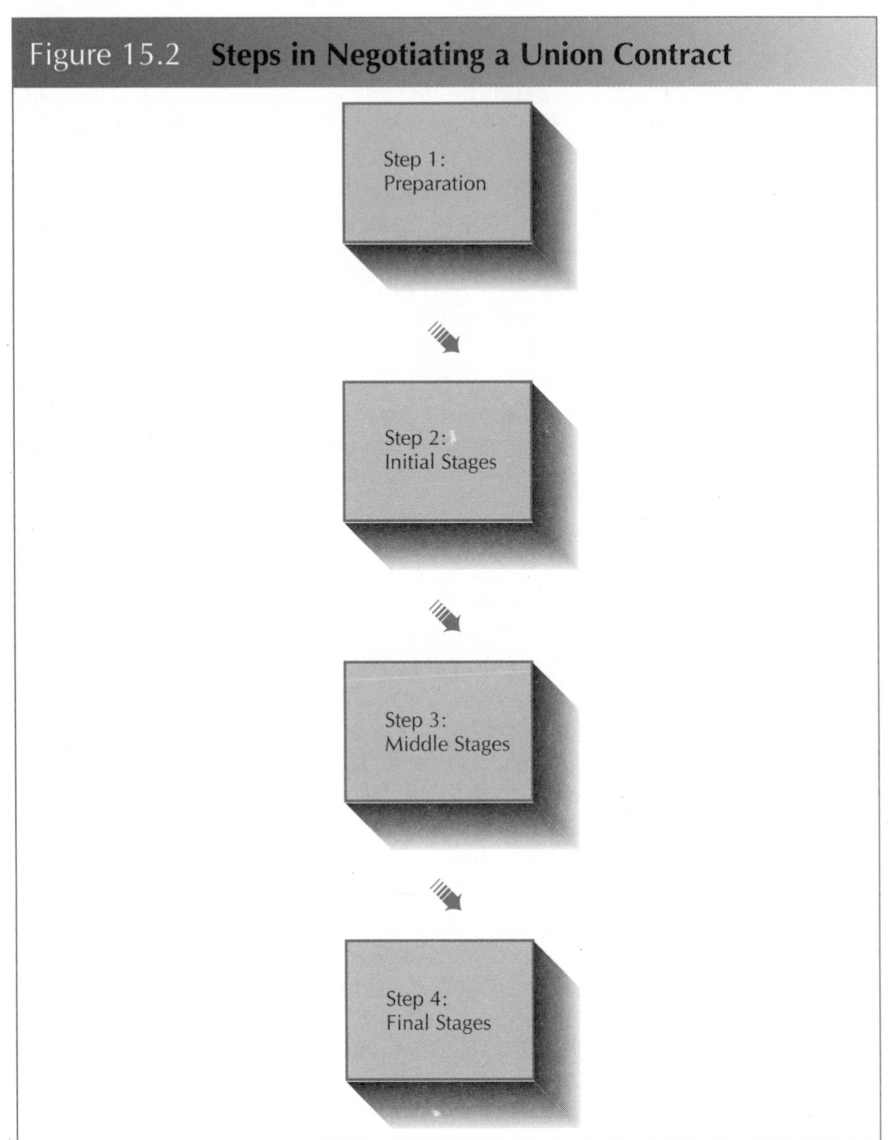

just one industry. Third, the job itself may be treated differently in different companies, or the pay package may differ from company to company. Union and management negotiators may, therefore, arrive at very different figures, based on which information they think is most relevant.

The second factor, the ability to pay, concerns the ability of the company to pay a particular wage. A major determinant of ability to pay is the company's profitability. As simple as this sounds, in practice, it too is far more complex. One reason for the complexity is that current profitability does not necessarily indicate future profitability. A company may, for example, be prospering currently, but indicators may suggest a downturn in the near future. Second, profits may be used for various capital improvements, which in turn provide less money for wages.

Whether this in fact is a better use of profits may be debatable. Finally, even if a company is quite profitable, a wage increase may drive up the cost of the product or service, which in turn may result in business loss. For example, in the major league baseball strike of 1993–1994, the owners claimed that the high average salary earned by players was driving some teams out of business and proposed a salary cap. In turn, the players' union argued that the more profitable owners should simply subsidize the less profitable owners. Even with the same information, union and management negotiators may arrive at very different conclusions as to the company's ability to pay.[4]

The final factor used to determine the appropriate wage is the cost of living. Unions, in particular, believe that a fair wage is one that enables the workers to live in a reasonably comfortable fashion. Various governmental agencies, such as the Bureau of Labor Statistics, provide information as to how much it costs to live at a reasonable standard in different parts of the country. In addition, because the cost of living can be expected to rise over the term of the contract, both sides will attempt to estimate the future inflation rate. Again, there are different sources of information with which to base estimates, which can lead to different conclusions. Of course, in industries that are experiencing serious economic problems, cost-of-living increases may not be possible. In 1994, for example, union workers at United Airlines agreed to wage cuts over a six-year period; in exchange, however, workers would obtain partial ownership of the company.[5]

Aside from negotiating the basic wage, rules for modifying the basic wage may be adopted in the contract. For example, some union contracts may include an automatic adjustment, referred to as an escalator clause, that adjusts wages (both up and down), depending on the cost of living. Another type of rule, the wage reopener, permits renegotiation of the contract if requested by either the union or management. Clearly, much preparation is required by both sides in order to arrive at a contract that will be acceptable to all relevant parties.

Escalator clause
A clause included in some union contracts that adjusts wages (both up and down), depending on the cost of living.

Besides obtaining relevant information for each issue, management should obtain information from supervisors and managers as to what specific problems have arisen with previous contracts. From the union's perspective, it is important to communicate with members to determine what issues and concerns they have, so that a contract can be negotiated that they will endorse. Once preparation has been concluded by both sides, they are ready to move to the actual bargaining process.

Initial Negotiation Stages

Frequently, there is an initial meeting between union and management that focuses on exchanging information on each party's position. In most cases, the union provides a list of its positions on such issues as pay increase, benefits, and so forth. These positions may be highly unrealistic, the main goal from the union's perspective being to satisfy members that the union is doing its best. Both parties often invite a number of guests, who attend in a ceremonial role. Unions, for example, may have members of other unions attend their initial meetings.

Middle Stages of the Bargaining Process

At this intermediate stage, both union and management should have a fairly good idea as to the key objectives of the other side. Each side secretly determines what it will concede on each issue, as well as its key objectives. Based on this information, serious negotiations begin. In 1994, for example, unions at General Electric (GE) Company began the negotiation process with high expectations because GE had had excellent profits. The company, however, was very reluctant to give in to the union demands. The high expectations of the union coupled with GE management's resistance led to diminished progress as the expiration date of the contract drew near.[6]

Two strategies often used are the trading point procedure and the counterproposal approach. Each of these is explained in greater detail next.

Trading Point Procedure. This technique is much like the "horse trading" approach you may have used at various times. Essentially, the trading point procedure involves one side saying to the other, "We'll concede on this issue (such as wage increases), if you concede on this other issue (for example, overtime pay).

Trading point procedure
The trading point procedures involve one side saying to the other: "We'll concede on this issue (e.g., wage increases), if you concede on this other issue (e.g., overtime pay)."

Counterproposal. This technique involves making an offer in response to the other side's offer. For example, the union may ask for a $1.00-per-hour raise. Management may then make a counterproposal of a $.50 raise, along with double overtime. Counterproposals are actually used by the National Labor Relations Board as evidence of good faith bargaining, which is required under the National Labor Relations Act (see Chapter 14).

Counterproposal
This technique involves making an offer in response to the other side's offer.

In sum, the middle stages of contract negotiation involve serious discussion and activity. The final stages of the negotiation process are often the most important ones, though.

Final Stages of Contract Negotiations

In many cases, the contract negotiations will go down to the wire as both sides often wait until the old contract runs out or a strike is about to occur. An imminent strike deadline may, in fact, force both parties to reconsider their priorities. In the 1994 GE example, the contract negotiations were concluded shortly before a strike deadline. In the final agreement, the union received the highest wage increase and best improvement in pension funds in years, but it received few gains in other

Contract negotiation meetings often begin on friendly terms as the two sides meet together to resolve issues affecting union and management alike. Shown is the opening of the 1984 UAW-GM negotiations, with UAW president Owen Bieber (left) shaking hands with GM's Al Warren.

areas, such as job security. In fact, the union contract even required employees to pay more for health benefits than in previous years.[7]

In order to avoid a strike, two mechanisms are often used: joint study groups and mediation.

Joint study groups
A joint study group is a task force, composed of both management and union representatives, and often third parties as well, for the purpose of examining issues of particular concern in a nonadversarial setting.

Joint Study Groups. As suggested by the term, a joint study group is a task force, composed of both management and union representatives (and often third parties as well) for the purpose of examining issues of particular concern in a nonadversarial setting. The group is often established immediately after a contract is negotiated, so that both sides are able to discuss controversial issues well before a new contract is negotiated. With sufficient time, many problem areas may be worked out before the next set of negotiations takes place.

Mediation
In mediation, a neutral party meets with the union and management to work out an agreement (the mediator's suggestions are not binding on either party).

Mediation. In mediation, a neutral party meets with the union and management to work out an agreement. It is important to note that the mediator's suggestions are not binding on either party. That is, either side may choose to reject the mediator's proposals. The purpose of mediation, then, is to involve an independent, neutral party who can generate new solutions for a negotiation impasse. In many cases, a mediator has indeed been helpful in resolving an impasse. The United States government operates the Federal Mediation and Conciliation Service, which provides mediators for businesses that are experiencing difficulty in contract negotiations. Many states also provide similar services. During the major league baseball strike of 1993–1994, President Clinton appointed William Usery to serve as a mediator.

Research has shown that the most effective mediators are highly experienced in the mediation process and work very hard to generate new, creative solutions. As one very effective mediator stated it, "Mediation doesn't start until both of the parties have told the mediator there's no more room for compromise."[8]

When No Contract Can Be Negotiated

Strike
When workers refuse to go to work.

When a contract cannot be successfully negotiated, workers may choose to go on strike, or refuse to go to work. Although relatively rare, a strike can be quite disruptive to an organization. This is particularly true for a large organization, where a strike at one plant may force other plants and facilities to slow down or even close as a result. For example, if an automobile manufacturer experiences a strike at the brake production facility, it may not be possible to continue to build cars at other facilities because no brakes are available. The strike, or the threat of one, is the union's ultimate weapon against the company. That is one reason why, in recent times, as businesses increasingly hire replacement workers (often referred to as "scabs") to replace striking workers, union power has diminished significantly. Recent attempts to pass congressional laws limiting a company's right to hire replacement workers have failed, much to the chagrin of unions.

Replacement workers
Often called "scabs," replacement workers are hired to replace striking personnel.

Another reason why the threat of a strike has diminished in value to the union is that companies have developed extensive backup plans. For example, in coping with the 1994 strike by the United Automobile Workers (UAW), Caterpillar used a variety of strategies, such as utilizing replacement, temporary, and management workers to operate its manufacturing facilities; shifting work to nonunion production sites; and making extensive use of automation.[9]

Despite the broad publicity when a strike occurs, such events are relatively rare in the United States. In the first ten months of 1994, for example, there were

Box 15.1 Some Important Clues for Predicting Which Plants Will Strike

Tales from the Trenches

A comparison of plants that have gone on strike with plants that did not go on strike suggests a number of clues that can be used to predict the strike decision. One major difference between the striking and nonstriking plants was the number of grievances filed and the number of days it took to settle a grievance. On average, striking plants had about 50 grievances over a three-month period, while nonstriking plants had around 10. Moreover, it took roughly three times longer to resolve a grievance at the striking plants. A second major difference was the number of complaints filed by the third shift. At striking plants, the third shift typically had many more complaints than at the nonstriking plants. Why should the number of complaints by the third shift be an important clue? The third shift may be a critical indicator of problems because being at work at night (generally from 11 P.M. to 7 A.M.), these employees generally have the least contact with management (top management rarely is around at night), the least experienced supervisors (the most senior supervisors will prefer day work), and the most equipment-related problems (support services are usually the most limited at this time). The third shift therefore is often the best indicator of union-management friction. Another important clue was the amount of overtime. Among the striking plants, overtime was generally required by the union contract, with penalties for workers who refused the request. By contrast, in the nonstriking plants, provisions for easing the burden of overtime work were provided, such as rotation among departments and extra rewards (such as tickets to local sports events) for those working overtime. Striking plants also gave much more power to supervisors, including the right to terminate, while nonstriking plants gave much less power to supervisors. Finally, plants differed with regard to organizational structure. Striking plants tended to be one of many plants in the company or division, while nonstriking plants tended to be the only plant in the division or company. While the precise reason for this finding is not clear, the multiplant arrangement means that top management has much less awareness of employee relations problems. Furthermore, many human resource practices may be established at the company and division level, which may not be appropriate for all of the plants. It may be that lack of specific attention to each plant results in more labor strife.

For plants interested in reducing the likelihood of a strike, these clues should be carefully monitored, and where problems are indicated, steps should be taken to address them.

Source: Adapted from W. Imberman, "Who Strikes—and Why?" *Harvard Business Review,* November/December 1983, 18–28.

only 44 work stoppages involving 1,000 or more workers. During the same period in 1993, there were only 32 work stoppages.[10]

Should Public-Sector Employees Be Allowed to Strike?

One of the most controversial issues regarding public-sector employees concerns the right to strike. Currently, only about ten states legally permit public-sector employees to strike, and even these states apply restrictions (police and firefighters are typically prohibited from striking, for example). Nevertheless, public-sector employees do sometimes go on strike, even when illegal. In 1988, for example, there were nine major strikes by public-sector employees, involving some 16,000 workers. Over the years, the vast majority of the strikes have occurred in education settings (in fact, you may have had additional vacation from school as a result), with the next largest number occurring in the mass transit area.[11]

Should public-sector employees have the right to strike? What do you think? Here are some of the basic reasons for permitting them to strike.[12]

1. Few Public-Sector Jobs Are Really Essential. Aside from police and firefighters, one could argue that few public-sector jobs are critical for proper functioning. For example, many jobs could be subcontracted with private firms, such as trash removal and bus driving. With few exceptions (perhaps police and firefighters), there is no reason the public couldn't function effectively without these workers.
2. Preventing Strikes Leads to Other Forms of Protest. Even if the employees are prohibited from striking, they can usually use other means to express their discontent. For example, police can refuse to issue tickets, firefighters can refuse to carry out certain routine work (such as conduct inspections), and so forth. According to this argument, prohibiting strikes simply means the workers will use other approaches to express their displeasure with the terms and conditions of work.
3. Penalties for Striking Create Other Problems. As just noted, public-sector employees often strike, even if prohibited. The penalties for such illegal actions, however, may create more problems. For example, an illegal New York prison guard strike resulted in 8,000 employees having their pay cut. The guards then appealed the penalties on an individual basis, requiring more than 2,500 hearings. The hearings required the state to spend substantial amounts of time and money. This argument suggests that the costs of prohibiting strikes outweigh any gains.

Here are some of the arguments *against* permitting public-sector workers to strike:

1. Public Employees Have Unfair Control. Compared to their private-sector counterparts, the "employer" in the public sector has relatively little power to respond to a strike. The employer in the public sector cannot lock out the employees and cannot lose customers or revenue. Because most public-sector organizations have a monopoly on their product or service (for example, public transportation, public schools), the customers have little or no choice but to encourage management to settle. Under this argument, there is an essential difference between the public and private sectors, and therefore strikes should not be permitted in the public sector.
2. Penalties for Strikes Must Be Enforced in Order to Work. In response to the third reason given in favor of allowing public-sector employees to strike, some argue that enforcement of penalties for striking has simply been too lax to be meaningful. According to this argument, then, consistently applied penalties for striking would definitely inhibit illegal strikes.

Clearly, there are important points on both sides of the argument regarding the right of public-sector employees to strike. Whether laws change in the future remains to be seen.

Current Trends in Contract Negotiations

In recent years, contract negotiations have produced relatively small increases in workers' pay. In 1994, despite a growing economy, wages on average increased

Box 15.2 Handling a Union Strike: A Management Perspective

Tales from the Trenches

According to experts, it takes a minimum of one month for management to prepare for a strike. One central committee and three subcommittees should be formed. The three subcommittees are as follows:

1. A production committee.
2. A production support committee.
3. A strike control center committee.

The production committee, as suggested by the title, is charged with maintaining production or service during the strike. One of the issues that this committee considers is how the production line or service schedule will be staffed, depending on how many workers go on strike. In addition, this committee is responsible for clarifying vendors' rights and responsibilities (for example, issues concerning delivery across picket lines), stockpiling inventory, maintaining equipment schedules, and so forth.

The production support committee has a number of responsibilities, including staffing, security, and facility services. For example, this committee will be responsible for ensuring that striker replacements are hired as needed and that supervisors are trained on what to say and what not to say to employees regarding the strike. For instance, supervisors must not make threats regarding the pending strike (statements such as, "If you join the strike, I'll make sure you never get a job in this town again," are clearly illegal). It is essential that supervisors be given thorough instructions about what they can and cannot say and do.

The production support committee is also in charge of security matters. For obvious reasons, this is a critical issue when a strike takes place. Because sabotage of machinery and equipment, and even violence, can occur, it is essential to have a carefully developed security plan to cover all areas. For example, it will be useful to have prepared a plan for safely transporting employees who are coming to work. There are also laws that affect security measures. For instance, movie cameras can only be used to record mass picketing, violence, or other illegal activities. Legal picketing and distribution of literature cannot be videotaped, because this constitutes an infringement of employee rights. Finally, this committee is responsible for maintaining facility services. Utility companies, for example, should be notified of an impending strike to ensure continued service (the utility companies may also wish to protect their equipment). Contingency plans should be made in case various services (for instance, water) are lost.

Finally, the strike control center committee serves to coordinate all activities during the strike. Any questions, issues, or problems must be reported to this group, which operates on a 24-hour basis. The strike control center should have several telephones, lists of all employees along with their telephone numbers, and a wide variety of supplies (including a copying machine, food, and two-way radios). This committee is responsible for recording and documenting all strike-related activities (for example, when the strike begins, this committee would document any complaints of unfair striker activities), preparing all news releases, observing picket lines, and other related issues.

Given the complexity of a strike, careful planning is necessary. By assembling a team and assigning responsibilities to knowledgeable employees, a great deal of trouble can be spared.

Source: Adapted from W. Mullins, *Strike Defense Manual* (Houston: Gulf Publishing, 1980).

only 2 percent for the first year covered by the contract, representing one of the smallest increases on record. More than 20 percent of the contracts provided *no* raise for workers during the first year covered. Over the life of the contract, bargaining agreements covering 1,000 or more workers in the private sector averaged annual pay increases of 2.3 percent, compared to 2.1 percent, 3 percent, and 3.2 percent, in 1993, 1992, and 1991, respectively. At the same time, some contract negotiations focused on areas besides wage increases. In the health service industry, for example, the National Health and Human Care Employees Union negotiated a contract that guaranteed jobs of all covered workers with at least two years of service. Layoffs created by financial emergency would be decided by a four-person committee, composed of two union members and two management personnel. Terminated employees would be given as much as 80 percent of their salaries and family health insurance for one year. Management also agreed to give the union 30 days' notice of any proposed job changes, thus providing an opportunity for the union to respond.[13] In today's world, where job security is relatively low, contract provisions providing protection from layoffs may be more valuable to union members than large pay increases are.

In sum, successfully negotiating a union contract is a complicated, potentially lengthy task. Although many contracts are negotiated with little conflict, other contracts are only resolved after considerable negotiation or even a strike.

Administering the Union Contract

Once a contract has been successfully negotiated, the major task becomes administration of the contract. While negotiating the contract may seem difficult and time-consuming, administering the contract can be far more difficult and time-consuming. The reason for this is twofold: first, the contract cannot anticipate every possible situation or issue that will arise, second, many situations will be less than clear-cut as to how they fit within the language of the contract. In many cases, questions will arise as to whether management has violated the contract. Virtually all union contracts, therefore, include a grievance procedure. As described in the opening case, a grievance procedure provides a mechanism for the employee or union to dispute a decision that is believed to be in violation of the contract. Because of the importance of the grievance procedure, it will be discussed in greater detail next.

Grievance procedure
A grievance procedure provides a mechanism for the employee or union to dispute a decision that is believed to be in violation of the contract.

The Grievance Procedure

Although there is no one grievance procedure that is used by all companies, most grievance procedures have the following steps:[14]

1. The employee, with assistance from the union steward, files the necessary forms to initiate a grievance. At this stage, the employee and the shop steward meet with the first-line supervisor to resolve the dispute. About 20 percent of grievances are resolved at this step.[15]

2. If the employee is not satisfied with the solution proposed by the first-line supervisor, he or she can go to the next level of supervision (such as the shift supervisor) to resolve the conflict. At this stage, the union's business representative may represent the grievant. Approximately 34 percent of grievances are resolved at this step.[16]

3. If the employee is not satisfied with the decision in Step 2, he or she may seek resolution at the next level of management, which may involve the plant manager. At this step, the employee would probably be represented by a higher-level union representative, such as the local union's vice president. Nearly one-third of grievances are resolved in Step 3.[17]

Box 15.3 Union Changes: An International Perspective

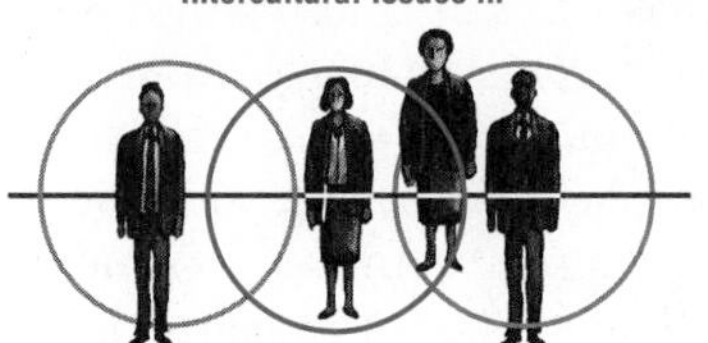

Unions are undergoing many changes, not only in the United States, but in the world. In some countries, unions are experiencing the same loss of workers as in the United States. Great Britain, for example, has experienced a decline in the number of trade employees represented by a union, as a result of workforce reductions and plant shutdowns. In other areas of the world, changes in unions have been much more profound. The Republic of Korea, for example, has experienced a myriad of changes in the last ten years. Major labor law reforms in 1987 resulted in a large increase in the number of union members in just two years, followed by a small decline in the next two years. A variety of bills to provide further labor reforms, including allowing public-sector employees to unionize, were vetoed by the president in the early 1990s. In 1992, the government attempted to pass legislation weakening the unions, whom it blamed for economic problems. Concerted opposition from Korean unions, as well as from the International Labour Organization, which Korea joined in 1991, prevented passage of this legislation. Union activists hope that additional laws, more favorable toward unions, can be passed in the coming years.

The situation for unions is quite different in mainland China. Recent changes in standards of living have led to much greater awareness of workplace problems. Large numbers of workers are employed in low-paying, dangerous factory settings. Fires often break out, leading to many deaths. For example, explosions in mines during the first three months of 1994 resulted in the deaths of more than 750 workers. Some human rights groups and international unions are clamoring for sanctions against China until workplace conditions are improved. There is only one legal union in China, the All-China Federation of Trade Unions, which does little to prevent these problems. Some dissidents have considered establishing a new union, called the League for the Protection of Workers' Rights. Another response has been an increase in strikes. Although illegal, the number of strikes has increased to more than 8,000 in 1993. How Chinese unions will fare in the future is unknown.

Sources: Adapted from P.B. Beaumont, and R.I.D. Harris. "Trade Union Recognition and Employment Contraction. Britain, 1980–1984," *British Journal of Industrial Relations* 29 (1991), 49–58; Y. Park, "Industrial Relations and Labour Law Developments in the Republic of Korea," *International Labor Review* 132 (1993) 581–82; and M.W. Brauchli and J. Kahn, "Toil and Trouble," *The Wall Street Journal,* May 19, 1994, A1, A4.

4. If the employee is still not satisfied with the outcome, he or she has the right to request an arbitration hearing. An arbitration hearing involves a neutral third party or arbitrator, who will listen to the arguments of both sides and make a ruling. Unlike decisions made by a mediator, which either party may reject, both parties must accept the arbitration decision. Just over 10 percent of grievances proceed all the way to arbitration.[18]

Employee's Perspective on the Grievance Procedure

Why would the union encourage you to file a grievance? Three reasons may be offered. First, the union may feel that the terms of the contract have been violated. For example, the union may believe that your supervisor disciplined you without just cause. Second, the union may be fulfilling its obligation to represent you in a fair manner, having you file a grievance will serve as evidence that the union is fulfilling this legal obligation. Third, the union may encourage you to file a grievance for political reasons, such as a need to seem tough with management and stand up for its members.[19]

You may be wondering what the chances are that you will be victorious if your grievance proceeds all the way to the arbitration stage. Research indicates that the nature of the grievance is a decisive factor. If you are involved in a discharge, you have a 50 percent chance of losing the case and approximately a 33 percent chance of having a compromise being awarded (for example, you might be suspended for one week without pay). If you are filing a grievance for a lesser discipline action (such as a one-day suspension), you have slightly more than a 1-out-of-3 chance of completely winning your case, a similar probability of completely losing, and slightly less than a 1-out-of-3 chance of obtaining a compromise. In most cases, then, it is in your best interests as an employee to file a grievance if you are in a unionized facility and feel mistreated.[20]

We turn now to a more detailed examination of the arbitration stage of the grievance process, which plays an important role in management-union relations.

Arbitration Process

Arbitration process Resembles a courtroom hearing, but the rules are not as formalized. An arbitrator is selected, and that person is responsible for making a final ruling after considering all of the relevant evidence and testimony, and provide a decision and explanation in a written report.

The arbitration process is referred to as a "quasi-legal" proceeding because it resembles a courtroom hearing, but the rules are not as formalized. For example, a contract may state that only one person will serve as an arbitrator or that a mutually agreed-upon arbitrator will be used. There is no one standard procedure as to how the hearing will proceed. Although there are no specific rules for the arbitration process, some common features exist. We will discuss two areas in greater detail: the selection and the role of the arbitrator and the arbitration hearing.[21]

Selection and Role of the Arbitrator. There are three basic procedures for choosing an arbitrator:

1. One person is chosen to serve on all arbitration hearings.
2. There is a panel of arbitrators, who serve on a rotating basis.
3. The parties obtain a list of possible arbitrators from the American Arbitration Association or Federal Mediation and Conciliation Service, and ultimately choose one.

The role of the arbitrator is twofold. First, the arbitrator must conduct the hearing in an appropriate fashion. He or she must provide a fair opportunity for both sides to present their case, ensure proper procedures are followed, and make decisions about what evidence may be presented. Second, the arbitrator is responsible for making the final ruling. In this capacity, the arbitrator must consider all of the relevant evidence and testimony, and provide a decision and explanation in a written report.

Arbitration Hearing. The arbitrator serves as the judge during the hearing. Both sides make an opening statement, followed by the introduction of relevant evidence. Either party may show exhibits, which may contain information such as the relevant contractual statements (recall in the opening case that the arbitrator paid close attention to the exact wording of the union contract). Following the exhibits, both sides will call witnesses to testify. The witnesses generally testify under oath. After testifying on behalf of one side (for example, management), the witnesses may be cross-examined by the other side (such as the union). The arbitrator may also ask questions of the witnesses. At times, the union, management, or arbitrator may request an actual visit to the location where the incident occurred. Following testimony by witnesses, both parties provide their closing arguments, which may be delivered either orally, in writing, or both.

Although the arbitration process is lengthy and time-consuming, it is a highly regarded and relatively efficient means of resolving disagreements. Perhaps that is one reason why arbitration is being used in many more areas today, including settlement of consumer complaints and employment discrimination charges. As demonstrated in the opening case, the precise wording in a bargaining agreement is extremely important. Failure by the organization to have an appropriate contract can lead to many subsequent grievances and, ultimately, important management decisions may be overturned.

Eliminating the Union

Once a union is elected to represent the employees, is it a permanent fixture? The answer is no. Just as the workers may decide to vote in a union to represent them, the workers may choose to vote out the union. This latter process is referred to as

Box 15.4 **So You Want to Be a Labor Arbitrator?**

Your Turn

Did reading about arbitration stimulate your interest in becoming a labor arbitrator? If so, here is some information that will help you decide whether this is a viable career option. First, you should know that many arbitrators are members of the National Academy of Arbitrators (NAA), which requires either substantial experience as a labor arbitrator or more limited experience in labor arbitration coupled with other activities such as writing in the area of labor-management relations. If you have had experience working on behalf of unions or management dealing with union issues, you may not be able to join the NAA. Given this information, you should not be surprised that few people begin their careers as arbitrators. Rather, most current arbitrators started in a law, teaching, or industrial relations career, and then began doing arbitration on a part-time basis.

In terms of the arbitrator's career stages, initial entry appears to be the most difficult. Because no licensing or certification is needed to be a labor arbitrator, and given the way in which they are selected, there is a major emphasis on age and experience. Most labor arbitrators are in their late 40s when they work on their first case. As one labor arbitrator put it, there are two ways to deal with one's early career stage: having a full-time job to pay one's bills or having a great deal of patience. Moreover, most arbitrators work in this capacity only on a part-time basis. Not surprisingly, then, a large percentage of part-time arbitrators are lawyers or teachers, careers that allow them to do arbitration while maintaining a full-time job.

As indicated above, many arbitrators are members of the NAA. In fact, some management-union contracts require that only NAA members be used as arbitrators. It will not surprise you, then, that NAA arbitrators average more than three times as many cases annually (57 on average) than non-NAA arbitrators (17 on average).

By now you are probably wondering whether it is financially worth becoming a labor arbitrator. In 1986, the average fee per case was slightly over $1,000. The average NAA member reported earnings of about $65,000, while the average non-NAA member (who is probably doing this activity on a part-time basis) earned roughly $15,000 annually.

With all of these facts in mind, it is clearly difficult to become a labor arbitrator, and few people make a great deal of money doing arbitration. Clearly, this is not a career most people should plan on having.

Source: Adapted from M. Bognanno, C. Coleman, eds., *Labor Arbitration in America* (New York: Praeger, 1992).

Decertification campaign
Just as the workers may decide to vote in a union to represent them, the workers may choose to vote out the union.

a **decertification campaign**. In the political context, this is similar to impeachment. The process of decertification is much like the representation campaign. At least 30 percent of the employees in the bargaining unit must indicate an interest in an election before the actual election will be held. After the National Labor Relations Board approves the petition, an election will be held to determine the status of the union. As in the representation campaign, a simple majority of the employees (50 percent + 1) voting against the union will eliminate union representation.[22]

Just as there are a number of restrictions as to what management can do during the representation campaign, there are a number of restrictions as to what management can do during the decertification campaign. These restrictions are quite similar to the ones described in Table 14.6.[23]

Given the continuing decline of unionized workers in the United States, it should not surprise you that the number of decertification elections has increased over the years, from about 100 annually in the 1950s to more than 1,000 each year

Box 15.5 Why One Company Decertified the Union

Northeast Color Research, Inc., a custom photography lab located in Massachusetts, became unionized when it grew from 2 to 25 employees. Like many small companies, however, lack of clear human resource policies and a shortage of skilled supervisors led to discontent among the employees. Of the 12 employees who were eligible to vote for representation by the United Food and Commercial Workers Union, 9 voted yes.

Tales from the Trenches

From the start, Joanne Frederick, CEO of Northeast, resented the interference of a union. At the same time, she admitted that the union was helpful to her in certain ways. For example, union rules enabled the company to more easily enforce discipline procedures. Nonetheless, Frederick consulted with a labor attorney for advice on how to legally counter the union. As a result of the attorney's suggestions, Frederick did a number of things. First, she began to improve certain aspects of the workplace, such as the employee lounge, that were not covered by the union contract (what advantage do you think this provided?). Second, she began to replace supervisors who had poor management skills with more effective supervisors. Third, she accepted union provisions in the contract that she knew employees would not like, such as narrow job descriptions (which the employees would find too restrictive because they wanted to gain as much experience as possible).

Many of the employees began to dislike the union rules. For example, the highly skilled employees resented the union's emphasis on seniority rather than qualifications. Ten months after the contract was signed, the employees met with Frederick to discuss various company issues. When the employees asked why a broken machine had yet to be replaced, she replied that the costs associated with the union had prevented it from being fixed. The employees became upset and realized that there were certain drawbacks to the union. She then mentioned that employees could contact the National Labor Relations Board regarding decertification. Within hours, the employees called to tell her they had initiated a decertification effort. Based on a straw vote indicating little support for keeping the union, the union withdrew, thereby avoiding a humiliating election.

Although decertification is still relatively rare, it is most common in small businesses. In the case of Northeast Color, the union faced several disadvantages, particularly a lack of understanding of the nature of this type of business. Accordingly, the union was removed shortly after being voted in.

Source: Adapted from R.C. Wood, "The Decline and Fall of a Union," *Inc.*, October 1982, 134.

in the 1990s. Moreover, the union is losing roughly 75 percent of the time and rarely is able to be reinstated.[24]

We conclude this chapter with some suggestions that may help organizations to maintain effective labor-management relationships.

Developing Harmonious Labor-Management Relations: Suggestions for Employers

Management can take several steps to improve its relationships with the union.

1. Reconsider the Nature of Labor-Management Relationships. As described in the previous chapter, although union-management relationships have generally been acrimonious in the United States, some unions and companies have attempted to form a completely different relationship. The implications of this new relationship for the union, and how it compares with the traditional role unions play, are provided in Table 15.1. As you can see, the role of unions in the future may be to serve as a partner with, rather than adversary to, management.[25]

   The 1992 contract negotiated between AT&T and the Communications Workers of America (CWA) exemplifies this new relationship. Described as the "Workplace of the Future," the contract creates a multilevel partnership between the union and management. As shown in Table 15.2, this contract establishes a number of task forces and committees, with union and management representatives, that will enable both sides to work together on important issues that face the organization. What is particularly interesting about this contract is that the union has a far greater role in long-term human resource planning, as well as in general business issues, than unions have had in the past. Other companies that have developed such innovative relationships with the union include a Shell Oil plant in Ontario, Canada, and the United Auto Workers and General Motors in the Toyota plant in Fremont, California. In these latter instances, which were new or radically redesigned plants, the union played an active role with management in planning and implementing new management approaches.[26] Whether such contracts become commonplace remains to be seen.[27]

Table 15.1 **The Traditional Role versus the New Role Unions May Play**

Topic	Traditional Role	New Role
1. Corporate policy	No role	Represents workforce
2. Organizational effectiveness	No role	Facilitates and inputs
3. Work design	Bargaining issue	Participates
4. Rewards	Bargaining issue	Bargains for and helps administer and design
5. Quality of work life	Bargaining, grievances	Facilitates, monitors

Source: Adapted from E.E. Lawler and S.A. Mohrman, "Unions and the New Management," *Academy of Management Executive* 1 (1987), 293–300.

Table 15.2 **Components of the New CWA and AT&T Contract**

1. **Local Level:** CWA and AT&T managers agree on various mechanisms to be implemented (information sharing, self-managed teams, etc.).
2. **Business Division Planning Councils:** CWA and AT&T representatives establish and monitor new technologies and work structures, and jointly engage in human resource planning.
3. **Constructive Relationship Council:** Addresses corporation-level issues and resolves issues brought by local-level and business division planning councils.
4. **Human Resources Board:** Composed of three top executives, two union officers, and two outside human resource experts, this component is responsible for human resource issues from a long-term perspective.

Source: Adapted from M. Bahr, "Communications Workers of America," *Quality Progress* 26 (1993), 59–60.

2. Implement Programs to Improve Labor-Management Relations. As described in Chapter 12, many companies have implemented programs to increase employee empowerment while improving productivity and quality. These programs, as well as information meetings between union officials, employees, and plant managers, have been found to reduce grievances and the need for disciplinary actions. Managers must be educated as to the importance of harmonious labor-management relationships in ensuring high labor efficiency and outstanding product quality. Indeed, research shows that positive labor relationships do improve the bottom line.[28]

3. Improve the Grievance Process. Maintaining an effective, fair grievance procedure is an important aspect of the labor-management relationship. Companies are therefore encouraged to examine the efficacy of the grievance procedure on an ongoing basis. Some organizations, for example, have introduced an additional, half step in the traditional four-step system that involves an informal meeting between the affected parties in attempt to avoid arbitration. Other organizations have established special boards for the purpose of reducing case backlogs. Some organizations also have found that supervisors are poorly trained in handling and responding to grievances, and that supervisors often have only limited understanding of the collective bargaining agreement. To address these shortcomings, companies have developed training programs for supervisors, thereby leading to fewer grievances and more effective responses.[29]

Conclusion

In conclusion, unions play a major role in the human resource area. By requiring that virtually all terms and conditions of employment are determined with its input, the union has established itself as a major factor in the human resource function of the company. Once a union is elected, a contract governing all aspects of the employment relationship between workers and management will be written, and a great deal of managerial decision making and discretion over such matters as pay increases, terminations, and job assignments is eliminated. A grievance procedure is included, enabling workers to appeal management decisions. Failure on the part of management to deal effectively with the union ultimately increases conflict and reduces organizational productivity and quality.

Applying Core Concepts

1. Do you work in a union facility? If not, ask a friend or relative who does to answer these questions. What is the name of your business steward? Your business representative? What is the name of the local union? What national or international union does it belong to? Does it belong to any federation? You may wish to obtain more information from a federation office. The AFL-CIO, for example, maintains a web page on the World Wide Web (WWW.AFLCIO.ORG).
2. Find information about a recent situation in which the union accepted a contract after a strike (for example, the major league baseball strike of 1993–1994). What were some of the factors that produced an acceptable contract? In your opinion, which party (management or union) gave in?
3. Explain why you think the typical grievance procedure works well. Why would a union want to have a grievance system?
4. What are the barriers to a widespread, radical change in the way union-management relationships operate in the United States? Can you think of any outside forces (for example, the changing business environment) that might alter the traditional relationship between unions and management?
5. Given what you read in Chapters 14 and 15, what are your ideas about the relevance and value of unions? If you are covered in your current job or were covered in a previous job by a union contract, do you think things would have been better for you without the union? What about for the company? If you were not covered by a union contract, would you have preferred to have one? Why or why not?

Key Terms

- Union structure
- Business representative
- Union steward
- Escalator clause
- Trading point procedure
- Counterproposal
- Joint study groups
- Mediation
- Strike
- Replacement workers
- Grievance procedure
- Arbitration process
- Decertification campaign

Chapter 15: Experiential Exercise

Labor Arbitration

I. *Objectives:*
   1. To familiarize you with the arbitration process.
   2. To give you practice in presenting a case before others.
   3. To examine issues relating to contract administration.

II. *Out-of-Class Preparation Time:* 40–50 minutes

III. *Procedures:* Either at the beginning of or before class each student should read the exercise. To start the exercise, the instructor will divide the class into the following three groups:
   1. Union representatives (approximately five individuals)
   2. Company representatives (approximately five individuals)
   3. Arbitrators (all remaining participants, divided into groups of three to five members)

The union representatives should meet together and carefully examine "The Union Position" and prepare to argue and defend this position. The company representatives

Contributed by Gerald E. Calvasina, The University of North Carolina at Charlotte.
Source: S. Nkomo, M. Fottler, R. McAfee. *Applications in Human Resource Management* (Cincinnati, OH: South-Western, 1996).

should do the same with reference to "The Company Position." Meanwhile the arbitrators should read both the union position and the company position and discuss among themselves the arguments for and against each position.

After both the union and company representatives have prepared their position statements, each should present their case to the arbitrators. Each group will be allowed five minutes for their presentation, then an additional five minutes to counter the other group's position.

After all presentations are complete, each group of arbitrators will be given ten minutes to discuss the case and reach a decision. These decisions should be presented, along with the reasoning behind them, to all participants.

Finally, the instructor may (optionally) present the arbitrator's actual decision in this case.

The Issue

Was the grievant discharged for just cause? The company claimed the employee's negligence of duty resulted in the discharge and the union claimed poor performance was the issue. If the union is right, what should be the remedy?

Pertinent Provisions of the Union Agreement

Article I. Purpose of the Agreement. The management of the company and the direction of the working force, including the right to plan, direct, and control operations, the right to hire, suspend, transfer, or discharge for just and sufficient cause, to relieve employees from duties because of lack of work or for other legitimate business reasons and the right to introduce new or improved methods or facilities of production is vested exclusively in the company; provided, however, that such rights shall not be exercised for the purpose of discriminating against any employee, and such rights shall not conflict with the provisions of this agreement.

Article 33. Discipline and Discharge. 33.1. In cases of poor job performance, the following procedure dealing with discipline will be accomplished with written notification to the Union:

a. Formal written warning in the first instance with copy to the employee.
b. In subsequent instances, formal written warning and/or suspension without pay for a period not to exceed five working days.
c. In the event three or more instances occur, one of which results in a suspension, within any two-year period, discharge for just cause will be accomplished.

33.1.1. For purposes of this article, job performance shall include consideration of the following factors:

1. Attendance record, including absenteeism, tardiness, and proven abuse of sick leave.
2. Adherence to industrial safety rules.
3. Adherence to Company house rules.
4. Ability to perform assigned tasks satisfactorily.

33.2. In cases of personal misconduct, the disciplinary action taken, including discharge, will be consistent with the gravity of the offense.

Background

The grievant was employed as a service technician for the ABC Petroleum/Gas Company from August 1984 to April of 1993. On January 26, 1993, grievant was dispatched to a customer who reported a strong odor. Grievant's service report showed that he spent 26 minutes on the call, that no leaks were found, and that no repairs were made. The grievant did not take a pressure/manometer test.

Later that same day, in response to a second call, another technician was sent to the customer's home. The second technician checked the gas tank and gauge readings, added some gas, used the track, and did the pressure/manometer test. He tested the lines and isolated the source of the gas odor at a leak in the heater connector after the shutoff valve on the heater. The leak was located less than two feet from the pilot light on the water heater, which was lit. The technician replaced the heater connector and put the old one in the back of his truck. Subsequently, the grievant's immediate supervisor talked with the second technician and examined the damaged heater connector. On January 28, 1993, the supervisor met with the grievant and informed him that he was being suspended, pending an investigation. The reason for the suspension was "Negligent in responding to report of gas odor on January 26, failure to perform leak investigation according to company procedures/leaving party with hazardous condition." By letter on April 16, 1993, grievant was notified that he was being terminated based on the company's findings indicating that "the incident was of such serious nature that we would be remiss in continuing your employment as a technician."

The Company's Position

The company contends that the grievant failed to follow normal procedures necessary to determine whether there was a gas leak, and that leaving the customer in a hazardous condition constituted just cause for discharge. The grievant's failure to find or repair the gas leak was not poor performance but negligence of duty. The company defined poor performance as involving a lack of skills or intelligence and that the grievant's behavior was not caused by a lack of skills or innate inability. The company specifically refers to Article 1.3 which permits the company to discharge an employee for "just cause" and that under Article 1.3, no prior warnings are required. The company also noted in its presentation that the employee was previously suspended for 5 days in 1990, and that he has been reprimanded on numerous occasions for various infractions.

The Union's Position

The union contends that the grievant should have been disciplined under section 33.1 for poor job performance. The union contends that grievant performed three of the four tests usually performed and that at worst used poor judgement in not pressure testing the system. Further, the union contends that the company failed to give grievant adequate notice of the rule or the consequences of his action. The grievant did not have knowledge that he could be discharged for negligence in performance of his duties. Further, the union claimed that the company did not conduct a proper investigation and relied solely on the report of the second technician sent to the customer's home. The company made no attempt to visit the job site to determine firsthand if grievant had followed company rules.

Chapter 15 References

1. A. Sloane and F. Witney, *Labor Relations* (Englewood Cliffs, NJ: Prentice-Hall, 1977).
2. Ibid.
3. M. Cimini and C. Muhl, "Labor-Management Bargaining in 1994," *Monthly Labor Review,* January 1994, 23–39.
4. Ibid.
5. Ibid.
6. Ibid.
7. Ibid.
8. S. Briggs and D. Koys, "What Makes Labor Mediators Effective?" *Labor Law Journal* 40 (1989), 517–20.
9. Cimini and Muhl "Labor-Management."
10. Ibid.
11. C.J. Coleman, *Managing Labor Relations in the Public Sector* (San Francisco: Jossey-Bass, 1990).
12. Ibid.
13. L. Williamson and P. Brown, "Collective Bargaining in Private Industry, 1994," *Monthly Labor Review,* June 1995, 3–12.
14. A. Zack, *Grievance Arbitration* (Lexington, MA: Lexington Books, 1989).
15. J. Davy and G. Bohlander, "Recent Findings and Practices in Grievance-Arbitration Procedures," *Labor Law Journal,"* March 1992, 184–90.
16. Ibid.
17. Ibid.
18. Ibid.
19. Ibid.
20. P. Breslin and P. Zirkel, "Arbitrator Impartiality and the Burden of Proof," *Labor Law Journal,* June 1993, 381–84.

21. Zack, *Grievance Arbitration.*
22. D. Savino and N. Bruning, "Decertification Strategies and Tactics: Management and Union Perspectives," *Labor Law Journal* April 1992, 201–10.
23. A. Bethke, R. Mondy, and S. Premeaux, "Decertification: The Role of the First-Line Supervisor," *Supervisory Management,* February 1986, 21–23.
24. Savino and Bruning, "Decertification Strategies."
25. E. Lawler and S. Mohrman, "Unions and the New Management," *Academy of Management Executive* 1, (1987), 293–300.
26. Lawler and Mohrman, "Unions and the New Management."
27. I. Lobel, "Labor-Management Cooperation: A Critical View," *Labor Law Journal,* May 1992, 281–89.
28. H. Katz, T. Kochan, and M. Weber, "Assessing the Effects of Industrial Relations Systems and Efforts to Improve the Quality of Working Life on Organizational Effectiveness," *Academy of Management Journal* 28 (1985), 509–26.
29. M. Gordon and S. Miller, "Grievances: A Review of Research and Practice," *Personnel Psychology* 37 (1984), 117–46.

Employee Rights

chapter 16

Core Concepts

After reading this chapter, you should be capable of

1. Understanding the conditions under which you may be protected from a termination.
2. Explaining when you can examine your personnel file.
3. Determining whether or not your company can search your desk, briefcase, or other work areas.
4. Recognizing the problems associated with a workplace romance.
5. Discussing different types of work schedules.

Opening Case

Yesterday, you found yourself in a rather interesting discussion with several of your coworkers during lunchtime regarding the company, On-Line Books, Inc. The discussion began when Linda mentioned that last month she noticed that her desk seemed to have been searched over the weekend. Although nothing was taken, several items in the drawers had been moved and the papers on her desk had been scattered. Because she locks her desk every night, she wondered who might have opened the drawers. When she mentioned it to her supervisor, he acted somewhat embarrassed, and mumbled something about security having a copy of everyone's desk keys. "Now why would they search *my* desk?" asked Linda. Jim replied, "I don't know why your desk would be searched, but someone in my office (whose name will go unmentioned) feels he has been turned down for promotions because eight years ago he was charged with sexual harassment. Although the charges were investigated and proven false, he worries that the allegations are still listed in his personnel file and have left a permanent stain on his career." Jean then spoke up and said, "Do any of you remember Bill Norris? Do you know why he left?" Someone in the group mumbled, "Because of a personality clash with top management?" Jean shook her head and whispered: "I heard that Bill had an extramarital affair with one of the secretaries in the executive suite. Our CEO believes that such affairs are immoral, and so he fired Bill." After looking around to make sure no one else was in earshot, Philip replied in a hushed tone, "If you think that's bad, there is an employee in my department who was fired suddenly without any forewarning. No one had any idea why, because his performance appraisals had been excellent during his four years with On-Line Books. The only thing he could think of was that he had been interviewed on TV about his views on abortion two days before the termination. And we all know how the executive vice president of operations feels about abortion issues! So, the only explanation for his being fired seemed to be his views on abortion."

As you think about some of the comments that were made yesterday, you wonder whether these stories are true, and if they are true, can a company really take these actions? You are especially concerned about the employee who was allegedly fired for his views on abortion, because the implication is that anyone could be fired simply on the grounds that one's supervisor holds a different opinion on some matter. As you consider your own experience both in this company and at previous jobs, you can recall certain management actions that seemed wrong to you at the time. At one company, you found your supervisor reading a personal letter addressed to you that had mistakenly been sent to the workplace. The letter revealed some private things about your life, and you noticed that your boss was much more uncomfortable with you after that and never asked you to go to lunch again. When you worked for a different company, you found out that one of the vice presidents had been listening in on certain employees' phone calls, even though some of these calls were of a personal nature.

You are probably wondering by now whether companies actually have the legal right to engage in activities like the ones described. Can you, for example, be terminated for expressing your opinion regarding abortion? Can an employer search your desk or locker without permission? What about access to your personnel files to make sure they are accurate? Does your employer have the right to restrict your romantic relationships? Can your boss read your mail and listen to your phone conversations? These, and other related issues, will be discussed in much greater detail in this chapter. Employee rights, as you will see, is an evolving and changing area of law. You will also see that, in many instances, what is legal depends on the state where you work.

The remainder of this chapter is divided into several sections. First, you will read about your legal rights if you are terminated, followed by a discussion of your rights to examine personnel records. Third, we will discuss your protection from being searched by your employer. Fourth, you will read about current organizational approaches to workplace romances, followed by an overview of disciplinary procedures. Finally, you will read about your rights regarding hours of work and various organizational programs to increase work schedule flexibility. We begin with a discussion of your legal rights if you are terminated.

Terminations: For Good Cause, Bad Cause, or No Cause at All

Recall in the opening case of this chapter that Philip talked about an employee who was terminated, perhaps because of his televised statements about abortion. Can you be fired for a reason like that? It may come as a surprise to you that many employees are employed "at will," that is, at the will or discretion of the company. The **employment at will** (or EAW) concept in the United States goes back more than 100 years ago to a court case in New York. In that case, the court ruled that an employee could be fired for any reason at all, regardless of whether the reason was a good one (for example; if the employee stole company equipment), a bad one (perhaps the supervisor did not like the color of the employee's tie), or there was no reason at all (maybe the supervisor just felt like firing someone). If employment at will seems completely unfair to you, consider the matter from a completely different perspective—that of the company. In other words, how would you feel if you were a manager in the following situation. In the middle of the busiest season of the year (for instance, you work for a tax accounting firm and it is two days before April 15), one of your three employees announces that she is quitting. Would you have the legal right to force her to continue working? Of course not. Well, according to the courts in the 19th century, it seemed quite logical that if an employee could leave the work relationship at any time he or she desired, an employer should have the right to terminate an employee at any time. The principle that you could be terminated at any time is generally referred to as employment at will.[1]

Employment at will When employees are employed "at will," or at the will or discretion of the company. This means that if an employee can leave the work relationship at any time he or she desires, an employer has the same right.

During the 1970s and the 1980s, however, the employment-at-will principle was challenged in many state courts. In these cases, the plaintiffs argued that a wrongful discharge had occurred. Such cases received much attention in the popular media. One widely publicized study, for example, found that employees in California won nearly 70 percent of the wrongful discharge cases, and average awards to plaintiffs were well over $500,000![2] As you will see next, the likelihood that you will win a wrongful discharge suit depends much on the state in which you are employed. You will read first about exceptions to employment at will, followed by suggestions for what companies can do to reduce the chances they will be successfully sued for wrongful discharge.

Exceptions to Employment at Will

What does it take for an employee to win a wrongful discharge lawsuit? Let us begin by discussing the various legal considerations that are used to show the employee was wrongfully discharged. These may be sorted into six categories:

1. Civil rights and labor laws.
2. Written contracts.

3. Implied contracts.
4. Covenant of good faith and fair dealing.
5. Public policy.
6. Statutory law.

It is important to note that the third, fourth, and fifth categories are not based on specific, written laws. Rather, they are legal principles that have been applied to the employment-at-will area. Therefore, they are subject to change from time to time. Furthermore, their applicability varies from state to state. As you can see from Table 16.1, California courts have accepted all three of these exceptions; em-

Table 16.1 **States That Recognize Exceptions to Employment at Will**

State	Implied Contract*	Whistleblower/ Public Policy	Good Faith
Alabama	√	N	X
Alaska	√	N	√
Arizona	√	√	N
Arkansas	√	√	N
California	√	√	√
Colorado	√	N	N
Connecticut	√	√	√
Delaware	X	N	N
Dist. of Columbia	√	√	N
Florida	N	X	N
Georgia	N	X	N
Hawaii	N	√	X
Idaho	√	√	N
Illinois	√	√	X
Indiana	X	√	X
Iowa	N	√	√
Kansas	√	√	X
Kentucky	N	√	N
Louisiana	N	N	N
Maine	√	N	X
Maryland	N	√	X
Massachusetts	N	√	√
Michigan	√	√	N
Minnesota	√	N	X
Mississippi	√	N	N
Missouri	N	√	N
Montana	N	√	√
Nebraska	N	√	N
Nevada	N	√	√

(continued)

Table 16.1 **States That Recognize Exceptions to Employment at Will**
(continued from previous page)

State	Implied Contract*	Whistleblower/ Public Policy	Good Faith
New Hampshire	√	√	√
New Jersey	√	√	N
New Mexico	√	√	X
New York	√	N	X
North Carolina	X	√	N
North Dakota	N	N	√
Ohio	√	N	N
Oklahoma	√	N	X
Oregon	√	√	X
Pennsylvania	√	√	X
Rhode Island	N	√	N
South Carolina	√	√	N
South Dakota	√	√	N
Tennessee	X	√	N
Texas	N	√	N
Utah	N	N	N
Vermont	N	N	N
Virginia	N	√	N
Washington	√	√	N
West Virginia	√	√	X
Wisconsin	N	√	X
Wyoming	√	N	N

*An "implied contract" is one formed by oral statements, employee handbooks, or conduct of the parties.
√ Courts in this jurisdiction have generally recognized this exception to the doctrine of employment at will (where either party may terminate the relationshp at any time and for any reason).
X Courts in this jurisdiction have generally not recognized this exception to employment at will.
N Courts in this jurisdiction, though they may or may not have heard cases on this issue, have failed to reach a definitive conclusion or establish a clear precedent regarding this exception to employment at will.

Source: L.G. Joel, *Every Employee's Guide to the Law* (New York: Pantheon Books, pp. 61–62, 1993).

ployees in the state of California therefore have considerable protection from wrongful discharge. At the other extreme, Utah courts probably would not accept any of the exceptions. In that state, employers have the upper hand. Each of these six categories will now be discussed in greater detail.[3]

Civil Rights and Labor Laws. As you have read in previous chapters, there are many laws—such as the Civil Rights Act of 1964, and the Age Discrimination in Employment Act, to name but two—that protect employees from discrimination on the basis of their sex, race, religion, age, and other characteristics. If an employee can show that he or she was fired on this basis, the employee can win the job back, back wages, and possibly other forms of relief (such as attorney's fees). Because these are federal laws, they apply in all states.[4]

Written Contracts. Some workers have written contracts or agreements, which specify the terms and conditions under which a termination may take place. Can you think of any occupations where a written contract might be commonly used? Many professional sports, for example, provide players with a written contract. Most tenured faculty have a written contract that specifies the terms and conditions of a termination. Also as described in Chapters 14 and 15, unionized employees usually have written contracts that specify in great detail the causes for termination, as well as the procedures for disputing a termination. Nevertheless, the vast majority of employees do not have written contracts. As with the first category, written contract laws apply in all states.[5]

Implied contract
An implied agreement between employer and employee regarding an aspect of the job, such as the statement "Once you pass the probationary period, your job is guaranteed for life." Employee handbooks can also be considered implied contracts.

Implied Contract. Even if you were not given a written contract, you may be able to demonstrate that the company made an implied contract with you. There are many ways in which a company may have made an implied contract. As one example, what if the interviewer said to you, "Once you pass the probationary period, your job is guaranteed for life." In some court cases, this statement or similar statements have been taken as implied contracts and are grounds for victory by the plaintiff. Another example of an implied contract involves the employee handbook. Many employee handbooks, for example, describe a progressive disciplinary procedure wherein an employee would be warned of any performance problems, followed by counseling. Only if the problem was still not resolved would the employee be terminated. But there have been cases in which the company did not follow its handbook procedures; the employee was often terminated without any warning or opportunity to improve. In certain states, the courts have ruled that the company had, on those grounds, violated an implied contract.[6]

Some implied contract arguments may sound rather weak to you, but were successful in court. Consider the following actual court cases:

Written contracts are fairly common in some industries such as professional sports, but they are not always employment contracts. Shown here is soccer player Carlos Valderrama signing a contract to endorse Umbro sports products and merchandise.

1. An employee terminated before one year of employment had a letter, stating the salary as an annual sum; the court recognized this as an implied contract lasting one year.
2. An employee who worked for one company for many years moved to another state to work for another employer. He was terminated after a short period of time. Given that he left a secure position he had held for many years to work for this new firm, the court held this to be an implied contract.[7]

Covenant of Good Faith and Fair Dealing
An exception to employment at will that may be used when the reason for the termination was clearly inappropriate or the conditions under which the firing was made were extremely inconsiderate of the employee.

Covenant of Good Faith and Fair Dealing. This exception to employment at will may be used when the reason for the termination was clearly inappropriate or the conditions under which the firing was made were extremely inconsiderate of the employee. With regard to the first situation, an employee with 25 years of seniority was terminated just before a customer made a $25 million order. The court decided that the real reason for the termination was so that the company would not have to give the employee the large commission he would have earned. As an example of the second situation, the classic case concerns a restaurant owner who

Box 16.1 Written Contracts: An Employee Perspective

Your Turn

Now that you have read that a written contract can provide you some protection from being terminated, you may want to know more about getting one. In fact, a written contract or a similar agreement is much more common for middle-level managers than was true in the past. It is estimated that about 25 percent of middle-level managers are getting some type of written agreement, up from only 5 percent just a few years ago. Aside from the protection from being terminated, there are other reasons for trying to get a contract. Take, for example, Arnold Margolis. In the summer of 1992, Sweet Life Foods hired Margolis as director of health and beauty aids at an annual salary of $72,000. Although he received a letter stipulating this agreement, the company withdrew the offer without explanation several days before he would begin. In the meantime, not only had he resigned from his previous job, but he had already moved from New York to Connecticut. Over a year later, Margolis still had not yet found a suitable job. If he had insisted on a written contract, he would have fared better.

In general, the greater the demand for your skills and expertise, the more likely you are to obtain a written agreement. One financial executive was able to negotiate a written agreement stipulating that if he left the company, he would be provided continued medical benefits until he found employment at a company offering the same level of benefits. Why was he able to negotiate this kind of agreement? "They wanted the guy a lot," explains a headhunter. Aside from that general principle, if you are moving from another part of the country to accept the new job, you should be in a better position to get a written agreement. For example, a senior manager living in Chicago accepted a job in a town in Iowa with fewer than 20,000 residents. One condition for accepting the job was a written agreement stating that he would be reimbursed for moving back to Chicago if he stopped working for the company. Most top managers joining a financially troubled business insist on a written agreement providing a guaranteed income if the company fails.

Some companies require the employee to give something in return for the written agreement. Oftentimes, this is an advance warning of quitting. In certain industries, the employee must agree to a no-compete clause, with which the employee agrees not to work for a competing firm for a certain period of time, even after he or she has left the company.

Should you get a written contract, be sure the document states that the agreement is binding. You may also wish to consult with an attorney.

Source: Adapted from J. Lublin, "Before You Take That Great Job, Get It in Writing," *The Wall Street Journal*, February 9, 1994, B1.

lined up the waitresses, and terminated them one at a time when they did not indicate who was stealing.[8]

Public policy
An exception to employment at will in which the employee has either committed an action, or refused to commit an action, that is in the interest of the common public good.

Public Policy. This exception to employment at will may surprise you because it seems obvious that an employee would win; in turn, this should indicate to you how pervasive the notion of employment at will was until about 20 years ago. In a public policy exception to employment at will, the employee has either committed an action, or refused to commit an action, that is in the interest of the common public good. Some examples include participating in jury duty, reporting the company's violation of some rule or regulation (often referred to as *whistleblowing*), or refusing to commit a violation of the law (such as refusing to dump toxic waste). Does it surprise you that in years past the company had a legal right to terminate you for those actions? The fact that in many cases your company had such a right indicates how well-entrenched employment at will was in the United States.[9]

Statutory Law. Recall that the three exceptions you just read about are not written, or statutory laws. Rather, they are legal principles that have been applied to the employment-at-will area. Only one state, Montana, has a formal, written law regarding wrongful discharge. Passed in 1987, the Wrongful Discharge From Employment Act was designed to strike a balance between workers' rights and companies' rights. This law specifies that a wrongful discharge has occurred in any of the following instances:[10]

1. The termination was connected to a public policy issue (for example, the employee refused to do an illegal act).
2. The termination was not for good cause and the employee had passed probation.
3. The company violated its written human resource policies.

While there have been attempts in other states, such as California and Wisconsin, as well as on the federal level, to pass similar legislation, so far these attempts have been unsuccessful. Some states do, however, have much more limited statutes, protecting whistleblowers or other public policy exceptions.[11]

Recommendations for Organizations

Companies are encouraged to take the following precautions to limit their liability in wrongful discharge cases:[12]

1. Review the Employee Handbook and Modify as Needed. Companies are encouraged to review their employee handbooks for any language suggestive of promises or guarantees of employment. Expressions like "permanent employee" and "you will be fired only for just cause" should be eliminated. On the other hand, the handbook should include a statement like the following: "This handbook is only intended as a source of information, not as a binding employment contract, and the provisions contained herein are subject to change without notice."

2. Train Supervisors and Hiring Managers. All personnel that are responsible for hiring and firing should be given information about the nature of implied contracts and other exceptions to employment at will.

3. Consider Including a Statement in the Application Blank to Clarify the Company's Liability. Most application blanks contain a statement like, "I under-

stand that my employment is at the will of the company, and that I may be terminated at any time for any reason."

4. Examine any Other Policies That Might Be Interpreted as an Implied Contract. Some companies initially hire employees on a probationary status. At the end of this period, some companies refer to successful employees as being "permanent." In some courts, this designation has been accepted as an implied contract. This and similar policies should be carefully examined and changed if necessary. In general, any proposed termination should be carefully reviewed by the human resource manager or company attorney before action is taken.

Personnel Files

In the opening case of this chapter, one of the employees mentioned that a coworker may have been denied promotions because of earlier sexual harassment charges. Although the charges had proven to be false, the concern was that the charges had created a permanent mark on the worker's personnel file. Do you think employees should have the right to examine their records or files? Do you think employees should have the right to correct their records or files? Most employees believe they should have both of these rights. Legally, however, your right to examine and correct your personnel file depends on where you work. If you are a federal government employee, you will have more rights than most other employees do. We will begin, then, with the rights of federal government employees, and then move on to other workers.

Federal Government Employees and Access to Personnel Files

If you are a federal employee, you have a right to your personnel files under the Privacy Act of 1974. This law only covers federal administrative agencies (for instance, the Food and Drug Administration), and it allows individuals who work at these agencies the right to examine their records and to correct any mistakes in the records. If you are not an employee covered by the Privacy Act of 1974 (for example, if you work for the private sector), there are other laws that may grant you the right to review your file. These are discussed next.[13]

Privacy Act of 1974
The law that gives federal employees a right to their personnel files (this law covers federal administrative agencies and allows individuals who work at these agencies the right to examine their records and the right to correct any mistakes in the records).

Private Sector, and State and Local Government Employees

While no comprehensive national laws cover employee rights to their personnel files, many states have enacted such laws. Table 16.2 contains a summary of these laws for each state. As you can see, 27 states have a law that grants employees the right to review their personnel records, and some states have laws that provide you with access to your company's medical records. Your legal right to see your personnel files, then, depends on where you work. If you work in Mississippi, for instance, you have no *legal* right to examine your personnel records.[14]

Because these laws are written by each state, they differ from one another in many ways. We will discuss these laws in greater detail, with attention to how they differ from state to state.[15]

Are All Organizations Covered? The state laws differ widely in terms of which organizations are covered and which are exempt. If, for example, you work in Minnesota and your organization employs only 15 workers, you would have no legal

Table 16.2 **States Providing Access to Personnel Records**

State	Personnel Files	Medical Records	Remove/Explain
Alaska	√	—	—
Arizona	public employees	—	—
Arkansas	√	√	—
California	√	—	—
Connecticut	√	√	√
Delaware	√	√	√
District of Columbia	District Employees	—	√
Illinois	√	—	√
Iowa	√	—	—
Kentucky	public employees	—	—
Louisiana	—	√	—
Maine	√	—	—
Massachusetts	√	—	√
Michigan	√	—	√
Minnesota	√	—	√
Nebraska	public employees	—	—
Nevada	√	—	employer's option
New Hampshire	√	—	√
North Dakota	public employees	—	—
Ohio	—	√	—
Oklahoma	—	√	—
Oregon	√	—	—
Pennsylvania	√	—	√
Rhode Island	√	—	—
South Dakota	public employees	—	—
Tennessee	public employees	—	—
Texas	public safety personnel	—	—
Utah	public employees	—	—
Washington	√	—	—
Wisconsin	√	—	√

Personnel Files: √ indicates that, in general, both public and private employees are covered by the law requiring access to personnel files. "Public employees" means only public employees must be given access to their files and that private employers are not expressly covered.
Medical Records: √ indicates that medical records are expressly included among the records to which employees must be given access. (A √ under *Medical Records* only indicates that the law refers to medical records specifically and not to personnel records in general.)
Remove/Explain: √ indicates that employees are allowed to request that their employer remove erroneous or dated material with which the employee does not agree; or in the alternative, the employee has a right to insert an explanation, which must remain a permanent part of the file.
Note: States not listed do not have specific laws regarding access to personnel files.

Source: L. Joel, *Every Employee's Guide to the Law* (New York: Pantheon Books, p. 164, 1993).

right to your personnel files. That is because the law only covers organizations with 20 or more employees. If you worked in Illinois, however, you would have the legal right to see your files, because the law in this state covers organizations with 5 or more employees.

Which Employees Can View Their Files? Some states, such as Washington, permit only current employees to view their personnel files. Other states, such as Pennsylvania, also permit employees on leave and employees on layoff (as long as they are eligible for recall) to review their files. Several states, including Connecticut, Illinois, and Nevada, permit former employees to review their records, but only up to a certain time (for example, Nevada allows an employee to review records only up to 60 days after leaving the company).

What May Be Seen as Part of a Personnel File? The state laws differ in terms of what is considered part of the personnel file. A handful of states, such as Michigan, ban certain information from appearing in the file, such as political affiliations, publications, and other nonwork-related items. The Americans with Disabilities Act specifically requires that medical information be kept separate from the personnel file. Aside from this, states differ in terms of what information in the personnel file may legally be concealed from the employee. In most states, you, as an employee, have no right to see documents that involve a third party. Can you think of such a document that you might have a keen interest in seeing? The best example might be a letter of reference, written by a professor or former employer. Most states do not give you the right to examine those documents. Generally, employees also do not have the right to examine information that will be used in criminal investigations. Some of these laws even permit the company to conceal documents regarding investigations of alleged violations of employment laws. To return to the opening case, depending on the state in which On-Line Books was located, the anonymous employee may or may not have had the legal right to review the materials about alleged sexual harassment.

How Do Employees Initiate a Request to Review Their Files? By now you may be wondering just what you need to do to obtain a copy of your personnel file. The answer depends somewhat on where you are. In some states (such as Maine and Michigan), your request must be in writing, that is, you would need to draft a letter stating your interest in reviewing your personnel file. In some states, you would also need to indicate which documents you wish to see (as is the case in Michigan) and/or the purpose of the inspection (as in Delaware).

What Can You Do If There Is an Error in Your File? Now that you have reviewed your personnel file, you may believe that it contains a mistake. Perhaps a previous performance rating is lower than it was supposed to be, or the number of absences from work is wrong. Most state laws require that you, as an employee, first inform the company of the error. If the organization disagrees with you, you will be required to submit a written statement explaining your assessment. A few states, such as Illinois, Michigan, and Minnesota, provide the employee with a legal recourse for removing false information.

What If Your Company Denies You the Right to Review Your Files? Your company may deny you access to your personnel file for two reasons. First, your company may simply be unaware of your rights. Second, your company may not wish to share information with you. In either case, the penalty and the law to enforce your rights differ from state to state. In states such as Wisconsin, employers that deny you access to your file may be fined up to $100 each day. Other states (such as

Illinois and Michigan) allow you, as an employee, to sue the company. In some cases, you may even be able to collect damages and court costs. Again, the exact procedures and penalties will differ from state to state.

So far, we have been discussing your *legal* rights with regard to personnel files. Some companies have established internal regulations, beyond legal requirements, that provide access to personnel files if an employee requests a review. Why do you think an organization would open itself up to that kind of scrutiny, as well as extra time and expense? There are probably two answers to that question. First, from a self-preservation standpoint, some companies feel they are best off developing internal regulations. They feel that failure to impose their own regulations will lead to government-imposed requirements, which will create greater problems. Second, some companies feel that internal regulations promote a greater sense of fairness on the part of employees, which in turn will improve employee satisfaction and commitment to the organization. Whether the federal government will impose future regulations covering access to personnel files of private-sector organizations remains to be seen. In sum, depending on your employer and the state where you work, you may have a legal right to examine and correct your personnel files. In many cases, however, you will only be able to access this information as part of a civil rights lawsuit or charge under the Occupational Safety and Health Act.[16]

Searches and Seizures

In the opening case of this chapter, Linda mentioned that her desk apparently had been searched over the weekend, perhaps by the company. Do you think an organization should have the right to search your purse, clothing, car, or other areas? As you will see, the U.S. Constitution may provide some protection from unfair searches and seizures. In many cases, however, your only protection will be what is referred to as "common law privacy." These two sources of protection from your company in connection with searches and seizures are described in greater detail next.

U.S. Constitution

Perhaps you have heard people talk about their "constitutional rights." What are they referring to by this expression? If they are talking about privacy, they probably mean the Fourth Amendment of the U.S. Constitution, which protects you from unreasonable searches and seizures.[17] But the U.S. Constitution only protects you from the government. If you are working for a private-sector organization, the Constitution will not protect you from your employer. If you are a government employee, however, the U.S. Constitution can provide you some degree of protection from searches and seizures. The key word is "reasonable." For certain government jobs, such as a Federal Bureau of Investigation (FBI) agent, it may be quite reasonable for the organization to sometimes search private work areas, such as desks, purses, and so forth, to ensure proper security. Consider, for example, a case in which a package of jewels was reported missing in a customs office. To find the package, a customs-service supervisor searched the jacket of an employee who had handled the package earlier in the day. The package was indeed found in the jacket. Do you think this constituted a reasonable or an unreasonable search? The court ruled that under the circumstances it was a reasonable search. But what if you are not a government employee? In that case, there is a common-law privacy concept that might be helpful to you.[18]

Common Law Privacy

Only a few states have written laws protecting you from searches and seizures if you work for a nongovernmental organization. But there is a general principle, referred to as **common law privacy**, that does provide you some measure of protection. The notion goes back to a paper published in the *Harvard Law Review* in 1890, which describes several aspects of the right to privacy, including the right to be free from searches of one's property and body. Recall that in the opening case of this chapter, Linda was concerned that her desk had been searched. A key factor for the courts in determining whether one's common law rights have been violated is whether the employees had an expectation that their desks might be searched. If, for example, the organization had posted notices in the facility indicating that desks and lockers could be subject to searches, the employee would be expected to know that this could happen. On the other hand, consider a case that took place in Texas at a privately owned business. Employees were provided lockers and told they could use their own locks for privacy purposes. Nevertheless, the company searched some lockers. Because the employees were led to believe the lockers were private and presumably would not be searched, the jury awarded $100,000 to the employee for violation of common law privacy. A second consideration is the reasonableness of the search. For example, are the employees working in an occupation where money or goods are stolen? Would drugs create hazards at work? Under these conditions, an employer would have greater latitude in conducting searches.[19]

Common law privacy
A general principle that protects an employee from searches and seizures in a non-governmental organization.

The laws are somewhat more vague when it comes to one's personal property, such as purses and clothing. In a New Jersey ruling, the court permitted a casino to search employees because of the amount of money handled and the opportunity for theft. In general, though, companies must have stronger arguments for the need to search personal property than are required for them to search company property.

In sum, employees do have some protection from unfair searches and seizures. If an organization intends to retain the right to conduct searches, employees should be made aware of the possibility that company property could be inspected at any time. Returning to the opening case of this chapter, then, Linda may have had grounds for a lawsuit, particularly if she could show that employees did not expect to have their desks searched.

Workplace Romance

Compared to years past, romantic relationships at work are much more common today. In the opening case of this chapter, one of the employees commented that Bill Norris was fired because of an extramarital affair he had with a secretary in the company. Does that sound fair to you? Have you ever had a romantic relationship with someone at work? How would you feel if you were terminated for such a

Box 16.2 Can Your Supervisor Listen to Your Phone Calls or Read Your Mail?

Does your supervisor have the legal right to listen in on your phone calls? If you recall Chapter 7, you may remember that many companies monitor and eavesdrop on employee phone conversations with customers. You may have wondered how this practice is legal under the federal law that prohibits wiretapping or interception of telephone conversations. The answer is that this law provides several exceptions, including the right for the employer to listen in during the course of routine business. For the most part, supervisors have the right to listen in on your business-related phone calls. On the other hand, your supervisor's right to listen to personal phone conversations is far more limited. While a supervisor can safely listen long enough to determine whether or not the employee is engaged in a personal call, it is generally recommended that the supervisor not listen any more than is necessary to determine the nature of the call. It is the company's right, however, to restrict excessive personal phone calls.

How about reading an employee's mail? It depends on the nature of the mail. If the mail is business related, the company has the right to open and read it. If the mail appears to be personal, however, no one should read it, other than the employee to whom it is addressed. The company does have the right, however, to prohibit personal mail from being sent to the office or facility and to return such letters to the post office.

In the last few years, there has been a proliferation of new forms of electronic transmission, including electronic mail (E-mail) and fax machines. The general principle is that because it is company equipment and on company premises, supervisors do have the right to examine this material. At times, however, it may not be readily apparent whether the communication is personal or business related. In that case, a supervisor should read only as much as is necessary to determine whether it is personal or not, and then he or she should take the document or letter to an authorized person (such as the company attorney or human resource manager) for assistance. When in doubt, supervisors should contact the appropriate personnel. In general, then, companies do have the right to examine any business-related communications to employees. However, management should not examine personal communications. The use of company equipment for personal communications can be prohibited.

Source: Adapted from G. Webster, "Respecting Employee Privacy," *Association Management,* January 1994, 142–43, 146.

relationship? In this section we first examine why companies are concerned about these relationships, then we look at employees' rights in workplace romances. We will conclude with a description of current organizational policies regarding workplace romance.

Romantic Relationships: Why Companies Are Concerned

You may remember from Chapter 2 that sexual harassment could occur in two ways. One way is a quid pro quo situation, in which a supervisor requests sexual favors from another employee in exchange for pay increases, promotions, and similar personnel actions. Alternatively, sexual harassment charges could be brought if the employee can prove that the workplace is stressful owing to the sexual behavior that occurs (hostile environment). Under the quid pro quo approach, a workplace romance may end with the subordinate claiming that she (or he) was forced into this relationship in order to receive pay raises or promotions. Under the hostile environment approach, one employee actually won a lawsuit when she demonstrated that she was treated poorly because other coworkers were having romantic relationships with their supervisors, while she refused to engage in such behavior. In short, one major concern organizations have with romantic relationships on the job is the possibility they will turn into sexual harassment lawsuits.[20]

A second concern on the part of organizations is that romantic relationships are disruptive. First, romantic relationships may create tension in the workplace, as the couple exchanges whispers, glances, and so forth. Matters may become even worse when the relationship ends, and the two employees begin avoiding one another. Second, it is often feared that favoritism will occur or perhaps will be suspected of occurring. During the early 1980s, for example, William Agee, then CEO of Bendix Corporation, became romantically involved with Mary Cunningham (who was in her 20s). In a much publicized story, Mary Cunningham rose quickly to upper management ranks, and the two spent many hours together. According to Agee and Cunningham, their time was spent working on business-related matters; but various parties, including the board of directors, became outraged, and eventually Mary Cunningham was forced to leave.[21]

Despite the concern about the disruptive nature of romantic relationships, there is anecdotal evidence to the contrary. Consider Pam and Lou Shuckman, both recruiters for Accountants on Call, a temp service for accountants. Now married, they met at a company-sponsored junket. They believe that being married makes them much more productive, as they are able to share their knowledge and ideas with one another. The company seems to agree. A recent company newsletter announced, "The couple that bills together, thrills together." And there is no scientific evidence indicating that work romances reduce productivity.[22]

Aside from these reasons, many companies are simply conservative. They may especially frown upon extramarital affairs, if only out of religious or moral convictions. Romances between unmarried employees may be discouraged if there is any public display of affection.

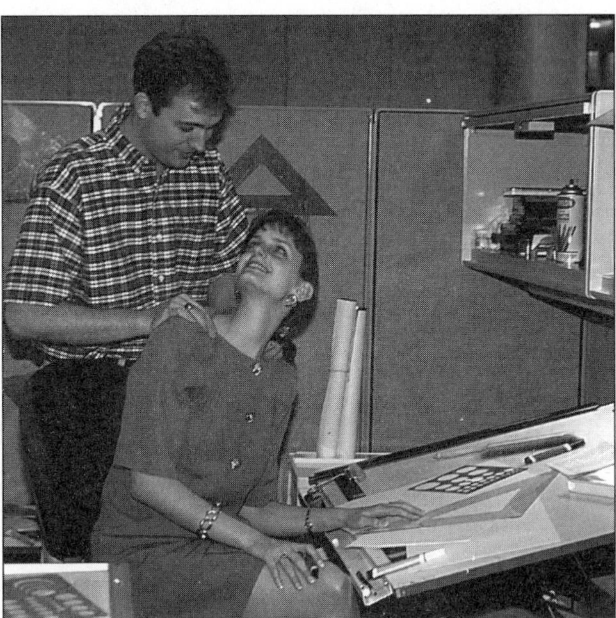

Workplace romances can be disruptive to other workers if displays of affection occur publicly or frequently. Embracing, hand-holding, intimate conversations, and the like are not appropriate in a professional setting.

Box 16.3 Your Attitude toward Workplace Romances

To examine your attitude toward romance in the workplace, indicate whether you agree (A) or disagree (D) with each of the following statements. When you finish filling in your answers, compare your answers with the responses of 200 CEOs.

1. Office romances increase the possibility of favoritism or the appearance of favoritism. ________
2. Office romances can create an unbusinesslike appearance. ________
3. Office romances expose the company to sexual harassment suits. ________
4. Given the number of hours managers spend in the office nowadays, office romances are inevitable. ________
5. The incidence of office romance has increased in the past ten years. ________
6. In the long run, office romances inevitably result in problems for the company. ________
7. When an office romance develops, one of the parties should leave the company voluntarily. ________

Now, compare your answers with the results of a survey of 200 CEOs.

Your Turn

Item Number	% Agree	% Disagree	% Not Sure
1	86	13	1
2	78	21	1
3	77	20	3
4	51	46	3
5	35	39	26
6	21	75	4
7	17	78	5

Do the percentages from the survey of CEOs surprise you? How do your answers compare?

Adapted from A.B. Fisher, "Getting Comfortable with Couples in the Workplace," *Fortune*, October 10, 1994, 138–42, 144.

Workplace Romances: Your Legal Rights

Now that you have read about companies' concerns, you may wonder whether employees have any rights regarding workplace romances. Recall that while private-sector employees do not enjoy a right-to-privacy law, there are some common-law right-to-privacy principles. One such concept, referred to as "intrusion upon seclusion," might provide a right for employees to engage in workplace romances.

Some states also prohibit discrimination on the basis of marital status. It is possible that such a law could be used to prove discrimination against unmarried persons engaged in a workplace romance. Finally, recall that in the Agee-Cunningham story, the woman was forced to leave the organization. Indeed, in past years, some organizations had a written policy requiring that the employee in the romantic relationship with less status leave the organization. But this often resulted in sex discrimination, as a woman typically holds the lower-level job. If your company's policy discriminates against you on the basis of marital status or gender, you may have grounds for a lawsuit.[23]

Organizational Policies Regarding Workplace Romances

In the last few years, most companies have chosen to implement limited policies regarding workplace romances. Yet some companies retain what may seem to you to be rather broad restrictions. For example, Wal-Mart Stores decided several years ago to terminate two employees who had sex with one another. This decision was based on Wal-Mart's official policy to terminate any employee who commits adultery. As it turns out, the woman, who was legally separated from her husband, had sex with a single male employee. Sound extreme? Technically, adultery is illegal in every state. But New York state law guarantees employees the right to privacy outside of the workplace, as long as the activity is not illegal. Since adultery is illegal, Wal-Mart may have gotten away with this action, except for one catch: someone who is legally separated is not committing adultery. The attorney general of New York was therefore able to sue Wal-Mart Stores for a violation of state laws.

Relatively few companies have policies that are as restrictive as the one at Wal-Mart. In fact, a recent survey showed that 70 percent of companies permit workplace romances, while 28 percent permit, but discourage it. Only 2 percent of companies surveyed banned workplace romances. Many companies do have a policy that people romantically involved with each other cannot have a supervisor-subordinate relationship. Apple Computer, for example, specifically states in its handbook that no direct reporting or contractual relationship can be formed with a member of your immediate family, relative, or individual with whom you have a "significant personal relationship." Other companies have tried to educate employees with regard to the potential problems associated with workplace romances. Du Pont, for example, addresses the issue as part of sexual harassment training. Du Pont has an official policy that if an employee has a personal relationship that could negatively affect the company, the employee has an obligation to inform management and pursue ways to prevent any negative consequences.[24]

If a company is considering adopting or reviewing a workplace romance policy, the following guidelines should be considered.[25]

1. Rather than having a blanket statement restricting or banning workplace romances, restrictions should only apply to cases in which the relationship might interfere with the work activity, such as when a supervisory-subordinate romance exists or when one of the parties has influence over the other party with regard to pay, promotions, and so forth.
2. The policy should not be restricted to workplace romances alone; it should cover any type of personal relationship, including parent-child relationships and relationships between spouses.
3. If there is a chance that one of the covered situations might materialize, the parties involved should be given a sufficient time period (perhaps a week) to resolve the problem.
4. Employees should be given advance notice of the policy before it is implemented in order for them to prepare for any changes that will be necessary.

In short, current thinking is that companies can have only limited control over workplace romances. Above all, companies are advised to ensure that the policy is reasonable, job related, and does not unfairly discriminate against one type of relationship over others. Going back to the opening case of this chapter, then, firing Bill Norris because he had allegedly had an extramarital affair could be quite difficult to defend in court.

Finally, in addition to the areas already addressed, many states grant additional protection to employees with regard to legal behavior off the job (such as smoking) and, in some cases, even your political activities (for example, expressing your support for a particular political candidate). Many states have a law protecting employees from employment discrimination based on their use of tobacco and alcohol products after work hours. Stay tuned to more changes and additional laws in this area.[26]

Box 16.4 What You Say *Can* Hurt You

Tales from the Trenches

Do you enjoy talking with your peers at work? Ever talk with your coworkers after work about the job, your family, or personal problems? Have you ever attended your company's employee assistance program (EAP) for counseling? If you have done any of these things, or thought about it, be careful what you say. It can hurt you. Consider the story of Lewis Hubble, who worked at Kmart's distribution center for nearly 30 years. When Hubble met Al, a new employee at the center, they became instant friends. They ate lunch together, and even went drinking occasionally after work. But Al was really an undercover investigator, working with several others posing as new employees. They allegedly wrote reports about what employees said and did. According to a lawsuit filed by the employees claiming a violation of their rights, the report included information about their drinking habits, sexual preferences, personal problems, as well as other non-job-related information. A Kmart spokesperson will only say that the undercover agents were looking for a crime ring suspected of operating through the distribution center.

But it's not just undercover agents who may tell the company what you have said. A legal assistant in Oregon filed a workers' compensation claim for wrist pain she claimed was caused by her job. At an administrative hearing to contest her claim, lawyers for the company claimed her injury wasn't caused by the job at all. Rather, they argued that her pain was caused by emotional stress and hormonal problems induced by an abortion. How did the lawyers learn about her abortion? They had interviewed her coworkers, several of whom she had talked with about the abortion.

Some companies are trying to make it even easier for coworkers to provide such information. Merck & Co., Northern Telecom, and Boise Cascade are among the companies that have a 24-hour confidential, toll-free number for employees to call when they have information on such illegal activities as stealing and drug use.

Such practices, not surprisingly, have led to countersuits by employees. Pamela Black, for example, was suspected of on-the-job drug use by her employer, Freedom Newspapers Inc. According to Black, she was suspected of drug use because she was taking drops for an eye inflammation problem. Based on telephone calls from employees, the company launched a surveillance operation, which culminated in a seven-hour interrogation of Black. In her lawsuit, Black maintains the company asked her a variety of personal questions, including relationships with her children and men. She was then fired, allegedly for poor performance.

So whom can you trust? Many people think that company counselors, frequently working for the employee assistance program (EAP), are safe. In fact, your company may even tell you that the content of your discussions with your counselor is confidential. The reality may be quite different. For instance, Donnie Burgess, a computer specialist at a greeting-card company, used his company's EAP in 1988. In 1992, when suing the company for breach of contract, the company's lawyers used his EAP file to bring evidence that Burgess had certain personality problems. Well, you might think, don't EAP counselors have any personal ethics? Garth Elliott, director of an EAP program, had personal ethics and refused to hand over files for his organization to use against employees. The result? The company seized the files anyhow, and demoted him.

Not all companies are disingenuous about the uses of EAP information. Morgan Stanley, known as having one of the most ethical and well-run EAPs, tells employees that information they provide to the EAP may be made available to management if the employee sues the company. The bottom line is you should be cautious in talking with coworkers and company representatives.

Sources: E. Schultz, "Employee Beware: The Boss May Be Listening," *The Wall Street Journal,* July 29, 1994, C1, C16; and E. Schultz, "If You Use Firm's Counselors, Remember Your Secrets Could Be Used against You," *The Wall Street Journal,* May 26, 1994, C1, C20.

Now that you have read about some major areas of employee rights, we will discuss employee disciplinary procedures. As you will see, managers and supervisors should determine and communicate disciplinary actions in a suitable manner.

Employee Disciplinary Procedures

Although disciplinary procedures are relatively infrequently used, the way in which they are made and communicated may affect employees' perceptions of their supervisor. Among the most common reasons for disciplining employees are absenteeism and tardiness problems, performance deficiencies, drug use on the job, negligence, misconduct (such as fighting at work or playing pranks), and insubordination. Most organizations today use two key concepts in meting out disciplinary action: progressive discipline and due process. Each of these terms is explained in greater detail next.[27]

Progressive Discipline

Recall from Chapter 7 that both professional and legal standards encourage companies to give employees sufficient warning and opportunity to correct performance problems. The same notions underlie progressive discipline. In a progressive discipline system, the employee is given ample warning of performance or other work-related problems. Failure to change his or her behavior is accompanied by increasingly harsher disciplinary action. Thus, a typical progressive disciplinary system will have four basic steps:[28]

Progressive discipline
In a progressive discipline system, the employee is given ample warning of performance or other work-related problems. Failure to change his or her behavior is accompanied by increasingly harsher disciplinary action.

1. The employee is notified of the problem and warned that disciplinary action will be taken if the problem is not solved.
2. If the problem is not solved, the employee is reminded that the problem remains, and a written warning is placed into his or her file.
3. If the problem is still not solved, the employee is suspended (temporarily barred from working) without pay for a short period of time.
4. Finally, if the problem is not solved, the employee is terminated.

While harsher disciplinary action is generally appropriate, there are instances where more immediate action is needed. For example, an employee who walks through the workplace carrying a firearm may need to receive more than just a verbal warning; in that case, immediate suspension without pay may be the most appropriate action while a thorough investigation is undertaken to determine whether a termination is in order.

Due Process

Due process is based on the notion that employees have the right to be treated fairly, particularly when being disciplined. Generally, due process involves these four features:

Due process
The notion that employees have the right to be treated fairly, particularly when being disciplined.

1. Employees are aware of the company's expectations and the consequences of not meeting those expectations (for instance, employees are aware of the conditions under which termination will occur).
2. Consequences are predictable and consistent.
3. Disciplinary actions are based on facts that are obtained from an investigation.
4. Employees have an opportunity to hear the facts and explain the situation from their perspective.[29]

Organizations that incorporate these features in their disciplinary procedures will experience better employee relations and reduce legal liability.

Taking Disciplinary Action

For most managers and supervisors, communicating the need for disciplinary action is one of the least pleasant aspects of their job. If you review Chapter 7, you will see that it describes a set of steps for giving informal feedback and indicates the appropriate place for a mention of disciplinary action. In addition to the steps outlined in Chapter 7, the following suggestions are offered:[30]

1. Explain to the Employee Precisely What the Action Is, Why It Is Necessary, and When the Action Will Take Place. Employees need to know that actions will be taken in order for them to feel the subsequent action is fair.
2. Complete a Thorough, Careful, and Neutral Investigation of the Facts before Deciding to Discipline. Document your investigation, and be sure to have witnesses sign their names to statements.
3. Check Company Policies. Many companies have written policies about disciplinary actions. For some situations (such as fighting on the job), immediate termination may be required. Failure to follow company policies may have negative consequences for managers and supervisors.

Although taking disciplinary action is not a pleasant task, it is critical for maintaining motivation in the workplace and ensuring that rules and regulations are followed. If the organization is sued or a union grievance is filed, adherence to these suggestions will be critical for defending the company's disciplinary actions.

Next, you will read about hours of work and what employees' rights are in that regard. You will also learn about some of the programs companies have used to increase work schedule flexibility.

Employee Rights and Work Hours

Did you ever have a job where you worked more than 40 hours per week? Did you wonder whether you had a legal right to refuse to work more than 40 hours per week? Following a discussion of that issue, you will learn more about several work schedule programs that companies have implemented to give employees greater flexibility and control over their work hours, such as flextime, compressed workweeks, and job sharing. First, we address the issue of the number of hours an organization can require you to work.

Working More Than 40 Hours per Week: Your Rights

There are few laws restricting the number of hours your company can require you to work. Aside from the Fair Labor Standards Act (FLSA), which requires companies to pay nonexempt workers an overtime wage, there is little regulation of the hours worked by adults in the United States. The major exception to this general rule occurs at the state level, wherein some states have limits on the number of consecutive hours or days that workers in certain occupations (primarily transportation-related jobs) can work. About two dozen states also have certain break requirements, such as a required 30-minute meal period for every five hours of a six-hour workday. Interestingly, certain other countries, such as Sweden, do have national laws that affect the hours of work. The Working Hours Act in Sweden, for

Box 16.5 **Do You Work Enough Hours?**

Do you think you work enough hours? One way to determine whether you are putting in enough hours at the job is to examine the number of hours people work in other parts of the world. Consider the work hours in two of the world's greatest industrial nations: Germany and Japan. While the number of hours worked by manufacturing workers has actually declined over the last 35 years in these two countries, it has increased in the United States. In fact, West German production workers average only about 1,500 hours of work annually, while U.S. workers average nearly 2,000 hours of work annually (Japanese workers average more than 2,100 hours of work each year). Part of the reason for the relatively fewer number of hours worked by German workers is a law that requires West German companies to give at least five weeks' paid vacation annually. Another reason German workers work fewer hours is their attitude toward work. As one German supervisor stated it, "Work hard when you're on the job and get out as fast as you can." And, unlike many U.S. workers who work overtime on a regular basis or who work a second job, German workers tend to avoid working overtime or second jobs. In fact, German law prohibits workers from working during their paid vacations. Does Germany sound like a better place to work? As an employee it might be. But you should also know that on average, U.S. workers have bigger homes and more cars than both German and Japanese workers. From a manager's perspective, neither Germany nor Japan may sound quite so good either—U.S. workers are more productive than either German and Japanese workers.

But even in the United States, some companies are becoming increasingly considerate about the number of hours their employees work. Consider Mary McCarthy-Coyle, a fast-track employee at Deloitte & Touche, the accounting firm. When McCarthy-Coyle recently met with her mentor, Denise Buonopane, she was given one major message: reduce your work hours. McCarthy-Coyle routinely works 100 hours each week. So why has Deloitte & Touche told her to slack off? Primarily because turnover at Deloitte & Touche had reached epidemic levels, as high as 25 percent annually among female employees. Partners at the company are also being encouraged to set an example. Buonopane, herself a mother of three young children, occasionally works a seven-day week. But she sets her limits in other ways. For example, she will not travel over the weekend.

Not all firms encourage their workers to reduce work hours. Consider a suit brought against the law firm Cleary, Gottlieb, Steen & Hamilton, which was filed after a new attorney committed suicide. The lawsuit, filed by the employee's father, charges the company forced the employee to work long hours (often 20-hour days) with impossible deadlines. Law firms are notorious for their long hours—some New York law firms allegedly require up to 3,000 billable hours each year. Because not all work hours are billable, an attorney may need to work 4,000 hours to reach that goal, or an average of about 80 hours per week!

Sources: Adapted from A. Stevens, "Suit over Suicide Raises Issue: Do Associates Work Too Hard?" *The Wall Street Journal,* April 15, 1994, B1; S. Shellenbarger, "A Crucible in Balancing Job and Family," *The Wall Street Journal,* December 14, 1994, B1; D. Benjamin and T. Horwitz, "German View: 'You Americans work too hard—and for what?'" *The Wall Street Journal,* July 14, 1994, B1, B5; and M. Magnet, "The Truth about the American Worker," *Fortune,* May 4, 1992, 48–65.

example, specifies that the workweek must not average more than 40 hours for a four-week period. Moreover, work between midnight and 5 A.M. is restricted, and there are limitations on overtime.[31]

If you live in the United States then, you have little legal control over your hours of work. As you will see next, some companies require employees to work shiftwork. Other companies, however, have implemented programs that provide employees with some control over their work schedule.

Shiftwork

Shiftwork
Any type of schedule in which the majority of the work hours occur between 4 P.M. and 7 A.M.

Shiftwork is any type of schedule in which the majority of the work hours occur between 4 P.M. and 7 A.M. Workers who work the third shift (usually from 11 P.M. to 7 A.M.), for example, would be considered shiftworkers.[32] Some employees work on a rotating shift schedule: they work the morning shift (perhaps 7 A.M. to 3 P.M.) during the first week, the second shift (3 P.M. to 11 P.M.) during the next week, and the night shift (11 P.M. to 7 A.M.) during the third week. Shiftwork has a negative connotation; most workers do not like it because it interferes with leisure activities and conflicts with our natural biological sleeping cycles or circadian patterns.[33]

Organizations that use shiftwork generally do so because of economic or business necessity. Can you think of some types of organizations that might use shiftwork? Hospitals, law enforcement agencies, and all-night convenience stores are a few of the organizations that must use shiftwork. Many production facilities also use shiftwork; the cost of shutting down and starting up again or leaving the plant idle is simply too high.

Research on the effects of shiftwork has supported the concerns many employees have with this schedule. Studies have indicated that employees who have shiftwork tend to experience less sleep, suffer from more sleep interruptions, and feel more weariness than other workers. In terms of general health, shiftworkers have been found to have more appetite problems, greater levels of tension, higher blood pressure, and decreased physical fitness. Shiftwork schedules are often cited as the reason for high turnover, decreased job performance, and higher divorce rates. On the other hand, some studies also report beneficial advantages of shiftwork. To some extent, the effects depend on individual characteristics. People who like late hours (so-called "night owls") may actually prefer shiftwork over the standard workday schedule.[34]

Flextime

Flextime
Deciding which hours of the day you will work. The basic purpose of flextime is to decrease employees' conflicts between work and personal schedules.

Do you have the right to decide which hours of the day you work? If so, you are probably the beneficiary of a flextime program. The earliest flexible work hours program was introduced in France in the mid-1950s. The concept spread to many other European cities in the 1960s, and it was rapidly adopted by companies in Germany, Switzerland, and France. Flextime caught on later in the United States. The first major company to implement flextime in the United States was Control Data Corporation, which began its program in 1972. Although currently only about 10 percent of workers in the United States participate in a flextime program, many more companies are beginning to recognize the value of flexible work hours.[35] Harris Bank of Chicago, for example, recently implemented a flextime program that provides much greater flexibility to employees. One result of the program is that the evening hours, traditionally disliked by all employees, are covered much better now that staff members have more flexibility to set their own schedules.[36]

There are several different versions of flextime.[37] They differ in terms of whether the schedule can change on a daily basis, whether a working day can vary in terms of hours worked, and whether the employees must be present for core time every working day. Figure 16.1 illustrates different types of flextime programs.

Figure 16.1 Types of Flextime Programs

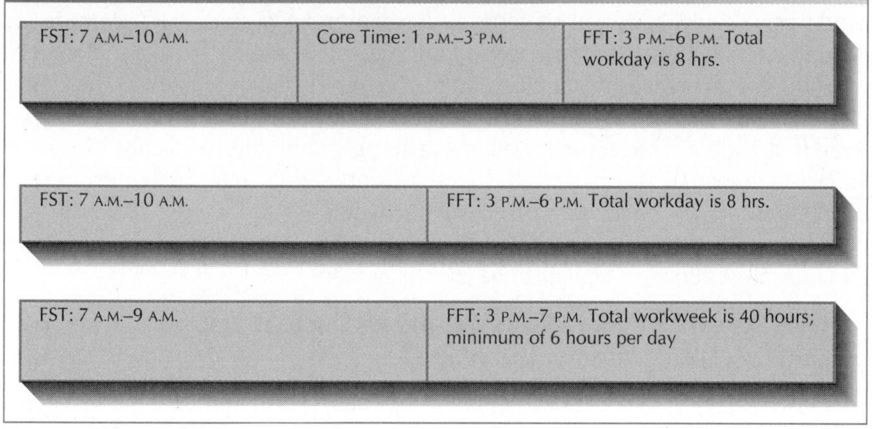

FST: 7 A.M.–10 A.M.	Core Time: 1 P.M.–3 P.M.	FFT: 3 P.M.–6 P.M. Total workday is 8 hrs.

FST: 7 A.M.–10 A.M.	FFT: 3 P.M.–6 P.M. Total workday is 8 hrs.

FST: 7 A.M.–9 A.M.	FFT: 3 P.M.–7 P.M. Total workweek is 40 hours; minimum of 6 hours per day

Note: FST is flexible starting time; FFT is flexible finishing time. Core time is the hours that all employees must be present.

The basic purpose of a flextime schedule is to decrease conflicts between an employee's work and personal schedules. Some workers, for example, may be responsible for taking their children to school and therefore may be unable to arrive at work before 9 A.M. Other workers may simply prefer to finish work at 4 P.M. rather than 5 P.M. every day. Yet other workers may prefer to sleep later, arrive at work at 10 A.M., and finish work at 6 P.M.

In general, anecdotal evidence indicates that most employees and supervisors strongly favor flextime programs. But do flextime programs really make a difference from the organization's perspective? In terms of job attitudes, research shows that flextime programs have a consistently positive effect. Moreover, once employees begin a flextime program, they rarely wish to return to a standard work schedule. Tardiness also tends to drop dramatically; some companies report that tardiness virtually disappears. However, flextime has much less of an effect on productivity and performance, which are unlikely to decline—some studies show no change in productivity and performance. One explanation is that productivity only increases when work groups previously had to share equipment, a practice that flexible hours can help to eliminate. Otherwise, flextime has no effect on productivity.[38]

Despite the positive effects of flextime, two problems often arise:

1. Supervisor Resistance. About 20 percent of supervisors express displeasure with flextime. Their dissatisfaction usually stems from the need to expend more time and effort to schedule workers and greater difficulty in communicating with employees, who may not always be present at the same time.

2. Increased Overhead Costs. Because the total workday may be longer (some workers arrive as early as 7 A.M. while others work as late as 7 P.M.), utility and other overhead costs may rise slightly.[39]

Despite these difficulties, flextime appears to offer many advantages. You will read next about a different type of work schedule that attempts to provide more flexibility to employees: the compressed workweek.

Compressed Workweek

Compressed workweek A workweek in which the work hours are reallocated so that they are completed in less than five days, for example, a four-day, 40-hour workweek.

How many days should there be in the workweek? Many people assume that a workweek should be five days long. But some organizations use a compressed workweek, in which employees work a full week in less than five days. Mobil and Gulf Oil, the first reported company to use a compressed workweek in the United States, adopted a four-day 40-hour workweek in 1940. It was not until 1960, however, that another U.S. company adopted this program. Approximately 25 percent of large companies in the United States currently either offer or require certain employees to work on a compressed work schedule.[40]

Although there are many different types of compressed workweek schedules, the four most common appear to be the following:[41]

1. 4/40. Employees work 10 hours each day for four days; employees are off work for three days, usually over the weekend.
2. Floating 4/40. Employees work four 10-hour days, with four days off, in a cycle.
3. 4½/40. Employees work four 9-hour days and one 4-hour day, with two and a half days off.
4. 5/45–4/36. Employees work 9-hour days, alternating between five-day and four-day weeks.

The key feature of the compressed workweek, then, is that the work hours are reallocated so that they are completed in fewer than five days. Unlike flextime, employees do not have a choice in the times they work.

The purpose of the compressed workweek is to provide a schedule that is better suited to either the workers' or the organization's schedule. Under what circumstances do you think that workers might desire a compressed work schedule? Consider employees who must commute long distances to arrive at work (for example, in California some workers may spend two hours commuting each way). In other cases, a compressed work schedule will meet the needs of both the employees and the organization. Consider the following situation in which all of a police department's patrol officers wished to take their vacations during the summer. Administration, however, was concerned about understaffing during peak vacation times. The solution was to implement a compressed workweek, in which each police officer worked a 12-hour, four-day schedule followed by four days off from work.[42]

In terms of the effects of the compressed workweek, the results are somewhat mixed. While many employees favor the opportunity to have more leisure time, the workers who are most favorably predisposed are those who are least satisfied with their jobs. The likely explanation is that if you don't like your job, a schedule that reduces the number of days you must come to work is quite appealing. While a compressed workweek may reduce tardiness, some research also indicates the opposite effect; perhaps some workers have difficulty adjusting to earlier starting times on workdays. Of greatest concern, though, is that the effects of the compressed workweek on productivity are quite mixed. Those organizations that reported no change in productivity have attributed this effect to worker fatigue (in one study, as many as 45 percent of the workers reported being tired) or workers taking on a second job during their off days. Finally, a compressed workweek can lead to greater scheduling problems, overtime payment problems, and conflict with personal schedules.[43]

Box 16.6 Telecommuting: The Ultimate in Flexibility

There are more than seven million workers in the United States who telecommute or work at home. Surveys indicate that large numbers of employees would like to telecommute. Would you like a job that enables you to work at home? If you answered yes, you have plenty of company—and the majority of people who do telecommute are satisfied with this arrangement. But a recent study conducted in the state of Washington found that about 33 percent of the telecommuters ended the arrangement. Telecommuters experience discomfort for several basic reasons. First, some feel isolated from their friends at work. As one telecommuter stated it, "Every day is the same. You put in your eight hours and there isn't anybody to talk to, and you miss what's going on in the outside world." A second problem experienced by some telecommuters is the increased pressure. Perhaps because a telecommuter is able to work 24 hours a day at home, some find it difficult to stop working. A third problem is that telecommuting can reduce communication between the employee and the boss. Some telecommuters also suffer from distractions at home, especially children, who may not understand that Mom or Dad are really "at work" and are not to be disturbed. Finally, many telecommuters worry about reduced visibility with top management, thereby harming their chances for promotions. Some research suggests these fears are unfounded. One study, for example, reported that telecommuters actually were promoted more rapidly than nontelecommuters. However, these results may not generalize to other situations, as the telecommuters were probably high performers to begin with. Employees who are successful working at home tend to fit the following profile:

- They have little need for face-to-face contact with coworkers and customers.
- They have quiet offices at home where they will not be disturbed.
- They have the necessary equipment (such as a fax machine).
- They need no direct supervision.
- They have a supervisor who is results oriented and not concerned about amount of time at work.
- They have a trusting relationship with their supervisor.

If you do not meet these criteria, telecommuting may not work for you.

Sources: Adapted from S. Shellenbarger, "Some Thrive, but Many Wilt Working at Home," *The Wall Street Journal,* December 14, 1993, B1, B10; and S. Shellenbarger, "I'm Still Here! Home Workers Worry They're Invisible." *The Wall Street Journal,* December 16, 1993, B1, B6.

Conclusion

You have read about different aspects of employee rights. As you can see, employees are slowly gaining more rights with regard to terminations, access to personnel files, searches, workplace romances, and legal behaviors outside of work. Much will depend, however, on the state where the employee lives. With regard to work schedules, employees have relatively fewer rights. Many companies, however, have begun to introduce their own flexible work schedule programs to give employees greater choice and control. Compared with the workplace even 30 years ago, employees have many more rights today than in the past.

Applying Core Concepts

1. You show up to work tomorrow and your boss says, "I hate your hairstyle; you are fired." Can he or she do this to you? Under what circumstances might you be able to sue successfully?
2. You would like to see your personnel file. When you ask your boss, he or she says, "No way!" What can you do?

3. Can your company search your desk? Explain your answer.
4. Could your company terminate a coworker who was not married and who had a workplace romance with your supervisor? What about if the romance was between two coworkers? Why might it make a difference?
5. Given your current or anticipated job, what type of work schedule would you like most? Why?

Key Terms

- Employment at will
- Implied contract
- Covenant of Good Faith and Fair Dealing
- Public policy
- Privacy Act of 1974
- Common law privacy
- Progressive discipline
- Due process
- Shiftwork
- Flextime
- Compressed workweek

Chapter 16: Experiential Exercise

Employee Rights Case

Presented below are four situations involving employees' *potential* misconduct. Your task is to decide for each case what to do with the employee. Your decision can be doing nothing at all, immediate termination, suspension until further investigation, or anything else you think is appropriate.

In each case, you should consider the rights of all relevant parties including the employee, the supervisor, the company, coworkers, and customers. Among your considerations should be: (a) ethics, (b) employee rights, (c) company image, (d) employer rights. If you are discussing this in groups, have one person in the group represent the employee, one person the supervisor, one person the coworker, customer, or whomever the complaining party is, and one person represent top management.

Finally, you should consider each situation in terms of: (1) what should be done without consideration of the law; and (2) what should be done given the laws that pertain. Be sure to identify the laws that might pertain in each situation.

Situation 1 One Saturday night, a vice chancellor of a private, prestigious university sees the manager of external relations leaving a bar that is well known for drugs and prostitution. The manager is walking with several people dressed in leather jackets and torn-up jeans. From the way the manager is walking, she seems to be intoxicated. She is saying crude obscenities as she walks.

Situation 2 One Friday evening, two mid-level managers of a large computer products firm are seen posting signs announcing an upcoming meeting of the American Nazi Party on telephone poles (this is being done on their own time). The evidence is provided in a videotape taken by a customer of this firm, who is threatening to provide the videotape to television stations.

Situation 3 One of your employees accidentally left an invitation on his desk that he wrote for an orgy he is holding at his house for homosexual men only. The coworker says he found the invitation on the employee's desk. The coworker noticed the content of this invitation, which included sexually explicit statements, as well as pictures. The coworker is demanding that the employee be terminated, given the offensive nature of the invitation.

Situation 4 A manager of information systems at a grocery store chain was recently arrested and charged with making and selling pornographic pictures and movies of children. He is out on bail, and would very much like to continue working at your company. He has always performed very well on the job, and has never had any kind of problem at work. However, a well-known ultraconservative citizens' group that operates in the small town where the store is located has written a letter to the store manager demanding he be fired immediately or they will boycott the chain.

Chapter 16 References

1. K. Sovereign, *Personnel Law* (Reston, VA: Reston Publishing, 1984).
2. S. Youngblood and L. Bierman, "Employment-at-Will: New Developments and Research Implications," in *Research in Personnel and Human Resource Management,* vol. 12, ed. G. Ferris (Greenwich, CT: JAI Press, 1994).
3. L.G. Joel III, *Every Employee's Guide to the Law* (New York: Pantheon Books, 1993).
4. M. Rothstein, C. Craver, E. Schroeder, E. Shoben, and L. Vander Velde, *Employment Law* (St. Paul, MN: West, 1994).
5. Joel, *Every Employee's Guide.*
6. Ibid.
7. Sovereign, *Personnel Law.*
8. Ibid.
9. Rothstein et al., *Employment Law.*
10. Youngblood and Bierman, "Employment-at-Will."
11. D. Koys, S. Briggs, and J. Grenig, "State Court Disparity on Employment-at-Will," *Personnel Psychology* 40 (1987), 565–77.
12. Joel, *Every Employee's Guide.*
13. D. Bennett-Alexander and L. Pincus, *Employment Law for Business* (Chicago: Irwin, 1995).
14. Joel, *Every Employee's Guide.*
15. J. Coil and C. Rice, "Determining Whether Employees Have a Right to Review Personnel Records," *Employment Relations Today* 19 (Autumn 1992), 335–46.
16. Sovereign, *Personnel Law.*
17. D. McWhirter, *Your Rights at Work* (New York: John Wiley, 1993).
18. McWhirter, *Your Rights at Work.*
19. Joel, *Every Employee's Guide.*
20. L. Jenner, "Office Dating Policies: Is There a Workable Way?" *HR Focus,* November 1993, 5.
21. A.B. Fisher, "Getting Comfortable with Couples in the Workplace," *Fortune,* October 3, 144, 138–42.
22. Ibid.
23. J. Segal, "Love: What's Work Got to Do with It?" *HR Magazine,* June 1993, 36–41.
24. Jenner, "Office Dating Policies."
25. Ibid.
26. Rothstein et al., *Employment Law;* Joel, *Every Employee's Guide.*
27. R. Arvey, G. Davis, and S. Nelson, "Use of Discipline in an Organization: A Field Study," *Journal of Applied Psychology* 69 (1984), 448–60.
28. J. Redeken, *Employee Discipline: Policies and Practices* (Washington: Bureau of National Affairs, 1989).
29. Ibid.
30. G. Latham and K. Wexley, *Increasing Productivity through Performance Appraisal* (Reading, MA: Addison-Wesley, 1981).
31. U. Weigelt, "On the Road to a Society of Free Choice: The Politics of Working Time in Sweden," in *Working Time in Transition,* ed. K. Hinrichs, W. Roche, and C. Sirianni (Philadelphia: Temple University Press, 1991).
32. S. Nollen, *New Work Schedules in Practice* (New York: Van Nostrand Reinhold, 1982).
33. T. Akerstedt, "Adjustment of Physiological Circadian Rhythms and the Sleep-Wake Cycle to Shiftwork," in *Hours of Work: Temporal Factors in Work-Scheduling,* ed. S. Folkard and T. Monk (Chichester, England: John Wiley, 1985).
34. M. Frese and K. Okonek, "Reasons to Leave Shiftwork and Psychological and Psychosomatic Complaints of Former Shiftworkers," *Journal of Applied Psychology* 69 (1984), 509–14.

35. J. Pierce, J. Newstrom, R. Dunham, and A. Barber, *Alternative Work Schedules,* (Boston: Allyn & Bacon, 1989).
36. S. Shellenbarger, "More Companies Experiment with Workers' Schedules, *The Wall Street Journal,* January, 13, 1994, B1, B6.
37. Nollen, *New Work Schedules in Practice.*
38. D. Ralston, W. Anthony, and D. Gustafson, "Employees May Love Flextime, but What Does It Do to the Organization's Productivity?" *Journal of Applied Psychology* 70 (1985), 272–79; and C. Orpen, "Effect of Flexible Working Hours on Employee Satisfaction and Performance," *Journal of Applied Psychology* 66 (981), 113–15.
39. Pierce et al., *Alternative Work Schedules.*
40. Ibid.
41. Nollen, *New Work Schedules in Practice.*
42. J. Pierce and R. Dunham, "The 12-Hour Work Day: A 48-Hour, Eight-Day Work Week," *Academy of Management Journal* 35 (1992), 1086–98.
43. Nollen, *New Work Schedules in Practice.*

appendix 1 A Brief History of Human Resource Management

Prior to the 20th century, the management of employees was the responsibility of each supervisor and manager, and there was no systematic approach to human resources (HR). This was partly due to the fact that most production was performed under a craft system, in which the work was completed by small teams of employees under the direction of a master craftsman. However, following the Industrial Revolution, production work became increasingly performed by large companies, which in turn created a greater need for formal, carefully conceived methods of managing employees.[1]

The early part of the 20th century witnessed the development of two approaches to managing HR. One approach, scientific management or Taylorism, sought to design jobs to maximize efficiency. Under this approach, the company would identify the appropriate number of employees needed, determine the most effective way to perform each task, and provide training to the workers where necessary.[2]

The second approach that emerged in the beginning of the 20th century was personnel psychology, which emphasized testing of people's abilities to identify the best employees for each job. The Bureau of Salesmanship Research, for example, was established in 1915 and among its major projects was the development of a test battery for a selection of salespeople. Compared with scientific management, then, personnel psychology emphasized choosing the appropriate employees to fit the demands of the job.[3]

Within a few years, interest in HR grew rapidly. Columbia University offered the first HR course in 1920, around the same time that Ford Motor company adopted the first formal HR system.

The next major event in the HR field was a series of workplace studies that was completed in the 1930s. Generally referred to as the Hawthorne studies (after Western Electric's Hawthorne plant where some of this research was performed), the investigators examined the effects of illumination, pay incentives, and rest breaks on work productivity. Much to their surprise, they found that social relationships, including team development, informal work group norms, and supervision, had a far greater impact on productivity. This research, along with a series of studies examining job attitudes, marked the beginning of the human relations era, which emphasized the psychological and sociological aspects of work.[4]

The demand for human resource management programs heightened during World War II, as a result of the mass drafting of men by the armed forces and the large numbers of women who were placed in manufacturing jobs previously occupied by these men. Tests were developed for the armed forces to place draftees into the most appropriate positions. Extensive use was made of training technologies to enable women to succeed at jobs in which they had not previously worked. After the war, both government and industry continued to use these and other HR programs and practices.[5]

During the 1950s and continuing until the mid-1960s, quality of work life (QWL) became a major concern by business and industry. Studies by Dr. Herzberg and Drs. Hackman and Oldham indicating the importance of intrinsic job satisfaction, led to programs that modified jobs to increase workers' responsibility, recognition, and enjoyment. In subsequent years, the QWL movement spawned HR practices such as quality circles, employee involvement, and the team concept.[6]

Although there were many significant events that took place in the United States during the 1960s, HR was most dramatically affected by the passage of the Civil Rights Act of 1964. Up until this time, there were few laws governing human resource management and those that did exist were simple and straightforward. The Civil Rights Act of 1964, however, banned discrimination in the employment context on the basis of race, sex, religion, and national origin. As a result, every manager was now responsible for a whole new set of concerns and issues. Since passage of the Civil Rights Act of 1964, many more laws have been passed that affect HR, and their complexity continued to grow on a yearly basis.[7]

By the mid-1970s, global competition had become a serious issue for businesses in the United States. Partly as a response to this trend and partly due to a growing awareness of the need to utilize all available resources, HR became an increasingly important function in organizations.[8] At the same time, the development of various formulas to quantify both the costs and the benefits of any HR program or practice enabled organizations to hold human resource staff increasingly accountable. Increased awareness of the importance continued into the next decade as well. By the late 1980s, HR function was no longer viewed as merely an administrative and advisory function. Rather, HR was increasingly viewed as a partner in developing business strategy and a key player in major organizational restructurings.[9]

We are now more than half-way through the 1990s. While HR issues remain of vital importance to organizations, the trend towards reengineering has led to serious questions about the appropriate role of the HRM *function*. Some feel that the HRM function should be radically modified or perhaps done away with completely, leaving most of the HR responsibilities with line managers and outsourcing other programs, such as benefits. Despite these questions, it is clear that HR activities will remain of interest and concern to both employees and organizations in the 21st century.[10]

References

1. J. Butler, G. Ferris, & N. Napier. "Strategy and Human Resources Management." (Cincinnati, OH; South-Western, 1991).
2. Ibid.
3. R. Katzell and J. Austin, "From Then to Now: The Development of Industrial-Organizational Psychology in the United States," *Journal of Applied Psychology* 77, (1992): 803-825.
4. Ibid.
5. J. Bender, T. Urban, M. Galang, D. Frink and G. Ferris, "Developing Human Resources Professionals at ARCO Oil and Gas Company," In G. Ferris and M. R. Buckley (Eds.),

"Human Resources Management: Perspectives, Context, Functions, and Outcomes." (Englewood Cliffs, NJ: Prentice-Hall, 1996).

6. Katzell and Austin, "From Then to Now"
7. J. Ledvinka and V. Scarpello, "Federal Regulation of Personnel and Human Resource Management.: (Boston: PWS-Kent, 1991).
8. M. Beer, B. Spector, P. Lawrence, D. Q. Mills and R. Walton, "Managing Human Assets.: (New York: Free Press, 1984).
9. Butler, Ferris, Napier "Strategy and HRM"
10. T. Stewart, "Human Resources Bites Back," *Fortune,* May 13, 1996, volume 133, 175-176.

GLOSSARY

360 Degree Feedback Information is gathered from a variety of sources, including subordinates, who complete performance appraisals, and the results are summarized for the employee and areas needing improvement are discussed.

401(k) A type of savings program that has become quite popular since its introduction in 1981. The 401(k) program permits employees to place about $9000 each year into a retirement fund tax-free until it is withdrawn.

Add-on plan A cafeteria plan in which all existing benefits are maintained.

Adverse impact The employer treats the group as a whole in a discriminatory manner.

Affirmative action Emphasis on recruitment of traditionally underrepresented groups; altering managerial and supervisory attitudes to eliminate prejudice; removing discriminatory barriers in hiring and promotions; and using a quota, or giving preferential treatment in hiring and promotion, to groups that have been underrepresented in the organization's workforce.

Age Discrimination in Employment Act of 1967 Prohibits age discrimination. When first passed, it applied only to individuals between the ages of 40 and 65. In 1978, it was changed to include individuals under 70 years of age. In subsequent years, Congress abolished the age cap in subsequent years for almost all jobs.

Ambiguity of appraisal forms The wide difference of appraisals and opinions where the scales may be vague or unclear.

Americans with Disabilities Act of 1990 Prohibits most other employers from discriminating against the disabled. Also addressed the definition of what disability means. Also required that employers offer reasonable accommodations.

Amount of learning Refers to the knowledge, skills, and abilities that were acquired by the trainees from the program. The amount of learning is measured in the context of the training program, not on the job.

Applicant flow A method of assessing whether the plaintiff's group was adversely affected by the selection procedures that involves comparison of the hiring rate of the plaintiff's group to the hiring rate of the majority group.

Apprenticeship A formal program involving a combination of classroom instruction and hands-on practice and training, primarily in the skilled crafts such as carpentry.

Arbitration Process Resembles a courtroom hearing, but the rules are not as formalized. An arbitrator is selected, and that person is responsible for making a final ruling after considering all of the relevant evidence and testimony, and provide a decision and explanation in a written report.

Assessment center An extended work sample.

Authorization card The equivalent of obtaining sufficient numbers of signatures of eligible voters for a political candidate to appear on the ballot, at least 30% of the relevant employees must sign these cards

Bargaining Unit Refers to the employees who will be voting in the election, and if the union wins, these are the employees who will be represented by the union.

Behavior Observation Scales A behaviorally-based approach that has the rater evaluate the frequency with which the employee engages in various behaviors.

Behavioral changes This aspect of program success refers to the degree to which the trainees' behavior on the job has been affected by the training program.

Behaviorally-Anchored Rating Scales A rating system that defines the dimension and organizational skills in terms of behavior, and where the points on the scale are defined, or anchored, in behavioral terms.

Behaviorally-based scales Developed as a response to the shortcomings of the graphic scale approach, the behaviorally-based scale provides a set of scales that are defined in a precise, behavioral fashion.

Benchmark jobs Jobs that are similar or comparable in content across firms.

Benchmarking Involves comparing an organization's human resource practices and programs to other organizations.

Biographical information blank Utilizes a broader range of questions on an application blank, particularly those pertaining to past achievements and personal goals and aspirations, which are scored with a standardized key.

Bona fide occupational qualification (BFOQ) Suitable defense against a discrimination charge only where age, religion, sex or national origin is an actual qualification for performing the job.

Bottom up forecast Involves the department managers making estimates of future human resource demands based on issues such as new positions needed, positions to be eliminated, expected overtime, hours worked by temporary, part-time, or independent contractors, and expected changes in workload by department.

Broadbanding A pay structure that contains relatively few grades, with much greater range in each as compared to the traditional pay structure.

Business strategy Refers to the approach that companies take in conducting business.

Business Representative The business representative's primary responsibility is to represent the union in contract negotiations, and also is responsible for collecting union dues, paying union bills, and interacting with the national union.

Cafeteria benefits A benefits plan that resembles a cafeteria, for which the customer pays a flat monthly fee, and has a choice between taxable (usually cash) and nontaxable elements of compensation (such as health insurance).

Carpal tunnel syndrome First identified in the 1980s, this injury involves pressure on the median nerve, which is located in the wrist, and often requires surgery.

Cases Involves a written description of an organizational situation.

Central Tendency An alternative to the leniency effect where raters rate practically all employees about average.

Civil Rights Act of 1866 The first of many laws banning race discrimination in private companies, unions, and employment agencies, passed in 1866.

Civil Rights Act of 1964 A comprehensive law banning workplace discrimination (which covers race, color, religion, sex, and national origin) passed in 1964.

Civil Rights Act of 1991 A further delineation of civil rights, resulting from several controversial Supreme Court decisions during the late 1980s. Some of the key changes include: making it easier for employees and job applicants to win lawsuits; prohibiting the use of different norms, based on race or sex, for scoring tests; permitting use of jury trials; expanding coverage of discrimination laws to US citizens working for US companies based in other countries; and allowing employees and job applicants to win punitive damages in certain circumstances.

Closed internal recruitment system Employees are unaware of job openings and therefore do not have the opportunity to formally apply.

Coaching Informal, unplanned training and development activities provided by supervisors and peers.

COBRA The Consolidated Omnibus Budget Reconciliation Act (COBRA) of 1985 requires companies with 20 or more employees to offer continued coverage of health insurance to participants who would otherwise no longer be eligible to participate in the health insurance plan.

Cognitive ability test Intelligence tests given to applicants.

College campus recruitment A method of recruiting by visiting and participating in college campuses and their placement centers. Advantages include a new source of applicants, the placement center helps locate applicants and provides resumes to organizations, applicants can be prescreened, applicants will not have to be enticed away from a current job, and lower salary expectations.

Common Law Privacy A general principle that protects an employee from searches and seizures in a non-governmental organization.

Comparable worth The concept that jobs of equal worth or value should be paid the same, even if the jobs are completely different.

Comparative approaches Rating forms that require the rater to compare each employee to the other employees, also known as the bell-shaped curve that is particularly common in freshman and sophomore college courses.

Compensable factor The determinants of job worth.

Compensation Wages and salaries, bonuses, and benefits such as health insurance, vacation time, and pension programs given to employees for services rendered to the organization.

Compressed work week A work week in which the work hours are reallocated so that they are completed in less than five days, for example, a 4-day, 40-hour work week.

Computer-based training Computers are used to present material to trainees, either on a need-to-know basis, at their own pace, or in their own offices.

Concrete results Address training program success in terms of the "bottom line" outcomes such as increased productivity, reduced accident rate, or whatever the objectives of the training program are.

Contamination When a rating form has additional, irrelevant performance dimensions that may contaminate the performance appraisal.

Content validity Another method of demonstrating job relatedness, where the selection procedure should: comprise a simulation of the job, have scores based on concrete and observable behavior by the test taker, represent important aspects of the job, and assess activities for which the person will not receive training if hired.

Continuous Improvement Emphasizes ongoing efforts to improve productivity and quality.

Constructive confrontation Useful in helping supervisors prompt employees to seek treatment from the EAP, constructive confrontation involves four steps: 1) the supervisor confronts the employee with evidence of unsatisfactory performance; 2) the supervisor provides coaching to improve the employee's performance; 3) at the same time, the supervisor encourages the employee to contact the EAP; and 4) the supervisor continues to inform the employee of the consequences of continued unsatisfactory performance.

Copayment Refers to the amount of money the employee must pay for the specific health service.

Correlation coefficient A statistic that summarizes the relationship between two variables or measures.

Cost savings (gain-sharing) plan Provides a payout when productivity improvements occur.

Counterproposal This technique involves making an offer in response to the other side's offer.

Covenant of Good Faith and Fair Dealing An exception to employment at will which may be used when the reason for doing the termination was clearly inappropriate or the conditions under which the firing was made were extremely inconsiderate of the employee.

Criterion-related validity study One method of demonstrating that a selection procedure is job-related. The organization would use the selection method, or predictor, with a large number of applicants or current employees to obtain measures of job behavior, then use statistics to calculate the relationship between the predictor and the criteria.

Decertification Campaign Just as the workers may decide to vote in a union to represent them, the workers may choose to vote out the union.

Defamation Slander or libel which can result in a lawsuit.

Deferred profit-sharing The contributions are usually made only by the employer, and are determined by the profitability of the company.

Deficiency When a performance appraisal form is missing key aspects of job performance.

Defined benefit pension program Described in terms of what the employee will receive upon retirement, the plan relies on a formula, which determines exactly what the employee will receive upon retirement.

Defined contribution pension program In this program, each participating employee has an individual fund into which contributions may be made by the company, the employee, or both, depending on the specific type of plan.

Demand-control model of stress The theory that states that an employee will experience the most stress when the job has high demands and little control.

Diamond career advancement system A relatively new career advancement system, the diamond system is used in an organization that is project-based, and involves few upward, but potentially many sideways, moves.

Disability income If an employee were to become completely disabled and unable to work, social security would provide monthly social security payments.

Disparate treatment When an employer treats people differently or evaluates them by different standards, depending on their age, sex, race or other protected categories.

Distributed training A training session that is conducted over a longer period of time, such as one hour per week for sixteen weeks.

Due process The notion that employees have the right to be treated fairly, particularly when being disciplined.

Employee assistance program An organization-sponsored program that helps identify workers in need of counseling, motivates them to obtain the needed counseling, and provides the proper counseling sources.

Employee empowerment Refers to how much decision-making power and authority employees at the lowest level of the organization acquire as a result of the work design available to organizations.

Employee Polygraph Protection Act of 1988 Prohibits most private-sector organizations from having you take a polygraph test as a condition of employment.

Employee referral An excellent source of job applicants, employee referral means using personal contacts to locate job opportunities

Employee Retirement Income Security Act (ERISA) An act instituted in 1974 to eliminate pension mismanagement and abuse.

Employee stock ownership plan (ESOP) The ESOP provides employees with company stock while at the same time allowing the company to borrow money from a bank at a reduced tax rate.

Employment agencies Organizations that serve as a third party, matching applicants to jobs.

Employment at will When employees are employed "at will," or at the will or discretion of the company. This means that if an employee can leave the work relationship at any time he or she desires, an employer has the same right.

Entry stage The point at which the individual begins a new job.

Equipment simulators Used for jobs or tasks where use of actual equipment would pose a danger to the trainee (or others) or the risk of substantial financial loss exists.

Equal Employment Opportunity Commission (EEOC) Created by Title VII of the Civil Rights Act of 1964 and is the agency that processes discrimination charges and writes regulations pertinent to Congressional laws.

Equal Pay Act of 1963 An amendment to the Fair Labor Standards Act of 1938 that attempts to eliminate sex discrimination in pay.

Escalator Clause A clause included in some union contracts that adjusts wages (both up and down), depending on the cost of living.

Evaluation Assessing employees for several different reasons, including determining pay raises, giving feedback, and assessing training programs.

Evil intent An earlier practice, where employers would refuse to hire applicants of a particular race, religion, or gender simply out of prejudice.

Executive Order 11246 A law passed by President Lyndon B. Johnson in 1965

that prohibits discrimination on the basis of race, color, religion, sex and national origin.

Exempt employees Employees who are not covered by the law's provision that requires companies to pay time and a half for overtime, often applies to executive, administrative, and professional employees.

External environment Refers to conditions that are outside of the organization, including business conditions, workforce characteristics, laws, unions, and technology.

External issue Events or trends outside of the organization, such as workforce demographics and technology.

External recruitment sources Tap applicants from outside of the organization. Advantages include new perspectives by bringing in new employees, offers a large pool of applicants, and may be necessary for increasing minority and female representation in the workforce.

Fair Credit Reporting Act Requires an employer to notify the applicant, in writing within three days of requesting a credit check.

Fair Labor Standards Act of 1938 A Congressional law passed with the intent of improving working conditions and living standards.

False positive Occurs when you are mistakenly identified as a drug user even though you do not use drugs.

Family and Medical Leave Act Passed in 1993, this act requires companies that have at least 50 employees to grant an unpaid leave to employees who meet any of the following conditions: the employee has become responsible for a child; is providing care for a child, parent or spouse with a serious health condition; or the employee is experiencing a serious health condition that leaves him or her unable to perform the job.

Fee-for-service The traditional health-insurance program in which the employee and/or the employer pay for each medical service provided.

Fiduciary A person to whom property or power is entrusted for the benefit of another, such as a person who has authority over the pension plan management, assets, or administration.

Flexible spending account FSAs allow an employee to pay for health care expenses or dependent care assistance expenses on a "before-tax" basis.

Flextime Deciding which hours of the day you work. The basic purpose of flextime is to decrease employees' conflicts between work and personal schedules.

"For Cause" Means if there is good reason to believe you may have been under the influence of drugs during work, your company may require you to take a drug test.

Functional arrangement The traditional arrangement of organizational structure that is organized by departments and work is organized by task and job similarity.

Funding rules Requires the pension plan to have sufficient funds so that promised benefits will be available to employees when they retire.

General Duty Clause OSHA guidelines that require compliance with basic standards, as well as the responsibility of providing a workplace that is free from recognized safety and health hazards.

Glass ceiling Refers to an invisible barrier preventing women from advancing to higher levels within the organization.

Grade overlap The amount of overlap that exists between grades.

Graphic scales A type of performance evaluation form that uses broad, relatively ambiguous work dimensions, such as quality, leadership, and reliability.

Graphology Handwriting analysis.

Green circle rates Refer to employees whose salaries are below the minimum of their respective grade.

Grievance Procedure A grievance procedure provides a mechanism for the employee or union to dispute a decision that is believed to be in violation of the contract.

Guaranteed investment contract A type of fund offered by most companies that is similar to bank-sponsored accounts, guaranteed investment contracts have one major difference: GICs are usually held by insurance companies.

Halo This error occurs when one aspect of the subordinate's performance affects the rater's evaluation of other performance dimensions.

Hay Plan A pre-established job evaluation plan that is widely used for evaluating executive, managerial and professional positions.

Hazard Communication Standard of 1985 A regulation that covers all hazardous chemicals. As of 1987, companies covered by the OSH Act must meet the requirements of the Hazard Communication Standard.

Health maintenance organization (HMO) A network of medical professionals and hospitals that provide health care for participants.

Honesty test Two types of honesty tests: overt and personality-based. The overt test asks questions that directly address test-takers' perceptions and feelings about honesty, while personality-based tests tend to be somewhat less obvious as to what they are assessing, and focus on personality traits associated with dishonesty.

Hostile environment sexual harassment An environment created by unwelcome sexual advances, requests for sexual favors, and other verbal or physical conduct of a sexual nature.

Human resource demand The procedure for predicting the number of employees that will be needed in the future, usually by using quantitative and qualitative methods.

Human Resource Management The programs, policies, and practices for managing an organization's workforce.

Human resource planning The process of examining an organization's or individual's future human resource needs compared to future human resource capabilities, and developing human resource policies and practices to address potential problems.

Human resource supply The number of employees the company is likely to have in the future.

Immigration Reform and Control Act Provides additional protection against discrimination on the basis of national origin, and even protects certain non-citizens of the US, such as individuals who are permanent residents of the US or have declared an intention to gain citizenship in the US.

Implied contract An implied agreement between employer and employee regarding an aspect of the job, such as the statement, "Once you pass the probationary period, your job is guaranteed for life." Employee handbooks can also be considered implied contracts.

Improshare Stands for Improved Productivity through Sharing, and focuses on the number of hours of work. Improshare also involves a formula which compares input to output, where input is the number of hours that it should take to complete the work compared with the number of hours it actually took to do the work.

In-network A list of medical professionals that are associated with the plan (POS, HMO, PPO).

Individual incentive The payout is based on the individual employee's performance, and performance is evaluated using an objective standard.

Internal issue Events or trends within the organization, such as business strategy, organizational structure, and company profitability.

Internal environment Refers to those factors that are within the organization and under its control, such as the work structure and business strategy.

Internship A program providing work experience prior to graduation from an academic program.

Internal recruitment sources Provide applicants who already are employed by the organization. Advantages include less expense, greater speed in completing the recruitment process, less orientation time for new employees, and an effective motivator for employees.

Job analysis The process of collecting information about two basic issues: what the job entails, and what knowledge, skills, abilities and other requirements are needed to perform the work.

Job burnout A sense of emotional exhaustion, lack of energy, feeling of depersonalization towards coworkers or clients, a sense of personal failure and limited progress at work are all characteristics of burnout. One cause lies within the individual employee, whereas a second cause lies in the nature of the work.

Job classification Categories or classes are defined in terms of responsibility for subordinates, contact with other departments, amount of education required, and technical skills involved.

Job enlargement Involves increasing the number of tasks performed by each employee, and having jobs that are somewhat less specialized.

Job enrichment Increasing job satisfaction by using such intrinsic factors as achievement, recognition, and the work itself instead of enforcing extrinsic factors such as company policy and supervision.

Job evaluation A systematic, objective procedure for determining the value of a group of jobs for the organization.

Job grades A manager may choose to sort jobs into a smaller number of grades or classes, usually into 10-20 different grades.

Job posting system When an organization publicizes job openings on bulletin boards, electronic media, and similar outlets.

Job relatedness Refers to whether the selection procedure is related to job requirements or job outcomes.

Job rotation A formal, planned program involving assignment of trainees to varying job assignments in different parts of the organization.

Joint Study Groups A joint study group is a task force, composed of both management and union representatives, and often third-parties as well, for the purpose of examining issues of particular concern in a nonadversarial setting.

Judgment errors Errors made due to poor judgment, decision making, and biases.

Labor market survey Provides information as to what other organizations who compete for employees are paying, and is used to determine what other companies are paying employees so that an organization can effectively recruit and retain its workers.

Landrum-Griffin Act (Labor-Management Reporting and Disclosure Act) Passed in 1959, this act's major purpose was to protect employees from unions.

Lecture training Involves an instructor verbally presenting material to a group of trainees.

Leniency Many raters give higher performance evaluations than deserved, often created by organizational policies and practices.

Long-term care An insurance program that pays for medical care at home or in a nursing home.

Long-term disability insurance Insurance that covers long-term disabilities, usually for periods of time greater than six months.

Management-by-objectives An evaluation system that uses clearly defined objectives or goals, with a specified time frame in which they will be reached.

Market pricing An approach to developing a pay structure that essentially downplays internal value and relies almost exclusively on external value to determine pay.

Markov analysis A quantitative procedure of determining supply that uses historical rates of promotion, transfer, and turnover to estimate future availabilities in the workforce.

Massed training A training session that is conducted in a compacted timetable, such as in a lengthy two-day program.

Mastery stage The next stage after entry, this is when employees seek to attain a high degree of success in their work.

Maximum-out-of-pocket annual payment Refers to the most that an employee would have to pay for medical expenses in a single year.

McDonnell-Douglas vs. Green standards A case in 1973 that outlined a more elaborate three-step process for examining hiring or promotion discrimination under the disparate treatment concept.

Mediation In mediation, a neutral party meets with the union and management to work out an agreement (the mediator's suggestions are not binding on either party).

Mentor A person who is higher up the organization and who can provide career advice and support to a less senior employee.

Merit pay The payout is based on the individual employee's performance, performance is evaluated in a subjective fashion, and the payout is added to the employee's base salary.

Meta-analysis Developed by Frank Schmidt and John Hunter, this is a statistical procedure for summarizing past research, and have indicated that cognitive ability tests have adequate validity across virtually all jobs.

Modular plan A cafeteria plan in which the employee is offered a choice of several benefit "packages" or modules.

National Institute for Occupational Safety and Health NIOSH provides research and training support for OSHA. The research focuses on developing new safety and health standards; the training is for OSHA inspectors and other staff involved with OSH Act enforcement.

National Labor Relations Board Established by the Wagner Act, this board is responsible for administering and interpreting the act.

Negligent hiring A finding that an employer is responsible for using poor selection procedures after an employee inflicts harm on the customer or other third party.

Newspaper advertisements A method of job recruitment by advertising in newspapers. Advantages include quick placement of ads, flexibility in terms of information, and can target a specific geographic area.

No SPITting rule The legal requirements that stipulate what management cannot do to employees who are unionizing: spy on union activities, promise changes in personnel practices, interrogate employees, or threaten employees.

Non-exempt employees Employees who are covered by the law's provision that requires companies to pay time and a half for each hour that an employee works more than forty hours per week, as long as the job is covered by the law.

Occupational Safety and Health Act of 1970 Passed by Congress in 1970, this law's purpose was to reduce the high rate of workplace accidents, injuries, and deaths in the U.S.

Occupational Safety and Health Administration (OSHA) The major agency created to administer and oversee the OSH Act, including establish safety standards, permit variances, or exceptions, to those standards, conduct inspections of workplaces, and issue citations, indicating a violation of OSH Act regulations.

Occupational Safety and Health Review Commission The purpose of the OSHRC is to review appeals from companies that have been issued a citation by OSHA.

Off-the-job training Involves training that is conducted away from the worksite.

Office of Federal Contract Compliance Programs (OFCCP) Wrote and enforces a document referred to as "Revised Order No. 4" which contains the guidelines for affirmative action to remedy underutilization of women and minorities in firms that have government contracts and subcontracts.

On-the-job training Involves training that is provided at the worksite.

One-on-one instruction A person who serves as a trainer for the organization meets with the employee at the workplace and instructs the trainee.

Open internal recruitment system Employees are made aware of potential openings and have the opportunity to formally apply.

Organization-wide incentive The payout is based on the performance of the plant, division, or organization, and performance is evaluated using an objective standard.

Organizational analysis The purpose of this analysis is to examine the organization, unit, or department and determine its basic business strategy, objectives, and goals.

Organizational structure Refers to how work tasks are assigned, who reports to whom, and how decisions are made.

OSHA Form No. 101 Employees who use Form No. 200 must also complete this form, which requires detailed information about work-related injuries and illnesses, including the circumstances of the incident, a description of the injury or illness, and the name of the doctor and hospital that provided treatment.

OSHA Form No. 200 This form must be used by most employers with more than 10 workers. This form records information about workers who are injured or become ill as a result of the job and if the injury or illness resulted in death, days off from work, transfer, termination, medical treatment, unconsciousness, or work/motion restrictions.

OSHA variance In certain cases, an employer may request either a temporary or permanent exception to an OSHA standard, and must seek a variance. OSHA would inspect and possibly hold a hearing on the proposed deviation. If OSHA agrees to the modification, a variance would be granted, thus permitting this deviation.

Out-of-network Any medical professional not associated with the plan (POS, HMO, PPO). If an employee chooses a doctor that is out-of-network, the cost will be higher than using an in-network professional.

Outsourcing When companies contract their work to other companies and individuals to save money.

Paid time off Includes vacation, holidays, and personal absences.

Panel interview A group of interviewers interviewing a candidate at the same time. This type of interview is used to reduce personal biases any individual interviewer may have.

Passage stage Refers to the point during which the employee prepares to change jobs or employers.

Pay range The range of pay a manager chooses within each grade, usually depending on seniority, performance, or other relevant factors.

Pay structure Designates the base pay for each job.

Pension Benefit Guaranty Corporation Serves as an insurance program whereby pension plan participants are guaranteed at least some benefits even if the fund is terminated before being fully funded.

Person analysis Addresses the question of whether there are certain employees who are deficient in the important tasks/KSAs, and whether training would address these deficiencies.

Personal absences Allowed on certain days in which the employee is unable to come to work for reasons beyond their control, such as jury duty, family death, military duty, divorce hearings, and doctor visits.

Personality test A test given to an applicant that will supposedly predict the type of personality a candidate has, and how that personality will affect job performance.

Planning The steps an organization and its managers take to achieve its goals for the long-term and short-term of the company.

Planned job rotation model A carefully designed plan by the organization for employees to gain experience in specific functions for a predetermined amount of time.

Point method job evaluation One of the most commonly used job evaluation procedures that involves forming a committee, selecting and defining compensable factors, establishing and defining levels for each compensable factor, determining the total number of points for the system, dividing total points among compensable factors, distributing points to each level on every factor, and evaluating the jobs.

Point-of-service (POS) A plan that attempts to combine the advantages of the HMO with the advantages of the PPO.

Position allocation and control procedure A more traditional approach to estimating the demand for employees, position allocation and control procedure uses rules determined by top management in estimating future needs.

Pre-existing condition An illness, injury or pregnancy that an individual has prior to becoming covered by the health insurance plan.

Preferred-provider organization (PPO) A network of medical professionals and hospitals that have agreed to give discounted services. Unlike the HMO, participants may go to any medical professional or hospital they wish.

Pregnancy Discrimination Act of 1978 An amendment to the Civil Rights Act of 1964, states that an employer: cannot require maternity leave of a particular length; must provide the same terms and conditions for a leave of absence for childbirth as is provided for other medical conditions; and must offer those returning from medical leave the same or equivalent job and employment conditions.

Prevailing wage laws Require companies with government contracts to pay workers the standard wage for the area, either the wage paid to a majority of workers in the area or a wage based on a weighted formula, which may be used if there is no single wage for the area.

Primary-care physician The physician chosen through an HMO that decides what kind of treatment is needed, and provides referrals to the appropriate specialists within the HRM.

Privacy Act of 1974 The law that gives federal employees a right to their personnel files (covers federal administrative agencies and allows individuals who work at these agencies the right to examine their records, and the right to correct any mistakes in the records).

Process arrangement The arrangement of an organization that is organized by activities that provide value to the customer.

Product market survey Provides information as to what other organizations providing the same product or service are paying their employees, and is used to make sure that the organization's payroll costs are not higher than its business competitor.

Profit-sharing plan Performance is linked to some index of profitability.

Progressive discipline In a progressive discipline system, the employee is given ample warning of performance or other work-related problems. Failure to change his or her behavior is accompanied by increasingly harsher disciplinary action.

Psychological assessment Conducted by a psychologist, this assessment lasts between 4 to 8 hours, and involves an hour and a half interview as well as personality and cognitive ability tests.

Public policy An exception to employment at will in which the employee has either committed an action, or refused to commit an action, that is in the interest of the common public good.

Quality circle Originating in Japan in the early 1960s, the quality circle usually has between 3 and 15 members who meet on a regular basis, and their purpose is to identify, discuss, and solve production or business-related problems within the members' work area.

Quid-pro-quo sexual harassment A Latin phrase meaning something in exchange for something else, such as a supervisor offering an employee a promotion or raise or other personnel action in exchange for sexual favors.

Race norming A method used to eliminate adverse impact by separating norms for different racial and gender groups.

Ratio analysis Involves comparison of the number of employees to some index of work load.

Reasonable accommodation A modification or adjustment to a job, the work environment, or the way things usually are done that enables a qualified individual with a disability to enjoy an equal employment opportunity.

Reasonable cause Based on their initial investigation, the EEOC may feel that a case has merit, or reasonable cause, to pursue a settlement or a suit.

Red circle rates Refer to employees whose salaries exceed the maximum of their respective grade.

Regression analysis Relies on factors or predictors that determine the demand for employees, such as revenues, degree of automation, and so forth.

Rehabilitation Act of 1973 Prohibited discrimination against disabled individuals, applying only to government employers or businesses having contracts with the federal government.

Repetitive stress injury First identified in the 1990s, this injury is a form of muscle strain, usually not crippling.

Replacement planning A method of forecasting human resource supply which involves an assessment of potential candidates to replace existing executives and other high level managers, as they retire or leave for other organizations.

Replacement Workers Often called "scabs," replacement workers are hired to replace striking personnel.

Right-to-sue notice A notice issued from the EEOC that gives you the right to have a lawyer take your case in a discrimination suit.

Role-plays A technique which involves trainees acting out an assigned role in a hypothetical situation.

Rucker plan A variant to the Scanlon plan, this plan replaces sales as the measure of output with something called "value added," which is the sales value of production after subtracting non-labor costs.

SAWNOF approach "Sit And Watch Nellie Or Fred" method of training, in which the employee is instructed to go sit and watch Nellie or Fred (usually, experienced workers).

Scanlon plan Relies on a formula which contains two factors: a monetary index of output, reflecting how much was produced, and a measure of input or what it might cost the company to produce this output. The goal of the plan is to lower the input relative to output.

Scientific management The classical approach to job design, which concentrates on such principles as specialization and simplification, repetitiveness, mechanical pacing, limited interpersonal interaction, and predetermined work techniques.

Severity A bias in the opposite direction, in which a supervisor has a tendency to rate too harshly.

Sick building syndrome Caused by either bacteria/fungi contamination of the heating/cooling ducts or vehicle fumes from outside air, the symptoms include skin and mucous membrane irritations, headaches and fatigue, and are thought to be caused by working in a modern office building.

Shiftwork Any type of schedule in which the majority of the work hours occur between 4pm and 7am.

Short-term disability insurance Insurance that covers short-term disabilities, usually for a period of six months or less.

Skill-based pay An approach that represents a significant departure from the traditional pay structure, this procedure rewards workers for the skills or knowledge they have mastered.

Social loafing The phenomenon in which one or two team members fail to do their "fair share," leaving other team members to compensate for their lack of performance.

Social Security/Medicare Two government programs that receive funding from employees and their companies, which are used for retirement, disability, survivor benefits, and health care expenses.

Staffing Refers to recruiting, hiring, promotions, and termination processes.

Stock analysis An alternative approach for showing the selection procedure had an adverse effect is to compare the percentage of the protected group members in the organization's workforce to the percentage of the protected group members in the labor market.

Stress interview An interview technique that is an attempt by the interviewer to see how a candidate fares under duress.

Strike When workers refuse to go to work.

Structured interview Uses a predetermined set of questions that are clearly job-related, such as the behavior description interview and situational interview.

Succession planning Similar to replacement planning, except that it is more long-term and developmentally- oriented, and is likely to involve input from several managers and the recommendation of various developmental activities for the candidates to ensure ability to fill positions as they open.

Summary plan description A certain type of report that details the fiscal health and outlines the company's pension plan, and must be available to all new participants.

Survivor benefits Depending on the age and status of an employee's spouse and children, they may be eligible for monthly social security benefits if the employee dies.

Taft-Hartley Act (Labor-Management Relations Act) Passed in 1947, this act was a pro-management law designed to protect employers from unfair union practices.

Task/KSA analysis Involves obtaining information from the organizational analysis to analyze the tasks performed in each job, and then determining the knowledge, skills, and abilities needed to effectively perform these tasks.

Task/LSAO Inventory A job analysis technique that focuses on both the tasks performed in the job and the KSAOs needed to perform them.

Team incentive The payout is based on the team's level of performance, and performance is evaluated using an objective standard.

Television and radio ads Methods of job recruitment by advertising open positions using television and radio spots. Advantages include these ads are more likely to reach individuals who are not actively seeking employment, ads are more likely to stand out, enables the organization to target the audience more carefully, and a considerable amount of creativity can be used in designing the ad.

Temporary employees Employees who are hired for short term projects or to fill a position created by personnel who are on leave, etc. Temporary employees are often less expensive for businesses, can be added or dropped without having to terminate them, and the task of recruiting, hiring, disciplining, and so forth is the responsibility of the placement agency, not the company.

Total Quality Management TQM emphasizes a business objective (quality), and articulates various policies, practices, and management philosophies, to support that objective, and enhance product or service quality.

Trading Point Procedure The trading point procedure involves one side saying to the other: "We'll concede on this issue (e.g., wage increases), if you concede on this other issue (e.g., overtime pay)."

Traditional interview The most common type of interview, which allows the interviewer a great deal of discretion in terms of which questions are asked and in what order.

Trainee reactions An important index of program success, trainees are asked to record their reactions by means of a survey or questionnaire at the end of the training session.

Training and development Planned efforts by organizations to increase employees' knowledge, skills and abilities (KSAs).

Training needs analysis An assessment by the organization of what the training needs are of its employees.

Transfer of training The principle that employees transfer the KSAs learned in the training period over into their jobs.

Trunk and branch career advancement system This model allows employees to move between different functions and areas, just as a tree has trunk and many branches, which turn off into other branches.

Tuition reimbursement A fairly recent benefit, tuition reimbursement programs vary in terms of the amount of reimbursement they provide, but usually provide 75 to 100% reimbursement contingent on a passing grade.

Undue hardship Exists if the accommodation to enable a qualified individual with a disability to enjoy an equal employment opportunity would involve considerable expense or difficulty to the company.

Union Election The process used to establish a union within an organization. The union election begins by contact between the workers and the union, then at least 30% of the relevant employees must sign authorization cards, then it may petition the NMRB for permission to hold an election.

Unemployment compensation Provides payments to an employee who is terminated by such means as a layoff (not for being fired or quitting).

Union An organization of workers whose purpose is to represent the employees in their dealings with management.

Union Steward The union steward plays a key role in day-to-day relationships with management, usually performing the union-related work on a part-time basis.

Union Structure Labor unions have three major levels in their structure: the local unions form the first layer; national and international unions form the next level; and federations represent the top of the union structure.

Urinalysis A urine sample that is tested for drugs.

Utility Refers to the benefits versus costs of using a particular selection procedure.

Utility analysis A relatively recent approach to choosing which, if any, human resource programs should be implemented, utility analysis considers the financial benefits versus the costs of any human resource program, and attempts to base the choice of program on its dollar value to the organization.

Utilization analysis A method of affirmative action planning, where the employer must compare the race, sex and ethnic composition of the workforce to the race, sex, and ethnic composition of the labor market.

Utilization review Refers to a process by which medical services are analyzed and reviewed.

Vacancy analysis Similar to the Markov analysis, except that it is based on managerial judgments of the probabilities of promotion, transfer, and turnover rates.

Validation study A method of demonstrating that a test is valid is by statistically examining its relationship with job performance.

Vertical career advancement system Characterized by job advancement up a clearly delineated path within a specific functional area.

Vesting Refers to the rights an employee has to the pension benefits if employment is terminated prior to retirement.

Videotape training A videotape is used to present material to a group of trainees; the most popular training technique today.

Wagner Act (National Labor Relations Act) Passed in 1935, this law gives workers the right to organize and participate in union activities, prohibits various management tactics that would discourage unions, outlaws company-sponsored unions, and forbids the company from discriminating against employees for participating in union activities.

Weighted application blank An objectively scored application blank.

Wellness programs Some organizations have implemented worksite wellness programs to improve the overall physical and mental health of their workforce. They typically involve a series of educational and behavioral change courses designed to encourage smoking cessation, proper diet and nutrition, and improved physical fitness.

Work samples A brief simulation of major job activities.

Work team The typical work team consists of between 3 and 30 employees, with one person assigned as the team leader. The team may have anywhere from some control to complete control over the project or problem.

Workers' compensation A benefit that provides income and payments for workers injured, disabled, or killed on the job.

PHOTO CREDITS

Chapter 1

4 Image 7113 ©1995 PhotoDisc, Inc.

13 Image 1394 ©1995 PhotoDisc, Inc.

Chapter 2

34 ©Jean Higgins/Unicorn Stock Photos

49 ©Steven Lunetta/StockUp

Chapter 3

67 ©Doug Menuez/SABA

68 Courtesy of International Business Machines Corporation

70 James Walker, 'Human Resource Strategy,' 1992, p. 225. Reprinted by permission of McGraw-Hill

79 FORTUNE, July 12, 1993, "The Jobs Americans Hold," W. Woods, pg 54–55. Reprinted with permission of Fortune Magazine. ©1993 Time Inc. All rights reserved.

Chapter 4

99 HB Photo/Annette Coolidge

103 ©Dennis Mac Donald/Unicorn Stock Photos

Chapter 5

126 Ernest J. McCormick, P.R. Jeanneret, and Robert C. Mecham, Position Analysis Questionnaire, © 1969 by Purdue Research Foundation, West Lafayette, Ind. 47907.

133 ©W.B. Sponbarg/PhotoEdit

135–36 Sample Application for Employment. Reprinted by permission of Rediform Office Products, Coppell, Texas

140 Annette Coolidge/HB Photo

Chapter 6

161 Career Anchors: Discovering Your Real Values by E.H. Schein. ©1990 by Pfeiffer & Company, San Diego, CA. Used with permission.

163 ©Michael Newman/PhotoEdit

178 ©Amy C. Etra/PhotoEdit

Chapter 7

199 Image 1370 ©1995 PhotoDisc, Inc.

210 Image 7194 ©1995 PhotoDisc, Inc.

Chapter 8

219 Chase Cotton Mill in Burlington, VT., May 1909. Photographed by Lewis Hine. Reproduced from the collection of the Library of Congress.

228 'Sample Evaluation: Know-How from Hay Plan,' from Hay Group, Inc. All rights reserved. Reprinted with permission.

230 Adapted from A. Bennett , 'Managers' Incomes aren't Worlds Apart', The Wall Street Journal, October 12, 1992, B1. Reprinted by permission of The Wall Street Journal, ©1992 Dow Jones & Company, Inc. All Rights Reserved Worldwide.

232-33 Survey Report, Organization Resources Counselors, Inc.

234 Image 7015 ©1995 PhotoDisc, Inc.

Chapter 9

251 Image 21100 ©1995 PhotoDisc, Inc.

262 Annette Coolidge/HB Photo

267 Formula for 'Executive Officer Performance Bonus Plan'. Used with permission from Saloman Inc.

Chapter 10

288 Image 7323 ©1995 PhotoDisc, Inc.

298 Image 72059, Series 72000 © Corel Corporation.

Chapter 11

308 Adapted from P. Froiland, 'Who's Getting Trained?' Training, October, 1993. Reprinted with permission from TRAINING Magazine, ©1993. Lakewood Publications, Minneapolis, MN. All rights reserved. Not for resale.

314–15 G. Rummler, 'Human Performance Problems and Their Solutions,' from Human Resource Management Journal, Winter, 2–10. Reprinted by permission of Human Resource Management Journal, Fort Collins, CO.

318 'Who's Getting Trained?' by P. Froiland from Training, October, 1993. Reprinted with permission from TRAINING Magazine, ©1993. Lakewood Publications, Minneapolis, MN. All rights reserved. Not for resale.

322 ©Dick Young/Unicorn Stock Photos

323 Image14152 ©1995 PhotoDisc, Inc.

Chapter 12

338 Image 7305 ©1995 PhotoDisc, Inc.

347 Photo courtesy of Honda, Marysville Ohio

Chapter 13

367 Adapted from B. Marsh, 'Workers at risk,' Wall Street Journal, February 3, 1994, p. A1 & A5. Reprinted by Permission of The Wall Street Journal, ©1994 Dow Jones & Company, Inc. All Rights Reserved Worldwide.

368 ©Jeff Greenberg/PhotoEdit

377 John R. Hollenbeck, Daniel R. Ilgren, & Suzanne M. Crampton. Lower Back Pain Disability in Occupational Settings: A Review of the Literature from a Human Resource Management View. 'Personnel Psychology', V.45, p. 247–248. Used by permission.

378 Annette Coolidge/HB Photo

381 Robert Karasek & Tores Theorell, 'Healthy Work: Stress, Productivity, and the Reconstruction of Working Life', ©1990 by Robert Karasek.Basic Books: NY. Reprinted by permission of BasicBooks, a division of HarperCollins Publishers, Inc.

Chapter 14

398 Adapted from M. Ybarra, 'Waking Dramatic', The Wall Street Journal, March 21, 1994, p. A1 & A9. Reprinted by permission of The Wall Street Journal, © 1994 Dow Jones & Company, Inc. All Rights Reserved.

402 ©1994 Jim West

405 Authorization Card for AFL-CIO CLC Membership. Reprinted with permission of The American Federation of Labor & Congress of Industrial Organizations.

Chapter 15

408 ©Harvey Finkle

421 ©1994 Jim West

Chapter 16

442 ©Allsport USA

443 Adapted from J. Lublin, 'Before You Take That Great Job, Get it in Writing,' The Wall Street Journal, February 9, 1994, B1. Reprinted by permission of The Wall Street Journal, ©1994 Dow Jones & Company, Inc. All Rights Reserved.

451 ©Annette Coolidge/HB Photo

452 Adapted from 'Respecting Employee Privacy,' by G. Webster, from Association Management, Jan. 1994, p. 142–143, 146. Reprinted with permission from ASSOCIATION MANAGEMENT, ©1994, American Society of Association Executives, Washington, D.C.

INDEX